T0366473

EARLY GREEK PHILOSOPHY

V

LCL 528

EARLY GREEK PHILOSOPHY

VOLUME V

WESTERN GREEK THINKERS
PART 2

EDITED AND TRANSLATED BY
ANDRÉ LAKS AND GLENN W. MOST

IN COLLABORATION WITH
GÉRARD JOURNÉE

AND ASSISTED BY
LEOPOLDO IRIBARREN

HARVARD UNIVERSITY PRESS
CAMBRIDGE, MASSACHUSETTS
LONDON, ENGLAND
2016

Library of Congress Control Number 2015957358
CIP data available from the Library of Congress

ISBN 978-0-674-99706-6

*Composed in ZephGreek and ZephText by
Technologies 'N Typography, Merrimac, Massachusetts.
Printed on acid-free paper and bound by
The Maple-Vail Book Manufacturing Group*

CONTENTS

THE ELEATICS

19. PARMENIDES [PARM.]

The tradition that goes back to Apollodorus of Athens gives Parmenides' *floruit* as 504/500 BC, which would imply that he was born ca. 540. Plato asserts that he visited Athens once at a date that is incompatible with the chronology (see **P4**), and he is said, like other philosophers, to have been invited to act as a legislator. A stela of a statue discovered at Velia (the ancient Elea), Parmenides' native city, claims that he belonged to a family of doctors, the Ouliads, who were probably connected with the cult of Apollo Oulios ('Healer of Wounds'). This might be no more than a legend projected back onto Parmenides by a guild of doctors who revered him as their heroic founder; but in any case it is instructive that Parmenides, often considered in ancient as in modern times to have been a thinker who neglected research on nature for the sake of ontology, could have been commemorated on this stela (as elsewhere in various testimonia) as a natural philosopher (*phusikos*).

Parmenides is the author of a single poem in dactylic hexameters. Its text was preserved in its entirety at least until the time of Simplicius (sixth century AD), who seems to have recognized that he was making more probable its survival, at least in part, by citing large extracts from it. One hundred sixty-one lines have reached us, the vast

3

majority of these thanks to him. We possess almost the entirety of the introduction (or "proem"), a very large part (90 percent, according to Diels) of the first of the two grand sections announced at the end of this introduction, and a small fraction (barely 10 percent, again according to Diels) of the second part. It is probable that the whole poem did not exceed the length of one of the shorter books of Homer's epics, between three hundred and four hundred lines.

The interpretative problems raised by this work, which has played a determining role in the history of Western philosophy, are of an enormous complexity, because of the reflection it undertakes on the term 'to be.' We cannot discuss these in depth in this introduction any more than we enter into the problems of interpretation in the other chapters; but nevertheless in this case some specific indications are indispensable.

The first twenty-three lines of the poem describe in the first person a cosmic journey in which a young man is conveyed on a chariot guided by the daughters of the Sun to the place where the gates of Day and Night are located (cf. **COSM. T8–T9**). Once he has entered into a palace—doubtless that of the Night—he is welcomed by an anonymous goddess who displays her benevolence to him by instructing him in "everything," namely, "the truth" (the doctrine of being and its attributes that constitute the first part of the poem) and "the opinions of mortals" (the cosmology and physiology that make up its second part).

The goddess distinguishes between two "roads of investigation," "is" and "is not," of which the latter is immediately discarded. There is considerable disagreement

about the possible subject of this "is," and this has implications for the translation. One often finds translators and commentators supplying either "being" or "this" or "it" (scil. that which is at issue). The interpretation that we have adopted goes back to G. Calogero: it preserves the initial indeterminacy of the verb 'to be' conjugated in the third person ("is") and accepts that the analysis of the predicates that are suitable for this verbal form gradually leads to the determination of its subject ("what is," "a being"). But this proposal has its own difficulties, and it is not the only one possible. As for the discussion regarding the meaning of the verb 'to be' in Parmenides, it is doubtless futile to try to determine, in the wake of scholarship of an analytic inspiration, whether it is existential *or* predicative *or* veridical. Parmenides' usage is likely to have been underdetermined, since, as Eudemus already remarked (**R50**), the idea of a plurality of meanings of the term 'to be' did not appear before Plato.

The course of the road of truth culminates in the celebrated comparison of being, at the conclusion of its determination, with a "well-rounded ball" that condenses within itself the totality of its predicates. Situated at the intersection between "the truth," of which this is the final statement, and "the opinions of mortals," which it announces by its visualizable character, this phrase constitutes at the same time a border and a transition between two discourses that differ both in their ontological presuppositions and in their pretention to truth. According to the interpretation of the term *eoikota* in **D8.65**—that is the most plausible one (despite its Platonic connotations)— the world is the "resemblance" of being.

Although we possess only few verses originally belonging to the second part of the poem, two programmatic passages (**D8, D9**) and the doxographic reports give us a fairly precise idea of its contents. This part was in any case Parmenides' attempt to improve on his predecessors' attempts to explain the world. His starting point is constituted by two principles, which he calls "forms" (*morphai*), Fire (or Light) and Night, which mortals are said to have posited (this implies a certain arbitrariness). Each principle is in a relation of identity to itself, in the image of being, but it is also opposed to the other one: the fire of day is mild and light, the night is dense and heavy. Their mixture, out of which the world has progressively issued, is the work of a divinity with a demiurgic function. The domain covered by the explanations given was broad, reaching from the nature of the stars and their trajectories to the reproduction of living beings. It is understandable that antiquity could have considered Parmenides as a full-fledged "natural philosopher," despite the Platonic-Aristotelian tendency to consider only the first part of his poem and to treat his cosmophysiology as being at best secondary. It is true that Parmenides' immediate disciples, Zeno and Melissus, renounced all explanation bearing on the world, which they considered simply inconsequential from the point of view of the doctrine of being.

In the case of Parmenides, the major interpretative traditions, most often determined by Plato and Aristotle, are passed along from one author to another, so that a purely chronological arrangement of the **R** section would not only have resulted in many repetitions but would also have given a false impression about a distinctive characteristic

of that very reception: the recurrence of similar statements is, as it were, the counterpart of the indelible mark
that Parmenides left on Greek thought. In this chapter, as
in certain other ones that present analogous characteristics in this regard (this is especially the case for the Atomists and the Pythagoreans), we have treated the material
with resolute selectiveness and have organized it themati-
cally.

BIBLIOGRAPHY

Editions and Translations

J. Bollack. *Parménide, de l'étant au monde* (Paris, 2006).

B. Cassin. *Parménide: Sur la nature ou sur l'étant. La
langue de l'être* (Paris, 1998).

A. H. Coxon. *The Fragments of Parmenides. A Critical
Text with Introduction and Translation, the Ancient Testimonia and a Commentary* (Assen, 1986); revised and
expanded edition with new translations by R. McKira-
han (Las Vegas, 2009).

H. Diels. *Parmenides. Lehrgedicht. Mit einem Anhang
über griechische Thüren und Schlösser* (Berlin, 1897;
Sank Augustin, 2003).

D. Gallop. *Parmenides of Elea. Fragments. A Text and
Translation* (Toronto, 1984).

D. O'Brien. *Le poème de Parménide,* texte, traduction,
essai critique, in P. Aubenque, ed., *Études sur Parménide,* vol. I (Paris, 1987).

L. Tarán. Parmenides. *A Text with Translation, Commentary, and Critical Essays* (Princeton, 1965; 3rd ed.
1971).

Studies

On the Eleatic School in General

G. Calogero. *Studi sull'Eleatismo* (Rome, 1932; repr. Florence, 1977).

P. Curd. *The Legacy of Parmenides. Eleatic Monism and Later Presocratic Thought* (Princeton, 1998; 2nd ed. Las Vegas, 2004).

On Parmenides in General

J. Mansfeld. *Die Offenbarung des Parmenides und die menschliche Welt* (Assen, 1964).

A. P. D. Mourelatos. *The Route of Parmenides. A Study of Word, Image, and Argument in the Fragments* (New Haven, 1970; 2nd ed. Las Vegas, 2007).

J. A. Palmer. *Parmenides and Presocratic Philosophy* (Oxford, 2009).

On the Proem

W. Burkert. "Das Proömium des Parmenides und die Katabasis des Pythagoras," *Phronesis* 14 (1969): 1–30.

On Being and Its Attributes

J. Barnes, "Parmenides and the Eleatic One," *Archiv für Geschichte der Philosophie* 61 (1979): 1–21.

C. H. Kahn. *The Verb 'Be' in Ancient Greek* (Dordrecht, 1973; Indianapolis, 2003).

PARMENIDES

On *Nous* and *Noein*

J. H. Lesher, "Parmenides' Critique of Thinking," *Oxford Studies in Ancient Philosophy* 2 (1984): 1–30.

On the Cosmology

J. Bollack, "La cosmologie parménidienne de Parménide," in R. Brague and J.-F. Courtine, eds., *Herméneutique et ontologie: Mélanges en hommage de Pierre Aubenque* (Paris, 1990), pp. 17–53.

On the Reception of Parmenides in Plato

J. A. Palmer. *Plato's Reception of Parmenides* (Oxford, 1999).

OUTLINE OF THE CHAPTER

P

Chronology (P1–P4)
Family (cf. P8, P23b)
Philosophical Lineages (P5–P11)
    Xenophanes or Anaximander? (P5–P7)
    Ameinias and the Pythagoreans (P8–P11)
Influences, Disciples, Lovers (P12–P19)
Parmenides as the Legislator of Elea (P20–P22)
Statue and Iconography (P23)

D

Only One Treatise (D1)
Poetical Form (D2)
The Traditional Title (D3)

9

PARMENIDES

PARMENIDES [28 DK]

P

Chronology (P1–P4)

P1 (< A1) Diog. Laert. 9.23 (Apollod. *FGrHist* 244 F341)

ἤκμαζε δὲ κατὰ τὴν ἐνάτην καὶ ἑξηκοστὴν Ὀλυμπιάδα.

P2 (cf. A11) Eus. *Chron.*

a Hier. *Chron.*, p. 111.21–22

[ad Ol. 81 = 456/52] Empedocles et Parmenides physici
philosophi notissimi habentur.

b *Chron. Pasch.*, p. 306.3

[ad Ol. 80.3 = 458/7] Ἐμπεδοκλῆς καὶ Παρμενίδης φυσικοὶ φιλόσοφοι ἐγνωρίζοντο.

PARMENIDES

Chronology (P1–P4)

P1 (< A1) Diogenes Laertius

He was in his maturity during the 69th Olympiad [= 504/500].

P2 (cf. A11) Eusebius, *Chronicle*

a Jerome, *Chronicle*

[Ol. 81 = 456/52] Empedocles and Parmenides, natural philosopher, are considered very well known.

b *Chronicon Paschale*

[Ol. 80.3 = 458/7] Empedocles and Parmenides, natural philosophers, were well known.

P3 (cf. A11) Eus. *Chron.*

a Hier. *Chron.*, p. 114.7–10

[ad Ol. 86.1 = 436/5] Democritus Abderites et Empedocles et Hippocrates medicus Gorgias Hippiasque et Prodicus et Zeno et Parmenides philosophi insignes habentur.

b (≠ DK) Cyrill. Alex. *Jul.* 1.15

[Ol. 86 = 436/32] ὀγδοηκοστῇ ἕκτῃ Ὀλυμπιάδι γενέσθαι φασὶ τὸν Ἀβδηρίτην Δημόκριτον, Ἐμπεδοκλέα τε καὶ Ἱπποκράτην, καὶ Πρόδικον, Ζήνωνα καὶ Παρμενίδην.

P4 (< A5)

a Plat. *Parm.* 127a–c

[ΚΕ.] ἔφη δὲ δὴ ὁ Ἀντιφῶν λέγειν τὸν Πυθόδωρον ὅτι ἀφίκοιντό ποτε εἰς Παναθήναια τὰ μεγάλα Ζήνων τε καὶ Παρμενίδης. τὸν μὲν οὖν Παρμενίδην εὖ μάλα ἤδη πρεσβύτην εἶναι, σφόδρα πολιόν, καλὸν δὲ κἀγαθὸν τὴν ὄψιν, περὶ ἔτη μάλιστα πέντε καὶ ἑξήκοντα· Ζήνωνα δὲ ἐγγὺς τῶν τετταράκοντα τότε εἶναι [. . . cf. **P12a**]· Σωκράτη δὲ εἶναι τότε σφόδρα νέον.

b Athen. *Deipn.* 11.113 505F

Παρμενίδῃ μὲν γὰρ καὶ ἐλθεῖν εἰς λόγους τὸν τοῦ Πλάτωνος Σωκράτην μόλις ἡ ἡλικία συγχωρεῖ, οὐχ ὡς καὶ τοιούτους εἰπεῖν ἢ ἀκοῦσαι λόγους [. . . = **P12c**].

16

P3 (cf. A11) Eusebius, *Chronicle*

a Jerome, *Chronicle*

[Ol. 86.1 = 436/5] Democritus of Abdera, Empedocles, Hippocrates the doctor, Gorgias and Hippias, Prodicus, Zeno, and Parmenides are considered famous philosophers.

b (≠ DK) Cyril of Alexandria, *Against Julian*

They say that Democritus of Abdera, Empedocles and Hippocrates, and Prodicus, Zeno, and Parmenides were alive in the 86th Olympiad [= 436/32].

P4 (< A5)

a Plato, *Parmenides*

[Cephalus:] Antiphon reported that Pythodorus had said that Zeno and Parmenides once came to the Great Panathenaic festival; and that Parmenides was already quite old, with very white hair, but was a fine man to look upon, around sixty-five years old, while Zeno was near forty at that time [. . .]; Socrates was very young at the time.[1]

[1] In 454, Socrates was sixteen years old; this date would be compatible with Jerome's chronology (cf. **P2a**) if we suppose that Parmenides was born around 520 (cf. also **P3a**). The Apollodoran tradition represented by **P1** presupposes instead a date of birth around 540, which would make this meeting impossible.

b Athenaeus, *Deipnosophists*

His age scarcely permits Plato's Socrates to have conversed with Parmenides, let alone to have said or heard such speeches [. . .].

Family

See **P8, P23a**

Philosophical Lineages (P5–P11)
Xenophanes or Anaximander? (P5–P7)

P5 (> A6) Arist. *Metaph.* A5 986b21–22

Ξενοφάνης δὲ πρῶτος τούτων ἑνίσας (ὁ γὰρ Παρμενίδης τούτου λέγεται μαθητής[1]) [. . .].

[1] μαθητής E: γενέσθαι μαθητής A[b]

P6

a (< A1) Diog. Laert. 9.21

Ξενοφάνους δὲ διήκουσε[1] Παρμενίδης Πύρητος Ἐλεάτης (τοῦτον Θεόφραστος ἐν τῇ Ἐπιτομῇ [Frag. 227D
FHS&G] Ἀναξιμάνδρου φησὶν ἀκοῦσαι).

[1] Ξενοφάνους δὲ διήκουσε ut huic loco alienum secl.
Dorandi

b (< A2) *Suda* Π.675

Παρμενίδης Πύρητος Ἐλεάτης φιλόσοφος, μαθητὴς
γεγονὼς Ξενοφάνους τοῦ Κολοφωνίου, ὡς δὲ Θεόφραστος [cf. app. Frag. 227D FHS&G] Ἀναξιμάνδρου τοῦ
Μιλησίου [. . .].

PARMENIDES

Family

See **P8, P23a**

Philosophical Lineages (P5–P11)
Xenophanes or Anaximander? (P5–P7)

P5 (> A6) Aristotle, *Metaphysics*

[. . .] Xenophanes, the first of those [scil. together with Parmenides and Melissus] to have taught the One (for Parmenides is said to have been his pupil) [. . .] [cf. **XEN. R2**].

P6

a (< A1) Diogenes Laertius

Parmenides of Elea, son of Pyres, studied with Xenophanes (Theophrastus says in his *Epitome* that he [i.e. probably Parmenides] studied with Anaximander).

b (< A2) *Suda*

Parmenides of Elea, son of Pyres, philosopher, was a disciple of Xenophanes of Colophon, but, as Theophrastus says, of Anaximander of Miletus.[1]

---

[1] The word order in **P6a** suggests that 'he' there should refer to Parmenides, and this is how the *Suda* understands it. Many scholars have doubted that Theophrastus could have said that Parmenides studied with Anaximander and therefore refer 'he' to Xenophanes; but there are other cases of claims for intellectual affiliation that are impossible chronologically. T. Dorandi, *Elenchos* 30 (2009): 347–53, on the basis of a reexamination of the mss., suggests that the words 'studied with Xenophanes' do not belong here.

P7 (< A7) Alex. *In Metaph.*, p. 31.7–9

περὶ Παρμενίδου καὶ τῆς δόξης αὐτοῦ καὶ Θεόφραστος ἐν τῷ πρώτῳ Περὶ τῶν φυσικῶν οὕτως λέγει
[Frag. 227C FHS&G] "τούτῳ δὲ ἐπιγενόμενος Παρμενίδης Πύρητος ὁ Ἐλεάτης" (λέγει δὲ¹ Ξενοφάνην) [. . .].

    ¹ καὶ post δὲ del. Diels

Ameinias and the Pythagoreans (P8–P11)

P8 (< A1) Diog. Laert. 9.21

ὅμως δ' οὖν ἀκούσας καὶ Ξενοφάνους οὐκ ἠκολούθη-
σεν αὐτῷ. ἐκοινώνησε δὲ καὶ Ἀμεινίᾳ Διοχάρτα¹ τῷ
Πυθαγορικῷ [**PYTH. b T35**], ὡς ἔφη Σωτίων [Frag. 27
Wehrli], ἀνδρὶ πένητι μέν, καλῷ δὲ καὶ ἀγαθῷ. ᾧ καὶ
μᾶλλον ἠκολούθησε καὶ ἀποθανόντος ἡρῷον ἱδρύ-
σατο γένους τε ὑπάρχων λαμπροῦ καὶ πλούτου, καὶ
ὑπ' Ἀμεινίου ἀλλ' οὐχ ὑπὸ Ξενοφάνους εἰς ἡσυχίαν
προετράπη.

    ¹ Διοχάρτα Bechtel: διοχαίτη BP: καὶ διοχέτη F: Διοχαίτα
Diels, alii alia

P9 (< A12) Strab. 6.1.1

[. . .] οἱ δὲ νῦν Ἐλέαν ὀνομάζουσιν· ἐξ ἧς Παρμενίδης
καὶ Ζήνων ἐγένοντο, ἄνδρες Πυθαγόρειοι [. . . = **P21**].

P7 (< A7) Alexander of Aphrodisias, *Commentary on Aristotle's* Metaphysics

About Parmenides and his opinion Theophrastus too, in the first book of his *On Physics,* speaks as follows: "Parmenides of Elea, son of Pyres, who came after him," (he means Xenophanes) [. . .].

Ameinias and the Pythagoreans (P8–P11)

P8 (< A1) Diogenes Laertius

Although he studied with Xenophanes too, nonetheless he did not follow him. But as Sotion says, he also associated with Ameinias the Pythagorean, son of Diochartas, a poor man but of a noble character (*kalos kagathos*). It was this man that he preferred to follow, and when he died he founded a heroic shrine for him, as he was of noble birth and wealth, and it was by Ameinias, and not by Xenophanes, that he was guided toward tranquility.

P9 (< A12) Strabo, *Geography*

[. . .] people now call [scil. this city] Elea; it is from here that Parmenides and Zeno came, Pythagorean men.

P10 (< A4) Procl. *In Parm.*, p. 619.5–8

[. . .] διδάσκαλος μὲν ὁ Παρμενίδης ὤν, μαθητὴς δὲ ὁ Ζήνων, Ἐλεάται δὲ ἄμφω, καὶ οὐ τοῦτο μόνον, ἀλλὰ καὶ τοῦ Πυθαγορικοῦ διδασκαλείου μεταλαβόντε, καθάπερ που καὶ ὁ Νικόμαχος[1] ἱστόρησεν.

[1] Νικόμαχος Σg: Καλλίμαχος A

P11 (< 58.A) Iambl. *VP* 267

Ἐλεάτης Παρμενίδης

Influences, Disciples, Lovers (P12–P19)

P12 (< A5)

a Plat. *Parm.* 127b

[KE.] [. . .] Ζήνωνα [. . . cf. **P4**], εὐμήκη δὲ καὶ χαρίεντα ἰδεῖν, καὶ λέγεσθαι αὐτὸν παιδικὰ τοῦ Παρμενίδου γεγονέναι.

b Diog. Laert. 9.25

ὁ δὴ Ζήνων διακήκοε Παρμενίδου καὶ γέγονεν αὐτοῦ παιδικά.

P10 (< A4) Proclus, *Commentary on Plato's* Parmenides

[. . .] Parmenides being the teacher, and Zeno his disciple, both of them from Elea, and not only this, but also both having taken part in the Pythagorean teaching, as Nicomachus [scil. of Gerasa] has reported somewhere.

P11 (< 58.A) Iamblichus, *Life of Pythagoras*

From Elea: Parmenides [cf. **PYTH. b T30 [4]**].

See also **R66–R70**

Influences, Disciples, Lovers (P12–P19)

P12 (< A5)

a Plato, *Parmenides*

[Cephalus:] Zeno was [. . . cf. **P4**] tall and attractive in appearance, and it was said that he had been Parmenides' beloved.

b Diogenes Laertius

Zeno studied with Parmenides and became his beloved.

23

c Athen. *Deipn.* 11.113 505F

[. . . = **P4b**] τὸ δὲ πάντων σχετλιώτατον[1] καὶ τὸ εἰπεῖν
οὐδεμιᾶς κατεπειγούσης χρείας ὅτι παιδικὰ γεγόνοι
τοῦ Παρμενίδου Ζήνων ὁ πολίτης αὐτοῦ.

   [1] σχετλιώτερον ms., corr. Musurus

P13 (< 31 A2) *Suda* E.1002

ἠκροάσατο δὲ πρώτου Παρμενίδου, οὗτινος, ὥς φησι
Πορφύριος ἐν τῇ φιλοσόφῳ ἱστορίᾳ [Frag. 208F
Smith], καὶ ἐγένετο παιδικά.

P14 (A9) Diog. Laert. 8.55

ὁ δὲ Θεόφραστος Παρμενίδου φησὶ [Frag. 227B
FHS&G] ζηλωτὴν αὐτὸν γενέσθαι καὶ μιμητὴν ἐν τοῖς
ποιήμασι· καὶ γὰρ ἐκεῖνον ἐν ἔπεσι τὸν Περὶ φύσεως
ἐξενεγκεῖν λόγον.

P15 (≠ DK) Diog. Laert. 8.56

Ἀλκιδάμας δ᾽ ἐν τῷ Φυσικῷ φησι [Frag. 8 Avezzù]
κατὰ τοὺς αὐτοὺς χρόνους Ζήνωνα καὶ Ἐμπεδοκλέα
ἀκοῦσαι Παρμενίδου [. . .].

P16 (< A3) Diog. Laert. 2.3

Ἀναξιμένης [. . .] Μιλήσιος ἤκουσεν Ἀναξιμάνδρου.
ἔνιοι δὲ καὶ Παρμενίδου φασὶν ἀκοῦσαι αὐτόν.[1]

c Athenaeus, *Deipnosophists*

[. . .] the most shameful thing of all is that he [i.e. Plato] says, without being compelled by any necessity, that Parmenides' fellow citizen Zeno was his beloved.

P13 (< 31 A2) *Suda*

He [i.e. Empedocles] studied with Parmenides first, of whom, as Porphyry says in his *Philosophical History,* he also became the beloved.

P14 (A9) Diogenes Laertius

Theophrastus says that he [i.e. Empedocles] became Parmenides' rival and imitator in his poems; for he too published his text *On Nature* in verse.

P15 (≠ DK) Diogenes Laertius

Alcidamas in his *On Nature* says that Zeno and Empedocles studied with Parmenides at the same time [. . .].

P16 (< A3) Diogenes Laertius

Anaximenes [. . .] from Miletus studied with Anaximander; some say that he also studied with Parmenides.[1]

---

[1] This indication has no chronological value; cf. n. 1 at **ANAXIMEN. P1.**

---

[1] ἔνιοι . . . αὐτόν secl. Marcovich ut gloss. ex 9.21 (Παρμενί-δην et αὐτοῦ corr. Marcovich ex Volkmann)

P17 (< 30 A1) Diog. Laert. 9.24

οὗτος ἤκουσε Παρμενίδου.

P18 (< A8) Simpl. *In Phys.*, p. 28.4–6 (= Theophr. Frag. 229 FHS&G)

Λεύκιππος δὲ ὁ Ἐλεάτης ἢ Μιλήσιος (ἀμφοτέρως γὰρ λέγεται περὶ αὐτοῦ) κοινωνήσας Παρμενίδῃ τῆς φιλοσοφίας, οὐ τὴν αὐτὴν ἐβάδισε Παρμενίδῃ καὶ Ξενοφάνει περὶ τῶν ὄντων ὁδόν, ἀλλ᾽ ὡς δοκεῖ τὴν ἐναντίαν [. . . = **ATOM. D32**].

P19 (≠ DK) Anon. *Proleg. in Plat. Philos.* 1.3.15

ἐφοίτησε δὲ καὶ Κρατύλῳ τῷ Ἡρακλειτείῳ καὶ Ἑρμο-γένει[1] τῷ Παρμενιδείῳ, τὰ Ἡρακλείτου καὶ Παρμενί-δου δόγματα μαθεῖν βουλόμενος.

   [1] Ἑρμογένει coni. Westermann: Ἑρμίππῳ ms.

Parmenides as the Legislator of Elea (P20–P22)

P20 (< A1) Diog. Laert. 9.23

λέγεται δὲ καὶ νόμους θεῖναι τοῖς πολίταις, ὥς φησι Σπεύσιππος ἐν τῷ Περὶ φιλοσόφων [Frag. 3 Tarán].

P21 (< A12) Strab. 6.1.1

[. . . = **P9**] δοκεῖ δέ μοι καὶ δι᾽ ἐκείνους καὶ ἔτι πρότε-ρον εὐνομηθῆναι [. . .]

P17 (< 30 A1) Diogenes Laertius

He [i.e. Melissus] studied with Parmenides.

P18 (< A8) Theophrastus in Simplicius, *Commentary on Aristotle's* Physics

Leucippus, from Elea or Miletus (for both are reported for him), after having shared in Parmenides' philosophy, did not follow the same road as Parmenides and Xenophanes regarding the things that exist, but the opposite one, as it seems [. . .].

P19 (≠ DK) Anonymous, *Life of Plato*

He [i.e. Plato] spent time with Cratylus, Heraclitus' disciple, and Hermogenes, Parmenides' disciple, since he wanted to learn the doctrines of Heraclitus and Parmenides.

Parmenides as the Legislator of Elea (P20–P22)

P20 (< A1) Diogenes Laertius

And he is said to have established laws for his fellow citizens, as Speusippus says in his *On Philosophers*.

P21 (< A12) Strabo, *Geography*

[. . .] it [i.e. Elea] seems to me to have had good laws both because of these men [scil. Parmenides and Zeno, cf. **ZEN. P13–P16**] and also even earlier [. . .]

P22 (A12) Plut. *Adv. Col.* 32 1126A–B

Παρμενίδης δὲ τὴν ἑαυτοῦ πατρίδα διεκόσμησε νόμοις ἀρίστοις, ὥστε τὰς ἀρχὰς καθ᾽ ἕκαστον ἐνιαυτὸν
ἐξορκοῦν τοὺς πολίτας ἐμμενεῖν τοῖς Παρμενίδου νόμοις.

Statue and Iconography (P23)

P23 (≠ DK) *SEG* XXXVIII 1020

a

ΠΑ[Ρ]ΜΕΝΕΙΔΗΣ ΠΥΡΗΤΟΣ
ΟΥΛΙΑΔΗΣ ΦΥΣΙΚΟΣ

P22 (A12) Plutarch, *Against Colotes*

Parmenides put his country in order by means of optimal laws, so that the citizens make the magistrates swear an oath every year that they will respect Parmenides' laws.

Statue and Iconography (P23)

P23 (≠ DK)

a Stela of a headless statue found at Elea, dated after ca. AD 50

> Parmenides, son of Pyres,
> Of the family of the Ouliads, natural philosopher[1]

[1] The Ouliads of Elea seem to have been a caste of healers and priests of Apollo (*oulios* is an epithet of Apollo in his quality as healer), and they may have revered Parmenides (who was represented by the statue on the base of which this inscription was written, found in the ruins of their building at Elea) as their heroic patron and presumed ancestor. But it should be noted that Ouliadês is a widely distributed personal name in ancient Greek (cf. *LGPN* 1.355, 2.355, 5A.351, 5B.335–36), and the implications of this inscription remain uncertain.

b cf. Koch, "Ikonographie," in Flashar, Bremer, Rechenauer (2013), I.1, p. 222.

PARMENIDES [28 DK]

D

Only One Treatise (D1)

D1 (< A13) Diog. Laert. 1.16

οἱ δὲ ἀνὰ ἓν συγγράψαντες[1] [. . .] Παρμενίδης [. . .].

> [1] συγγράψαντες BP, γρ. F[2]: σύγγραμμα F[1]

Poetical Form (D2)

D2 (< A1) Diog. Laert. 9.22

καὶ αὐτὸς δὲ διὰ ποιημάτων φιλοσοφεῖ, καθάπερ Ἡσίοδός τε καὶ Ξενοφάνης καὶ Ἐμπεδοκλῆς.

The Traditional Title (D3)

D3 (< A14) Simpl. *In Cael.*, p. 556.25–26

[. . .] Περὶ φύσεως ἐπέγραφον τὰ συγγράμματα καὶ Μέλισσος καὶ Παρμενίδης [. . .] [cf. **MEL. D1b**].

PARMENIDES

D

Only One Treatise (D1)

D1 (< A13) Diogenes Laertius

[. . .] others, who wrote only one treatise: [. . .] Parmenides [. . .].

Poetical Form (D2)

D2 (< A1) Diogenes Laertius

He too expresses his philosophy in verse, like Hesiod, Xenophanes, and Empedocles.

The Traditional Title (D3)

D3 (< A14) Simplicius, *Commentary on Aristotle's* On the Heavens

[. . .] Both Melissus and Parmenides entitled their treatises *On Nature* [. . .] [cf. **MEL. D1b**].

See also **ALCM. D2**

The Proem of the Poem (D4)

D4 (B1) v. 1–30: Sext. Emp. *Adv. Math.* 7.111 (et al.); v. 28–32: Simpl. *In Cael.*, pp. 557.25–558.2 (et al.)

ἐναρχόμενος γοῦν τοῦ Περὶ φύσεως γράφει τοῦτον τὸν τρόπον·

ἵπποι ταί με φέρουσιν, ὅσον τ᾽ ἐπὶ θυμὸς ἱκάνοι,
πέμπον ἐπεί μ᾽ ἐς ὁδὸν βῆσαν πολύφημον ἄγουσαι
δαίμονος, ἣ κατὰ πάντ᾽ ἄστη φέρει εἰδότα φῶτα·
τῇ φερόμην· τῇ γάρ με πολύφραστοι φέρον ἵπποι

5   ἅρμα τιταίνουσαι, κοῦραι δ᾽ ὁδὸν ἡγεμόνευον.
ἄξων δ᾽ ἐν χνοίῃσιν ἵει σύριγγος ἀϋτήν
αἰθόμενος (δοιοῖς γὰρ ἐπείγετο δινωτοῖσιν
κύκλοις ἀμφοτέρωθεν), ὅτε σπερχοίατο πέμπειν
Ἡλιάδες κοῦραι, προλιποῦσαι δώματα Νυκτός

10   εἰς φάος, ὠσάμεναι κράτων ἄπο χερσὶ καλύπτρας.

3 πάντ᾽ ἄστη (falso) legit Mutschmann: παντατη (cum variis accentibus) mss.: alii aliter   6 χνοίῃσιν ἵει Diels post Karsten: χνοίῃσινι N: χνοιῇσιν LEABVR   10 κράτων Mullach post Karsten: κρατερῶν mss.

PARMENIDES

The Proem of the Poem (D4)

D4 (B1) Sextus Empiricus, *Against the Logicians*

At the beginning of his *On Nature* he writes as follows:

> [The journey to the goddess]
> **The mares that carry me as far as ardor might
> go**
> **Were bringing me onward, after having led me
> and set me down on the divinity's many-
> worded**
> **Road, which carries through all the towns** (?)
> **the man who knows.**
> **It was on this road that I was being carried: for
> on it the much-knowing horses were carrying
> me,**
> **Straining at the chariot, and maidens were**   5
> **leading the way.**
> **The axle in the naves emitted the whistle of a
> flute**
> **As it was heated (for it was pressed hard by two
> whirling**
> **Wheels, one on each side), while the maidens of
> the Sun**
> **Hastened to bring me, after they had left
> behind the palace of Night**
> **Towards the light[1] and had pushed back the**   10
> **veils from their heads with their hands.**

[1] Interpreters have often understood "hastened to bring me . . . toward the light," not "after they had left behind . . . toward the light."

ἔνθα πύλαι Νυκτός τε καὶ Ἤματός εἰσι
   κελεύθων,
καί σφας ὑπέρθυρον ἀμφὶς ἔχει καὶ λάϊνος
   οὐδός·
αὐταὶ δ' αἰθέριαι πλῆνται μεγάλοισι θυρέτροις·
τῶν δὲ Δίκη πολύποινος ἔχει κληῖδας ἀμοιβούς.
15   τὴν δὴ παρφάμεναι κοῦραι μαλακοῖσι λόγοισιν
πεῖσαν ἐπιφραδέως, ὥς σφιν βαλανωτὸν ὀχῆα
ἀπτερέως ὤσειε πυλέων ἄπο· ταὶ δὲ θυρέτρων
χάσμ' ἀχανὲς ποίησαν ἀναπτάμεναι
   πολυχάλκους
ἄξονας ἐν σύριγξιν ἀμοιβαδὸν εἰλίξασαι
20   γόμφοις καὶ περόνῃσιν ἀρηρότε· τῇ ῥα δι'
   αὐτέων
ἰθὺς ἔχον κοῦραι κατ' ἀμαξιτὸν ἅρμα καὶ
   ἵππους.
καί με θεὰ πρόφρων ὑπεδέξατο, χεῖρα δὲ χειρί
δεξιτερὴν ἕλεν, ὧδε δ' ἔπος φάτο καί με
   προσηύδα·
ὦ κοῦρ' ἀθανάτοισι συνάορος ἡνιόχοισιν,
25   ἵπποις ταί σε φέρουσιν ἱκάνων ἡμέτερον δῶ,

14 Δίκη Scaliger: δίκην mss.

That is where the gate of the paths of Night and
    Day is,[2]
And a lintel and a stone threshold hold it on
    both sides.
Itself ethereal, it is occupied by great doors,
And much-punishing Justice holds its
    alternating keys.
The maidens, cajoling her with gentle words,   15
Wisely persuaded her to thrust quickly back for
    them
The bolted bar from the gate. And when it flew
    open
It made a gaping absence of the doors, after
    rotating in turn
In their sockets the two bronze pivots
Fastened with pegs and rivets. There, through   20
    them,
The maidens guided the chariot and horses
    straight along the way.
And the goddess welcomed me graciously, took
    my right hand
In her own hand, and spoke these words,
    addressing me:

    [The beginning of the goddess' speech]
Young man, companion of deathless charioteers,
    you who
Have come to our home by the mares that carry   25
    you,

[2] Cf. **COSM. T8, T9.**

χαῖρ', ἐπεὶ οὔτι σε μοῖρα κακὴ προὔπεμπε
    νέεσθαι
τήνδ' ὁδόν (ἦ γὰρ ἀπ' ἀνθρώπων ἐκτὸς πάτου
    ἐστίν),
ἀλλὰ Θέμις τε Δίκη τε. χρεὼ δέ σε πάντα
    πυθέσθαι
ἠμὲν Ἀληθείης εὐπειθέος ἀτρεμὲς ἦτορ
    30   ἠδὲ βροτῶν δόξας, ταῖς οὐκ ἔνι πίστις ἀληθής.
ἀλλ' ἔμπης καὶ ταῦτα μαθήσεαι, ὡς τὰ
    δοκοῦντα
χρῆν δοκίμως εἶναι διὰ παντὸς πάντα περῶντα.

29 εὐπειθέος Plut. *Adv. Col.* 1114D, Clem. Alex. *Strom.*
5.59.6, Diog. Laert. 9.22: εὐκυκλέος Simpl.: εὐφεγγέος Procl. *In
Tim.* 2. 105b   post v. 30 hab. Sextus D8.2–6a = B7.2–6
D.–K.   32 χρῆν DE: χρὴν A: χρὴ Karsten   περῶντα
A: περ ὄντα DEF

*Fragments from the First Part, on Truth, and
Transition to the Second Part (D5–D8)*

D5 (B5) Procl. *In Parm.*, p. 708.10–11

– ∪ ∪ | – ∪ ∪ | – ∪ ∪ | – ξυνὸν δέ μοί ἐστιν,
ὁππόθεν ἄρξωμαι· τόθι γὰρ πάλιν ἵξομαι αὖθις.

I greet you [or: Rejoice!]: for it is no evil fate that
    has sent you to travel
This road (for indeed it is remote from the
    paths of men),
But Right and Justice. It is necessary that you
    learn everything,
Both the unshakeable heart of well-convincing
    (*eupeitheos*) **truth**
And the opinions of mortals, in which there is   30
    no true belief (*pistis*).
But nonetheless you will learn this too: how
    opinions
Would have to be acceptable, forever
    penetrating all things (?).[3]

[3] The text of the second half of the line is uncertain.

Fragments from the First Part, on Truth, and
Transition to the Second Part (D5–D8)

D5 (B5) Proclus, *Commentary on Plato's* Parmenides

        In common, for me, is
The point from which I shall begin: for I shall
    return there once again later.

D6 (B2, B3) v. 1–8a: Procl. *In Tim.*, 2.105b13–22; v. 3–8a: Simpl. *In Phys.*, pp. 116.28–117.1 (et al.); v. 8b: Clem. Alex. *Strom.* 6.23.3 (et al.)

[B2]　εἰ δ᾽ ἄγ᾽ ἐγὼν ἐρέω, κόμισαι δὲ σὺ μῦθον
　　　　ἀκούσας,
　　αἵπερ ὁδοὶ μοῦναι διζήσιός εἰσι νοῆσαι·
　　ἡ μὲν ὅπως ἔστιν τε καὶ ὡς οὐκ ἔστι μὴ εἶναι,
　　πειθοῦς ἐστι κέλευθος (ἀληθείη γὰρ ὀπηδεῖ),
5　　ἡ δ᾽ ὡς οὐκ ἔστιν τε καὶ ὡς χρεών ἐστι μὴ
　　　　εἶναι,
　　τὴν δή τοι φράζω παναπευθέα ἔμμεν ἀταρπόν·
　　οὔτε γὰρ ἂν γνοίης τό γε μὴ ἐὸν (οὐ γὰρ
　　　　ἀνυστόν)
[B3]　οὔτε φράσαις. τὸ γὰρ αὐτὸ νοεῖν ἐστίν τε καὶ
　　　　εἶναι.

1 ἄγ᾽ ἐγὼν Karsten: ἄγε τῶν mss.　　　3 ὡς Simpl.: om. Procl.　　　6 παναπευθέα Simpl. EF: παραπεύθεα Simpl. D: παναπειθέα Procl. P: παραπειθέα Procl. N　　　7 ἀνυστόν Simpl.: ἐφικτόν Procl.

D6 (B2) Proclus, *Commentary on Plato's* Timaeus (et al.)
+ (B3) Clement of Alexandria, *Stromata* (et al.).

Well then, as for me, I shall say—and as for you, [B2]
    have a care for this discourse when you have
    heard it—
What are the only roads of investigation for
    thought (*noêsai*):
The one, that "is," and that it is not possible
    that "is not,"
Is the path of conviction (*peithô*), for it
    accompanies truth;
The other, that "is not," and that it is necessary   5
    that "is not"—
I show you that it is a path that cannot be
    inquired into at all.
For you could not know that which is not (for
    this is impracticable)
Nor could you show it.
                For it is the same, to [B3]
think (*noein*) and also to be.[1]

[1] This phrase is transmitted separately from the preceding
lines, but it completes them in meaning and meter, and it is
plausibly attached to them by scholars. For the meaning, cf.
D8.39–41.

D7 (B6) v. 1–2a (. . . ἔστιν): Simpl. *In Phys.*, p. 86.27–28;
v. 1b (ἔστι . . .)–9: Simpl. *In Phys.*, p. 117.4–13; v. 8–9a
(. . . ταὐτόν): Simpl. *In Phys.*, p. 78.3–4

χρὴ τὸ λέγειν τε νοεῖν τ' ἐὸν ἔμμεναι· ἔστι γὰρ
εἶναι·
μηδὲν δ' οὐκ ἔστιν· τά γ' ἐγὼ φράζεσθαι
ἄνωγα.
πρώτης γάρ σ' ἀφ' ὁδοῦ ταύτης διζήσιος
⟨εἴργω⟩,
αὐτὰρ ἔπειτ' ἀπὸ τῆς, ἣν δὴ βροτοὶ εἰδότες
οὐδέν
5   πλάττονται, δίκρανοι· ἀμηχανίη γὰρ ἐν αὐτῶν
στήθεσιν ἰθύνει πλαγκτὸν νόον· οἱ δὲ φοροῦνται
κωφοὶ ὁμῶς τυφλοί τε, τεθηπότες, ἄκριτα φῦλα,
οἷς τὸ πέλειν τε καὶ οὐκ εἶναι ταὐτὸν
νενόμισται
κοὐ ταὐτόν, πάντων δὲ παλίντροπός ἐστι
κέλευθος.

1 τε Karsten: τὸ mss.   τεὸν F: τὸ ὂν DE, corr. Brandis
2 τά γ' ἐγὼ D: τά γε F: τοῦ ἐγὼ E: τά σε ed. Ald.: τά σ' ἐγὼ
Bergk   3 σ' mss. optimi: τ' scrips. Cordero cum mss. BC
⟨εἴργω⟩ Diels: ⟨ἄρξει⟩ Cordero: ⟨ἄρξω⟩ Nehamas   5 πλάττονται mss.: πλάζονται ed. Ald.

D7 (B6) Simplicius, *Commentary on Aristotle's* Physics

> It is necessary to say and to think that this is
>   being;[1] for it is possible that it is,[2]
> While nothing is not: that is exactly what I bid
>   you to meditate.
> For such is the first road of investigation from
>   which ⟨I keep⟩ you ⟨away⟩,
> But then also from this one,[3] which mortals who
>   know nothing
> Invent (*plattontai*),[4] two-headed [scil. creatures]!   5
>   For the helplessness in their
> Breast directs their wandering (*plankton*)
>   thought; and they are borne along,
> Deaf and likewise blind, stupefied, tribes
>   undecided [or: without judgment],
> Who suppose that "this is and is not" [or: that to
>   be and not to be] is the same
> And not the same, and that of all things [or: for
>   all] the path is backward-turning.[5]

[1] Or else: "It is necessary to say and to think this: that being [i.e. that which is] is." Several recent editors accept the transmitted text, translating either "It is necessary to say that this, and to think that this, is being," or "It is necessary to say this and to think this, viz. that being is."   [2] Or: "for being is" vel sim. But it is difficult to suppose that a nonsubstantivized infinitive could be the subject of a verb.   [3] Or, adopting other supplements instead of Diels': "for such is the first road of investigation [i.e. the one indicated in lines 1–2a] by which ⟨you [or: I] will begin⟩, / But then also from this one [scil. corresponding to the latter part of the poem]."   [4] Or: "where mortals . . . wander."   [5] Probably an allusion to Heraclitus, cf. **HER. D65, R15.**

D8 (B7 et B8) v. 1–2: Plat. *Soph.* 237a et 258d; Simpl. *In Phys.*, pp. 244.1–2, 135.21–22, 143.30–144.1 (et al.); v. 1: Arist. *Metaph.* N2 1089a4; v. 2–7a (. . . λείπεται): Sext. *Adv. Math.* 7.111 (et al.); v. 6b (μόνος . . .)–57: Simpl. *In Phys.*, pp. 145.1–146.25 (et al.); v. 48–50: Plat. *Soph.* 244e; v. 55–66: Simpl. *In Phys.*, pp. 38.30–39.9; v. 58–64: Simpl. *In Phys.*, pp. 30.23–31.2, 180.1–7 (et al.)

[B7.1]   οὐ γὰρ μήποτε τοῦτο δαμῇ εἶναι μὴ ἐόντα·
           ἀλλὰ σὺ τῆσδ᾽ ἀφ᾽ ὁδοῦ διζήσιος εἶργε νόημα
           μηδέ σ᾽ ἔθος πολύπειρον ὁδὸν κατὰ τήνδε
              βιάσθω
           νωμᾶν ἄσκοπον ὄμμα καὶ ἠχήεσσαν ἀκουήν
     5   καὶ γλῶσσαν, κρῖναι δὲ λόγῳ πολύδηριν
              ἔλεγχον
           ἐξ ἐμέθεν ῥηθέντα. [B8] μόνος δ᾽ ἔτι μῦθος
              ὁδοῖο
           λείπεται ὡς ἔστιν· ταύτῃ δ᾽ ἐπὶ σήματ᾽ ἔασι
           πολλὰ μάλ᾽, ὡς ἀγένητον ἐὸν καὶ ἀνώλεθρόν
              ἐστιν,
           οὖλον μουνογενές τε καὶ ἀτρεμὲς ἠδ᾽ ἀτέλεστον·
10 [B8.5] οὐδέ ποτ᾽ ἦν οὐδ᾽ ἔσται, ἐπεὶ νῦν ἔστιν ὁμοῦ
              πᾶν,

1 τοῦτο δαμῇ Ar. EJ, Simpl. *In Phys.* p. 135 (E), p. 143 (DE), p. 244 (E): τοῦτ᾽ οὐ δαμῇ (vel τοῦτ᾽ οὐδαμῇ vel -ῇ) Plat., Ar. Aᵇ, Simpl. p. 244 (F)   9 οὖλον μουνογενές Clem. Alex. *Strom.* 5.112.2; Simpl. (μονογενές) *In Cael.* p. 556, *In Phys.* p. 29 (DE), p. 120 (D), p. 145 (E), al.: ἔστι γὰρ οὐλομελές Plut. *Adv. Col.* 1114C: μοῦνον, μουνογενές Eus. *PE* 13.13.39 et al.: alii alia

D8 (B7, B8)[1] Plato, *Sophist;* Sextus Empiricus, *Against the Logicians;* Simplicius, *Commentary on Aristotle's Physics* (et al.)

For never at all could you master this: that things that are not are.	[B7.1]
But as for you, keep your thought away from this road of investigation	
And do not let much-experienced [or: much-experiencing] **habit force you down onto this road,**	
To wield an aimless eye and an echoing ear	
And tongue—no, by the argument (*logos*) **decide the much-disputed refutation** (*elenkhos*)	5
Spoken by me. [B8] There only remains the word of the path [scil. that says]:	
"Is." On this one there are signs,	
Very many of them: that being, it [or: that what is] **is ungenerated, indestructible,**	
Complete, single-born, untrembling and unending [scil. probably: in time].[2]	
And was not, nor will it be at some time, since it is now, together, whole,	10 [B8.5]

[1] The two fragments were separated by Diels despite the citation by Sextus, which allows them to be combined.   [2] Given that Parmenides' being is elsewhere considered to be limited ("not . . . incomplete," **D8.37**), many interpreters consider this term to be corrupt.

ἀτέλεστον Simpl. *In Phys.* p. 30, p. 78 (ἀτέλευτον ed. Ald.): ἀγένητον Simpl. *In Cael.* p. 556, *In Phys.* p. 120, Plut. *Adv. Col.* 1114C, Clem. Alex. *Strom.* 5.112.2, Eus. *PE* 13.13.39, al.

ἕν, συνεχές· τίνα γὰρ γένναν διζήσεαι αὐτοῦ;
πῇ πόθεν αὐξηθέν; οὔτ' ἐκ μὴ ἐόντος ἐάσω
φάσθαι σ' οὐδὲ νοεῖν· οὐ γὰρ φατὸν οὐδὲ
    νοητόν
ἔστιν ὅπως οὐκ ἔστι. τί δ' ἄν μιν καὶ χρέος
    ὦρσεν
15   ὕστερον ἢ πρόσθεν, τοῦ μηδενὸς ἀρξάμενον,
[B8.10]   φῦν;
οὕτως ἢ πάμπαν πέλεναι χρεών ἐστιν ἢ οὐχί.
οὐδέ ποτ' ἐκ μὴ ἐόντος ἐφήσει πίστιος ἰσχύς
γίγνεσθαί τι παρ' αὐτό· τοῦ εἵνεκεν οὔτε
    γενέσθαι
οὔτ' ὄλλυσθαι ἀνῆκε Δίκη χαλάσασα πέδησιν,
20   ἀλλ' ἔχει· ἡ δὲ κρίσις περὶ τούτων ἐν τῷδ'
[B8.15]   ἔστιν·
ἔστιν ἢ οὐκ ἔστιν· κέκριται δ' οὖν, ὥσπερ
    ἀνάγκη,
τὴν μὲν ἐᾶν ἀνόητον ἀνώνυμον (οὐ γὰρ ἀληθής
ἔστιν ὁδός), τὴν δ' ὥστε πέλειν καὶ ἐτήτυμον
    εἶναι.
πῶς δ' ἂν ἔπειτα πέλοι τὸ ἐόν; πῶς δ' ἄν κε
    γένοιτο;

17 ἐκ μὴ ἐόντος Diels: ἐκ (vel ἔκ γε) μὴ ὄντος Simpl. *In Phys.* p. 78, 145: ἐκ τοῦ ἐόντος Karsten   24 ἔπειτα πέλοι τὸ mss. (πέλοιτο F): ἔπειτ' ἀπόλοιτο Kranz post Karsten et Stein

---

[3] Many interpreters, relying especially on the paraphrase that Simplicius seems to be making of this passage (cf. **R21**), correct to "out of what is."

44

One, continuous. For what birth could you seek
    for it?
How, from what could it have grown? Not from
    what is not—I shall not allow
You to say nor to think this: for it cannot be said
    nor thought
That "is not"; and what need could have
    impelled it
To grow later rather than sooner, if it had had   15
    nothing for its beginning?   [B8.10]
So it is necessary that it either be completely or
    not at all.
And neither will any force of belief (*pistis*) ever
    affirm that out of what is not[3]
Something is born besides itself. That is why
    Justice
Has not, loosening its fetters, allowed it either
    to be born or to be destroyed,
But holds it fast. The decision (*krisis*) on these   20
    matters depends upon this: [B8.15]
"Is" or "is not"? Well, it has been decided, as is
    necessary,
To abandon the one [scil. road] as unthinkable,
    unnameable (for it is not
The true road), and [scil. deciding] thereby that
    the other, by consequence, exists and is
    real.[4]
How then could what is exist afterward? And
    how could it be born?

---

[4] Or: "to admit that the one [scil. road] is unthinkable . . . and
[scil. to admit] thereby that the other exists. . . ."

25
[B8.20] εἰ γὰρ ἔγεντ᾽, οὐκ ἔστ᾽ οὐδ᾽ εἴ ποτε μέλλει
        ἔσεσθαι.
        τὼς γένεσις μὲν ἀπέσβεσται καὶ ἄπυστος
        ὄλεθρος.
        οὐδὲ διαιρετόν ἐστιν, ἐπεὶ πᾶν ἐστιν ὁμοῖον·
        οὐδέ τι τῇ μᾶλλον, τό κεν εἴργοι μιν
        συνέχεσθαι,
        οὐδέ τι χειρότερον, πᾶν δ᾽ ἔμπλεόν ἐστιν
        ἐόντος.
30
[B8.25] τῷ ξυνεχὲς πᾶν ἐστιν· ἐὸν γὰρ ἐόντι πελάζει.
        αὐτὰρ ἀκίνητον μεγάλων ἐν πείρασι δεσμῶν
        ἔστιν ἄναρχον ἄπαυστον, ἐπεὶ γένεσις καὶ
        ὄλεθρος
        τῆλε μάλ᾽ ἐπλάχθησαν, ἀπῶσε δὲ πίστις
        ἀληθής.
        ταὐτὸν τ᾽ ἐν ταὐτῷ τε μένον καθ᾽ ἑαυτό τε
        κεῖται
35
[B8.30] χοὕτως ἔμπεδον αὖθι μένει· κρατερὴ γὰρ
        Ἀνάγκη
        πείρατος ἐν δεσμοῖσιν ἔχει, τό μιν ἀμφὶς
        ἐέργει,
        οὕνεκεν οὐκ ἀτελεύτητον τὸ ἐὸν θέμις εἶναι·
        ἔστι γὰρ οὐκ ἐπιδευές· ἐὸν δ᾽ ἂν παντὸς ἐδεῖτο.
        ταὐτὸν δ᾽ ἐστὶ νοεῖν τε καὶ οὕνεκεν ἔστι νόημα.

38 ἐπιδευές Simpl. *In Phys.* p. 30 (EF), p. 40 (E[a] ed. Ald.),
p. 146: ἐπιδεές Simpl. p. 40 (DEF), p. 30 (DE)   μὴ post
ἐπιδευές del. Bergk

46

For if it was born, it is not, not any more than if 25
    it is going to be someday. [B8.20]
In this way birth is extinguished, and
    unknowable destruction.
Nor is it divisible, since as a whole it is similar,
Nor at all more here, which would prevent it
    from cohering,
Nor at all weaker, but as a whole it is full of
    being.
That is why as a whole it is continuous: for what 30
    is is adjacent to what is. [B8.25]
Moreover, motionless within the limits of its
    great bonds,
It is without beginning, without ending, since
    birth and destruction
Went wandering very far away—true belief
    (*pistis*) thrust them away.
Remaining the same and in the same [scil. place],
    it rests in itself
And thus remains stable there; for powerful 35
    Necessity [B8.30]
Holds it fast within the bonds of the limit, which
    confines it on all sides [or: keeps it separate].
That is why it is not allowed that what is (*to eon*)
    be incomplete.
For it is not lacking [scil. something]; if it were, it
    would lack everything.
This is the same: to think and the thought that
    "is."

40
[B8.35]

οὐ γὰρ ἄνευ τοῦ ἐόντος, ἐν ᾧ πεφατισμένον
     ἐστίν,
εὑρήσεις τὸ νοεῖν· οὐδὲν γὰρ ⟨ἢ⟩ ἔστιν ἢ ἔσται
ἄλλο πάρεξ τοῦ ἐόντος, ἐπεὶ τό γε Μοῖρ᾽
     ἐπέδησεν
οὖλον ἀκίνητόν τ᾽ ἔμεναι· τῷ πάντ᾽ ὄνομ᾽ ἔσται,
ὅσσα βροτοὶ κατέθεντο πεποιθότες εἶναι ἀληθῆ,

45
[B8.40]

γίγνεσθαί τε καὶ ὄλλυσθαι, εἶναί τε καὶ οὐχί,
καὶ τόπον ἀλλάσσειν διά τε χρόα φανὸν
     ἀμείβειν.
αὐτὰρ ἐπεὶ πεῖρας πύματον, τετελεσμένον ἐστί
πάντοθεν, εὐκύκλου σφαίρης ἐναλίγκιον ὄγκῳ,
μεσσόθεν ἰσοπαλὲς πάντη· τὸ γὰρ οὔτε τι
     μεῖζον

50
[B8.45]

οὔτε τι βαιότερον πελέναι χρεών ἐστι τῇ ἢ τῇ.
οὔτε γὰρ οὐκ ἐὸν ἔστι, τό κεν παύοι μιν
     ἱκνεῖσθαι
εἰς ὁμόν, οὔτ᾽ ἐὸν ἔστιν ὅπως εἴη κεν ἐόντος
τῇ μᾶλλον τῇ δ᾽ ἧσσον, ἐπεὶ πᾶν ἐστιν ἄσυλον·
οἷ γὰρ πάντοθεν ἶσον, ὁμῶς ἐν πείρασι κύρει.

41 οὐδὲν γὰρ Simpl. *In Phys.* p. 86: οὐδ᾽ εἰ χρόνος ἐστὶ
Simpl. p. 146: οὐδὲ χρόνος Coxon   ⟨ἢ⟩ Preller   43 ὄνομ᾽
ἔσται Simpl. *In Phys.* p. 87 (F): οὔνομα ἔσται (D): ὄνομ᾽ ἐστὶν
p. 146 ed. Ald.; cf. ὄνομ᾽ εἶναι Plat. *Theaet.* 180e et al.: ὀνόμασται Simpl. *In Phys.* p. 87 (E), p. 146 (DE): ὠνόμασται p. 146
(F)   50 χρεών Simpl. p. 146, p. 52, p. 89, Plat. *Soph.* 244e YW:
χρεόν Plat. BT   52 κεν Brandis: καὶ ἐν mss.: κενὸν ed. Ald.

---

5 Or, with another reading: "it is in virtue of this [scil. of that
which is] that all things have been named."

For without what is, in which it [scil. thinking] **is spoken,**   40
                                                                          [B8.35]
You will not find thinking. For nothing else
     ‹**either**› **is or will be**
Besides what is, since Destiny has bound this
To be whole and unmovable: so that a [scil. mere] **name will be all the things**[5]
About which mortals have established, convinced that they are true,
That they are born and are destroyed,[6] **are and are not,**   45
                                                                       [B8.40]
Change their place and modify their bright color.
Moreover, since its limit is most distant, it is completed
On every side, similar to the volume of a well-rounded ball,
Everywhere balanced equally starting from its center: for it must be
Neither at all bigger nor at all smaller here than there.   50
                                                                   [B8.45]
For neither is there nonbeing (*ouk eon*), **which could stop it from reaching**
What is similar to it; nor is there being so that of being there would be
More here and less there, since as a whole it is inviolable.
For, equal to itself on every side, it maintains itself in its limits, similarly.

---

[6] Or: "all the things that mortals have posited, convinced that they are true, / Are born and are destroyed. . . ."

55
[B8.50]

ἐν τῷ σοι παύω πιστὸν λόγον ἠδὲ νόημα
ἀμφὶς ἀληθείης· δόξας δ' ἀπὸ τοῦδε βροτείας
μάνθανε κόσμον ἐμῶν ἐπέων ἀπατηλὸν ἀκούων.
μορφὰς γὰρ κατέθεντο δύο γνώμας ὀνομάζειν·
τῶν μίαν οὐ χρεών ἐστιν (ἐν ᾧ πεπλανημένοι
εἰσίν),

60
[B8.55]

ἀντία δ' ἐκρίναντο δέμας καὶ σήματ' ἔθεντο
χωρὶς ἀπ' ἀλλήλων, τῇ μὲν φλογὸς αἰθέριον
πῦρ,
ἤπιον ὄν, μέγ' ἐλαφρόν, ἑωυτῷ πάντοσε τωὐτόν,
τῷ δ' ἑτέρῳ μὴ τωὐτόν· ἀτὰρ κἀκεῖνο κατ' αὐτό
τἀντία νύκτ' ἀδαῆ, πυκινὸν δέμας ἐμβριθές τε.

65
[B8.60]

τόν σοι ἐγὼ διάκοσμον ἐοικότα πάντα φατίζω,
ὡς οὐ μή ποτέ τίς σε βροτῶν γνώμη
παρελάσσῃ.

58 γνώμας Simpl. p. 39: γνώμαις p. 30 (p. 39 ed. Ald.)
60 ἀντία Simpl. (ἐναντία p. 30 DE): τἀντία Diels (cf. v. 64)
62 post μέγ' habet ἀραιὸν Simpl. p. 30, del. (ut gloss.) Diels
65 φατίζω Simpl.: φατίσω Karsten

[Transition to the second part of the poem]

At this point, for you I stop the argument 55
    worthy of belief (*piston*) **and the thought** [B8.50]
    (*noêma*)
About truth; from here on learn mortal opinions
By listening to the deceptive arrangement of my
    words.
For they have established two forms to name
    their views,
Of which the one is not necessary[7]—**in this they**
    wander in error—
And they have divided their body into opposites 60
    and posited signs [B8.55]
Separate from each other: for the one, the
    ethereal fire of flame,
Being mild, very light in weight, the same as
    itself everywhere,
And not the same as the other one; and that one
    too, in itself,
The opposite, night without knowledge [or:
    without light]**, a dense and heavy body.**
I tell you this arrangement of the world, 65
    adapted (*eoikos*)[8] **in every point,** [B8.60]
So that no conception (*gnômê*) **of mortals might**
    ever get past you.

[7] The construction and meaning are controversial. We understand that the error of mortals consists in their relating the two forms distinguished to that which is and to that which is not, whereas both of them ought to be related to that which is.

[8] 'Adapted' or 'resembling' or both.

*Fragments and Reports from the Second Part of
the Poem: The Opinions of Mortals (D9–D62)
An Overview of the Contents of the
Second Part (D9)*

D9 (cf. ad B10) Plut. *Adv. Col.* 13 1114B–C

[. . .] Παρμενίδης [. . . = **R53a**] καὶ διάκοσμον πεποίη-
ται, καὶ στοιχεῖα μιγνύς, τὸ λαμπρὸν καὶ σκοτεινόν,
ἐκ τούτων τὰ φαινόμενα πάντα καὶ διὰ τούτων ἀποτε-
λεῖ. καὶ γὰρ περὶ γῆς εἴρηκε πολλὰ καὶ περὶ οὐρανοῦ
καὶ ἡλίου καὶ σελήνης καὶ ἄστρων καὶ γένεσιν ἀνθρώπων ἀφήγηται.[1]

[1] ἀφήρηται mss., corr. Wyttenbach

A Methodological Exhortation (D10)

D10 (B4) Clem. Alex. *Strom.* 5.15.5 (et al.)

λεῦσσε δ' ὅμως ἀπεόντα νόῳ παρεόντα
  βεβαίως·
οὐ γὰρ ἀποτμήξει τὸ ἐὸν τοῦ ἐόντος ἔχεσθαι
οὔτε σκιδνάμενον πάντῃ πάντως κατὰ κόσμον
οὔτε συνιστάμενον. ∪ ∪ | – ∪ ∪ | – ∪ ∪ | – –

1 λεῦσσε Theod. *Cur.* 1.72 (BL): λεῦσε ms.

PARMENIDES

*Fragments and Reports from the Second Part of
the Poem: The Opinions of Mortals (D9–D62)
An Overview of the Contents of the
Second Part (D9)*

D9 (cf. ad B10) Plutarch, *Against Colotes*

Parmenides [. . .] has also described in his poem the arrangement of the world, and after he has mixed the elements, the bright and the dark, he produces all the phenomena out of them and by means of them. For he has
said many things about the earth, the heavens, the sun, the
moon and the heavenly bodies, and he recounts the origin
of human beings.

A Methodological Exhortation (D10)

D10 (B4) Clement of Alexandria, *Stromata* (et al.)

**See these things, which, remote though they
  are, are firmly present to thought** (*noos*).
For you [or: it] **will not cut off what is from
  cohering with what is,**
**Whether it is dispersed completely everywhere
  throughout the world**
Or is collected together.

Announcements of the Explanation of
Heavenly Bodies (D11–D12)

D11 (B11) Simpl. *In Cael.*, p. 559.20–27

Παρμενίδης δὲ περὶ τῶν αἰσθητῶν "ἄρξασθαί" φησι
"λέγειν"

– ∪ ∪ | – πῶς γαῖα καὶ ἥλιος ἠδὲ σελήνη
αἰθήρ τε ξυνὸς γάλα τ᾽ οὐράνιον καὶ Ὄλυμπος
ἔσχατος ἠδ᾽ ἄστρων θερμὸν μένος ὡρμήθησαν
γίγνεσθαι ∪ ∪ | – ∪ ∪ | – ∪ ∪ | – ∪ ∪ | – –

καὶ τῶν γινομένων καὶ φθειρομένων μέχρι τῶν μορίων
τῶν ζῴων τὴν γένεσιν παραδίδωσι.[1]

[1] παραδίδωσι DE: παραδεδώκασι A

D12 (B10) Clem. Alex. *Strom.* 5.138.1

εἴσῃ δ᾽ αἰθερίαν τε φύσιν τά τ᾽ ἐν αἰθέρι πάντα
σήματα καὶ καθαρᾶς εὐαγέος ἠελίοιο
λαμπάδος ἔργ᾽ ἀΐδηλα καὶ ὁππόθεν ἐξεγένοντο,
ἔργα τε κύκλωπος πεύσῃ περίφοιτα σελήνης
5   καὶ φύσιν, εἰδήσεις δὲ καὶ οὐρανὸν ἀμφὶς
        ἔχοντα

---

[1] The term can mean 'destructive,' 'completely visible,' or else 'hidden.'   [2] The heavens, in the restricted sense that Parmenides gives the term (**D23**, cf. **D18**), separate Olympus on high from the lower regions.

Announcements of the Explanation of
Heavenly Bodies (D11–D12)

D11 (B11) Simplicius, *Commentary on Aristotle's* On the Heavens

Regarding the sensibles, Parmenides says that he "begins to say"[1]

> **How the earth, the sun and the moon,**
> **The aether in common and the heavenly milk, farthest**
> **Olympus and the hot strength of the stars strove**
> **To be born**

and he teaches the origin of the things that are born and are destroyed, all the way to the parts of animals.

[1] Simplicius surely paraphrases the words that preceded the lines he is about to cite.

D12 (B10) Clement of Alexandria, *Stromata*

> **You will know the aethereal nature, and in the aether all**
> **The signs, and of the pure torch of the brilliant sun**
> **The blinding works,[1] and from where they are born,**
> **And you will learn the recurrent [or: wandering] works of the round-eyed moon**
> **And its nature, and you will also know from where the sky, which is on both sides,[2]**   5

ἔνθεν ἔφυ τε καὶ ὥς μιν ἄγουσ᾽ ἐπέδησεν
  Ἀνάγκη
πείρατ᾽ ἔχειν ἄστρων. ∪ ∪ | – ∪ ∪ | – ∪ ∪ | – –

6 μὲν γὰρ post ἔνθεν hab. ms.: del. Sylburg

Light and Night (D13)

D13 (B9) Simpl. *In Phys.*, p. 180.9–12

αὐτὰρ ἐπειδὴ πάντα φάος καὶ νὺξ ὀνόμασται
καὶ τὰ κατὰ σφετέρας δυνάμεις ἐπὶ τοῖσί τε καὶ
  τοῖς,
πᾶν πλέον ἐστὶν ὁμοῦ φάεος καὶ νυκτὸς
  ἀφάντου
ἴσων ἀμφοτέρων, ἐπεὶ οὐδετέρῳ μέτα μηδέν.

1 ὀνόμασται F¹: ὠνόμασται DE F²

The Beginnings of the Cosmogonic Process: The Wreaths, the Cosmogonic Divinity, and Other Gods (D14–D17)

D14 (B12)

a Simpl. *In Phys.*, p. 39.12–13

μετ᾽ ὀλίγα [scil. **D8.66**] δὲ πάλιν περὶ τῶν δυεῖν στοιχείων εἰπὼν ἐπάγει καὶ τὸ ποιητικὸν λέγων οὕτως [. . .
= **D14b.1–3**].

Was born and how Necessity led and enchained
   it
To maintain the limits of the heavenly bodies.

Light and Night (D13)

D13 (B9) Simplicius, *Commentary on Aristotle's* Physics

But since all things have been named light and
   night
And what belongs to their powers is assigned to
   these and to those,
The whole is altogether full of light and of
   ungleaming night,
Both of them equal, since nothing is amidst
   either of them.

*The Beginnings of the Cosmogonic Process: The
Wreaths, the Cosmogonic Divinity, and Other
Gods (D14–D17)*

D14 (B12)

a Simplicius, *Commentary on Aristotle's* Physics

A little after, having spoken once again about the two elements, he introduces the efficient [scil. cause] too, saying
[. . . = **D14b.1–3**].

b v. 1–3: Simpl. *In Phys.*, p. 39.14–16; v. 2–6: Simpl. *In Phys.*, p. 31.13–17

αἱ γὰρ στεινότεραι πλῆντο πυρὸς ἀκρήτοιο,
αἱ δ' ἐπὶ ταῖς νυκτός, μετὰ δὲ φλογὸς ἵεται
αἶσα·
ἐν δὲ μέσῳ τούτων δαίμων ἣ πάντα κυβερνᾷ·
πάντων γὰρ στυγεροῖο τόκου καὶ μίξιος ἄρχει
5   πέμπουσ' ἄρσενι θῆλυ μιγῆν τό τ' ἐναντίον
αὖτις
ἄρσεν θηλυτέρῳ. ∪ ∪ | – ∪ ∪ | – ∪ ∪ | – –

1 πλῆντο Bergk: παηντο Eᵃ: πάηντο D¹: πύηντο D²E: om.
F   ἀκρήτοιο Stein: ἀκρήτοις D Eᵃ: ἀκρίτοις EF: ἀκρίτοιο
ed. Ald.   4 πάντων γὰρ W: πάντα γὰρ DEF: πάντῃ γὰρ
Mullach: πᾶσιν γὰρ Stein: πάντα γὰρ ⟨ἣ⟩ Diels   ἄρχει
DE: ἀρχὴ F   5 μιγῆν Bergk et Stein: μιγέν mss.

D15 (< A37)

a Aët. 2.7.1 (Stob., Ps.-Plut. usque στερεὸν ὑπάρχειν)
[περὶ τάξεως τοῦ κόσμου]

Παρμενίδης στεφάνας εἶναι περιπεπλεγμένας ἐπαλλήλους,¹ τὴν μὲν ἐκ τοῦ ἀραιοῦ, τὴν δὲ ἐκ τοῦ πυκνοῦ·
μικτὰς δὲ ἄλλας² ἐκ³ φωτὸς καὶ σκότους μεταξὺ
τούτων· καὶ τὸ περιέχον δὲ πάσας τείχους δίκην στερεὸν ὑπάρχειν, ὑφ' ᾧ πυρώδης στεφάνη· καὶ τὸ με-
σαίτατον πασῶν περὶ ὃ⁴ πάλιν πυρώδης· τῶν δὲ συμ-
μιγῶν τὴν μεσαιτάτην ἁπάσαις †τε καὶ†⁵ πάσης

b Simplicius, *Commentary on Aristotle's* Physics

**For the narrower ones were filled with unmixed
fire,**
**The next ones with night, and afterward [or:
among these] there rushes a portion of flame.**
**And in the middle of these, the divinity who
steers all things.**
**For she begins the hateful birth and mingling of
all things,**
Leading the female to mingle with the male and 5
again, in the opposite direction,
The male with the female.

D15 (< A37)

a Aëtius

Parmenides: there are wreaths intertwined with one another, the one made out of the thin [scil. element], the
other out of the dense one; and others, mixed out of light
and darkness, are between these. What surrounds them
all like a rampart is solid, under this is a fiery [scil. wreath];
and this is also the case of the most central point of them
all, around which once again there is a fiery [scil. wreath].
The most central of the mixed [scil. wreaths] is for all of

---

¹ ἐπαλλήλους Stob. Plut MΠ: ἐπ' ἀλλήλας Plut. m: ἐπ' ἀλ-
λήλαις Plut. Laur. 31.37   ² ἀλλήλας Plut. mss. (sed ἄλλας
Eus. *PE* 15.38.1)   ³ ἐκ Plut., deest in Stob.   ⁴ περὶ ὅ
Boeckh: περὶ ὄν F: περὶ ὧν P: post πασῶν coni. lac. Diels
⁵ locus corruptus: ἁπάσαις τοκέα Davis: ἁπάσαις αἰτίαν
Krische: ἀρχὴν τε καὶ αἰτίαν Diels: alii alia

κινήσεως καὶ γενέσεως ὑπάρχειν, ἥντινα καὶ δαίμονα
κυβερνῆτιν καὶ κληροῦχον[6] ἐπονομάζει, δίκην τε καὶ
ἀνάγκην [. . . = **D18**].

⁶ κληροῦχον mss.: κληδοῦχον Fülleborn

b Cic. *Nat. deor.* 1.28

nam Parmenides quidem commenticium[1] quiddam: coro-
nae similem[2] efficit (στεφάνην appellat), continentem
ardorum[3] lucis[4] orbem, qui cingit caelum, quem appellat
deum [. . . = **D17**].

¹ commenticium *dett. Rom. Ven.*, conventicium *ADHPOB
FM*, conventium *N*   ² simile *OM²*, similitudinem *P*
³ ardorum *B¹*, ardorem *cett.*   ⁴ lucis *del. Pease*

D16 (B13) Simpl. *In Phys.*, p. 39.17–19

ταύτην καὶ θεῶν αἰτίαν εἶναί φησι λέγων

πρώτιστον μὲν Ἔρωτα θεῶν μητίσατο πάντων

καὶ τὰ ἑξῆς [. . . = **D61**].

D17 (< A37) Cic. *Nat. deor.* 1.28

[. . . = **D15b**] multaque eiusdem monstra, quippe qui
bellum, qui discordiam, qui cupiditatem, ceteraque generis eiusdem ad deum revocat [. . .]; eademque de sideribus
[. . . cf. **R59**].

them ⟨cause?⟩ of all movement and generation, which he also calls 'the divinity who steers' and 'the portion holder,'[1] 'justice' and 'necessity.'

[1] Or, emending: 'the key holder' (cf. **D4.14**).

b Cicero, *On the Nature of the Gods*

For Parmenides [scil. produces] a fiction: something similar to a wreath (he calls it *stephanê*), a continuous circle of the flames of [or: of the heat of the] light that encircles the heaven; he calls this god [. . .].

D16 (B13) Simplicius, *Commentary on Aristotle's* Physics (et al.[1])

He says that it [i.e. the divinity of **D14b.3**] is also the cause of the gods, when he says:

> **She[2] devised Eros as the very first of all the gods**

and what follows [. . .].

[1] This line is also cited by Plato and Aristotle, among others; see **R56–R57.**   [2] Plutarch identifies this divinity with Aphrodite; see **R58.**

D17 (< A37) Cicero, *On the Nature of the Gods*

[. . .] and there are many monstrosities of the same man, for he assigns war, discord, greed, and the other things of this sort to a god [. . .]; and the same for the stars [. . .].

Genesis and Order of the World:
A General Summary (D18)

D18 (< A37) Aët. 2.7.1 (Stob.) [περὶ τάξεως τοῦ κόσμου]

[. . . = **D15a**] καὶ τῆς μὲν γῆς ἀπόκρισιν εἶναι τὸν ἀέρα, διὰ τὴν βιαιοτέραν αὐτῆς ἐξατμισθέντα πίλησιν, τοῦ δὲ πυρὸς ἀναπνοὴν τὸν ἥλιον καὶ τὸν γαλαξίαν κύκλον· συμμιγῆ δ' ἐξ ἀμφοῖν εἶναι τὴν σελήνην, τοῦ τ' ἀέρος καὶ τοῦ πυρός. περιστάντος δ' ἀνωτάτω πάντων τοῦ αἰθέρος ὑπ' αὐτῷ τὸ πυρῶδες ὑποταγῆναι τοῦθ' ὅπερ κεκλήκαμεν οὐρανόν, ὑφ' ᾧ[1] ἤδη τὰ περίγεια.

[1] ᾧ Krische: οὐ mss.

Genesis and Order of the World:
The Constitutive Parts (D19–D39)
Heavens (D19)

D19 (< A38) Aët. 2.11.4 (Stob.) [περὶ τῆς οὐρανοῦ οὐσίας]

Παρμενίδης [. . .] πύρινον εἶναι τὸν οὐρανόν.

Heavenly Bodies (D20)

D20 (< A39) Aët. 2.13.8 (Stob.) [περὶ οὐσίας ἄστρων]

Παρμενίδης [. . .] πιλήματα πυρὸς τὰ ἄστρα.

Genesis and Order of the World:
A General Summary (D18)

D18 (< A37) Aëtius

[. . .] The air has separated out from the earth; it has evaporated because of the very violent pressure exerted upon it, while the sun and the Milky Way are an exhalation of fire. The moon is a mixture of both of them, of air and of fire. The aether occupies in a circle the highest position of all; below it is arranged the fiery [scil. region], which is what we call the sky; and under this finally are located the [scil. regions] that surround the earth.

Genesis and Order of the World:
The Constitutive Parts (D19–D39)
Heavens (D19)

D19 (< A38) Aëtius

Parmenides [. . .]: the heavens are fiery.

Heavenly Bodies (D20)

D20 (< A39) Aëtius

Parmenides [. . .]: the heavenly bodies are concentrations of fire.

Fixed Stars (D21)

D21 (< A40) Anon. *Introd. Arat.* 14

[. . .] τῶν μὲν ἀπλανῶν [. . .] τὰ μὲν ἀκατονόμαστα
ἡμῖν καὶ ἀπερίληπτα, ὡς καὶ Παρμενίδης ὁ φυσικὸς
εἴρηκε [. . .].

The Evening Star—The Morning Star (Venus)
(D22–D23)

D22 (< A1, cf. A40a) Diog. Laert. 9.23

καὶ δοκεῖ πρῶτος πεφωρακέναι τὸν αὐτὸν εἶναι Ἕσπερον καὶ Φωσφόρον, ὥς φησι Φαβωρῖνος ἐν πέμπτῳ
Ἀπομνημονευμάτων [Frag. 54 Amato]· οἱ δὲ Πυθαγόραν.

D23 (A40a) Aët. 2.15.7 (Stob.) [περὶ ταξέως ἀστέρων]

Παρμενίδης πρῶτον μὲν τάττει τὸν ἑῷον, τὸν αὐτὸν δὲ
νομιζόμενον ὑπ' αὐτοῦ καὶ ἕσπερον, ἐν τῷ αἰθέρι· μεθ'
ὃν τὸν ἥλιον, ὑφ' ᾧ τοὺς ἐν τῷ πυρώδει ἀστέρας, ὅπερ
οὐρανὸν καλεῖ.

Milky Way (D24)

D24 (A43a) Aët. 3.1.4 (Ps.-Plut.) [περὶ τοῦ γαλαξίου
κύκλου]

Παρμενίδης τὸ τοῦ πυκνοῦ καὶ ἀραιοῦ μίγμα γαλα-
κτοειδὲς ἀποτελέσαι χρῶμα.

Fixed Stars (D21)

D21 (< A40) Anonymous Introduction to Aratus' *Phaenomena*

[. . .] of the fixed stars [. . .], some are not named by us and cannot be apprehended [or: counted], as Parmenides the natural philosopher says too [. . .].

The Evening Star—The Morning Star (Venus) (D22–D23)

D22 (< A1, cf. A40a) Diogenes Laertius

He seems to have been the first person to have discovered that the evening star and the one that brings the light are the same, as Favorinus says in the fifth book of his *Memoirs;* others say that it was Pythagoras [cf. **PYTH. c D14**].

D23 (A40a) Aëtius

Parmenides puts in first place the morning star, which he considers to be the same as the evening star, in the aether; after this the sun, and under this latter the heavenly bodies of the fiery [scil. region], which he calls **'sky'** [cf. **D11**].

Milky Way (D24)

D24 (A43a) Aëtius

Parmenides: the mixture of the dense and the thin produces the milky color [scil. of the Milky Way].

Birth of the Sun and Moon (D25)

D25 (A43) Aët. 2.20.8a (Stob.) [περὶ οὐσίας ἡλίου]

Παρμενίδης τὸν ἥλιον καὶ τὴν σελήνην ἐκ τοῦ γαλαξίου κύκλου ἀποκριθῆναι, τὸν μὲν ἀπὸ τοῦ ἀραιοτέ-
ρου μίγματος, ὃ δὴ θερμόν, τὴν δὲ ἀπὸ τοῦ πυκνο-
τέρου, ὅπερ ψυχρόν.

The Sun: Its Nature (D26)

D26 (< A41) Aët. 2.20.8 (Stob.) [περὶ οὐσίας ἡλίου]

Παρμενίδης [. . .] πύρινον ὑπάρχειν τὸν ἥλιον.

The Moon: Its Nature, Size, and Appearance
(D27–D31)

D27 (B14) Plut. *Adv. Col.* 15 1116A

[. . .] τὴν σελήνην [. . .] κατὰ Παρμενίδην

   **νυκτὶ φάος περὶ γαῖαν ἀλώμενον ἀλλότριον
   φῶς**

   νυκτὶ φάος mss.: νυκτιφαὲς Scaliger

D28 (B15) Plut. *Fac. orb. lun.* 16.6 929B

   αἰεὶ παπταίνουσα πρὸς αὐγὰς ἠελίοιο

PARMENIDES

Birth of the Sun and Moon (D25)

D25 (A43) Aëtius

Parmenides: the sun and the moon were separated out
from the Milky Way, the former from the thinner mixture,
which is hot, the latter from the denser one, which is cold.

The Sun: Its Nature (D26)

D26 (< A41) Aëtius

Parmenides [. . .]: the sun is fiery.

The Moon: Its Nature, Size, and Appearance
(D27–D31)

D27 (B14) Plutarch, *Against Colotes*

[. . .] the moon [. . .] according to Parmenides,

> **A light (*phaos*) in the night wandering around
> the earth, a light (*phôs*) from elsewhere**[1]

[1] *Phôs* is a homonym of the Homeric term designating a mortal in the formula *allotrion phôs* ('a man from elsewhere').

D28 (B15) Plutarch, *On the Face in the Moon*

> **Always gazing toward the rays of the sun**

D29 (A42) Aët. 2.26.2 (Ps.-Plut.) [περὶ μεγέθους σελή-
νης]

Παρμενίδης ἴσην τῷ ἡλίῳ, καὶ ἀπ᾽ αὐτοῦ φωτίζεσθαι.

D30 (A42) Aët. 2.25.3 (Stob.; cf. Theod.) [περὶ σελήνης
οὐσίας]

Παρμενίδης πυρίνην.

D31 (B21) Aët. 2.30.4 (Stob.) [περὶ ἐμφάσεως αὐτῆς]

Παρμενίδης διὰ τὸ παραμεμῖχθαι τῷ περὶ αὐτὴν πυρώδει τὸ ζοφῶδες, ὅθεν ψευδοφανῆ[1] τὸν ἀστέρα καλεῖ.

[1] ψευδοφανῆ mss: ψευδοφαῆ Meineke

The Earth (D32–D39)
Its Birth (D32)

D32 (< A22) Ps.-Plut. *Strom.* 5 (Eus. *PE* 1.8.5)

λέγει δὲ τὴν γῆν τοῦ πυκνοῦ καταρρυέντος ἀέρος γεγονέναι.

Its Shape and Position (D33–D35)

D33 Diog. Laert.

a (< A1) 9.21

πρῶτος δὲ οὗτος τὴν γῆν ἀπέφαινε σφαιροειδῆ καὶ ἐν
μέσῳ κεῖσθαι.

D29 (A42) Aëtius

Parmenides: [the moon is] equal in size to the sun, and it is illuminated by it.

D30 (A42) Aëtius

Parmenides: [the moon is] fiery.

D31 (B21) Aëtius

Parmenides: [scil. the fact that the moon seems to be similar to the earth is] because the dark is mixed with the fiery that surrounds it, and this is why he calls that heavenly body **'false-shining.'**

The Earth (D32–D39)
Its Birth (D32)

D32 (< A22) Ps.-Plutarch, *Stromata*

He says that the earth came to be when the dense air flowed down.

Its Shape and Position (D33–D35)

D33 Diogenes Laertius

a (< A1)

He was the first to assert that the earth is spherical in shape and rests in the center.

b (< A44) 8.48

ἀλλὰ μὴν καὶ τὸν οὐρανὸν πρῶτον ὀνομάσαι κόσμον καὶ τὴν γῆν στρογγύλην, ὡς δὲ Θεόφραστος [Frag. 227E FSH&G] Παρμενίδην [. . .].

D34 (≠ DK) Schol. in Bas. *Hex.* 26

τὴν γῆν ἀκίνητον ἔφη Παρμενίδης ὁ Ἐλεάτης [. . .].

D35 (B15a) Schol. in Bas. *Hex.* 25

Παρμενίδης ἐν τῇ στιχοποιίᾳ ὑδατόριζον εἶπεν τὴν γῆν.

Earthquakes (D36)

D36 (< A44) Aët. 3.15.7 (Ps.-Plut.) [περὶ σεισμῶν γῆς]

Παρμενίδης [. . .] διὰ τὸ πανταχόθεν ἴσον ἀφεστῶσαν μένειν ἐπὶ τῆς ἰσορροπίας, οὐκ ἔχουσαν αἰτίαν δι’ ἣν δεῦρο μᾶλλον ἢ ἐκεῖσε ῥέψειεν ἄν· διὰ τοῦτο μόνον μὲν κραδαίνεσθαι μὴ κινεῖσθαι δέ.

Zones (D37–39)

D37 (cf. A44a) Ach. Tat. *Introd. Arat.* 31

πρῶτος δὲ Παρμενίδης ὁ Ἐλεάτης τὸν[1] περὶ τῶν ζωνῶν ἐκίνησε λόγον.

---

[1] ὁ Ἐλεάτης τὸν Maass: ὁ στεατήν τον V, om. M

b (< A44)

He [i.e. Pythagoras] was the first to call the heavens *kosmos* [i.e. a beautiful organized whole] and the earth 'round' [cf. **PYTH. c D13**]; but according to Theophrastus, it was Parmenides [. . .].

D34 (≠ DK) Scholia on Basil's *Hexameron*

Parmenides of Elea said that the earth is immobile [. . .].

D35 (B15a) Scholia on Basil's *Hexameron*

Parmenides in his poem called the earth **'water-rooted.'**

Earthquakes (D36)

D36 (< A44) Aëtius

Parmenides [. . .]: it [i.e. the earth] stays in place because it is equally distant from everywhere on account of its balance, having no reason why it should incline more in one direction than in another. It is for this reason that it is only shaken, but not moved.

Zones (D37–39)

D37 (cf. A44a) Achilles Tatius, *Introduction to Aratus' Phaenomena*

Parmenides of Elea was the first to discuss the topic of the zones.

D38 (< A44a) Strabo 2.2.2

φησὶ δὴ ὁ Ποσειδώνιος [Frag. F49 Kidd] τῆς εἰς πέντε
ζώνας διαιρέσεως ἀρχηγὸν γενέσθαι Παρμενίδην·
ἀλλ᾽ ἐκεῖνον μὲν σχεδόν τι διπλασίαν ἀποφαίνειν τὸ
πλάτος τὴν διακεκαυμένην τῆς μεταξὺ τῶν τροπικῶν,[1]
ὑπερπίπτουσαν[2] ἑκατέρων τῶν τροπικῶν εἰς τὸ ἐκτὸς
καὶ πρὸς ταῖς εὐκράτοις [. . .].

[1] τῆς . . . τροπικῶν secl. Kramer   [2] ὑπερπίπτουσαν
Brequigny: -πιπτούσης mss.: -πίπτουσαν καὶ Groskurd

D39 (A44a) Aët. 3.11.4 (Ps.-Plut.) [περὶ θέσεως γῆς]

Παρμενίδης πρῶτος ἀφώρισε τῆς γῆς τοὺς οἰκουμέ-
νους τόπους ὑπὸ ταῖς δυσὶ ζώναις ταῖς τροπικαῖς.

Physiology (D40–D60)
Generation of Living Creatures (D40–D50)
The Role of Heat (D40–D43)

D40 (< A1) Diog. Laert. 9.22

γένεσίν τ᾽ ἀνθρώπων ἐξ ἡλίου[1] πρῶτον γενέσθαι· αὐτὸν[2] δὲ ὑπάρχειν τὸ θερμὸν καὶ τὸ ψυχρόν, ἐξ ὧν τὰ
πάντα συνεστάναι.

[1] ἡλίου mss.: ἰλύος Frobenius   [2] αὐτὸν mss.: αἴτια
Diels

D38 (< A44a) Strabo, *Geography*

Posidonius says that Parmenides was the initiator of the division into five zones; but that he asserted that the torrid zone was almost twice as large as the one lying between the tropics, extending beyond each of the two tropics outward into the temperate zones.

D39 (A44a) Aëtius

Parmenides was the first to define the inhabited parts of the earth below the two tropical zones.

Physiology (D40–D60)
Generation of Living Creatures (D40–D50)
The Role of Heat (D40–D43)

D40 (< A1) Diogenes Laertius

The genesis of human beings came about in the beginning from the sun; but he himself [i.e. the human being?] is[1] the hot and the cold, out of which all things are constituted.

[1] Or, emending: "the causes are . . ."

D41 (< A51) Cens. *Die nat.* 4.8

haec eadem opinio etiam in Parmenide Veliensi[1] fuit
pauculis exceptis ab Empedocle dissensis.[2]

[1] Veliensi *vel* Veliate *edd.*: *locus corruptus*   [2] *locus incertus*

D42 (A53) Aët. 5.7.2 (Ps.-Plut.) [πῶς ἄρρενα γεννᾶται
καὶ θήλεα]

Παρμενίδης ἀντιστρόφως· τὰ μὲν πρὸς τοῖς ἄρκτοις
ἄρρενα βλαστῆναι, τοῦ γὰρ πυκνοῦ μετέχειν[1] πλείο-
νος· τὰ δὲ πρὸς ταῖς μεσημβρίαις θήλεα παρὰ τὴν
ἀραιότητα.

[1] μετέχει mss., corr. Diels

D43 (< A52) Arist. *PA* 2.2 648a29–31

[. . .] Παρμενίδης τὰς γυναῖκας τῶν ἀνδρῶν θερμο-
τέρας εἶναί φησι καὶ ἕτεροί τινες, ὡς διὰ τὴν θερ-
μότητα καὶ πολυαιμούσαις γινομένων τῶν γυναικείων
[. . . = **EMP. D173b**].

Seed (D44–D45)

D44 (< 24 A13) Cens. *Die nat.* 5.4

illud quoque ambiguam facit inter auctores opinionem,
utrumne ex patris tantummodo semine partus nascatur
[. . .] an etiam ex matris, quod [. . .] Parmenidi [. . .] visum
est.

D41 (< A51) Censorinus, *The Birthday*

The same opinion [scil. as Empedocles', cf. **EMP. D172**] was held by Parmenides of Elea, with a very few exceptions in which he differed from Empedocles.

D42 (A53) Aëtius

It is the opposite for Parmenides [scil. from Empedocles, cf. **EMP. D174**]: males grow in the north, for they have a greater share in what is dense; females in the south, because of the thinness.

D43 (< A52) Aristotle, *Parts of Animals*

[. . .] Parmenides and some other people say that women are warmer than men, on the supposition that menstruation comes about because of heat and for women with abundant blood [. . .].[1]

1 Cf. Arist. *GA* 4.1 765b17–26.

Seed (D44–D45)

D44 (< 24 A13) Censorinus, *The Birthday*

The following question too causes a difference of opinion among the authorities: whether the child is born only from the father's seed [. . .] or also from the mother's, which is the opinion of [. . .] Parmenides [. . .].

D45 (A53) Cens. *Die nat.* 5.2

Parmenides enim tum ex dextris tum e laevis partibus id
ire[1] putavit.

> [1] *verba* id ire *fortasse corrupta*: oriri *ed. Rostoch.*

Determination of the Sex (D46–D48)

D46 (B17) Gal. *In Hipp. Epid.* 6.2.46, p. 119.12–15

τὸ μέντοι ἄρρεν ἐν τῷ δεξιῷ μέρει τῆς μήτρας κυΐσκε-
σθαι καὶ ἄλλοι τῶν παλαιοτάτων ἀνδρῶν εἰρήκασιν.
ὁ μὲν γὰρ Παρμενίδης οὕτως ἔφη,

> δεξιτεροῖσιν μὲν κούρους, λαιοῖσι δὲ κούρας

δεξιτεροῖσι mss., corr. Karsten   δὲ Karsten: δ᾽ αὖ mss.

D47 (< A53) Aët. 5.7.4 (Ps.-Plut.) [πῶς ἄρρενα γεννᾶται
καὶ θήλεα]

[. . .] Παρμενίδης τὰ μὲν ἐκ τῶν δεξιῶν καταβάλλε-
σθαι εἰς τὰ δεξιὰ μέρη τῆς μήτρας, τὰ δ᾽ ἐκ τῶν ἀρι-
στερῶν εἰς τὰ ἀριστερά· εἰ δ᾽ ἐναλλαγείη τὰ τῆς κα-
ταβολῆς, γίνεσθαι θήλεα.

D48 (A54) Cens. *Die nat.* 6.5

at inter se certare feminae et maris,[1] et penes utrum
victoria sit, eius habitum referri auctor est Parmenides.

D45 (A53) Censorinus, *The Birthday*

Parmenides thought that it [i.e. the seed] comes (?) sometimes from the right side, sometimes from the left.

Determination of the Sex (D46–D48)

D46 (B17) Galen, *Commentary on Hippocrates'* Epidemics

That the male is conceived in the right part of the womb has also been said by other very ancient men. For Parmenides said as follows:

On the right the boys, on the left the girls

D47 (< A53) Aëtius

[. . .] Parmenides: the ones [scil. seeds] that come from the right side are expelled into the right side of the womb, the ones from the left side into the left side. But if the expulsion is reversed, females are born.

D48 (A54) Censorinus, *The Birthday*

Parmenides established the doctrine that those [scil. probably: the seeds] of the female and of the male fight against each other and that it is the condition of the one that wins that is reproduced.

---

[1] feminae et maris *plerique*: feminas et mares V[2] (et *recc.*): mares et foeminas *L*: <semina> feminae *Giusta*

Determination of the Character (D49)

D49 (B18) Cael. Aurel. *Tard. Pass.* 4.9.134–35

Parmenides libris, quos de natura scripsit, eventu inquit conceptionis molles aliquando seu subactos homines generari. [. . .]

> femina, virque simul Veneris cum germina miscent,
> venis informans diverso ex sanguine virtus
> temperiem servans bene condita corpora fingit.
> nam si virtutes permixto semine pugnent
> 5   nec faciant unam permixto in corpore dirae,
> nascentem gemino vexabunt semine sexum.

2 informans *edd.*: conformans *coni. Diels*   4 nam *ed. Bas.*: at *edd. Lug. Hal.*   5 permixto *ed. Bas.*: virtutem *Bendz*: vim mixto *coni. ed. Lug.*: mixtae uno *coni. Th. Gomperz*

Resemblances (D50)

D50 (A54) Aët. 5.11.2 (Ps.-Plut.) [πόθεν γίνονται τῶν γονέων αἱ ὁμοιώσεις καὶ τῶν προγόνων]

Παρμενίδης· ὅταν μὲν ἀπὸ τοῦ δεξιοῦ μέρους τῆς μήτρας ὁ γόνος ἀποκριθῇ, τοῖς πατράσιν· ὅταν δ᾽ ἀπὸ τοῦ ἀριστεροῦ, ταῖς μητράσιν.

PARMENIDES

Determination of the Character (D49)

D49 (B18) Caelius Aurelianus, *On Chronic Diseases*

In the books that he wrote on nature, Parmenides says that
at the moment of conception soft or submissive men are
sometimes generated. [. . .]

When the woman and the man mix together the
    seeds of Venus,
The power that is formed in the veins out of the
    different kinds of blood
Fashions well constructed bodies if it maintains a
    balance.
For if the powers fight when the seed is thoroughly
    mixed
And, dreadful, are not unified in a thoroughly mixed   5
    body,
They will disturb the newborn sex with a double
    seed.[1]

[1] What follows paraphrases this passage, restricting its explanation of character in general to the case of homosexuality.

Resemblances (D50)

D50 (A54) Aëtius

Parmenides: when the seed is separated from the right
side of the womb, [scil. the children resemble] the fathers;
when it is from the left side, the mothers.

Thought and Sensation (D51–D57)
General Principles (D51–D52)

D51 (B16) Arist. *Metaph.* Γ5 1009b22–25; Theophr. *Sens.* 3

ὡς γὰρ ἕκαστοτ᾽ ἔχει κρᾶσιν μελέων
πολυπλάγκτων,
τὼς νόος ἀνθρώποισι παρέστηκεν· τὸ γὰρ αὐτό
ἔστιν ὅπερ φρονέει μελέων φύσις ἀνθρώποισιν
καὶ πᾶσιν καὶ παντί· τὸ γὰρ πλέον ἐστὶ νόημα.

1 ἑκάστοτ᾽ Arist. E¹J, Theophr. (ἑκάστοτε): ἕκαστος Arist.
E²: ἑκάστῳ Arist. Aᵇ   πολυπλάγκτων Theophr.: πολυ-
κάμπτων Arist.   2 παρέστηκεν Theophr.: παρίσταται Arist.

D52 (< A46) Theophr. *Sens.* 1 et 3–4

[1] [. . .] Παρμενίδης [. . .] τῷ ὁμοίῳ [. . .] [3] Παρμενίδης μὲν γὰρ ὅλως οὐδέν ἀφώρικεν ἀλλὰ μόνον ὅτι
δυοῖν ὄντοιν στοιχείοιν κατὰ τὸ ὑπερβάλλον ἐστὶν ἡ
γνῶσις. ἐάν γὰρ ὑπεραίρῃ τὸ θερμὸν ἢ τὸ ψυχρόν,
ἄλλην γίνεσθαι τὴν διάνοιαν, βελτίω δὲ καὶ καθαρω-
τέραν τὴν διὰ τὸ θερμόν· οὐ μὴν ἀλλὰ καὶ ταύτην
δεῖσθαί τινος συμμετρίας [. . . = **D51**]· [4] τὸ γὰρ αἰσθάνεσθαι καὶ τὸ φρονεῖν ὡς ταὐτὸ λέγει, διὸ καὶ τὴν
μνήμην καὶ τὴν λήθην ἀπὸ τούτων γίνεσθαι διὰ τῆς
κράσεως [. . . = **R61**]· ὅτι δὲ καὶ τῷ ἐναντίῳ καθ᾽ αὑτὸ
ποιεῖ τὴν αἴσθησιν φανερόν, ἐν οἷς φησι τὸν νεκρὸν
φωτὸς μὲν καὶ θερμοῦ καὶ φωνῆς οὐκ αἰσθάνεσθαι

Thought and Sensation (D51–D57)
General Principles (D51–D52)

D51 (B16) Aristotle, *Metaphysics;* Theophrastus, *On Sensations*

> **For just as it possesses each time the mixture of**
> **much-wandering limbs,**[1]
> **So too thinking** (*noos*) **presents itself to humans:**
> **for it is the same**
> **That the nature of the limbs apprehends**
> **(*phronein*) in humans,**
> **Both in all and in each; for the full** [or: the more]
> **is thought** (*noêma*).

[1] According to the text of Aristotle: "with numerous curvings."

D52 (< A46) Theophrastus, *On Sensations*

[1] Parmenides [. . .] [scil. explains sensation] by the similar [. . .]. [3] Parmenides did not define anything at all except that, the elements being two in number, knowledge is in accordance with the one that prevails. For when the hot or the cold dominates, the thought becomes different. The better and the purer one of the two is the one produced by what is hot; but this one too requires a certain commensurability. [. . .] [4] For he speaks of sensation and thinking as being the same thing: this is why, for him, both memory and forgetting come about from these elements, by their mixture. [. . .] But the fact that he also explains sensation by one of the contraries taken by itself is clear from the passages in which he says that a corpse does not perceive light, heat, and sound, because fire has with-

διὰ τὴν ἔκλειψιν τοῦ πυρός, ψυχροῦ δὲ καὶ σιωπῆς καὶ τῶν ἐναντίων αἰσθάνεσθαι, καὶ ὅλως δὲ πᾶν τὸ ὂν ἔχειν τινὰ γνῶσιν [. . . = **R61**].

Doxographies Concerning the Soul,
Knowledge, and Sensations (D53–D57)
The Nature and Seat of the Soul (D53–D56)

D53

a (< A1) Diog. Laert. 9.22

καὶ τὴν ψυχὴν καὶ τὸν νοῦν ταὐτὸν εἶναι, καθὰ μέμνηται καὶ Θεόφραστος ἐν τοῖς Φυσικοῖς [Frag. 227D FHS&G].

b (< A45) Aët. 4.5.12 (Stob.) [περὶ τοῦ ἡγεμονικοῦ]

Παρμενίδης [. . .] ταὐτὸν νοῦν καὶ ψυχήν[1] [. . .].

   [1] νοῦς καὶ ψυχὴ mss., corr. Diels

D54 (< A45) Aët. 4.3.4 (Stob.) [εἰ σῶμα ἡ ψυχὴ καὶ τίς ἡ οὐσία αὐτῆς]

Παρμενίδης [. . .] πυρώδη.

D55 (A45) Macr. *In Somn.* 1.14.20

Parmenides ex terra et igne.

drawn, but does perceive cold, silence, and the contraries, and in general that everything that exists possesses some knowledge.

Doxographies Concerning the Soul,
Knowledge, and Sensations (D53–D57)
The Nature and Seat of the Soul (D53–D56)

D53

a (< A1) Diogenes Laertius

The soul and the intellect are identical, as Theophrastus reports in his *Physics* [. . .].

b (< A45) Aëtius

Parmenides [. . .]: the intellect and the soul are identical [. . .].

D54 (< A45) Aëtius

Parmenides [. . .]: it [scil. the soul] is fiery.

D55 (A45) Macrobius, *Commentary on Cicero's* Dream of Scipio

Parmenides: [the soul is made] of earth and fire.

D56 (< A45) Aët. 4.5.5 (Ps.-Plut.) [περὶ τοῦ ἡγεμονικοῦ]

Παρμενίδης [. . .] ἐν ὅλῳ τῷ θώρακι.

Sensations (D57)

D57 (< A47) Aët. 4.9.6 (Stob.; cf. Ps.-Plut.) [εἰ ἀληθεῖς αἱ αἰσθήσεις]

Παρμενίδης[1] [. . .] παρὰ[2] τὰς συμμετρίας τῶν πόρων τὰς κατὰ μέρος αἰσθήσεις γίνεσθαι τοῦ οἰκείου, τῶν αἰσθητῶν ἑκάστου[3] ἑκάστῃ[4] ἐναρμόττοντος.[5]

[1] Παρμενίδης om. Plut.   [2] παρὰ Plut.: περὶ Stob.
[3] ἑκάστου om. Plut.   [4] ἑκάστῃ Plut.: ἑκάστην Stob.
[5] ἐναρμόττοντος Diels: ἀναρμόττοντος Stob.: ἁρμόζοντος Plut.

Physiological Phenomena (D58–D60)
Appetite (D58)

D58 (< A50) Aët. 4.9.14 (Stob.) [εἰ ἀληθεῖς αἱ αἰσθήσεις]

Παρμενίδης [. . .] ἐλλείψει τροφῆς τὴν ὄρεξιν.[1]

[1] post ὄρεξιν lac. posuit Meineke

Sleep (D59)

D59 (< A46b) Tert. *An.* 43.2

[. . .] Parmenides refrigerationem.

D56 (< A45) Aëtius

Parmenides: [scil. the directive part of the soul is located] in the whole chest.

Sensations (D57)

D57 (< A47) Aëtius

Parmenides [. . .]: the particular perceptions of what is appropriate for them come about thanks to the commensurability of the passages, each of the perceptibles adapting itself to each of them.[1]

[1] It is possible that the idea of the commensurability of the passages is the result of a retroactive projection.

Physiological Phenomena (D58–D60)
Appetite (D58)

D58 (< A50) Aëtius

Parmenides [. . .]: appetite [scil. comes about] from lack of food.[1]

[1] This notice is found in a chapter entitled "Whether sensations are truthful," in a section specifically dedicated to the sensations of pleasure and pain (cf. **EMP. D203a**); it may be lacunose.

Sleep (D59)

D59 (< A46b) Tertullian, *On the Soul*

[. . .] Parmenides: [scil. sleep] is a cooling down [. . .].

Old Age (D60)

D60 (A46a) Aët. 5.30.4 (Stob.) [περὶ ὑγείας καὶ νόσου καὶ γήρως]

Παρμενίδου· γῆρας γίγνεσθαι παρὰ τὴν τοῦ θερμοῦ ὑπόλειψιν.

An Eschatology: The Circulation of Souls? (D61)

D61 (cf. B13) Simpl. *In Phys.*, p. 39.19–20

[. . . = **D16**] καὶ τὰς ψυχὰς πέμπειν ποτὲ μὲν ἐκ τοῦ ἐμφανοῦς[1] εἰς τὸ ἀειδές, ποτὲ δὲ ἀνάπαλίν φησιν.

　[1] ἐμφανοῦς FE[2]: ἀφανοῦς DE[1]

The End of Parmenides' Poem? (D62)

D62 (B19) Simpl. *In Cael.*, p. 558.7–11

παραδοὺς δὲ τὴν τῶν αἰσθητῶν διακόσμησιν ἐπήγαγε πάλιν·

οὕτω τοι κατὰ δόξαν ἔφυ τάδε καί νυν ἔασι
καὶ μετέπειτ᾽ ἀπὸ τοῦδε τελευτήσουσι τραφέντα·
τοῖς δ᾽ ὄνομ᾽ ἄνθρωποι κατέθεντ᾽ ἐπίσημον
ἑκάστῳ.

Old Age (D60)

D60 (A46a) Aëtius

Parmenides: old age comes about from lack of heat.

An Eschatology: The Circulation of Souls? (D61)

D61 (cf. B13) Simplicius, *Commentary on Aristotle's* Physics

[. . .] And he says that she [i.e. the divinity of **D14b**] sends the souls sometimes from the visible to the invisible, sometimes in the opposite direction.

The End of Parmenides' Poem? (D62)

D62 (B19) Simplicius, *Commentary on Aristotle's* On the Heavens

After he has explained the organization of the perceptibles, he has added once again:

> **In this way, according to opinion, these things
>   have been born and now they are,
> And later, having grown strong, starting from
>   that point they will come to their end.
> For these things, humans have established a
>   name that designates each one.**[1]

[1] This may well be the end of the goddess' speech, and perhaps indeed also of the poem as a whole.

PARMENIDES [28 DK]

R

Judgments on Parmenides' Poetry (R1–R5)

R1 (21 A25) Cic. *Acad.* 2.74

Parmenides Xenophanes minus bonis quamquam versibus
sed tamen illi versibus increpant eorum adrogantiam quasi
irati, qui cum sciri nihil possit audeant se scire dicere.

R2 Plut.

a (< A15) *Aud. poet.* 2 16C

τὰ δ' Ἐμπεδοκλέους ἔπη καὶ Παρμενίδου [. . .] λόγοι
εἰσὶ κεχρημένοι παρὰ ποιητικῆς ὥσπερ ὄχημα τὸν
ὄγκον καὶ τὸ μέτρον, ἵνα τὸ πεζὸν διαφύγωσιν.

b (< A16) *Aud.* 13 45A–B

μέμψαιτο δ' ἄν τις [. . .] Παρμενίδου [. . .] τὴν στιχο-
ποιίαν [. . .].

PARMENIDES

R

Judgments on Parmenides' Poetry (R1–R5)

R1 (21 A25) Cicero, *Prior Academics*

Parmenides and Xenophanes, although in less good verses [scil. than Empedocles'], but nonetheless in verses, attack, almost in anger, the arrogance of those who dare to say that they know, when nothing can be known.

R2 Plutarch

a (< A15) *How the Young Man Should Read Poetry*

The verses of Empedocles and Parmenides [. . .] are discourses that borrow from poetry its weight and meter like a chariot in order to avoid the pedestrian character of prose.

b (< A16) *How to Listen*

One could rebuke [. . .] Parmenides for his versification [. . .].

See also **XEN. R28**

R3 (> A20) Men. Rh. *Div. epid.*

a pp. 333.12–14, 337.1–7

φυσικοὶ δὲ οἵους οἱ¹ περὶ Παρμενίδην² καὶ Ἐμπεδοκλέα ἐποίησαν,³ τίς ἡ τοῦ Ἀπόλλωνος φύσις, τίς ἡ τοῦ
Διός, παρατιθέμενοι. [. . .] εἰσὶ δὲ τοιοῦτοι,⁴ ὅταν
Ἀπόλλωνος ὕμνον λέγοντες ἥλιον αὐτὸν εἶναι φάσκω-
μεν, καὶ περὶ τοῦ ἡλίου τῆς φύσεως διαλεγώμεθα, καὶ
περὶ Ἥρας ὅτι ἀήρ, καὶ Ζεὺς τὸ θερμόν· οἱ γὰρ τοιοῦτοι ὕμνοι φυσιολογικοί. καὶ χρῶνται δὲ τῷ τοιούτῳ
τρόπῳ Παρμενίδης τε καὶ Ἐμπεδοκλῆς ἀκριβῶς [. . .].

¹ οἵους οἱ Bursian: τοι ὅσοι ms.   ² περὶ Παρμενίδην
Heeren: παρὰ πᾶν μέρος ms.   ³ ἐποίησαν Bernhardy:
ἐτίμησαν ms.   ⁴ τοιοῦτοι edd.: de ms. non liquet

b p. 337.9–13

αὐτῶν δὲ τῶν φυσικῶν οἱ μὲν ἐξηγητικοί, οἱ δὲ ἐν
βραχεῖ προαγόμενοι· πλεῖστον γὰρ διαφέρει, ὡς εἰδότα ἀναμιμνήσκειν συμμέτρως, ἢ ὅλως¹ ἀγνοοῦντα
διδάσκειν. Παρμενίδης μὲν γὰρ καὶ Ἐμπεδοκλῆς ἐξ-
ηγοῦνται, Πλάτων δὲ ἐν βραχυτάτοις ἀνυμνεῖ.

¹ ὅλως Ricc. 1: ὀλίγως ms. optimus

R4 (> A18) Procl. *In Parm.*, p. 665.12–21

[. . .] καὶ αὐτὸς ὁ Παρμενίδης ἐν τῇ ποιήσει, καίτοι δι᾽
αὐτὸ δήπου τὸ ποιητικὸν εἶδος χρῆσθαι μεταφοραῖς

R3 (> A20) Menander Rhetor, *On Epideictic Speeches*

a

Physical are the ones [i.e. hymns] that Parmenides and
Empedocles composed, explaining what Apollo's nature
is, what is Zeus'. [. . .] It is ones of this sort, whenever,
reciting a hymn to Apollo, we declare that he is the sun,
and discuss the nature of the sun, and [scil. we say] that
Hera is the air, and Zeus is heat. For hymns of this sort are
a form of natural philosophy. Parmenides and Empedocles make use of this kind in a precise way [. . .].

b

Among the philosophers of nature, some use an explana-
tory style, others proceed with brevity. For there is a great
difference between reminding, in a measured way, someone who supposedly already knows, and teaching someone
who does not know at all. For Parmenides and Empedocles
explain, while Plato proclaims as briefly as possible.

R4 (> A18) Proclus, *Commentary on Plato's* Parmenides

[. . .] In his poetry, Parmenides himself [scil. like Plato],
though obliged by his poetic genre to make use of meta-

ὀνομάτων καὶ σχήμασι καὶ τροπαῖς ὀφείλων, ὅμως τὸ
ἀκαλλώπιστον καὶ ἰσχνὸν καὶ καθαρὸν εἶδος τῆς ἀπ-
αγγελίας ἠσπάσατο· δηλοῖ δὲ τοῦτο ἐν τοῖς τοιούτοις·

ἐὸν γὰρ ἐόντι πελάζει· [**D8.30**]

καὶ πάλιν·

ἐπεὶ νῦν ἔστιν ὁμοῦ· [cf. **D8.10**]

καὶ πάλιν·

οὔτε τι μεῖζον
οὔτε τι βαιότερον πελέναι χρεών ἐστι. [**D8.49–
50**]

καὶ πᾶν ὅτι τοιοῦτον· ὥστε μᾶλλον πεζὸν εἶναι δοκεῖν
ἢ ποιητικὸν λόγον.

R5 Simpl. *In Phys.*

a (≠ DK) p. 7.1–3

Ξενοφάνης δὲ ὁ Κολοφώνιος καὶ ὁ τούτου μαθητὴς
Παρμενίδης καὶ οἱ Πυθαγόρειοι τελεωτάτην μὲν περί
τε τῶν φυσικῶν καὶ τῶν ὑπὲρ τὴν φύσιν, ἀλλ’ αἰ-
νιγματώδη τὴν ἑαυτῶν φιλοσοφίαν παραδεδώκασιν.

b (> A20) pp. 146.29–147.7

εἰ δ’ “εὐκύκλου σφαίρης ἐναλίγκιον ὄγκῳ” [**D8.48**]
τὸ ἓν ὄν φησι, μὴ θαυμάσῃς· διὰ γὰρ τὴν ποίησιν

phorical terms, figures, and tropes, nevertheless gives a friendly welcome to the unadorned, dry, and pure style of announcement. He shows this in verses like the following ones:

for what is is adjacent to what is. [**D8.30**]

and again:

since it is now, together, whole. [cf. **D8.10**]

and again:

**it must be
Neither at all bigger nor at all smaller.** [**D8.49–
50**]

and everything else of this sort. So that his discourse seems to be more prosaic than poetic.

R5 Simplicius, *Commentary on Aristotle's* Physics

a (≠ DK)

Xenophanes of Colophon, his disciple Parmenides, and the Pythagoreans have transmitted a philosophy that is perfect, both about nature and about what is beyond nature, but also enigmatic.

b (> A20)

If he says that what is one is **"similar to the volume of a well-rounded ball"** [**D8.48**], don't be surprised: be-

καὶ μυθικοῦ τινος παράπτεται πλάσματος. τί οὖν δι-
έφερε τοῦτο εἰπεῖν ἢ ὡς Ὀρφεὺς εἶπεν "ᾠεὸν ἀργύ-
φεον" [Frag. 114F Bernabé; cf. **COSM. T24**]· καὶ δῆλον
ὅτι τινὰ μὲν τῶν εἰρημένων ὁλοσχερέστερον λεγόμενα
καὶ ἄλλοις ἐφαρμόττει τοῖς μετ᾽ αὐτό· ὥσπερ τὸ "**ἀγένητον καὶ ἀνώλεθρον**" [**D8.8**] καὶ τῇ ψυχῇ καὶ τῷ νοῒ
προσήκει καὶ τὸ "**ἀκίνητον**" [**D8.31, 43**] καὶ "**ἐν ταὐτῷ
μένον**" [**D8.34**] τῷ νοῒ· πάντα δὲ ἅμα καὶ εἰλικρινῶς
ἀκουόμενα ἐκείνῳ πρέπει. κἂν γὰρ κατά τι σημαινό-
μενον ἀγένητός ἐστιν ἡ ψυχὴ καὶ ὁ νοῦς, ἀλλὰ πρὸς
τοῦ νοητοῦ παρήχθη.

Plato on Parmenides' Authority (R6)

R6 (< A5) Plat. *Theaet.* 183e

[ΣΩ.] [. . . = **MEL. R2b**] Παρμενίδης δέ μοι φαίνεται,
τὸ τοῦ Ὁμήρου, "αἰδοῖός τέ μοι" εἶναι ἅμα "δεινός τε."

An Interpretation of the Traditional Title (R7)

R7 (> A14) Simpl. *In Cael.*, p. 556.24–27, 28–30

καὶ τί κωλύει, φαίη ἄν τις, μὴ λέγεσθαι φυσικοὺς
ἐκείνους μηδὲ ὡς φυσικοὺς εὐθύνεσθαι; ἢ ὅτι Περὶ
φύσεως ἐπέγραφον τὰ συγγράμματα καὶ Μέλισσος
καὶ Παρμενίδης; [. . .] καὶ γὰρ [. . .] καὶ τὴν τῶν ὄντων
φύσιν λέγομεν, καὶ μέντοι οὐ περὶ τῶν ὑπὲρ φύσιν
μόνον, ἀλλὰ καὶ περὶ τῶν φυσικῶν ἐν αὐτοῖς τοῖς

cause he is writing poetry, he has recourse as well to a certain kind of mythic fiction. What is the difference then between saying this or, as Orpheus said, "a silver-shining egg"? And it is clear that some of his expressions are formulated more generally and accord with others that come later: as **"ungenerated, indestructible"** [**D8.8**] is appropriate both for the soul and for the mind, and **"motionless"** [**D8.31, 43**] and **"remaining in the same"** [**D8.34**] for the mind. But all of these expressions, heard all together in their purity, are appropriate to it. For even if in a certain sense the soul and the mind are ungenerated, it is starting from the intelligible that the term has been introduced.

Plato on Parmenides' Authority (R6)

R6 (< A5) Plato, *Theaetetus*

[Socrates:] To me Parmenides seems, to use Homer's expression, "venerable and terrifying to me" [Helen speaking about Priam, *Il.* 3.172].

An Interpretation of the Traditional Title (R7)

R7 (> A14) Simplicius, *Commentary on Aristotle's* On the Heavens

And what prevents them, one might say, from being called natural philosophers and from being refuted as natural philosophers? Did not both Melissus and Parmenides entitle their treatises *On Nature?* [cf. **MEL. D1**] For [. . .] we speak also of 'the nature of the things that are'; and in those very treatises they have spoken not only about what

συγγράμμασι διελέγοντο, καὶ διὰ τοῦτο ἴσως οὐ παρ-
ῃτοῦντο Περὶ φύσεως ἐπιγράφειν.

The Proem (R8–R10)
Sextus Empiricus' Allegorical Interpretation (R8)

R8 (cf. ad B1) Sext. *Adv. Math.* 7.112–14

[112] ἐν τούτοις γὰρ [i.e. **D4**] ὁ Παρμενίδης ἵππους μέν
φησιν αὐτὸν **φέρειν** [**v. 1**] τὰς ἀλόγους τῆς ψυχῆς ὁρμάς τε καὶ ὀρέξεις, κατὰ δὲ τὴν **πολύφημον ὁδὸν** τοῦ
δαίμονος [**v. 2–3**], πορεύεσθαι τὴν κατὰ τὸν φιλόσοφον λόγον θεωρίαν, ὃς λόγος προπομποῦ δαίμονος
τρόπον ἐπὶ τὴν ἁπάντων ὁδηγεῖ γνῶσιν. **κούρας** [**v. 5**]
δ' αὐτοῦ προάγειν τὰς αἰσθήσεις, ὧν τὰς μὲν ἀκοὰς
αἰνίττεται ἐν τῷ λέγειν

> δοιοῖς γὰρ ἐπείγετο δινωτοῖσι
> **κύκλοις** [**v. 7–8**],

τουτέστι τοῖς τῶν ὤτων, τὴν φωνὴν δι' ὧν καταδέχον-
ται, [113] τὰς δὲ **ὁράσεις Ἡλιάδας κούρας** κέκληκε,
δώματα μὲν **Νυκτὸς** ἀπολιπούσας, **ἐς** ⟨**δὲ**⟩[1] **φάος ὠσα-
μένας** [**v. 9–10**], διὰ τὸ μὴ χωρὶς φωτὸς γίνεσθαι τὴν
χρῆσιν αὐτῶν. ἐπὶ δὲ τὴν **πολύποινον** [**v. 14**] ἐλθεῖν
Δίκην καὶ **ἔχουσαν κληῖδας ἀμοιβούς** [**v. 14**], τὴν διά-

---

[1] ⟨δὲ⟩ Bekker

transcends nature but also about natural objects, and perhaps this is why they did not refuse to entitle them *On Nature.*

The Proem (R8–R10)
Sextus Empiricus' Allegorical Interpretation (R8)

R8 (cf. ad B1) Sextus Empiricus, *Against the Logicians*

[112] In these verses [i.e. **D4**], Parmenides calls **"the mares that carry"** him [**v. 1**] the impulses and irrational desires of the soul; along **"the divinity's many-worded / Road"** [**v. 2–3**] proceeds theoretical knowledge in conformity with philosophical reason, which, like a tutelary divinity, leads to the knowledge of all things; the **"maidens"** [**v. 5**] that lead him are the sensations—he hints allegorically at hearing when he says,

> **it was pressed hard by two whirling Wheels** [**v. 7–8**],

that is by those of the ears, by which sound is apprehended; [113] the organs of sight he has called **"maidens of the Sun,"** [**v. 9**], who on the one hand have left **"the palace of Night"** and on the other hand **"toward the light have pushed back"** [cf. **v. 9–10**],[1] because one cannot make use of them without light. They arrive at **"much-punishing Justice"** that **"holds its alternating**

---

[1] We cannot tell from Sextus' paraphrase how he understood lines 9–10a of Parmenides' text. Its very obscurity may suggest that some ancient readers had wondered how to construe *eis phaos* (see note on **D4.10**).

νοιαν ἀσφαλεῖς ἔχουσαν τὰς τῶν πραγμάτων κατα-
λήψεις. [114] ἥτις αὐτὸν ὑποδεξαμένη ἐπαγγέλλεται
δύο ταῦτα διδάξειν,

ἠμὲν Ἀληθείης εὐπειθέος ἀτρεμὲς² ἦτορ [v. 29],

ὅπερ ἐστὶ τὸ τῆς ἐπιστήμης ἀμετακίνητον βῆμα, ἕτερον δὲ

βροτῶν δόξας, ταῖς οὐκ ἔνι πίστις ἀληθής
   [v. 30],

τουτέστι τὸ ἐν δόξῃ κείμενον πᾶν, ὅτι ἦν ἀβέβαιον.
καὶ ἐπὶ τέλει προσδιασαφεῖ τὸ μὴ δεῖν ταῖς αἰσθήσεσι προσέχειν ἀλλὰ τῷ λόγῳ·

μὴ γάρ σε, φησίν, ἔθος πολύπειρον ὁδὸν κάτα
   τήνδε βιάσθω
νωμᾶν ἄσκοπον ὄμμα καὶ ἠχήεσσαν ἀκουήν
καὶ γλῶσσαν, κρῖναι δὲ λόγῳ πολύπειρον
   ἔλεγχον
ἐξ ἐμέθεν ῥηθέντα. [= D8.3–6a]

ἀλλ' οὗτος μὲν καὶ αὐτός, ὡς ἐκ τῶν εἰρημένων συμ-
φανές, τὸν ἐπιστημονικὸν λόγον κανόνα τῆς ἐν τοῖς
οὖσιν ἀληθείας ἀναγορεύσας ἀπέστη τῆς τῶν αἰσθήσεων ἐπιστάσεως.

---

² ἀτρεμὲς NLE: ἀτρεκὲς ABVR

keys" [v. 14], i.e. thought, which possesses the sure apprehensions of things. [114] After she has welcomed him, she announces that she will teach him these two things:

> **Both the unshakeable heart of well-convincing truth [v. 29],**

that is, the unmovable foundation of knowledge, and then

> **the opinions of mortals, in which there is no true belief [v. 30],**

that is, everything that resides in opinion, because it is essentially uncertain. And at the end he makes the further clarification that one must rely not upon sensations but upon reason: he says,

> **And do not let much-experienced habit force you down onto this road,**
> **To wield an aimless eye and an echoing ear**
> **And tongue—no, by the argument decide the much-disputed refutation**
> **Spoken by me.** [= D8.3–6a]

Well, he himself, as is made clear from what I have said, has evoked scientific reason as the criterion of the truth in the things that are and he has kept far away from attention directed to sensations.

EARLY GREEK PHILOSOPHY V

References to Particular Points (R9–R10)

R9 (≠ DK) Herm. Alex. *in Phaedr.* 2.11, p. 127.31–33

οὐ πρῶτος δὲ ὁ Πλάτων ἡνίοχον καὶ ἵππους παρέλα-
βεν, ἀλλὰ πρὸ αὐτοῦ οἱ ἔνθεοι τῶν ποιητῶν, Ὅμηρος,
Ὀρφεύς, Παρμενίδης· ἀλλ' ὑπ' ἐκείνων μὲν ἅτε ἐνθέων
ἄνευ αἰτίας εἴρηται· ἐνθουσιῶντες γὰρ ἔλεγον [. . .].

R10

a (≠ DK) Porph. *Antr.* 23

τῶν δύο πυλῶν τούτων μεμνῆσθαι καὶ Παρμενίδην ἐν
τῷ Φυσικῷ φησὶ[1] [i.e. probably Numenius, Frag. 31 Des
Places] [. . .].

[1] φησὶ V: om. M: φασὶ Lascaris

b (≠ DK) Procl. *In Parm.*, p. 640.26–28

[. . .] ἐκεῖνο δὲ πρεσβυτικῆς εἶναι διανοίας καθορᾶν
καὶ οὐδὲ ἀνθρωπίνης, ὡς ἐν τοῖς ποιήμασί φησιν,
ἀλλὰ νύμφης ὑψιπύλης τινός.

References to Particular Points (R9–R10)

R9 (≠ DK) Hermias of Alexandria, *Commentary on Plato's* Phaedrus

It was not Plato who was the first person to use a driver and horses [*Phaedrus* 246a], but before him those divinely inspired poets, Homer, Orpheus, Parmenides; but these latter said this without giving the reason, since they were divinely inspired—for they spoke being full of the divinity [. . .].

R10 (≠ DK)

a Porphyry, *The Cave of the Nymphs*

He [i.e. probably Numenius] says that Parmenides too mentions these two gates [i.e. the ones of which Homer speaks, *Od.* 13.109–112] in his *Physics* [cf. **D4.11–21**].[1]

[1] Porphyry interprets these gates as the passageway of the 'immortals,' i.e. of the gods and souls [cf. **D61**].

b Proclus, *Commentary on Plato's* Parmenides

[. . .] to see this belongs to an elderly intelligence and not to a human one either, as he says in his poem, but to a certain goddess (*numphê*) of the lofty gate.[1]

[1] The adjective *hupsipulês*, which refers to the celestial gate of the goddess' palace (cf. **D4.11–21**), is Homeric and in principle could go back to Parmenides.

EARLY GREEK PHILOSOPHY V

The Two Parts of the Body of the Poem (R11–R18)
Aristotle (R11–R12)

R11 (cf. ad B8) Arist. *Phys.* 1.5 188a19–22

πάντες δὴ τἀναντία ἀρχὰς ποιοῦσιν οἵ τε λέγοντες ὅτι
ἓν τὸ πᾶν καὶ μὴ κινούμενον (καὶ γὰρ Παρμενίδης
θερμὸν καὶ ψυχρὸν ἀρχὰς ποιεῖ, ταῦτα δὲ προσαγορεύει πῦρ καὶ γῆν) [. . .].

R12 (> A24) Arist. *Metaph.* A5 986b27–987a2

[. . . = **XEN. R12**] Παρμενίδης δὲ μᾶλλον βλέπων ἔοικέ
που λέγειν· παρὰ γὰρ τὸ ὂν τὸ μὴ ὂν οὐθὲν ἀξιῶν
εἶναι, ἐξ ἀνάγκης ἓν οἴεται εἶναι τὸ ὂν καὶ ἄλλο οὐθέν
[. . .], ἀναγκαζόμενος δ' ἀκολουθεῖν τοῖς φαινομένοις,
καὶ τὸ ἓν μὲν κατὰ τὸν λόγον πλείω δὲ κατὰ τὴν αἴσθησιν ὑπολαμβάνων εἶναι, δύο τὰς αἰτίας καὶ δύο
τὰς ἀρχὰς πάλιν τίθησι, θερμὸν καὶ ψυχρόν, οἷον
πῦρ καὶ γῆν λέγων· τούτων δὲ τὸ μὲν κατὰ τὸ ὂν τὸ
θερμὸν[1] τάττει θάτερον δὲ κατὰ τὸ μὴ ὄν.

[1] τὸ θερμὸν secl. Primavesi ut glossam ad τὸ μὲν spectantem

Theophrastus (R13)

R13 (< A7) Alex. *In Metaph.*, p. 31.7–14

περὶ Παρμενίδου καὶ τῆς δόξης αὐτοῦ καὶ Θεόφραστος ἐν τῷ πρώτῳ Περὶ τῶν φυσικῶν οὕτως λέγει

The Two Parts of the Body of the Poem (R11–R18)
Aristotle (R11–R12)

R11 (cf. ad B8) Aristotle, *Physics*

They all make the contraries principles, both those who
say that the whole is one and that it does not move (for
Parmenides too makes the hot and the cold principles, but
he calls them fire and earth) [. . .].

R12 (> A24) Aristotle, *Metaphysics*

[. . .] But as for Parmenides, he seems to speak on the
basis of more attentive consideration: for thinking that
nonbeing is nothing next to being, he believes that necessarily being is one and that nothing else [scil. is] [. . .]; but
being obliged to follow the phenomena, and supposing
that according to reason the one exists, but according to
sensation the multiple does, he posits again that the causes
are two and the principles two, the hot and the cold,
speaking of them as fire and earth. And among these, he
places the hot on the side of being and the other one on
the side of nonbeing.

Theophrastus (R13)

R13 (< A7) Alexander of Aphrodisias, *Commentary on
Aristotle's* Metaphysics

Concerning Parmenides and his opinion, Theophrastus
too speaks as follows in the first book of his *On Physics:*

"τούτῳ δὲ ἐπιγενόμενος Παρμενίδης [. . .] ἐπ' ἀμφοτέρας ἦλθε τὰς ὁδούς. καὶ γὰρ ὡς ἀίδιόν ἐστι τὸ πᾶν
ἀποφαίνεται καὶ γένεσιν ἀποδιδόναι πειρᾶται τῶν
ὄντων, οὐχ ὁμοίως περὶ ἀμφοτέρων δοξάζων, ἀλλὰ
κατ' ἀλήθειαν μὲν ἓν τὸ πᾶν καὶ ἀγένητον καὶ σφαιροειδὲς ὑπολαμβάνων, κατὰ δόξαν δὲ τῶν πολλῶν εἰς
τὸ γένεσιν ἀποδοῦναι τῶν φαινομένων δύο ποιῶν τὰς
ἀρχάς, πῦρ καὶ γῆν, τὸ μὲν ὡς ὕλην τὸ δὲ ὡς αἴτιον
καὶ ποιοῦν" [Frag. 227C FHS&G].

Proclus (R14–R15)

R14 (≠ DK) Procl. *In Tim.* 2.105a–b (I, pp. 344–345
Diehl)

πρότερον μὲν δύο ἡγούμενα ἐποίει, νοητὸν καὶ γενητὸν ἢ παράδειγμα καὶ εἰκόνα, καὶ δύο τούτοις ἀνάλογον ἐλάμβανεν, ἐπιστήμην καὶ εἰκοτολογίαν ἢ
ἀλήθειαν καὶ πίστιν· ὡς ἀλήθειαν πρὸς τὸ νοητὸν
παράδειγμα, οὕτω πίστιν πρὸς τὴν γενητὴν εἰκόνα.
[. . .] ὁ δέ γε Παρμενίδης, καίτοι διὰ ποίησιν ἀσαφὴς
ὤν, ὅμως καὶ αὐτὸς ταῦτα ἐνδεικνύμενός φησιν· [. . .
= **D4.29–30, D6.1–8a**].

R15 (≠ DK) Procl. *In Tim.* 2.77c (I, p. 252.1–4 Diehl)

[. . .] καὶ ὁ ἐν ⟨τοῖς ἔπεσι⟩ Παρμενίδη⟨ς⟩¹ τὴν περὶ
τῶν αἰσθητῶν πραγματείαν διὰ τοῦτο Πρὸς Δόξαν

"Coming after him [i.e. Xenophanes] [. . .], Parmenides went on both paths. For at the same time he asserts that the whole is eternal and he tries to explain the genesis of the things that are; but he does not judge in the same way about both of these points: he supposes that according to the truth the whole is one, ungenerated, and spherical in shape, while according to the opinion of the many he accepts, in order to explain genesis, that the principles are two, fire and earth, the one as matter and the other as cause and agent."

Proclus (R14–R15)

R14 (≠ DK) Proclus, *Commentary on Plato's* Timaeus

Earlier he [i.e. Plato] posited two principal [scil. kinds of things], intelligible and generated, or model and image, and he assumed two [scil. modes of knowledge] analogous to these, science and plausible discourse, or truth and belief; as truth is to the intelligible model, so belief is to the generated image. [. . .] And Parmenides himself, though he is obscure because he is writing poetry, nonetheless indicates this too when he says, [. . . = **D4.29–30, then D6.1–8a**].

R15 (≠ DK) Proclus, *Commentary on Plato's* Timaeus

[. . .] It is for this reason that Parmenides in ⟨his verses⟩ entitled his treatment of perceptibles *Regarding* [or:

---

¹ suppl. Bäumker

ἐπέγραψεν ὡς τῶν αἰσθητῶν δοξαστῶν ὄντων κατὰ
τὴν ἑαυτῶν φύσιν.

Simplicius (R16–R18)

R16 (cf. ad B1, B19) Simpl. *In Cael.*, pp. 557.20–558.18

[. . .] οἱ δὲ ἄνδρες ἐκεῖνοι διττὴν ὑπόστασιν ὑπετίθεντο, τὴν μὲν τοῦ ὄντως ὄντος τοῦ νοητοῦ, τὴν δὲ τοῦ
γινομένου τοῦ αἰσθητοῦ, ὅπερ οὐκ ἠξίουν καλεῖν ὂν
ἁπλῶς, ἀλλὰ δοκοῦν ὄν· διὸ περὶ τὸ ὂν ἀλήθειαν εἶναί
φησι, περὶ δὲ τὸ γινόμενον δόξαν. λέγει γοῦν ὁ Παρμενίδης [. . . = **D4.28–32**]· ἀλλὰ καὶ συμπληρώσας τὸν
περὶ τοῦ ὄντως ὄντος λόγον καὶ μέλλων περὶ τῶν αἰσθητῶν διδάσκειν ἐπήγαγεν· [. . . = **D8.55–57**]· παραδοὺς δὲ τὴν τῶν αἰσθητῶν διακόσμησιν ἐπήγαγε
πάλιν· [. . . = **D62**].

R17 (A34) Simpl. *In Phys.*, p. 39.10–12

δοξαστὸν οὖν καὶ ἀπατηλὸν [**D8.57**] τοῦτον καλεῖ τὸν
λόγον [scil. **D8.55–66**] οὐχ ὡς ψευδῆ ἁπλῶς, ἀλλ᾽ ὡς
ἀπὸ τῆς νοητῆς ἀληθείας εἰς τὸ φαινόμενον καὶ δοκοῦν τὸ αἰσθητὸν ἐκπεπτωκότα.

Against?] *Opinion,*[1] on the idea that the perceptibles, by their very nature, are objects of opinion.

[1] This title, which is not authentic, refers to **D8.56.**

Simplicius (R16–R18)

R16 (cf. ad B1, B19) Simplicius, *Commentary on Aristotle's* On the Heavens

[. . .] those men [i.e. Parmenides and Melissus] accepted two kinds of existence, one of what truly is, the intelligible, and another of what becomes, the sensible, of which they did not think it right to say simply that it "is," but that it "seems to be." That is why what concerns being is truth and what concerns becoming is opinion. Parmenides says at any rate, [. . . = **D4.28–32**]. Moreover, after he has concluded the discussion about true being and is preparing to communicate his teaching about the perceptibles, he adds, [. . . = **D8.55–57**]. And after he has explained the organization of perceptibles in the world, he adds once again, [. . . = **D62**].

R17 (A34) Simplicius, *Commentary on Aristotle's* Physics

He says about this discussion [scil. **D8.55–66**] that it belongs to opinion and is **deceptive** [**D8.57**], not because it is purely and simply false, but because it has fallen away from the intelligible truth toward appearance and what is the object of opinion, the perceptible.

EARLY GREEK PHILOSOPHY V

R18 (cf. ad B8) Simpl. *In Phys.*, p. 179.31–33

καὶ γὰρ οἱ ἓν τὸ ὂν καὶ ἀκίνητον λέγοντες, ὥσπερ
Παρμενίδης, καὶ οὗτοι τῶν φυσικῶν ἐναντίας ποιοῦσι
τὰς ἀρχάς. καὶ γὰρ οὗτος ἐν τοῖς πρὸς δόξαν θερμὸν
καὶ ψυχρὸν ἀρχὰς ποιεῖ. ταῦτα δὲ προσαγορεύει πῦρ
καὶ γῆν καὶ φῶς καὶ νύκτα ἤτοι σκότος. λέγει γὰρ
μετὰ τὰ περὶ ἀληθείας· [. . . = **D8.58–64, D13**].

Arguments Against Generation (R19–R21)

R19 (≠ DK) Arist. *Phys.* 1.8 191a24–33

ζητοῦντες γὰρ οἱ κατὰ φιλοσοφίαν πρῶτοι τὴν ἀλήθειαν καὶ τὴν φύσιν τῶν ὄντων ἐξετράπησαν οἷον
ὁδόν τινα ἄλλην ἀπωσθέντες ὑπὸ ἀπειρίας, καί φασιν
οὔτε γίγνεσθαι τῶν ὄντων οὐδὲν οὔτε φθείρεσθαι διὰ
τὸ ἀναγκαῖον μὲν εἶναι γίγνεσθαι τὸ γιγνόμενον ἢ ἐξ
ὄντος ἢ ἐκ μὴ ὄντος, ἐκ δὲ τούτων ἀμφοτέρων ἀδύνατον εἶναι· οὔτε γὰρ τὸ ὂν γίγνεσθαι (εἶναι γὰρ ἤδη)
ἔκ τε μὴ ὄντος οὐδὲν ἂν γενέσθαι· ὑποκεῖσθαι γάρ τι
δεῖν.[1] καὶ οὕτω δὴ τὸ ἐφεξῆς συμβαῖνον αὔξοντες οὐδ᾽
εἶναι πολλά φασιν ἀλλὰ μόνον αὐτὸ τὸ ὄν.

[1] δεῖν Bonitz ex Simpl. *In Phys.*, p. 1140.24: δεῖ mss.

R18 (cf. ad B8) Simplicius, *Commentary on Aristotle's* Physics

For those who say that what is is one and immobile, like Parmenides, also admit contrary principles for natural objects. For in the section dedicated to opinion, he makes hot and cold the principles; but he calls them fire and earth, and light and night or darkness. For he says after the section that discusses the truth, [. . . = **D8.58–64, D13**].

Arguments Against Generation (R19–R21)

R19 (≠ DK) Aristotle, *Physics*

For the first people to seek philosophically the truth and the nature of beings were turned aside, as though they had been pushed back to another road by inexperience, and they say that none of the things that are either comes about or is destroyed, since it is necessary that what comes about come about either out of what is or out of what is not, and that it is impossible that this happen out of either of these: for what is cannot come about (for it already is); and out of what is not, nothing could come about, for there must be some substrate. And in this way, exaggerating the consequence that immediately follows, they say that the multiple does not exist either, but only being itself.[1]

[1] The monist natural philosophers are meant just as much as is Parmenides.

R20 (≠ DK) Simpl. *In Cael.*, p. 136.30–137.2

τὸ γὰρ γινόμενον καὶ ὡς ἐξ ὑποκειμένου νομίζοντες
γίνεσθαι καὶ ὑπὸ ποιητικοῦ αἰτίου εἰκότως ἔλεγον ἐκ
τοῦ μὴ ὄντος μηδὲν γίνεσθαι μήτε ὡς ἐκ στοιχείου
μήτε ὡς ἐκ ποιητικοῦ αἰτίου. καὶ γὰρ Παρμενίδης ὁ
πρῶτος, ὧν ἀκοῇ ἴσμεν, τοῦτον τὸν λόγον ἐρωτῶν ἐν
τοῖς ἔπεσι περὶ τοῦ ἀγένητον εἶναι τὸ ὂν τάδε γέ-
γραφε· [. . . = **D8.11b–14a**].

R21 (cf. ad B8) Simpl. *In Phys.*, p. 78.24–29

ταῦτα δὴ περὶ τοῦ κυρίως ὄντος λέγων ἐναργῶς ἀποδείκνυσιν, ὅτι ἀγένητον τοῦτο τὸ ὄν· οὔτε γὰρ ἐξ ὄντος, οὐ γὰρ προϋπῆρχεν ἄλλο ὄν· οὔτε ἐκ τοῦ μὴ
ὄντος, οὐδὲ[1] γὰρ ἔστι τὸ μὴ ὄν. καὶ διὰ τί δὴ τότε,
ἀλλὰ μὴ καὶ πρότερον ἢ[2] ὕστερον ἐγένετο; ἀλλ᾿ οὐδὲ
ἐκ τοῦ πῆ μὲν ὄντος πῆ δὲ μὴ ὄντος, ὡς τὸ γενητὸν
γίνεται· οὐ γὰρ ἂν τοῦ ἁπλῶς ὄντος προϋπάρχοι τὸ
πῆ μὲν ὂν πῆ δὲ μὴ ὄν, ἀλλὰ μετ᾿ αὐτὸ ὑφέστηκε.

---

[1] οὔτε mss., corr. Diels   [2] ἢ suprascr. D: om. EF

*Interpretations of Being and
Its Attributes (R22–R38)
Being, Interpreted as a Principle (R22)*

R22 (≠ DK) Arist. *Phys.* 1.2 184b15–17

ἀνάγκη δ᾿ ἤτοι μίαν εἶναι τὴν ἀρχὴν ἢ πλείους, καὶ

R20 (≠ DK) Simplicius, *Commentary on Aristotle's* On the Heavens

It is understandable that those who thought that what comes about comes about both from a certain substrate and from an efficient cause said that nothing comes about out of nonbeing, neither as from an element nor as from an efficient cause. For Parmenides was the first person of whom we have heard tell who, raising in his verses the question whether being is ungenerated, has written as follows: [. . . = **D8.11b–14a**].

R21 (cf. ad B8) Simplicius, *Commentary on Aristotle's* Physics

By saying this [i.e. **D8.8–19**] about what is in the primary sense, he demonstrates clearly that this being is ungenerated. For neither is it from being, for no other being preceded it; nor is it from nonbeing, for what does not exist does not exist either. And why then was it at this precise moment that it came about, and not also earlier or later? But neither is it from what in a certain way is but in a certain way is not, as comes about what comes about; for what in a certain way is but in a certain way is not could not precede what is in the simple sense, but appeared later than it [cf. ad **D8.18**].

Interpretations of Being and
Its Attributes (R22–R38)
Being, Interpreted as a Principle (R22)

R22 (≠ DK) Aristotle, *Physics*

It is necessary that the principle be either one or multiple;

111

εἰ μίαν, ἤτοι ἀκίνητον, ὥς φησι[1] Παρμενίδης καὶ Μέλισσος, ἢ κινουμένην, ὥσπερ οἱ φυσικοί [. . .].

[1] φησι EF: φασιν IJ

Being, Interpreted as the Whole (R23–R32)
Plato (R23–R26)

R23 (≠ DK) Plat. *Parm.* 128a–b

[ΣΩ.] σὺ μὲν γὰρ ἐν τοῖς ποιήμασιν ἓν φῂς εἶναι τὸ
πᾶν, καὶ τούτων τεκμήρια παρέχῃ καλῶς τε καὶ εὖ.

R24 (cf. ad B8) Plat. *Theaet.* 180d–e

[ΣΩ.] ὀλίγου δὲ ἐπελαθόμην, ὦ Θεόδωρε, ὅτι ἄλλοι αὖ
τἀναντία τούτοις ἀπεφήναντο,

†οἷον ἀκίνητον τελέθει τῷ παντὶ ὄνομ᾽ εἶναι†[1]

καὶ ἄλλα ὅσα Μέλισσοί τε καὶ Παρμενίδαι ἐναντιού-
μενοι πᾶσι τούτοις διισχυρίζονται, ὡς ἕν τε πάντα
ἐστὶ καὶ ἕστηκεν αὐτὸ ἐν αὑτῷ οὐκ ἔχον χώραν ἐν ᾗ
κινεῖται.

[1] cf. app. ad D8.43

R25

a (< A26) Plat. *Theaet.* 181a

[ΣΩ.] [. . .] οἱ τοῦ ὅλου στασιῶται [. . .].

and if it is one, either immobile, as Parmenides and Melissus say, or in motion, as the natural philosophers say [. . .].

Being, Interpreted as the Whole (R23–R32)
Plato (R23–R26)

R23 (≠ DK) Plato, *Parmenides*

[Socrates:] For you say in your poem that the whole is one, and you do a fine job of furnishing proofs of this.

R24 (cf. ad B8) Plato, *Theaetetus*

[Socrates:] I almost forgot, Theodorus, that other people have asserted the contrary of these [i.e. the partisans of movement], for example [. . . = inaccurate quotation of **D8.43**], and everything that the Melissuses and Parmenideses maintain in opposition to all of them: viz., that all things are one and that it [i.e. this one] remains itself in itself, since it does not have a place in which it could move [cf. **MEL. D10 [112]**].

R25

a (< A26) Plato, *Theaetetus*

[Socrates:] [. . .] the immobilizers of the whole [. . .].

b (≠ DK) Schol. in Plat. *Theaet.* ad 181a

'στασιῶται'] γλυκεῖα λέξις καὶ ἐγκωμιαστικὴ τῶν
ἀμφὶ Παρμενίδην.

R26 (cf. ad B8) Plat. *Soph.* 244d–e

[ΞΕ.] τί δέ; τὸ ὅλον ἕτερον τοῦ ὄντος ἑνὸς ἢ ταὐτὸν
φήσουσι τούτῳ;
[ΘΕ.] πῶς γὰρ οὐ φήσουσί τε καὶ φασίν;
[ΞΕ.] εἰ τοίνυν ὅλον ἐστίν, ὥσπερ καὶ Παρμενίδης
λέγει [. . . = **D8.48–50**], τοιοῦτόν γε ὂν τὸ ὂν μέσον τε
καὶ ἔσχατα ἔχει, ταῦτα δὲ ἔχον πᾶσα ἀνάγκη μέρη
ἔχειν.

Theophrastus and Eudemus (R27)

R27 (< A28) Simpl. *In Phys.*, p. 115.11–14

τὸν Παρμενίδου λόγον, ὡς ὁ Ἀλέξανδρος ἱστορεῖ, ὁ
μὲν Θεόφραστος οὕτως ἐκτίθεται ἐν τῷ πρώτῳ τῆς
Φυσικῆς ἱστορίας· "τὸ παρὰ τὸ ὂν οὐκ ὄν· τὸ οὐκ ὂν
οὐδέν· ἓν ἄρα τὸ ὄν" [Frag. 234 FHS&G], Εὔδημος δὲ
οὕτως "τὸ παρὰ τὸ ὂν οὐκ ὄν, ἀλλὰ καὶ μοναχῶς λέγεται τὸ ὄν· ἓν ἄρα τὸ ὄν" [Frag. 43 Wehrli] [. . . = **R50**].

b (≠ DK) Scholia on Plato's *Theaetetus*

'immobilizers': a pleasant and eulogistic expression for the followers of Parmenides.

R26 (cf. ad B8) Plato, *Sophist*

[The stranger from Elea:] Well then? Will they say that the whole is different from the being that is one, or that it is identical with it?

[Theaetetus:] How will they not say it? And indeed, they do say it.

[The stranger from Elea:] If then it is a whole, as Parmenides says, [. . . = **D8.48–50**], being, since it is of this sort, possesses a center and extremities; and possessing these, it must necessarily possess parts.

Theophrastus and Eudemus (R27)

R27 (< A28) Simplicius, *Commentary on Aristotle's* Physics

As Alexander reports, Theophrastus sets out Parmenides' argument in the first book of his *Physical Investigation* in the following way: "what is next to being does not exist; what does not exist is nothing; hence being is [scil. only] one"; and Eudemus in this way: "what is next to being does not exist; but being is spoken of in only one way; hence being is [scil. only] one."

Three Doxographies of Theophrastean Origin
(R28–R30)

R28 (A29) Aët. 1.24.1 (Ps.-Plut.) [περὶ γενέσεως καὶ φθορᾶς]

Παρμενίδης Μέλισσος Ζήνων ἀνῄρουν γένεσιν καὶ φθορὰν διὰ τὸ νομίζειν τὸ πᾶν ἀκίνητον.

R29 (< A22) Ps.-Plut. *Strom.* 5 (Eus. *PE* 1.8.5)

Παρμενίδης δὲ ὁ Ἐλεάτης [. . .] ἀΐδιον μὲν γὰρ τὸ πᾶν καὶ ἀκίνητον ἀποφαίνεται καὶ[1] κατὰ τὴν τῶν πραγμά-των ἀλήθειαν· εἶναι γὰρ αὐτὸ [. . . = **D8.9,** with textual variants]· γένεσιν δὲ τῶν καθ᾽ ὑπόληψιν ψευδῆ δοκούν-των εἶναι καὶ τὰς αἰσθήσεις ἐκβάλλει ἐκ τῆς ἀλη-θείας. φησὶ δὲ ὅτι εἴ τι παρὰ τὸ ὂν ὑπάρχει, τοῦτο οὐκ ἔστιν ὄν· τὸ δὲ μὴ ὂν ἐν τοῖς ὅλοις οὐκ ἔστιν. οὕτως οὖν τὸ ὂν ἀγένητον ἀπολείπει.

[1] καὶ del. Diels

R30 (< A23) (Ps.-?) Hippol. *Ref.* 1.11

καὶ γὰρ καὶ Παρμενίδης ἓν μὲν τὸ πᾶν ὑποτίθεται ἀΐδιόν τε καὶ ἀγέννητον[1] καὶ σφαιροειδές, οὐδ᾽ αὐτὸς ἐκφεύγων τὴν τῶν πολλῶν δόξαν, πῦρ λέγων καὶ γῆν τὰς τοῦ παντὸς ἀρχάς, τὴν μὲν γῆν ὡς ὕλην, τὸ δὲ πῦρ ὡς αἴτιον καὶ ποιοῦν. [. . .] ὁ αὐτὸς δὲ εἶπεν ἀΐδιον εἶναι τὸ πᾶν καὶ οὐ γενόμενον καὶ σφαιροειδὲς καὶ ὅμοιον, οὐκ ἔχον δὲ τόπον[2] ἐν ἑαυτῷ, καὶ ἀκίνητον καὶ πεπερασμένον.

Three Doxographies of Theophrastean Origin
(R28–R30)

R28 (A29) Aëtius

Parmenides, Melissus, and Zeno abolished genesis and destruction because they thought that the whole is immobile.

R29 (< A22) Ps.-Plutarch, *Stromata*

Parmenides of Elea [. . .] says that the whole is eternal and immobile and in conformity with the truth of things: for it is [. . . = **D8.9**]. He expels from the truth the generation of the things that seem, by a false conception, to exist, and sensations. He says that if anything exists next to what is, it is not a being; now, what is not does not exist in the universe. In this way then he accepts that what is is ungenerated.

R30 (< A23) (Ps.-?) Hippolytus, *Refutation of All Heresies*

As for Parmenides, he supposes that the whole is one, eternal and ungenerated and spherical in shape, but he too did not escape from the opinion of the many, since he says that the principles of the whole are fire and earth, earth as matter, and fire as cause and agent. [. . .] The same man said that the whole is eternal, not generated, spherical in shape, and homogeneous, and that, not having any place within itself, it is immobile and limited.

---

¹ ἀγέννητον mss.: ἀγένητον Diels   ² τύπον mss., corr. Brandis

Plotinus (R31)

R31 (≠ DK) Plot. 5.1.8

ἥπτετο μὲν οὖν καὶ Παρμενίδης πρότερον τῆς τοιαύτης
δόξης καθόσον εἰς ταὐτὸ συνῆγεν ὂν καὶ νοῦν, καὶ τὸ
ὂν οὐκ ἐν τοῖς αἰσθητοῖς ἐτίθετο "τὸ γὰρ αὐτὸ νοεῖν
ἐστίν τε καὶ εἶναι" [**D6.8b**] λέγων· καὶ "ἀκίνητον"
[**D8.31**] λέγει τοῦτο καίτοι προστιθεὶς τὸ νοεῖν, σω-
ματικὴν πᾶσαν κίνησιν ἐξαιρῶν ἀπ᾽ αὐτοῦ, ἵνα μένῃ
ὡσαύτως, καὶ ὄγκῳ σφαίρας [**D8.48**] ἀπεικάζων, ὅτι
πάντα ἔχει περιειλημμένα καὶ ὅτι τὸ νοεῖν οὐκ ἔξω,
ἀλλ᾽ ἐν ἑαυτῷ. ἓν [**D8.11**] δὲ λέγων ἐν τοῖς ἑαυτοῦ
συγγράμμασιν αἰτίαν εἶχεν ὡς τοῦ ἑνὸς τούτου πολλὰ
εὑρισκομένου.

An Alchemical Tradition (R32)

R32 (≠ DK) Ps.-Olymp. *Ars sacra* 27

ὁμοίως καὶ ὁ Χήμης τῷ Παρμενίδῃ ἀκολουθήσας φη-
σίν· "ἓν τὸ πᾶν, δι᾽ οὗ τὸ πᾶν· τοῦτο γὰρ εἰ μὴ ἔχοι
τὸ πᾶν, οὐδὲν τὸ πᾶν."

Being, Interpreted as the World (R33–R35)

R33 (≠ DK) Theod. *Cur.* 2.108

Παρμενίδης δὲ ὁ Ἐλεάτης καὶ τὸν κόσμον ἀγέννητον
εἶναι λέγων βοᾷ· [. . . = **D8.9,** with textual variants].

PARMENIDES

Plotinus (R31)

R31 (≠ DK) Plotinus, *Enneads*

Parmenides too earlier [scil. than Plato] touched upon an opinion of this sort, inasmuch as he identified being and mind (*nous*) and did not place being among the sensibles, when he said, **"For it is the same, to think and also to be"** [**D6.8b**].[1] And he says that it [i.e. being] is **"motion-less"** [**D8.31**]—in spite of the fact that he adds to it thinking (*noein*)—removing from it all bodily movement, so that it stays in the same condition, and comparing it to **"the volume of a ball"** [**D8.48**], since it contains everything englobed within it and because thinking is not outside, but within it. But by calling it **"one"** [**D8.11**] in his writings, he exposed himself to the accusation that this one reveals itself to be multiple.

[1] Plotinus cites this partial verse several times: *Enneads* 1.4.10, 3.8.8, 5.9.5.

An Alchemical Tradition (R32)

R32 (≠ DK) Ps.-Olympiodorus, *On the Sacred Art*

Similarly, Chemes, following Parmenides, says, "The whole is one, and by virtue of this it is the whole; for if the whole did not possess this, the whole would be nothing."

Being, Interpreted as the World (R33–R35)

R33 (≠ DK) Theodoret, *Cure of the Greek Maladies*

Parmenides of Elea, saying that the world too is ungenerated, cries out, [. . . = **D8.9**].

R34 (< A36) Aët. 2.4.11 (Stob.) [εἰ ἄφθαρτος ὁ κόσμος]

[. . .] Παρμενίδης [. . .] ἀγένητον καὶ ἀίδιον καὶ ἄφθαρτον τὸν κόσμον.

R35 (< A36) Aët. 2.1.2 (Stob.) [περὶ κόσμου]

[. . .] Παρμενίδης [. . .] ἕνα τὸν κόσμον.

Being, Interpreted as God (R36–R38)

R36 (A31) Aët. 1.7.26 (Stob.) [περὶ θεοῦ]

Παρμενίδης τὸ ἀκίνητον καὶ πεπερασμένον σφαιροειδές.

R37 (cf. ad B8) Clem. Alex. *Strom.* 5.112.2

Παρμενίδης δὲ ὁ μέγας, ὥς φησιν ἐν Σοφιστῇ Πλάτων, ὧδέ πως περὶ τοῦ θεοῦ γράφει· [. . . = **D8.8–9**].

R38 (≠ DK) Ps.-Olymp. *Ars sacra* 20

μίαν δὲ ἀκίνητον πεπερασμένην δύναμιν ἔλεγεν ὁ Παρμενίδης τὸ θεῖον, καὶ αὐτὸς λέγων ἀρχήν· τοῦτο γὰρ [. . .] καὶ ἕν ἐστιν, καὶ ἀκίνητον, καὶ πεπερασμένη ἡ ἀπ᾽ αὐτοῦ ἐνέργεια.

textus incertus

R34 (< A36) Aëtius

[. . .] Parmenides [. . .]: the world is ungenerated, eternal, and indestructible.

R35 (< A36) Aëtius

[. . .] Parmenides [. . .]: the world is [scil. only] one.[1]

  [1] This notice might not refer to the first part of the poem but instead be (correct) information about its second part: in effect, for Parmenides there is only one world.

Being, Interpreted as God (R36–R38)

R36 (A31) Aëtius

Parmenides: [scil. god is] what is immobile and limited, spherical in shape.

R37 (cf. ad B8) Clement of Alexandria, *Stromata*

The great Parmenides, as Plato says in the *Sophist* [cf. 237a = **R41**], writes about god more or less as follows: [. . . = **D8.8–9**].

R38 (≠ DK) Ps.-Olympiodorus, *On the Sacred Art*

Parmenides said that the divine is a potency, one, immobile, limited, and he also called it a principle; for it [. . .] is one and immobile, and the activity that comes from it is limited.

The Criterion of Truth (R39–R40)

R39 (cf. ad B1) Sext. Emp. *Adv. Math.* 7.111

Παρμενίδης τοῦ μὲν δοξαστοῦ λόγου κατέγνω, φημὶ
δὲ τοῦ ἀσθενεῖς ἔχοντος ὑπολήψεις, τὸν δ᾽ ἐπιστημο-
νικόν, τουτέστι τὸν ἀδιάπτωτον, ὑπέθετο κριτήριον,
ἀποστὰς καὶ ‹αὐτὸς›[1] τῆς τῶν αἰσθήσεων πίστεως
[. . . = **D4.1–30**].

[1] ‹αὐτὸς› Heintz

R40 (< A1; cf. ad B7) Diog. Laert. 9.22

κριτήριον δὲ τὸν λόγον εἶπε· τάς τε αἰσθήσεις μὴ
ἀκριβεῖς ὑπάρχειν. φησὶ γοῦν· [. . . = **D8.3–5**].

Criticisms of Parmenides' Ontology (R41–R50)
Plato (R41–R43)

R41 (≠ DK) Plat. *Soph.* 237a

[ΞΕ.] τετόλμηκεν ὁ λόγος οὗτος ὑποθέσθαι τὸ μὴ ὂν
εἶναι· ψεῦδος γὰρ οὐκ ἂν ἄλλως ἐγίγνετο ὄν. Παρμενίδης δὲ ὁ μέγας, ὦ παῖ, παισὶν ἡμῖν οὖσιν ἀρχό-
μενός τε[1] καὶ διὰ τέλους τοῦτο ἀπεμαρτύρατο, πεζῇ τε
ὧδε ἑκάστοτε λέγων καὶ μετὰ μέτρων [. . . = **D8.1–2**].

[1] τε Heindorf: γε W: δὲ BT

PARMENIDES

The Criterion of Truth (R39–R40)

R39 (cf. ad B1) Sextus Empiricus, *Against the Logicians*

Parmenides condemned the discourse (*logos*) of opinion,
I mean the one that includes weak suppositions, while he
took as the criterion scientific discourse (*logos*), that is, the
one that is infallible, keeping ‹himself› too away from the
belief that comes from sensations [. . .].

R40 (‹ A1; cf. ad B7) Diogenes Laertius

He said that reason (*logos*) is the criterion, and that sensations are not exact. For he says, [. . . = **D8.3–5**].

Criticisms of Parmenides' Ontology (R41–R50)
Plato (R41–R43)

R41 (≠ DK) Plato, *Sophist*

[The stranger from Elea:] This assertion [scil. that it is
possible to speak and judge falsely] dares to suppose that
nonbeing is not. For otherwise the false could not exist.
But great Parmenides, speaking each time both in ordinary language [i.e. in his oral teaching, cf. **R62**] and in
verse, testified from beginning to end for us when we were
children, my child, that [. . . = **D8.1–2**].

R42 (cf. ad B7) Plat. *Soph*. 258c–d

[ΞΕ.] οἶσθ᾽ οὖν ὅτι Παρμενίδῃ μακροτέρως τῆς ἀπορ-
ρήσεως ἠπιστήκαμεν;
[ΘΕ.] τί δή;
[ΞΕ.] πλεῖον ἢ ᾽κεῖνος ἀπεῖπε σκοπεῖν, ἡμεῖς εἰς τὸ
πρόσθεν ἔτι ζητήσαντες ἀπεδείξαμεν αὐτῷ.
[ΘΕ.] πῶς;
[ΞΕ.] ὅτι ὁ μέν πού φησιν [. . . = **D8.1–2,** with textual
variants].
[ΘΕ.] λέγει γὰρ οὖν οὕτως.
[ΞΕ.] ἡμεῖς δέ γε οὐ μόνον τὰ μὴ ὄντα ὡς ἔστιν ἀπε-
δείξαμεν, ἀλλὰ καὶ τὸ εἶδος ὃ τυγχάνει ὂν τοῦ μὴ
ὄντος ἀπεφηνάμεθα.

R43 (≠ DK) Simpl. *In Phys.*, p. 134.14–18

τὸν οὖν Πλάτωνά φασιν ἐνδοῦναι τῇ προτάσει τῇ λε-
γούσῃ τὸ παρὰ τὸ ὂν οὐκ ὄν (καὶ γὰρ τὴν κίνησιν καὶ
τὴν στάσιν καὶ ταὐτὸν καὶ ἕτερον ἐν Σοφιστῇ ἕτερα
τοῦ ὄντος εἶναί φησι), τὸ δὲ οὐκ ὂν οὐδὲν οὐκέτι συγ-
χωρεῖν· καὶ γὰρ τὰ ἕτερα τοῦ ὄντος, κἂν μὴ ὄντα ᾖ,
ἀλλ᾽ ὅμως εἶναί φησι καὶ ταύτῃ τὸ μὴ ὂν εἰσάγει.

Aristotle (R44–R49)

R44 (≠ DK) Arist. *GC* 1.8 325a2–23

ἐνίοις γὰρ τῶν ἀρχαίων ἔδοξε τὸ ὂν ἐξ ἀνάγκης ἕν

R42 (cf. ad B7) Plato, *Sophist*

[The stranger from Elea:] You know that our distrust for Parmenides is much greater than his prohibition.
[Theaetetus:] How so?
[The stranger:] By continuing to investigate further, we have demonstrated to him more than what he prohibited us from examining.
[Theaet.:] How?
[The stranger:] For he says, [. . . = **D8.1–2**].
[Theaet.:] This is what he says.
[The stranger:] But as for us, we have not only demonstrated that the things that are not are, but we have also shown the kind of nonbeing that it [scil. the nature of the other] happens to be.

R43 (≠ DK) Simplicius, *Commentary on Aristotle's Physics*

They say that Plato accepts the premise according to which what is next to being is not (for he says in *The Sophist* that movement, rest, the same, and the other are different from being), but that he no longer agrees that what is not is nothing [cf. *Soph.* 250a–c, 254d–258b]. For he says that the things that are different from being, even if they are not beings, nonetheless exist, and in this way he introduces nonbeing.

Aristotle (R44–R49)

R44 (≠ DK) Aristotle, *On Generation and Corruption*

Some of the ancients held the view that what is is of neces-

εἶναι καὶ ἀκίνητον· [. . . cf. **ATOM. D30**] ὑπερβαίνοντες[1] τὴν αἴσθησιν καὶ παριδόντες αὐτὴν ὡς τῷ λόγῳ
δέον ἀκολουθεῖν ἓν καὶ ἀκίνητον τὸ πᾶν εἶναί φασι.
[. . .] οἱ μὲν οὖν οὕτως καὶ διὰ ταύτας τὰς αἰτίας ἀπεφήναντο περὶ τῆς ἀληθείας· ἐπεὶ δὲ ἐπὶ τῶν λόγων
μὲν δοκεῖ ταῦτα συμβαίνειν, ἐπὶ δὲ τῶν πραγμάτων
μανίᾳ παραπλήσιον εἶναι τὸ δοξάζειν οὕτως· οὐδένα
γὰρ τῶν μαινομένων ἐξεστάναι τοσοῦτον ὥστε τὸ πῦρ
ἓν εἶναι δοκεῖν καὶ τὸν κρύσταλλον, ἀλλὰ μόνον τὰ
καλὰ καὶ τὰ φαινόμενα διὰ συνήθειαν, ταῦτ᾽ ἐνίοις
διὰ τὴν μανίαν οὐθὲν δοκεῖ διαφέρειν.

[1] ὑπερβαίνοντες ELM: ὑπερβάντες FHJVW

R45 (≠ DK) Arist. *Phys.* 8.3 253a32–b2

τὸ μὲν οὖν πάντ᾽ ἠρεμεῖν, καὶ τούτου ζητεῖν λόγον
ἀφέντας τὴν αἴσθησιν, ἀρρωστία τίς ἐστιν διανοίας,
καὶ περὶ ὅλου τινὸς ἀλλ᾽ οὐ περὶ μέρους ἀμφισβήτη-
σις· οὐδὲ μόνον πρὸς τὸν φυσικόν, ἀλλὰ πρὸς πάσας
τὰς ἐπιστήμας ὡς εἰπεῖν καὶ πάσας τὰς δόξας διὰ τὸ
κινήσει χρῆσθαι πάσας.

R46 (≠ DK) Arist. *Phys.* 1.2 184b25–185a5

τὸ μὲν οὖν εἰ ἓν καὶ ἀκίνητον τὸ ὂν σκοπεῖν οὐ περὶ
φύσεώς ἐστι σκοπεῖν· ὥσπερ γὰρ καὶ τῷ γεωμέτρῃ
οὐκέτι λόγος ἔστι πρὸς τὸν ἀνελόντα τὰς ἀρχάς, ἀλλ᾽
ἤτοι ἑτέρας ἐπιστήμης ἢ πασῶν κοινῆς, οὕτως οὐδὲ

sity one and immobile. [. . .] Going beyond sensation and disregarding it on the idea that one ought to follow reason (*logos*), they say that the whole is one and immobile. [. . .]. So it is in this way and for these reasons that some people have made assertions about the truth; but even if this seems to be the case when what is involved are arguments, to hold this opinion when what is involved are facts is very similar to madness. For no madman is so insane as to think that fire and ice are the same thing, but it is only between what is beautiful and what seems to be beautiful because of habit that it seems to some people, because of their madness, that they do not differ at all.

R45 (≠ DK) Aristotle, *Physics*

To say that all things are at rest, and to seek an argument for this, dismissing sensation, is a kind of infirmity of thought, and the dispute is about the whole and not about a part: it concerns not only natural philosophy, but virtually all the sciences and all opinions, since they all have recourse to motion.

R46 (≠ DK) Aristotle, *Physics*

To investigate whether what is is one and immobile is not to investigate about nature: for just as the geometer no longer has any argument against someone who denies his principles, but this [scil. sort of argument] belongs either to a different science or to a science common to all the sciences, so too the same thing happens to someone [scil.

τῷ περὶ ἀρχῶν· οὐ γὰρ ἔτι ἀρχὴ ἔστιν, εἰ ἓν μόνον
καὶ οὕτως ἓν ἔστιν. ἡ γὰρ ἀρχὴ τινὸς ἢ τινῶν.

R47 (> A25) Arist. *Cael.* 3.1 298b12–24

οἱ μὲν γὰρ αὐτῶν ὅλως ἀνεῖλον γένεσιν καὶ φθοράν·
οὐθὲν γὰρ οὔτε γίγνεσθαί φασιν οὔτε φθείρεσθαι τῶν
ὄντων, ἀλλὰ μόνον δοκεῖν ἡμῖν, οἷον οἱ περὶ Μέλισ-
σόν τε καὶ Παρμενίδην, οὕς, εἰ καὶ τἆλλα λέγουσι
καλῶς, ἀλλ᾽ οὐ φυσικῶς γε δεῖ νομίσαι λέγειν· τὸ γὰρ
εἶναι ἄττα τῶν ὄντων ἀγένητα καὶ ὅλως ἀκίνητα μᾶλ-
λόν ἐστιν ἑτέρας καὶ προτέρας ἢ τῆς φυσικῆς σκέ-
ψεως. ἐκεῖνοι δὲ διὰ τὸ μηθὲν μὲν ἄλλο παρὰ τὴν τῶν
αἰσθητῶν οὐσίαν ὑπολαμβάνειν εἶναι, τοιαύτας δέ
τινας νοῆσαι πρῶτοι φύσεις, εἴπερ ἔσται τις γνῶσις
ἢ φρόνησις, οὕτω μετήνεγκαν ἐπὶ ταῦτα τοὺς ἐκεῖθεν
λόγους.

R48 (≠ DK) Arist. *Phys.* 1.3 186a22–32

[. . . = **MEL. R10**] καὶ πρὸς Παρμενίδην δὲ ὁ αὐτὸς
τρόπος τῶν λόγων, καὶ εἴ τινες ἄλλοι εἰσὶν ἴδιοι· καὶ
ἡ λύσις τῇ μὲν ὅτι ψευδὴς τῇ δὲ ὅτι οὐ συμπεραίνε-
ται, ψευδὴς μὲν ᾗ ἁπλῶς λαμβάνει τὸ ὂν λέγεσθαι,
λεγομένου πολλαχῶς, ἀσυμπέραντος δὲ ὅτι, εἰ μόνα
τὰ λευκὰ ληφθείη, σημαίνοντος ἓν τοῦ λευκοῦ, οὐθὲν

who investigates] about principles. For there is no longer
a principle, if there is only one thing and it is one in this
way. For a principle is [scil. a principle] of something or
of some things.

R47 (> A25) Aristotle, *On the Heavens*

Some of them [i.e. of the earlier philosophers] completely
abolished generation and destruction. For they say that
none of the things that are either comes about or is destroyed, but that this only seems to us to be the case, like
Melissus and Parmenides, who should not be thought to
be speaking in terms of physics, even if otherwise they
speak quite well. For that certain beings are ungenerated
and in general immobile belongs to a kind of investigation that is different from and anterior to physics. But
since they did not posit anything outside of the substance
of the perceptibles, and since they were the first to think
of natures of this sort, if knowledge or thought were to
exist, they transferred to these realities arguments deriving from over there.

R48 (≠ DK) Aristotle, *Physics*

[. . .] The same kind of objection [scil. as against Melissus]
can be made against Parmenides, and other ones if there
are any that are specific. And the solution is in part that it
[i.e. the argument by which being is one] is false and in
part that it is inconclusive. It is false insofar as it supposes
that being is spoken of in only one way, although in fact it
is spoken of in multiple ways; and it is inconclusive because, if one considered only white things, and white
means only one thing, nonetheless the white things would

ἧττον πολλὰ τὰ λευκὰ καὶ οὐχ ἕν· [. . .] ἀλλὰ τοῦτο
Παρμενίδης οὔπω συνεώρα.

R49 (≠ DK) Arist. *Metaph.* A3 984b1–4

τῶν μὲν οὖν ἓν μόνον[1] φασκόντων εἶναι τὸ πᾶν οὐθενὶ
συνέβη τὴν τοιαύτην συνιδεῖν[2] αἰτίαν πλὴν εἰ ἄρα
Παρμενίδῃ, καὶ τούτῳ κατὰ τοσοῦτον ὅσον οὐ μόνον
ἓν ἀλλὰ καὶ δύο πως τίθησιν αἰτίας εἶναι.

[1] μόνον om. A[b]   [2] συνιδεῖν E: ἰδεῖν A[b]

Eudemus (R50)

R50 (< A28) Simpl. *In Phys.*, pp. 115.14–116.1

[. . . = **R27**] τοῦτο δὲ εἰ μὲν ἀλλαχοῦ που γέγραφεν
οὕτως σαφῶς Εὔδημος, οὐκ ἔχω λέγειν· ἐν δὲ τοῖς
Φυσικοῖς περὶ Παρμενίδου τάδε γράφει, ἐξ ὧν ἴσως
συναγαγεῖν τὸ εἰρημένον δυνατόν. "Παρμενίδης δὲ οὐ
φαίνεται δεικνύειν ὅτι ἓν τὸ ὄν, οὐδὲ εἴ τις αὐτῷ συγ-
χωρήσειε μοναχῶς λέγεσθαι τὸ ὄν. [. . .] ὥσπερ δὲ εἰ
πάντα εἴη τὰ ὄντα καλὰ καὶ μηθὲν εἴη λαβεῖν ὃ οὐκ
ἔστι καλόν, καλὰ μὲν ἔσται πάντα, οὐ μὴν ἕν γε τὸ
καλὸν ἀλλὰ πολλά (τὸ μὲν γὰρ χρῶμα καλὸν ἔσται
τὸ δὲ ἐπιτήδευμα τὸ δὲ ὁτιδήποτε), οὕτω δὴ καὶ ὄντα
μὲν πάντα ἔσται, ἀλλ' οὐχ ἓν οὐδὲ τὸ αὐτό· ἕτερον μὲν
γὰρ τὸ ὕδωρ, ἄλλο δὲ τὸ πῦρ. Παρμενίδου μὲν οὖν
⟨οὐκ ἂν⟩[1] ἀγασθείη τις ἀναξιοπίστοις ἀκολουθήσαν-

still be multiple and not only one. [. . .] But Parmenides did not yet see this.

R49 (≠ DK) Aristotle, *Metaphysics*

Among those who say that the whole is only one, no one has managed to see this cause [scil. the efficient cause] except Parmenides, and he does so only insofar as he does not posit a single cause but in a certain way two [cf. **D14**].

Eudemus (R50)

R50 (< A28) Eudemus in Simplicius, *Commentary on Aristotle's* Physics

[. . .] Whether Eudemus wrote this so clearly somewhere else, I cannot say. But in his *Physics* he writes about Parmenides the following (from which probably the preceding statement [i.e. the one in **R27**] can be extracted): "Parmenides does not seem to demonstrate that being is [scil. only] one, not even if one were to grant him that being is spoken of in only one way. [. . .] Just as, if everything that is were beautiful and it were not possible to find anything that was not beautiful, everything would be beautiful without the beautiful thereby being just one (in fact it will be multiple: for colors will be beautiful, activity, and everything else), so too all beings will be beings, without being one nor the same. For water is one thing, fire another. So one should ⟨not⟩ be surprised that Parmenides

---

[1] ⟨οὐκ ἄν⟩ Diels

τος λόγοις καὶ ὑπὸ τοιούτων ἀπατηθέντος, ἃ οὔπω
τότε διεσαφεῖτο (οὔτε γὰρ τὸ πολλαχῶς ἔλεγεν οὐδείς, ἀλλὰ Πλάτων πρῶτος τὸ δισσὸν εἰσήγαγεν,
οὔτε τὸ καθ᾽ αὑτὸ καὶ κατὰ συμβεβηκός)· [. . .]" [Frag.
43 Wehrli].

Three Defenses of Parmenides (R51–R53)
Simplicius Against Aristotle and Other
Predecessors (R51–R52)

R51 (> A19) Simpl. *In Phys.*, pp. 36.25–37.8

ἐπειδὴ δὲ καὶ Ἀριστοτέλους ἐλέγχοντος ἀκουσόμεθα
τὰς τῶν προτέρων φιλοσόφων δόξας καὶ πρὸ τοῦ Ἀριστοτέλους ὁ Πλάτων τοῦτο φαίνεται ποιῶν καὶ πρὸ
ἀμφοῖν ὅ τε Παρμενίδης καὶ Ξενοφάνης, ἰστέον ὅτι
τῶν ἐπιπολαιότερον ἀκροωμένων οὗτοι κηδόμενοι τὸ
φαινόμενον ἄτοπον ἐν τοῖς λόγοις αὐτῶν διελέγχου-
σίν, αἰνιγματωδῶς[1] εἰωθότων τῶν παλαιῶν τὰς ἑαυτῶν ἀποφαίνεσθαι γνώμας. δηλοῖ δὲ ὁ Πλάτων θαυ-
μάζων οὕτως τὸν Παρμενίδην, ὃν διελέγχειν δοκεῖ,
καὶ βαθέος κολυμβητοῦ δεῖσθαι λέγων τὴν διάνοιαν
αὐτοῦ. καὶ Ἀριστοτέλης δὲ τὸ βάθος αὐτοῦ τῆς σο-
φίας ὑπονοῶν φαίνεται, ὅταν λέγῃ "Παρμενίδης δὲ
<μᾶλλον βλέπων>[2] ἔοικέ που λέγειν." καὶ οὗτοι οὖν
ποτὲ μὲν τὸ παραλελειμμένον ἀναπληροῦντες, ποτὲ δὲ

[1] καὶ ante αἰνιγματωδῶς hab. DE   [2] <μᾶλλον βλέ-
πων> Diels ex *Metaph.* A5 986b27 (= **R12**)

132

has subscribed to untrustworthy arguments: he has been deceived by difficulties of a kind that at that time had not yet been clarified. For no one spoke of the multiple mode, seeing as Plato was the first to introduce the double meaning, nor of the in-itself and of the contingent."

Three Defenses of Parmenides (R51–R53)
Simplicius Against Aristotle and Other
Predecessors (R51–R52)

R51 (> A19) Simplicius, *Commentary on Aristotle's* Physics

Since we shall also hear Aristotle refuting the opinions of earlier philosophers, and, before Aristotle, Plato is seen to be doing likewise, and, before both of them, Parmenides and Xenophanes, one must know that these men, in their care for more superficial readers, refute what seems absurd in their writings, given that the ancients had the habit of revealing their thoughts in an enigmatic way. But it is clear that Plato, even though he seems to refute Parmenides, expresses his great admiration for him when he says that his thought requires a deep-sea diver.[1] And Aristotle evidently recognized the profundity of his wisdom when he writes, "But Parmenides seems to speak ‹on the basis of more attentive consideration›" [cf. **R12**]. And therefore these men—while they sometimes com-

---

[1] In fact Plato does not say this; but others said it about Heraclitus (cf. **HER. R5**).

τὸ ἀσαφῶς εἰρημένον σαφηνίζοντες, ποτὲ δὲ τὸ ἐπὶ
τῶν νοητῶν εἰρημένον ὡς μὴ δυνάμενον τοῖς φυσικοῖς
ἐφαρμόττειν διακρίνοντες ὡς ἐπὶ τῶν ἓν τὸ ὂν καὶ
ἀκίνητον λεγόντων, ποτὲ δὲ τὰς εὐκόλους ἐκδοχὰς
τῶν ἐπιπολαιοτέρων προαναστέλλοντες, οὕτως ἐλέγ-
χειν δοκοῦσι. καὶ πειρασόμεθα τούτοις καὶ ἡμεῖς ἐφιστάνειν ἐν ταῖς πρὸς ἕκαστον τοῦ Ἀριστοτέλους ἀντι-
λογίαις.

R52 (cf. ad B1, B19) Simpl. *In Cael.*, pp. 557.19–558.17

ἀλλ᾽ ὁ μὲν Ἀριστοτέλης, ὡς ἔθος αὐτῷ, πρὸς τὸ φαινόμενον καὶ νῦν τῶν λόγων ὑπήντησε προνοῶν τοῦ μὴ
τοὺς ἐπιπολαιοτέρους παραλογίζεσθαι, οἱ δὲ ἄνδρες
ἐκεῖνοι διττὴν ὑπόστασιν ὑπετίθεντο, [. . . = **R16**]. πῶς
οὖν τὰ αἰσθητὰ μόνον εἶναι Παρμενίδης ὑπελάμβα-
νεν ὁ περὶ τοῦ νοητοῦ τοιαῦτα φιλοσοφήσας, ἅπερ
νῦν περιττόν ἐστι παραγράφειν; πῶς δὲ τὰ τοῖς νοητοῖς ἐφαρμόζοντα μετήνεγκεν ἐπὶ τὰ αἰσθητὰ ὁ χωρὶς
μὲν τὴν ἕνωσιν τοῦ νοητοῦ καὶ ὄντως ὄντος παραδούς,
χωρὶς δὲ τὴν τῶν αἰσθητῶν διακόσμησιν ἐναργῶς καὶ
μηδὲ ἀξιῶν τῷ τοῦ ὄντος ὀνόματι τὸ αἰσθητὸν καλεῖν;

plete what has been omitted, sometimes clarify what has been expressed unclearly, sometimes separate what is said about the intelligibles, on the idea that this cannot apply adequately to natural objects, as in the case of those who say that what is is one and immobile, sometimes forestall the easy interpretations of the more superficial [scil. readers]—do not refute except in appearance. And we too shall endeavor to consider these points attentively with regard to the arguments that Aristotle advances against each of them.

R52 (cf. ad B1, B19) Simplicius, *Commentary on Aristotle's* On the Heavens

But Aristotle, as is his custom, here too has formulated his response considering the appearance of the words, taking care not to mislead his more superficial [scil. readers]. Yet those men [i.e. Parmenides and Melissus] accepted two kinds of existence [. . .]. How then could Parmenides have supposed "that only the perceptibles exist" [scil. as Aristotle claims in **R47**], given that regarding the intelligible he gives a philosophical account which it is superfluous to transcribe now? And how could he have transferred to the perceptibles what accords with the intelligibles, given that he taught on the one hand the unification of the intelligible and of what really is and on the other hand the organization of the world, treating these two clearly as separate matters, and did not think it right to call the perceptible by the name of being?

EARLY GREEK PHILOSOPHY V

Plutarch Against Colotes (R53)

R53 Plut. *Adv. Col.* 13

a (cf. ad B10) 1114B

ἀλλ᾽ ὅ γε Παρμενίδης οὔτε πῦρ ἀνήρηκεν οὔθ᾽ ὕδωρ
οὔτε κρημνὸν[1] οὔτε πόλεις, ὥς φησι Κωλώτης, ἐν Εὐ-
ρώπῃ καὶ Ἀσίᾳ κατοικουμένας [. . . = **D9**].

[1] κρημνὸν] κόσμον coni. Rasmus

b (> A34) 1114C–D

ἐπεὶ δὲ καὶ Πλάτωνος καὶ Σωκράτους ἔτι πρότερος
συνεῖδεν ὡς ἔχει τι δοξαστὸν ἡ φύσις ἔχει δὲ καὶ
νοητόν, ἔστι δὲ τὸ μὲν δοξαστὸν ἀβέβαιον καὶ πλα-
νητὸν ἐν πάθεσι πολλοῖς καὶ μεταβολαῖς τῷ φθίνειν
καὶ αὔξεσθαι καὶ πρὸς ἄλλον ἄλλως ἔχειν καὶ μηδ᾽
ἀεὶ πρὸς τὸν αὐτὸν ὡσαύτως τῇ αἰσθήσει, τοῦ νοητοῦ
δ᾽ ἕτερον εἶδος· ἔστι γὰρ οὐλομελές τε καὶ ἀτρεμὲς
ἠδ᾽ ἀγένητον [**D8.9,** with textual variants] ὡς αὐτὸς
εἴρηκε, καὶ ὅμοιον ἑαυτῷ καὶ μόνιμον ἐν τῷ εἶναι,
ταῦτα συκοφαντῶν ἐκ τῆς φωνῆς ὁ Κωλώτης καὶ τῷ
ῥήματι διώκων οὐ τῷ πράγματι τὸν λόγον ἁπλῶς
φησι πάντ᾽ ἀναιρεῖν τῷ ἓν ὂν ὑποτίθεσθαι τὸν Παρμενίδην. ὁ δ᾽ ἀναιρεῖ μὲν οὐδετέραν φύσιν, ἑκατέρᾳ δ᾽
ἀποδιδοὺς τὸ προσῆκον εἰς μὲν τὴν τοῦ ἑνὸς καὶ
ὄντος ἰδέαν τίθεται τὸ νοητόν, ὂν μὲν ὡς ἀίδιον καὶ
ἄφθαρτον ἐν δ᾽ ὁμοιότητι πρὸς αὐτὸ καὶ τῷ μὴ δέχε-

Plutarch Against Colotes (R53)

R53 Plutarch, *Against Colotes*

a (cf. ad B10)

But as for Parmenides, he abolished neither fire nor water, nor cliff (?) nor, as Colotes claims, the inhabited cities in Europe and Asia [. . .].

b (> A34)

But since he [i.e. Parmenides] understood even before Plato and Socrates that nature possesses one part that belongs to opinion and another part that is intelligible, and that the part that belongs to opinion is unstable and errs, subject to multiple affections and changes, because of diminution, growth, the different relations of things to other ones, and the fact that they are never identical for sensation, not even for the same individual, while the kind that is intelligible is different—for it is **"Complete and untrembling and unborn"** [**D8.9**], as he himself has said—and similar to itself and remaining at rest in its being, Colotes, playing the slanderer in what he says and pursuing the argument at the level of the words and not of the things, says that Parmenides simply abolishes all things by positing that being is one. But he [i.e. Parmenides] does not abolish either of the two natures, but assigns to each one what is appropriate to it: he places the intelligible in the category of the one and of being (since he has called being eternal and indestructible, and one by virtue of its similarity to itself and because it does not

137

σθαι διαφορὰν προσαγορεύσας, εἰς δὲ τὴν ἄτακτον
καὶ φερομένην τὸ αἰσθητόν.

References to Particular Points of the
Cosmology (R54–R60)
The Elements as Divine (R54)

R54 (A33) Clem. Alex. *Protr.* 5.64.2

Παρμενίδης δὲ ὁ Ἐλεάτης θεοὺς εἰσηγήσατο πῦρ καὶ
γῆν.

The Cosmogonic Divinity (R55)

R55

a (A32) Aët. 1.25.3 (Ps.-Plut.) [περὶ ἀνάγκης]

Παρμενίδης [. . .] πάντα κατ᾽ ἀνάγκην· τὴν αὐτὴν δ᾽
εἶναι εἱμαρμένην καὶ δίκην καὶ πρόνοιαν καὶ κοσμο-
ποιόν.

b (≠ DK) Theod. *Cur.* 6.13

ὁ δὲ Παρμενίδης τὴν ἀνάγκην καὶ Δαίμονα κέκληκε
καὶ Δίκην καὶ Πρόνοιαν.

admit difference), and the sensible in the category of what is disordered and in motion.

References to Particular Points of the Cosmology (R54–R60)
The Elements as Divine (R54)

R54 (A33) Clement of Alexandria, *Protreptic*

Parmenides of Elea introduced fire and earth as gods.

The Cosmogonic Divinity (R55)

R55

a (A32) Aëtius

Parmenides [. . .]: everything happens according to necessity; and fate, justice, providence, and the creator of the world are identical.

b (≠ DK) Theodoret, *Cure of the Greek Maladies*

Parmenides called necessity Divinity (*daimôn*), Justice, and Providence.

Eros (R56–R58)

R56 Plat. *Symp.*

a (cf. ad B13) 178a–b

τὸ γὰρ ἐν τοῖς πρεσβύτατον εἶναι τὸν θεὸν τίμιον, ἦ
δ᾽ ὅς, τεκμήριον δὲ τούτου· [. . .] Παρμενίδης δὲ τὴν
γένεσιν λέγει [. . . = **D16**].

b (≠ DK) 195b–c

[ΑΓ.] ἐγὼ δὲ Φαίδρῳ πολλὰ ἄλλα ὁμολογῶν τοῦτο
οὐχ ὁμολογῶ, ὡς Ἔρως Κρόνου καὶ Ἰαπετοῦ ἀρχαι-
ότερός ἐστιν, ἀλλά φημι νεώτατον αὐτὸν εἶναι θεῶν
καὶ ἀεὶ νέον, τὰ δὲ παλαιὰ πράγματα περὶ θεούς, ἃ
Ἡσίοδος καὶ Παρμενίδης λέγουσιν, Ἀνάγκῃ καὶ οὐκ
Ἔρωτι γεγονέναι, εἰ ἐκεῖνοι ἀληθῆ ἔλεγον· οὐ γὰρ ἂν
ἐκτομαὶ οὐδὲ δεσμοὶ ἀλλήλων ἐγίγνοντο καὶ ἄλλα
πολλὰ καὶ βίαια, εἰ Ἔρως ἐν αὐτοῖς ἦν, ἀλλὰ φιλία
καὶ εἰρήνη, ὥσπερ νῦν, ἐξ οὗ Ἔρως τῶν θεῶν βασι-
λεύει.

R57 (cf. ad B13) Arist. *Metaph.* A4 984b23–31

ὑποπτεύσειε δ᾽ ἄν τις Ἡσίοδον πρῶτον ζητῆσαι τὸ
τοιοῦτον, κἂν εἴ τις ἄλλος ἔρωτα ἢ ἐπιθυμίαν ἐν τοῖς
οὖσιν ἔθηκεν ὡς ἀρχήν, οἷον καὶ Παρμενίδης· καὶ

Eros (R56–R58)

R56 Plato, *Symposium*

a (cf. ad B13)

"The fact that he [i.e. Eros] is the oldest among them [i.e. the gods] is honorable," he [i.e. Phaedrus] said, "and here is proof of this [. . .][1] As for Parmenides, he speaks of his birth: [. . . = **D16**]."

> [1] Phaedrus cites here Hesiod, *Th.* 116–17 and 120 [= **COSM. T11**] and Acusilaus 9 B2 DK, for whom Eros was never begotten.

b (≠ DK)

[Agathon:] As for me, although I agree with Phaedrus on many other points, I do not agree with him on this one, that Eros is more ancient than Cronus and Iapetus. On the contrary, I say that he is the youngest of the gods and is always young, and that the ancient matters regarding the gods about which Hesiod and Parmenides speak[1] came about because of Necessity and not because of Eros, if they were speaking the truth. For there would not have been castrations, enchainments of each other, and many other deeds of violence, if Eros had been among them, but instead there would have been friendship and peace, as there is now, ever since Eros reigns over the gods.

> [1] This indication regarding Parmenides is without parallel.

R57 (cf. ad B13) Aristotle, *Metaphysics*

One might suspect that Hesiod was the first to have sought this kind of cause [scil. the efficient cause], or anyone else who placed love or desire among beings as a principle—

141

γὰρ οὗτος κατασκευάζων τὴν τοῦ παντὸς γένεσιν [. . .
= **D16**] φησιν [. . .] Ἡσίοδος δὲ [. . .], ὡς δέον ἐν τοῖς
οὖσιν ὑπάρχειν τινὰ αἰτίαν ἥτις κινήσει καὶ συνάξει
τὰ πράγματα.

R58 (cf. ad B13) Plut. *Amat.* 756E

διὸ Παρμενίδης μὲν ἀποφαίνει τὸν Ἔρωτα τῶν Ἀφροδίτης ἔργων πρεσβύτατον ἐν τῇ κοσμογονίᾳ γράφων
[. . . = **D16**].

An Epicurean Criticism of the
Cosmotheology (R59)

R59 (< A37) Cic. *Nat. deor.* 1.28

[. . . = **D15b**] in quo neque figuram divinam neque
sensum quisquam suspicari potest. multaque eiusdem
monstra, quippe qui bellum, qui discordiam, qui cupiditatem, ceteraque generis eiusdem ad deum revocat,
quae vel morbo vel somno vel oblivione vel vetustate
delentur; eademque de sideribus, quae reprehensa in alio
iam in hoc omittantur.

A Report about the Future of the World (R60)

R60 (< A23) (Ps.-?) Hippol. *Ref.* 1.11

τὸν ⟨δὲ⟩[1] κόσμον ἔφη φθείρεσθαι, ᾧ δὲ τρόπῳ, οὐκ
εἶπεν.

1 ⟨δὲ⟩ Diels

like Parmenides too, for he says when he is explaining the generation of the whole [. . . = **D16**], and Hesiod [incomplete citation of *Th.* 116–120 = **COSM. T11**], on the idea that among beings there must be a certain cause that will move things and bring them together.

R58 (cf. ad B13) Plutarch, *Dialogue on Love*

That is why Parmenides asserts that Eros is the most ancient of the works of Aphrodite[1] when he writes in his cosmogony, [. . . = **D16**].

---

[1] It is uncertain whether Parmenides himself gave this name to the divinity of **D16**.

An Epicurean Criticism of the Cosmotheology (R59)

R59 (< A37) Cicero, *On the Nature of the Gods*

[. . .] but in this [scil. heaven that Parmenides calls god in **D15b**], no one could suspect either a divine shape or sensation. And he has many monsters too, for he assigns to a god war, discord, greed, and the other things of this sort, which are destroyed by sickness, sleep, forgetting, or old age; and the same for the stars, which I can omit here because I have already criticized them elsewhere.

A Report about the Future of the World (R60)

R60 (< A23) (Ps.-?) Hippolytus, *Refutation of All the Heresies*

He said that the world will be destroyed, but he did not say in what way [cf. **D62**].

*A Theophrastean Criticism of the
Theory of Cognition (R61)*

R61 (< A46) Theophr. *Sens.* 4

[. . .= **D52**] ἂν δ᾽ ἰσάζωσι τῇ μίξει, πότερον ἔσται
φρονεῖν ἢ οὔ, καὶ τίς ἡ διάθεσις, οὐδὲν ἔτι διώρικεν
[. . .]. οὕτω μὲν οὖν αὐτὸς ἔοικεν ἀποτέμνεσθαι τῇ
φάσει τὰ συμβαίνοντα δυσχερῆ διὰ τὴν ὑπόληψιν.

Three Images of Parmenides (R62–R72)
Parmenides and Dialectic (R62–R65)
Parmenides as the Father of Dialectic (R62–R63)

R62 (> A5) Plat. *Soph.* 217c

[ΣΩ.] πότερον εἴωθας ἥδιον αὐτὸς ἐπὶ σαυτοῦ μακρῷ
λόγῳ διεξιέναι λέγων τοῦτο ὃ ἂν ἐνδείξασθαί τῳ βου-
ληθῇς, ἢ δι᾽ ἐρωτήσεων, οἷόν ποτε καὶ Παρμενίδῃ
χρωμένῳ καὶ διεξιόντι λόγους παγκάλους παρεγενό-
μην ἐγὼ νέος ὤν, ἐκείνου μάλα δὴ τότε ὄντος πρε-
σβύτου;

R63 (≠ DK) Sext. Emp. *Adv. Math.* 7.7

Παρμενίδης δὲ οὐκ ἂν δόξαι τῆς διαλεκτικῆς ἀπείρως
ἔχειν, ἐπείπερ πάλιν Ἀριστοτέλης τὸν γνώριμον αὐτοῦ Ζήνωνα διαλεκτικῆς ἀρχηγὸν ὑπείληφεν.

A Theophrastean Criticism of the
Theory of Cognition (R61)

R61 (< A46) Theophrastus, *On Sensations*

[. . .] But for the case in which these two [scil. the hot and the cold] are in equality in the mixture, he no longer indicates at all whether there will be thought or not, and what will be the corresponding condition [. . .]. Thus he himself seems to remove by this statement [scil. that in certain cases one of the contraries taken on its own has sensation] the difficulties that result from his hypothesis.

Three Images of Parmenides (R62–R72)
Parmenides and Dialectic (R62–R65)
Parmenides as the Father of Dialectic (R62–R63)

R62 (> A5) Plato, *Sophist*

[Socrates speaking to the stranger from Elea:] When you want to explain something to someone, is it your habit to explain it by yourself alone in a long speech, or by means of questions—as once, when I was present, Parmenides made use of them and worked out some very fine arguments; I was young, and at that time he was very old.

R63 (≠ DK) Sextus Empiricus, *Against the Logicians*

Parmenides would not seem to be inexperienced in dialectic, since Aristotle in turn considered that his companion Zeno was the founder of dialectic [cf. **ZEN. R4**].

Attributions of Zenonian Arguments to
Parmenides (R64–R65)

R64 (< A1) Diog. Laert. 9.23 (cf. 9.29)

καὶ πρῶτος ἐρωτῆσαι τὸν Ἀχιλλέα λόγον, ὡς Φαβωρῖνος ἐν Παντοδαπῇ ἱστορίᾳ [Frag. 80 Amato].

R65 (≠ DK) Simpl. *In Phys.*, p. 139.24–27

ὁ μέντοι Πορφύριος καὶ τὸν ἐκ τῆς διχοτομίας λόγον
Παρμενίδου φησὶν εἶναι ἓν τὸ ὂν ἐκ ταύτης πειρωμέ-
νου δεικνύναι. γράφει δὲ οὕτως· [Frag. 135F Smith]
"ἕτερος δὲ ἦν λόγος τῷ Παρμενίδη ὁ διὰ τῆς διχοτομίας οἰόμενος δεικνύναι τὸ ὂν ἓν εἶναι μόνον καὶ
τοῦτο ἀμερὲς καὶ ἀδιαίρετον [. . .]."

Parmenides as a Pythagorean (R66–R70)

R66 (> A4) Phot. *Bibl.* 249, p. 439a35–38 Bekker

τῆς δὲ λογικῆς σπέρματα καταβαλεῖν αὐτῷ Ζήνωνα
καὶ Παρμενίδην τοὺς Ἐλεάτας· καὶ οὗτοι δὲ τῆς Πυ-
θαγορείου ἦσαν διατριβῆς.

R67 (A4) Iambl. *VP* 166

[. . .] καὶ περὶ τῶν φυσικῶν ὅσοι τινὰ μνείαν πεποίη-
νται, πρῶτον Ἐμπεδοκλέα καὶ Παρμενίδην τὸν Ἐλεάτην προφερόμενοι τυγχάνουσιν [. . .].

*Attributions of Zenonian Arguments to
Parmenides (R64–R65)*

R64 (< A1) Diogenes Laertius

He was the first person to raise the question of the argument of Achilles [cf. **ZEN. D15a**], as Favorinus reports in his *Miscellaneous History*.

R65 (≠ DK) Simplicius, *Commentary on Aristotle's Physics*

Porphyry says that the argument of dichotomy [cf. **ZEN. D14**] too belongs to Parmenides, who was trying to demonstrate on this basis that being is one. He writes as follows: "Parmenides had another argument, the one by means of dichotomy, which aims to show that being is only one and that it is without parts and indivisible [. . .]."

Parmenides as a Pythagorean (R66–R70)

R66 (> A4) Photius, *Library*

Zeno and Parmenides, the Eleatics, sowed the seeds of logic for him [i.e. Plato]; these men too belonged to the Pythagorean school.

R67 (A4) Iamblichus, *Life of Pythagoras*

[. . .] among those [i.e. the Pythagoreans in Italy] who became celebrated for natural philosophy, Empedocles and Parmenides of Elea are distinguished first of all [. . .].

R68 (< A1) Diog. Laert. 9.23

καὶ δοκεῖ πρῶτος πεφωρακέναι τὸν αὐτὸν εἶναι Ἕσπερον καὶ Φωσφόρον [. . . cf. **D22**]· οἱ δὲ Πυθαγόραν·
Καλλίμαχος δέ φησι μὴ εἶναι αὐτοῦ τὸ ποίημα.

R69 (< A48) Aët. 4.13.10 (Stob.) [περὶ ὁράσεως]

ἔνιοι καὶ Πυθαγόραν τῇ δόξῃ ταύτῃ συνεπιγράφου-
σιν, ἅτε δὴ βεβαιωτὴν τῶν μαθημάτων· καὶ πρὸς
τούτῳ Παρμενίδην ἐμφαίνοντα τοῦτο διὰ τῶν ποιημάτων.

R70 (≠DK) Ps.-Ceb. *Tab.* 2.2

ἀλλὰ ξένος τις πάλαι ποτὲ ἀφίκετο δεῦρο, ἀνὴρ ἔμ-
φρων καὶ δεινὸς περὶ σοφίαν, λόγῳ τε καὶ ἔργῳ Πυ-
θαγόρειόν τινα καὶ Παρμενίδειον ἐζηλωκὼς βίον
[. . .].

Parmenides as a Christian (R71–R72)

R71 (≠DK) Clem. Alex. *Strom.* 5.59.6

ὅ τ᾽ Ἐλεάτης Παρμενίδης ὁ μέγας διττῶν εἰσηγεῖται
διδασκαλίαν ὁδῶν ὧδέ πως γράφων [. . . = **D4.29–30,**
with textual variants].

R68 (< A1) Diogenes Laertius

He seems to have been the first person to have discovered that the evening star and the star that brings the light are the same [. . .]; but others say that it was Pythagoras. But Callimachus says that the poem [scil. of Parmenides] is not by him [i.e. probably: Pythagoras].

R69 (< A48) Aëtius

Certain people attach the name of Pythagoras too to this opinion [i.e. that of Hipparchus regarding the mechanism of vision] as being the authority for scientific knowledge; and besides him, Parmenides, who states this in his poem.[1]

[1] Hipparchus thought, in the tradition of Plato's *Timaeus,* that visual rays depart from the eyes "like hands." Nothing of this sort is preserved among the verses of Parmenides.

R70 (≠ DK) Ps.-Cebes, *The Tablet*

A long time ago, a stranger arrived here one day, an intelligent man and expert in wisdom, who pursued in word and deed a certain Pythagorean and Parmenidean way of life [. . .].

Parmenides as a Christian (R71–R72)

R71 (≠ DK) Clement of Alexandria, *Stromata*

The great Parmenides of Elea introduced the doctrine of the two roads [i.e. that of the revealed truth of the New Testament and the initiation for the whole coming from the Old Testament], when he wrote as follows: [. . . = **D4.29–30**].

149

R72 (cf. ad B4) Clem. Alex. *Strom.* 5.15.5–16.1

ἀλλὰ καὶ Παρμενίδης ἐν τῷ αὐτοῦ ποιήματι περὶ τῆς
Ἐλπίδος αἰνισσόμενος τὰ τοιαῦτα λέγει· [. . . = **D10**].
ἐπεὶ καὶ ὁ ἐλπίζων, καθάπερ ὁ πιστεύων, τῷ νῷ ὁρᾷ
τὰ νοητὰ καὶ τὰ μέλλοντα.

The Rarity of the Text of Parmenides in the
6th Century AD (R73)

R73 (A21) Simpl. *In Phys.*, p. 144.25–28

καὶ εἴ τῳ μὴ δοκῶ γλίσχρος, ἡδέως ἂν τὰ περὶ τοῦ
ἑνὸς ὄντος ἔπη τοῦ Παρμενίδου μηδὲ πολλὰ ὄντα
τοῖσδε τοῖς ὑπομνήμασι παραγράψαιμι διά τε τὴν
πίστιν τῶν ὑπ᾽ ἐμοῦ λεγομένων καὶ διὰ τὴν σπάνιν
τοῦ Παρμενιδείου συγγράμματος.

R72 (cf. ad B4) Clement of Alexandria, *Stromata*

But Parmenides too in his poem refers allegorically to Hope when he says, [. . . = **D10**], since the man who hopes, like the one who believes, sees intelligible things and future ones with his mind.

See also **R37**

The Rarity of the Text of Parmenides in the 6th Century AD (R73)

R73 (A21) Simplicius, *Commentary on Aristotle's* Physics

And without wanting to seem overly insistent to anyone, I would like to cite in this commentary Parmenides' verses on the One that is—they are not many—both in order to make what I say more plausible and because of the rarity of Parmenides' text.

20. ZENO [ZEN.]

If we combine the indications furnished by the chronographer Apollodorus of Athens and those that can be derived from Plato's *Parmenides*—however uncertain the historical exactness of these latter might be—we can conclude that Zeno, a citizen of Elea like his teacher Parmenides, was born around 504/500 BC. The ancient tradition records his attachment to his city (which may lend a particular significance to his visit to Athens in the company of Parmenides to attend the Panathenaic festival), his admiration for Pericles, and his opposition to tyranny.

Plato states that his treatise was composed of a series of arguments intended to defend Parmenides' thesis on the unicity of being, arguments whose particular character was that they did not offer a positive demonstration (of the sort found in Melissus) but instead developed the aporias inherent in the contrary hypothesis of plurality, in order to demonstrate its impossibility by reason of the contradictory conclusions deriving from it. Other arguments of Zeno's refuted the existence of movement (four, according to Aristotle, see **D1, D14–D19**) and of place (**D13**). In late sources (Proclus, **D2;** Elias, **D3**), the total number of arguments increases to forty.

The procedure adopted by Zeno involves a novelty that Aristotle identified in making Zeno the inventor of dialectic, that is, a technique of contradictory argumentation in

which the starting point is found not among premises that are necessary or have been demonstrated previously but among reputable opinions. It is also on this basis that certain scholars, who have ancient antecedents, have been able to interpret Zeno's intention not as the indirect defense of Parmenides but as a skeptical nihilism deriving from the possibility of arguing legitimately in favor both of a thesis and of its contrary. The existence of an argument apparently directed not against multiplicity but against unity (see **R10–R15**) has been read in this way. In any case, the influence of Zeno's arguments has been immense, if only by reason of the refutations that philosophers have been obliged to seek for them (beginning with Aristotle, in the exposition of his doctrine of the continuous in Books 4 and 6 of his *Physics*), but it is due less to the philosophical position he defended than to the logical challenges that his paradoxes posed. Modern theoreticians of mathematics and physics have continued to find these interesting.

BIBLIOGRAPHY

Editions

M. Untersteiner. *Zenone. Testimonianze e frammenti*, (Florence, 1963).

Studies

M. Caveing. *Zénon d'Élee: prolégomènes aux doctrines du continu. Étude historique et critique des fragments et témoignages* (Paris, 1982).

See also, in the introduction to Parmenides, the works of G. Calogero and of P. Curd.

OUTLINE OF THE CHAPTER

ZENO [29 DK]

P

Chronology (P1–P3)

P1

a (< A1) Diog. Laert. 9.29

ἤκμαζε δὲ οὗτος κατὰ τὴν ἐνάτην[1] ‹καὶ ἑβδομηκοστὴν›[2] Ὀλυμπιάδα [= Apollod. *FGrHist* 244 F30].

    [1] ἐνάτην B: θ΄ P[1](Q): om. F   [2] ‹καὶ ἑβδομηκοστὴν›
Aldobrandinus

b (< A2) *Suda* Z.77

Ζήνων, Τελευταγόρου, Ἐλεάτης, φιλόσοφος τῶν ἐγ-
γιζόντων Πυθαγόρᾳ καὶ Δημοκρίτῳ κατὰ τοὺς χρόνους (ἦν γὰρ ἐπὶ τῆς οη΄ Ὀλυμπιάδος) [. . .].

P2 (< A3) Eus. *Chron.* (Hier. *Chron.*, p. 111.23)

[ad Ol. 81.1] Zeno [. . .] agnoscitur.

    Ol. 81.1] *vel* 81.2 *mss. quidam*

158

ZENO

P

Chronology (P1–P3)

P1

a (< A1) Diogenes Laertius

He attained his full maturity in the ‹7›9th Olympiad [= 464/60].

b (< A2) *Suda*

Zeno of Elea, son of Teleutagoras, one of the philosophers chronologically close[1] to Pythagoras and Democritus. For he lived during the 78th Olympiad [= 468/64].

[1] If this indication is not erroneous, it must be understood very broadly, as referring to an 'epoch.'

P2 (< A3) Eusebius, *Chronicle*

[Olympiad 81.1 = 456] Zeno [. . .] is recognized.

P3 (≠ DK) al-Šahrazūrī, *Nuzhat al-arwāḥ wa-rawḍat al-afrāḥ,* p. 32.40 Rosenthal

مات وله ثمانٍ وسبعون سنة.

Parmenides, Zeno's Intellectual
Father and Lover (P4–P5)

P4 (< A1) Diog. Laert. 9.25

Ζήνων Ἐλεάτης. τοῦτον Ἀπολλόδωρός φησιν [*FGrHist* 244 F30a] εἶναι ἐν Χρονικοῖς[1] φύσει μὲν Τελευταγόρου, θέσει δὲ Παρμενίδου.

[1] post Χρονικοῖς hab. mss. πύρητος τὸν δὲ Παρμενίδην, secl. Rossi: τὸν δὲ Παρμενίδην Πύρητος post Παρμενίδου add. Karsten

P5

a (< A11) Plat. *Parm.* 127b

[. . .] καὶ λέγεσθαι αὐτὸν παιδικὰ τοῦ Παρμενίδου γεγονέναι.

b (A11) Athen. *Deipn.* 11.113 505F

τὸ δὲ πάντων σχετλιώτατον[1] καὶ τὸ εἰπεῖν οὐδεμιᾶς κατεπειγούσης χρείας ὅτι παιδικὰ γεγόνοι τοῦ Παρμενίδου Ζήνων ὁ πολίτης αὐτοῦ.

[1] σχετλιώτερον A, corr. Musurus

P3 (≠ DK) al-Šahrazūrī, *The Pleasure Place of Spirits and the Garden of Rejoicing,* entry on "Zeno"

He died at the age of seventy-eight years.[1]

[1] Translated by Germana Chemi.

Parmenides, Zeno's Intellectual Father and Lover (P4–P5)

P4 (< A1) Diogenes Laertius

Apollodorus says in his *Chronicles* that he was by nature Teleutagoras' son but by adoption Parmenides'.

P5

a (< A11) Plato, *Parmenides*

[. . .] It was said that he had been Parmenides' beloved.

b (A11) Athenaeus, *Deipnosophists*

The most shameful thing of all is that he [i.e. Plato] says, without being compelled by any necessity, that Parmenides' fellow citizen Zeno was his beloved.

Zeno at Athens (P6–P8)

His Visit to the Great Panathenaic Festival (P6)

P6 (< A11) Plat. *Parm.* 127a–c

[ΚΕ.] ἔφη δὲ δὴ ὁ Ἀντιφῶν λέγειν τὸν Πυθόδωρον ὅτι ἀφίκοιντό ποτε εἰς Παναθήναια τὰ μεγάλα Ζήνων τε καὶ Παρμενίδης [. . . cf. **PARM. P4**]. Ζήνωνα δὲ ἐγγὺς τῶν[1] τετταράκοντα τότε εἶναι, εὐμήκη δὲ καὶ χαρίεντα ἰδεῖν [. . . = **P5a**]. καταλύειν δὲ αὐτοὺς ἔφη παρὰ τῷ Πυθοδώρῳ ἐκτὸς τείχους ἐν Κεραμεικῷ· οἳ δὴ καὶ ἀφικέσθαι τόν τε Σωκράτη καὶ ἄλλους τινὰς μετ᾽ αὐτοῦ πολλούς, ἐπιθυμοῦντας ἀκοῦσαι τῶν τοῦ Ζήνωνος γραμμάτων—τότε γὰρ αὐτὰ πρῶτον ὑπ᾽ ἐκείνων κομισθῆναι—Σωκράτη δὲ εἶναι τότε σφόδρα νέον.

[1] τῶν GW: ἐτῶν BT

Zeno and Pericles (P7–P8)

P7 (< A4) Plut. *Per.* 4.5

διήκουσε δὲ Περικλῆς καὶ Ζήνωνος τοῦ Ἐλεάτου [. . . = **R6**].

P8 (A17) Plut. *Per.* 5.3

[. . .] τοὺς δὲ τοῦ Περικλέους τὴν σεμνότητα δοξοκοπίαν τε καὶ τῦφον ἀποκαλοῦντας ὁ Ζήνων παρεκάλει καὶ αὐτούς τι τοιοῦτο δοξοκοπεῖν, ὡς τῆς προσποιήσεως αὐτῆς τῶν καλῶν ὑποποιούσης τινὰ λεληθότως ζῆλον καὶ συνήθειαν.

Zeno at Athens (P6–P8)
His Visit to the Great Panathenaic Festival (P6)

P6 (< A11) Plato, *Parmenides*

[Cephalus:] Antiphon reported that Pythodorus had said that Zeno and Parmenides once came to the Great Panathenaic festival [. . .]. Zeno was near forty at that time, tall and attractive in appearance [. . .]. He said that they stayed at Pythodorus' house outside the city walls in the Kerameikos; it was there that Socrates went together with many others desiring to hear what Zeno had written—for this was the first time that they had brought the book with them. Socrates was very young at the time.[1]

[1] See the note on **PARM. P4.**

Zeno and Pericles (P7–P8)

P7 (< A4) Plutarch, *Pericles*

Pericles also studied with Zeno of Elea [. . .].

P8 (A17) Plutarch, *Pericles*

[. . .] those who criticized Pericles' solemnity as being an ambition for glory and mere vanity Zeno called upon to be ambitious themselves for this kind of glory, since he thought that the very imitation of fine things gradually produces, without being noticed, a zeal for them and a habit.

Character (P9–P10)

P9 (< A1) Diog. Laert. 9.26

γέγονε δὲ ἀνὴρ γενναιότατος καὶ ἐν φιλοσοφίᾳ καὶ ἐν
πολιτείᾳ. φέρεται γοῦν αὐτοῦ βιβλία πολλῆς συνέ-
σεως γέμοντα.

P10 (< A1) Diog. Laert. 9.28

γέγονε δὲ τά τε ἄλλα ἀγαθὸς ὁ Ζήνων, ἀλλὰ καὶ ὑπε-
ροπτικὸς τῶν μειζόνων κατ' ἴσον Ἡρακλείτῳ· καὶ γὰρ
οὗτος τὴν πρότερον μὲν Ὕελην,[1] ὕστερον δὲ Ἐλέαν,
Φωκαέων οὖσαν ἀποικίαν, αὐτοῦ[2] δὲ πατρίδα, πόλιν
εὐτελῆ καὶ μόνον ἄνδρας ἀγαθοὺς τρέφειν ἐπισταμέ-
νην, ἠγάπησε μᾶλλον τῆς Ἀθηναίων μεγαλαυχίας,
οὐκ ἐπιδημήσας τὰ πολλὰ[3] πρὸς αὐτούς, ἀλλ' αὐτόθι
καταβιούς.

---

[1] Ὕελην Casaubon: ὕλην mss.   [2] αὐτοῦ mss., corr. Cobet
[3] τὰ πολλὰ mss.: πώμαλα Diels

Emoluments (P11)

P11 (< A4) (Ps.-?) Plat. *Alc. 1* 119a

[. . .] Πυθόδωρον τὸν Ἰσολόχου καὶ Καλλίαν τὸν Καλ-
λιάδου, ὧν ἑκάτερος Ζήνωνι ἑκατὸν μνᾶς τελέσας σο-
φός τε καὶ ἐλλόγιμος γέγονεν.

ZENO

Character (P9–P10)

P9 (< A1) Diogenes Laertius

He was a man of great nobility both in philosophy and in politics. For books of his full of much intelligence are in circulation.[1]

> [1] The plural may imply the existence of apocryphal writings (cf. **R35–R36**). On Zeno's political nobility, see **P13–P16**.

P10 (< A1) Diogenes Laertius

Zeno was a fine man in other regards, but he was also disdainful of the great, exactly as Heraclitus was [cf. **HER. P9**]. For he loved his own country—at first called Hyele, then Elea, a colony of the Phocaeans, a simple town that knew how to do nothing other than to raise fine men— more than the splendor of Athens; he did not travel there often, but passed his whole life in the same place.

Emoluments (P11)

P11 (< A4) (Ps.-?) Plato, *First Alcibiades*

[. . .] Pythodorus, son of Isolochus, and Callias, son of Calliades, became wise and famous because they had each paid a hundred minas to Zeno.

A Story of Injustice (P12)

P12 (A5) Arist. *Rhet.* 1.12 1372b3–5

[. . .] καὶ οἷς τοὐναντίον τὰ μὲν ἀδικήματα εἰς ἔπαινόν τινα, οἷον εἰ συνέβη ἅμα τιμωρήσασθαι ὑπὲρ πατρὸς ἢ μητρός, ὥσπερ Ζήνωνι [. . .].

The Philosopher and the Tyrant (P13–P16)

P13 (A6) Diod. Sic. 10.18.2–6

[2] ὅτι τυραννουμένης τῆς πατρίδος ὑπὸ Νεάρχου σκληρῶς, ἐπιβουλὴν κατὰ τοῦ τυράννου συνεστή-σατο.[1] καταφανὴς δὲ γενόμενος, καὶ κατὰ τὰς ἐν ταῖς βασάνοις ἀνάγκας διερωτώμενος ὑπὸ τοῦ Νεάρχου τίνες ἦσαν οἱ συνειδότες, ὤφελον γάρ, ἔφησεν, ὥσπερ τῆς γλώττης εἰμὶ κύριος, οὕτως ὑπῆρχον καὶ τοῦ σώματος. [3] τοῦ δὲ τυράννου πολὺ μᾶλλον ταῖς βα-σάνοις προσεπιτείναντος, ὁ Ζήνων μέχρι μέν τινος διεκαρτέρει· μετὰ δὲ ταῦτα σπεύδων ἀπολυθῆναί ποτε τῆς ἀνάγκης καὶ ἅμα τιμωρήσασθαι τὸν Νέαρχον, ἐπενοήσατό τι τοιοῦτον. [4] κατὰ τὴν ἐπιτονωτάτην ἐπίτασιν[2] τῆς βασάνου προσποιηθεὶς ἐνδιδόναι τὴν ψυχὴν ταῖς ἀλγηδόσιν ἀνέκραγεν, ἄνετε, ἐρῶ γὰρ πᾶ-

---

[1] κατεστήσατο ms., corr. Dindorf   [2] ἐπίστασιν ms., corr. Valois

A Story of Injustice (P12)

P12 (A5) Aristotle, *Rhetoric*

[. . .] and those whose unjust actions are considered praise-worthy, as for example if it happens that at the same time one takes vengeance for one's father or mother, as in the case of Zeno [. . .].[1]

[1] Aristotle is listing situations in which one does not hesitate to commit an unjust action. His reference to Zeno seems likely to be to the philosopher; the circumstances to which he is alluding are unknown.

The Philosopher and the Tyrant (P13–P16)[1]

[1] This episode is reported (with variations) by a number of other authors (Diogenes Laertius, Plutarch, Clement of Alexandria, Philostratus).

P13 (A6) Diodorus Siculus

[2] Because his country was ruled harshly by the tyrant Nearchus, he organized a conspiracy against the despot. But he was discovered, and when he was interrogated under the constraint of torture regarding the identity of his accomplices, he said, "If only I were master of my body as I am of my tongue" [cf. **P15**]. [3] The tyrant increased the torture greatly, but Zeno held out for a while; but then, wanting to be freed from the pain and at the same time to be avenged upon Nearchus, he had the following idea: [4] when the torture reached its greatest intensity, he pretended that he was dying because of the pain and cried out, "Stop! I will tell you the whole truth." And when they

σαν ἀλήθειαν. ὡς δ᾽ ἀνῆκαν,[3] ἠξίωσεν αὐτὸν ἀκοῦσαι
κατ᾽ ἰδίαν προσελθόντα· πολλὰ γὰρ εἶναι τῶν λέγεσθαι μελλόντων ἃ συνοίσει τηρεῖν ἐν ἀπορρήτῳ. [5]
τοῦ δὲ τυράννου προσελθόντος ἀσμένως καὶ τὴν
ἀκοὴν τῷ στόματι παραβαλόντος, ὁ Ζήνων τοῦ δυνά-
στου περιχανὼν τὸ οὖς ἐνέπρισε τοῖς ὀδοῦσι. τῶν δὲ
ὑπηρετῶν ταχὺ προσδραμόντων, καὶ πᾶσαν τῷ βα-
σανιζομένῳ προσφερόντων τιμωρίαν εἰς τὸ χαλάσαι
τὸ δῆγμα, πολὺ μᾶλλον προσενεφύετο. [6] τέλος δ᾽ οὐ
δυνάμενοι τἀνδρὸς νικῆσαι τὴν εὐψυχίαν, παρεκέντησαν[4] αὐτὸν ἵνα διίῃ τοὺς ὀδόντας. καὶ τοιούτῳ τεχνή-
ματι τῶν ἀλγηδόνων ἀπελύθη καὶ παρὰ τοῦ τυράννου
τὴν ἐνδεχομένην ἔλαβε τιμωρίαν.

  [3] ἀνῆκαν Reiske: ἀνῆκεν ms.   [4] παρεκέντησαν Döhner:
παρεκάλεσαν ms.

P14 (< A15) Elias *In Cat.*, p. 109.12–15

[. . . = **R9**] ἐρωτηθεὶς γὰρ οὗτός ποτε ὑπό του τυράννου
τίνες εἰσὶν οἱ μάλιστα ἐπιβουλεύοντες τῇ τυραννίδι
αὐτοῦ, τοὺς δορυφόρους ἔδειξεν· ὁ δὲ πεισθεὶς καὶ
ἀνελὼν αὐτοὺς διεφθάρη· ἀγαθὸν γὰρ ἐνόμισε τὸ ψεύ-
σασθαι διὰ τὴν τοῦ τυράννου ἀναίρεσιν.

P15 (A19) Tert. *Apol.* 50.9

Zeno Eleates consultus a Dionysio quidnam philosophia
praestaret, cum respondisset: "impassibilem fieri,"[1] fla-
gellis tyranni subiectus[2] sententiam suam ad mortem usque signabat.

had stopped, he told him to come close to him so that he would be the only one to hear: for many of the things that he was going to say would be better kept secret. [5] The tyrant was pleased and, coming close to him, placed his ear beside the mouth of Zeno, who seized the despot's ear with his teeth and bit it. The servants ran up quickly and inflicted all kinds of further suffering upon the tortured man in order to make him stop biting, but instead he bit all the more firmly. [6] In the end they were unable to overcome this man's courage, and they stabbed him to death to make him loosen his bite. And it was by this stratagem that he was freed from his pains and took the vengeance he could upon the tyrant.

P14 (< A15) Elias, *Commentary on Aristotle's* Categories

[. . .] For when he was asked one day by the tyrant who were the people who were conspiring most again his tyranny, he indicated the bodyguards; the other was convinced, killed them—and was assassinated. For he thought it was a good thing to tell a lie in order to overthrow a tyrant.

P15 (A19) Tertullian, *Apology*

When Dionysius asked Zeno of Elea what it was that philosophy could provide, he answered, "to become indifferent to suffering"; when he was condemned by the tyrant to be whipped, he set a seal upon his opinion to the point of death.

---

[1] impassibilem fieri *F*: contemptu mortis inpassibilis *S*, contemptum mortus inpassibilis *vulg.*, contemptu mortis impassibilem fieri *coni. Haverkamp*   [2] subiectus *F*: obiectus *vulg.*, abiectus *dett.*

P16 (A20) Stob. 3.7.37

Ζήνων ὁ Ἐλεάτης ὑπὸ τοῦ τυράννου στρεβλούμενος,
ὅπως εἴποι τοὺς συνωμότας· "εἰ γὰρ ἦσαν," εἶπεν,
"<οὐκ ἂν>[1] ἐτυράννεις."

[1] <οὐκ ἂν> Meineke

Another Apothegm (P17)

P17 (< A1) Diog. Laert. 9.29

τοῦτόν φασι λοιδορούμενον ἀγανακτῆσαι· αἰτιασαμέ-
νου δέ τινος, φάναι· "ἐὰν μὴ λοιδορούμενος[1] προσ-
ποιῶμαι, οὐδὲ ἐπαινούμενος αἰσθήσομαι."

[1] μὴ λοιδορούμενος BP¹Φh: μὴ om. F¹, expunxit Pˣ: λοιδορούμενος μὴ Iunius: λοιδορούμενος μὴ <ἀχθῆναι> Marcovich

P16 (A20) Stobaeus, *Anthology*

When Zeno of Elea was tortured by the tyrant so that he would name his accomplices, he said, "If there were any, you would not be tyrant."

Another Apothegm (P17)

P17 (< A1) Diogenes Laertius

They say that when he was vilified he became very angry; and when someone criticized him, he said, "If I do not pretend [scil. to be angry] when I am vilified, then I will not notice either when I am being praised" [cf. **EMP. P28a**].

Iconography (P18)

P18 (≠ DK) Richter I, pp. 108–9; Koch, "Ikonographie," in Flashar, Bremer, Rechenauer (2013), I.1, p. 222.

ZENO [29 DK]

D

Writings

Cf. **R2, R35–R36**

The Number of Zeno's Arguments (D1–D3)

D1 (< A25) Arist. *Phys.* 6.9 239b9–11

τέτταρες δ᾽ εἰσὶν οἱ λόγοι περὶ κινήσεως Ζήνωνος οἱ
παρέχοντες τὰς δυσκολίας τοῖς λύουσιν.

D2 (< A15) Procl. *In Parm.*, p. 694.17–19

πολλῶν δὲ εἰρημένων ὑπὸ τοῦ Ζήνωνος λόγων καὶ
τετταράκοντα ὄντων[1] πάντων, ἕνα τῶν πρώτων ὁ Σω-
κράτης ἀπολαβὼν ἀπορεῖ πρὸς αὐτόν [. . .].

---

[1] ὄντων Steel ex Moerbeke (entibus): τῶν ΑΣ

D3 (< A15) Elias *in Cat.*, p. 109.15–20

καὶ τῷ οἰκείῳ διδασκάλῳ ποτὲ Παρμενίδῃ ἓν λέγοντι

ZENO

D

Writings

Cf. **R2, R35–36**

The Number of Zeno's Arguments (D1–D3)

D1 (< A25) Aristotle, *Physics*

There are four arguments by Zeno about motion [cf. **D14–D19**], which present difficulties for those who try to solve them.

D2 (< A15) Proclus, *Commentary on Plato's* Parmenides

Of the many arguments stated by Zeno, which were forty in all, Socrates has chosen one of the first ones and raises a difficulty with regard to it [. . .].

D3 (< A15) Elias, *Commentary on Aristotle's* Categories

And in favor of his former personal teacher, Parmenides,

173

τὸ ὂν κατὰ[1] τὸ εἶδος, ἐκ τῆς ἐναργείας[2] πολλὰ τὰ ὄντα,
συντίθησιν ἐκ τεσσαράκοντα ἐπιχειρημάτων ὅτι ἓν τὸ
ὄν, ἀγαθὸν νομίσας τῷ οἰκείῳ συμμαχεῖν διδασκάλῳ.
καί ποτε πάλιν τῷ αὐτῷ συνηγορῶν διδασκάλῳ
ἀκίνητον λέγοντι τὸ ὄν, διὰ πέντε ἐπιχειρημάτων κα-
τασκευάζει ὅτι ἀκίνητον τὸ ὄν.

[1] καὶ mss., corr. Kranz   [2] ἐναργείας Diels: ἐνεργείας
mss.

The Contents of the Arguments
Preserved (D4–D19)
Arguments Against Plurality (D4–D12)
The First Argument: Similar and Dissimilar (D4)

D4 (A12 Untersteiner) Plat. *Parm.* 127d–128a

τὸν οὖν Σωκράτη ἀκούσαντα πάλιν τε κελεῦσαι τὴν
πρώτην ὑπόθεσιν τοῦ πρώτου λόγου ἀναγνῶναι, καὶ
ἀναγνωσθείσης, πῶς, φάναι, ὦ Ζήνων, τοῦτο λέγεις;
εἰ πολλά ἐστι τὰ ὄντα, ὡς ἄρα δεῖ αὐτὰ ὅμοιά τε εἶναι
καὶ ἀνόμοια, τοῦτο δὲ δὴ ἀδύνατον· οὔτε γὰρ τὰ
ἀνόμοια ὅμοια οὔτε τὰ ὅμοια ἀνόμοια οἷόν τε εἶναι.
οὐχ οὕτω λέγεις; οὕτω, φάναι τὸν Ζήνωνα. οὐκοῦν εἰ
ἀδύνατον τά τε ἀνόμοια ὅμοια εἶναι καὶ τὰ ὅμοια
ἀνόμοια, ἀδύνατον δὴ καὶ πολλὰ εἶναι· εἰ γὰρ πολλὰ
εἴη, πάσχοι ἂν τὰ ἀδύνατα.

who said that being is one according to its form, but that beings are multiple according to the evidence, he concludes on the basis of forty arguments that being is one, since he thought it a good thing to defend his own teacher. And agreeing once again with this same teacher, who said that being is immobile, he establishes on the basis of five[1] arguments that being is immobile.

[1] Aristotle (**D1**) says 'four.'

The Contents of the Arguments
Preserved (D4–D19)
Arguments Against Plurality (D4–D12)
The First Argument: Similar and Dissimilar (D4)

D4 (≠ DK) Plato, *Parmenides*

After he had listened, Socrates asked him [i.e. Zeno] to read again the first hypothesis (*hupothesis*) of the first argument; and, when it had been read, he said, "What are you saying, Zeno? If beings are multiple, then it is necessary that the same things be both similar and dissimilar; but this is certainly impossible: for it is not possible that dissimilar things be similar nor that similar ones be dissimilar. Is this not what you are saying?"

"Yes," said Zeno.

"And so, if it is not possible that dissimilar things be similar nor that similar things be dissimilar, it is certainly also impossible that they be multiple. For if they were multiple, what would happen to them would be impossibilities."

Argument by Magnitude:
Small and Large (D5–D10)

D5 (< B1) Simpl. *In Phys.*, p. 141.1–2

εἰ μὴ ἔχοι[1] μέγεθος τὸ ὂν οὐδ' ἂν εἴη.

[1] ἔχοι DF: ἔχει E ed. Ald.

D6 (< B1) Simpl. *In Phys.*, p. 141.2–8

εἰ δὲ ἔστιν, ἀνάγκη ἕκαστον[1] μέγεθός τι ἔχειν καὶ
πάχος καὶ ἀπέχειν αὐτοῦ τὸ ἕτερον ἀπὸ τοῦ ἑτέρου.
καὶ περὶ τοῦ προύχοντος ὁ αὐτὸς λόγος. καὶ γὰρ
ἐκεῖνο ἕξει μέγεθος καὶ προέξει αὐτοῦ τι. ὅμοιον δὴ
τοῦτο ἅπαξ τε εἰπεῖν καὶ ἀεὶ λέγειν· οὐδὲν γὰρ
αὐτοῦ τοιοῦτον ἔσχατον ἔσται οὔτε ἕτερον πρὸς ἕτερον οὐκ ἔσται. οὕτως εἰ πολλά ἐστιν, ἀνάγκη αὐτὰ
μικρά τε εἶναι καὶ μεγάλα, μικρὰ μὲν ὥστε μὴ ἔχειν
μέγεθος, μεγάλα δὲ ὥστε ἄπειρα εἶναι.

[1] τὸ ὄν post ἕκαστον hab. F

D7 (B2) Simpl. *In Phys.*, p. 139.9–15

ἐν δὴ τούτῳ δείκνυσιν ὅτι οὗ μήτε μέγεθος μήτε πάχος μήτε ὄγκος μηθείς ἐστιν, οὐδ' ἂν εἴη τοῦτο. "εἰ
γὰρ[1] ἄλλῳ ὄντι, φησί, προσγένοιτο, οὐδὲν ἂν μεῖζον
ποιήσειεν· μεγέθους γὰρ μηδενὸς ὄντος, προσγενο-
μένου δὲ[2] οὐδὲν οἷόν τε εἰς μέγεθος ἐπιδοῦναι. καὶ

Argument by Magnitude:
Small and Large (D5–D10)

D5 (< B1) Simplicius, *Commentary on Aristotle's* Physics

If what exists did not have magnitude, it would not exist either.

D6 (< B1) Simplicius, *Commentary on Aristotle's* Physics

But if it exists, it is necessary that each thing possess some magnitude and thickness and that one part of it be distinct from something else. And the same argument applies to what is more. For it too will possess a magnitude and one part of it will be more. Now, it is the same thing to say this one time and to say it forever. For no part of such a thing will be the last one, nor will there be any part of it that will not be in relation with another. Thus if many things exist, it is necessary that they be both small and large, so small that they do not have any size, and so large that they are unlimited.

D7 (B2) Simplicius, *Commentary on Aristotle's* Physics

In this argument he shows that what does not possess any magnitude or thickness or volume could not exist either. He says, **"For if it were added to another thing that exists, this would not make it any larger. For if a magnitude is nothing, when it is added it is not possible to progress toward magnitude. And already in**

---

[1] εἰ γὰρ D: οὐ γὰρ EF: οὐ γὰρ εἰ ed. Ald.   [2] προσγε-
νομένου δὲ obl. D, δὲ del. Zeller

οὕτως ἂν ἤδη τὸ προσγινόμενον οὐδὲν εἴη. εἰ δὲ
ἀπογινομένου τὸ ἕτερον μηδὲν ἔλαττόν ἐστι, μηδὲ
αὖ προσγινομένου αὐξήσεται, δῆλον ὅτι τὸ προσ-
γενόμενον οὐδὲν ἦν οὐδὲ τὸ ἀπογενόμενον."[3]

[3] ἀπογενόμενον ed. Ald.: ἀπογινόμενον DEF

D8 (A21) Arist. *Metaph.* B4 1001b7–13

ἔτι εἰ ἀδιαίρετον αὐτὸ τὸ ἕν, κατὰ μὲν τὸ Ζήνωνος
ἀξίωμα οὐθὲν ἂν εἴη (ὃ γὰρ μήτε προστιθέμενον μήτε
ἀφαιρούμενον ποιεῖ μεῖζον μηδὲ ἔλαττον,[1] οὔ φησιν
εἶναι τοῦτο τῶν ὄντων, ὡς δηλονότι ὄντος μεγέθους
τοῦ ὄντος· καὶ εἰ μέγεθος, σωματικόν· τοῦτο γὰρ
πάντῃ ὄν· τὰ δὲ ἄλλα πῶς μὲν προστιθέμενα ποιήσει
μεῖζον, πῶς δ' οὐθέν, οἷον ἐπίπεδον καὶ γραμμή,
στιγμὴ δὲ καὶ μονὰς οὐδαμῶς) [. . . = **R24**].

[1] μηδὲ ἔλαττον Aᵇ: om. EJ

D9 (< A22) Simpl. *In Phys.*, p. 138.3–6

τὸν δὲ [. . .] λόγον τὸν ἐκ τῆς διχοτομίας τοῦ Ζήνωνος
εἶναί φησιν ὁ Ἀλέξανδρος λέγοντος ὡς εἰ μέγεθος
ἔχοι τὸ ὂν καὶ διαιροῖτο, πολλὰ τὸ ὂν καὶ οὐχ ἓν ἔτι
ἔσεσθαι, καὶ διὰ τοῦτο[1] δεικνύντος ὅτι μηδὲν τῶν
ὄντων ἔστι τὸ ἕν.

[1] τοῦτο E: τούτου cett.

this way, what is added would be nothing. And if, when it is removed, the other thing is not at all smaller, and if when it is added it does not make it larger, then it is clear that what is added is nothing, and so too what is taken away."

D8 (A21) Aristotle, *Metaphysics*

Furthermore, if the one itself is indivisible, according to Zeno's axiom, it would be nothing: for that which, if added or removed, makes neither larger nor smaller, he says that this does not belong to the things that exist, as he evidently supposes that what exists is a magnitude, and if it is a magnitude it is corporeal. For this is what exists absolutely; while the other things, if they are added, will make it larger in a certain way, but in another way not at all, like the surface and line; but the point and the unit, not at all [. . .].

D9 (< A22) Simplicius, *Commentary on Aristotle's* Physics

Alexander says that the [. . .] argument derived from dichotomy [Aristotle, *Physics* 187a1–3] comes from Zeno, who says that if what exists had a magnitude and were divided, what exists would be multiple and no longer one, and who shows thereby that the one is not any of the things that exist [cf. **R10a, R13**].

D10 (A16) Simpl. *In Phys.*, p. 97.12–13 (= Eudem. Frag. 37a Wehrli)

καὶ Ζήνωνά φασι λέγειν, εἴ τις αὐτῷ τὸ ἓν ἀποδοίη τί ποτέ ἐστιν, ἕξειν τὰ ὄντα λέγειν.

Limited and Unlimited (D11)

D11 (B3) Simpl. *In Phys.*, p. 140.28–33

πάλιν γὰρ δεικνὺς ὅτι εἰ πολλά ἐστι, τὰ αὐτὰ πεπερασμένα ἐστὶ καὶ ἄπειρα, γράφει ταῦτα κατὰ λέξιν ὁ
Ζήνων· "εἰ πολλά ἐστιν, ἀνάγκη τοσαῦτα εἶναι ὅσα
ἐστὶ καὶ οὔτε πλείονα αὐτῶν οὔτε ἐλάττονα. εἰ δὲ
τοσαῦτά ἐστιν ὅσα ἐστί, πεπερασμένα ἂν εἴη.[1] εἰ
πολλά ἐστιν, ἄπειρα τὰ ὄντα ἐστίν. ἀεὶ γὰρ ἕτερα
μεταξὺ τῶν ὄντων ἐστί, καὶ πάλιν ἐκείνων ἕτερα
μεταξύ. καὶ οὕτως ἄπειρα τὰ ὄντα ἐστί."

[1] post ἂν εἴη add. καὶ πάλιν ed. Ald.

A Corollary? The Grain of Millet (D12)

D12

a (< A29) Arist. *Phys.* 8.5 250a19–22

ὁ Ζήνωνος λόγος [. . .] ὡς ψοφεῖ τῆς κέγχρου ὁτιοῦν
μέρος [. . . = **R16**].

ZENO

D10 (A16) Simplicius, *Commentary on Aristotle's* Physics

They report that Zeno said that if someone explained to him what the one might be, he would be able to say what the things that exist [scil. are].

Limited and Unlimited (D11)

D11 (B3) Simplicius, *Commentary on Aristotle's* Physics

For after he has shown again that, if many things exist, the same things are limited and unlimited, Zeno writes what follows, which I cite in his own words: **"If many things exist, it is necessary that they be as numerous as they are, and neither superior to them in number nor inferior in number. But if they are as numerous as they are, they will be limited. If many things exist,[1] then the things that exist are unlimited. For between the things that exist there are always other things, and then again others between those. And thus the things that exist are unlimited."**

[1] This sentence is not connected to the preceding one in the Greek. Perhaps a connecting particle was lost in the course of transmission, but it is also possible that Zeno's arguments were presented in the form of a list.

A Corollary? The Grain of Millet (D12)

D12

a (< A29) Aristotle, *Physics*

[. . .] Zeno's argument, which says that any part of a grain of millet makes a sound [. . .].

b (< A29) Simpl. *In Phys.*, p. 1108.14–29

[. . .] λύει καὶ τὸν Ζήνωνος τοῦ Ἐλεάτου λόγον, ὃν
ἤρετο Πρωταγόραν τὸν σοφιστήν. "εἰπὲ γάρ μοι,"
ἔφη, "ὦ Πρωταγόρα, ἆρα ὁ εἷς κέγχρος καταπεσὼν
ψόφον ποιεῖ ἢ τὸ μυριοστὸν τοῦ κέγχρου"; τοῦ δὲ εἰπόντος μὴ ποιεῖν "ὁ δὲ μέδιμνος," ἔφη, "τῶν κέγχρων
καταπεσὼν ποιεῖ ψόφον ἢ οὔ"; τοῦ δὲ ψοφεῖν εἰπόντος
τὸν μέδιμνον "τί οὖν," ἔφη ὁ Ζήνων, "οὐκ ἔστι λόγος
τοῦ μεδίμνου τῶν κέγχρων πρὸς τὸν ἕνα καὶ τὸ μυριοστὸν τὸ τοῦ ἑνός"; τοῦ δὲ φήσαντος εἶναι "τί οὖν,"
ἔφη ὁ Ζήνων, "οὐ καὶ τῶν ψόφων ἔσονται λόγοι πρὸς
ἀλλήλους οἱ αὐτοί; ὡς γὰρ τὰ ψοφοῦντα, καὶ οἱ ψό-
φοι· τούτου δὲ οὕτως ἔχοντος, εἰ ὁ μέδιμνος τοῦ κέγχρου ψοφεῖ, ψοφήσει καὶ ὁ εἷς κέγχρος καὶ τὸ μυριοστὸν τοῦ κέγχρου."

Argument Against the Existence of Place (D13)

D13

a (> A24) Arist. *Phys.* 4.1 209a23–26

ἔτι δὲ καὶ αὐτὸς εἰ ἔστι τι τῶν ὄντων, ποῦ[1] ἔσται; ἡ
γὰρ Ζήνωνος ἀπορία ζητεῖ τινὰ λόγον· εἰ γὰρ πᾶν τὸ
ὂν ἐν τόπῳ, δῆλον ὅτι καὶ τοῦ τόπου τόπος ἔσται, καὶ
τοῦτο εἰς ἄπειρον.[2]

[1] ποῦ] ποὺ Ross   [2] ἄπειρον EV: ἄπειρον πρόεισιν Λ

b (< A29) Simplicius, *Commentary on Aristotle's* Physics

[. . .] he [i.e. Aristotle] resolves the argument of Zeno of Elea, which he posed as a question to the sophist Protagoras. For he said, "Tell me, Protagoras, does one grain of millet make a sound when it falls or does the thousandth part of the grain of millet?" When the other answered that it did not, he said, "Does a medimnus[1] of grains of millet make a sound or not when it falls?" When the other answered that it did make a noise, Zeno said, "Well then, is there not a proportion between a medimnus of grains of millet and a single grain and the thousandth part of that one grain?" And when the other answered that there was one, Zeno said, "Well then, will there not be the same proportions between the sounds with regard to one another? For just as the things are that make a sound, so too are their sounds; and since that is so, if a medimnus of millet makes a sound, a single grain of millet will make a sound too, and so too the thousandth part of that grain."

[1] A unit of measure equivalent to fifty-two liters.

Argument Against the Existence of Place (D13)

D13

a (> A24) Aristotle, *Physics*

Moreover, if it [i.e. place] is one of the things that are, where will it be? For Zeno's aporia requires some argumentation. For if every thing that exists is in a place, it is clear that there will also be a place of the place, and this will go on to infinity.

b (Nachtrag I, p. 498) Simpl. *In Phys.*, p. 562.3–6

ὁ Ζήνωνος λόγος ἀναιρεῖν ἐδόκει τὸ εἶναι[1] τὸν τόπον ἐρωτῶν οὕτως· "εἰ ἔστιν ὁ τόπος, ἔν τινι ἔσται· πᾶν γὰρ ὂν ἔν τινι· τὸ δὲ ἔν τινι καὶ ἐν τόπῳ. ἔσται ἄρα καὶ[2] ὁ τόπος ἐν τόπῳ καὶ τοῦτο ἐπ' ἄπειρον· οὐκ ἄρα ἔστιν ὁ τόπος."

[1] τὸ εἶναι E: om. F   [2] καὶ om. E

Arguments Against Motion (D14–D19)
First Argument, Called That of Dichotomy (D14)

D14 (< A25) Arist. *Phys.* 6.9 239b11–14

[. . . = **D1**] πρῶτος μὲν ὁ περὶ τοῦ μὴ κινεῖσθαι διὰ τὸ πρότερον εἰς τὸ ἥμισυ δεῖν ἀφικέσθαι τὸ φερόμενον ἢ πρὸς τὸ τέλος [. . .].

Second Argument, Called Achilles (D15)

D15

a (A26) Arist. *Phys.* 6.9 239b14–20

δεύτερος δ' ὁ καλούμενος Ἀχιλλεύς· ἔστι δ' οὗτος, ὅτι τὸ βραδύτατον[1] οὐδέποτε καταληφθήσεται θέον ὑπὸ τοῦ ταχίστου· ἔμπροσθεν γὰρ ἀναγκαῖον ἐλθεῖν τὸ

[1] βραδύτατον E: βραδύτερον ΚΛ

b (Nachtrag I, p. 498) Simplicius, *Commentary on Aristotle's* Physics

Zeno's argument seemed to abolish the existence of place by asking as follows: "If place is, it will be in something. For everything that is is in something; now, in something is also in a place; so the place too will be in a place, and this will go on to infinity. So place does not exist."

Arguments Against Motion (D14–D19)[1]

[1] For the number of arguments, see **D3**.

First Argument, Called That of Dichotomy (D14)

D14 (< A25) Aristotle, *Physics*

[. . .] the first [scil. argument] is that there is no motion, because what is displaced must arrive at the half before arriving at the end [. . .].

Second Argument, Called Achilles (D15)

D15

a (A26) Aristotle, *Physics*

The second [scil. argument] is the one called "Achilles." It consists of saying that what is slowest will never be overtaken when it runs by what is fastest. For before that can happen, it is necessary that the pursuer arrive at the

διῶκον ὅθεν ὥρμησεν τὸ φεῦγον, ὥστε ἀεί τι προέχειν
ἀναγκαῖον τὸ βραδύτερον. ἔστιν δὲ καὶ οὗτος ὁ αὐτὸς
λόγος τῷ διχοτομεῖν, διαφέρει δ' ἐν τῷ διαιρεῖν μὴ
δίχα τὸ προσλαμβανόμενον μέγεθος [. . . = **R19**].

b (≠ DK) Them. *In Phys.*, p. 199.23–29

δεύτερος δέ ἐστιν ὁ λόγος ὁ καλούμενος Ἀχιλλεὺς
τετραγῳδημένος καὶ τῷ ὀνόματι· οὐ γάρ, ὅπως φησίν,
τὸν Ἕκτορα καταλήψεται ὁ ποδωκέστατος Ἀχιλλεύς,
ἀλλ' οὐδὲ τὴν βραδυτάτην χελώνην. εἰ γὰρ τὸν διώκοντα ἀνάγκη[1] πρότερον ἐλθεῖν ἐπὶ τὸ πέρας τοῦ
διαστήματος, οὗ τὸ φεῦγον προελήλυθεν, ἀδύνατον
ἄλλο ὑπ' ἄλλου καταληφθῆναι. ἐν ᾧ γὰρ ὁ διώκων
τοῦτο δίεισι τὸ διάστημα, δῆλον ὡς ὁ φεύγων ἕτερόν
τι προστίθησιν· εἰ γὰρ καὶ ἔλαττον ἀεὶ τῷ βραδύτε-
ρος ὑποκεῖσθαι, ἀλλ' οὖν προστίθησί γέ τι.

[1] τὸν διώκοντα ἀνάγκη L: τὸν διώκοντα MCS: δεῖ τὸν διώκοντα Laur. 85, 14: τὸ διῶκον ἀνάγκη Schenkl (cf. Simpl. *In
Phys.* 1014.14–15)

Third Argument, Called That of the Arrow
(D16–D17)

D16

a (< A27) Arist. *Phys.* 6.9 239b5–7

εἰ γὰρ αἰεί, φησίν, ἠρεμεῖ πᾶν[1] ὅταν ᾖ κατὰ τὸ ἴσον,
ἔστιν δ' αἰεὶ τὸ φερόμενον ἐν τῷ νῦν,[2] ἀκίνητον τὴν
φερομένην εἶναι ὀϊστόν.

place from which the pursued started out, so that it is necessary that the slower one always be somewhat ahead. This argument too is the same as the one by the procedure of dichotomy, but it differs in that the supplementary magnitude is not divided in half [. . .].

b (≠ DK) Themistius, *Paraphrase of Aristotle's* Physics

The second is the one called "Achilles," grandiloquent in its title too. For, as he says, Achilles, who is the swiftest of foot, will not overtake Hector, but also not even the tortoise, which is the slowest of all. For if it is necessary that the pursuer first reach the limit of the distance that the pursued has already traversed, it is impossible that the one can ever be overtaken by the other. For during the time that the pursuer traverses this distance, it is clear that the pursued adds some other distance. For even if each time it is smaller, owing to the fact that it is slower, nonetheless it does indeed add something.

Third Argument, Called That of the Arrow
(D16–D17)

D16

a (< A27) Aristotle, *Physics*

If, he says, everything is always at rest when it is in an equal [scil. space], and what moves is always in the present moment, then the arrow that is displaced is immobile.

---

¹ ἢ κινεῖται post πᾶν hab. mss.: secl. Zeller: coni. οὐ κινεῖται Ross, alii aliter   ² ἐν τῷ νῦν EHIJK: ἐν τῷ νῦν τῷ κατὰ τὸ ἴσον fecit F, Zeller (τῷ omisso): ἐν τῷ νῦν, πᾶν δὲ κατὰ τὸ ἴσον ἐν τῷ νῦν Diels

b (< A27) Arist. *Phys.* 6.9 239b30

τρίτος δ᾽ ὁ νῦν ῥηθείς, ὅτι ἡ ὀϊστὸς φερομένη ἕστηκεν
[. . . = **R20**].

D17 (B4) Diog. Laert. 9.72

Ζήνων δὲ τὴν κίνησιν ἀναιρεῖ λέγων "τὸ κινούμενον
οὔτε ἐν ᾧ ἔστι τόπῳ κινεῖται οὔτε ἐν ᾧ μὴ ἔστι."

Fourth Argument, Called That of the Stadium
(D18–D19)

D18 (< A28) Arist. *Phys.* 6.9 239b33–240a1

τέταρτος δ᾽ ὁ περὶ τῶν ἐν τῷ¹ σταδίῳ κινουμένων ἐξ
ἐναντίας ἴσων ὄγκων παρ᾽ ἴσους, τῶν μὲν ἀπὸ² τέλους
τοῦ σταδίου τῶν δ᾽ ἀπὸ μέσου, ἴσῳ τάχει, ἐν ᾧ συμβαίνειν οἴεται ἴσον εἶναι χρόνον τῷ διπλασίῳ τὸν
ἥμισυν [. . . = **R21**].

¹ τῷ E: om. ΚΛ   ² ἀπὸ] ἀπὸ τοῦ FHIJ²K

D19 (A25) Arist. *Top.* 8.8 160b7–9

πολλοὺς γὰρ λόγους ἔχομεν ἐναντίους ταῖς δόξαις,
οὓς χαλεπὸν λύειν, καθάπερ τὸν Ζήνωνος ὅτι οὐκ ἐνδέχεται κινεῖσθαι οὐδὲ τὸ στάδιον διελθεῖν [. . .].

b (< A27) Aristotle, *Physics*

The third [scil. argument] has just been mentioned [cf. **D16a**]: it consists of saying that the arrow that is displaced is immobile [. . .].

D17 (B4) Diogenes Laertius

Zeno abolishes motion by saying, **"What is moved does not move either in the place in which it is nor in the one in which it is not."**

Fourth Argument, Called That of the Stadium
(D18–D19)

D18 (< A28) Aristotle, *Physics*

The fourth [scil. argument] is the one about bodies of the same dimensions that move at an equal speed in a stadium and pass alongside other bodies of the same dimensions in the opposite direction, the ones starting from the end of the stadium, the others from the middle, in which case, he thinks, one half of a period of time is equal to its double [. . .].

D19 (A25) Aristotle, *Topics*

There are many arguments contrary to opinions that are difficult to resolve, like Zeno's that consists of saying that it is not possible for there to be motion nor a traversal of the stadium [. . .].

ZENO [29 DK]

R

The First Mention of Zeno

See **DOX. T7** (Isocrates)

Attested Writings about Zeno (R1)

R1 (I, p. 252.2–3) Diog. Laert.

a (5.25 = Arist.)

Πρὸς τὰ Ζήνωνος α'.

b (5.87 = Heracl. Pont.)

Πρὸς τὰ[1] Ζήνωνος α'.

[1] τὸ mss., corr. Stephanus

The Intention of Zeno's Text: The Defense of Parmenides (R2)

R2 (> A12) Plat. *Parm.* 127e–128e

[ΣΩ.] ἆρα τοῦτό ἐστιν ὃ βούλονταί σου οἱ λόγοι, οὐκ

ZENO

R

The First Mention of Zeno

See **DOX. T7** (Isocrates)

Attested Writings about Zeno (R1)

R1 (I, p. 252.2–3) Diogenes Laertius
a Aristotle
Against Zeno's Doctrines, one book.

b Heraclides of Pontus
Against Zeno's Doctrines, one book.

The Intention of Zeno's Text:
The Defense of Parmenides (R2)

R2 (˃ A12) Plato, *Parmenides*
[Socrates:] Is this the intention of your arguments, nothing

ἄλλο τι ἢ διαμάχεσθαι παρὰ πάντα τὰ λεγόμενα ὡς
οὐ πολλά ἐστι; καὶ τούτου αὐτοῦ οἴει σοι τεκμήριον
εἶναι ἕκαστον τῶν λόγων, ὥστε καὶ ἡγῇ τοσαῦτα τεκμήρια παρέχεσθαι, ὅσουσπερ λόγους γέγραφας, ὡς
οὐκ ἔστι [128a] πολλά; οὕτω λέγεις, ἢ ἐγὼ οὐκ ὀρθῶς
καταμανθάνω;

[ΖΗ.] οὔκ, ἀλλά, φάναι τὸν Ζήνωνα, καλῶς συνῆκας
ὅλον τὸ γράμμα ὃ βούλεται.

[ΣΩ.] μανθάνω, εἰπεῖν τὸν Σωκράτη, ὦ Παρμενίδη, ὅτι
Ζήνων ὅδε οὐ μόνον τῇ ἄλλῃ σου φιλίᾳ βούλεται
ᾠκειῶσθαι, ἀλλὰ καὶ τῷ συγγράμματι. ταὐτὸν γὰρ
γέγραφε τρόπον τινὰ ὅπερ σύ, μεταβάλλων δὲ ἡμᾶς
πειρᾶται ἐξαπατᾶν ὡς ἕτερόν τι λέγων. σὺ μὲν γὰρ ἐν
τοῖς ποιήμασιν ἓν φῂς εἶναι [b] τὸ πᾶν, καὶ τούτων
τεκμήρια παρέχῃ καλῶς τε καὶ εὖ· ὅδε δὲ αὖ οὐ πολλά
φησιν εἶναι, τεκμήρια δὲ καὶ αὐτὸς πάμπολλα καὶ
παμμεγέθη παρέχεται. τὸ οὖν τὸν μὲν ἓν φάναι, τὸν
δὲ μὴ πολλά, καὶ οὕτως ἑκάτερον λέγειν ὥστε μηδὲν
τῶν αὐτῶν εἰρηκέναι δοκεῖν σχεδόν τι λέγοντας
ταὐτά, ὑπὲρ ἡμᾶς τοὺς ἄλλους φαίνεται ὑμῖν τὰ εἰρημένα εἰρῆσθαι.

[ΖΗ.] ναί, φάναι τὸν Ζήνωνα, ὦ Σώκρατες, σὺ δ᾽ οὖν
τὴν ἀλήθειαν τοῦ γράμματος οὐ πανταχοῦ ᾔσθησαι.
καίτοι [c] ὥσπερ γε αἱ Λάκαιναι σκύλακες εὖ μεταθεῖς
τε καὶ ἰχνεύεις τὰ λεχθέντα· ἀλλὰ πρῶτον μέν σε
τοῦτο λανθάνει, ὅτι οὐ παντάπασιν οὕτω σεμνύνεται
τὸ γράμμα, ὥστε ἅπερ σὺ λέγεις διανοηθὲν γραφῆ-
ναι, τοὺς ἀνθρώπους δὲ ἐπικρυπτόμενον ὥς τι μέγα

other than to struggle, against everything that is said, to establish that things are not multiple? And you think that each of your arguments is a proof (*tekmêrion*) of this very thing, so that you think you are supplying just as many proofs as you have written arguments that things are not [128a] multiple? Is this what you mean, or have I not understood correctly?

[Zeno:] But no, you have understood well what the intention of the whole text is.

[Socrates:] I understand, Parmenides, that Zeno here desires to be close to you not only by his friendship in general, but also by his text. For in a certain way he has written the same thing as you; but by introducing a change he is trying to fool us into believing that he is saying something different. For in your poem you say that the whole [b] is one, and for this you supply excellent and fine proofs. But this man, inversely, says that things are not multiple, and he too supplies very many and very lengthy proofs. But that the one man says 'one' and the other 'not multiple,' and that each of them speaks in such a way that they do not seem to be speaking at all about the same things, while they are saying practically the same things—it seems that what you have said goes over the heads of the rest of us.

[Zeno:] Yes, but you still have not entirely perceived the true nature of the text, [c] despite the fact that, like young Spartan dogs, you are pursuing and tracking the traces of what is said in it. First of all, you do not see that the text does not pride itself at all on having been written with the intention you describe and concealing it from people, as though this were some great accomplishment. No, what

193

διαπραττόμενον· ἀλλὰ σὺ μὲν εἶπες τῶν συμβεβη-
κότων τι, ἔστι δὲ τό γε ἀληθὲς βοήθειά τις ταῦτα¹ τῷ
Παρμενίδου λόγῳ πρὸς τοὺς ἐπιχειροῦντας [d] αὐτὸν
κωμῳδεῖν ὡς εἰ ἕν ἐστι, πολλὰ καὶ γελοῖα συμβαίνει
πάσχειν τῷ λόγῳ καὶ ἐναντία αὑτῷ. ἀντιλέγει δὴ οὖν
τοῦτο τὸ γράμμα πρὸς τοὺς τὰ πολλὰ λέγοντας, καὶ
ἀνταποδίδωσι ταὐτὰ² καὶ πλείω, τοῦτο βουλόμενον
δηλοῦν, ὡς ἔτι γελοιότερα πάσχοι ἂν αὐτῶν ἡ ὑπόθε-
σις, εἰ πολλά ἐστιν, ἢ ἡ τοῦ ἓν εἶναι, εἴ τις ἱκανῶς
ἐπεξίοι. διὰ τοιαύτην δὴ φιλονικίαν ὑπὸ νέου ὄντος
ἐμοῦ ἐγράφη, καί τις αὐτὸ ἔκλεψε γραφέν, ὥστε οὐδὲ
βουλεύσασθαι ἐξεγένετο [e] εἴτ᾽ ἐξοιστέον αὐτὸ εἰς τὸ
φῶς εἴτε μή. ταύτῃ οὖν σε λανθάνει, ὦ Σώκρατες, ὅτι
οὐχ ὑπὸ νέου φιλονικίας οἴει αὐτὸ γεγράφθαι, ἀλλ᾽
ὑπὸ πρεσβυτέρου φιλοτιμίας· ἐπεί, ὅπερ γ᾽ εἶπον, οὐ
κακῶς ἀπήκασας.

¹ post ταῦτα hab. mss. τὰ γράμματα: secl. Burnet
² ταὐτὰ Schleiermacher: ταῦτα B: om. T

The Dialectician (R3–R9)
From Eleatism to Dialectic (R3–R5)

R3 (A13) Plat. *Phaedr.* 261d

τὸν οὖν Ἐλεατικὸν Παλαμήδην λέγοντα οὐκ ἴσμεν
τέχνῃ, ὥστε φαίνεσθαι τοῖς ἀκούουσι τὰ αὐτὰ ὅμοια
καὶ ἀνόμοια, καὶ ἓν καὶ πολλά, μένοντά τε αὖ καὶ
φερόμενα;

you have spoken of is a secondary effect, but in truth these writings constitute a defense of Parmenides' argument against those who undertake [d] to make fun of him on the idea that if the One exists, it must by reason of that argument undergo many things that are absurd and that are contrary to it. Thus this text contradicts those who affirm multiplicity and it pays them back the same and more, with the intention of showing that their thesis (*hupothesis*), that there is multiplicity, undergoes things which are even more absurd than does the thesis that the One exists, if someone examines the matter sufficiently. It was written by me out of a kind of contentiousness (*philonikia*) when I was young; and someone stole it when it had been written, so that I did not have a chance to reflect [e] on whether I should publish it or not. This is how you misunderstand it, Socrates, for you think that it was written not out of a young man's contentiousness (*philonikia*) but out of an older man's ambitiousness (*philotimia*). And yet, as I said, the image you gave of it was not entirely mistaken.

The Dialectician (R3–R9)
From Eleatism to Dialectic (R3–R5)

R3 (A13) Plato, *Phaedrus*

[. . .] As for the Eleatic Palamedes,[1] do we not know that he speaks artfully so that the same things appear to listeners to be similar and dissimilar, one and many, and again at rest and in motion?

[1] Palamedes, the Greek warrior at Troy accused of treason by Odysseus (cf. **GORG. D25**), was also considered to have invented games, calculation, and other things (cf. **DRAM. T56, T62**).

R4 (A10) Diog. Laert. 8.57

Ἀριστοτέλης δ᾽ ἐν τῷ Σοφιστῇ [Frag. 65 Rose] φησι πρῶτον Ἐμπεδοκλέα ῥητορικὴν εὑρεῖν, Ζήνωνα δὲ διαλεκτικήν.

R5 (A23) Ps.-Plut. *Strom.* 6 (= Eus. *PE* 1.8.6)

Ζήνων δὲ ὁ Ἐλεάτης ἴδιον μὲν οὐδὲν ἐξέθετο, διηπόρησεν δὲ περὶ τούτων ἐπὶ πλεῖον.

Antilogy (R6)

R6 (< A4) Plut. *Per.* 4.5

[. . . = **P7**] καὶ Ζήνωνος τοῦ Ἐλεάτου πραγματευομένου[1] περὶ φύσιν ὡς Παρμενίδης, ἐλεγκτικὴν δέ τινα καὶ δι᾽ ἀντιλογίας εἰς ἀπορίαν κατακλείουσαν ἐξασκήσαντος ἕξιν [. . .].

[1] πραγματευομένου ‹μὲν› Reiske

*Zeno's Amphoteroglossia and
Its Interpretations (R7–R9)*

R7 (< A1) Timon in Diog. Laert. 9.25 [= Frag. 45 Di Marco]

ἀμφοτερογλώσσου τε μέγα σθένος οὐκ
  ἀλαπαδνόν
Ζήνωνος πάντων ἐπιλήπτορος [. . . = **MEL. R19**].

R4 (A10) Aristotle in Diogenes Laertius

Aristotle says in his *Sophist* that Empedocles was the first person to have discovered rhetoric, and Zeno dialectic.

R5 (A23) Ps.-Plutarch, *Stromata*

Zeno of Elea did not set forth anything of his own, but developed further the difficulties on these subjects [scil. the doctrines of Parmenides].

Antilogy (R6)

R6 (< A4) Plutarch, *Pericles*

[. . .] Zeno of Elea, who studied nature, like Parmenides,[1] but practiced an attitude of a refutative kind and locked [scil. his interlocutor] into an aporia by means of antilogy [. . .].

[1] If this indication is not mistaken (cf. **R39**), it presupposes, in the case of Zeno, that 'nature' be understood as 'that which is.'

*Zeno's Amphoteroglossia and
Its Interpretations (R7–R9)*

R7 (< A1) Timon of Phlius in Diogenes Laertius

The great force, not easy to overpower, of two-
    tongued
Zeno who catches everyone by surprise [. . .].

---

1 ἀλαπαδνὸν MA: ἀπατηλὸν SU

R8 (≠ DK) Simpl. *In Phys.*, p. 139.3–4

[. . .] τὸν Ζήνωνα ὡς ἐφ' ἑκάτερα γυμναστικῶς ἐπιχειροῦντα (διὸ καὶ 'ἀμφοτερόγλωσσος' λέγεται) [. . . = **R12**].

R9 (< A15) Elias, *In Cat.*, p. 109.10–12

ἀμφοτερόγλωσσος δ' ἐκλήθη οὐχ ὅτι διαλεκτικὸς ἦν, ὡς ὁ Κιττιεύς, καὶ τὰ αὐτὰ ἀνεσκεύαζε καὶ κατεσκεύαζεν, ἀλλ' ὅτι τῇ ζωῇ διαλεκτικὸς ἦν ἄλλα μὲν λέγων ἄλλα δὲ φρονῶν [. . . = **P14**].

The One as a Problem and Its Interpretative
Consequences (R10–R15)
The Interpretation of Eudemus and of
Alexander (R10)

R10 (≠ DK) Simpl. *In Phys.*

a (p. 138.18–22)

ταῦτα τοῦ Ἀλεξάνδρου λέγοντος ἐφιστάνειν ἄξιον πρῶτον μέν, εἰ Ζήνωνος οἰκεῖον τοῦτο τὸ μηδὲν τῶν ὄντων λέγειν τὸ ἕν. ὅς γε τοὐναντίον πολλὰ γέγραφεν ἐπιχειρήματα τὸ πολλὰ εἶναι ἀναιρῶν, ἵνα διὰ τῆς τῶν πολλῶν ἀναιρέσεως τὸ ἓν εἶναι πάντα βεβαιωθῇ, ὅπερ καὶ ὁ Παρμενίδης ἐβούλετο.

R8 (≠ DK) Simplicius, *Commentary on Aristotle's* Physics

[. . .] Zeno, who tried to argue as an exercise in both directions (that is why he is called 'two-tongued') [. . .].

R9 (< A15) Elias, *Commentary on Aristotle's* Categories

He [scil. Zeno of Elea] was called 'two-tongued' not because he was a dialectician, like the one [i.e. Zeno] from Citium, and demonstrated and refuted the same things, but because he was a dialectician in his way of life, saying one thing and thinking another [. . .].[1]

[1] Elias supports the interpretation that makes Zeno a defender of Parmenides, as in Plato's *Parmenides* (**R2**), against the one that makes him a dialectician *in utramque partem,* which goes back to Plato's *Phaedrus* (**R3**).

The One as a Problem and Its Interpretative
Consequences (R10–R15)
The Interpretation of Eudemus and of
Alexander (R10)

R10 (≠ DK) Simplicius, *Commentary on Aristotle's* Physics

a

Since Alexander says this [cf. **D9**], it is worth stopping to consider first of all whether saying that the One is not any of the things that exist does indeed belong to Zeno, who on the contrary wrote many arguments to abolish the existence of the multiplicity of things, so that thanks to the suppression of that multiplicity it would be confirmed that all things are one, which was just what Parmenides wanted [. . .].

b (pp. 138.29–139.3, cf. p. 97.11–16)

ἀλλ' ἔοικεν ἀπὸ τῶν Εὐδήμου λόγων ὁ Ἀλέξανδρος
δόξαν περὶ τοῦ Ζήνωνος λαβεῖν ὡς ἀναιροῦντος τὸ ἕν·
λέγει γὰρ ὁ Εὔδημος ἐν τοῖς Φυσικοῖς [Frag. 37a
Wehrli, p. 25.21–25] "ἆρα οὖν τοῦτο μὲν οὐκ ἔστιν,[1]
ἔστι δέ τι ἕν; τοῦτο γὰρ ἠπορεῖτο. καὶ Ζήνωνά φασιν
λέγειν, εἴ τις αὐτῷ τὸ ἓν ἀποδοίη τί ποτέ ἐστιν, ἕξειν
τὰ ὄντα λέγειν. ἠπόρει δὲ ὡς ἔοικε διὰ τὸ τῶν μὲν
αἰσθητῶν ἕκαστον κατηγορικῶς τε πολλὰ λέγεσθαι
καὶ μερισμῷ, τὴν δὲ στιγμὴν μηθὲν[2] τιθέναι. ὃ γὰρ
μήτε προστιθέμενον αὔξει μήτε ἀφαιρούμενον μειοῖ,
οὐκ ᾤετο τῶν ὄντων εἶναι."

[1] οὐκ ἔστιν ἕν p. 97.11, an recte? (ἕν secl. Diels)
[2] μηθὲν DE: μηδὲν F: μηδ' ἕν p. 97.15

Simplicius' Hypotheses (R11–R13)

R11 (> A21) Simpl. *In Phys.*, p. 99.7–18 [= Eudem. Frag.
37a Wehrli, p. 27.7–17]

ἐν ᾗ ὁ μὲν τοῦ Ζήνωνος λόγος ἄλλος τις ἔοικεν οὗτος
εἶναι παρ' ἐκεῖνον τὸν ἐν βιβλίῳ φερόμενον, οὗ καὶ ὁ
Πλάτων ἐν τῷ Παρμενίδῃ μέμνηται. ἐκεῖ μὲν γὰρ ὅτι
πολλὰ οὐκ ἔστι δείκνυσι βοηθῶν ἐκ τοῦ ἀντικειμένου
τῷ Παρμενίδῃ ἓν εἶναι[1] λέγοντι· ἐνταῦθα δέ, ὡς ὁ Εὔ-
δημός φησι, καὶ ἀνῄρει τὸ ἕν (τὴν γὰρ στιγμὴν ὡς

[1] εἶναι post ἓν add. ed. Ald.

b

But it seems to have been from what Eudemus said that Alexander derived the opinion according to which Zeno abolishes the One. For Eudemus says in his *Physics*, "Well then, is it that this is not,[1] but that there exists a certain One? For that was the difficulty. And they say that Zeno maintained that if someone could explain to him just what can be the One, he would be able to say [scil. what are] the things that are. The aporia seems to derive from the fact that on the one hand each of the perceptibles is called multiple both by reference to the categories and in virtue of division, while on the other hand he established that the point absolutely does not exist.[2] For he did not think that something that, when added, does not cause to increase and which, when removed, does not cause to diminish, belongs to the things that are."

[1] Or: "is it that this is not one," if we adopt the text transmitted in an earlier citation of the same passage (p. 97.11).

[2] Or: "does not even exist," according to the text of p. 97.15.

Simplicius' Hypotheses (R11–R13)

R11 (> A21) Simplicius, *Commentary on Aristotle's* Physics

In this passage [i.e. the text corresponding to Eudemus Frag. 37 Wehrli], Zeno's argument seems to be different from the one that is transmitted in the book, and that Plato too mentions in the *Parmenides* [cf. **R2**]. For there he demonstrates that the multiple does not exist, coming on the basis of the contrary hypothesis to the aid of Parmenides, who says that the one exists; while here, as Eudemus says, he also abolishes the One (for he speaks of the

τὸ ἓν λέγει), τὰ δὲ πολλὰ εἶναι συγχωρεῖ. ὁ μέντοι
Ἀλέξανδρος καὶ ἐνταῦθα τοῦ Ζήνωνος ὡς τὰ πολλὰ
ἀναιροῦντος μεμνῆσθαι τὸν Εὔδημον οἴεται. "ὡς γὰρ
ἱστορεῖ, φησίν, Εὔδημος, Ζήνων ὁ Παρμενίδου γνώ-
ριμος ἐπειρᾶτο δεικνύναι ὅτι μὴ οἷόν τε τὰ ὄντα
πολλὰ εἶναι τῷ μηδὲν εἶναι ἐν τοῖς οὖσιν ἕν, τὰ δὲ
πολλὰ πλῆθος εἶναι ἑνάδων." καὶ ὅτι μὲν οὐχ ὡς τὰ
πολλὰ ἀναιροῦντος τοῦ Ζήνωνος Εὔδημος μέμνηται
νῦν, δῆλον ἐκ τῆς αὐτοῦ λέξεως· οἶμαι δὲ μηδὲ[2] ἐν τῷ
Ζήνωνος βιβλίῳ τοιοῦτον ἐπιχείρημα φέρεσθαι, οἷον
ὁ Ἀλέξανδρός φησι.

2 μηδὲ Zeller: μήτε mss.

R12 (> ad B2) Simpl. *In Phys.*, p. 139.3–23

καὶ εἰκὸς μὲν ἦν τὸν Ζήνωνα ὡς ἐφ᾽ ἑκάτερα γυμναστικῶς ἐπιχειροῦντα [. . . = **R8**] καὶ τοιούτους ἐκφέρειν
λόγους περὶ τοῦ ἑνὸς ἀποροῦντα· ἐν μέντοι τῷ συγγράμματι αὐτοῦ πολλὰ ἔχοντι ἐπιχειρήματα καθ᾽
ἕκαστον δείκνυσιν ὅτι τῷ πολλὰ εἶναι λέγοντι συμβαίνει τὰ ἐναντία λέγειν· ὧν ἕν ἐστιν ἐπιχείρημα, ἐν
ᾧ δείκνυσιν ὅτι "εἰ πολλά ἐστι [. . .] ὥστε μηθὲν ἔχειν
μέγεθος" [cf. **D6** with textual variants]. ἐν δὴ τούτῳ δείκνυσιν ὅτι οὗ μήτε μέγεθος μήτε πάχος μήτε ὄγκος
μηθείς ἐστιν, οὐδ᾽ ἂν εἴη τοῦτο. [. . . = **D7**]. καὶ ταῦτα
οὐχὶ τὸ ἓν ἀναιρῶν ὁ Ζήνων λέγει, ἀλλ᾽ ὅτι μέγεθος
ἔχει ἕκαστον τῶν πολλῶν καὶ ἀπείρων τῷ πρὸ τοῦ

point as of the One), while he concedes that the multiple exists. However, Alexander thinks that Eudemus mentions Zeno here too as abolishing the multiple; he says, "as Eudemus reports, Zeno, the companion of Parmenides, tried to demonstrate that it is not possible for the multiple to exist, from the fact that there is nothing that is one among the things that are, while the multiple is a quantity of unities." And the fact that Eudemus in the present case does not mention Zeno as abolishing the multiple is clear from his own words. But I think that no such argument as Alexander reports is to be found in Zeno's book either.

R12 (> ad B2) Simplicius, *Commentary on Aristotle's Physics*

Now it would be plausible that Zeno, insofar as he tried to argue in both directions as an exercise [. . .], would have also produced arguments of this sort, formulating difficulties about the One. However, in his treatise, which contains many arguments, he shows in each one that anyone who says that multiple things exist ends up contradicting himself. One of these arguments is the one in which he shows that **"if many things exist** [. . .] **as to have no magnitude whatsoever"** [cf. **D6**]; now in this one [i.e. **D7**] he shows that what possesses neither any magnitude nor thickness nor volume could not exist either [. . .]. Zeno says this not in order to abolish the One, but because each of the things that are multiple and unlimited possesses a magnitude because, by reason of division to infinity, there

λαμβανομένου ἀεί τι εἶναι¹ διὰ τὴν ἐπ᾽ ἄπειρον το-
μήν·² ὃ δείκνυσι προδείξας ὅτι οὐδὲν ἔχει μέγεθος ἐκ
τοῦ ἕκαστον τῶν πολλῶν ἑαυτῷ ταὐτὸν εἶναι καὶ ἕν.
καὶ ὁ Θεμίστιος δὲ τὸν Ζήνωνος λόγον ἓν εἶναι τὸ ὂν
κατασκευάζειν φησὶν ἐκ τοῦ συνεχές τε αὐτὸ εἶναι καὶ
ἀδιαίρετον· εἰ γὰρ διαιροῖτο, φησίν, οὐδὲ³ ἔσται ἀκριβῶς ἓν διὰ τὴν ἐπ᾽ ἄπειρον τομὴν τῶν σωμάτων [cf.
Them. in Phys., p. 12.1–4]. ἔοικε δὲ μᾶλλον ὁ Ζήνων
λέγειν ὡς οὐδὲ πολλὰ ἔσται.

¹ τῷ πρὸ . . . ἀεί τι εἶναι D: μέγεθος, τὸ πρὸ . . . ἀεί τι
εἶναι EF   ² post τομήν add. ed. Ald. δεῖ δὲ ἓν εἶναι
³ οὐδὲ Themistius: οὐδὲν mss.

R13 (≠ DK) Simpl. In Phys., p. 141.8–11

μήποτε οὖν Ζήνωνος μέν ἐστιν ὁ ἐκ τῆς διχοτομίας
λόγος, ὡς Ἀλέξανδρος βούλεται, οὐ μέντοι τὸ ἓν ἀναιροῦντος ἀλλὰ τὰ πολλὰ μᾶλλον τῷ τἀναντία συμβαίνειν τοῖς ὑποτιθεμένοις αὐτὰ καὶ ταύτῃ τὸν Παρμενίδου λόγον βεβαιοῦντος ἓν εἶναι λέγοντα τὸ ὄν.

Interpretative Consequences (R14–R15)
Nihilist (R14)

R14 (< A21) Sen. Epist. 88.45

si Parmenidi, nihil est praeter unum; si Zenoni, ne unum
quidem.

always exists something before what is taken away; this is what he shows, after he has shown earlier that nothing has magnitude from the fact that each of the multiple things is identical with itself and is one. And Themistius too says that Zeno's argument establishes the thesis that what is is one on the basis of the fact that it is both continuous and indivisible. He [i.e. Themistius, paraphrasing Zeno] says, "For if it were divided, it will not be one in the precise sense, by reason of the division of bodies to infinity." But Zeno seems instead to be saying that multiple things will not exist either.

R13 (≠ DK) Simplicius, *Commentary on Aristotle's* Physics

Perhaps then it is indeed the case that the argument based upon the dichotomy belongs to Zeno, as Alexander suggests [cf. **D9**], but that he [i.e. Zeno] is not abolishing the One but rather the plurality, since those who posit the latter are forced to contradict themselves, and in this way he is confirming Parmenides' argument which states that what is is one.

Interpretative Consequences (R14–R15)
Nihilist (R14)

R14 (< A21) Seneca, *Letters to Lucilius*

If [scil. I believe] Parmenides, nothing exists, except the One; if Zeno, not even the One.

Proto-Skeptic (R15)

R15 (ad B4) Diog. Laert. 9.72

οὐ μὴν ἀλλὰ καὶ Ξενοφάνης καὶ Ζήνων ὁ Ἐλεάτης καὶ Δημόκριτος κατ᾽ αὐτοὺς σκεπτικοὶ τυγχάνουσιν.

Criticism of Zeno's Arguments (R16–R27)
Theoretical Refutations (R16–R26)
Aristotle's Criticisms (R16–R21)
The Argument of the Grain of Millet, D12 (R16)

R16 (A29) Arist. *Phys.* 8.5 250a19–22

διὰ τοῦτο ὁ Ζήνωνος λόγος οὐκ ἀληθής, ὡς ψοφεῖ τῆς κέγχρου ὁτιοῦν μέρος· οὐδὲν γὰρ κωλύει μὴ κινεῖν τὸν ἀέρα ἐν μηδενὶ χρόνῳ τοῦτον ὃν ἐκίνησεν πεσὼν[1] ὁ ὅλος[2] μέδιμνος.

[1] πεσὼν HJΣ: ἐνπεσὼν E: ἐμπεσὼν FIK   [2] ὅλος ὁ K: ὅλος H

The Arguments about Motion (R17–R20)
Against the First Argument (D14, Dichotomy)
(R17–R18)

R17 (A25) Arist. *Phys.* 6.2 233a21–31

διὸ καὶ ὁ Ζήνωνος λόγος ψεῦδος λαμβάνει τὸ μὴ ἐν-δέχεσθαι τὰ ἄπειρα διελθεῖν ἢ ἅψασθαι τῶν ἀπείρων καθ᾽ ἕκαστον ἐν πεπερασμένῳ χρόνῳ. διχῶς γὰρ λέ-γεται καὶ τὸ μῆκος καὶ ὁ χρόνος ἄπειρον, καὶ ὅλως

ZENO

Proto-Skeptic (R15)

R15 (ad B4) Diogenes Laertius

According to them [i.e. the Pyrrhonians], Xenophanes, Zeno of Elea, and Democritus are skeptics.

Criticism of Zeno's Arguments (R16–R27)
Theoretical Refutations (R16–R26)
Aristotle's Criticisms (R16–R21)
The Argument of the Grain of Millet, D12 (R16)

R16 (A29) Aristotle, *Physics*

That is why Zeno's argument, which says that any part of a grain of millet makes a sound, is not true. For nothing prevents it from not moving, in any period of time, this air, which the whole medimnus[1] moved when it fell.

  [1] Fifty-two liters.

The Arguments about Motion (R17–R20)
Against the First Argument (D14, Dichotomy)
(R17–R18)

R17 (A25) Aristotle, *Physics*

That is why Zeno's argument accepts falsely that it is not possible to traverse things that are unlimited [scil. in number] nor to touch individually things that are unlimited [scil. in number] within a limited time. For it is in two ways that both length and time, and in general everything con-

πᾶν τὸ συνεχές, ἤτοι κατὰ διαίρεσιν ἢ τοῖς ἐσχάτοις. τῶν μὲν οὖν κατὰ τὸ ποσὸν ἀπείρων οὐκ ἐνδέχεται ἅψασθαι ἐν πεπερασμένῳ χρόνῳ, τῶν δὲ κατὰ διαίρεσιν ἐνδέχεται· καὶ γὰρ αὐτὸς ὁ χρόνος οὕτως ἄπειρος. ὥστε ἐν τῷ ἀπείρῳ καὶ οὐκ ἐν τῷ πεπερασμένῳ συμβαίνει διιέναι τὸ ἄπειρον, καὶ ἅπτεσθαι τῶν ἀπείρων τοῖς ἀπείροις, οὐ τοῖς πεπερασμένοις.

R18 (≠ DK) Arist. *Phys.* 8.8 263a4–11

τὸν αὐτὸν δὲ τρόπον ἀπαντητέον καὶ πρὸς τοὺς ἐρωτῶντας τὸν Ζήνωνος λόγον,[1] εἰ ἀεὶ τὸ ἥμισυ διιέναι δεῖ, ταῦτα δ' ἄπειρα, τὰ δ' ἄπειρα ἀδύνατον διεξελθεῖν, ἢ ὡς τὸν αὐτὸν τοῦτον λόγον τινὲς ἄλλως ἐρωτῶσιν, ἀξιοῦντες ἅμα τῷ κινεῖσθαι τὴν ἡμίσειαν πρότερον ἀριθμεῖν καθ' ἕκαστον γιγνόμενον τὸ ἥμισυ, ὥστε διελθόντος τὴν ὅλην ἄπειρον συμβαίνει ἠριθμηκέναι ἀριθμόν· τοῦτο δ' ὁμολογουμένως ἐστὶν ἀδύνατον.

[1] post λόγον habent mss. καὶ ἀξιοῦντας: secl. Ross

Against the Second Argument (D15, Achilles) (R19)

R19 (≠ DK) Arist. *Phys.* 6.9 239b20–29

[. . . = **D15**] τὸ μὲν οὖν μὴ καταλαμβάνεσθαι τὸ βραδύτερον συμβέβηκεν ἐκ τοῦ λόγου, γίγνεται δὲ παρὰ ταὐτὸ τῇ διχοτομίᾳ (ἐν ἀμφοτέροις γὰρ συμβαίνει μὴ ἀφικνεῖσθαι πρὸς τὸ πέρας διαιρουμένου πως τοῦ με-

tinuous, are said to be unlimited [scil. in number]: either by division or with regard to their extremities. Now it is not possible to touch things that are unlimited [scil. in number] according to quantity within a limited time, but it is possible to do so with regard to those that are so according to division. For time itself is unlimited in this way. So that what happens is that it is within an unlimited [scil. time], and not a limited one, that one succeeds in traversing what is unlimited, and that it is by unlimited things, and not by limited ones, that one touches unlimited ones.

R18 (≠ DK) Aristotle, *Physics*

One must also reply in the same way to those [cf. **R32–R34**] who pose the question of Zeno's argument, viz. that it is always necessary to traverse the half, and these [i.e. halves] are unlimited [scil. in number], and it is impossible to traverse to the very end things that are unlimited [scil. in number], or as others formulate differently the question that is posed by this same argument, when they think that within the same time as the motion covers the half, one must first count the half that happens each time, so that when one has entirely traversed the totality, it comes about that one will have counted an unlimited number. But this is generally agreed to be impossible.

Against the Second Argument (D15, Achilles) (R19)

R19 (≠ DK) Aristotle, *Physics*

That the slower one is not overtaken ensues from the argument, but it happens for the same reason as for the dichotomy (for in both cases it comes about that one does not arrive at the limit when the magnitude is divided in a cer-

γέθους· ἀλλὰ πρόσκειται ἐν τούτῳ ὅτι οὐδὲ τὸ τάχι-
στον τετραγῳδημένον ἐν τῷ διώκειν τὸ βραδύτατον[1]),
ὥστ᾽ ἀνάγκη καὶ τὴν λύσιν εἶναι[2] τὴν αὐτήν. τὸ δ᾽
ἀξιοῦν ὅτι τὸ προέχον οὐ καταλαμβάνεται, ψεῦδος·
ὅτε γὰρ προέχει, οὐ καταλαμβάνεται· ἀλλ᾽ ὅμως καταλαμβάνεται, εἴπερ δώσει διεξιέναι τὴν πεπερασμένην.

[1] βραδύτερον FHK   [2] post εἶναι hab. ἑκατέρων E

Against the Third Argument (D16–D17, The Arrow) (R20)

R20 (≠ DK) Arist. *Phys.* 6.9 239b31–33

[. . . = **D16b**] συμβαίνει δὲ παρὰ τὸ λαμβάνειν τὸν
χρόνον συγκεῖσθαι ἐκ τῶν νῦν· μὴ διδομένου γὰρ
τούτου οὐκ ἔσται ὁ συλλογισμός.

Against the Fourth Argument (D18–D19, The Stadium) (R21)

R21 (< A28) Arist. *Phys.* 6.9 240a1–17

[. . . = **D18**] ἔστι δ᾽ ὁ παραλογισμὸς ἐν τῷ τὸ μὲν
παρὰ κινούμενον τὸ δὲ παρ᾽ ἠρεμοῦν τὸ ἴσον μέγεθος
ἀξιοῦν τῷ ἴσῳ τάχει τὸν ἴσον φέρεσθαι χρόνον· τοῦτο
δ᾽ ἐστὶ ψεῦδος. οἷον ἔστωσαν οἱ ἑστῶτες ἴσοι ὄγκοι
ἐφ᾽ ὧν τὰ ΑΑ,[1] οἱ δ᾽ ἐφ᾽ ὧν τὰ ΒΒ[2] ἀρχόμενοι ἀπὸ τοῦ
μέσου,[3] ἴσοι τὸν ἀριθμὸν τούτοις ὄντες καὶ τὸ μέγε-

tain way; but what is added in this one is that it will not even be the same in the dramatic case of the fastest one pursuing the slowest), so that it is necessary that the solution be the same. But to think that the one that is ahead is not overtaken is false; for as long as it is ahead it is not overtaken; but all the same it is overtaken, if one grants that it is possible to traverse completely a limited [scil. distance].

Against the Third Argument (D16–D17, The Arrow) (R20)

R20 (≠ DK) Aristotle, *Physics*

It comes about from supposing that time is composed of instants; for if this is not granted, there will not be an argument [i.e. the conclusion will not follow].

Against the Fourth Argument (D18–D19, The Stadium) (R21)

R21 (< A28) Aristotle, *Physics*

The paralogism consists in supposing that a body of the same dimension moving at an equal speed moves during the same time alongside a moving body as alongside a body at rest. But this is false. For example, let the bodies of the same dimension at rest be AA; let BB be those that start from the middle [scil. of the stadium[1]], which are equal to the former in number and in magnitude; and let

---

[1] Or, according to several mss.: of the A's.

---

[1] $\alpha\alpha$ EP: $\alpha\alpha\alpha$ FHJK: $\alpha\alpha\alpha\alpha$ I   [2] $\beta\beta$ EP: $\beta\beta\beta\beta$ F: β HIJK   [3] $\mu\acute{\epsilon}\sigma o\nu$ EHIJ[1]: $\mu\acute{\epsilon}\sigma o\nu$ $\tau\hat{\omega}\nu$ α FJ[2]K

θος, οἱ δ᾽ ἐφ᾽ ὧν τὰ ΓΓ[4] ἀπὸ τοῦ ἐσχάτου,[5] ἴσοι τὸν
ἀριθμὸν ὄντες τούτοις καὶ τὸ μέγεθος, καὶ ἰσοταχεῖς
τοῖς Β. συμβαίνει δὴ τὸ πρῶτον Β ἅμα ἐπὶ τῷ ἐσχάτῳ
εἶναι καὶ τὸ πρῶτον Γ, παρ᾽[6] ἄλληλα κινουμένων.
συμβαίνει δὲ τὸ Γ παρὰ πάντα[7] τὰ Β διεξεληλυθέναι,[8]
τὸ δὲ Β παρὰ τὰ ἡμίση· ὥστε ἥμισυν εἶναι τὸν χρό-
νον· ἴσον γὰρ ἑκάτερόν ἐστιν παρ᾽ ἕκαστον. ἅμα δὲ
συμβαίνει τὸ Β[9] παρὰ πάντα τὰ Γ παρεληλυθέναι·
ἅμα γὰρ ἔσται[10] τὸ πρῶτον Γ καὶ τὸ πρῶτον Β ἐπὶ
τοῖς ἐναντίοις ἐσχάτοις, ἴσον[11] χρόνον παρ᾽ ἕκαστον
γιγνόμενον τῶν Β ὅσον περ[12] τῶν Α,[13] ὥς φησιν,[14] διὰ
τὸ ἀμφότερα ἴσον χρόνον παρὰ τὰ Α[15] γίγνεσθαι. ὁ
μὲν οὖν λόγος οὗτός ἐστιν, συμβαίνει δὲ παρὰ τὸ
εἰρημένον ψεῦδος.

[4] γ ΚΛ   [5] ἐσχάτου] ἐσχάτου β Α: ἐσχάτου τῶν β F
[6] γ ἐπὶ τῶ ἐσχάτω β παρ᾽ Η   [7] post πάντα hab. HI τὰ β:
secl. Ross: β E[1]: τὰ α E[2]FJK   [8] post ἴσον χρόνον παρ᾽
ἕκαστον γιγνόμενον τῶν Β ὅσον περ τῶν Α (cf. infra 14)
collocanda ci. Alex. in Simpl. *In Phys.*, p. 1019.27–30   [9] τὸ β]
τὸ πρῶτον β Cornford: τὸ α Ε: τὰ ΚΛ   [10] ἔσται ΕJ: ἐστι
FHIK   [11] παραληλυθέναι (ἅμα γὰρ . . . ἐσχάτοις), ἴσον
Lachelier   [12] τῶν Γ, ὅσον περ <τὸ Γ> Lachelier   [13] α
ΚΛ: αα Ε   [14] ἴσον . . . φησιν secl. Ross (cf. supra 8)
[15] α ΚΛ: αα Ε

Peripatetic Criticisms of the Argument on Place, D13 (R22–R23)

R22 (A24) Arist. *Phys.* 4.3 210b22–25

ὁ δὲ Ζήνων ἠπόρει, ὅτι εἰ ὁ τόπος ἐστί τι, ἔν τινι[1]

CC be those that start from the end [scil. of the stadium],[2] which are equal to these in number and in magnitude, and equal in speed to the B's. It follows that, when they move alongside one another, the first B and the first C are at the end at the same time; and it also follows that the C has crossed all of the B's, and the B's only half, so that the time is one half, since each one passes beside the other for an equal time. And at the same time it follows that [scil. the first] B has crossed all the C's; for the first C and the first B will arrive at the last [scil. bodies] located at opposite extremities at the same time, as [scil. the first C] is alongside each of the B's and each of the A's for an equal time, as he says,[3] because both of them are beside the A's for an equal time. This then is the argument, and it arises from the falsehood that I have indicated.[4]

2 Or of the last B, according to the text of two mss. 3 The passage 'as [scil. the first C] . . . says' is considered an intrusive gloss by some editors. 4 The text of this passage is difficult to establish and the reconstruction of its argument controversial.

Peripatetic Criticisms of the Argument on
Place, D13 (R22–R23)

R22 (A24) Aristotle, *Physics*

The aporia that Zeno formulated, viz. that if place is some-

1 ἔν τινι Simpl. *In Phys.*, p. 562.4: ἐν τίνι mss.

ἔσται, λύειν οὐ χαλεπόν· οὐδὲ γὰρ κωλύει ἐν ἄλλῳ
εἶναι τὸν πρῶτον² τόπον, μὴ μέντοι ὡς ἐν τόπῳ ἐκείνῳ
[. . .].

² πρώτως EJ

R23 (< A24) Eudem. in Simpl. *In Phys.*, p. 563.23–28 [=
Frag. 78 Wehrli, p. 37.23–27]

πρὸς δὲ Ζήνωνα φήσομεν πολλαχῶς τὸ ποῦ λέγε-
σθαι· εἰ μὲν οὖν ἐν τόπῳ ἠξίωκεν εἶναι τὰ ὄντα, οὐ
καλῶς ἀξιοῖ· οὔτε γὰρ ὑγείαν οὔτε ἀνδρίαν οὔτε ἄλλα
μυρία φαίη τις ἂν ἐν τόπῳ εἶναι. οὐδὲ δὴ ὁ τόπος
τοιοῦτος ὢν οἷος εἴρηται. εἰ δὲ ἄλλως τὸ ποῦ, κἂν ὁ
τόπος εἴη ποῦ· τὸ γὰρ τοῦ σώματος πέρας ἐστὶ τοῦ
σώματος ποῦ· ἔσχατον γάρ.

Arguments about the One:
Peripatetic Solutions (R24–R26)

R24 (≠ DK) Arist. *Metaph.* B4 1001b13–16

[. . . = **D8**] ἀλλ᾽ ἐπειδὴ¹ οὗτος² θεωρεῖ φορτικῶς, καὶ³
ἐνδέχεται εἶναι ἀδιαίρετόν τι⁴ ὥστε⁵ καὶ πρὸς ἐκεῖνόν
τιν᾽ ἀπολογίαν ἔχειν (μεῖζον μὲν γὰρ οὐ ποιήσει
πλεῖον δὲ προστιθέμενον τὸ τοιοῦτον).

¹ ἐπειδὴ EJ: εἰ δὴ Aᵇ   ² οὗτος EJ: οὕτως Aᵇ   ³ καὶ
Aᵇ: καὶ οὐκ EJ   ⁴ τι Aᵇ: om. EJ   ⁵ post ὥστε hab. mss.
καὶ οὕτως, secl. Ross: καὶ οὕτως ὥστε coni. Christ: καὶ οὕτως
Lasson

thing, it will be in something, is not difficult to resolve. For nothing prevents the first place from being in something else, but not in the sense of being in that place [. . .].

R23 (< A24) Eudemus in Simplicius, *Commentary on Aristotle's* Physics

Against Zeno we shall say that 'where' is said in multiple senses. If then he thought that the things that are are in a place, he is not thinking correctly. For no one would say that health, courage, or a thousand other things are in a place; and certainly not place either, if it is of the sort that has been said. But if 'where' is taken in a different sense, place too could be somewhere; for the limit of a body is a 'where' of the body; for it is an extremity.

> *Arguments about the One:*
> *Peripatetic Solutions (R24–R26)*

R24 (≠ DK) Aristotle, *Metaphysics*

[. . .] But since he considers things crudely, it is also possible that there exist something indivisible, so that in this way there is some defense [scil. of this hypothesis] even against him; for something of this sort, if it is added, will make the thing not bigger but more numerous [cf. **D8**].[1]

[1] The sentence is obscure in both syntax and meaning.

R25 (≠ DK) Arist. *SE* 33 182b26–27

οἱ δὲ τὸν Ζήνωνος λόγον καὶ Παρμενίδου λύουσι διὰ
τὸ πολλαχῶς φάναι τὸ ἓν λέγεσθαι καὶ τὸ ὄν.

R26 (≠ DK) Eudem. in Simpl. *In Phys.*, p. 99.1–5 [=
Frag. 37a Wehrli, p. 27.3–5]

εἰ δὲ παρῆν ἡμῖν Ζήνων, ἐλέγομεν ἂν πρὸς αὐτὸν περὶ
τοῦ ἑνὸς ἐνεργείᾳ ὅτι οὐκ ἔστι πολλά· τὸ μὲν γὰρ
κυρίως αὐτῷ ὑπάρχει, τὰ δὲ κατὰ δύναμιν. οὕτως οὖν
ἓν καὶ πολλὰ τὸ αὐτὸ γίνεται, ἐνεργείᾳ δὲ θάτερον
μόνον, ἅμα δὲ ἄμφω οὐδέποτε.

Practical Refutations: The Cynics (R27)

R27

a (≠ DK) Simpl. *in Phys.*, p. 1012.22–26

[. . .] ὥστε καὶ Διογένη τὸν κύνα τῶν ἀποριῶν ποτε
τούτων ἀκούσαντα μηδὲν μὲν εἰπεῖν πρὸς αὐτάς, ἀνα-
στάντα δὲ βαδίσαι καὶ διὰ τῆς ἐναργείας αὐτῆς λῦ-
σαι τὰ ἐν τοῖς λόγοις σοφίσματα [Frag. V B 481 G²].

b (< A15) Elias *In Cat.*, p. 109.20–23

οἷς ἀντειπεῖν μὴ δυνηθεὶς Ἀντισθένης ὁ Κυνικὸς ἀνα-
στὰς ἐβάδισε, νομίσας ἰσχυροτέραν εἶναι πάσης τῆς
διὰ λόγων ἀντιλογίας τὴν διὰ τῆς ἐνεργείας ἀπόδειξιν. [Frag. V A 159 G²]

R25 (≠ DK) Aristotle, *Sophistic Refutations*

Other people resolve the argument of Zeno and Parmenides by asserting that 'one' and 'being' are said in multiple ways.

R26 (≠ DK) Eudemus in Simplicius, *Commentary on Aristotle's* Physics

If Zeno were here with us, we would reply to him by saying about the One in actuality that it is not multiple. For this [scil. to be one] belongs to it properly speaking, while the multiple does so in potentiality. So it is in this way that the same thing is one and multiple, but in actuality is only one of the two, and it is never both at the same time.

Practical Refutations: The Cynics (R27)

R27

a (≠ DK) Simplicius, *Commentary on Aristotle's* Physics

[. . .] so that Diogenes the Cynic, having heard tell one day about these aporias [scil. Zeno's], did not say anything against them, but stood up and started walking, providing a solution by the evidence (*enargeia*) itself to the sophisms contained in the arguments.

b (< A15) Elias, *Commentary on Aristotle's* Categories

Since he had nothing with which he could reply [scil. to Zeno's arguments], Antisthenes the Cynique stood up and started walking, thinking that the demonstration by act (*energeia*) was more effective than any contradiction by argument.

Positive Uses of Zeno's Arguments (R28–R34)
The Platonic Tradition (R28–R29)
Plato's Parmenides *Inspired by*
Zeno's Arguments (R28)

R28 (≠ DK) Procl. *In Parm.*, pp. 631.25–632.9

πολλαχῶς γὰρ ἐκείνου καταβαλεῖν[1] ἐγχειρήσαντος
τοὺς πολλὰ τὰ ὄντα τιθεμένους, ὡς καὶ μέχρι τετταράκοντα λόγων τὰ ἀντικείμενα συγκρουόντων προ-
ελθεῖν αὐτῷ τὸν ἔλεγχον, αὐτὸν[2] πρὸς τὸ ἓν ποιήσασθαι τὴν παντοδαπὴν ταύτην τῶν ἐπιχειρημάτων
ἐπίδειξιν, ἁμιλλώμενον πρὸς τὸν κατὰ τοῦ πλήθους
τῶν ὄντων γυμνασάμενον, δεικνύντα τὸν ὅμοιον τρόπον ἐκείνῳ τὰ ἀντικείμενα περὶ ταὐτόν· καὶ ὡς ἐκεῖνος
ἤλεγχε τὰ πολλά, δεικνὺς αὐτὰ καὶ ὅμοια καὶ ἀνόμοια,
καὶ ταὐτὰ καὶ ἕτερα, καὶ ἴσα ὄντα καὶ ἄνισα, κατὰ τὰ
αὐτὰ δὴ καὶ αὐτὸν ἀποφαίνειν τὸ ἓν ὅμοιον καὶ ἀνόμοιον [. . .].

[1] καταβαλεῖν Y (deicere Moerbeke): καταλαβεῖν ΑΣ
[2] αὐτὸν ΑΣ: ipsorum Moerbeke

The Neoplatonists (R29)

R29 (≠ DK) Procl. *In Parm.*, p. 769.22–39

ἐπεὶ καὶ ὁ Ζήνων, οὐ μόνον ἐξ ἐκείνων, ἀλλὰ καὶ ἐκ
τῆς τούτων ἀκολουθίας ἀπήλεγχε τὴν ἀτοπίαν τῶν τὰ
πολλὰ τοῦ ἑνὸς χωριζόντων· οὐ γὰρ μόνον ἐκ τοῦ

Positive Uses of Zeno's Arguments (R28–R34)
The Platonic tradition (R28–R29)
Plato's Parmenides *Inspired by*
Zeno's Arguments (R28)

R28 (≠ DK) Proclus, *Commentary on Plato's* Parmenides

For, since he [i.e. Zeno] had tried in many ways to refute those people who posit the multiplicity of the things that are, so that his refutation went as far as forty arguments that knock the contraries against one another, he [i.e. Plato] has put this manifold display of arguments at the service of the One, competing against the man who opposed the multiplicity of the things that are and establishing, in the same way as he did, the contraries with regard to the same thing,. And just as the former man refuted multiplicity by showing that the same things are similar and dissimilar, the same and different, and equal and unequal, so too the latter one stated that the One is similar and dissimilar [. . .].

The Neoplatonists (R29)

R29 (≠ DK) Proclus, *Commentary on Plato's* Parmenides

For Zeno refuted the absurdity of those people who separate the multiple from the One not only on the basis of these arguments, but so too on the basis of their conse-

ὁμοίου καὶ ἀνομοίου ἐπεποίητο τὴν ἐπιχείρησιν, οὐδὲ
αὖ μόνον ἐκ τοῦ ἑνὸς καὶ τοῦ πλήθους, ἀλλ᾽ ἤδη καὶ
ἀπὸ στάσεως καὶ κινήσεως. τὸ γὰρ αὐτὸ καὶ κατὰ τὸ
αὐτὸ καὶ ἱστάμενον καὶ κινούμενον ἀπέφηνεν, εἰ τὰ
πολλὰ μὴ μετέχοι τοῦ ἑνός· πᾶν τὸ ἱστάμενον ἔν τινι
ἐστιν ἑνί, καὶ πᾶν τὸ κινούμενον ἐξίσταται τοῦ ἑνός,
ὥστε τὰ πολλὰ εἰ μὴ μετέχοι τινὸς ἑνὸς ἄστατά ἐστι·
καὶ πάλιν εἰ αὐτὸ τοῦτο ἔχοι κοινὸν τὸ μὴ μετέχειν
τινός,[1] ἔν τινι[2] ἔσται· ταύτῃ οὖν πάλιν ἀκίνητα· τὰ
αὐτὰ ἄρα καὶ κινούμενα ἔσται καὶ ἑστῶτα· οὐκ ἄρα
πολλά ἐστιν ἔρημα πάντῃ τοῦ ἑνός.

[1] τινὸς ‹ἑνός› Taylor ex g)   [2] τινι ‹ἑνὶ› Luna-Segonds

The Xenocratean Tradition (R30–R31)

R30 (A22) Ps.-Arist. *Lin.* 968a18–23

ἔτι δὲ κατὰ τὸν τοῦ Ζήνωνος λόγον ἀνάγκη τι μέγεθος ἀμερὲς εἶναι, εἴπερ ἀδύνατον μὲν ἐν πεπερασμένῳ
χρόνῳ ἀπείρων ἅψασθαι, καθ᾽ ἕκαστον ἁπτόμενον,
ἀνάγκη δ᾽ ἐπὶ τὸ ἥμισυ πρότερον ἀφικνεῖσθαι τὸ κινούμενον, τοῦ δὲ μὴ ἀμεροῦς πάντως ἔστιν[1] ἥμισυ.

[1] ἔσται LHᵃUᵃ

quences. For he had developed his argumentation not only on the basis of the similar and the dissimilar, nor again only on that of the one and the multiple, but also on that of rest and motion. For he stated that the same thing, according to the same relation, would be at the same time at rest and in motion, if the multiple did not participate in the One: everything that is at rest is in a certain One, and everything that is in motion departs from the One, so that if the multiple did not participate in a certain One it would be instable; and again, if this same thing had in common not to participate in anything, it will be in something. In this way, it [i.e. multiplicity] is once again immobile. It follows that the same things are at the same time in motion and at rest. Therefore the multiple is not entirely deprived of the One.

The Xenocratean Tradition (R30–R31)

R30 (A22) Ps.-Aristotle, *On Indivisible Lines*

Furthermore, according to Zeno's argument it is necessary that there exist a certain indivisible magnitude, if indeed it is true that it is impossible in a limited time to touch things that are unlimited [scil. in number] by touching each of them, and that it is necessary that what is moved arrive earlier at the half, and that of what is not deprived of parts there exists in any case a half.

R31 (cf. A22) Alex. Aphr. in Simpl. *In Phys.*, p. 138.10–18

τούτῳ δὲ τῷ λόγῳ, φησί, τῷ περὶ τῆς διχοτομίας ἐνδοῦναι Ξενοκράτη τὸν Καλχηδόνιον [Frag. 42 Heinze]
δεξάμενον μὲν τὸ πᾶν τὸ διαιρετὸν πολλὰ εἶναι (τὸ
γὰρ μέρος ἕτερον εἶναι τοῦ ὅλου) καὶ τὸ μὴ δύνασθαι
ταὐτὸν ἕν τε ἅμα καὶ πολλὰ εἶναι διὰ τὸ μὴ συναλη-
θεύεσθαι τὴν ἀντίφασιν, μηκέτι δὲ συγχωρεῖν πᾶν
μέγεθος διαιρετὸν εἶναι καὶ μέρος ἔχειν· εἶναι γάρ
τινας ἀτόμους γραμμάς, ἐφ’ ὧν οὐκέτι ἀληθεύεσθαι
τὸ πολλὰς ταύτας εἶναι. οὕτως γὰρ ᾤετο τὴν τοῦ ἑνὸς
εὑρίσκειν φύσιν καὶ φεύγειν τὴν ἀντίφασιν διὰ τοῦ
μήτε τὸ διαιρετὸν ἓν εἶναι ἀλλὰ πολλά, μήτε τὰς ἀτόμους γραμμὰς πολλὰ ἀλλ’ ἓν μόνον.

Megarians and Related Figures (R32–R34)

R32 (≠ DK) Cic. *Acad.* 2.129

Megaricorum fuit nobilis disciplina. cuius ut scriptum
video princeps Xenophanes [. . .] deinde eum secuti Parmenides et Zeno [. . .].

R33 (≠ DK) Sext. Emp. *Pyrrh. Hyp.* 3.71

εἰ κινεῖταί τι, ἤτοι ἐν ᾧ ἔστι τόπῳ κινεῖται ἢ ἐν ᾧ οὐκ
ἔστιν. οὔτε δὲ ἐν ᾧ ἔστιν· [. . .] οὔτε ἐν ᾧ μὴ ἔστιν·
[. . .] οὐκ ἄρα κινεῖταί τι. οὗτος δὲ ὁ λόγος ἔστιν μὲν
Διοδώρου τοῦ Κρόνου [cf. **D17**].

R31 (cf. A22) Simplicius, *Commentary on Aristotle's* Physics

It was to this argument about dichotomy, he [i.e. Alexander] says, that Xenocrates of Chalcedon yielded when he accepted that a whole that is divisible is multiple (for the part is different from the whole) and that it is not possible that the one and the multiple be identical because the contradictory cannot be true at the same time; but he does not grant additionally that every magnitude is divisible and possesses a part. For there are certain indivisible lines about which it is no longer true that these are multiple. For he thought that in this way he had discovered the nature of the one and escaped the contradictory, because what is divisible is not one but multiple, and indivisible lines are not multiple but only one.

Megarians and Related Figures (R32–R34)

R32 (≠ DK) Cicero, *Prior Academics*

The teaching of the Megarians was noble: as I find written, their initiator was Xenophanes [. . .] who was then followed by Parmenides and Zeno [. . .].

R33 (≠ DK) Sextus Empiricus, *Outlines of Pyrrhonism*

If something moves, either it moves in the place in which it is or in the place in which it is not; but it does not in the place in which it is [. . .]; nor in the place in which it is not; [. . .] hence nothing moves. This argument comes from Diodorus Cronus.

R34 (≠ DK) Schol. in Arist. *Metaph.*, p. 778b17

(ad Θ3 1046b29, οἱ Μεγαρικοί κτλ.): οἱ περὶ Ζήνωνα.

Suspect Reports (R35–R39)
Alleged Titles and Characterizations of Zeno's
Books Deriving from the Interpretation of His
Arguments (R35–R36)

R35 (< A2) *Suda* Z.77

ἔγραψεν Ἔριδας, Ἐξήγησιν τῶν Ἐμπεδοκλέους, Πρὸς τοὺς φιλοσόφους, Περὶ φύσεως.

R36 (< A14) Diog. Laert. 3.48

διαλόγους τοίνυν φασὶ πρῶτον γράψαι Ζήνωνα τὸν Ἐλεάτην.

A Doxographical Inference (R37)

R37 (cf. A23) Aët. 4.9.1 (Stob.) [εἰ ἀληθεῖς αἱ αἰσθήσεις]

[. . .] Ζήνων [. . .] ψευδεῖς εἶναι τὰς αἰσθήσεις [cf. **MEL. D18**].

A Theologization of the One (R38)

R38 (A30) Aët. 1.7.27 (Stob.) [περὶ θεοῦ]

Μέλισσος καὶ Ζήνων τὸ ἓν καὶ πᾶν καὶ μόνον ἀίδιον καὶ ἄπειρον.

R34 (≠ DK) Scholia on Aristotle's *Metaphysics*

The Megarians: the followers of Zeno.

Suspect Reports (R35–R39)
Alleged Titles and Characterizations of Zeno's
Books Deriving from the Interpretation of His
Arguments (R35–R36)

R35 (< A2) *Suda*

He wrote *Quarrels, Interpretation of* [scil. *the Works of*]
Empedocles, Against the Philosophers, On Nature.

R36 (< A14) Diogenes Laertius

They say that Zeno of Elea was the first person to write
dialogues.

A Doxographical Inference (R37)

R37 (cf. A23) Aëtius

[. . .] Zeno [. . .]: sensations are deceptive.

A Theologization of the One (R38)

R38 (A30) Aëtius

Melissus and Zeno: [scil. god is] the One and the whole,
and he alone is eternal and unlimited.

An Erroneous Attribution (R39)

R39 (< A1) Diog. Laert. 9.29

ἀρέσκει δ' αὐτῷ τάδε· κόσμον[1] εἶναι κενόν τε μὴ εἶναι·
γεγενῆσθαι δὲ τὴν τῶν πάντων[2] φύσιν ἐκ θερμοῦ καὶ
ψυχροῦ καὶ ξηροῦ καὶ ὑγροῦ, λαμβανόντων αὐτῶν εἰς
ἄλληλα τὴν μεταβολήν· γένεσίν τε ἀνθρώπων ἐκ γῆς
εἶναι, καὶ ψυχὴν κρᾶμα ὑπάρχειν ἐκ τῶν προειρημέ-
νων κατὰ μηδενὸς τούτων ἐπικράτησιν.

[1] κόσμον Φh: κόσμος BP[1](Q): κόσμους FP[4]   [2] πάν-
τωνBPF: ὑδάτων Φh

An Erroneous Attribution (R39)

R39 (< A1) Diogenes Laertius

These are his opinions: the worlds exist, and the void does not exist. The nature of all things has come about from the warm and the cold, the dry and the wet, when these are transformed into one another. The genesis of human beings is from the earth, and the soul is a mixture of the things mentioned earlier, without there being a preponderance of any of these.

21. MELISSUS [MEL.]

Melissus came from Samos and was a contemporary of Empedocles, Anaxagoras, and Herodotus: Apollodorus' chronology set his *floruit* during the 84th Olympiad (444/40 BC), coinciding with the apogee of the Periclean age. The date is manifestly deduced from the victorious naval battle (441/40) in which he acted as commander for the Samians against the Athenian fleet (in which Sophocles participated), before Pericles finally subjugated the island. The biographical tradition makes Melissus a disciple of Parmenides; this can scarcely be doubted with regard to his doctrine, but the chronology makes any direct contact between the two men highly improbable.

Melissus was the author of a single work. Our information about his doctrine depends above all on Simplicius, who in his commentary to Aristotle's *Physics* cites all the verbal fragments that have survived. Melissus' treatise differed from Parmenides' work in three regards: its form, as Melissus wrote in prose, not in verse; its program, as he spoke solely about the nature of being, to the exclusion of any cosmology; and its ontological doctrine, as he systematized and clarified the Parmenidean series of predicates of being, partially modifying the list and its meaning and in particular declaring being 'unlimited.'

Aristotle felt very little respect for Melissus, whose

paralogisms he denounces and whom he regards as a vulgar thinker. But Melissus surely merits such contempt just as little as he deserves Simplicius' spectacular rehabilitation [cf. **R21**]. Melissus' greatest interest resides in the fact that he provides us, by recomposing Parmenides' poem, with the earliest critical reading of it.

BIBLIOGRAPHY

Editions

G. Reale. *Melisso: Testimonianze e frammenti* (Florence, 1970).

R. Vitali. *Melisso di Samo. Sul mondo o sull'essere* (Urbino, 1973).

Studies

J. A. Palmer. "Melissus and Parmenides," *Oxford Studies in Ancient Philosophy* 26 (2004): 19–54.

See also, in the introduction to Parmenides, the works of G. Calogero and of P. Curd.

OUTLINE OF THE CHAPTER

P

231

MELISSUS [30 DK]

P

Chronology (P1–P4)

P1 (< A1) Diog. Laert. 9.24

Μέλισσος Ἰθαιγένους Σάμιος [. . .]. φησὶ δ᾽ Ἀπολλόδωρος [*FGrHist* 244 F72] ἠκμακέναι αὐτὸν κατὰ τὴν
τετάρτην καὶ ὀγδοηκοστὴν Ὀλυμπιάδα.

P2 (cf. A1) Eus. *Chron.* (= Hier. *Chron.*, p. 113.19)

[ad Ol. 84.1] Melissus physicus agnoscitur.

P3 (< A2) *Suda* M.496

[. . .] καὶ ἦν ἐπὶ τῶν Ζήνωνος τοῦ Ἐλεάτου καὶ Ἐμπεδοκλέους χρόνων [. . . = **P7**].

P4 (A3) Plut. *Them.* 2

καίτοι Στησίμβροτος Ἀναξαγόρου τε διακοῦσαι τὸν
Θεμιστοκλέα φησὶ [*FGrHist* 107 F1] καὶ περὶ Μέλισσον σπουδάσαι τὸν φυσικόν, οὐκ εὖ τῶν χρόνων

MELISSUS

P

Chronology (P1–P4)

P1 (< A1) Diogenes Laertius

Melissus, son of Ithaegenes, from Samos [. . .]. Apollodorus says that he reached maturity during the 84th Olympiad [= 444/40].

P2 (cf. A1) Eusebius, *Chronicle*

[1st year of the 84th Olympiad:] Melissus, the natural philosopher, is celebrated.

P3 (< A2) *Suda*

[. . .] he lived during the time of Zeno of Elea and Empedocles [. . .].[1]

   [1] This sentence is erroneously included in an entry about Meletus, but what follows (cf. **P7**) shows that it refers to Melissus.

P4 (A3) Plutarch, *Themistocles*

Stesimbrotus says that Themistocles studied with Anaxagoras and also spent time with Melissus, the natural philosopher; but he has not grasped the chronology correctly.

ἁπτόμενος· Περικλεῖ γάρ, ὃς πολὺ νεώτερος ἦν Θεμι-
στοκλέους, Μέλισσος μὲν ἀντεστρατήγει πολιορκοῦ-
ντι Σαμίους, Ἀναξαγόρας δὲ συνδιέτριβε [. . . = **SOPH.
R4**].

Philosophical Lineage and Relations (P5)

P5 (‹ A1) Diog. Laert. 9.24

οὗτος ἤκουσε Παρμενίδου· ἀλλὰ καὶ εἰς λόγους ἦλθεν
Ἡρακλείτῳ· ὅτε καὶ συνέστησεν αὐτὸν τοῖς Ἐφεσίοις
ἀγνοοῦσι, καθάπερ Ἱπποκράτης Δημόκριτον Ἀβδη-
ρίταις.

Participation in Politics and War (P6–P8)

P6 (‹ A1) Diog. Laert. 9.24

γέγονε δὲ καὶ πολιτικὸς ἀνὴρ καὶ ἀποδοχῆς παρὰ
τοῖς πολίταις ἠξιωμένος· ὅθεν ναύαρχος αἱρεθεὶς ἔτι
καὶ μᾶλλον ἐθαυμάσθη διὰ τὴν οἰκείαν ἀρετήν.

For it was against Pericles, who was much younger than Themistocles, that Melissus fought as a general when he [i.e. Pericles] besieged Samos [cf. **P8**], and it was with him [i.e. Pericles] that Anaxagoras associated [. . .] [cf. **ANAXAG. P18–P22**].

Philosophical Lineage and Relations (P5)

P5 (< A1) Diogenes Laertius

He studied with Parmenides; but he also went to Heraclitus for discussions; on this occasion he presented him to the Ephesians (who did not know him), just as Hippocrates [scil. presented] Democritus to the Abderitans [cf. **ATOM. P47**].[1]

---

[1] Any meeting between Melissus and Heraclitus is chronologically impossible. What matters is the homage paid to the philosopher of becoming (cf. **D11**).

Participation in Politics and War (P6–P8)

P6 (< A1) Diogenes Laertius

He was also a man engaged in politics and was considered worthy of favor by his fellow citizens. That is why, after he had been chosen commander of the fleet, he became the object of even greater admiration because of his personal moral virtue.

P7 (< A2) *Suda* M.496

[. . . = **P3**] [. . .] καὶ ἀντεπολιτεύσατο δὲ Περικλεῖ· καὶ
ὑπὲρ Σαμίων στρατηγήσας ἐναυμάχησε πρὸς Σοφο-
κλῆν τὸν τραγικόν, Ὀλυμπιάδι ὀγδοηκοστῇ τετάρτῃ.

P8 (< A3) Plut. *Per.* 26–27

[26] πλεύσαντος[1] γὰρ αὐτοῦ, Μέλισσος ὁ Ἰθαγένους,
ἀνὴρ φιλόσοφος στρατηγῶν τότε τῆς Σάμου, κατα-
φρονήσας τῆς ὀλιγότητος τῶν νεῶν καὶ[2] τῆς ἀπειρίας
τῶν στρατηγῶν, ἔπεισε τοὺς πολίτας ἐπιθέσθαι τοῖς
Ἀθηναίοις. καὶ γενομένης μάχης νικήσαντες οἱ Σάμιοι
καὶ πολλοὺς μὲν αὐτῶν ἄνδρας ἑλόντες, πολλὰς δὲ
ναῦς διαφθείραντες, ἐχρῶντο τῇ θαλάσσῃ καὶ παρ-
ετίθεντο τῶν ἀναγκαίων πρὸς τὸν πόλεμον ὅσα μὴ
πρότερον εἶχον. ὑπὸ δὲ τοῦ Μελίσσου καὶ Περικλέα
φησὶν αὐτὸν Ἀριστοτέλης [Frag. 577 Rose] ἡττηθῆναι
ναυμαχοῦντα πρότερον. [. . .] [27] πυθόμενος δ᾽ οὖν ὁ
Περικλῆς τὴν ἐπὶ στρατοπέδου συμφοράν, ἐβοήθει
κατὰ τάχος, καὶ τοῦ Μελίσσου πρὸς αὐτὸν ἀντιταξα-
μένου κρατήσας καὶ τρεψάμενος τοὺς πολεμίους εὐθὺς
περιετείχιζε [. . .].

---

[1] ἀποπλεύσαντος Cobet   [2] ἢ mss., corr. Κοραῒς

P7 (< A2) *Suda*

[. . .] and he was a political opponent of Pericles; and as a general for the Samians he fought a naval battle against Sophocles, the tragedian, during the 84th Olympiad [= 444/40].

P8 (< A3) Plutarch, *Pericles*

[26] When the fleet [i.e. of Pericles] had sailed out [scil. against the allies of the Samians], Melissus, son of Ithagenes, a philosopher who was general of Samos at that time, disregarding the small number of the ships and the inexperience of the generals, persuaded his fellow citizens to attack the Athenians. And when they met in battle, the Samians were victorious, and after they had captured many men and destroyed many ships, they dominated the sea and laid up a store of the necessities for war such as they had not had before. And Aristotle says that Pericles himself was defeated by Melissus in an earlier sea battle. [. . .] [27] When Pericles heard about his army's disaster, he came rapidly to its assistance; and after he had defeated Melissus, who had arrayed his army in battle against him, and put the enemy to flight, he immediately laid siege [scil. to Samos] [. . .].

MELISSUS [30 DK]

D

Only One Treatise, and Its Traditional Title (D1)

D1

a (< 28 A13) Diog. Laert. 1.16

[. . .] οἱ δὲ ἀνὰ ἓν συγγράψαντες·[1] Μέλισσος [. . .].

  [1] συγγράψαντες BP, γρ. F²: σύγγραμμα F¹

b (A4) Simpl. *In Phys.*, p. 70.16–17

[. . .] ὁ Μέλισσος καὶ τὴν ἐπιγραφὴν οὕτως ἐποιήσατο τοῦ συγγράμματος Περὶ φύσεως ἢ περὶ τοῦ ὄντος.

MELISSUS

D

Only One Treatise, and Its Traditional Title (D1)

D1

a (< 28 A13) Diogenes Laertius

[. . .] others, who wrote only one treatise: Melissus [. . .].

b (A4) Simplicius, *Commentary on Aristotle's* Physics

[. . .] Melissus also entitled his treatise *On Nature or on Being* [cf. **R22** and **PARM. D3**].

See also **ALCM. D2**

EARLY GREEK PHILOSOPHY V

The Attributes of Being: The Preserved Fragments
in Their Probable Order (D2–D10)
Ungenerated (D2)

D2

a (B1) Simpl. *In Phys.*, p. 162.23–26

καὶ Μέλισσος δὲ τὸ ἀγένητον τοῦ ὄντος ἔδειξε τῷ
κοινῷ τούτῳ χρησάμενος ἀξιώματι. γράφει δὲ οὕτως·
"ἀεὶ ἦν ὅ τι ἦν καὶ ἀεὶ ἔσται. εἰ γὰρ ἐγένετο, ἀναγ-
καῖόν ἐστι πρὶν γενέσθαι εἶναι μηδέν. †εἰ τύχοι
νῦν†[1] μηδὲν ἦν, οὐδαμὰ ἂν γένοιτο οὐδὲν[2] ἐκ μηδενός."

[1] εἰ τύχοι νῦν E: εἰ τύχη νῦν D: εἰ τοίνυν F: ὅτε τοίνυν prop.
Diels, alii alia   [2] οὐδὲν DE: μηδὲν F

b (≠ DK) Arist. *Phys.* 1.8 191a24–31

ζητοῦντες γὰρ οἱ κατὰ φιλοσοφίαν πρῶτοι τὴν ἀλήθειαν καὶ τὴν φύσιν τῶν ὄντων [. . .] φασιν οὔτε γίγνεσθαι τῶν ὄντων οὐδὲν οὔτε φθείρεσθαι διὰ τὸ
ἀναγκαῖον μὲν εἶναι γίγνεσθαι τὸ γιγνόμενον ἢ ἐξ
ὄντος ἢ ἐξ μὴ ὄντος, ἐκ δὲ τούτων ἀμφοτέρων ἀδύνατον εἶναι· οὔτε γὰρ τὸ ὂν γίγνεσθαι (εἶναι γὰρ ἤδη)
ἔκ τε μὴ ὄντος οὐδὲν ἂν γενέσθαι· ὑποκεῖσθαι γάρ τι
δεῖν.[1]

[1] δεῖ mss., corr. Bonitz

240

*The Attributes of Being: The Preserved Fragments
in Their Probable Order (D2–D10)
Ungenerated (D2)*

D2

a (B1) Simplicius, *Commentary on Aristotle's* Physics

Melissus too [i.e. like Parmenides] has shown that what is
is ungenerated, by making use of this common axiom [i.e.
that nothing comes from what is not]. He writes as follows:
**"What was has always been and always will be. For
if it came to be, it is necessary that it was nothing
before it came to be. †But if it happened to be now†
was nothing (?), nothing would have come to be out
of what is not."**

b (≠ DK) Aristotle, *Physics*

For the first people who sought according to philosophy
the truth and the nature of the things that are [. . .] say
that none of the things that are either comes to be or is
destroyed, because it is necessary that what comes to be
come to be either out of what is or out of what is not, but
that it is impossible [scil. for it to come to be] out of either
of these two: for neither can what is come to be (for it
already is) and out of what is not nothing can come to be,
for there has to be something as a substrate.

Unlimited (D3–D5)

D3 (B2) Simpl. *In Phys.*, p. 109.20–25 (et al.)

ὅτε τοίνυν οὐκ ἐγένετο, ἔστι δέ,[1] ἀεὶ ἦν καὶ ἀεὶ
ἔσται[2] καὶ ἀρχὴν οὐκ ἔχει οὐδὲ τελευτήν, ἀλλ᾽ ἄπειρόν ἐστιν. εἰ μὲν γὰρ ἐγένετο, ἀρχὴν ἂν εἶχεν (ἤρξατο γὰρ ἄν ποτε γινόμενον[3]) καὶ τελευτήν (ἐτελεύτησε γὰρ ἄν ποτε γινόμενον[4])· εἰ δὲ μήτε ἤρξατο
μήτε ἐτελεύτησεν ἀεί τε ἦν καὶ ἀεὶ ἔσται,[5] οὐκ ἔχει
ἀρχὴν οὐδὲ τελευτήν· οὐ γὰρ ἀεὶ εἶναι ἀνυστὸν ὅ τι
μὴ πᾶν ἐστι.

  [1] δέ p. 109: τε καὶ p. 29   [2] ἀεὶ ἔσται p. 109: ἔσται
p. 29   [3–4] γινόμενον mss.: γενόμενον Diels   [5] καὶ ἀεὶ
ἔσται p. 109: om. p. 29

D4 (B3) Simpl. *In Phys.*, p. 109.31–32

ἀλλ᾽ ὥσπερ ἔστιν ἀεί, οὕτω καὶ τὸ μέγεθος ἄπειρον
ἀεὶ χρὴ εἶναι.

D5 (B4) Simpl. *In Phys.*, p. 110.3–4

ἀρχήν τε καὶ τέλος ἔχον οὐδὲν οὔτε ἀίδιον οὔτε
ἄπειρόν ἐστιν.

Unlimited (D3–D5)

D3 (B2) Simplicius, *Commentary on Aristotle's* Physics

Since therefore it did not come about, but is, it always was and always will be, and has neither a beginning nor an end, but is unlimited. For if it came about, it would have a beginning (for it would have begun if it had come about at some time) and an end (for it would have come to an end if it had come about at some time). But if it has neither begun nor come to an end, always was and always will be, then it has neither a beginning nor an end. For it is impossible, for what is not entirely, to be forever.

D4 (B3) Simplicius, *Commentary on Aristotle's* Physics

But just as it always is, in the same way it is necessary that it also always unlimited in magnitude.

D5 (B4) Simplicius, *Commentary on Aristotle's* Physics

Nothing that has a beginning and an end is either eternal or unlimited.

One (D6–D7)

D6 (B6) Simpl. *In Cael.*, p. 557.16–17

εἰ γὰρ εἴη, ἓν εἴη ἄν· εἰ γὰρ δύο εἴη, οὐκ ἂν δύναιτο
ἄπειρα εἶναι, ἀλλ᾽ ἔχοι ἂν πείρατα πρὸς ἄλληλα.[1]

  [1] γράφεται ἄλλως· εἰ γὰρ οὕτως ἓν ἔσται, δύναιντ᾽ ἂν
ἄπειρα εἶναι ἀλλ᾽ ἔχοι ἂν πείρατα πρὸς ἄλληλα E[2] in marg.

D7 (B5) Simpl. *In Phys.*, p. 110.5–6

εἰ μὴ ἓν εἴη, περανεῖ[1] πρὸς ἄλλο.

  [1] περανοῖ E

Without Shape (D8)

D8 (< B9) Simpl. *In Phys.*, p. 110.1–2 (et al.)

εἰ μὲν ὂν εἴη,[1] δεῖ αὐτὸ ἓν εἶναι· ἓν δὲ ὂν δεῖ αὐτὸ
σῶμα μὴ ἔχειν.[2]

  [1] ὂν εἴη D: οὖν εἴη EF: ὂν ἔστι Brandis   [2] ἓν δὲ . . .
ἔχειν] ἓν ἐόν, φησί, δεῖ αὐτὸ σῶμα μὴ ἔχειν. εἰ δὲ ἔχοι πάχος, ἔχοι ἂν μόρια καὶ οὐκέτι ἕν εἴη p. 87.6

Indivisible and Immobile (D9)

D9 (B10) Simpl. *In Phys.*, p. 109.33–34

εἰ γὰρ διῄρηται, φησί, τὸ ἐόν, κινεῖται. κινούμενον
δὲ οὐκ ἂν εἴη.

One (D6–D7)

D6 (B6) Simplicius, *Commentary on Aristotle's* On the Heavens

For if it existed, it would have to be one. For if it were two, it could not be unlimited, but they would limit each other.

D7 (B5) Simplicius, *Commentary on Aristotle's* Physics

If it were not one, it will have a limit against another.

Without Shape (D8)

D8 (< B9) Simplicius, *Commentary on Aristotle's* Physics

If it were something that is, it must be one. But if it is one, it must not have a body.[1]

---

[1] Not to have a 'body' does not mean to be incorporeal, as Simplicius understands it (cf. **R21b**), but rather not to have a definite shape. In another passage in Simplicius, this fragment is followed by a sentence ("If it possessed thickness, it would have parts, and would no longer be one") that Diels attributes to Melissus.

Indivisible and Immobile (D9)

D9 (B10) Simplicius, *Commentary on Aristotle's* Physics

For if what is is divided, he says, **it moves. But if it moved it would not exist.**

Further Attributes (D10)

D10 (B7) Simpl. *In Phys.*, pp. 111.18–112.15

λέγει δ᾽ οὖν ὁ Μέλισσος οὕτως τὰ πρότερον εἰρημένα συμπεραινόμενος καὶ οὕτως τὰ περὶ τῆς κινήσεως ἐπάγων.

οὕτως οὖν ἀίδιόν ἐστι καὶ ἄπειρον καὶ ἓν καὶ ὅμοιον πᾶν καὶ οὔτ᾽ ἂν ἀπόλοιτο οὔτε μεῖζον γίνοιτο οὔτε μετακοσμέοιτο οὔτε ἀλγεῖ οὔτε ἀνιᾶται. εἰ γάρ τι τούτων πάσχοι, οὐκ ἂν ἔτι ἓν εἴη. εἰ γὰρ ἑτεροιοῦται, ἀνάγκη τὸ ἐὸν μὴ ὅμοιον εἶναι, ἀλλὰ ἀπόλλυσθαι τὸ πρόσθεν ἐόν, τὸ δὲ οὐκ ἐὸν γίνεσθαι. εἰ τοίνυν τριχὶ μιῇ μυρίοις ἔτεσιν ἑτεροῖον γίνοιτο τὸ πᾶν, ὀλεῖται¹ ἂν² ἐν τῷ παντὶ³ χρόνῳ.

ἀλλ᾽ οὐδὲ μετακοσμηθῆναι ἀνυστόν· ὁ γὰρ κόσμος ὁ πρόσθεν ἐὼν οὐκ ἀπόλλυται οὔτε ὁ μὴ ἐὼν γίνεται. ὅτε δὲ μήτε προσγίνεται μηδὲν μήτε ἀπόλλυται μήτε ἑτεροιοῦται, πῶς ἂν μετακοσμηθὲν τῶν ἐόντων τι ᾖ; εἰ μὲν γάρ⁴ τι ἐγίνετο ἑτεροῖον, ἤδη ἂν καὶ μετακοσμηθείη.

οὐδὲ ἀλγεῖ· οὐ γὰρ ἂν πᾶν εἴη ἀλγέον· οὐ γὰρ ἂν δύναιτο ἀεὶ εἶναι χρῆμα ἀλγέον οὐδὲ

¹ de forma ὀλεῖται cum ἄν dub. edd. (sed cf. Kühner-Gerth 2.1³.209): ὄλοιτο Mullach: ὀλεῖσθαι Schulteß ² γίνοιτο τὸ πᾶν, ὀλεῖται ἂν mss.: γίνοιτο, ὀλεῖται πᾶν Diels ³ παντὶ] παρόντι F ⁴ γάρ ed. Ald.: γε DF et in lit. E

Further Attributes (D10)

D10 (B7) Simplicius, *Commentary on Aristotle's* Physics

This then is what Melissus says in conclusion to what he said earlier, adding his statements about motion as follows:

> In this way therefore it is eternal, unlimited, one, and entirely similar, and it could not either be destroyed, nor increase in size, nor change its arrangement, nor suffer either pain or distress. For if it underwent any of these affections, it would no longer be one. For if it becomes different, it is necessary that what is not be similar, but that what was before be destroyed, and what is not come to be. If then the whole had become different by a single hair in the course of thousands of years, it would have been destroyed in the whole of this time.
>
> But neither is it possible that it change its arrangement. For the arrangement that was before is not destroyed, and the one that is not does not come to be. But since nothing is added nor is destroyed nor becomes different, then how could any of the things that are change its arrangement? For only if it became something of a different sort, could it then change its arrangement.
>
> Nor does it feel pain: for it could not feel pain as a whole. For a thing could not always

ἔχει ἴσην δύναμιν τῷ ὑγιεῖ· οὔτ' ἂν ὅμοιον
εἴη, εἰ ἀλγέοι· ἀπογινομένου γάρ τευ ἂν ἀλ-
γέοι ἢ προσγινομένου, κοὐκ ἂν ἔτι ὅμοιον εἴη.
οὐδ' ἂν τὸ ὑγιὲς ἀλγῆσαι δύναιτο· ἀπὸ γὰρ ἂν
ὄλοιτο τὸ ὑγιὲς καὶ τὸ ἐόν, τὸ δὲ οὐκ ἐὸν γένοιτο. καὶ περὶ τοῦ ἀνιᾶσθαι ωὑτὸς λόγος τῷ
ἀλγέοντι.

ουδὲ κενεόν ἐστιν οὐδέν· τὸ γὰρ κενεὸν οὐδέν ἐστιν· οὐκ ἂν οὖν εἴη τό γε μηδέν. οὐδὲ
κινεῖται· ὑποχωρῆσαι γὰρ οὐκ ἔχει οὐδαμῇ,
ἀλλὰ πλέων ἐστίν. εἰ μὲν γὰρ κενεὸν ἦν, ὑπ-
εχώρει ἂν εἰς τὸ κενόν· κενοῦ δὲ μὴ ἐόντος οὐκ
ἔχει ὅκη ὑποχωρήσει. πυκνὸν δὲ καὶ ἀραιὸν
οὐκ ἂν εἴη· τὸ γὰρ ἀραιὸν οὐκ ἀνυστὸν πλέων
εἶναι ὁμοίως τῷ πυκνῷ, ἀλλ' ἤδη τὸ ἀραιόν γε
κενεώτερον γίνεται τοῦ πυκνοῦ. κρίσιν δὲ ταύτην χρὴ ποιήσασθαι τοῦ πλέω καὶ τοῦ μὴ
πλέω· εἰ μὲν οὖν χωρεῖ τι ἢ εἰσδέχεται, οὐ
πλέων· εἰ δὲ μήτε χωρεῖ μήτε εἰσδέχεται,
πλέων. ἀνάγκη τοίνυν πλέων εἶναι, εἰ κενὸν
μὴ ἔστιν. εἰ τοίνυν πλέων ἐστίν, οὐ κινεῖται.

ταῦτα μὲν οὖν τὰ τοῦ Μελίσσου.

feel pain, nor [scil. when it feels pain] **does it
have the same capacity as what is healthy. Nor
would it be similar, if it felt pain; for it would
be because something left it or were added
that it would feel pain, and then it would no
longer be similar. What is healthy would not
be able to feel pain either: for what is healthy
and what is would be destroyed, and what is
not would come to be. And the same argument
applies to distress as to pain.**

**And there is not any void. For the void is
nothing. But what is nothing could not exist.
Nor does it move. For it has nowhere it can
recede to, but it is full; for if there were void,
it would recede toward the void; but since the
void does not exist, it has nowhere to recede
to. And it could not be either dense or rarefied;
for it is not possible that what is rarefied be full
in the same way as the dense is, but the rarefied, itself, must come to be more void than
the dense. The question whether it is full or
not full must be decided in this way: if something goes out or penetrates into it, it is not
full; but if nothing either goes out or penetrates into it, it is full. Hence it is necessary
that it be full, if there is no void. Hence if it is
full, it does not move.**

This then is what Melissus says.

The Senses Err (D11)

D11 (B8) Simpl. *In Cael.*, pp. 558.21–559.12

εἰπὼν γὰρ περὶ τοῦ ὄντος, ὅτι ἕν ἐστι καὶ ἀγένητον
καὶ ἀκίνητον καὶ μηδενὶ κενῷ διειλημμένον, ἀλλ᾽ ὅλον
ἑαυτοῦ πλῆρες, ἐπάγει·

> μέγιστον μὲν οὖν σημεῖον οὗτος ὁ λόγος, ὅτι
> ἓν μόνον ἔστιν, ἀτὰρ καὶ τάδε σημεῖα· εἰ γὰρ
> ἦν πολλά, τοιαῦτα χρὴ αὐτὰ εἶναι, οἷόν περ
> ἐγώ φημι τὸ ἓν εἶναι· εἰ γὰρ ἔστι γῆ καὶ ὕδωρ
> καὶ ἀὴρ καὶ σίδηρος καὶ χρυσὸς καὶ πῦρ καὶ
> τὸ μὲν ζῶον, τὸ δὲ τεθνηκός, καὶ μέλαν καὶ
> λευκὸν καὶ τὰ ἄλλα, ὅσα φασὶν οἱ ἄνθρωποι
> εἶναι ἀληθῆ, εἰ δὴ ταῦτα ἔστι, καὶ ἡμεῖς ὀρ-
> θῶς ὁρῶμεν καὶ ἀκούομεν, εἶναι χρὴ ἕκαστον
> τοιοῦτον, οἷόν περ τὸ πρῶτον ἔδοξεν ἡμῖν, καὶ
> μὴ μεταπίπτειν μηδὲ γίνεσθαι ἑτεροῖον, ἀλλὰ
> ἀεὶ εἶναι ἕκαστον, οἷόν πέρ ἐστιν. νῦν δέ φα-
> μεν ὀρθῶς ὁρᾶν καὶ ἀκούειν καὶ συνιέναι, δο-
> κεῖ δὲ ἡμῖν τό τε θερμὸν ψυχρὸν γίνεσθαι καὶ
> τὸ ψυχρὸν θερμὸν καὶ τὸ σκληρὸν μαλθακὸν
> καὶ τὸ μαλθακὸν σκληρὸν καὶ τὸ ζῶον ἀπο-
> θνήσκειν καὶ ἐκ μὴ ζῶντος γίνεσθαι, καὶ
> ταῦτα πάντα [559] ἑτεροιοῦσθαι καὶ ὅ τι ἦν τε
> καὶ ὃ νῦν οὐδὲν ὅμοιον εἶναι, ἀλλ᾽ ὅ τε σίδη-
> ρος σκληρὸς ἐὼν τῷ δακτύλῳ κατατρίβεσθαι

The Senses Err (D11)

D11 (B8) Simplicius, *Commentary on Aristotle's* On the Heavens

After he has said about what is that it is one, ungenerated, immobile, and not separated by any void, but as a whole full of itself, he continues:

> **The greatest proof** (*sêmeion*) **that it is only one is this argument, but these following ones are also proofs. For if many things existed, they would have to be exactly like what I myself say that the one is. For if earth exists and water, air, iron, gold, fire, the living and the dead, black and white, and the other things of which humans say that they are true, if then all these things exist, and we see and hear correctly, then it is necessary that each thing of this sort be as it first seemed to us, and that it not change or become different, but that each one always be as it is. But as it is, we say that we see, hear, and understand correctly, but it seems to us that what is hot becomes cold and what is cold hot, what is hard soft and what is soft hard, that what is living dies and that it comes to be out of what is not living, and that all these things [559] become different, and that what was and what is now are not at all similar, but that iron, although it is hard, is rubbed away by the finger and at the same time flows, and**

ὁμοῦ ῥέων[1] καὶ χρυσὸς καὶ λίθος καὶ ἄλλο ὅ
τι ἰσχυρὸν δοκεῖ εἶναι πᾶν, ἐξ ὕδατός τε γῆ
καὶ λίθος γίνεσθαι,[2] ὥστε συμβαίνει μήτε
ὁρᾶν μήτε τὰ ὄντα γινώσκειν. οὐ τοίνυν ταῦτα
ἀλλήλοις ὁμολογεῖ· φαμένοις γὰρ εἶναι πολλὰ
καὶ ἀΐδια καὶ εἴδη τε καὶ ἰσχὺν ἔχοντα πάντα
ἑτεροιοῦσθαι ἡμῖν δοκεῖ καὶ μεταπίπτειν ἐκ
τοῦ ἑκάστοτε ὁρωμένου· δῆλον τοίνυν, ὅτι οὐκ
ὀρθῶς ἑωρῶμεν, οὐδὲ ἐκεῖνα πολλὰ ὀρθῶς δοκεῖ εἶναι· οὐ γὰρ ἂν μετέπιπτεν, εἰ ἀληθῆ ἦν,
ἀλλ᾽ ἦν, οἷόν περ ἐδόκει ἕκαστον, τοιοῦτον·
τοῦ γὰρ ἐόντος ἀληθινοῦ κρεῖσσον οὐδέν, ἢν
δὲ μεταπέσῃ, τὸ μὲν ἐὸν[3] ἀπώλετο, τὸ δὲ οὐκ
ἐὸν γέγονεν. οὕτως οὖν, εἰ πολλὰ εἴη, τοιαῦτα
χρὴ εἶναι, οἷόν περ τὸ ἕν.

σαφῶς οὖν οὗτος καὶ τὴν αἰτίαν εἶπε, δι᾽ ἣν τὰ αἰσθητὰ οὐκ εἶναι λέγουσιν ἀλλὰ δοκεῖν εἶναι.

---

[1] ὁμοῦ ῥέων ADEF: ὁμουρέων Bergk: ‹καὶ› ὁμοῦ ῥέειν coni.
Heiberg   [2] ἐξ ὕδατός τε γῆ καὶ λίθος γίνεσθαι post ὥστε
συμβαίνει μήτε ὁρᾶν μήτε τὰ ὄντα γινώσκειν habent ADEF:
transp. Heiberg (post Karsten)   [3] μὲν ἐὸν Brandis: μέσον
ADEF

likewise gold, stone, and everything else that seems to be resistant, and that earth and stone come to be out of water, so that the result is that we neither see nor know the things that are. Hence these [scil. statements] do not agree with one another. For although we say that they are many, eternal, that they possess forms and force, it seems to us that they all become different and change out of what is seen each time. Hence it is clear that we do not see correctly, and that it is not correctly that these things seem to us to be many. For they would not change if they were true, but they would be just as each one seemed to us to be. For there is nothing stronger than what truly is; but if it changed, then what is would be destroyed, while what is not would come to be. In this way, therefore, if many things existed, they would have to be exactly like the one.

Thus this man has also clearly stated the reason why they [scil. Parmenides and Melissus] say that the perceptibles do not exist but seem to exist.

Echoes of Melissus' Treatise in the Testimonia
(D12–D20)
Testimonia (D12–D18)

D12 (A8) Arist.

a *Phys.* 4.6 213b12–14

Μέλισσος μὲν οὖν καὶ δείκνυσιν ὅτι τὸ πᾶν ἀκίνητον
ἐκ τούτων· εἰ γὰρ κινήσεται, ἀνάγκη εἶναι, φησί, κενόν, τὸ δὲ κενὸν οὐ τῶν ὄντων.

b *GC* 325a2–16

ἐνίοις γὰρ τῶν ἀρχαίων ἔδοξε τὸ ὂν ἐξ ἀνάγκης ἓν
εἶναι καὶ ἀκίνητον· τὸ μὲν γὰρ κενὸν οὐκ ὄν, κινηθῆναι δ' οὐκ ἂν δύνασθαι μὴ ὄντος κενοῦ κεχωρισμένου,
οὐδ' αὖ πολλὰ εἶναι μὴ ὄντος τοῦ διείργοντος· τοῦτο
δὲ μηδὲν διαφέρειν, εἴ τις οἴεται μὴ συνεχὲς εἶναι τὸ
πᾶν ἀλλ' ἅπτεσθαι διῃρημένον, τοῦ φάναι πολλὰ καὶ
μὴ ἓν εἶναι καὶ κενόν. εἰ μὲν γὰρ πάντῃ διαιρετόν,
οὐθὲν εἶναι ἕν, ὥστε οὐδὲ πολλά, ἀλλὰ κενὸν τὸ ὅλον·
εἰ δὲ τῇ μὲν τῇ δὲ μή, πεπλασμένῳ τινὶ τοῦτ' ἐοικέναι·
μέχρι πόσου γὰρ καὶ διὰ τί τὸ μὲν οὕτως ἔχει τοῦ
ὅλου καὶ πλῆρές ἐστι, τὸ δὲ διῃρημένον; ἔτι[1] ὁμοίως[2]
ἀναγκαῖον μὴ εἶναι κίνησιν. ἐκ μὲν οὖν τούτων τῶν
λόγων [. . .] ἓν καὶ ἀκίνητον τὸ πᾶν εἶναί φασι καὶ

[1] ἔτι E: ἔτι δ' FHJVLMW   [2] ὁμοίως φάναι FHLW

Echoes of Melissus' Treatise in the Testimonia
(D12–D20)
Testimonia (D12–D18)

D12 (A8) Aristotle

a *Physics*

Melissus also shows on the basis of these [scil. arguments]
that the whole is immobile: for if it moves, he says, it is
necessary that there be void, but the void does not belong
to the things that are.

b *On Generation and Corruption*

Some of the ancients thought that what is must necessarily
be one and immobile; for the void is something that does
not exist, and what is could not move if there is no separate
void, nor could many things exist, if there is not something
that separates them; and if one thinks that the whole is not
continuous but, being divided, [scil. its parts] are in contact, this is not at all different from saying that many things
exist and not only one, and that the void exists. For if it is
divisible everywhere, there is nothing that is one, so that
they are not many either, but all is void; but if it is [scil.
divisible] here but not there, this seems to be like a fiction.
For up to what point [scil. is it divisible], and for what
reason is one part of the whole like this and full, while
another part is divided? Moreover, in the same way it is
necessary, according to them, that there not be motion.
On the basis of these arguments [. . .], they say therefore
that the whole is one and immobile; and certain people

ἄπειρον ἔνιοι· τὸ γὰρ πέρας περαίνειν ἂν πρὸς τὸ
κενόν.

D13 (≠ DK) Eudem. in Simpl. *In Phys.*, p. 111.13–14
(cf. Frag. 42 Wehrli)

[. . .] πλῆρες δέ, ὅτι οὐκ ἔστιν[1] ἄπειρον κενοῦ μετέχον
[cf. **R16**].

[1] ἔστιν DF: ἔσται E

D14 (A14) Philod. *Rhet.* vol. 2, p. 169.8–11

[. . .] Παρ[μ]εν[ίδη κ]αὶ Μέλισσον ἐν τὸ πᾶ[ν λέ-
γον]τας εἶναι καὶ διὰ τὸ [τὰς] αἰσ[θήσ]εις ψευδε[ῖς εἶναι . . .

D15 (A9) Cic. *Acad.* 2.37.118

[. . .] Melissus hoc[1] quod esset infinitum et inmutabile et
fuisse semper et fore.

[1] hoc] omne *Plasberg*

D16 (≠ DK) Alex. Aphr. in Simpl. *In Phys.*, p. 110.13–20

"ὁ Μέλισσος δείξας τὸ ἄπειρον ἐκ τοῦ μήτε ἀρχὴν
μήτε τέλος ἔχειν, ἐκ δὲ τοῦ ἀπείρου τὸ ἓν εἶναι, ἐφεξῆς καὶ ὅτι ἀκίνητον δείκνυσιν [. . .] τῷ τὸ κινούμενον
ἢ διὰ πλήρους ὀφείλειν κινεῖσθαι ἢ διὰ κενοῦ (οὕτω
δὲ καὶ ἄλλο τι ἔσεσθαι). ὅτι δὲ διὰ μὲν πλήρους οὐχ

[i.e. Melissus] say that it is unlimited, for the limit would limit it by relation to the void.[1]

[1] Although only the last sentence distinguishes Melissus, the whole preceding train of thought also reflects his doctrine. Melissus' argument is implicitly attributed to Parmenides.

D13 (≠ DK) Eudemus in Simplicius, *Commentary on Aristotle's* Physics

[. . .] it is full, because there is nothing unlimited that participates in the void.

D14 (A14) Philodemus, *Rhetoric*

[. . .] Parmenides and Melissus, who say that the whole is one, also because sensations are false . . .

D15 (A9) Cicero, *Prior Academics*

[. . .] Melissus [scil. says that] this [scil. universe], which is unlimited and immutable, both was forever and will be.

D16 (≠ DK) Alexander in Simplicius, *Commentary on Aristotle's* Physics

"Melissus, having shown that it is unlimited because it has neither a beginning nor an end, and that it is one because it is unlimited, goes on to show that it is also immobile [. . .] on the grounds that what moves must move either through what is full or through the void (but in this way something else will also exist). But because it is not pos-

οἷόν τέ τι κινηθῆναι, κενὸν δὲ μὴ δύνασθαι ἐν τοῖς
οὖσιν εἶναι (μηδὲν γὰρ εἶναι τὸ κενόν, ὄντος τε μηκέτι
ἔσεσθαι ἄπειρον τὸ ὄν· εἰ γὰρ εἴη μεθίστασθαι δυνάμενον ἐν[1] ἑαυτῷ, δῆλον ὡς μεῖζον ἂν αὐτοῦ εἴη,[2] οὐδὲν
δὲ μεῖζον τοῦ ἀπείρου) . . ."[3] ταῦτα μὲν οὖν οὕτως αὐτῇ
λέξει φησὶν ὁ Ἀλέξανδρος [. . . = **R23a**].

[1] ἐν F: om. E   [2] εἴη Torstrik: ᾗ mss.   [3] deest
apodosis

D17 (< A1) Diog. Laert. 9.24

ἐδόκει δὲ αὐτῷ τὸ πᾶν ἄπειρον εἶναι καὶ ἀναλλοίωτον
καὶ ἀκίνητον καὶ ἓν ὅμοιον ἑαυτῷ καὶ πλῆρες· κίνησίν
τε μὴ εἶναι, δοκεῖν δὲ εἶναι. [. . . = **R27**]

D18 (29 A23) Aët. 4.9.1 (Stob.) [εἰ ἀληθεῖς αἱ αἰσθή-
σεις]

[. . .] Παρμενίδης, [. . .], Μέλισσος [. . .] ψευδεῖς εἶναι
τὰς αἰσθήσεις.

*Two Comprehensive Expositions Reflecting the
Order of Melissus' Treatise (D19–D20)*

D19 (< A5) Ps.-Arist. *MXG* 1.1–8 (974a1–b7)

[1] ἀΐδιον εἶναί φησιν εἴ τι ἔστιν, εἴπερ μὴ ἐνδέχεσθαι

multa menda quae praesertim in ms. R exhibentur omittimus

sible for something to move through what is full, and the
void cannot be among the things that are (for the void is
nothing, and if it exists then what is will no longer be unlimited; for if it were capable of moving [or: changing] in
itself, it is clear that it would be bigger than it, but nothing
is bigger than the unlimited) . . ."[1] This is what Alexander
says literally [. . .].

[1] Simplicius' citation from Alexander's text breaks off before
the main clause.

D17 (< A1) Diogenes Laertius

He thought that the whole[1] is unlimited, unchangeable,
immobile, one similar to itself, and full; and that movement does not exist, but seems to exist [. . .].

[1] In the doxographic tradition concerning the Eleatics, 'the
whole' is often substituted for 'what is' (cf. **R24**).

D18 (29 A23) Aëtius

[. . .] Parmenides, [. . .], Melissus, [. . .]: sensations are
deceptive [cf. **ZEN. R37**].

*Two Comprehensive Expositions Reflecting the
Order of Melissus' Treatise (D19–D20)*

D19 (< A5) Ps.-Aristotle, *On Melissus, Xenophanes, and Gorgias*

[1] He says that if something is, it is eternal, if it is true

γενέσθαι μηδὲν ἐκ μηδενός· εἴτε γὰρ ἅπαντα γέγονεν
εἴτε μὴ πάντα, ἀίδια[1] ἀμφοτέρως·

ἐξ οὐδενὸς γὰρ γενέσθαι ἂν αὐτὰ[2] γιγνόμενα.
ἁπάντων τε γὰρ γιγνομένων οὐδὲν ⟨ἂν⟩[3] προϋπάρ-
χειν· εἴτ᾽ ὄντων τινῶν ἀεὶ ἕτερα προσγίγνοιτο, πλέον
ἂν καὶ μεῖζον τὸ ὄν[4] γεγονέναι· ᾧ δὲ[5] πλέον καὶ μεῖζον,
τοῦτο γενέσθαι ἂν ἐξ οὐδενός· ⟨ἐν⟩[6] τῷ γὰρ ἐλάττονι
τὸ πλέον οὐδ᾽[7] ἐν τῷ μικροτέρῳ τὸ μεῖζον οὐχ ὑπάρχειν.

[2] ἀίδιον δὲ ὂν ἄπειρον εἶναι, ὅτι οὐκ ἔχει ἀρχὴν
ὅθεν ἐγένετο, οὐδὲ τελευτὴν εἰς ὃ γιγνόμενον ἐτελεύ-
τησέ ποτε.

[3] πᾶν δὲ καὶ ἄπειρον ὂν ⟨ἓν⟩[8] εἶναι· εἰ γὰρ δύο ἢ
πλέω[9] εἴη, πέρατ᾽ ἂν[10] εἶναι ταῦτα πρὸς ἄλληλα.

[4] ἓν δὲ ὂν ὅμοιον εἶναι πάντη· εἰ γὰρ ἀνόμοιον,
πλείω ὄντα οὐκ ἂν ἔτι ἓν εἶναι ἀλλὰ πολλά.

[5] ἀίδιον δὲ ὂν ἄμετρόν τε καὶ ὅμοιον πάντη ἀκίνητον εἶναι τὸ ἕν· οὐ γὰρ ἂν κινηθῆναι μὴ εἴς τι ὑπο-
χωρῆσαν. ὑποχωρῆσαι δὲ ἀνάγκην εἶναι ἤτοι εἰς
πλῆρες ἰὸν[11] ἢ εἰς κενόν· τούτων δὲ τὸ μὲν οὐκ ἂν
δέξασθαι,[12] τὸ δὲ οὐκ εἶναι οὐδέν.[13]

[6] τοιοῦτον δὲ ὂν τὸ ἓν ἀνώδυνόν τε καὶ ἀνάλγητον

---

[1] ἀδύνατον Bonitz   [2] αὐτὰ Apelt: αὐτῶν mss.: ἀεὶ τὰ
Wendland   [3] ⟨ἂν⟩ Diels   [4] ὂν L: ἕν R   [5] δὴ
mss., corr. Susemihl   [6] ⟨ἐν⟩ Beck   [7] ⟨ὡς⟩ οὐδ᾽
Wendland   [8] ⟨ἓν⟩ Kern   [9] πλέω (πλέον R) ἢ δύο
mss.: transp. Susemihl   [10] πέραιαν R, περὶ λίάν L: corr.
edd.

that it is not possible that anything can come to be out of nothing. For whether all things have come to be, or not all things, in either case they are eternal.

For these things, if they came to be, would come to be out of nothing. For if all things came to be, nothing would exist previously [cf. **D2**]. And if some things existed and others came to be by being added later, then what is would become more numerous and larger. But what it would be more numerous and larger by, would come to be out of nothing: for the more numerous does not exist ⟨in⟩ the less numerous, nor the larger in the smaller.

[2] But if it is eternal, it is unlimited, because it does not have a beginning starting from which it could come to be, nor an end toward which it would ever be terminated [cf. **D3**].

[3] But being all and unlimited, it is ⟨one⟩. For if things were two or more, they would limit each other [cf. **D6–D7**].

[4] But if it is one, it is in every way similar to itself; for if it were dissimilar, then things, being a plurality, would be no longer one, but multiple [cf. **D8, D10**].

[5] But if it is eternal, immense, and everywhere similar, the One is immobile. For it could not move without receding into something. Now, it is necessary, in order to recede, to penetrate either into what is full or what is void. But of these two, the one could not receive it while the other is nothing [cf. **D9**].

[6] But if it is of this kind, the One is free from suffering

---

11 ὄν mss., corr. Bekker   12 τὸ πλῆρες post δέξασθαι hab. mss., del. Diels   13 ἢ τὸ κενὸν post οὐδὲν hab. mss., del. Apelt

ὑγιές τε καὶ ἄνοσον εἶναι, οὔτε μετακοσμούμενον θέσει οὔτε ἑτεροιούμενον εἴδει οὔτε μιγνύμενον ἄλλῳ·
κατὰ πάντα γὰρ ταῦτα πολλά τε τὸ ἓν γίγνεσθαι καὶ
τὸ μὴ ὂν τεκνοῦσθαι καὶ τὸ ὂν φθείρεσθαι ἀναγκάζε-
σθαι· ταῦτα δὲ ἀδύνατα εἶναι.

[7] καὶ γὰρ εἰ τὸ μεμῖχθαί τι ἓν ἐκ πλειόνων λέγοιτο,[14] καὶ εἴη πολλά τε καὶ κινούμενα εἰς ἄλληλα τὰ
πράγματα, καὶ ἡ μίξις ἢ ὡς ἐν ἑνὶ σύνθεσις εἴη τῶν
πλειόνων ἢ τῇ ἐπαλλάξει[15] οἷον ἐπιπρόσθησις[16] γίγνοιτο τῶν μιχθέντων· ἐκείνως μὲν ἂν διάδηλα χωρὶς
ὄντα[17] εἶναι τὰ μιχθέντα, ἐπιπροσθήσεως δ᾽ οὔσης ἐν
τῇ τρίψει γίγνεσθαι ἂν ἕκαστον φανερόν, ἀφαιρουμένων [974b1] τῶν πρώτων τὰ ὑπ᾽ ἄλληλα τεθέντα τῶν
μιχθέντων· ὧν οὐδέτερον συμβαίνειν.

[8] διὰ τούτων δὲ τῶν τρόπων κἂν εἶναι πολλὰ κἂν
ἡμῖν ᾤετο[18] φαίνεσθαι μόνως.[19] ὥστε ἐπειδὴ οὐχ οἷόν
τε οὕτως, οὐδὲ πολλὰ δυνατὸν εἶναι τὰ ὄντα, ἀλλὰ
ταῦτα δοκεῖν οὐκ ὀρθῶς. πολλὰ γὰρ καὶ ἄλλα κατὰ
τὴν αἴσθησιν φαντάζεσθαι·[20] λόγον δ᾽ οὔτ᾽ ἐκείν᾽ αἱ-
ρεῖν[21] τὰ αὐτὰ[22] γίγνεσθαι, οὔτε πολλὰ εἶναι τὸ ὄν,
ἀλλὰ ἓν[23] ἀίδιόν τε καὶ ἄπειρον καὶ πάντῃ ὅμοιον
αὐτὸ αὑτῷ.

[14] τὸ μεμῖχθαί τι ἓν . . . λέγοιτο] τὸ μεμῖχθαι γίγνεσθαί
ἓν . . . λέγοιτο prop. Diels: τῷ μεμῖχθαι τι . . . γένοιτο
Bonitz   [15] ἀπαλλάξει mss., corr. Mullach   [16] ἐπι-
πρόσθεσις L, -θέσεις R: corr. Bekker   [17] χωρίζοντα L, -των
R: corr. Apelt   [18] ᾤ.ετ L, ὡς τὸ R: corr. Diels   [19] μόνων
coni. Apelt

and pain, healthy and without illness, it neither undergoes rearrangement in its position nor change in its shape nor mixture with anything else. For in all of these processes it is necessary that the one become multiple, that what is not be generated, and that what is be destroyed. Now, these are impossibilities [cf. **D10**].

[7] For even if one said that one thing is a mixture of many things—that real things were many and moved toward each other, and the mixture were either the combination of many things in one or else were produced by the exchange of the things mixed, like a superposition—then in the former case the mixed things would be manifest, being separate; while if there were superposition, each one would become visible as a result of rubbing, the lower parts of the mixture being revealed when the higher ones are removed. But neither of these is what happens.

[8] In these ways, he thought, there could be plurality and also this would only be for us in appearance (?). So that since this is not possible in this way, it is not possible either that the things that are be many, but it is incorrectly that this appears to us to be the case. For we imagine many other things as well on the basis of sensation [cf. **D11**]. But the argument shows that neither do the identical things become these [i.e. other?], nor is what multiple, but instead one, eternal and unlimited, and similar to itself in every way.

²⁰ ἀπατᾷ (L) vel ἄπασαν (R) post φαντάζεσθαι hab. mss.: ἀπατᾶν corr. Spalding, quod Diels del.: φαντάζεσθαι del. Spalding   ²¹ οὔταικεινaιρει R, οὔτεειαιρεῖν L: corr. Bonitz   ²² τὰ αὐτὰ mss.: τὰ ὄντα Bonitz: ταῦτα Diels   ²³ ἕν om. R

D20 (I, pp. 268–273) Simpl. *In Phys.*, pp. 103.13–104.17

νῦν δὲ τὸν Μελίσσου λόγον ἴδωμεν [. . .]. τοῖς γὰρ τῶν φυσικῶν ἀξιώμασι χρησάμενος ὁ Μέλισσος περὶ γενέσεως καὶ φθορᾶς ἄρχεται τοῦ συγγράμματος οὕτως·

εἰ μὲν μηδὲν ἔστι, περὶ τούτου [15] τί ἂν λέγοιτο ὡς ὄντος τινός; εἰ δέ τι ἐστίν, ἤτοι γινόμενόν ἐστιν ἢ ἀεὶ ὄν. ἀλλ᾽ εἰ γενόμενον, ἤτοι ἐξ ὄντος ἢ ἐξ οὐκ ὄντος· ἀλλ᾽ οὔτε ἐκ μὴ ὄντος οἷόν τε γενέσθαι τι (οὔτε ἄλλο μὲν οὐδὲν ὄν, πολλῷ δὲ μᾶλλον τὸ ἁπλῶς ὄν) οὔτε ἐκ τοῦ ὄντος. εἴη γὰρ ἂν οὕτως καὶ οὐ γίνοιτο. οὐκ ἄρα γινόμενόν ἐστι τὸ ὄν. ἀεὶ ὂν ἄρα ἐστίν. οὐδὲ[1] φθαρήσεται τὸ ὄν. οὔτε [20] γὰρ εἰς τὸ μὴ ὂν οἷόν τε τὸ ὂν μεταβάλλειν (συγχωρεῖται γὰρ καὶ τοῦτο ὑπὸ τῶν φυσικῶν) οὔτε εἰς ὄν. μένοι γὰρ ἂν πάλιν οὕτω γε καὶ οὐ φθείροιτο. οὔτε ἄρα γέγονε τὸ ὂν οὔτε φθαρήσεται· ἀεὶ ἄρα ἦν τε καὶ ἔσται.

ἀλλ᾽ ἐπειδὴ τὸ γενόμενον ἀρχὴν ἔχει, τὸ μὴ γενόμενον ἀρχὴν οὐκ ἔχει, τὸ δὲ ὂν οὐ γέγονεν, οὐκ ἂν ἔχοι[2] ἀρχήν. ἔτι δὲ τὸ φθειρόμενον τε-

---

[1] οὔτε mss., corr. Diels   [2] ἂν ἔχοι] ἄρ᾽ ἔχει Diels

---

[1] Simplicius' formulation leads one to expect a literal citation; but the passage is generally considered to be a paraphrase. Burnet considers the initial sentence to be a genuine fragment of Melissus (Frag. 1A).

D20 (I, pp. 268–73) Simplicius, *Commentary on Aristotle's* Physics

Now let us consider Melissus' argument [. . .]. For Melissus, making use of the axioms of the natural philosophers regarding generation and destruction [scil. of nongeneration out of nonbeing and of nondestruction into nonbeing], begins his treatise as follows:[1]

If nothing is, what could [15] one say about it, as if it were something? But if something is, either it comes to be, or it always is. But if it comes to be, then that is either out of something that is, or out of something that is not. But it is not possible for anything—neither what is in general, nor all the more what is in absolute terms—to come about either out of what is not [cf. **D2**] nor out of what is. For in that case, it would be and would not come about. Therefore, what is does not come to be. Therefore, it always is, and what is will never be destroyed. For [20] it is not possible, for what is, to be changed either into what is not (for this too is granted by the natural philosophers) nor into what is. For once again, if this were so, it would remain and would not be destroyed. Therefore what is has not come to be and will not be destroyed. Therefore, it always was and always will be [cf. **D5**].

But since what comes about has a beginning, what does not come about does not have a beginning [cf. **D3**]. Now, what is has not come about: it could not have a beginning. Furthermore, what is

λευτὴν [25] ἔχει. εἰ δέ τί ἐστιν ἄφθαρτον, τελευτὴν οὐκ ἔχει. τὸ ὂν ἄρα ἄφθαρτον ὂν τελευτὴν
οὐκ ἔχει.

τὸ δὲ μήτε ἀρχὴν ἔχον μήτε τελευτὴν ἄπειρον
τυγχάνει ὄν. ἄπειρον ἄρα τὸ ὄν.

εἰ δὲ ἄπειρον, ἕν. εἰ γὰρ δύο εἴη, οὐκ ἂν δύναιτο ἄπειρα εἶναι, ἀλλ' ἔχοι ἂν πέρατα πρὸς
ἄλληλα. ἄπειρον δὲ τὸ ὄν· οὐκ ἄρα πλείω τὰ
ὄντα· ἓν ἄρα τὸ ὄν.

ἀλλὰ μὴν εἰ ἕν, καὶ ἀκίνητον. [30] τὸ γὰρ ἓν
ὅμοιον ἀεὶ ἑαυτῷ· τὸ δὲ ὅμοιον οὔτ' ἂν ἀπόλοιτο
οὔτ' ἂν μεῖζον γίνοιτο οὔτε μετακοσμέοιτο οὔτε
ἀλγεῖ οὔτε ἀνιᾶται. εἰ γάρ τι τούτων [104.1] πάσχοι, οὐκ ἂν ἓν εἴη. τὸ γὰρ ἡντιναοῦν κίνησιν
κινούμενον ἔκ τινος καὶ εἰς ἕτερόν τι μεταβάλ-
λει. οὐθὲν δὲ ἦν ἕτερον παρὰ τὸ ὄν· οὐκ ἄρα
τοῦτο κινήσεται.

καὶ κατ' ἄλλον δὲ τρόπον οὐδὲν κενόν ἐστι
τοῦ ὄντος. τὸ γὰρ κενὸν οὐδέν ἐστιν. οὐκ ἂν οὖν
εἴη τό γε μηδέν. οὐ κινεῖται οὖν τὸ [5] ὄν. ὑποχωρῆσαι γὰρ οὐκ ἔχει οὐδαμῇ κενοῦ μὴ ὄντος.
ἀλλ' οὐδὲ εἰς ἑαυτὸ συσταλῆναι δυνατόν. εἴη
γὰρ ἂν οὕτως ἀραιότερον αὑτοῦ καὶ πυκνότε-
ρον. τοῦτο δὲ ἀδύνατον. τὸ γὰρ ἀραιὸν ἀδύνατον ὁμοίως πλῆρες εἶναι τῷ πυκνῷ. ἀλλ' ἤδη τὸ
ἀραιόν γε κενότερον γίνεται τοῦ πυκνοῦ· τὸ δὲ

destroyed has [25] an end. But if something is indestructible, it does not have an end. Therefore, what
is, being indestructible, does not have an end.

Now, what has neither a beginning nor an end
turns out to be unlimited. Therefore, what is is unlimited [cf. **D6** and **D7**].

But if it is unlimited, it is one. For if there were
two, they could not be unlimited, but they would
limit each other. Now, what is is unlimited. Therefore it is not the case that there exist a plurality of
the things that are. Therefore what is is one [cf.
D8].

But again, if it is one, it is also immobile. [30] For
the one is always similar to itself. But the similar
could not either be destroyed nor increase in size
nor change its arrangement nor does it suffer pain
or distress. For if it were [104.1] affected in one of
these ways, it would not be one. For what moves in
any way whatsoever is transformed from one thing
into another. But there was nothing else outside of
what is, therefore this will not move [cf. **D10**].

And according to another mode [scil. of argu-
ment], nothing of what is is void. For the void is
nothing. And what is nothing could therefore not
exist. Therefore, being does not [5] move. For, if
there is no void, it cannot recede in any way. But
neither can it contract itself into itself. For in this
way it would be more rarefied and denser than itself. Now, this is impossible. For it is impossible that
the rarefied be as full as the dense; but what is rarefied is more void than what is dense. Now, the
void does not exist [cf. **D10**]. As for the question

267

κενὸν οὐκ ἔστιν. εἰ δὲ πλῆρές ἐστι τὸ ὂν ἢ μή, κρίνειν χρὴ τῷ εἰσδέχεσθαί [10] τι αὐτὸ ἄλλο ἢ μή· εἰ γὰρ μὴ εἰσδέχεται, πλῆρες. εἰ δὲ εἰσ- δέχοιτό τι, οὐ πλῆρες. εἰ οὖν μὴ ἔστι κενόν, ἀνάγκη πλῆρες εἶναι· εἰ δὲ τοῦτο, μὴ κινεῖσθαι, οὐχ ὅτι μὴ δυνατὸν διὰ πλήρους κινεῖσθαι, ὡς ἐπὶ τῶν σωμάτων λέγομεν, ἀλλ' ὅτι πᾶν τὸ ὂν οὔτε εἰς ὂν δύναται κινηθῆναι (οὐ γὰρ ἔστι τι παρ' αὐτό) οὔτε εἰς τὸ μὴ ὄν· οὐ γὰρ ἔστι τὸ μὴ ὄν.

whether what is is full or not, that must be decided on the basis of whether it accepts [10] something else into itself or not. For if it does not accept anything into itself, it is full; but if it could accept something into itself, it would not be full. Therefore, if there is no void, it must necessarily be full. But if that is so, it does not move, not because it is not possible for it to move through what is full, as we say regarding bodies, but because everything that is can move neither toward what is (for there is nothing outside of it) nor toward what is not. For what is not does not exist.

MELISSUS [30 DK]

R

The Earliest Attestation:
The Hippocratic Corpus (R1)

R1 (A6) Hipp. *Nat. hom.* 1

[. . . = **MED. T6**] ἀλλ' ἔμοιγε δοκέουσιν οἱ τοιοῦτοι ἄνθρωποι αὐτοὶ ἑωυτοὺς καταβάλλειν ἐν τοῖσιν ὀνόμασι τῶν λόγων ‹τῶν› ἑωυτῶν[1] ὑπὸ ἀσυνεσίης, τὸν δὲ Μελίσσου λόγον ὀρθοῦν.

> [1] ‹τῶν› ἑωυτῶν Jouanna: αὐτῶν A: αὐτέων MV

Isocrates

See **DOX. T6–T7**

Plato (R2)

R2 Plat. *Theaet.*

a (cf. ad 28 B8) 180e

[. . .] καὶ ἄλλα ὅσα Μέλισσοί τε καὶ Παρμενίδαι ἐν-

MELISSUS

R

The Earliest Attestation:
The Hippocratic Corpus (R1)

R1 (A6) Hippocrates, *On the Nature of Man*

[. . .] As for me, people like this [i.e. monist natural philosophers] seem, because of their lack of understanding, to refute themselves in the terms of their arguments, and to justify the argument of Melissus.

Isocrates

See **DOX. T6–T7**

Plato (R2)

R2 Plato, *Theaetetus*

a (cf. ad 28 B8)

[Socrates:] [. . .] and everything that the Melissuses and

αντιούμενοι πᾶσι τούτοις διισχυρίζονται, ὡς ἕν τε
πάντα ἐστὶ καὶ ἕστηκεν αὐτὸ ἐν αὑτῷ οὐκ ἔχον χώραν
ἐν ᾗ κινεῖται [cf. **PARM. R24**].

b (≠ DK) 183e

[ΣΩ.] Μέλισσον μὲν καὶ τοὺς ἄλλους, οἳ ἓν ἑστὸς λέγουσι τὸ πᾶν, αἰσχυνόμενος μὴ φορτικῶς σκοπῶμεν,
ἧττον αἰσχύνομαι ἢ ἕνα ὄντα Παρμενίδην [. . . =
PARM. R6].

Aristotle's Book Against Melissus (R3)

R3 (ad A5) Diog. Laert. 5.25 (= Arist.)

Πρὸς τὰ Μελίσσου α′

Aristotle's General Negative Judgment (R4–R5)

R4 (≠ DK) Arist. *Phys.* 1.2 185a5–12

ὅμοιον δὴ τὸ σκοπεῖν εἰ οὕτως ἓν καὶ πρὸς ἄλλην
θέσιν ὁποιανοῦν διαλέγεσθαι τῶν λόγου ἕνεκα λεγομένων [. . .] ἢ λύειν λόγον ἐριστικόν, ὅπερ ἀμφότεροι
μὲν ἔχουσιν οἱ λόγοι, καὶ ὁ Μελίσσου καὶ ὁ Παρμενί-
δου· καὶ γὰρ ψευδῆ λαμβάνουσι καὶ ἀσυλλόγιστοί
εἰσιν· μᾶλλον δ᾽ ὁ Μελίσσου φορτικὸς καὶ οὐκ ἔχων
ἀπορίαν, ἀλλ᾽ ἑνὸς ἀτόπου δοθέντος τὰ ἄλλα συμβαί-
νει· τοῦτο δὲ οὐδὲν χαλεπόν.

Parmenideses maintain in opposition to all of them [scil. the partisans of movement]: viz., that all things are one and that it [i.e. this one] remains itself in itself, since it does not have a place in which it could move.

b (≠ DK)

[Socrates:] Although I feel a sense of respectful embarrassment about examining in a vulgar manner Melissus and the others, who say that the whole is one and stable, I feel that way less with regard to them than I do with regard to Parmenides, who is only one man [. . .].

Aristotle's Book Against Melissus (R3)

R3 (ad A5) Diogenes Laertius [Catalog of Aristotle's works]

Against Melissus' Doctrines, one book.

Aristotle's General Negative Judgment (R4–R5)

R4 (≠ DK) Aristotle, *Physics*

To consider whether it [i.e. what is] is one in this sense [scil. unique] is like arguing against any other position maintained only for the sake of argument [. . .], or providing the solution for an eristical argument, a characteristic of both arguments, Melissus' as much as Parmenides'. For not only are their premises false, but their conclusions are also invalid. Or rather, Melissus' [scil. argument] is vulgar and does not present a genuine difficulty: if one absurdity is granted, the rest follows—but this is not at all difficult.

R5 (< A7) Arist. *Metaph.* A5 986b25–28

οὗτοι μὲν οὖν [. . .] ἀφετέοι πρὸς τὴν νῦν ζήτησιν, οἱ
μὲν δύο καὶ πάμπαν ὡς ὄντες μικρὸν ἀγροικότεροι,
Ξενοφάνης καὶ Μέλισσος· Παρμενίδης δὲ μᾶλλον
βλέπων ἔοικέ που λέγειν [. . .].

Specific Peripatetic Criticisms (R6–R18)
Aristotle (R6–R12)
Criticism of the Unicity and Immobility of
Being (R6–R9)

R6 (≠DK) Arist. *Top.* 1.11 104b19–24

θέσις δέ ἐστιν ὑπόληψις παράδοξος τῶν γνωρίμων
τινὸς κατὰ φιλοσοφίαν, οἷον [. . .] ὅτι ἓν τὸ ὄν,¹ καθάπερ Μέλισσός φησιν [. . .].

¹ ὄν (Λ): πᾶν C, corr. C²

Interpretation and Criticisms of the Unlimited
Character of Being (R7–R11)

R7 (< 21 A30) Arist. *Metaph.* A5 986b18–21

Παρμενίδης μὲν γὰρ ἔοικε τοῦ κατὰ τὸν λόγον ἑνὸς
ἅπτεσθαι, Μέλισσος δὲ τοῦ κατὰ τὴν ὕλην (διὸ καὶ ὁ
μὲν πεπερασμένον ὁ δ' ἄπειρόν φησιν εἶναι αὐτό).

R5 (< A7) Aristotle, *Metaphysics*

So [. . .] for the purposes of the present investigation [scil. the investigation of the first causes], these men [i.e. Xenophanes, Parmenides, and Melissus] should be disregarded—and two of them, Xenophanes and Melissus, completely, since they are a bit too unsophisticated; but as for Parmenides, he seems to speak on the basis of more attentive consideration [. . .] [cf. **PARM. R12; XEN. R12**].

Specific Peripatetic Criticisms (R6–R18)
Aristotle (R6–R12)
Criticism of the Unicity and Immobility of
Being (R6–R9)

R6 (≠ DK) Aristotle, *Topics*

A thesis is a paradoxical idea that is maintained by some famous philosopher, like [. . .] "what is is one," as Melissus says [. . .].

See also **PARM. R44, R47**

Interpretation and Criticisms of the Unlimited
Character of Being (R7–R11)

R7 (< 21 A30) Aristotle, *Metaphysics*

Parmenides seems to have discussed the one according to its definition, Melissus according to the matter (this is why the former says that it is limited, the latter that it is unlimited).

R8 (ad 28 B8) Arist. *Phys.* 3.6 207a15–17

διὸ βέλτιον οἰητέον Παρμενίδην Μελίσσου εἰρηκέναι·
ὁ μὲν γὰρ τὸ ἄπειρον[1] ὅλον φησίν, ὁ δὲ τὸ ὅλον πεπεράνθαι [. . .].

[1] τὸ ἄπειρον mss.: ἄπειρον τὸ Bonitz

R9 (> A10) Arist. *SE*

a 5.167b12–18

ὁμοίως δὲ καὶ ἐν τοῖς συλλογιστικοῖς, οἷον ὁ Μελίσσου λόγος ὅτι ἄπειρον τὸ ἅπαν, λαβὼν τὸ μὲν ἅπαν
ἀγένητον (ἐκ γὰρ μὴ ὄντος οὐδὲν ἂν γενέσθαι), τὸ δὲ
γενόμενον ἐξ ἀρχῆς γενέσθαι· εἰ μὴ οὖν γέγονεν, ἀρχὴν οὐκ ἔχειν[1] τὸ πᾶν, ὥστ᾽ ἄπειρον. οὐκ ἀνάγκη δὲ
τοῦτο συμβαίνειν· οὐ γὰρ εἰ τὸ γενόμενον ἅπαν ἀρχὴν ἔχει, καὶ εἴ τι ἀρχὴν ἔχει, γέγονεν [. . .].

[1] ἔχει mss., corr. Diels

b 6.168b27, 36–40

οἱ δὲ παρὰ τὸ ἑπόμενον μέρος εἰσὶ τοῦ συμβεβηκό-
τος· [. . .] ἐν τῷ Μελίσσου λόγῳ, τὸ αὐτὸ εἶναι λαμβάνει[1] τὸ γεγονέναι καὶ ἀρχὴν ἔχειν [. . .]. ὅτι γὰρ τὸ
γεγονὸς ἔχει ἀρχήν, καὶ τὸ ἔχον ἀρχὴν γεγονέναι
ἀξιοῖ, ὡς ἄμφω ταὐτὰ ὄντα τῷ ἀρχὴν ἔχειν, τό τε
γεγονὸς καὶ τὸ πεπερασμένον.

[1] λαμβάνει secl. Wallies

R8 (ad 28 B8) Aristotle, *Physics*

That is why we must think that Parmenides has spoken better than Melissus. For the latter says that the unlimited is a whole, the former that the whole is limited [. . .].

R9 (> A10) Aristotle, *Sophistic Refutations*

a

The same thing [scil. the error relating to the convertibility of the consequent] happens in deductions as well, as for example in Melissus' argument that the whole is unlimited, which assumes as premises on the one hand that the whole is ungenerated (for nothing could be generated out of what is not) and on the other that what is generated is generated out of a beginning. If therefore it has not been generated, the whole does not have a beginning, so that it is unlimited [cf. **D3**]. But it is not necessary that this happen. For even if everything that is generated has a beginning, it is not because something has a beginning that it has been generated [. . .].

b

The ones [scil. refutations] connected with the consequent are a part of those connected with the accident. [. . .] in Melissus' argument, one assumes that to be generated and to have a beginning are the same thing [. . .]. For because what has been generated has a beginning, one claims that what has a beginning has been generated, on the idea that the two things, to be generated and to be limited, are identical because they both have a beginning.

c 8.181a27–30

[. . .] παρ᾽ ὃ καὶ ὁ τοῦ Μελίσσου λόγος· εἰ γὰρ τὸ
γεγονὸς ἔχει ἀρχήν, τὸ[1] ἀγένητον ἀξιοῖ μὴ ἔχειν, ὥστ᾽
εἰ ἀγένητος ὁ οὐρανός, καὶ ἄπειρος. τὸ δ᾽ οὐκ ἔστιν·
ἀνάπαλιν γὰρ ἡ ἀκολούθησις.

[1] τὸ ABD: καὶ τὸ cu

R10 (cf. A10) Arist. *Phys.* 1.3 186a6–22

ἀμφότεροι γὰρ ἐριστικῶς συλλογίζονται, καὶ Μέλισσος καὶ Παρμενίδης. ὅτι μὲν οὖν παραλογίζεται Μέλισσος, δῆλον· οἴεται γὰρ εἰληφέναι, εἰ τὸ γενόμενον
ἔχει ἀρχὴν ἅπαν, ὅτι καὶ τὸ μὴ γενόμενον οὐκ ἔχει.
εἶτα καὶ τοῦτο ἄτοπον, τὸ παντὸς εἶναι[1] ἀρχήν—τοῦ
πράγματος καὶ μὴ τοῦ χρόνου, καὶ γενέσεως μὴ τῆς
ἁπλῆς ἀλλὰ καὶ ἀλλοιώσεως, ὥσπερ οὐκ ἀθρόας γιγνομένης[2] μεταβολῆς. ἔπειτα διὰ τί ἀκίνητον, εἰ ἕν;
ὥσπερ γὰρ καὶ τὸ μέρος ἓν ὄν, τοδὶ τὸ ὕδωρ, κινεῖται
ἐν ἑαυτῷ, διὰ τί οὐ καὶ τὸ πᾶν; ἔπειτα ἀλλοίωσις διὰ
τί οὐκ ἂν εἴη; ἀλλὰ μὴν οὐδὲ τῷ εἴδει οἷόν τε ἓν εἶναι,
πλὴν τῷ ἐξ οὗ (οὕτως δὲ ἓν καὶ τῶν φυσικῶν τινες
λέγουσιν, ἐκείνως δ᾽ οὔ)· ἄνθρωπος γὰρ ἵππου ἕτερον
τῷ εἴδει καὶ τἀναντία ἀλλήλων [. . . = **PARM. R48**].

[1] εἶναι F: οἴεσθαι εἶναι EIJ   [2] ἀθρόως γενομένης I

c

[. . .] to which [scil. those arguments by the consequent that imply the opposites] the argument of Melissus is connected. For if what has come to be has a beginning, he thinks that what has not come to be does not, so that if the world (*ouranos*) has not come to be, it is also unlimited. But that is not the case: for the [scil. valid] logical sequence holds to the inversion [scil. of the terms of the proposition: if what has come about has a beginning, then what does not have a beginning has not come about].

R10 (cf. A10) Aristotle, *Physics*

Both of them argue eristically, Melissus as well as Parmenides. Therefore it is clear that Melissus commits a paralogism. For [1st objection] he thinks that, if everything that has come to be has a beginning [cf. **D3**], he is also admitting that what has not come to be does not have one. Then [2nd objection] this too is absurd, that there be a beginning for everything and not for time [cf. **D3, D5**], and not only for generation in the simple sense but also for alteration, as though transformation never came about all at once. Then [3rd objection], why is it immobile, if it is one [cf. **D9, R21d**]? For just as the part that is one, like this water here, moves in itself, why does not the whole do so as well? Then [4th objection], why would there be no alteration [cf. **D10, R23a**]? And again [5th objection], it is not possible either that it be one in virtue of its form, unless it be by that of which it is made (some of the natural philosophers speak of the one in this way, and not in that one). For a human being is different from a horse in virtue of its form, and so too the contraries with regard to one another [cf. **R21e**].

R11 (> A11) Arist. *Phys.* 1.2 185a32–b5

Μέλισσος δὲ τὸ ὂν ἄπειρον εἶναί φησιν. ποσὸν ἄρα
τι τὸ ὄν· τὸ γὰρ ἄπειρον ἐν τῷ ποσῷ, οὐσίαν δὲ ἄπειρον εἶναι ἢ ποιότητα ἢ πάθος οὐκ ἐνδέχεται εἰ μὴ
κατὰ συμβεβηκός, εἰ ἅμα καὶ ποσὰ ἄττα εἶεν·[1] ὁ γὰρ
τοῦ ἀπείρου λόγος τῷ ποσῷ προσχρῆται, ἀλλ᾽ οὐκ
οὐσίᾳ οὐδὲ τῷ ποιῷ. εἰ μὲν τοίνυν καὶ οὐσία ἔστι καὶ
ποσόν, δύο καὶ οὐχ ἓν τὸ ὄν· εἰ δ᾽ οὐσία μόνον, οὐκ
ἄπειρον, οὐδὲ μέγεθος ἕξει οὐδέν· ποσὸν γάρ τι ἔσται.

[1] ἄττα ἂν εἶεν E: εἴη S

Criticism of the Denial of the Void (R12)

R12 (≠ DK) Arist. *Phys.* 4.7 214a26–31

οὐδεμία δ᾽ ἀνάγκη, εἰ κίνησις ἔστιν, εἶναι κενόν. ὅλως
μὲν οὖν πάσης κινήσεως οὐδαμῶς, δι᾽ ὃ καὶ Μέλισσον ἔλαθεν· ἀλλοιοῦσθαι γὰρ τὸ πλῆρες ἐνδέχεται.
ἀλλὰ δὴ οὐδὲ τὴν κατὰ τόπον κίνησιν· ἅμα γὰρ ἐνδέχεται ὑπεξιέναι ἀλλήλοις, οὐδενὸς ὄντος διαστήματος χωριστοῦ παρὰ τὰ σώματα τὰ κινούμενα.

Eudemus (R13–R16)
Criticism of D2 (R13)

R13 (≠ DK) Simpl. *In Phys.*, p. 105.21–27

ὁ μέντοι Εὔδημος καὶ διὰ τούτων τῶν λημμάτων οὐ-

MELISSUS

R11 (> A11) Aristotle, *Physics*

Melissus says that what is is unlimited. Hence what is is a certain quantity. For the unlimited belongs to [scil. the category of] quantity. But a substance, a quality, or an affection cannot be unlimited except contingently, if at the same time they were certain quantities. For the definition of what is unlimited makes use of quantity, but not of substance or quality. If then both substance and quantity exist, what is is two and not one; and if only substance exists, it is not unlimited, and it will not have any magnitude either: for it will be a certain quantity.

Criticism of the Denial of the Void (R12)

R12 (≠ DK) Aristotle, *Physics*

There is no necessity, if motion exists, that the void exist. Generally speaking, the argument does not at all concern every kind of motion (this is why Melissus did not notice this, for the full can undergo an alteration), but not motion according to place either. For things can reciprocally yield their places without there being any separate interval besides the bodies in motion.

Eudemus (R13–R16)
Criticism of D2 (R13)

R13 (≠ DK) Simplicius, *Commentary on Aristotle's* Physics

Eudemus says that by means of these premises, he [i.e.

δὲν ἄλλο δείκνυσθαί φησιν ἢ ὅπερ ἐξ ἀρχῆς, ὅτι τὸ
ὂν ἀγένητόν ἐστιν· ἡ γὰρ ὑγιὴς ἀντιστροφή ἐστι 'τὸ
μὴ ἔχον ἀρχὴν ἀγένητόν ἐστιν, τὸ δὲ ὂν οὐκ ἔχει
ἀρχήν'.

λέγεται[1] δὲ οὕτως· "οὐ γὰρ εἰ τὸ γενόμενον ἀρχὴν
ἔχει, τὸ μὴ γενόμενον ἀρχὴν οὐκ ἔχει, μᾶλλον δὲ τὸ
μὴ ἔχον ἀρχὴν οὐκ ἐγένετο· οὕτω γὰρ ἐπὶ τῶν ἀπο-
φάσεων ἡ ἀκολούθησις γίνεται. ἀγένητον οὖν αὐτῷ
γίνεται τὸ ὄν, οὐ γὰρ ἔχει ἀρχήν" [Frag. 38 Wehrli].

[1] λέγεται] λέγει ed. Ald.

Criticism of D3 (R14–R15)

R14 (≠ DK) Simpl. *In Phys.*, p. 108.8–13

καὶ συντίθεται καὶ Εὔδημος [Frag. 39 Wehrli] ὅτι κἂν
ἐπ' ἄλλων τινῶν ὀλίγων γενητῶν οὐκ εἰσὶν ἀρχαὶ αἱ
κατὰ τὸ πρᾶγμα, ἀλλ' ἐφ'[1] οὗ σημαινομένου λαμβάνει
Μέλισσός εἰσι. γράφει δὲ οὕτως· "ἀλλ' ἴσως ὀλίγων
μὲν οὔκ εἰσιν ἀρχαί, ἐφ' ὧν δὲ λαμβάνει εὔλογον εἶναι. διὸ τοῦτο μὲν παραχωρητέον, τὴν δὲ ἀκολούθη-
σιν ἐπισκεπτέον."

[1] ἐφ' ed. Ald.: ἀφ' DEF

R15 (≠ DK) Simpl. *In Phys.*, p. 108.26–30

καὶ Εὔδημος δὲ τὸ ἁπλῶς ὂν ἀγένητον εἶναι συγχωρεῖ
λέγων [Frag. 40 Wehrli] "τὸ μὲν γὰρ ἅπαν τὸ ὂν

Melissus] shows nothing other than what he shows from the beginning, viz. that what is has not come to be: for the valid conversion is 'what does not have a beginning has not come about; now, what is does not have a beginning.'

This is what is said [scil. by Eudemus]: "for it is not true that if what has come to be has a beginning, what has not come to be does not have one, but rather that what does not have a beginning has not come to be: for it is in this way that the logical sequence is produced in the case of negations. What he obtains, therefore, is that what is has not come to be, since it does not have a beginning."

Criticism of D3 (R14–R15)

R14 (≠ DK) Simplicius, *Commentary on Aristotle's Physics*

Eudemus too concludes that even if, with regard to some few cases of generated things, there are no beginnings concerning the thing [cf. **R10**], with regard to what Melissus is considering and is indicated, there certainly are. He writes as follows: "but perhaps, in a small number of cases, there are no beginnings, but for the objects that he is considering it is reasonable that there be some. This is why he must concede this point, but examine the logical sequence."

R15 (≠ DK) Simplicius, *Commentary on Aristotle's Physics*

Eudemus also [scil. like Aristotle] concedes that what purely and simply is is ungenerated, when he says, "it is

ἀθρόον¹ μὴ γίνεσθαι² καλῶς ἔχει συγχωρεῖν, ἐπειδὴ
οὐχ οἷόν τε ἐκ μὴ ὄντος αὐτὸ γίνεσθαι·³ ἀλλὰ κατὰ
μέρος γίνεσθαι πολλὰ καὶ φθείρεσθαι εὔλογον δήπου
ἐστὶ καὶ ὁρῶμεν τοῦτο."

¹ ἀθρόον DEF: ἀθρόως ed. Ald.: del. Torstrik   ² γενέσθαι Torstrik   ³ γίνεσθαι D: γενέσθαι EF

Criticism of D7 (R16)

R16 (≠ DK) Simpl. *In Phys.* p. 110.6–11

τοῦτο δὲ αἰτιᾶται Εὔδημος [Frag. 41 Werhli] ὡς ἀδιορίστως λεγόμενον γράφων οὕτως· "εἰ δὲ δὴ συγχωρή-
σειέ τις ἄπειρον εἶναι τὸ ὄν, διὰ τί καὶ ἓν ἔσται; οὐ
γὰρ δὴ διότι πλείονα, περανεῖ πῃ πρὸς ἄλληλα. δοκεῖ
γὰρ καὶ ὁ παρεληλυθὼς χρόνος ἄπειρος εἶναι περαί-
νων πρὸς τὸν παρόντα. πάντῃ μὲν οὖν ἄπειρα τὰ
πλείω τάχα οὐκ ἂν εἴη, ἐπὶ θάτερα δὲ φανεῖται¹ ἐνδέχεσθαι. χρὴ² οὖν διορίσαι πῶς ἄπειρα οὐκ ἂν εἴη, εἰ
πλείω."³

¹ φανεῖται] φαίνεται Torstrik   ² χρὴ] χρῆν Spengel
³ πλείω ed. Ald.: πλείονα D: πλεῖον E

correct to concede that everything that is does not come about all at once, since it is not possible that it come to be from what is not; but it is evidently reasonable that many things come to be and are destroyed part by part, and this is what we see happening."

Criticism of D7 (R16)

R16 (≠ DK) Simplicius, *Commentary on Aristotle's Physics*

Eudemus criticizes this statement [scil. **D7**] as being said indefinitely; he writes as follows: "If one conceded that what is is unlimited, why will it also be one? It is certainly not because things are multiple that they will somehow limit each other. For past time too seems to be unlimited even though it has as its limit the present time. Therefore perhaps it is not in an absolute sense that multiple things would be unlimited, but they will seem to be able to be this either on the one side or on the other. Therefore it is necessary to define in what way they would not be unlimited, if they are multiple."

See also **R22**

The Anonymous Treatise On Melissus,
Xenophanes, and Gorgias: *A Selection (R17)*

R17 (<A5) Ps.-Arist. *MXG*

a 1.9, 12, 14 (974b 8–14; b26–29; 975a7–11)

[1.9] ἆρ᾿ οὖν δεῖ πρῶτον μὲν μὴ πᾶσαν λαβόντα δόξαν ἄρχεσθαι, ἀλλ᾿ αἳ μάλιστά εἰσι βέβαιοι; ὥστ᾿ εἰ
μὲν ἅπαντα τὰ δοκοῦντα μὴ ὀρθῶς ὑπολαμβάνεται,
οὐθὲν ἴσως προσήκει οὐδὲ τούτῳ προσχρῆσθαι τῷ
δόγματι, <ὅτι>¹ οὐκ ἄν ποτε οὐδὲν γένοιτο ἐκ μηδενός.
μία γάρ τίς ἐστι δόξα, καὶ αὕτη τῶν οὐκ ὀρθῶν, ἣν
ἐκ τοῦ αἰσθάνεσθαί πως ἐπὶ πολλῶν πάντες² ὑπειλή-
φαμεν. [. . .] [12] τυγχάνομεν³ δὲ ἔχοντες ἀμφοτέρας
τὰς ὑπολήψεις ταύτας, καὶ ὡς ἂν οὐ γένοιτ᾿ ἂν οὐδὲν
ἐκ μηδενὸς ὄντος⁴ <καὶ ὡς>⁵ πολλά τε καὶ κινούμενά
ἐστι τὰ ὄντα. ἀμφοῖν δὲ πιστὴ μᾶλλον αὕτη, καὶ θᾶττον ἂν πρόοιντο πάντες ταύτης ἐκείνην⁶ τὴν δόξαν.
[. . .] [14] λέγεταί τε καὶ σφόδρα ὑπὲρ αὐτῶν γίγνεσθαί τε τὰ μὴ ὄντα, καὶ δὴ⁷ γεγονέναι πολλὰ ἐκ μὴ
ὄντων, καὶ οὐχ ὅτι οἱ τυγχάνοντες, ἀλλὰ καὶ τῶν δο-
ξάντων τινὲς εἶναι σοφῶν εἰρήκασιν.

multa menda quae praesertim in ms. R exhibentur omittimus
¹ <ὅτι> Spalding   ² πάντες L: ὄντες R: πάντως Diels
³ τυγχανόμενα mss., corr. Mullach   ⁴ ὄντος del. Diels
⁵ <καὶ ὡς> Mullach   ⁶ ταύτην ἐκείνης mss., corr. Bonitz
⁷ μὴ mss., corr. Bonitz

The Anonymous Treatise On Melissus, Xenophanes, and Gorgias: A Selection (R17)

R17 (<A5) Ps.-Aristotle, *On Melissus, Xenophanes, and Gorgias*

a [On the proper use of common opinions]

[1.9] Is it not necessary first of all to begin by accepting not every opinion, but those that are most firmly established? So that if it is correct not to admit all opinions, it is perhaps not right either to make use of this opinion, <viz. that> nothing could ever come to be out of nothing. For this is just one opinion, and it is one of those that are not correct, which we all admit because, in a certain way, we perceive it in many cases. [. . .] [12] But it happens that we have these two opinions, both that nothing could come to be out of what is nothing, <and that> the things that are are many and in motion. Of these two, the latter one is more credible, and everyone would give up the former opinion more quickly than this one. [. . .] [14] It is also vigorously asserted about these, both that things that are not come to be and that many things come to be out of things that are not, and this is asserted not only by ordinary people but also by some of those who have the reputation of being sages.

b 2.2, 6 (975a21–25; a38–39)

[2.2] καὶ πρῶτον τεθέντος, ὃ πρῶτον λαμβάνει, μηδὲν γενέσθαι ἂν ἐκ μὴ ὄντος, ἆρα ἀνάγκη ἀγένητα ἅπαντα εἶναι, ἢ οὐδὲν κωλύει γεγονέναι ἕτερα ἐξ ἑτέρων, καὶ τοῦτο εἰς ἄπειρον ἰέναι; [3] ἢ καὶ ἀνακάμπτειν κύκλῳ [. . .]; [6] [. . .] τί κωλύει τὰ μὲν γενόμενα αὐτῶν εἶναι, τὰ δ᾽ ἀίδια [. . .];

c 2.13–14 (975b34–39; 976a2–3)

[13] εἰ δὲ καὶ ταῦτά τις συγχωροίη, καὶ εἴη τι[1] καὶ ἀγένητον εἴη, τί μᾶλλον ἄπειρον δείκνυται; ἄπειρον γὰρ εἶναί φησιν, εἰ ἔστι μέν, μὴ γέγονε δέ·[2] πέρατα γὰρ εἶναι τὴν τῆς γενέσεως ἀρχήν τε καὶ τελευτήν. [14] [. . .] τί δὴ κωλύει καὶ εἰ μὴ ἐγένετο, ἔχειν ἀρχήν, οὐ μέντοι γε ἐξ ἧς ἐγένετο, ἀλλὰ καὶ ἑτέραν, καὶ εἶναι περαίνοντα πρὸς ἄλληλα ἀίδια ὄντα;

[1] τε mss., corr. edd.   [2] γεγονέναι mss., corr. Sylburg

d 2.19–21 (976a21–22; a28–30; a31)

[19] ἔτι εἰ ἀίδιόν τε καὶ ἄπειρόν ἐστι, πῶς ἂν εἴη ἓν σῶμα ὄν; [. . .] [20] εἰ δὲ μήτε σῶμα μήτε πλάτος μήτε μῆκος ἔχον μηδέν, πῶς ἂν ἄπειρον ⟨τὸ⟩ ἓν[1] εἴη; ⟨ἢ⟩[2] τί κωλύει πολλὰ[3] καὶ ἀνάριθμα[4] τοιαῦτα εἶναι; [21] ⟨ἔτι⟩[5] τί κωλύει καὶ πλείω ὄντα ἑνὸς μεγέθει ἄπειρα εἶναι;

b [On the eternity of what is]

[2.2] And if one begins by positing what he takes for a first premise, viz. that nothing could come to be out of what is not, is it necessary that all things be ungenerated, or does nothing prevent one thing from having come to be out of another, and that this go on to infinity? [3] Or that they recur in a cycle [. . .]? [6] What prevents some of them from coming to be, while others are eternal [. . .]?;

c [On the unlimitedness of what is]

[2.13] But even if one were to concede this, both that it is and that it is ungenerated, how does this thereby more show it to be unlimited? For he says that it is unlimited, if it is but has not come to be, for the beginning and the end of generation are limits. [. . .] [14] But what prevents it, even if it has not come to be, from having a beginning—not the one starting from which it has come to be, but another one—and that eternal things limit each other?

d [On the unity of what is]

[2.19] Moreover, if it is eternal and unlimited, how would it be one, if it is a body? [. . .] [20] And if it does not possess a body nor breadth nor length, how would ⟨the⟩ One be unlimited? ⟨Or⟩ what is there that prevents such things from being multiple and innumerable? [21] ⟨Moreover,⟩ what prevents things, being more than one, from being unlimited in magnitude?

---

[1] ⟨τὸ⟩ ἕν Diels: ἂν mss.: del. Mullach   [2] ⟨ἢ⟩ Wilson
[3] πολλὰ om. L   [4] ἀνάριθμα Bern. 402: ἐνάριθμα R: ἐν ἀριθμῷ L   [5] ⟨ἔτι⟩ Wilson

e 2.22 (976a37–b4)

[22] ἔτι ἓν ὂν οὐδὲν ἄτοπον, εἰ μὴ πάντῃ ὅμοιόν ἐστιν. εἰ γάρ ἐστιν ὕδωρ ἅπαν ἢ πῦρ ἢ ὅτι δὴ ἄλλο τοιοῦτον, οὐδὲν κωλύει πλείω εἰπεῖν τοῦ ὄντος ἑνὸς εἴδη, ἰδίᾳ[1] ἕκαστον ὅμοιον αὐτὸ ἑαυτῷ. [23] καὶ γὰρ μανόν, τὸ δὲ πυκνὸν εἶναι, μὴ ὄντος ἐν τῷ μανῷ κενοῦ, οὐδὲν κωλύει.[2]

> [1] δι᾽ R, δεῖ L: corr. Apelt   [2] κωλύειν mss., corr. Bonitz

f 2.25–27 (976b12–15, 19)

[25] ἀκίνητον δ᾽ εἶναί φησιν, εἰ κενὸν μὴ ἔστιν· ἅπαντα γὰρ κινεῖσθαι τῷ ἀλλάττειν τόπον. [26] πρῶτον μὲν οὖν τοῦτο πολλοῖς οὐ συνδοκεῖ, ἀλλ᾽ εἶναί τι κενόν, οὐ μέντοι τοῦτό γέ τι σῶμα εἶναι [. . .]. [27] ἀλλὰ δὴ καὶ εἰ μὴ ἔστι κενὸν μηδέν, τί ἧσσον ἂν κινοῖτο;

A Criticism by Aristocles:
Melissus Refutes Himself (R18)

R18 (A14) Aristocl. in Eus. *PE* 14.17.7–8 (cf. Frag. 7 Chiesara)

[7] ὅ γέ τοι Μέλισσος ἐθέλων ἐπιδεικνύναι διότι τῶν φαινομένων καὶ ἐν ὄψει τούτων οὐδὲν εἴη τῷ ὄντι, διὰ τῶν φαινομένων ἀποδείκνυσιν αὐτῶν· φησὶ γοῦν· "εἰ γάρ ἐστι γῆ καὶ ὕδωρ [. . .] καὶ τὸ μαλακὸν σκλη-

e [On the homogeneity of what is]

[2.22] Moreover, if it is one, it is not at all strange that it not be similar everywhere. For if it is all water or fire or anything else of this sort, nothing prevents one from saying that there are several kinds of what is one, each one being similar to itself in its own way. [23] For that it be rarefied, but here dense, given that there is no void in what is rarefied—nothing prevents this.

f [On the immobility of what is]

[2.25] He says that it is immobile if there is no void; for all things move by changing place. [26] But first of all, many people do not share this opinion but say that there is a void, without this being a body [. . .]. [27] But even if there is no void, why would it move any the less?

A Criticism by Aristocles:
Melissus Refutes Himself (R18)

R18 (A14) Aristocles in Eusebius, *Evangelical Preparation*

[7] Melissus, wishing to show that none of these phenomena that are visible really exists, demonstrates this by means of the phenomena themselves. At least he says, **"For if earth exists, water** [. . .] **and what is soft hard"**

ρόν" [cf. **D11**]. [8] ταῦτα δὲ καὶ ἄλλα πολλὰ τοιαῦτα
λέγοντος αὐτοῦ καὶ μάλα εἰκότως ἐπύθετό τις ἄν· ἆρ᾽
οὖν ὅτι[1] θερμόν ἐστι κἄπειτα τοῦτο γίνεται ψυχρόν,
οὐκ αἰσθόμενος ἔγνως; ὁμοίως δὲ καὶ περὶ τῶν ἄλλων.
ὅπερ γὰρ ἔφην, εὑρεθείη ἂν οὐδὲν ἀλλ᾽ ἢ τὰς αἰσθήσεις ἀναιρῶν καὶ ἐλέγχων διὰ τὸ μάλιστα πιστεύειν
αὐταῖς.

[1] ὅτι mss.: ὅτι ὁ νῦν Stephanus

The Skeptics: Timon of Phlius (R19)

R19 (< 29 A1) Timon in Diog. Laert. 9.25 (= Frag. 45 Di
Marco)

[. . . = **ZEN. R7**] ἠδὲ Μελίσσου[1]
πολλῶν φαντασμῶν ἐπάνω, παύρων γε μὲν
ἥσσω.[2]

[1] Μέλισσον Meineke   [2] γε . . . ἥσσω BP: δὲ . . . εἴσω F

Simplicius on Melissus (R20–R23)
Melissus' Stylistic Advantage
Over Parmenides (R20)

R20 (≠DK) Simpl. *In Cael.*, p. 558.17–19

ἀλλὰ καὶ Μέλισσος ὡς καταλογάδην γράψας σαφέ-
στερον ἔτι τὴν ἑαυτοῦ περὶ τούτων γνώμην ἐξέφηνε
δι᾽ ὅλου μὲν τοῦ λόγου, καὶ ἐν τούτοις δὲ οὐχ ἥκιστα
τοῖς ῥητοῖς· [. . . = **R22c**].

[cf. **D11**]. [8] One could quite reasonably ask him when he says this and many other things of this sort, "The fact that something that is now warm then comes to be cold—do you not know this by perceiving it?" And the same for the other things. For as I said, one would discover that he is doing nothing other than abolishing and refuting sense perceptions because he has the greatest confidence in them.

The Skeptics: Timon of Phlius (R19)

R19 (< 29 A1) Timon in Diogenes Laertius

[. . .] and that [scil. force] of Melissus,
Superior to many illusions, and defeated by very few.

Simplicius on Melissus (R20–R23)
Melissus' Stylistic Advantage
Over Parmenides (R20)

R20 (≠ DK) Simplicius, *Commentary on Aristotle's* On the Heavens

But Melissus, insofar as he writes in prose, has expressed his opinion on these questions [scil. the double existence] even more clearly [scil. than Parmenides] throughout his whole text, and above all in the following statements: [. . . cf. **R22c, D11**].

Simplicius Defends Melissus Against Aristotle's
and Alexander's Objections (R21–R22)
Replies to Aristotle's Objections in
Physics *1.3 (R21)*

R21 (≠DK) Simpl. *In Phys.*

a p. 107.29–31

καὶ ταῦτα μὲν καλῶς ὁ Ἀριστοτέλης ἀντείρηκε, πρὸς
τὸ φαινόμενον ὑπαντῶν. ἐπεὶ δὲ σοφὸς ἀνὴρ Μέλισσος, ὡς τοιούτου χρὴ καὶ τῆς ἐννοίας στοχαζόμενον
τὰ ἐπαχθέντα αὐτῷ ἐγκλήματα ἀπολύσασθαι.

b pp. 107.31–108.15

καὶ ὅτι μὲν οὐ σωματικὸν ἐλάμβανε τὸ ὄν, δῆλον ἐκ
τοῦ ἀκίνητον καὶ ἀδιαίρετον αὐτὸ δεικνύναι τῶν σωμάτων ἐναργῆ τὴν κίνησιν καὶ τὴν διαίρεσιν ἐμφαι-
νόντων. ἀλλ᾽ ἀντὶ μὲν τοῦ αἰσθητοῦ καὶ διαστατοῦ τὸ
γενητὸν παραλαμβάνει, ὥσπερ καὶ ὁ παρὰ Πλάτωνι
Τίμαιος λέγων "γέγονεν· ὁρατὸς γὰρ ἁπτός τέ ἐστι
καὶ σῶμα ἔχων," ἀντὶ δὲ τοῦ νοητοῦ καὶ ἀμεροῦς τὸ
ἀγένητον, ὡς καὶ τοῦτο πάλιν ὁ Πλάτων "τί τὸ ὂν ἀεί,
γένεσιν δὲ οὐκ ἔχον." ὅταν οὖν λέγῃ τὸ γενητὸν ἀρχὴν ἔχειν, τὸ αἰσθητόν φησι καὶ διαστατὸν ἅτε
περανθὲν ἀρχὴν ἔχειν καὶ πέρας· οὐ γάρ ἐστιν ἄπειρον σῶμα. [. . . = **R16**] ὅταν δὲ ὁ Μέλισσος ἐπιφέρῃ
"τὸ μὴ γενόμενον ἀρχὴν οὐκ ἔχει" [cf. **D20**], τότε
λέγει ὅτι τὸ ὄντως ὂν ἀμερές ἐστι καὶ οὔτε ἀρχὴν οὔτε
τελευτὴν ἔχει· διὸ καὶ ἄπειρον.

*Simplicius Defends Melissus Against Aristotle's
and Alexander's Objections (R21–R22)
Replies to Aristotle's Objections in*
Physics *1.3 (R21)*

R21 (≠ DK) Simplicius, *Commentary on Aristotle's*
Physics

a [Simplicius' reasons]

On the one hand Aristotle has formulated excellent objections, replying at the level of appearance. But since Melissus is a wise man, it is by aiming (*stokhazesthai*) at the thought too of a man of this sort that the objections that have been raised against him must be resolved.

b [Reply to the first objection = **R8 [1]**]

The fact that he did not consider what is as corporeal is clear from the fact that he shows that it is immobile and indivisible, whereas bodies clearly manifest change and division. But instead of 'perceptible' and 'extended,' he accepts 'generated,' just as Timaeus says in Plato, "it has come to be; for it is visible and tangible and has a body" [*Timaeus* 28b], and instead of 'intelligible' and 'without parts,' 'ungenerated,' as Plato once again says, "what is it that always is but has no generation?" [*Timaeus,* 27d]. Therefore, when he says that what has come to be has a beginning, he says that what is perceptible and extended, because it is limited, has a beginning and a limit. For there does not exist any unlimited body. [. . .] But when Melissus adds, **"what does not come about does not have a beginning"** [cf. **D20**], he is saying that what really is is without parts and that it has neither a beginning nor an end; and that is why it is unlimited.

EARLY GREEK PHILOSOPHY V

c p. 109.7–110.6

ἐγκαλεῖται δὲ ὁ Μέλισσος καὶ ὡς τῆς ἀρχῆς πολλαχῶς λεγομένης ἀντὶ τῆς κατὰ τὸν χρόνον ἀρχῆς, ἥτις
ὑπάρχει τῷ γενητῷ, τὴν κατὰ τὸ πρᾶγμα λαβών, ἥτις
καὶ τοῖς ἀθρόως μεταβάλλουσιν οὐχ ὑπάρχει. ἔοικε
δὲ αὐτὸς καὶ πρὸ τοῦ Ἀριστοτέλους τεθεᾶσθαι καλῶς
ὅτι πᾶν σῶμα, καὶ τὸ ἀΐδιον, πεπερασμένον ὑπάρχον
πεπερασμένην ἔχει δύναμιν καὶ ὅσον ἐφ' ἑαυτῷ ἀεὶ ἐν
τέλει χρόνου ἐστί, διὰ δὲ τὴν ἀεικίνητον τοῦ παράγον-
τος ἐπιστασίαν καὶ ἐν ἀρχῇ ἀεί ἐστι καὶ ἀΐδιον ὑπάρχει, ὥστε τὸ κατὰ μέγεθος ἀρχὴν καὶ τέλος ἔχον καὶ
κατὰ χρόνον ἔχει ταῦτα καὶ ἀνάπαλιν. τὸ γὰρ ἀρχὴν
ἔχον χρόνου καὶ τέλος οὐχ ἅμα πᾶν ἐστι. διὸ ποιεῖται
μὲν τὴν ἀπόδειξιν ἀπὸ τῆς κατὰ χρόνον ἀρχῆς καὶ
τελευτῆς. ἄναρχον δὲ οὕτως καὶ ἀτελεύτητον οὔ φησιν εἶναι ὃ μὴ πᾶν ἐστι, τουτέστιν ὃ μὴ ἅμα ὅλον
ἐστίν· ὅπερ τοῖς ἀμερέσιν ὑπάρχει καὶ τῷ ὄντι ἀπείροις, τῷ δέ γε ἁπλῶς ὄντι καὶ κυριώτατα· τῷ γὰρ ὄντι
πᾶν ἐκεῖνό ἐστι.

λέγει δὲ ταῦτα οὕτως ὁ Μέλισσος [. . . = **D3**]. καὶ
ὅτι μὲν τὸ "ποτὲ" χρονικόν ἐστι, δῆλον· ὅτι δὲ "γινόμενον" τὸ κατ' οὐσίαν γενητὸν εἶπεν, ὃ ἕως ἂν ᾖ γινόμενόν ἐστι καὶ οὐκ ὄν, δῆλον ἐκ τοῦ "ἐτελεύτησε
γὰρ ἄν ποτε γινόμενον ὄν" καὶ ἐκ τοῦ "οὐ γὰρ ἀεὶ
εἶναι ἀνυστὸν ὅ τι μὴ πᾶν ἐστι," ὡς τοῦ ἀεὶ ὄντος,

c [Reply to the second objection = **R8 [2]**]

The objection is also made to Melissus that, 'beginning' (*arkhê*) being spoken of in many ways, he accepts, instead of the beginning with regard to time, which happens for what is generated, the beginning according to the thing, which does not happen to what changes all at once [cf. **R14**, **R15**]. But he seems to have seen clearly himself, even before Aristotle, that every body, including the eternal body, has a limited power if it is limited, and that, as much as is possible for it, it always exists at the end of time, but that because of the always-moving supervision of what moves it, it is always in the beginning too and is eternal, so that what has a beginning and an end with regard to magnitude also has these with regard to time and inversely. For what has a beginning and an end in time does not exist all together. This is why he makes his demonstration on the basis of the beginning and end with regard to time. But he says that what is not a whole, i.e. what is not simultaneously an ensemble, is not in this way without a beginning and an end; this happens instead to what is without parts and is really unlimited, to what is purely and simply and in the proper sense of the term. For this is really a whole.

And this is how Melissus says this: [. . . = **D3**]. That **"at some time"** is temporal is clear; and that he applies the expression **"comes about"** to what is generated in its substance, which, until it exists, is in the course of coming about and does not exist, is clear from the phrase **"for it would have come to an end if it had come about at some time"** and from the phrase **"for it is impossible, for what is not entirely, to be forever,"** on the idea that

297

ὃ καὶ πᾶν ἐστιν, ἀντικειμένου τῷ γενητῷ. ὅτι δὲ
ὥσπερ τὸ "ποτὲ γενόμενον" πεπερασμένον τῇ οὐσίᾳ
φησίν, οὕτω καὶ τὸ ἀεὶ ὂν ἄπειρον λέγει τῇ οὐσίᾳ,
σαφὲς πεποίηκεν εἰπών [. . . = **D4**] μέγεθος δὲ οὐ τὸ
διαστατόν φησιν· αὐτὸς γὰρ ἀδιαίρετον τὸ ὂν δείκνυ-
σιν· [. . . = **D9**] μέγεθος τὸ διάρμα αὐτὸ λέγει τῆς
ὑποστάσεως. ὅτι γὰρ ἀσώματον εἶναι βούλεται τὸ ὄν,
ἐδήλωσεν εἰπών [. . . = **D8**]. καὶ ἐφεξῆς δὲ τῷ ἀιδίῳ τὸ
ἄπειρον κατὰ τὴν οὐσίαν συνέταξεν εἰπών [. . . = **D5**]
ὥστε τὸ μὴ ἔχον ἄπειρόν ἐστιν. ἀπὸ δὲ τοῦ ἀπείρου
τὸ ἓν συνελογίσατο ἐκ τοῦ [. . . = **D7**].

d p. 113.3–19

ὡς δὲ τοῦ ἑνὸς ἀλλοιοῦσθαι καὶ ἑτεροιοῦσθαι δυναμέ-
νου καὶ μένοντος ἔτι ἑνὸς κατὰ τὴν οὐσίαν, οὕτως νῦν
ὑπήντησεν ὁ Ἀριστοτέλης τὸ ἓν ὁλοσχερῶς κατὰ τὴν
συνήθειαν λαβών (λέγομεν γὰρ ἕνα καὶ τὸν αὐτὸν
μένοντα Σωκράτην ὀδυνᾶσθαί τε τὸ σκέλος καὶ ἀναπαύεσθαι), τοῦ Μελίσσου κυριώτερον τὸ ἓν λαβόντος
ἀλλ᾽ οὐχ ὁλοσχερέστερον, ὡς δηλοῖ τά τε ἄλλα τὰ
εἰρημένα καὶ οὐχ ἥκιστα τὸ "εἰ τοίνυν τριχὶ μιῇ μυρίοις ἔτεσιν ἑτεροῖον γίνοιτο τὸ πᾶν, ὀλεῖται ἂν ἐν
τῷ παντὶ χρόνῳ" [cf. **D10**], ὡς δέον ὂν εἰ ἕν ἐστι, καὶ
ὅμοιον[1] καὶ ἀίδιον κυρίως· ὥστε κατὰ πάντα μένον[2]
οὐκ ἂν ἔχοι τι καθ᾽ ὃ μεταβολὴν ὑποδέξεται. ἀνάγκη

[1] δέον ⟨τὸ⟩ ὂν εἰ ἕν ἐστι καὶ ὅμοιον ⟨εἶναι⟩ Torstrik
[2] μένειν mss., corr. ed. Ald

what always is, what also totally is, is opposed to what
comes to be. But the fact that, just as he says that what
"comes about at some time" is limited in its substance,
so too he says that what always is is unlimited in its substance—this he has made clear by saying, [. . . = **D4**]. By
"magnitude" he does not mean extent. For he himself
shows that being is indivisible: [. . . = **D9**]. By **"magnitude"** he means the very elevation (*diarma*) of existence.
For the fact that he means that what is is incorporeal—this
he has made clear by saying, [. . . = **D8**]. And right after
the determination 'eternal' he has placed 'unlimited according to substance,' saying, [. . . = **D5**], so that what does
not have it [scil. beginning and end] is unlimited. And he
has concluded from the unlimited to the one on the basis
of [. . . = **D7**].

d [Reply to the fourth objection, then to the third one =
R8 [4, 3]]

That the One can be altered and changed, while at the
same time still remaining one in its substance, Aristotle
has objected in this way, by taking 'one' globally, in conformity with its customary meaning (for we say that Socrates remains one and the same when he has pain in his
leg and when he recovers); whereas Melissus takes 'one'
in its proper sense and not globally, as other statements
show, and in particular, **"If then the whole had become
different by a single hair in the course of thousands
of years, it would have been destroyed in the whole
of this time"** [cf. **D10**], on the idea that it is necessary,
if it is one, that it be similar and eternal in the proper
sense; so that, remaining [scil. immobile] in every regard,

γὰρ ἦν τὸ ἀλλοιούμενον καὶ τὸ ἑτεροιούμενον ὁπω-
σοῦν ἀπ᾽ ἄλλης διαθέσεως εἰς ἄλλην μεταβάλλειν.
κατὰ τόπον δὲ εἰ κινοῖτο περιδινούμενον ὥσπερ τὸ
ὕδωρ, κενοῦ μὴ ὄντος ἀνάγκη σχῆμα ἔχειν περιφερές,
οἷον σφαιρικὸν ἢ κωνικὸν ἢ κυλινδρικόν· τὰ γὰρ
ἄλλα σχήματα περιδινούμενα ἄλλοτε ἄλλον τόπον
ἐπιλαμβάνει·[3] ἐσχηματισμένον δὲ πεπερασμένον ἂν
εἴη καὶ οὐκ ἄπειρον. εἰ δὲ ἀκίνητον πρότερον ὂν κινοῖτο ἐν τῷ αὐτῷ τόπῳ, ἀνάγκη πυκνουμένου καὶ
ἀραιουμένου μέρους τινὸς γίνεσθαι τὴν ἀρχὴν τῆς
κινήσεως. ὅλως δὲ σωμάτων κίνησις ἡ περιδίνησις·
ἀσώματον δὲ δέδεικται τὸ ὂν ὑπὸ Μελίσσου.

3 ἐπιλαμβάνει E: περιλαμβάνει DF

e p. 114.14–22

δῆλον δὲ ὅτι εἰ οὕτως εἶδός τις λέγει ὡς τὸ σύνθετον,
οὗ καὶ ὁ ὁρισμὸς σύνθετος ἀποδίδοται, οὐκ ἂν δέ-
ξαιτο Μέλισσος εἶδος εἶναι τὸ ὄν· εἰ δὲ οὕτως ὡς τὸ
ἄυλον καὶ ἁπλούστατον, τάχα ἂν δέξαιτο· πολλὰ γὰρ
αὐτοῦ καὶ αὐτὸς κατηγορεῖ, τὸ ἀγένητον, τὸ ἀκίνητον,
τὸ ἄπειρον καὶ ἄλλα πολλά. ἀλλ᾽ οὔτε οὕτως ἓν ὡς τὸ
ἐξ οὗ καὶ τὸ ὑλικὸν λέγοι ἂν Μέλισσος οὔτε ὡς οἱ
φυσικοί (ἀσώματον γὰρ λέγει τὸ ὄν) οὔτε κατὰ τὴν
κυρίως ὕλην, εἴπερ μήτε εἰσδέχεσθαί τι λέγει τὸ ὂν
μήτε μετακοσμεῖσθαι, ἡ δὲ ὕλη καὶ εἰσδέχεται καὶ

it would have nothing in regard to which it would admit transformation. For it is necessary that what is altered and changed in any way be transformed out of one disposition into another. And if it moved according to place, rotating like water, it is necessary, since there is no void, that it have a round shape, for example spherical, conical, or cylindrical. For the other shapes, when they rotate, occupy a different place each time. But if it had a shape, it would be limited and not unlimited. And if, being formerly immobile, it moved in the same place, it is necessary that the motion begin by the condensation or rarefaction of some part. And in general, rotation is a movement of bodies. But Melissus has shown that what is is incorporeal.

e [Reply to the fifth objection = **R8 [5]**]

It is clear that if one understands 'shape' in the sense of 'composed,' the definition of which is also presented as composed, Melissus would not accept that what is have a shape; but if it is in the sense of 'immaterial' and 'completely simple,' then perhaps he would accept it. For he himself predicates about it many determinations: 'ungenerated,' 'immobile,' 'unlimited,' and many others. But Melissus would not be able to understand the One either as what something is made of and what is material, nor like the natural philosophers (for he says that what is is incorporeal [cf. **D8**]) nor in conformity with matter in the proper sense of the term, since he says that what is neither lets anything penetrate into it nor changes its arrangement [cf. **D10**], while matter both lets itself be penetrated and

301

μετακοσμεῖται. ἔτι δὲ "τοῦ ἐόντος ἀληθινοῦ," φησί,
"κρεῖσσον οὐδέν." ἡ δὲ ὕλη τὸ χείριστον.

Simplicius' Reply to Aristotle's Criticism of the
Eleatics in On the Heavens *(R22)*

R22 (≠ DK) Simpl. *In Cael.*

a p. 557.1–15

ἀλλ᾽ ὅπερ Ἀριστοτέλης αὐτοῖς ἐγκαλεῖ τὴν αἰτίαν τῆς
διαμαρτίας ἐξελέγχων σκληρὸν ὄντως ἦν, εἴπερ ἀληθὲς ἦν· ἐκεῖνοι γάρ, φησίν, οὐδὲν μὲν ἄλλο παρὰ τὴν
τῶν αἰσθητῶν οὐσίαν ὑπολαμβάνοντες ἐν ὑποστάσει
εἶναι, πρῶτοι δὲ ἐννοήσαντες, ὅτι ἀνάγκη τοιαύτας
τινὰς¹ ἀγενήτους καὶ ἀκινήτους εἶναι φύσεις, εἴπερ
ἔστι γνῶσις ἐπιστημονική [. . .] μετήνεγκαν ἐπὶ τὰ
αἰσθητὰ καὶ γενητὰ τοὺς τοῖς νοητοῖς καὶ ἀκινήτοις
ἐφαρμόζοντας λόγους, εἴ γε περὶ φύσεως προτιθέμε-
νοι λέγειν τὰ ἐκείνοις προσήκοντα λέγουσι. καὶ εἰ
Περὶ φύσεως ἢ Περὶ τοῦ ὄντος ἐπέγραψε Μέλισσος,
δῆλον ὅτι τὴν φύσιν ἐνόμιζεν εἶναι τὸ ὂν καὶ τὰ φυσικὰ τὰ ὄντα, ταῦτα δέ ἐστι τὰ αἰσθητά. καὶ ταύτῃ
δὲ ἴσως ὁ Ἀριστοτέλης εἶπεν αὐτοὺς μηδὲν ἄλλο
παρὰ τὴν τῶν αἰσθητῶν οὐσίαν ὑπολαμβάνειν τῷ ἐν
λέγειν τὸ ὄν· τοῦ γὰρ αἰσθητοῦ ἐναργῶς εἶναι δοκοῦν-
τος, εἰ ἓν τὸ ὄν ἐστιν, οὐκ ἂν εἴη ἄλλο παρὰ τοῦτο.

¹ τοιαύτας τινὰς edd. (ex vers. lat. Moerb.): τοιαύτας DEF:
τινας A

changes its arrangement. Furthermore, he says, **"there is nothing stronger than what truly is"** [cf. **D10**], while matter is what is worst of all.

Simplicius' Reply to Aristotle's Criticism of the Eleatics in On the Heavens *(R22)*

R22 (≠ DK) Simplicius, *Commentary on Aristotle's* On the Heavens

a

But Aristotle's criticism of them [i.e. Parmenides and Melissus], in demonstrating the cause of their error, would be really harsh if it were true. For, he says, these men, thinking that nothing else existed outside of the substance of the perceptibles, but being the first to understand that, if there is to be any scientific knowledge, it is necessary that there exist natures of this sort, ungenerated and immobile, [. . .], transferred to perceptible and generated things the arguments that are appropriate for intelligible and immobile ones, if it is true that, proposing to speak about nature, what they say is appropriate for those [scil. other things]. And if Melissus also entitled his treatise *On Nature or on Being* [cf. **D1**], it is clear that he thought that what is is nature, and that the things that are are the natural things, that is, the perceptible things. And this is perhaps why Aristotle said that "they did not posit anything outside of the substance of the perceptibles" [cf. **PARM. R47**], because they said that what is is one. For since the sensible manifestly seems to exist, if what is is one, there would not be anything else outside of it.

EARLY GREEK PHILOSOPHY V

b p. 557.19–23

ἀλλ᾽ ὁ μὲν Ἀριστοτέλης, ὡς ἔθος αὐτῷ, πρὸς τὸ φαινόμενον καὶ νῦν τῶν λόγων ὑπήντησε προνοῶν τοῦ
μὴ τοὺς ἐπιπολαιοτέρους παραλογίζεσθαι, οἱ δὲ ἄνδρες ἐκεῖνοι διττὴν ὑπόστασιν[1] ὑπετίθεντο,[2] τὴν μὲν
τοῦ ὄντως ὄντος τοῦ νοητοῦ, τὴν δὲ τοῦ γινομένου τοῦ
αἰσθητοῦ, ὅπερ οὐκ ἠξίουν καλεῖν ὂν ἁπλῶς, ἀλλὰ
δοκοῦν ὄν.

[1] ὑπόστασιν DEF: ὑπόθεσιν A   [2] ὑπετίθεντο DE: πα-
ρετίθεντο A

c p. 558.17–21

ἀλλὰ καὶ Μέλισσος [. . . cf. **R20**] τὴν ἑαυτοῦ περὶ
τούτων γνώμην ἐξέφηνε [. . .] ἐν τούτοις [. . .] τοῖς ῥη-
τοῖς· εἰπὼν γὰρ περὶ τοῦ ὄντος, ὅτι ἕν ἐστι καὶ ἀγένητον καὶ ἀκίνητον καὶ μηδενὶ κενῷ διειλημμένον, ἀλλ᾽
ὅλον ἑαυτοῦ πλῆρες, ἐπάγει [. . . = **D11**].

d p. 559.12–14

[. . . cf. **D11**] σαφῶς οὖν οὗτος καὶ τὴν αἰτίαν εἶπε, δι᾽
ἣν τὰ αἰσθητὰ οὐκ εἶναι λέγουσιν ἀλλὰ δοκεῖν εἶναι.
πῶς οὖν ἄν τις αὐτοὺς ὑπολάβοι μόνον τὸ αἰσθητὸν
νομίζειν εἶναι;

b

But Aristotle, as is his custom, here too has formulated his response considering the appearance of the words, taking care not to mislead his more superficial [scil. readers]. Yet those men [i.e. Parmenides and Melissus] accepted two kinds of existence, the one of what really is, the intelligible, and the other of what comes to be, the perceptible, which they did not think they had to call "being" in the simple sense, but rather "seeming to be" [cf. **PARM. R52**].

c

But Melissus [. . . cf. **R20**] has expressed his opinion on these questions [scil. the double existence] [. . .] in the following statements. For having said that what is is one, ungenerated, immobile, and not separated by any void, but as a whole full of itself, he continues, [. . . = **D11**].

d

Therefore he [i.e. Melissus] has clearly explained the reason why they say that the sensibles are not but seem to be. Therefore how could one suppose that they [i.e. Parmenides and Melissus] think that only the perceptible exists?

*Simplicius Disputes Alexander's Reading of
Fragment D10 (R23)*

R23 (≠DK) Simpl. *In Phys.*

a p. 110.20–26

[. . . = **D16**] ὡς τὴν κατὰ τόπον κίνησιν ἀναιροῦντος
τοῦ Μελίσσου μόνην, οὐ μὴν καὶ τὴν ἀλλοίωσιν,
οὕτως ποιεῖται τὴν ἐξήγησιν διὰ τὸ ὑπὸ τοῦ Ἀριστοτέλους εἰρημένον τὸ ἔπειτα ἀλλοίωσις διὰ τί οὐκ ἂν
εἴη. ἐμοὶ δὲ δοκεῖ συμπεραινόμενος ὁ Μέλισσος τὰ
περὶ τοῦ ὄντος εἰρημένα, ὅτι ἀγένητον καὶ ἀίδιον καὶ
ἄπειρον καὶ ἓν καὶ ὅμοιον, ἐκ τούτων καὶ τὰς ἄλλας
πάσας κινήσεις τὰς περὶ[1] τὴν γένεσιν ἀφαιρεῖν ἀπὸ
τοῦ ὄντος [. . .].

[1] περὶ ed. Ald.: παρὰ mss.

b p. 111.11–19

ὅτι δὲ οὐχ ὡς ὁ Ἀλέξανδρος ἤκουσεν, οὕτως ἡ ἀπό-
δειξις προῆλθεν ἐκ τοῦ τὸ κινούμενον ἢ διὰ πλήρους
ὀφείλειν κινεῖσθαι ἢ διὰ κενοῦ, ἀλλ' ὅτι δεῖ αὐτὸ τὸ
ὂν πλῆρες εἶναι, δηλοῖ καὶ ὁ Εὔδημος λέγων [Frag. 42
Wehrli] "ἀκίνητον δὲ δὴ πῶς; ἢ ὅτι πλῆρες; πλῆρες δέ,
ὅτι οὐκ ἔστιν[1] ἄπειρον κενοῦ μετέχον." ἀλλ' ἐπειδὴ
κἂν ἀρχαιοπρεπῶς ἀλλ' οὐκ ἀσαφῶς ταῦτα καὶ ὁ
Μέλισσος ἔγραψε, παρακείσθω καὶ αὐτὰ τὰ ἀρχαῖα
γράμματα πρὸς τὸ δύνασθαι τοὺς ἐντυγχάνοντας

MELISSUS

Simplicius Disputes Alexander's Reading of Fragment D10 (R23)

R23 (≠ DK) Simplicius, *Commentary on Aristotle's* Physics

a

[. . .] Since he [i.e. Alexander] thinks that Melissus abolishes only motion according to place and not change as well, he develops an interpretation on the basis of what Aristotle says ("Then why would there be no alteration?") [cf. **R10**]. But to me it seems that Melissus, in concluding what he has said about what is, viz. that it is ungenerated, eternal, unlimited, one, and similar, on the basis of these determinations denies to what is all the other motions as well that concern generation [. . .].

b

The fact that, contrarily to what Alexander understood [cf. p. 110.13–10], the demonstration proceeded not from the fact that what moves ought to move either through what is full or through a void, but that it is necessary that what is be itself full—Eudemus makes this clear too when he says, "And why is it immobile? Is it not because it is full? But it is full, because there is not anything unlimited that participates in the void." But since Melissus too has written these things quite clearly, even if in an archaic manner, I shall cite these ancient writings themselves, so that read-

---

¹ ἔστιν DF: ἔσται E

ἀκριβεστέρους γίνεσθαι κριτὰς τῶν προσφυεστέρων ἐξηγήσεων. λέγει δ᾽ οὖν ὁ Μέλισσος οὕτως τὰ πρότερον εἰρημένα συμπεραινόμενος καὶ οὕτως τὰ περὶ τῆς κινήσεως ἐπάγων [. . . = **D10**].

*Doxographical Inflections and
Deformations (R24–R28)
Cosmologization of the One-All (R24)*

R24 Aët.

a (28 A29) 1.24.1 (Ps.-Plut.) [περὶ γενέσεως καὶ φθορᾶς]

Παρμενίδης Μέλισσος Ζήνων ἀνῄρουν γένεσιν καὶ φθορὰν διὰ τὸ νομίζειν τὸ πᾶν ἀκίνητον.

b (28 A36) 2.4.11 (Stob.) [εἰ ἔμψυχος ὁ κόσμος καὶ προνοίᾳ διοικούμενος]

Ξενοφάνης, Παρμενίδης, Μέλισσος ἀγένητον καὶ ἀίδιον καὶ ἄφθαρτον τὸν κόσμον.

c (28 A36) 2.1.2 (Stob.) [περὶ κόσμου]

[. . .] Παρμενίδης, Μέλισσος [. . .] ἕνα τὸν κόσμον.

d (< A9) 1.3.14 (Theod. *Cur.* 4. 8) [περὶ ἀρχῶν]

Μέλισσος [. . .] τὴν [. . .] παραδοθεῖσαν διδασκαλίαν ἀκήρατον οὐκ ἐτήρησεν· ἄπειρον γὰρ οὗτος ἔφη τὸν κόσμον, ἐκείνων φάντων πεπερασμένον.

ers can judge with greater precision which interpretation is the more appropriate one. This then is what Melissus says in conclusion of his earlier statements, adding what he has to say about motion as follows: [. . . = **D10**].

Doxographical Inflections and Deformations (R24–R28) Cosmologization of the One-All (R24)

R24 Aëtius

a (28 A29)

Parmenides, Melissus, and Zeno abolished genesis and destruction because they thought that the whole is immobile [= **PARM. R28**].

b (28 A36)

Xenophanes, Parmenides, Melissus: the world is ungenerated, eternal, and indestructible [= **PARM. R34**].

c (28 A36)

[. . .] Parmenides, Melissus: [. . .] the world is one.

d (< A9)

Melissus [. . .] did not preserve in its purity the teaching that had been transmitted [scil. by Parmenides] to him. For he said that the world is unlimited, while they said that it was limited [cf. **PARM. R36**].

e (< 64 A10) 2.1.6 (Stob.) [περὶ κόσμου]

[. . .] Μέλισσος τὸ μὲν πᾶν ἄπειρον, τὸν δὲ κόσμον πεπεράνθαι.

R25 (A12) Epiphan. *Pan.* 3.2.9.12

Μέλισσος [. . .] ἐν τὸ πᾶν ἔφη εἶναι, μηδὲν δὲ βέβαιον ὑπάρχειν τῇ φύσει, ἀλλὰ πάντα εἶναι φθαρτὰ ἐν δυνάμει.

Two Opposite Theological Readings (R26–R27)

R26 (A13) Aët. 1.7.27 (Stob.) [τίς ὁ θεός]

Μέλισσος καὶ Ζήνων τὸ ἐν καὶ πᾶν καὶ μόνον ἀίδιον καὶ ἄπειρον.

R27 (< A1) Diog. Laert. 9.24

[. . . = **D17**] ἀλλὰ καὶ περὶ θεῶν ἔλεγε μὴ δεῖν ἀποφαίνεσθαι· μὴ γὰρ εἶναι γνῶσιν αὐτῶν.

e (< 64 A10)

[. . .] Melissus: the whole is unlimited, but the world is limited [cf. **DIOG. R16**].

R25 (A12) Epiphanius, *Panarion*

Melissus [. . .] said that the whole is one, and that nothing stable exists by nature, but that everything is corruptible in potential.

Two Opposite Theological Readings (R26–R27)

R26 (A13) Aëtius

Melissus and Zeno: [scil. god is] one and all, and only he is eternal and unlimited.

R27 (< A1) Diogenes Laertius

But he also said about the gods that it is necessary not to make a pronouncement, for we do not have knowledge about them.[1]

---

[1] This statement has no echo in the surviving fragments, and its content is suspect.

A Medical Utilization of Melissus' Doctrine (R28)

R28 (< A6) Gal. *In Hipp. Nat. hom.* 1.3 (p. 17.20–25
Mewaldt)

[. . .] τὸν δὲ Μελίσσου λόγον ὀρθοῦσιν ἡγουμένου μὲν
ἓν εἶναι καὶ αὐτοῦ τοῦτο, οὐ μὴν ἐκ τῶν τεσσάρων γ᾽
ἕν τι τούτων, ἀέρος καὶ γῆς ὕδατός τε καὶ πυρός. ἔοικε
δὲ ὁ ἀνὴρ οὗτος ἐννοῆσαι μὲν εἶναί τινα οὐσίαν κοι-
νήν, ὑποβεβλημένην τοῖς τέσσαρσι στοιχείοις, ἀγέν-
νητόν τε καὶ ἄφθαρτον, ἣν οἱ μετ᾽ αὐτὸν ῾ὕλην᾽ ἐκά-
λεσαν, οὐ μὴν διηρθρωμένως γε δυνηθῆναι τοῦτο
δηλῶσαι. ταύτην δ᾽ οὖν αὐτὴν τὴν οὐσίαν ὀνομάζει
τὸ ἓν καὶ τὸ πᾶν.

The Interpretation by a Historian of Myths (R29)

R29 (> B11) Palaeph. *Incred.*, pp. 1.9–2.3 Festa

ὅσα δὲ εἴδη καὶ μορφαί εἰσι λεγόμεναι καὶ γενόμεναι
τότε, αἳ νῦν οὐκ εἰσί, τὰ τοιαῦτα οὐκ ἐγένετο. εἰ γάρ
ποτε καὶ ἄλλοτε ἐγένετο, καὶ νῦν τε γίνεται καὶ αὖθις
ἔσται. ἀεὶ δὲ ἔγωγε ἐπαινῶ τοὺς συγγραφέας Μέλισσον καὶ Λαμίσκον τὸν Σάμιον ἐν ἀρχῇ λέγοντας
"ἔστιν ἃ ἐγένετο νῦν καὶ <ἀεὶ>[1] ἔσται."

---

[1] νῦν καὶ <ἀεὶ> Kranz: καὶ νῦν mss.

A Medical Utilization of Melissus' Doctrine (R28)

R28 (< A6) Galen, *Commentary on Hippocrates'* On the
Nature of Man

[. . .] They [i.e. the monist philosophers] justify the argument of Melissus, who himself too thought that only one
thing exists, but not one of these four, air and earth, water
and fire. It seems that this man thought that there exists
a certain common substance underlying the four elements, ungenerated and indestructible, which his succes-
sors called 'matter,' but that he was not able to show this
in an articulate manner. Hence he calls this substance itself the one and the whole.

The Interpretation by a Historian of Myths (R29)

R29 (> B11) Palaephatos, *Incredible Stories*

All the kinds and forms [scil. of monsters] that people
say existed once but now do not exist—in fact these have
never existed. For if they existed at some other time, they
still exist now and will exist later. For my part, I always
praise the authors Melissus and Lamiscus of Samos who
said at the beginning, "What has come to be exists now
and ⟨always⟩ will exist."

An Aphorism Attributed to Melissus in
Syriac (R30)

R30 (cf. B12) *Studia Sinaitica* 1, p. 34

C = Cambridge univ. libr. Add. 2012, fol. 175v, Wright, cat. p. 538

S = Monastery of Saint Catherine on Mount Sinai, Syr. 16, fol. 147v

[1] C S   [2] C S

An Aphorism Attributed to Melissus in
Syriac (R30)

R30 (cf. B12) From a Syriac collection of Greek sayings

Melissus said, "I am deeply troubled by people's futile efforts. They exhaust themselves by staying awake at night for arduous journeys. They voyage through sea storms, and are tossed up and down, hanging between life and death. As strangers, they stay far away from their homes to amass money, although they do not even know who will inherit their money when they die. Yet they do not desire to acquire the glorious treasures of wisdom, of which they cannot be robbed: they can bequeath it to their friends, it accompanies them to the Underworld, and it is never away from them. Intelligent people testify to this by saying, 'The wise man has died, not his wisdom.'"[1]

[1] Translated from the French translation by Henri Hugonnard-Roche; revised by Peter E. Pormann.

22. EMPEDOCLES [EMP.]

Empedocles was born in Agrigentum (in Greek, Acragas) in Sicily. He belonged to a rich and illustrious family. According to the chronographer Apollodorus of Athens, he was forty years old in 444/43, the date of the foundation of the colony of Thurioi, for which Protagoras wrote the constitution (cf. **PROT. P12**). This is a construction, but it is the only element we have available, together with Aristotle's indication that he died at the age of sixty, to establish his dates of birth and death at 484/83–424/23. It is not entirely impossible that Empedocles had a more extensive literary production, but the numerous surviving fragments all derive from two works known in antiquity under the titles *On Nature* (the title is doubtless not original, cf. **ALCM. D2**) and *Purifications.*

Two questions, which involve the presentation of his texts no less than the interpretation of his thought, dominate the scholarly discussion on the work of Empedocles.

The first is whether the two transmitted titles correspond to two distinct works or refer to one and the same poem. Some scholars, relying essentially on the synthetic presentation that (Ps.-?) Hippolytus provides for Empedocles in his *Refutation of All Heresies* (**R89**), have embraced the hypothesis of a single poem, which seemed to receive support from the discovery, in fragments of a pa-

pyrus unknown before 1999, that two verses generally attributed to the *Purifications* are found in a practically identical form in an evidently cosmological context (**D34.1–2** = **D76.5–6**). But these grounds are not compelling, if we accept that the narrative about the origin and structure of the cosmos—from the heavens down to animals and plants, in the tradition going back to Anaximander—entertained relations of homology with a narrative of moral and religious orientation that reconfigured the traditional mythical theme of the punishment of guilty divinities and the Pythagorean doctrine of transmigration. In such a perspective, there is nothing surprising about textual echoes that can extend to the reiteration of whole verses, especially given that the repetition of verses or of groups of verses, identically or with slight variations, is a characteristic trait of Empedocles' style. As for the possible doubt, which remains, concerning the attribution of this fragment or that one to the one poem or the other, this does not constitute an argument against their distinction in principle. Besides, it is striking that Aristotle is interested only in Empedocles' physical narrative and says nothing at all about his eschatological views, while we owe our knowledge of this latter aspect essentially to citations by authors of a Platonic orientation, where this doctrine plays an important role. In choosing to present in section **D** the fragments of the *Purifications* before those of the poem on nature—following some other editors, like Mansfeld/Primavesi, but contrarily to DK—we wish to suggest a certain precedence, in Empedocles' thought, of the ethical dimension over the physical doctrine—a dimension that is visible in the physical poem itself, where the history of the world is directed by the two antagonistic

forces of Love and Strife—without this entailing any hypothesis about the chronology of the composition of the two poems.

The second question is that of reconstructing what is called Empedocles' 'cycle'—that is, the number, nature, and duration of the different stages that lead from the total domination of Love (or of Strife) to the total domination of Strife (or of Love)—a question itself connected with the question of knowing whether Empedocles envisioned a double zoogony, indeed a double cosmogony, corresponding to each of the two parts of the cycle. The data, difficult and contested, go rather in the direction of a double genesis and a double destruction (see in particular the beginning of **D73**); recently discovered scholia to Aristotle make it possible even to speculate on the duration of the different phases implied (**D84b2, R13b2**). But were these two geneses of a different nature? In spite of various attempts, it does not seem possible to distribute the known fragments to the one rather than to the other, and Aristotle says explicitly that Empedocles "omitted" the genesis under Love (**D83**). The consequences that can be derived from this dissymmetry between the principal program and its effective realization are doubtless important, but cannot be discussed here.

BIBLIOGRAPHY

Editions and Commentaries

J. Bollack. *Empédocle,* 4 vols. (Vol. 1, *Introduction à l'ancienne physique;* vol. 2, *Les Origines. Édition cri-*

tique; vol. 3, *Les Origines. Commentaires 1 et 2*) (Paris, 1965–1969; repr. 1992).

B. Inwood. *The Poem of Empedocles: A Text and Translation with an Introduction* (Toronto, 1992; 2nd ed. 2001).

A. Martin and O. Primavesi. *L'Empédocle de Strasbourg* (P. Strasb. gr. Inv. 1665–1666) (Strasbourg, 1999).

O. Primavesi. *Empedokles, Physika I* (Berlin-New York, 2008).

T. Vítek. *Empedoklés, II. Zlomsky* (Prague, 2006).

Studies

D. O'Brien. *Empedocles' Cosmic Cycle. A Reconstruction from the Fragments and Secondary Sources* (Cambridge, 1969).

O. Primavesi. "Empedokles," in H. Flashar, D. Bremer, G. Rechenauer, eds., *Ueberweg. Grundriss der Geschichte der Philosophie. Die Philosophie der Antike.* Bd. 1/2 *Frühgriechische Philosophie* (Basel, 2013), pp. 668–739.

OUTLINE OF THE CHAPTER

P

EMPEDOCLES

EMPEDOCLES [31 DK]

P

Chronology (P1–P6)

P1 (< A1) Diog. Laert. 8.74

ἤκμαζε δὲ κατὰ τὴν τετάρτην καὶ ὀγδοηκοστὴν
Ὀλυμπιάδα.

P2 (cf. A9) Eus. *Chron.* (= Hier., p. 111.20)

[Ol. 81] Empedocles et Parmenides physici philosophi
notissimi habentur.

P3 (< A1) Diog. Laert.

a 8.52

ὁ δὲ ‹τὴν›[1] μίαν καὶ ἑβδομηκοστὴν Ὀλυμπιάδα νενι-
κηκὼς

  κέλητι τούτου πάππος[2] ἦν ὁμώνυμος

ὥσθ᾽ ἅμα καὶ[3] τὸν χρόνον ὑπὸ τοῦ Ἀπολλοδώρου ση-
μαίνεσθαι [*FGrHist* 244 F32a].

EMPEDOCLES

P

Chronology (P1–P6)

P1 (< A1) Diogenes Laertius

He reached maturity during the 84th Olympiad [= 444/40 BC].[1]

> [1] 444 is the date of the foundation of Thourioi; cf. **P6**.

P2 (cf. A9) Jerome in Eusebius, *Chronicle*

[Ol. 81 = 456/52] Empedocles and Parmenides, natural philosophers, are considered very celebrated.

P3 (< A1) Diogenes Laertius

a Apollodorus' indication

The one [scil. the Empedocles] who was victorious at the 71st Olympic games [= 496]

> in the horse-race was his grandfather, of the same
> name,

so that at the same time Apollodorus also indicates the chronology.

---

[1] ⟨τὴν⟩ Cobet   [2] πάντως mss., corr. Karsten   [3] καὶ ⟨τούτου⟩ Jacoby

b 8.51

λέγει δὲ καὶ Ἐρατοσθένης ἐν τοῖς Ὀλυμπιονίκαις
[*FGrHist* 241 F7] τὴν πρώτην καὶ ἑβδομηκοστὴν
Ὀλυμπιάδα νενικηκέναι τὸν τοῦ Μέτωνος πατέρα,
μάρτυρι χρώμενος Ἀριστοτέλει [Frag. 71 Rose].

P4 (< A6) Arist. *Metaph.* A3 984a11–12

Ἀναξαγόρας δὲ ὁ Κλαζομένιος τῇ μὲν ἡλικίᾳ πρότερος ὢν τούτου [. . . cf. **ANAXAG. R8**].

P5 (< A1) Diog. Laert.

a 8.73

ὕστερον δὲ διά τινα πανήγυριν πορευόμενον ἐπ᾽ ἀμά-
ξης ὡς εἰς Μεσσήνην πεσεῖν καὶ τὸν μηρὸν κλάσαι·
νοσήσαντα δ᾽ ἐκ τούτου τελευτῆσαι ἐτῶν ἑπτὰ καὶ
ἑβδομήκοντα.

b 8.74

περὶ δὲ τῶν ἐτῶν Ἀριστοτέλης διαφέρεται· φησὶ γὰρ
[Frag. 71 Rose] ἐκεῖνος ἑξήκοντα ἐτῶν αὐτὸν τελευτῆ-
σαι· οἱ δὲ ἐννέα καὶ ἑκατόν.

P6 (< A1) Diog. Laert. 8.52

Ἀπολλόδωρος δ᾽ ὁ γραμματικὸς ἐν τοῖς Χρονικοῖς
φησιν ὡς [*FGrHist* 244 F32a]

b Eratosthenes' indication

Eratosthenes, invoking the testimony of Aristotle, also says in his *Olympic Victors* that the father of Meton [i.e. Empedocles' grandfather] had won in the 71st Olympics [= 496].

P4 (< A6) Aristotle, *Metaphysics*

Anaxagoras of Clazomenae, who was earlier in age than him [i.e. Empedocles] [. . .].

P5 (< A1) Diogenes Laertius

a

Later, when he was traveling in a carriage to Messina for some festival, he fell and broke his thigh. He became ill as a result of this and died at the age of seventy-seven years.

b

But Aristotle differs about the age; for he says that he died at sixty years. Others say at 109 years.[1]

[1] Like his disciple Gorgias according to Apollodorus (cf. **GORG. P25**).

P6 (< A1) Diogenes Laertius

Apollodorus the grammarian says in his *Chronology,*

ἦν μὲν Μέτωνος υἱός, εἰς δὲ Θουρίους
αὐτὸν νεωστὶ παντελῶς ἐκτισμένους
⟨ὁ⟩[1] Γλαῦκος ἐλθεῖν φησιν.

εἶθ᾽ ὑποβάς·

οἱ δ᾽ ἱστοροῦντες ὡς πεφευγὼς οἴκοθεν[2]
εἰς τὰς Συρακούσας μετ᾽ ἐκείνων ἐπολέμει
πρὸς τὰς Ἀθήνας ἀγνοεῖν τελέως ἐμοί[3]
δοκοῦσιν· ἢ γὰρ οὐκέτ᾽ ἦν ἢ παντελῶς
ὑπεργεγηρακώς, ὅπερ οὐχὶ[4] φαίνεται.

[1] ⟨ὁ⟩Cobet   [2] οἴκοθεν πεφευγὼς mss.: transp. Meineke
[3] πρὸς τὰς Ἀθήνας ἀγνοεῖν τελέως ⟨ἐ⟩μοι Bahnsch: πρὸς τοὺς
ἀθηναίους τελέως ἀγνοεῖν μοι mss.   [4] οὐ mss., corr.
Meineke

Origin (P7)

P7 (< A1) Diog. Laert. 8.54

ὅτι δ᾽ ἦν Ἀκραγαντῖνος ἐκ Σικελίας, αὐτὸς ἐναρχόμενος τῶν Καθαρμῶν φησιν· [. . . = **D4.1–2a**].

Family (P8)

P8 (< A1) Diog. Laert.

a 8.51

Ἐμπεδοκλῆς, ὥς φησιν Ἱππόβοτος [Frag. 15 Gigante],
Μέτωνος ἦν υἱὸς τοῦ Ἐμπεδοκλέους, Ἀκραγαντῖνος·

He was Meton's son, but Glaucus says
He came to Thourioi,
Which had just been founded. [= 444]

And then somewhat later,

Those who report that he was exiled from his
    homeland
To Syracuse and fought together with them
Against Athens seem to me to be completely
Ignorant. For either he was no longer alive or else
    had
Become extremely old, which does not seem to have
    been the case.

Origin (P7)

P7 (< A1) Diogenes Laertius

That he came from Agrigentum in Sicily, he himself says
at the beginning of the *Purifications:* [. . . = **D4.1–2a**].

Family (P8)

P8 (< A1) Diogenes Laertius

a

Empedocles, according to Hippobotus, was the son of
Meton, the son of Empedocles, and came from Agrigen-

τὸ δ᾽ αὐτὸ καὶ Τίμαιος ἐν τῇ πεντεκαιδεκάτῃ τῶν
Ἱστοριῶν ‹λέγει προσιστορῶν›[1] ἐπίσημον ἄνδρα γεγονέναι τὸν Ἐμπεδοκλέα τὸν πάππον τοῦ ποιητοῦ
[FGrHist 566 F26b]· ἀλλὰ καὶ Ἕρμιππος τὰ αὐτὰ
τούτῳ φησίν [Frag. 25 Wehrli] ὁμοίως καὶ Ἡρακλείδης
ἐν τῷ Περὶ νόσων [Frag. 76 Wehrli], ὅτι λαμπρᾶς ἦν
οἰκίας ἱπποτροφηκότος τοῦ πάππου.

   [1] ‹λέγει προσιστορῶν› Diels

b 8.53

Σάτυρος δὲ ἐν τοῖς Βίοις φησὶν [Frag. 12 Schorn] ὅτι
Ἐμπεδοκλῆς υἱὸς μὲν ἦν Ἐξαινέτου, κατέλιπε δὲ καὶ
αὐτὸς υἱὸν Ἐξαίνετον.

c 8.53

Τηλαύγης δ᾽ ὁ Πυθαγόρου παῖς ἐν τῇ πρὸς Φιλόλαον
ἐπιστολῇ φησι τὸν Ἐμπεδοκλέα Ἀρχινόμου εἶναι
υἱόν.

d 8.53

ἐγὼ δὲ εὗρον ἐν τοῖς Ὑπομνήμασι Φαβωρίνου [Frag.
56 Amato] ὅτι [. . .] ἀδελφὸν ἔσχε Καλλικρατίδην.

tum. Timaeus ‹says› the same thing in the fifteenth book of his *Histories,* ‹adding› that the poet's grandfather Empedocles had been a famous man; and Hermippus too says the same thing as he does, as does Heraclides in his *On Illnesses:* that he came from an illustrious family and that his grandfather raised horses.

b

Satyrus says in his *Lives* that Empedocles was the son of Exaenetus, and that he himself left a son named Exaenetus.

c

Telauges the son of Pythagoras says in his letter to Philolaus that Empedocles was the son of Archinomus.

d

I myself [i.e. Diogenes Laertius] found in the *Memoirs* of Favorinus that Empedocles [. . .] had a brother named Callicratides.

Lover (P9)

P9 (< A1) Diog. Laert. 8.60–61

ἦν δ᾽ ὁ Παυσανίας, ὥς φησιν Ἀρίστιππος [IV A 158
G²] καὶ Σάτυρος [Frag. 14 Schorn] ἐρώμενος αὐτοῦ, ᾧ
δὴ καὶ τὰ Περὶ φύσεως προσπεφώνηκεν οὕτως· [. . . =
D41].

Philosophical Genealogy (P10–P15)
Pythagoreans . . . (P10–P12)

P10 (< A1) Diog. Laert. 8.54

ἀκοῦσαι δ᾽ αὐτὸν Πυθαγόρου Τίμαιος διὰ τῆς ἐνάτης
ἱστορεῖ [FGrHist 566 F14], λέγων ὅτι καταγνωσθεὶς
ἐπὶ λογοκλοπίᾳ τότε [. . .] τῶν λόγων ἐκωλύθη μετέχειν. μεμνῆσθαι δὲ καὶ αὐτὸν Πυθαγόρου λέγοντα·
[. . . = **D38.1–2**]· οἱ δὲ τοῦτο εἰς Παρμενίδην αὐτὸν
λέγειν ἀναφέροντα.[1]

[1] οἱ δὲ . . . ἀναφέροντα om. F

P11 (< A8) Eus. *PE* 10.14.15

Τηλαύγους δὲ Ἐμπεδοκλῆς ἀκουστὴς γίνεται [. . .].

P12 (< A1) Diog. Laert. 8.55

φησὶ δὲ Νεάνθης [FGrHist 84 F26] ὅτι μέχρι Φιλολάου
καὶ Ἐμπεδοκλέους ἐκοινώνουν οἱ Πυθαγορικοὶ τῶν

Lover (P9)

P9 (< A1) Diogenes Laertius

Pausanias, as Aristippus and Satyrus say, was his beloved; it is to him that he has addressed his *On Nature* as follows: [. . . = **D41**].

Philosophical Genealogy (P10–P15)
Pythagoreans . . . (P10–P12)

P10 (< A1) Diogenes Laertius

Timaeus reports in his ninth book that he [i.e. Empedocles] studied with Pythagoras, and says that then, having been caught plagiarizing, he was forbidden [. . .] from participating in the discussions; and that he himself mentions Pythagoras when he says [. . . = **D38.1–2**]. But some people think that he says this with reference to Parmenides.

P11 (< A8) Eusebius, *Evangelical Preparation*

Empedocles was a student of Telauges [. . .].

P12 (< A1) Diogenes Laertius

Neanthes says that until Philolaus and Empedocles, the Pythagoreans shared their teachings among themselves.

λόγων. ἐπεὶ δ' αὐτὸς διὰ τῆς ποιήσεως ἐδημοσίωσεν
αὐτά, νόμον ἔθεντο μηδενὶ μεταδώσειν ἐποποιῷ. [. . .]
τίνος μέντοι γε αὐτῶν ἤκουσεν ὁ Ἐμπεδοκλῆς, οὐκ
εἶπε· τὴν γὰρ περιφερομένην πρὸς <Φιλόλαον>[1] Τηλαύγους ἐπιστολὴν ὅτι τε μετέσχεν Ἱππάσου καὶ
Βροτίνου, μὴ εἶναι ἀξιόπιστον.

[1] <Φιλόλαον> Roeper ex §53

. . . *Parmenides* . . . *(P13)*

P13 (< A1) Diog. Laert. 8.55

ὁ δὲ Θεόφραστος Παρμενίδου φησὶ [Frag. 227B
FHS&G] ζηλωτὴν αὐτὸν γενέσθαι καὶ μιμητὴν ἐν τοῖς
ποιήμασι· καὶ γὰρ ἐκεῖνον ἐν ἔπεσι τὸν Περὶ φύσεως
ἐξενεγκεῖν λόγον.

. . . *and Others (P14–P15)*

P14 (< A1) Diog. Laert. 8.56

Ἕρμιππος δὲ [Frag. 26 Wehrli] οὐ Παρμενίδου, Ξενοφάνους δὲ γεγονέναι ζηλωτήν, ᾧ καὶ συνδιατρῖψαι
καὶ μιμήσασθαι τὴν ἐποποιίαν· ὕστερον δὲ τοῖς Πυ-
θαγορικοῖς ἐντυχεῖν.

P15 (< A1) Diog. Laert. 8.56

Ἀλκιδάμας δ' ἐν τῷ Φυσικῷ φησι [Frag. 8 Avezzù]

But when he [i.e. Empedocles] divulged them in his poetry, they made the rule not to transmit them to any poet. [. . .] But with which of them Empedocles had studied, he [i.e. Neanthes] did not say. For the letter to ⟨Philolaus⟩ that is in circulation under the name of Telauges, in which he claims that he [i.e. Empedocles] participated [scil. in the teaching] of Hippasus and Brontinus, is not credible [cf. **HIPPAS. P3**].

. . . Parmenides . . . (P13)

P13 (< A1) Diogenes Laertius

Theophrastus says that he was an emulator of Parmenides and imitated him in his poems; for he too published his work *On Nature* in hexameters.

. . . and Others (P14–P15)

P14 (< A1) Diogenes Laertius

But Hermippus says that he was the emulator not of Parmenides but of Xenophanes, with whom he spent time and whose hexameter poetry he imitated; and that it was later that he encountered the Pythagoreans.

P15 (< A1) Diogenes Laertius

Alcidamas in his *Physics* says that Zeno and Empedocles

κατὰ τοὺς αὐτοὺς χρόνους Ζήνωνα καὶ Ἐμπεδοκλέα
ἀκοῦσαι Παρμενίδου, εἶθ᾽ ὕστερον ἀποχωρῆσαι, καὶ
τὸν μὲν Ζήνωνα κατ᾽ ἰδίαν φιλοσοφῆσαι, τὸν δὲ
Ἀναξαγόρου διακοῦσαι καὶ Πυθαγόρου· καὶ τοῦ μὲν
τὴν σεμνότητα ζηλῶσαι τοῦ τε βίου καὶ τοῦ σχήματος, τοῦ δὲ τὴν φυσιολογίαν.

The Thaumaturge (P16–P17)

P16 (< A1) Diog. Laert. 8.59–62

[59] τοῦτόν φησιν ὁ Σάτυρος [Frag. 13 Schorn] λέγειν
ὡς αὐτὸς παρείη τῷ Ἐμπεδοκλεῖ γοητεύοντι. ἀλλὰ καὶ
αὐτὸν διὰ τῶν ποιημάτων ἐπαγγέλλεσθαι τοῦτό τε
καὶ ἄλλα πλείω, δι᾽ ὧν φησι· [. . . = **D43**]. [60] φησὶ
δὲ καὶ Τίμαιος ἐν τῇ ὀκτωκαιδεκάτῃ[1] [FGrHist 566
F30] κατὰ πολλοὺς τρόπους τεθαυμάσθαι τὸν ἄνδρα.
καὶ γὰρ ἐτησίων ποτὲ σφοδρῶς πνευσάντων ὡς[2] τοὺς
καρποὺς λυμῆναι,[3] κελεύσας ὄνους ἐκδαρῆναι καὶ
ἀσκοὺς ποιῆσαι[4] περὶ τοὺς λόφους καὶ τὰς ἀκρωρείας
διέτεινε πρὸς τὸ συλλαβεῖν τὸ πνεῦμα· λήξαντος δὲ
Κωλυσανέμαν κληθῆναι. Ἡρακλείδης τε ἐν τῷ Περὶ
νόσων φησὶ [Frag.77 Wehrli] καὶ Παυσανίᾳ ὑφηγήσα-
σθαι αὐτὸν τὰ περὶ τὴν ἄπνουν. [. . .] [61] τὴν γοῦν
ἄπνουν ὁ Ἡρακλείδης[5] φησὶ [Frag. 77 Wehrli] τοιοῦτόν

---

[1] ὀκτωκαιδεκάτῃ BF: ιη′ P: ιβ′ Beloch   [2] ὡς BP: ὡς ἂν
F: ὡς καὶ Φ   [3] λυμήνασθαι Cobet   [4] ποιεῖσθαι
Cobet   [5] ἡράκλητος BF, ἡράκλειτος P, corr. Mercurialis

studied with Parmenides at the same time, that they then left him, and that Zeno went on to do philosophy on his own, while the other [i.e. Empedocles] continued to study with Anaxagoras and Pythagoras and emulated the latter's dignified way of life and bearing, and the former's study of nature.[1]

[1] A construction of intellectual affinities implying chronological impossibilities.

The Thaumaturge (P16–P17)[1]

[1] There are many other references to Empedocles' thaumaturgy.

P16 (< A1) Diogenes Laertius

[59] Satyrus says that he [i.e. Gorgias] asserted that he had been present while Empedocles performed magic [cf. **GORG. P5**], and that he himself in his poems proclaimed this and many other things, when he says [. . . = **D44**]. [60] Timaeus says in his 18th book that this man caused amazement in many ways. For one time, when the Etesian winds blew so strongly that they were ruining the crops, he ordered them to flay asses and to make bags [scil. out of their skins]; and he stretched these out around the hills and headlands in order to catch the wind; and when it stopped he was called "Wind-stopper" [cf. **D43.3–4**]. Heraclides in his *On Diseases* says that he also explained to Pausanias the case of the woman who had stopped breathing. [. . .] [61] Heraclides says that what happened with her was this:

τι εἶναι, ὡς τριάκοντα ἡμέρας συντηρεῖν ἄπνουν καὶ
ἄσφυκτον[6] τὸ σῶμα· ὅθεν εἶπεν αὐτὸν καὶ ἰητρὸν καὶ
μάντιν, λαμβάνων ἅμα καὶ ἀπὸ τούτων τῶν στίχων·
[62] [. . . = **D4.1–2, 4–11**].

6 ἄσφυκτον Mercurialis: ἄσηπτον BPF, ἄσιτον Φh

P17 (< A15) Iambl. *VP* 113

Ἐμπεδοκλῆς δέ σπασαμένου τὸ ξίφος ἤδη νεανίου
τινὸς ἐπὶ τὸν αὐτοῦ ξενοδόχον Ἄγχιτον [. . .] μεθαρ-
μοσάμενος ὡς εἶχε τὴν λύραν καὶ πεπαντικόν τι μέ-
λος καὶ κατασταλκτικὸν καταχειρισάμενος εὐθὺς ἀν-
εκρούσατο τὸ

    νηπενθές τ᾽ ἄχολόν τε, κακῶν ἐπίληθον ἁπάντων

κατὰ τὸν ποιητήν, καὶ τόν τε ἑαυτοῦ ξενοδόχον Ἄγχιτον θανάτου ἐρρύσατο καὶ τὸν νεανίαν ἀνδροφο-
νίας. ἱστορεῖται δ᾽ οὗτος τῶν Ἐμπεδοκλέους γνωρίμων ὁ δοκιμώτατος ἔκτοτε γενέσθαι.

Democratic Tendency (P18–P19)

P18 (< A1) Diog. Laert. 8.72

Νεάνθης δ᾽ ὁ Κυζικηνὸς [. . .] φησι [*FGrHist* 84 F28]
Μέτωνος τελευτήσαντος τυραννίδος ἀρχὴν ὑποφύε-
σθαι· εἶτα τὸν Ἐμπεδοκλέα πεῖσαι τοὺς Ἀκραγαντί-
νους παύσασθαι μὲν τῶν στάσεων, ἰσότητα δὲ πολι-
τικὴν ἀσκεῖν.

for thirty days he observed her body, which was without respiration or pulse [cf. **D43.9**]. For this reason he called him both a doctor and a seer, deriving this also from the following lines: [62] [. . . = **D4.1–2, 4–11**].

P17 (< A15) Iamblichus, *Life of Pythagoras*

When a young man had already drawn his sword against his host Anchitus [. . .], Empedocles changed the harmony of the lyre he was holding and, seizing upon a mellow and sedating tune, quickly struck up the line,

> that calms grief and anger and brings forgetfulness of all evils,

as the poet [i.e. Homer] says [*Odyssey* 4.221], and saved both his host Anchitus from dying and the young man from committing murder. It is reported that this man went on to become Empedocles' most celebrated disciple [cf. **D41**].

Democratic Tendency (P18–P19)

P18 (< A1) Diogenes Laertius

Neanthes of Cyzicus [. . .] says that after the death of Meton a tyranny was gradually beginning to develop, but that then Empedocles persuaded the Agrigentines to put an end to their dissensions and to practice political equality.

EARLY GREEK PHILOSOPHY V

P19 (< A1) Diog. Laert. 8.63–66

[63] φησὶ δ᾿ αὐτὸν καὶ Ἀριστοτέλης [Frag. 66 Rose]
ἐλεύθερον γεγονέναι καὶ πάσης ἀρχῆς ἀλλότριον, εἴ
γε τὴν βασιλείαν αὐτῷ διδομένην παρῃτήσατο, καθάπερ Ξάνθος ἐν τοῖς περὶ αὐτοῦ λέγει [FGrHist 765
F33], τὴν λιτότητα δηλονότι πλέον ἀγαπήσας. [64] τὰ
δ᾿ αὐτὰ καὶ Τίμαιος εἴρηκε [FGrHist 566 F134], τὴν
αἰτίαν ἅμα παρατιθέμενος τοῦ δημοτικὸν εἶναι τὸν
ἄνδρα. φησὶ γὰρ ὅτι κληθεὶς ὑπό τινος τῶν ἀρχόντων
καὶ¹ προβαίνοντος τοῦ δείπνου τὸ ποτὸν οὐκ εἰσεφέ-
ρετο, τῶν² ἄλλων ἡσυχαζόντων, μισοπονήρως διατε-
θεὶς ἐκέλευσεν εἰσφέρειν· ὁ δὲ κεκληκὼς ἀναμένειν
ἔφη τὸν τῆς βουλῆς ὑπηρέτην. ὡς δὲ παρεγένετο,
ἐγενήθη συμποσίαρχος, τοῦ κεκληκότος δηλονότι
καταστήσαντος, ὃς ὑπεγράφετο τυραννίδος ἀρχήν·
ἐκέλευσε γὰρ ἢ πίνειν ἢ καταχεῖσθαι τῆς κεφαλῆς.
τότε μὲν οὖν ὁ Ἐμπεδοκλῆς ἡσύχασε· τῇ δὲ ὑστεραίᾳ
εἰσαγαγὼν εἰς δικαστήριον ἀπέκτεινε καταδικάσας
ἀμφοτέρους, τόν τε κλήτορα καὶ τὸν συμποσίαρχον.
ἀρχὴ μὲν οὖν αὐτῷ³ τῆς πολιτείας ἥδε. [65] πάλιν δ᾿
Ἄκρωνος τοῦ ἰατροῦ τόπον αἰτοῦντος παρὰ τῆς βουλῆς εἰς κατασκευὴν πατρῴου μνήματος διὰ τὴν ἐν
τοῖς ἰατροῖς ἀκρότητα παρελθὼν ὁ Ἐμπεδοκλῆς
ἐκώλυσε, τά τε ἄλλα περὶ ἰσότητος διαλεχθεὶς καί τι
καὶ τοιοῦτον ἐρωτήσας· "τί δ᾿ ἐπιγράψομεν ἐλεγεῖον;
ἢ τοῦτο·

344

P19 (< A1) Diogenes Laertius

[63] Aristotle too says that he was free-spirited and averse to any political power, since he refused the kingship when it was offered to him, as Xanthus says in his work about him, evidently because he preferred a simple life. [64] Timaeus says the same thing, and at the same time adds the reason why this man had a democratic tendency. For he says that when he was invited to dinner by one of the magistrates and the dinner had gone on for a while but no wine had been brought in, the others remained silent, but he became irritated and ordered that it be brought in; but the host said that they were waiting for the servant of the Council. When he arrived, he was made symposiarch, evidently because this had been decided by the host, who was laying plans to seize power as a tyrant; for he ordered them either to drink the wine or to pour it onto their heads. At the time Empedocles remained silent; but the next day he brought both men to court, the host and the symposiarch, and had them condemned and executed,. And this was the beginning of his involvement in politics. [65] And again: when Acron the doctor asked the Council for a place in order to erect a monument for his father because of his eminence among doctors, Empedocles spoke up and prevented him, saying various things about equality and asking a question like this: "What inscription in elegiac verse shall we place on it? This?

---

¹ καὶ] ὡς Diels ² δ᾿ post τῶν del. Cobet ³ αὕτη mss., corr. Aldobrandinus: αὐτοῦ Huebner

ἄκρον ἰατρὸν Ἄκρων' Ἀκραγαντῖνον πατρὸς
   Ἄκρου
  κρύπτει κρημνὸς ἄκρος πατρίδος ἀκροτάτης;"

[. . .] [66] ὕστερον δ' ὁ Ἐμπεδοκλῆς καὶ τὸ τῶν χιλίων
ἄθροισμα κατέλυσε συνεστὸς ἐπὶ ἔτη τρία, ὥστε οὐ
μόνον ἦν τῶν πλουσίων, ἀλλὰ καὶ τῶν τὰ δημοτικὰ
φρονούντων [. . . = **P20**].

Wealth, Bearing, and Character (P20–P23)

P20 (< A1) Diog. Laert. 8.66

[. . . = **P19**] ὅ γέ τοι Τίμαιος ἐν τῇ πρώτῃ καὶ δευτέρᾳ[1]
(πολλάκις γὰρ αὐτοῦ μνημονεύει) φησὶν [*FGrHist* 566
F2] ἐναντίαν ἐσχηκέναι γνώμην αὐτὸν †τῇ τε πολιτείᾳ
φαίνεσθαι†,[2] ὅπου γε[3] ἀλαζόνα καὶ φίλαυτον ἐν τῇ
ποιήσει·[4] φησὶ γοῦν [. . . = **D4.4–5** (πωλεῦμαι)] καὶ τὰ
ἑξῆς.

   [1] πρώτῃ καὶ δευτέρᾳ (α' καὶ β') mss.: ια' καὶ ιβ' Beloch
[2] locus corruptus, alii aliter   [3] ὅπου γε Kuhn: ἔστι ὅπου γε
Richards: ἔστι γὰρ ὅπου γε Marcovich   [4] ἐν τῇ ποιήσει
del. Diels: post ἐν τῇ ποιήσει add. ἴδοι τις ἄν rec.

P21 (< A1) Diog. Laert. 8.73

ἔτι τε πολλὰς τῶν πολιτίδων ἀπροίκους ὑπαρχούσας
αὐτὸν προικίσαι διὰ τὸν παρόντα πλοῦτον· διὸ δὴ
πορφύραν τε ἀναλαβεῖν αὐτὸν καὶ στρόφιον ἐπιθέσθαι χρυσοῦν, ὡς Φαβωρῖνος ἐν Ἀπομνημονεύμασιν

Acron, the eminent (*akron*) doctor of Agrigentum
    (*Akragantinon*) (his father was Acros),
    Lies under the eminent (*akros*) peak of his most
        eminent (*akrotatês*) fatherland."

[. . .] [66] Later Empedocles dissolved the assembly of the
Thousand, which had been established for three years, so
that he belonged not only to the wealthy people but also
to those who favored the common people [. . .].

Wealth, Bearing, and Character (P20–P23)

P20 (< A1) Diogenes Laertius

[. . .] Timaeus says in his first and second books (in fact he
often mentions him) that he seems to have acquired the
opposite opinion †. . . political constitution . . .†, at least
wherever in his poetry [scil. he appears?] as a braggart and
narcissist;[1] for at least he says [. . . = **D4.4–5a**] and the
following lines.

  [1] The text of this phrase is very uncertain.

P21 (< A1) Diogenes Laertius

Moreover, by reason of his ample wealth he gave a dowry
to many girls of his city who did not have one. And this
was how he could dress in purple clothes and a gold sash,
as Favorinus says in his *Memoirs,* and also wear bronze

347

[Frag. 45 Amato]· ἔτι τε ἐμβάτας χαλκᾶς καὶ στέμμα
Δελφικόν. κόμη τε ἦν αὐτῷ βαθεῖα· καὶ παῖδες ἀκό-
λουθοι· καὶ αὐτὸς ἀεὶ σκυθρωπὸς ἐφ᾽ ἑνὸς σχήματος
ἦν. τοιοῦτος δὴ προῄει, τῶν πολιτῶν ἐντυχόντων καὶ
τοῦτο ἀξιωσάντων οἱονεὶ βασιλείας τινὸς παράση-
μον.

P22 (< A1) Diog. Laert. 8.70

Διόδωρος δὲ ὁ Ἐφέσιος περὶ Ἀναξιμάνδρου[1] γράφων
[FGrHist 1102 F1] φησὶν ὅτι τοῦτον ἐζηλώκει, τραγι-
κὸν ἀσκῶν τῦφον καὶ σεμνὴν ἀναλαβὼν ἐσθῆτα.

  [1] Ἀναξαγόρου Gigante ex 8.56

P23 (A17) Ps.-Arist. *Probl.* 30.1 953a26–28

τῶν δὲ ὕστερον Ἐμπεδοκλῆς καὶ Πλάτων καὶ Σω-
κράτης καὶ ἕτεροι συχνοὶ τῶν γνωρίμων [scil. φαίνον-
ται μελαγχολικοὶ ὄντες, cf. a12].

Doctor and Orator? (P24)

P24 (< A1) Diog. Laert. 8.58

φησὶ δὲ Σάτυρος ἐν τοῖς Βίοις [Frag. 13 Schorn] ὅτι καὶ
ἰατρὸς ἦν καὶ ῥήτωρ ἄριστος. Γοργίαν γοῦν[1] τὸν Λε-
οντῖνον αὐτοῦ γενέσθαι μαθητήν, ἄνδρα ὑπερέχοντα
ἐν ῥητορικῇ καὶ Τέχνην ἀπολελοιπότα [= **GORG. P5**].

  [1] γοῦν PF: δὲ B

shoes and a Delphic garland. He had luxuriant hair and a retinue of young attendants; and he was always gloomy and did not change his bearing. This is how he went along; and when his fellow citizens met him they regarded this as though it were a sign of a certain royalty [cf. **D4**].

P22 (< A1) Diogenes Laertius

Diodorus of Ephesus, writing about Anaximander, says that he [i.e. Empedocles] imitated him in cultivating a theatrical pomp and wearing pretentious clothes.

P23 (A17) Ps.-Aristotle, *Problems*

Among men who were later [scil. than a number of heroes], Empedocles, Plato, Socrates, and many other celebrated people [scil. were evidently melancholy].

Doctor and Orator? (P24)

P24 (< A1) Diogenes Laertius

Satyrus says in his *Lives* that he was a doctor and a first-rate orator, and that in any case Gorgias of Leontini was his disciple, a man who was preeminent in rhetoric and left behind a technical manual on this art.

Lost Works? (P25–P26)

P25 (< A1) Diog. Laert.

a 8.57–58

[57] ἐν δὲ τῷ Περὶ ποιητῶν φησιν ὅτι [Arist. Frag. 70 Rose] [. . . cf. **R1b**] γράψαντος αὐτοῦ καὶ ἄλλα ποιήματα τήν τε τοῦ Ξέρξου διάβασιν καὶ προοίμιον εἰς Ἀπόλλωνα, ταῦθ᾽ ὕστερον κατέκαυσεν ἀδελφή τις αὐτοῦ (ἢ θυγάτηρ, ὥς φησιν Ἱερώνυμος [Frag. 30 Wehrli]), τὸ μὲν προοίμιον ἄκουσα, τὰ δὲ Περσικὰ βουληθεῖσα διὰ τὸ ἀτελείωτα εἶναι. [58] καθόλου δέ φησι καὶ τραγῳδίας αὐτὸν γράψαι καὶ πολιτικούς· Ἡρακλείδης δ᾽ ὁ τοῦ Σαραπίωνος ἑτέρου φησὶν εἶναι τὰς τραγῳδίας [Frag. 6 Müller = *FHG* III.169]. Ἱερώνυμος δὲ τρισὶ καὶ τετταράκοντά φησιν [Frag. 30 Wehrli]) ἐντετυχηκέναι, Νεάνθης δὲ [*FGrHist* 84 F27] νέον ὄντα γεγραφέναι τὰς τραγῳδίας καὶ αὐτὸς¹ ἑπτὰ² ἐντετυχηκέναι.

¹ αὐτὸν mss., corr. Cobet: αὐτῶν Diels   ² ἔπειτα mss., corr. Diels

b 8.77 (= Lobon Frag. 12 Garulli)

[. . . = **D1**] ὁ δὲ Ἰατρικὸς λόγος εἰς ἔπη ἑξακόσια.

P26 (< A2) *Suda* E.1002

[. . . = **D2**] ἰατρικὰ καταλογάδην, καὶ ἄλλα πολλά.

Lost Works? (P25–P26)

P25 (< A1) Diogenes Laertius

a

[57] He [scil. Aristotle] also says in his *On the Poets* [. . .] that, after he had written other poems—*The Expedition of Xerxes* and the *Prelude to Apollo*—a sister of his (or daughter, as Hieronymus says) later burned them, the prelude involuntarily, but the Persian poem voluntarily, since it was unfinished. [58] And he says in general that he also wrote tragedies and political discourses. But Heraclides [i.e. Lembos], the son of Sarapion, says that the tragedies are by someone else. Hieronymus says that he had come across forty-three of them, Neanthes that he wrote the tragedies when he was young and that he himself had come across seven of them.

b

[. . .] his *Medical Treatise* [scil. extends] to six hundred lines.

P26 (< A2) *Suda*

[. . . scil. he composed . . .] medical writings in prose; and many other things.

Apothegms (P27–P28)

P27 (< A1) Diog. Laert. 8.63

ὅθεν τὸν Ἐμπεδοκλέα εἰπεῖν, τρυφώντων αὐτῶν· "Ἀκραγαντῖνοι τρυφῶσι μὲν ὡς αὔριον ἀποθανούμενοι, οἰκίας δὲ κατασκευάζονται ὡς πάντα τὸν χρόνον βιωσόμενοι."

P28 (A20) *Gnomol. Par.*

a 153

Ἐμπεδοκλῆς ἐρωτηθείς, διὰ τί σφόδρα ἀγανακτεῖ κακῶς ἀκούων, ἔφη· "ὅτι οὐδὲ ἐπαινούμενος ἡσθήσομαι, εἰ μὴ κακῶς ἀκούων λυπηθήσομαι."

b 158

Ἐμπεδοκλῆς πρὸς τὸν λέγοντα, ὅτι οὐδένα σοφὸν εὑρεῖν δύναμαι, "κατὰ λόγον" εἶπε· "τὸν γὰρ ζητοῦντα σοφὸν αὐτὸν πρῶτον εἶναι δεῖ σοφόν."

The Death of Empedocles (P29)

P29 (< A1) Diog. Laert. 8.67–72

[67] περὶ δὲ τοῦ θανάτου διάφορός ἐστιν αὐτοῦ λόγος.

[a] Ἡρακλείδης μὲν γὰρ [Frag. 83 Wehrli] τὰ περὶ τῆς ἄπνου διηγησάμενος, ὡς ἐδοξάσθη Ἐμπεδοκλῆς

EMPEDOCLES

Apothegms (P27–P28)

P27 (< A1) Diogenes Laertius

That is why [scil. because Agrigentum was very populous] Empedocles says, while they were living in luxury, "The Agrigentines live in luxury as though they were going to die tomorrow, but they build their houses as though they were going to live forever."

P28 (A20) *Paris Gnomology*

a

When Empedocles was asked why he was so annoyed by the bad things people said about him, he said, "Because I would not be pleased when I am praised either, if I were not aggrieved when they speak badly about me" [cf. **ZEN. P17**].

b

When someone said that he was not able to find any wise man, Empedocles replied, "That is reasonable: for whoever seeks a wise man must first be wise himself."

The Death of Empedocles (P29)[1]

P29 (< A1) Diogenes Laertius

[67] About his death there are various accounts.

[a] For Heraclides, telling, with regard to the woman who had stopped breathing [cf. **P16**], how Empedocles

---

[1] There are many other references to Empedocles' suicide.

ἀποστείλας τὴν νεκρὰν ἄνθρωπον ζῶσαν, φησὶν ὅτι
θυσίαν συνετέλει πρὸς τῷ Πεισιάνακτος ἀγρῷ. συν-
εκέκληντο δὲ τῶν φίλων τινές, ἐν οἷς καὶ Παυσανίας.
[68] εἶτα μετὰ τὴν εὐωχίαν οἱ μὲν ἄλλοι χωρισθέντες
ἀνεπαύοντο, οἱ μὲν ὑπὸ τοῖς δένδροις ὡς ἀγροῦ παρακειμένου, οἱ δ᾽ ὅπῃ βούλοιντο, αὐτὸς δ᾽ ἔμεινεν ἐπὶ τοῦ
τόπου ἐφ᾽ οὗπερ κατεκέκλιτο. ὡς δ᾽ ἡμέρας γενηθεί-
σης ἐξανέστησαν, οὐχ ηὑρέθη μόνος. ζητουμένου δὲ
καὶ τῶν οἰκετῶν ἀνακρινομένων καὶ φασκόντων μὴ
εἰδέναι, εἷς τις ἔφη μέσων νυκτῶν φωνῆς ὑπερμε-
γέθους ἀκοῦσαι προσκαλουμένης Ἐμπεδοκλέα, εἶτ᾽
ἐξαναστὰς ἑωρακέναι φῶς οὐράνιον καὶ λαμπάδων
φέγγος, ἄλλο δὲ μηδέν· τῶν δ᾽ ἐπὶ τῷ γενομένῳ ἐκ-
πλαγέντων, καταβὰς ὁ Παυσανίας ἔπεμψέ τινας ζη-
τήσοντας. ὕστερον δὲ ἐκώλυεν[1] πολυπραγμονεῖν, φάσκων εὐχῆς ἄξια συμβεβηκέναι καὶ θύειν αὐτῷ δεῖν
καθαπερεὶ γεγονότι θεῷ.

[69] [a1] Ἕρμιππος δέ φησι [Frag. 27 Wehrli; cf.
Heracl. Frag. 85 Wehrli] Πάνθειάν τινα Ἀκραγαντίνην
ἀπηλπισμένην ὑπὸ τῶν ἰατρῶν θεραπεῦσαι αὐτὸν καὶ
διὰ τοῦτο τὴν θυσίαν ἐπιτελεῖν· τοὺς δὲ κληθέντας
εἶναι πρὸς τοὺς ὀγδοήκοντα.

[a2] Ἱππόβοτος δέ φησιν [Frag. 16 Gigante] ἐξανα-
στάντα αὐτὸν ᾠδευκέναι ὡς ἐπὶ τὴν Αἴτνην, εἶτα
παραγενόμενον ἐπὶ τοὺς κρατῆρας τοῦ πυρὸς ἐναλέ-
σθαι καὶ ἀφανισθῆναι, βουλόμενον τὴν περὶ αὐτοῦ
φήμην βεβαιῶσαι ὅτι γεγόνοι θεός, ὕστερον δὲ γνω-
σθῆναι, ἀναρριπισθείσης αὐτοῦ μιᾶς τῶν κρηπίδων·

was famous for having sent that dead person back alive again, says that he was performing a sacrifice near the field belonging to Peisianax. Some of his friends, including Pausanias, had been invited. [68] Then after the banquet the others went off to rest, some under the trees, as the field was nearby, others wherever they wished; but he remained where he had been reclining. But when they got up at daybreak, he was the only one who could not be found. When they looked for him and the servants, when asked, said they knew nothing, someone said that in the middle of the night he had heard a very loud voice calling upon Empedocles, and that he had gotten up and seen a light in the sky and a gleam of torches, but nothing else. They were astounded by what had happened, and Pausanias ended up sending some people to look for him. But later he told them not to trouble themselves, saying that what had happened was worthy of prayer, and that they should sacrifice to him as though he had become a god.

[69] [a1] But Hermippus says that he had cured an Agrigentine woman, a certain Pantheia, whom the doctors had given up as a hopeless case, and that this was why he was performing a sacrifice. There were about eighty invited guests.

[a2] Hippobotus says that he got up and walked toward Aetna, and then, when he had arrived at the fiery craters, he threw himself in and vanished, since he wished to confirm the rumor that he had become a god; but that later the truth was discovered, when one of his shoes was

---

1 ἐκώλυεν Diels post Reiske: ἐκωλύθη mss.

χαλκᾶς γὰρ εἴθιστο ὑποδεῖσθαι. πρὸς τοῦτο ὁ Παυσανίας ἀντέλεγε. [. . . = **P22**] [70] τοῖς[2] Σελινουντίοις
ἐμπεσόντος λοιμοῦ διὰ τὰς ἀπὸ τοῦ παρακειμένου
ποταμοῦ δυσωδίας, ὥστε καὶ αὐτοὺς φθείρεσθαι καὶ
τὰς γυναῖκας δυστοκεῖν, ἐπινοῆσαι[3] τὸν Ἐμπεδοκλέα
καὶ δύο τινὰς ποταμοὺς τῶν σύνεγγυς ἐπαγαγεῖν
ἰδίαις δαπάναις· καὶ καταμίξαντα γλυκῆναι τὰ
ῥεύματα. οὕτω δὴ λήξαντος τοῦ λοιμοῦ καὶ τῶν Σελι-
νουντίων εὐωχουμένων ποτὲ παρὰ τῷ ποταμῷ, ἐπι-
φανῆναι τὸν Ἐμπεδοκλέα· τοὺς δ᾽ ἐξαναστάντας προσ-
κυνεῖν καὶ προσεύχεσθαι καθαπερεὶ θεῷ. ταύτην οὖν
θέλοντα βεβαιῶσαι τὴν διάληψιν εἰς τὸ πῦρ ἐναλέ-
σθαι.

[71] [b] τούτοις δ᾽ ἐναντιοῦται Τίμαιος [FGrHist 566
F6], ῥητῶς λέγων ὡς ἐξεχώρησεν εἰς Πελοπόννησον
καὶ τὸ σύνολον οὐκ ἐπανῆλθεν· ὅθεν αὐτοῦ καὶ τὴν
τελευτὴν ἄδηλον εἶναι. πρὸς δὲ τὸν Ἡρακλείδην
[Frag. 84 et 115 Wehrli] καὶ ἐξ ὀνόματος ποιεῖται τὴν
ἀντίρρησιν ἐν τῇ τετάρτῃ.[4] Συρακούσιόν τε γὰρ εἶναι
τὸν Πεισιάνακτα καὶ ἀγρὸν οὐκ ἔχειν ἐν Ἀκράγαντι·
Παυσανίαν τε μνημεῖον <ἂν>[5] πεποιηκέναι τοῦ φίλου,
τοιούτου διαδοθέντος λόγου, ἢ ἀγαλμάτιόν τι ἢ ση-
κὸν οἷα θεοῦ· καὶ γὰρ πλούσιον εἶναι. "πῶς οὖν," φησίν, "εἰς τοὺς κρατῆρας ἥλατο ὧν σύνεγγυς ὄντων

---

[2] τοῖς δὲ rec.   [3] <λύσιν> ἐπινοῆσαι Marcovich   [4] τετάρτῃ BF: δ᾽ P: ιδ᾽ Diels: δευτέρᾳ καὶ δεκάτῃ Jacoby   [5] <ἂν>
Mueller

hurled up again. For he had the habit of wearing bronze shoes. Pausanias[2] objected to this account. [...] [70] When a plague fell upon the inhabitants of Selinunte because of the miasmas coming from the neighboring river, so that they themselves were dying and the women were miscarrying, Empedocles understood and at his own expense diverted two nearby rivers to the city; and the mixture sweetened its streams. When the plague had stopped in this way, the Selinuntines were banqueting one day beside the river and Empedocles arrived. They got up and prostrated themselves before him and prayed to him as though he were a god. It was because he wished to confirm this belief that he threw himself into the fire.[3]

[71] [b] But Timaeus opposes these accounts, saying explicitly that he withdrew to the Peloponnese and never came back at all; and that this is why the manner of his death is unknown. It is expressly against Heraclides that he makes his refutation in his fourth book. For he says that Peisianax was from Syracuse and did not possess a field at Agrigentum; and that Pausanias would have erected a monument to his friend if a story like this had been in circulation, either a little statue or a shrine, as for a god—for he was rich. He says, "How then could he have thrown himself into craters which he never mentioned even once,

---

[2] Probably the Pausanias who was a character in Heraclides' dialogue.   [3] It is unclear whether the story about the plague at Selinunte still derives from Hippobotus or is yet a further version that coincides with the preceding one on certain points.

οὐδὲ μνείαν ποτὲ ἐπεποίητο; [72] τετελεύτηκεν οὖν ἐν
Πελοποννήσῳ. οὐδὲν δὲ παράδοξον τάφον αὐτοῦ μὴ
φαίνεσθαι· μηδὲ γὰρ ἄλλων πολλῶν." τοιαῦτά τινα
εἰπὼν ὁ Τίμαιος ἐπιφέρει· "ἀλλὰ διὰ παντός ἐστιν
Ἡρακλείδης τοιοῦτος παραδοξολόγος [. . .]."

Honors (P30–P31)

P30 (< A1) Diog. Laert. 8.72

Ἱππόβοτος δέ φησιν [Frag. 17 Gigante] ὅτι ἀνδριὰς
ἐγκεκαλυμμένος Ἐμπεδοκλέους ἔκειτο πρότερον μὲν
ἐν Ἀκράγαντι, ὕστερον δὲ πρὸ τοῦ Ῥωμαίων βουλευ-
τηρίου ἀκάλυφος δηλονότι μεταθέντων αὐτὸν ἐκεῖ
Ῥωμαίων· γραπταὶ μὲν γὰρ εἰκόνες¹ καὶ νῦν περι-
φέρονται.

¹ εἰκόνες Sturz: εἰσὶ τινὲς (sic) mss.: εἰκόνες ‹αὐτοῦ› Cobet

P31 (< A1) Diog. Laert. 8.73

εἶναι δ᾽ αὐτοῦ καὶ τάφον ἐν Μεγάροις.

although they were nearby? [72] Hence he died in the Peloponnese. And there is nothing strange in the fact that no tomb of his is to be found; the same is true for many other men." After saying something like this, Timaeus continues, "But Heraclides is always recounting this kind of absurdities [. . .]."

Honors (P30–P31)

P30 (< A1) Diogenes Laertius

Hippobotus says that a veiled statue of Empedocles was set up formerly in Agrigentum, then later without a veil in front of the Senate House in Rome, evidently because the Romans had transferred it there. And painted images are in circulation even now.

P31 (< A1) Diogenes Laertius

There is also a tomb of his in Megara.

EMPEDOCLES [31 DK]

D

Two Poems of Empedocles:
The Testimonia (D1–D3)

D1 (‹ A1) Diog. Laert. 8.77 (= Lobon Frag. 12 Garulli)

τὰ μὲν οὖν Περὶ φύσεως αὐτῷ καὶ οἱ Καθαρμοὶ εἰς
ἔπη τείνουσι πεντακισχίλια [. . . = **P25b**].

D2 (‹ A2) *Suda* E.1002

καὶ ἔγραψε δι᾽ ἐπῶν Περὶ φύσεως τῶν ὄντων βιβλία
β΄.[1] καὶ ἔστιν ἔπη ὡς δισχίλια [. . . = **P26**].

   [1] βιβλία β΄ mss.: βιβλία γ΄ ed. princ.: lac. post βιβλία conj.
Primavesi

D3 (A12) Athen. *Deipn.* 14.12 620D

τοὺς δ᾽ Ἐμπεδοκλέους Καθαρμοὺς ἐραψῴδησεν
Ὀλυμπίασι Κλεομένης ὁ ῥαψῳδός, ὥς φησιν Δικαί-
αρχος ἐν τῷ Ὀλυμπικῷ [Frag. 87 Wehrli].

EMPEDOCLES

D

Two Poems of Empedocles:
The Testimonia (D1–D3)[1]

[1] For other works attributed to Empedocles, see **P25–P26.**

D1 (< A1) Diogenes Laertius

His works *On Nature* and *The Purifications* extend to five thousand lines [. . .].

D2 (< A2) *Suda*

He wrote in hexameters *On the Nature of The Things that Are*[1] in two books, about two thousand lines [. . .].

[1] The notice in the *Suda* is unambiguous, but the fact that it does not mention the *Purifications* has led some scholars to postulate a lacuna, including perhaps an indication of length, in order to harmonize this information with **D1,** which is doubtless its source.

D3 (A12) Athenaeus, *Deipnosophists*

Cleomenes the rhapsode recited Empedocles' *Purifications* at Olympia, as Dicaearchus says in his *Olympic Dialogue.*

See also **ALCM. D2**

Purifications (D4–D40)
Proem (D4–D5)

D4 (B112) Diog. Laert. 8.54 (v. 1–2a) + 8.62 (v. 1–2, 4–11); Diod. Sic. 13.83.1 (v. 3); Clem. Alex. *Strom.* 6.30.1 (v. 10, 12)

[. . .] αὐτὸς ἐναρχόμενος τῶν Καθαρμῶν φησιν·

ὦ φίλοι, οἳ μέγα ἄστυ κατὰ ξανθοῦ
   Ἀκράγαντος
ναίετ᾽ ἀν᾽ ἄκρα πόλεος, ἀγαθῶν μελεδήμονες
   ἔργων,
ξείνων αἰδοῖοι λιμένες, κακότητος ἄπειροι,
χαίρετ᾽· ἐγὼ δ᾽ ὑμῖν θεὸς ἄμβροτος, οὐκέτι
   θνητός
5 πωλεῦμαι μετὰ πᾶσι τετιμένος, ὥσπερ ἔοικα,
ταινίαις τε περίστεπτος στέφεσίν τε θαλείοις·
τοῖσιν ἄμ᾽ εὖτ᾽ ἂν ἵκωμαι ἐς ἄστεα τηλεθάοντα,
ἀνδράσιν ἠδὲ γυναιξὶ σεβίζομαι· οἱ δ᾽ ἄμ᾽
   ἕπονται
μυρίοι ἐξερέοντες ὅπῃ πρὸς κέρδος ἀταρπός,
10 οἱ μὲν μαντοσυνέων κεχρημένοι, οἱ δ᾽ ἐπὶ
   νούσων
παντοίων ἐπύθοντο κλύειν εὐηκέα βάξιν
δηρὸν δὴ χαλεπῇσι πεπαρμένοι ⟨ἀμφ᾽ ὀδύνῃσι⟩.

3 om. Diog. Laert., add. Sturz ex Diod.   7 τοῖσιν ἄμ᾽
εὖτ᾽ ἂν ἵκωμαι P⁴: τοῖσιν ἄμα νίκωμαι BP¹F: ⟨πᾶσι δὲ⟩ τοῖς
ἂν ἵκωμαι Wilamowitz: ⟨πᾶσι δ᾽⟩ ἄμ᾽ εὖτ᾽ ἂν ἵκωμαι Wright
10 δ᾽ ἐπὶ Sturz ex Clem.: δέ τι BPF: δέ τε rec.

EMPEDOCLES

Purifications *(D4–D40)*
Proem *(D4–D5)*[1]

[1] Diels suggested that **D5** may have followed directly on **D4**. A more extensive reconstruction of the beginning of the *Purifications* is proposed by Rashed in *Elenchos* 29 (2008): 7–37.

D4 (B112) Diogenes Laertius (et al.)

[. . .] he himself says at the beginning of the *Purifications:*

> Friends, you who dwell in the great city beside
>   the yellow Acragas
> On the lofty citadel and who care for good
>   deeds,
> Respectful harbors for strangers, inexperienced
>   in wickedness,
> I greet you! I, who for you am an immortal god,
>   no longer mortal,
> I go among you, honored, as I am seen,   5
> Crowned with ribbons and with blooming
>   garlands.
> Whenever I arrive with these in the flourishing
>   cities,
> I am venerated by men and by women; they
>   follow me,
> Thousands of them, asking where is the road to
>   benefit:
> Some of them desire prophecies, others ask to   10
>   hear,
> For illnesses of all kinds, a healing utterance,
> Pierced for a long time by terrible ⟨*pains*⟩.

---

12 χαλεπῇσι πεπ. ⟨ἀμφ᾽ ὀδύνῃσι⟩ Bergk: χαλεποῖσι πεπ. Clem.: χαλεποῖσι πεπ. ⟨ἀμφὶ μόγοισιν⟩ Diels

363

D5 (B113) Sext. Emp. *Adv. Math.* 1.302

ἀλλὰ τί τοῖσδ' ἐπίκειμ' ὡσεὶ μέγα χρῆμά τι
    πράσσων,
εἰ θνητῶν περίειμι πολυφθερέων ἀνθρώπων;

*Communication of the Truth and
Access to Divinity (D6–D9)*

D6 (B114) Clem. Alex. *Strom.* 5.9.1

ὦ φίλοι, οἶδα μὲν οὕνεκ' ἀληθείη πάρα μύθοις
οὓς ἐγὼ ἐξερέω· μάλα δ' ἀργαλέη γε τέτυκται
ἀνδράσι καὶ δύσζηλος ἐπὶ φρένα πίστιος ὁρμή.

2 ἔγωγ' ms., corr. Sylburg

D7 (B131) (Ps.-?) Hippol. *Ref.* 7.31

εἰ γὰρ ἐφημερίων ἕνεκέν τινος, ἄμβροτε
    Μοῦσα,
ἡμετέρας μελέτας ⟨μέλε τοι⟩ διὰ φροντίδος
    ἐλθεῖν,
εὐχομένῳ νῦν αὖτε παρίστασο, Καλλιόπεια,
ἀμφὶ θεῶν μακάρων ἀγαθὸν λόγον ἐμφαίνοντι.

2 ⟨μέλε τοι⟩ Diels: ⟨ἅδε τοι⟩ Wilamowitz, alii alia
3 εὐχομένων ms., corr. Duncker-Schneidewin

D5 (B113) Sextus Empiricus, *Against the Professors*

> But why do I insist upon these things as though
>   I were doing something great,
> To be superior to mortals, men destructible in
>   many ways?

Communication of the Truth and
Access to Divinity (D6–D9)

D6 (B114) Clement of Alexandria, *Stromata*

> Friends, I know that truth is in the words
> That I shall speak out; but it is very irksome
> For men, and causes distrust, the impulse of
>   persuasion for the mind (*phrên*).

D7 (B131) (Ps.-?) Hippolytus, *Refutation of All Heresies*

> For if for the sake of one of the ephemeral
>   beings, immortal Muse,
> ⟨You took care⟩ that our worries traverse your
>   thought,
> Stand once again by my side as I pray to you,
>   Calliope,
> While I present an excellent speech about the
>   blessed gods.

D8 (B132) Clem. Alex. *Strom.* 5.140.5

ὄλβιος, ὃς θείων πραπίδων ἐκτήσατο πλοῦτον,
δειλὸς δ' ᾧ σκοτόεσσα θεῶν πέρι δόξα
μέμηλεν.

D9 (B133) Clem. Alex. *Strom.* 5.81.2; Theod. *Cur.* 1.74

οὐκ ἔστιν πελάσασθαι ἐν ὀφθαλμοῖσιν ἐφικτόν
ἡμετέροις ἢ χερσὶ λαβεῖν, ᾗπέρ τε μεγίστη
πειθοῦς ἀνθρώποισιν ἁμαξιτὸς εἰς φρένα
πίπτει.

The Punishment of Guilty Divinities (D10–D12)

D10 (B115) (Ps.-?) Hipp. *Haer.* 7.29, 14–24 (v. 1–2, 4–8, 9–12); Plut. *Exil.* 17 607C (v. 1, 3, 5–6, 9–12, 13); Philop. *In An.*, p. 73.32–33 (v. 13–14) (et al.)

ἔστιν Ἀνάγκης χρῆμα, θεῶν ψήφισμα παλαιόν,
ἀίδιον, πλατέεσσι κατεσφρηγισμένον ὅρκοις·
εὖτέ τις ἀμπλακίῃσι φόνῳ φίλα γυῖα μιήνῃ
– ∪ ∪ ὅς κ' ἐπίορκον ἁμαρτήσας ἐπομόσσῃ,
5 δαίμονες οἵτε μακραίωνος λελάχασι βίοιο,

1 ἔστιν Simp. *In Phys.* p. 1184.9: ἔστι τι Hipp. Plut.   ἀνάγκης Plut.: ἀνάγκη Hipp. Simpl.   ψήφισμα Hipp. Plut.: σφρήγισμα (vel σφράγισμα A) Simpl.
3 φόνῳ Stephanus: φόβῳ Plut.   μιήνῃ Stephanus: μιν Plut.   4 <νείκεῖ θ'> ὅς κ' Diels, alii alia   5 δαίμονες οἵτε Plut.: δαιμόνιοί τε Hipp.

D8 (B132) Clement of Alexandria, *Stromata*

> Happy he who possesses the wealth of divine
>   organs of thought (*prapides*);
> Wretched, he who cares for an obscure doctrine
>   about the gods.

D9 (B133) Clement of Alexandria, *Stromata*

> It is impossible to approach it [scil. probably: the
>   divine[1]], to attain it with our eyes
> Or to grasp it with hands—which is how the
>   greatest highway of
> Persuasion penetrates to the mind (*phrên*) of
>   men.

[1] This is suggested by the context of citation in Clement.

The Punishment of Guilty Divinities (D10–D12)

D10 (B115) (Ps.-?) Hippolytus, *Refutation of All Heresies*
(et al.)

> There is an oracle of Necessity, an ancient
>   decree of the gods,
> Eternal, sealed by broad oaths:
> Whenever by crimes some one [scil. of them]
>   pollutes his limbs, by murder
> ⟨. . .⟩ whoever commits a fault by perjuring
>   himself on oath,
> The divinities (*daimones*) who have received as   5
>   lot a long life,

τρίς μιν μυρίας ὥρας ἀπὸ μακάρων ἀλάλησθαι,
φυομένους παντοῖα διὰ χρόνου εἴδεα θνητῶν
ἀργαλέας βιότοιο μεταλλάσσοντα κελεύθους.
αἰθέριον μὲν γάρ σφε μένος πόντονδε διώκει,
10   πόντος δ' ἐς χθονὸς οὖδας ἀπέπτυσε, γαῖα δ' ἐς
      αὐγάς
ἠελίου φαέθοντος, ὁ δ' αἰθέρος ἔμβαλε δίναις·
ἄλλος δ' ἐξ ἄλλου δέχεται, στυγέουσι δὲ
      πάντες.
τῶν καὶ ἐγὼ νῦν εἰμι, φυγὰς θεόθεν καὶ ἀλήτης,
Νείκεϊ μαινομένῳ πίσυνος. ∪ ∪ | – ∪ ∪ | – –

7 φυομένους Hipp.: φυόμενον Stein   χρόνου Bergk:
χρόνον Hipp.   9 μὲν γάρ Plut. Vit. aer. alien 830F et Eus.
PE 5.5.2: γάρ Plut. Is. et Os. 361C: γε Hipp.   σφε Plut.:
om. Hipp.   10 πόντος δ' ἐς Plut.: πόντος δὲ Eus. Hipp.
11 φαέθοντος Hipp.: ἀκάμαντος Plut. (Vit. aer. alien 830E, Is.
et Os.)   13 τῶν Hipp.: τὴν Plut.: ὡς Philop.   νῦν om.
Hipp.: δεῦρο Philop.   εἰμι Hipp.: εἶμι Plut.

D11 (ad B115) Plut. Is. et Os. 361C

Ἐμπεδοκλῆς δὲ καὶ δίκας φησὶ διδόναι τοὺς δαίμονας ὧν ⟨ἂν⟩[1] ἐξαμάρτωσι καὶ πλημμελήσωσιν [. . . =
D10.9–12], ἄχρι οὗ κολασθέντες οὕτω καὶ καθαρθέν-
τες αὖθις τὴν κατὰ φύσιν χώραν καὶ τάξιν ἀπολά-
βωσι.

[1] ⟨ἂν⟩ Eus. PE 5.5.2

Must wander thrice ten thousand seasons far
    from the blessed ones,
Growing during this time in the different forms
    of mortal beings,
Exchanging the painful paths of life.
For the force of the aether chases them toward
    the sea,
The sea spits them out toward earth's surface,   10
    the earth toward the rays
Of the bright sun, and he [i.e. the sun] hurls
    them into the eddies of the aether.
Each one receives them from another, but all
    hate them.
Of them, I too am now one,[1] an exile from the
    divine and a wanderer,
I who relied on insane Strife.

[1] Or, with Plutarch's text: "It is this [scil. route] that I will now follow."

D11 (ad B115) Plutarch, *On Isis and Osiris*

Empedocles says that the divinities (*daimones*) are punished for whatever faults and offenses they commit [. . .] until, having been punished in this way and been purified, they once again take up their natural location and rank.

D12 (B142) P. Herc. 1012, Col. 40.7–10 (p. 59 Primavesi)

τὸν δ' οὔτ' ἄρ τε Διὸς τέγεοι δόμοι αἰγ[ιόχοιο]
οὔ]τε τ[ί π]ῃ Ἄιδου δέ[χεται πυ]κι[νὸ]ν στέγος
[–]δ[–]

1 αἰγ[ιόχοιο] Vogliano
2 rest. Martin, alii aliter   [ἔν]δ[ον] van der Ben

The Transmigrations of Living Beings (D13–D20)

D13 (B117) Diog. Laert. 8.77 (et al.)

ἤδη γάρ ποτ' ἐγὼ γενόμην κοῦρός τε κόρη τε
θάμνος τ' οἰωνός τε καὶ ἔξαλος ἔμπορος ἰχθύς.

2 ἔμπορος Hipp. *Haer.* 1.3.2, Athen. *Deipn.* 8.69: ἔμπυρος
Diog. Laert. mss.: ἔλλοπος Clem. Alex. *Strom.* 6.24.3

D14 (B118) Clem. Alex. *Strom.* 3.14.2

κλαῦσά τε καὶ κώκυσα ἰδὼν ἀσυνήθεα χῶρον.

D15 (B119) Plut. *Exil.* 17 607C

ἐξ οἵης τιμῆς τε καὶ ὅσσου μήκεος ὄλβου
. . .

D12 (B142) Herculaneum Papyrus

Him [i.e. the exiled demon] **neither do the covered abodes of aegis-bearing Zeus Receive nor in any way the dense palace of Hades** . . .

The Transmigrations of Living Beings (D13–D20)

D13 (B117) Diogenes Laertius (et al.)

For as for me, once I was already both a youth and a girl, A bush and a bird, and a sea-leaping, voyaging fish.

D14 (B118) Clement of Alexandria, *Stromata*

I wept and wailed when I saw an unaccustomed place.

D15 (B119) Plutarch, *On Exile* (et al.)

Far from what honor and from what abundance of bliss

. . .

D16 (B120) Porph. *Antr.* 8, p. 61.19

παρά τε γὰρ Ἐμπεδοκλεῖ αἱ ψυχοπομποὶ δυνάμεις
λέγουσιν

   ἠλύθομεν τόδ᾿ ὑπ᾿ ἄντρον ὑπόστεγον – ∪ ∪ | – –

D17 (B124) Clem. Alex. *Strom.* 3.14.2 (et al.)

   ὦ πόποι, ὦ δειλὸν θνητῶν γένος, ὦ
      δυσάνολβον,
   τοίων ἔκ τ᾿ ἐρίδων ἔκ τε στοναχῶν ἐγένεσθε.

   1 ὦ δειλὸν Scaliger: ἢ δειλὸν Clem.   2 τοίων Porph.
Abst. 3.27, Timon Frag. 10.2 Di Marco: οἵων Clem.

D18 (B125) Clem. Alex. *Strom.* 3.14.2

   ἐκ μὲν γὰρ ζωῶν ἐτίθει νεκρὰ εἴδε᾿ ἀμείβων.

D19 (B126) Plut. *Esu carn.* 2.4 998C

   σαρκῶν ἀλλογνῶτι περιστέλλουσα χιτῶνι

D20 (B148) Plut. *Quaest. conv.* 5.8 683E

   ἀμφιβρότην χθόνα [cf. **R4**]

      The World of Opposites (D21–D24)

D21 (B122) Plut. *Tranquil. an.* 15 474B (et al.)

   ἔνθ᾿ ἦσαν Χθονίη τε καὶ Ἡλιόπη ταναῶπις,
   Δῆρίς θ᾿ αἱματόεσσα καὶ Ἁρμονίη θεμερῶπις,

D16 (B120) Porphyry, *The Cave of the Nymphs*

In Empedocles, the powers that accompany the souls say,

We have arrived under the roof of this cave . . .

D17 (B124) Clement of Alexandria, *Stromata* (et al.)

**Alas! Wretched race of mortals, miserable race!
From such kinds of strife and from such groans
are you born!**

D18 (B125) Clement of Alexandria, *Stromata*

**Out of living beings he produced dead forms,
proceeding to the exchange.**

D19 (B126) Plutarch, *On the Eating of Flesh*

**[Scil. She,[1]] enveloping in an unfamiliar cloak of
flesh** . . .

[1] The subject here is feminine, unlike the masculine in **D18**.

D20 (B148) Plutarch, *Table Talk*

man-enveloping earth [cf. **R4**]

The World of Opposites (D21–D24)

D21 (B122) Plutarch, *On the Tranquility of the Soul* (et al.)

**The Earthly was there, and the farsighted Sun-
eyed,
Bloody Combat and calm-seeing Harmony,**

Καλλιστώ τ' Αἰσχρή τε, Θόωσά τε Δηναίη τε,
Νημερτής τ' ἐρόεσσα μελάγκαρπός τ' Ἀσάφεια.

4 μελάγκαρπός τ' Plut. W (μελαγκάρποτ' RSN): μελάγ-
κουρός τ' Tzetz. In Aristoph. Prolog. 1.115: μελάγκορον τ'
Tzetz. Chil. 12.573

D22 (B123) Corn. *Theol.* 17

Φυσώ τε Φθιμένη τε, καὶ Εὐναίη καὶ Ἔγερσις,
Κινώ τ' Ἀστεμφής τε, πολυστέφανός τε
    Μεγιστώ
καὶ †Φορίη, Σοφή† τε καὶ Ὀμφαίη ∪ ∪ | – –

3 versus restitutus valde incertus (cf. **R97**)   φορίη NB:
φορίην PVLXW (-ιήν M): φορύνη G: Ἀφορίη Bergk   σόφη
N (sine acc.) BG: σοφήν PMLX: σομφήν V: Σωπή Bergk   ὀμφαίη NBG: ὀμφαίην PMVLX   Ἀφορίη τε Σόφη τε καὶ
Ὀμφαίη ⟨σκοτόεσσα⟩ Picot, alii alia

D23 (B116) Plut. *Quaest. conv.* 9.5 745C

– ∪ ∪ | – ∪ ∪ | – στυγέει δύστλητον Ἀνάγκην.

D24 (B121) Hierocl. *In Carm. Aur.* 24.2–3 (et al.)

– ∪ ∪ | – ∪ ∪ | – ∪ ∪ | – ∪ ἀτερπέα χῶρον,
ἔνθα Φόνος τε Κότος τε καὶ ἄλλων ἔθνεα
    Κηρῶν
Ἄτης ἀν λειμῶνα κατὰ σκότος ἠλάσκουσιν.

2 post. hunc vers. habet αὐχμηραί τε νόσοι καὶ σήψιες ἔργα
τε ρευστά Procl. In Crat. p. 97, quod secl. edd. plerique

**Beauty and Ugliness, Quickness and Slowness,
Lovely Infallibility and black-fruited
Indistinctness.**

D22 (B123) Cornutus, *Greek Theology*

**Growth and Perishing, and Sleep and
Awakeness,
And Movement and Immovability, and many-
crowned Excellence
And †*Phoriê, Sophê*†[1] and Utterance . . .**

[1] The text and meaning of these two terms are very uncertain
(the former might suggest 'filth,' the latter 'wisdom'), and the
whole verse is reconstituted from words that Cornutus could also
have derived from the context (cf. **R97**).

D23 (B116) Plutarch, *Table Talk*

. . . [scil. Grace?] **hates intolerable Necessity.**

D24 (B121) Hierocles, *Commentary on Pythagoras'
Golden Verses*

. . . **a joyless place,
Where Murder, Rage, and the tribes of the
other Death-divinities
Wander in darkness along the meadow of
Destruction** (*Atê*).[1]

[1] In Proclus' citation of this passage in his commentary on
Plato's *Cratylus,* there is an additional verse after v. 2: "The desic-
cating illnesses, the putrefactions and the works of flux."

---

3 ἀνὰ λειμῶνα mss., corr. Bentley: ἐνὶ λειμῶνι Procl. *In Remp.*
2.157   ἠλάσκουσι mss.: ἱλάσκονται Procl. *In Remp.* 2.157

The Reign of Cypris (D25–D26)

D25 (B128) Athen. *Deipn.* 12 510C (v. 1–7); Porph. *Abst.*
2.21.2–4 (v. 1–3, 4–7), 27 (v. 8–10) (et al.)

οὐδέ τις ἦν κείνοισιν Ἄρης θεὸς οὐδὲ Κυδοιμός
οὐδὲ Ζεὺς βασιλεὺς οὐδὲ Κρόνος οὐδὲ
   Ποσειδῶν,
ἀλλὰ Κύπρις βασίλεια ∪ | – ∪ ∪ | – ∪∪ | – –
τὴν οἵγ᾽ εὐσεβέεσσιν ἀγάλμασιν ἱλάσκοντο
5   γραπτοῖς τε ζώοισι μύροισί τε δαιδαλεόδμοις
σμύρνης τ᾽ ἀκρήτου θυσίαις λιβάνου τε
   θυώδους,
ξανθῶν τε σπονδὰς μελιτῶν ῥίπτοντες ἐς οὖδας·
ταύρων δ᾽ ἀκρήτοισι φόνοις οὐ δεύετο βωμός,
ἀλλὰ μύσος τοῦτ᾽ ἔσκεν ἐν ἀνθρώποισι
   μέγιστον,
10 θυμὸν ἀπορραίσαντας ἐέδμεναι ἠέα γυῖα.

2 Ζεὺς. . . Κρόνος Ath.: ὁ Ζεὺς . . . ὁ Κρόνος Porph.
7 ξανθῶν. . . μελιτῶν Ath.: ξουθῶν. . . μελιττῶν Porph.
8 ἀκρήτοισι Scaliger: ἀκρίτοισι Porph.: ἀκράτοισι Eus. *PE*
4.14.7: ἀρρήτοισι Fabriciuss   10 ἐέδμεναι Eus. (ἐσμεναι A),
Cyrill. Alex. *Jul.* 9 p. 972D Migne: ἐέλμεναι Porph.: ἐνέδμεναι
Diels

D26 (B130) Schol. in Nic. *Ther.* 452c, p. 185

ἦσαν δὲ κτίλα πάντα καὶ ἀνθρώποισι προσηνῆ,
θῆρές τ᾽ οἰωνοί τε, φιλοφροσύνη τε δεδήει.

EMPEDOCLES

The Reign of Cypris (D25–D26)

D25 (B128) Porphyry, *On Abstinence* (et al.)

> There was neither some Ares for them as a god
>   nor Tumult,
> Nor Zeus king nor Cronus nor Poseidon,
> But Cypris queen . . . [1]
> She it was whose favor they won with pious
>   images,
> Painted animals and artfully scented perfumes,   5
> Sacrifices of unmixed myrrh and of fragrant
>   incense,
> Casting onto the ground libations of blond
>   honey.
> The altar was not drenched with the unmixed
>   blood of bulls,
> But this was among men the greatest pollution:
> To rip out the life and to devour the noble   10
>   limbs.

[1] 'Cypris queen' is created on the model of 'Zeus king.' As the verse is incomplete, we cannot know whether these men had her as their god, or whether 'Cypris' governed another verb.

D26 (B130) Scholia on Nicander's *Theriaca*

> All were tame and gentle to human beings,
> Wild beasts and birds, and benevolence blazed
>   forth.

---

2 οἰωνοί Sturz: ἄνθρωποί mss.

377

The Rule of Life (D27–D35)

D27

a (B135) Arist. *Rhet.* 1.13 1373b14–16

[. . .] καὶ ὡς Ἐμπεδοκλῆς λέγει περὶ τοῦ μὴ κτείνειν τὸ ἔμψυχον· τοῦτο γὰρ οὐ τισὶ μὲν δίκαιον τισὶ δ᾽ οὐ δίκαιον,

ἀλλὰ τὸ μὲν πάντων νόμιμον διά τ᾽
εὐρυμέδοντος
αἰθέρος ἠνεκέως τέταται διά τ᾽ ἀπλέτου αὐγῆς.

b (ad B135) Cic. *Rep.* 3.11.19

Pythagoras et Empedocles unam omnium animantium condicionem iuris esse denuntiant clamantque inexpiabilis poenas impendere iis a quibus violatum sit animal.

D28 (B136) Sext. Emp. *Adv. Math.* 9.129

οὐ παύσεσθε φόνοιο δυσηχέος; οὐκ ἐσορᾶτε
ἀλλήλους δάπτοντες ἀκηδείῃσι νόοιο;

D29 (B137) Sext. Emp. *Adv. Math.* 9.129

μορφὴν δ᾽ ἀλλάξαντα πατὴρ φίλον υἱὸν ἀείρας

The Rule of Life (D27–D35)

D27

a (B135) Aristotle, *Rhetoric*

[. . .] and as Empedocles says with regard to not killing what possesses life: for it is not the case that this is rightful in some cases but not rightful in others,

> **But what is lawful for all, through the wide-ruling**
> **Aether it extends continuously and through the boundless light.**

b (ad B135) Cicero, *On the Republic*

Pythagoras and Empedocles assert that there is a single legal condition for all living beings and they proclaim that inexpiable punishments await those who have done violence to an animal.

D28 (B136) Sextus Empiricus, *Against the Natural Philosophers*

> **Will you not desist from evil-sounding murder? Do you not see**
> **That you are devouring each other in the carelessness of your mind?**

D29 (B137) Sextus Empiricus, *Against the Natural Philosophers*

> **The father, lifting up his own son who has changed shape,**

σφάζει ἐπευχόμενος μέγα νήπιος· οἱ δ᾽
   ἀπορεῦνται
λισσόμενον θύοντες, ὁ δ᾽ αὖ νήκουστος
   ὁμοκλέων
σφάξας ἐν μεγάροισι κακὴν ἀλεγύνατο δαῖτα.
5   ὡς δ᾽ αὔτως πατέρ᾽ υἱὸς ἑλὼν καὶ μητέρα
   παῖδες
θυμὸν ἀπορραίσαντε φίλας κατὰ σάρκας
   ἔδουσιν.

2 οἶδα πορεῦνται N: οἱ δὲ πορεῦνται LEϛ, corr. Diels
3 λισσόμενον NLE: λισσόμενοι ϛ   θύοντος Hermann:
θύοντας Wilamowitz   ὅδ᾽ ἀνήκουστος mss., corr. Diels
6 ἀπορραίσσαντα mss., corr. Karsten

D30 (B145) Clem. Alex. *Protr.* 27.3

τοιγάρτοι χαλεπῇσιν ἀλύοντες κακότησιν
οὔποτε δειλαίων ἀχέων λωφήσετε θυμόν.

D31 (B141) Aul. Gell. *Noct.* 4.11.9

δειλοί, πάνδειλοι, κυάμων ἄπο χεῖρας ἔχεσθαι.

D32 (B140) Plut. *Quaest. conv.* 3.1 646D

δάφνης – ∪ ∪ τῶν φύλλων ἀπὸ πάμπαν ἔχεσθαι

τῶν] Φοιβείων Diels

Cuts his throat, with a prayer—fool that he is!
    The others are at a loss
While they sacrifice the suppliant; but he [scil.
    the father], deaf to the shouts,
Has cut the throat and prepared an evil meal in
    his house.
In the same way, a son seizes his father and   5
    children their mother,
And ripping out their life they devour the flesh
    of their dear ones.

D30 (B145) Clement of Alexandria, *Protreptic*

And so, driven mad by terrible crimes,
You will never rest your heart (*thumos*) from
    dreadful sufferings.

D31 (B141) Aulus Gellius, *Attic Nights*

Wretched, completely wretched, keep your
    hands away from beans!

D32 (B140) Plutarch, *Table Talk*

Keep yourselves completely away from . . . bay
    leaves.

D33 (B144) Plut. *Cohib. ira* 16 464B

– ∪ ∪ | – ∪ ∪ | – ∪ ∪ *νηστεῦσαι κακότητος.*

D34 (B139) Porph. *Abst.* 2.31.5 (cf. **D76.5–6**)

οἴμ᾽ ὅτι οὐ πρόσθεν με διώλεσε νηλεὲς ἦμαρ,
πρὶν σχέτλι᾽ ἔργα βορᾶς περὶ χείλεσι
μητίσασθαι.

1 οἴμοι ὅτ᾽ mss., corr. Nauck

D35 (B143) Theon Sm. *Exp.*, p. 15.10–11

κρηνάων ἄπο πέντε ταμών ∪ ἀτειρέι (?) χαλκῷ

ταμών restit. Picot ex ταμόντα (cf. **R99**)   ἀτειρέι dett.
quidam: ἀκηρέι lect. incerta in ms. (in ras.)

The Different Forms of Excellence (D36–D40)
Among Animals and Plants (D36–D37)

D36 (B127) Ael. *Nat. anim.* 12.7 (et al.)

ἐν θήρεσσι λέοντες ὀρειλεχέες χαμαιεῦναι
γίγνονται, δάφναι δ᾽ ἐνὶ δένδρεσιν ἠυκόμοισιν.

1 ἐν θήρεσσι Schol. in Aphthonium (Hermann, *Orphica*,
p. 511): ἐν θηρσὶ δὲ Ael.   2 ἐνὶ Ael.: ἐν Schol. in Aphth.

D33 (B144) Plutarch, *On Controlling Anger*

> ... **to abstain from evil.**[1]

[1] These words might also have stood at the beginning of the line.

D34 (B139) Porphyry, *On Abstinence*

> **Alas, that the pitiless day did not destroy me earlier,**
> **Before I contrived terrible deeds of feeding around my lips!**[1]

[1] These two verses (the second in a slightly different form) appear in the poem on nature (**D76.5–6**).

D35 (B143) Theon of Smyrna, *On Mathematics Useful for Understanding Plato*

> **Cutting from five sources ... with unwearying (?) bronze**[1]

[1] Text and meaning uncertain. This might be a ritual prescription. Theon gives the verse an allegorical interpretation of an epistemological nature (cf. **R99**).

The Different Forms of Excellence (D36–D40)
Among Animals and Plants (D36–D37)

D36 (B127) Aelian, *On the Nature of Animals*

> **Among wild beasts, they become mountain-bedded earth-couched lions,**
> **And laurels among beautiful-tressed trees.**

D37 (26 Mansfeld/Primavesi) Hdn. *Prosod. cath.*, Cod. Vind. Hist. gr. 10 (p. 36 Primavesi-Alpers)

παρὰ μέντοι Ἐμπεδοκλεῖ ἐν β′ Καθαρμῶν

τῶν γὰρ ὅσα ῥίζαις μὲν ἐπασσυτέρ᾽, [α]ὐτὰ[ρ
ὕ]περθε
μανοτέροις ὄρπηξι καταστῇ‹ι› τηλεθάο[ντα].

1–2 rest. et corr. Primavesi-Alpers

Among Humans (D38–D40)
One Extraordinary Man (D38)

D38 (B129) Porph. *VP* 30

ἦν δέ τις ἐν κείνοισιν ἀνὴρ περιώσια εἰδώς,
ὃς δὴ μήκιστον πραπίδων ἐκτήσατο πλοῦτον
παντοίων τε μάλιστα σοφῶν ἐπιήρανος ἔργων·
ὁππότε γὰρ πάσῃσιν ὀρέξαιτο πραπίδεσσιν,
5 ῥεῖά γε τῶν ὄντων πάντων λεύσσεσκεν ἕκαστα
καί τε δέκ᾽ ἀνθρώπων καί τ᾽ εἴκοσιν αἰώνεσσιν.

Varieties of Human Excellence (D39)

D39 (B146) Clem. Alex. *Strom.* 4.150.1

εἰς δὲ τέλος μάντεις τε καὶ ὑμνοπόλοι καὶ
ἰητροί
καὶ πρόμοι ἀνθρώποισιν ἐπιχθονίοισι πέλονται,
ἔνθεν ἀναβλαστοῦσι θεοὶ τιμῇσι φέριστοι.

D37 (≠ DK) Herodian, *General Prosody*

In Empedocles in the second book of the *Purifications:*

> Among these, all the ones whose roots are dense
>   but who in height
> Grow blossoming out in scattered branchings.

Among Humans (D38–D40)
One Extraordinary Man (D38)

D38 (B129) Porphyry, *Life of Pythagoras*

> There was among them a man, knowledgeable
>   beyond measure,
> Who possessed the greatest wealth of organs of
>   thought (*prapides*),
> And most of all a master in wise deeds of all
>   kinds.
> For whenever he stretched forth with all his
>   organs of thought (*prapides*),
> Easily he saw each one of all the things that are   5
> In ten lives of men, and in twenty.[1]

[1] According to Porphyry (**R45**), Empedocles is referring to Pythagoras; cf. also **P10**.

Varieties of Human Excellence (D39)

D39 (B146) Clement of Alexandria, *Stromata*

> At the end they become seers, hymn singers,
>   doctors,
> And leaders (*promoi*) for humans on the earth,
> And then they blossom up as gods, the greatest
>   in honors.

The End of the Purifications*? (D40)*

D40 (B147) Clem. Alex. *Strom.* 5.122.3 (et al.)

ἀθανάτοις ἄλλοισιν ὁμέστιοι, αὐτοτράπεζοι
ἐόντες, ἀνδρείων ἀχέων ἀπόκληροι, ἀτειρεῖς.

1 αὐτοτράπεζοι Eus. *PE* 13.13.49: ἔν τε τραπέζαις Clem.
2 ἐόντες] εὔνιες Scaliger

The Poem on Nature (D41–D256)
Programmatic Statements (D41–D43)

D41 (B1) Diog. Laert. 8.60–61

[. . .] ὁ Παυσανίας [. . .] ᾧ δὴ καὶ τὰ Περὶ φύσεως
προσπεφώνηκεν οὕτως·

Παυσανίη, σὺ δὲ κλῦθι, δαΐφρονος Ἀγχίτου υἱέ

Ἀγχίτεω Diels

D42 (B2) Sext. Emp. *Adv. Math.* 7.123 (et al.)

στεινωποὶ μὲν γὰρ παλάμαι κατὰ γυῖα
    κέχυνται·
πολλὰ δὲ δείλ᾽ ἔμπαια, τά τ᾽ ἀμβλύνουσι
    μερίμνας.
παῦρον δὲ ζωῆσι βίου μέρος ἀθρήσαντες
ὠκύμοροι καπνοῖο δίκην ἀρθέντες ἀπέπταν

3 δὲ mss.: δ᾽ ἐν Wilamowitz   ἀθρήσαντος LEABR:
ἀθροίσαντος NV, corr. Scaliger: ἀθροίσαντες Bollack

The End of the Purifications? *(D40)*

D40 (B147) Clement of Alexandria, *Stromata*

> **Sharing the hearth with other immortals, sitting**
> **at the same table,**
> **Without any share in men's sufferings,**
> **indestructible.**[1]

[1] The participle *eontes* ('being') has the grammatical func-
tional of a copulative; but its prominent position in enjambment
at the beginning of the line may further suggest the permanence
of this condition.

The Poem on Nature (D41–D256)
Programmatic statements (D41–D43)

D41 (B1) Diogenes Laertius

[. . .] Pausanias [. . .] to whom he has addressed his *On
Nature* as follows:

> **Pausanias, listen, you, son of wise-minded**
> **Anchitus**

D42 (B2) Sextus Empiricus, *Against the Logicians*

> **For narrow are the resources spread out along**
> **the limbs,**
> **And numerous the miseries that break in,**
> **blunting the thoughts.**
> **Having seen in their existences (*zôê*) only a small**
> **part of life (*bios*),**
> **They fly off, swift-fated, borne along like smoke,**

5   αὐτὸ μόνον πεισθέντες, ὅτῳ προσέκυρσεν
    ἕκαστος
    πάντοσ᾽ ἐλαυνόμενοι. τὸ δ᾽ ὅλον ⟨τίς ἄρ᾽⟩
    εὔχεται εὑρεῖν;
    οὕτως οὔτ᾽ ἐπιδερκτὰ τάδ᾽ ἀνδράσιν οὔτ᾽
    ἐπακουστά
    οὔτε νόῳ περιληπτά. σὺ ⟨δ᾽⟩ οὖν, ἐπεὶ ὧδ᾽
    ἐλιάσθης,
    πεύσεαι· οὐ πλεῖόν γε βροτείη μῆτις ὄρωρεν.

6 ⟨τίς ἄρ᾽⟩ Fränkel: ⟨πᾶς⟩ Bergk, alii alia
8 ⟨δ᾽⟩ Bergk   9 πλεῖόν γε] πλέον ἠὲ Diels

D43 (B111) Diog. Laert. 8.59 (et al.)

    φάρμακα δ᾽ ὅσσα γεγᾶσι κακῶν καὶ γήραος
    ἄλκαρ
    πεύσῃ, ἐπεὶ μούνῳ σοὶ ἐγὼ κρανέω τάδε πάντα.
    παύσεις δ᾽ ἀκαμάτων ἀνέμων μένος οἵ τ᾽ ἐπὶ
    γαῖαν
    ὀρνύμενοι πνοιαῖσι καταφθινύθουσιν ἀρούρας·
5   καὶ πάλιν, ἢν κ᾽ ἐθέλῃσθα, παλίντιτα πνεύματ᾽
    ἐπάξεις·
    θήσεις δ᾽ ἐξ ὄμβροιο κελαινοῦ καίριον αὐχμὸν
    ἀνθρώποις, θήσεις δὲ καὶ ἐξ αὐχμοῖο θερείου

1–3 desunt in B   3 παύσεις P¹: παύσῃ F   ἀκα-
μάτων P: ἐκ καμάτων F   4 ἀρούρας Clem. Alex. Strom.
6.30.1: ἄρουραν mss.

Convinced of whatever one thing each one of
    them has encountered, 5
Driven in every direction. But the whole, ‹who
    then› boasts that he has found it?
Thus these things are neither seen by men nor
    heard
Nor grasped by the mind (*noos*). But you, since
    you have withdrawn here,
You will learn; never has human intelligence
    (*mêtis*) soared further.

D43 (B111) Diogenes Laertius

As many as are the remedies for ills, and
    protection against old age—
You will learn them, since for you alone I myself
    will accomplish all this.
You will stop the force of tireless winds that,
    rushing down
Onto the earth, destroy the fields with their
    blasts;
And in turn, if you wish, you will bring back 5
    breezes in requital.
Out of a black rain cloud you will make an
    opportune dryness
For human beings, and you will also make out
    of a summer dryness

---

6 θήσεις F: τής εἰς B: στήσεις Ps   7 θερείου rec.: θε-
ρείοις F¹: θερίοις BP¹(Q)

ῥεύματα δενδρεόθρεπτα, τά τ' αἰθέρι ναιήσονται,
ἄξεις δ' ἐξ Ἀίδαο καταφθιμένου μένος ἀνδρός.

8 τάτ' αἰθέρι ναιήσονται P¹(Q): ταταιθεριναίης ὄντα B:
τάτε θέρει ναήσονται F: τάτ' ἐν θέρει ἔσονται Sud. A.3242:
τά τ' αἰθέρι ἀίσσονται Wilamowitz: τά τ' αἰθέρι ναιετάουσιν
Bollack

The Form of Empedocles' Poem (D44–D47)

D44 (B3) Sext. Emp. *Adv. Math.* 7.125 (et al.)

ἀλλὰ θεοὶ τῶν μὲν μανίην ἀποτρέψατε
γλώσσης,
ἐκ δ' ὁσίων στομάτων καθαρὴν ὀχετεύσατε
πηγήν.
καὶ σέ, πολυμνήστη λευκώλενε παρθένε Μοῦσα,
ἄντομαι, ὧν θέμις ἐστὶν ἐφημερίοισιν ἀκούειν,
5   πέμπε παρ' Εὐσεβίης ἐλάουσ' εὐήνιον ἅρμα.
μηδέ σέ γ' εὐδόξοιο βιήσεται ἄνθεα τιμῆς
πρὸς θνητῶν ἀνελέσθαι, ἐφ' ᾧ θ' ὁσίης πλέον
εἰπεῖν
θάρσεϊ—καὶ τότε δὴ σοφίης ἐπ' ἄκροισι θοάζει.
ἀλλ' ἄγ' ἄθρει πάσῃ παλάμῃ, πῇ δῆλον
ἕκαστον,

1 ἀποτρέψατε Stephanus: ἀπετρέψατε mss.
2 ὀχετεύσατε Stephanus: ὠχεύσατε N: ἐχεύσατε E: ὀχεύ-
σατε L⌐   7 ἐφ' ᾧ θ' ὁσίης Clem. Alex. *Strom.* 5.59.3: ἐφω-
θοείης mss.

EMPEDOCLES

**Streams nourishing trees that will dwell in the aether,
And you will bring out of Hades the strength of a man who has died.**

The Form of Empedocles' Poem (D44–D47)

D44 (B3) Sextus Empiricus, *Against the Logicians*

**But, gods, turn aside from my tongue their madness
And draw forth from pious lips a pure stream.
And you, Muse, much-wooed, white-armed virgin,
I beg you: the words that it is permitted for ephemeral beings to hear,
Send them from Piety while you drive the rein-obeying chariot.**   5
As for you [i.e. Pausanias], **may she** [i.e. the Muse]
**not compel you to gather the flowers
Of glorious honor from mortals, so as to speak more than is sanctioned** (*hosiê*),
In rash audacity: it is then indeed that she sits enthroned on the heights of wisdom (*sophiê*).[1]
But come, consider with every resource in what way each thing is evident,

[1] Lines 5–7 are difficult. We take Empedocles to be leaving open the possibility of a Muse deprived of wisdom—the one who has inspired other poets.

---

8 θοάζει mss. (et Procl. *In Tim.* 106F): θοάζειν Hermann: θοάσσεις Karsten   9 ἀλλ᾽ ἄγ᾽ ἄθρει πάσῃ Bergk: ἀλλὰ γὰρ ἄθρει πᾶς mss.

10   μήτε τιν' ὄψιν ἔχων πίστει πλέον ἢ κατ' ἀκουήν
      ἢ ἀκοὴν ἐρίδουπον ὑπὲρ τρανώματα γλώσσης,
      μήτε τι τῶν ἄλλων, ὁπόση πόρος ἐστὶ νοῆσαι,
      γυίων πίστιν ἔρυκε, νόει θ' ᾗ δῆλον ἕκαστον.

D45 (B25) Schol. in Plat. *Gorg.* 498e, et al.

   – ∪ ∪ | – καὶ δὶς γάρ, ὃ δεῖ, καλόν ἐστιν
   ἐνισπεῖν.

   ἐνισπεῖν] ἀκοῦσαι Plut. *Non posse suav.* 24 1103F

D46 (B24) Plut. *Def. orac.* 15 418C

   – ∪ ∪ | – κορυφὰς ἑτέρας ἑτέρῃσι προσάπτων
   μύθων, μήτε λέγειν ἀτραπὸν μίαν – ∪ ∪ | – –

   1 ἑτέρῃσι] ἑτέραις (-σι) mss., corr. Scaliger
   2 μήτε λέγειν] μὴ τελέειν Knatz

D47 (B4) Clem. Alex. *Strom.* 5.18.4

   ἀλλὰ κακοῖς μὲν κάρτα πέλει κρατέουσιν
      ἀπιστεῖν.
   ὡς δὲ παρ' ἡμετέρης κέλεται πιστώματα
      Μούσης,
   γνῶθι διατμηθέντος ἐνὶ σπλάγχοισι λόγοιο.

   1 πέλει] μέλει Schwartz   3 διατμηθέντος ms.: διασση-
   θέντος Diels: διατμισθέντος Wilamowitz

Without holding some vision in greater trust   10
    than what accords with hearing (*akouê*),
Nor a resonating sound (*akoê*) as superior to the
    clarities of the tongue,
And from none of the other limbs, in whatever
    way it provides a path for thought (*noêsai*),
Withhold your trust, but think (*noei*) in whatever
    way each thing is evident.

D45 (B25) Scholia on Plato's *Gorgias*

    . . . for it is a fine thing to state even twice what
    is fitting.

D46 (B24) Plutarch, *The Obsolescence of Oracles*

        . . . fitting onto each other the peaks
Of words, not to utter only a single path . . .

D47 (B4) Clement of Alexandria, *Stromata*

But base people greatly distrust (*apistein*)
    authority;
Whereas you, in what way the proofs (*pistômata*)
    coming from our Muse command—
Know this in your deepest heart, once the
    argument has been cut up [i.e. analyzed].

Ontology (D48–D55)
Being (D48–D50)

D48 (B12) Phil. *Aetern. mund.* 5, p. 74.7–8 (v. 1–2); Ps.-Arist. *MXG* 2 975a3–4

ἔκ τε γὰρ οὐδάμ᾽ ἐόντος ἀμήχανόν ἐστι
    γενέσθαι
τό τ᾽ ἐὸν ἐξαπολέσθαι ἀνήνυστον καὶ ἄπυστον·
αἰεὶ γὰρ τῇ γ᾽ ἔσται ὅπη κέ τις αἰὲν ἐρείδῃ.

1 ἔκ τε γὰρ οὐδάμ᾽ ἐόντος Diels: ἔκ τοῦ γὰρ οὐδαμῇ ὄντος Phil.: ἐκ τοῦ μὴ ὄντος Ps.-Arist. (L): ἔκ τοῦ γὰρ μὴ ἐόντος Bollack   2 τό τε ὂν mss., corr. Bollack: καί τ᾽ ἐὸν Diels   ἐξαπολέσθαι (-εῖσθαι) Phil.: ἐξόλλυσθαι Ps.-Arist.   ἄπυστον Mangey: ἄπαυστον Phil.: ἄπρηκτον Ps.-Arist.   3 τῇ γ᾽ ἔσται Panzerbieter: θήσεσθαι mss.: θησεῖται Bollack

D49 (B13) Aët. 1.18.2 (Stob., Theod. *Cur.* 4.14) [περὶ κενοῦ]

οὐδέ τι τοῦ παντὸς κενεὸν πέλει οὐδὲ περισσόν.

οὐδέ τι Stob., Theod. KBL: οὐδέν τι Theod. MC (τι om. V)   κενεὸν Theod.: κενὸν Stob.

D50 (B14) Ps.-Arist. *MXG* 2 976b25

τοῦ παντὸς δ᾽ οὐδὲν κενεόν· πόθεν οὖν τί κ᾽
    ἐπέλθοι;

κενεόν R: κεν (lac. 4 litt.) L   πόθον mss., corr. Spalding

394

Ontology (D48–D55)
Being (D48–D50)

D48 (B12) Philo of Alexandria, *On the Eternity of the World;* Ps.-Aristotle, *On Melissus, Xenophanes, and Gorgias*

> For from what is not at all, it is impossible that
>   something come about,
> And that what is be completely destroyed is
>   unfeasible and unheard of;
> For, wherever one presses each time, each time
>   it will be there.

D49 (B13) Aëtius

> And nothing, in the whole, is empty nor in
>   excess.

D50 (B14) Ps.-Aristotle *On Melissus, Xenophanes, and Gorgias*

> Of the whole, nothing is empty; so from where
>   could anything come to be added to it?

Mixture, Birth, and Death (D51–D55)

D51 (B11) Plut. *Adv. Col.* 12 1113C

νήπιοι· οὐ γάρ σφιν δολιχόφρονές εἰσι
   μέριμναι,
οἳ δὴ γίγνεσθαι πάρος οὐκ ἐὸν ἐλπίζουσιν
ἤ τι καταθνήσκειν τε καὶ ἐξόλλυσθαι ἁπάντη.

3 πάντη mss., corr. Xylander

D52 (B15) Plut. *Adv. Col.* 12 1113D

οὐκ ἂν ἀνὴρ τοιαῦτα σοφὸς φρεσὶ μαντεύσαιτο,
ὡς ὄφρα μέν τε βιῶσι, τὸ δὴ βίοτον καλέουσι,
τόφρα μὲν οὖν εἰσίν, καί σφιν πάρα δειλὰ καὶ
   ἐσθλά,
πρὶν δὲ πάγεν τε βροτοὶ καὶ ‹ἐπεὶ› λύθεν, οὐδὲν
   ἄρ' εἰσίν.

3 δεινὰ mss., corr. Bergk   4 ‹ἐπεὶ› λύθεν Reiske: λυ-
θέντ' mss.

D53 (B8) Aët. 1.30.1 (Ps.-Plut.) [περὶ φύσεως] (et al.)

ἄλλο δέ τοι ἐρέω· φύσις οὐδενός ἐστιν ἁπάντων
θνητῶν, οὐδέ τις οὐλομένου θανάτοιο τελευτή,
ἀλλὰ μόνον μῖξίς τε διάλλαξίς τε μιγέντων
ἐστί, φύσις δὲ βροτοῖς ὀνομάζεται
   ἀνθρώποισιν.

EMPEDOCLES

Mixture, Birth, and Death (D51–D55)

D51 (B11) Plutarch, *Against Colotes*

> The fools! They have no long-thinking concerns,
> Those who suppose that what was not before
>   comes about,
> Or that something dies and is completely
>   destroyed.

D52 (B15) Plutarch, *Against Colotes*

> A wise man would not surmise such things in his
>   mind:
> That so long as they live what they call a life,
> For so long they are, and evil things and good
>   ones are theirs,
> But that before mortals have coalesced and
>   ⟨*after*⟩ having dissolved, they are nothing.

D53 (B8) Aëtius

> Something else I will tell you: of nothing is
>   there birth, among all
> Mortal things, nor is there an ending coming
>   from baleful death,
> But only mixture and exchange of things mixed
> Exist, and 'birth' is a name given by mortal
>   humans.

---

1 ἁπάντων] ἐόντων Arist. *Metaph.* Δ4 1015a1: ἑκάστου Plut. *Adv. Col.* 10 1111F   2 οὐλομένου . . . τελευτή] οὐλομένη . . . γενέθλη Plut.   4 δὲ βροτοῖς] δ᾽ ἐπὶ τοῖς Arist. *Metaph.* Plut.

D54 (B9) Plut. *Adv. Col.* 11 1113A–B

οἱ δ' ὅτε μὲν κατὰ φῶτα μιγὲν φῶς αἰθέρι – –
ἢ κατὰ θηρῶν ἀγροτέρων γένος ἢ κατὰ θάμνων
ἠὲ κατ' οἰωνῶν, τότε μὲν τὸν – ∪ γενέσθαι·
εὖτε δ' ἀποκρινθῶσι, τὰ δ' αὖ δυσδαίμονα
πότμον,
5   ᾗ ⟨γε⟩ θέμις, καλέουσιν, ὁμῶς δ' ἐπίφημι καὶ
αὐτός.

1 μιγὲν φῶς αἰθέρι lac. 6–7 lit. E, 8 lit. B: μιγέντ' εἰς αἰθέρ'
ἵ⟨κωνται⟩ Diels: αἰθέριον ⟨βῇ⟩ Primavesi   3 post τὸν lac.
7 lit. E, 8 lit. B: τότε μὲν τὸ ⟨λέγουσι⟩ Reiske   4 ἀποκρι-
θῶσι mss.: corr. Panzerbieter   τὰ] τὸ Reiske   5 ᾗ (vel
ἡ vel ἦ) Plut. *Praec. Ger.* 28. 820F: εἶναι mss.: ἢ Diels: οὐ
Wilamowitz   ⟨γε⟩ Bollack: ⟨οὐ⟩ Bachet de Méziriac: ⟨ᾗ⟩
Wilamowitz   ὁμῶς nos: ὅμως vel ὅσω mss., Plut. 820F
plerique: νόμῳ Plut. 820F G[3]

D55 (B10) Plut. *Adv. Col.* 11 1113B

. . . θάνατον . . . ἀλοίτην

*The Four Elementary Roots and the Two
Fundamental Powers (D56–D65)*

D56 (< A33) Aët. 1.3.20 (Ps.-Plut.) [περὶ τῶν ἀρχῶν τί
εἰσιν]

Ἐμπεδοκλῆς [. . .] τέτταρα μὲν λέγει στοιχεῖα, πῦρ
ἀέρα ὕδωρ γῆν, δύο δ' ἀρχικὰς δυνάμεις, Φιλίαν τε
καὶ Νεῖκος· ὧν ἡ μέν ἐστιν ἑνωτικὴ τὸ δὲ διαιρετικόν.

D54 (B9) Plutarch, *Against Colotes*

**But they, when light mixed with aether in a
  human** (?) . . .
Or in the race of savage beasts or of bushes
Or of birds, then . . . **to be born;**
**But when they are separated apart, this in turn
  they call 'unfortunate destiny,'**
As is licit (*themis*)**, and I myself too apply it** [i.e.   5
this term] **in the same way.**[1]

[1] The text of this fragment is very corrupt.

D55 (B10) Plutarch, *Against Colotes*

. . . **death** . . . **vengeful**

*The Four Elementary Roots and the Two
Fundamental Powers (D56–D65)*

D56 (< A33) Aëtius

Empedocles [. . .] says that there are four elements (fire,
air, water, and earth) and two powers that are principles
(Love and Strife), of which the former unifies while the
latter divides.

D57 (B6) Aët. 1.3.20 (Ps.-Plut.) (et al.) [περὶ ἀρχῶν τι εἰσιν]

τέσσαρα τῶν πάντων ῥιζώματα πρῶτον ἄκουε·
Ζεὺς ἀργὴς Ἥρη τε φερέσβιος ἠδ᾿ Ἀϊδωνεύς
Νῆστίς θ᾿, ἣ δακρύοις τέγγει κρούνωμα
βρότειον.

1 τῶν Aët.; Sext. Emp. *Adv. Math.* 10.317; Clem. Alex. *Strom.*
6.17.3; Stob. 1.10.11a; Hippol. *Ref.* 7.29.3 et 10.7.3 et 4; Philop.
In Phys. 88.6 et 95.4–5: γὰρ Sext. Emp. *Adv. Math.* 9.362 et
10.315   2 ἀργὴς Sextus 9.362 et 10.315; Diog. Laert. 8.76
et alii: αἰθὴρ Aët.: ἀήρ Hippol. *Ref.* 10.7

D58 Simpl. *In Phys.*

a (ad B98) p. 32.3–4

καλεῖ δὲ τὸ μὲν πῦρ καὶ Ἥφαιστον καὶ ἥλιον καὶ
φλόγα, τὸ δὲ ὕδωρ ὄμβρον, τὸν δὲ ἀέρα αἰθέρα.

b (ad B21) p. 159.10–12

[. . .] ἐπάγει ἑκάστου τῶν εἰρημένων τὸν χαρακτῆρα,
τὸ μὲν πῦρ ἥλιον καλῶν, τὸν δὲ ἀέρα αὐγὴν καὶ
οὐρανόν, τὸ δὲ ὕδωρ ὄμβρον καὶ θάλασσαν. λέγει δὲ
οὕτως· [. . . = **D77**].

D59 (B7) Hesych. A.441

ἀγέννητα· στοιχεῖα. παρὰ Ἐμπεδοκλεῖ.

    ἀγένητα Diels

400

D57 (B6) Aëtius

> **Hear first of all the four roots of all things:**
> **Zeus the gleaming, Hera who gives life,**
>   **Aidoneus,**
> **And Nêstis, who moistens with her tears the**
>   **mortal fountain.** [cf. **R90–R92**]

D58 Simplicius, *Commentary on Aristotle's* Physics

a (ad B98)

He also calls the fire **'Hephaestus'** [cf. **D192**], **'sun,'** and **'flame,'** the water **'rain,'** the air **'aether.'**

b (ad B21)

[. . .] he introduces the characterization of each of the things [scil. the four elements] that he has mentioned [scil. in **D73.232–66**], calling the fire **'sun,'** the air **'gleam'** and **'sky,'** and the water **'rain'** and **'sea.'** He speaks as follows: [. . . = **D77**].

D59 (B7) Hesychius, *Lexicon*

Unborn: the elements, in Empedocles.

D60 (B23) Simpl. *In Phys.*, p. 160.1–11

ὡς δ' ὁπόταν γραφέες ἀναθήματα ποικίλλωσιν
ἀνέρες ἀμφὶ τέχνης ὑπὸ μήτιος εὖ δεδαῶτε,
οἵτ' ἐπεὶ οὖν μάρψωσι πολύχροα φάρμακα
    χερσίν,
ἁρμονίῃ μείξαντε τὰ μὲν πλέω, ἄλλα δ'
    ἐλάσσω,
5   ἐκ τῶν εἴδεα πᾶσιν ἀλίγκια πορσύνουσι,
δένδρεά τε κτίζοντε καὶ ἀνέρας ἠδὲ γυναῖκας
θῆράς τ' οἰωνούς τε καὶ ὑδατοθρέμμονας ἰχθῦς
καί τε θεοὺς δολιχαίωνας τιμῇσι φερίστους·
οὕτω μή σ' ἀπάτη φρένα καινύτω ἄλλοθεν εἶναι
10 θνητῶν, ὅσσα γε δῆλα γεγάασιν ἄσπετα,
    πηγήν,
ἀλλὰ τορῶς ταῦτ' ἴσθι, θεοῦ πάρα μῦθον
    ἀκούσας.

2 ἀμφὶ ed. Ald.: ἄμφω mss.   δεδαῶτε DE: δεδαῶτες F
4 μείξαντε Diels: μίξαντε EF: μίξαντες D   6 κτίζοντες D

D61 (B71) Simpl. *In Cael.*, p. 530.1–4

εἰ δέ τι σοι περὶ τῶνδε λιπόξυλος ἔπλετο
    πίστις,
πῶς ὕδατος γαίης τε καὶ αἰθέρος ἠελίου τε

D60 (B23) Simplicius, *Commentary on Aristotle's* Physics

As when painters color many-hued sacrificial
   offerings,
Both[1] men, by reason of their skill, very expert
   in their art,
They grasp many-colored pigments in their
   hands,
Then, having mixed them in harmony, the ones
   more, the others less,
Out of these they compose forms similar to all   5
   things,
Creating trees, men, and women,
Wild beasts and birds, water-nourished fish,
And long-lived gods, the greatest in honors:
In this way may your mind not succumb to the
   error that it is from elsewhere [scil. than from
   the four elementary roots]
That comes the source of all the innumerable   10
   mortal things whose existence is evident,
But know this exactly, once you have heard the
   word of a god.[2]

[1] The form of the participles in lines 4 and 6 suggests that
Empedocles is speaking about two painters.   [2] Perhaps the
Muse, perhaps Empedocles himself.

D61 (B71) Simplicius, *Commentary on Aristotle's* On the
Heavens

If your belief (*pistis*) about these things were
   ever lacking in firmness—
How from water, earth, aether, and sun

403

κιρναμένων εἴδη τε γενοίατο χροιά τε θνητῶν
τοῖ᾽ ὅσα νῦν γεγάασι συναρμοσθέντ᾽ Ἀφροδίτῃ,
. . .

D62 (cf. B19) Plut. *Prim. frig.* 16 952B (cf. **R93**)

a

Νεῖκός τ᾽ οὐλόμενον ∪ ∪ | – ∪ ∪ | – ∪ ∪ | – – [=
D73.250]

τ᾽ om. Plut., restituerunt edd. ex **EMP. D73.250**

b

– ∪ ∪ | – ∪ ∪ | – ∪ ∪ | – σχεδύνην Φιλότητα

D63 (B16) (Ps.-?) Hippol. *Ref.* 6.25.1

ἦ γὰρ καὶ πάρος ἦν ⟨τε⟩ καὶ ἔσσεται, οὐδέ
ποτ᾽, οἴω,
τούτων ἀμφοτέρων κενεώσεται ἄσπετος αἰών.

1 ἦ Miller: ἦν P: εἰ H et Hipp. 7.29 (P)   ἦν καὶ mss.,
corr. Duncker-Schneidewin   οὐδέ ποτ᾽ οἴω Hipp. 7.29 (H):
ἔσται οὐδέπω τοίω mss. et Hipp. 7.29 (P)   2 ἄσπετος
Miller: ἄσβεστος Hipp.

D64 (cf. B151) Plut. *Amat.* 13 756E

. . . ζείδωρον . . .

Mixed together, the forms and colors of mortal
    things come about,
As they all exist now, fitted together by
    Aphrodite,
. . .

D62 (cf. B19) Plutarch, *On the Principle of Cold* (cf.
R93)

a

And baleful Strife . . .

b

       . . . Love that holds together[1]

[1] The words might also have occurred earlier in the line.

D63 (B16) (Ps.-?) Hippolytus, *Refutation of all Heresies*

For certainly, she [scil. Love or Strife] was before
    and she will be, and never, I suppose,
Will the innumerable length of lifetime be
    empty of both of these.

D64 (cf. B151) Plutarch, *Dialogue on Love*

. . . life-giving [scil. Aphrodite] . . .

D65 (cf. B18) Plut. *Is. et Os.* 48 370D

Ἐμπεδοκλῆς δὲ τὴν ἀγαθουργὸν ἀρχὴν Φιλότητα καὶ Φιλίαν, πολλάκις δ᾽ Ἁρμονίαν καλεῖ θεμερῶπιν.

The Operation of the Two Fundamental Powers:
Unifications and Affinities (D66–D72)

D66 (< 146 Bollack) Arist. *EN* 8.2 1155b6–8

[. . .] ἐξ ἐναντίας δὲ τούτοις ἄλλοι τε καὶ Ἐμπεδοκλῆς, τὸ γὰρ ὅμοιον τοῦ ὁμοίου ἐφίεσθαι.

D67 (B37) Arist. *GC* 2.6 333b1–2

αὔξει δὲ χθὼν μὲν σφέτερον γένος, αἰθέρα δ᾽ αἰθήρ.

γένος ELMWF: δέμας HJ¹V

D68 (B90) Plut. *Quaest. conv.* 5.8.2 683E (et al.)

ὣς γλυκὺ μὲν γλυκὺ μάρπτε, πικρὸν δ᾽ ἐπὶ πικρὸν ὄρουσεν,
ὀξὺ δ᾽ ἐπ᾽ ὀξὺ ἔβη, δαερὸν δ᾽ ἐποχεῖτο δαηρῷ.

1 post μὲν hab. ἐπὶ Plut., om. Macrobius *Sat.* 7.5.17
2 δαερὸν δ᾽ ἐποχεῖτο δαηρῷ Diels: δαλερὸν δαλεροῦ λαβέτως Plut.: θερμὸν δ᾽ ἐποχεύετο θερμῷ Macr.: δαλερὸν δαλερῷ δ᾽ ἐποχεῦτο Karsten: ἀλερὸν δ᾽ ἐποχεύεθ᾽ ἀληρῷ Bollack

D65 (cf. B18) Plutarch, *On Isis and Osiris*

Empedocles calls the principle that produces what is good
Love (*Philotês*) and **Friendship** (*Philiê*), and often **calm-
seeing Harmony.**

The Operation of the Two Fundamental Powers:
Unifications and Affinities (D66–D72)[1]

[1] The six passages in this section certainly belonged to different episodes of the history of the world, but it is difficult or impossible to assign a precise place to them. We collect them here
because they illustrate a fundamental principle of Empedocles'
physics.

D66 (≠ DK) Aristotle, *Nicomachean Ethics*

[. . .] others, including Empedocles [scil. express a view]
the opposite to these [i.e. Euripides and Heraclitus, cf.
HER. D62]: for [scil. they say that] the similar desires the
similar.

D67 (B37) Aristotle, *On Generation and Corruption*

Earth increases its own kind, and aether aether.

D68 (B90) Plutarch, *Table Talk*

**Thus the sweet seized hold of the sweet, the
bitter rushed upon the bitter,
The pungent mounted the pungent, and the hot
(?) rode upon the hot (?).**

EARLY GREEK PHILOSOPHY V

D69 (B91) Alex. (?) *Quaest.* 2.23, p. 72.26

ὕδωρ οἴνῳ μᾶλλον ἐνάρθμιον, αὐτὰρ ἐλαίῳ
οὐκ ἐθέλει ∪ ∪ | – ∪ ∪ | – ∪ ∪ | – ∪ ∪ | – –

ὕδωρ οἴνῳ μᾶλλον] οἴνῳ <μὲν γὰρ> μᾶλλον coni. Diels,
qui ὕδωρ Emped. abiud. et Alex. attrib.   ἐναρίθμιον mss.,
corr. Karsten

D70 (B93) Plut. *Def. orac.* 41 433B

βύσσῳ δὲ γλαυκῆς †κρόκου† καταμίσγεται
ἀκτίς.

κρόκου F: κρόκον ΠΒ: κρόνου Gυ: κόκκος Diels: κόρκου
Bollack   ἀκτίς mss.: ἀκτῆς Wilamowitz

D71 (B34) Arist. *Meteor.* 4.4 382a1–2

ἄλφιτον ὕδατι κολλήσας ∪ ∪ | – ∪ ∪ | – –

D72 (B33) Plut. *Amic. mult.* 5 95A

ὡς δ' ὅτ' ὀπὸς γάλα λευκὸν ἐγόμφωσεν καὶ
ἔδησε

. . .

D69 (B91) Alexander of Aphrodisias, *Natural Questions*

> Water is more adapted to wine, but with olive
> oil
> It does not want [scil. probably: to mix]

D70 (B93) Plutarch, *The Obsolescence of Oracles*

> With linen is mixed the splendor of gleaming
> saffron (?).

D71 (B 34) Aristotle, *Meteorology*

> Having blended barley meal with water . . .

D72 (B33) Plutarch, *On the Number of Friends*

> As when fig juice curdles white milk and binds it
> . . .

The Alternation of Becoming (D73–D86)
Remains of the Original Sequence of the
Poem (D73–D74)

D73 (≠ DK) P. Strasb. gr. Inv. 1665–66, v. 232–308, ed.
Primavesi 2008;[1] v. 233–66 = B17 DK (Simpl. *In Phys.*,
pp. 158.1–159.4 et al.); v. 301–8 = B20 DK (Simpl. *In
Phys.*, p. 1124.12–18)

233
[B17.1]

δίπλ᾽ ἐρέω· τοτὲ μὲν γὰρ ἓν ηὐξήθη μόνον εἶναι
ἐκ πλεόνων, τοτὲ δ᾽ αὖ διέφυ πλέον᾽ ἐξ ἑνὸς
εἶναι.

235

δοιὴ δὲ θνητῶν γένεσις, δοιὴ δ᾽ ἀπόλειψις·
τὴν μὲν γὰρ πάντων ξύνοδος τίκτει τ᾽ ὀλέκει τε,

[B17.5]

ἡ δὲ πάλιν διαφυομένων θρεφθεῖσα διέπτη.
καὶ ταῦτ᾽ ἀλλάσσοντα διαμπερὲς οὐδαμὰ λήγει,
ἄλλοτε μὲν Φιλότητι συνερχόμεν᾽ εἰς ἓν
ἅπαντα,

240

ἄλλοτε δ᾽ αὖ δίχ᾽ ἕκαστα φορεύμενα Νείκεος
ἔχθει.

240a

⟨οὕτως ᾗ μὲν ἓν ἐκ πλεόνων μεμάθηκε
φύεσθαι,⟩

[1] The papyrus, which contains the remains of the end of Fr.
B17 DK and of what follows it, has in the margin a numerical
indication next to verse 300 that permits, for this fragment, exact
numbering of the verses of the poem. This numbering is
reproduced in the margins, as well as the correspondence with
the verses previously known. The difference for verses 233–240a
from the numbering of Primavesi's edition, which begins with

The Alternation of Becoming (D73–D86)
Remains of the Original Sequence of the
Poem (D73–D74)

D73 (≠ DK) Strasbourg Papyrus; (B17, B20) Simplicius,
Commentary on Aristotle's Physics

Twofold is what I shall say: for at one time they [i.e. the elements] **grew to be only one**	233 [B17.1]
Out of many, at another time again they separate to be many out of one.	
And double is the birth of mortal things, double their death.	235
For the one [i.e. birth] **is both born and destroyed by the coming together of all things,**	
While the other inversely, when they are separated, is nourished and flies apart (?).	[B17.5]
And these [scil. the elements] **incessantly exchange their places continually,**	
Sometimes by Love all coming together into one,	
Sometimes again each one carried off by the hatred of Strife.	240
⟨**Thus insofar as they have learned to grow as one out of many,**⟩	240a

---

verse 232, is due to our designating 240a as the verse inserted by
the editors, which he numbers 240.

236 ξύνοδος Martin-Primavesi (cf. v. 294, 300): σύνοδος
Simpl.

237 θρεφθεῖσα Panzerbieter: θρυφθεῖσα Simpl. F: δρυφθεῖσα Simpl. DE   διέπτη Scaliger: δρέπτη Simpl.

240a hunc versum (= **D77b.**8) post Bergk add. edd. plerique

[B17.10]   ἠδὲ πάλιν διαφύντος ἑνὸς πλέον᾽ ἐκτελέθουσι,
     τῆι μὲν γίγνονταί τε καὶ οὔ σφισιν ἔμπεδος
      αἰών·
     ἧι δὲ διαλλάσσοντα διαμπερὲς οὐδαμὰ λήγει,
     ταύτηι δ᾽ αἰὲν ἔασιν ἀκίνητοι κατὰ κύκλον.

245   ἀλλ᾽ ἄγε μύθων κλῦθι· μάθη γάρ τοι φρένας
     αὔξει·
[B17.15]   ὡς γὰρ καὶ πρὶν ἔειπα πιφαύσκων πείρατα
     μύθων,
     δίπλ᾽ ἐρέω· τοτὲ μὲν γὰρ ἓν ηὐξήθη μόνον εἶναι
     ἐκ πλεόνων, τοτὲ δ᾽ αὖ διέφυ πλέον᾽ ἐξ ἑνὸς
     εἶναι,
     πῦρ καὶ ὕδωρ καὶ γαῖα καὶ ἠέρος ἄπλετον ὕψος,
250   Νεῖκός τ᾽ οὐλόμενον δίχα τῶν, ἀτάλαντον
     ἁπάντηι,
[B17.20]   καὶ Φιλότης ἐν τοῖσιν, ἴση μῆκός τε πλάτος τε·
     τὴν σὺ νόωι δέρκευ, μηδ᾽ ὄμμασιν ἧσο
     τεθηπώς·
     ἥτις καὶ θνητοῖσι νομίζεται ἔμφυτος ἄρθροις,

241 ἠδὲ Karsten: ἧι δὲ Simpl.   244 ἀκίνητον Stein
245 μάθη γάρ τοι Bergk: μέθη γάρ τοι Simpl. DE: μέθυ γάρ
τοι Simpl. F: μάθησις γὰρ Stob. 2.31.6   249 ἠέρος Simpl.,
Sext. Emp. Adv. Math. 9.10, Athenag. 22: αἰθέρος Plut. Adul.
63C, Clem. Alex Strom. 6.17   ἄπλετον Simpl. Clem.:
ἤπιον Plut. Sext. Athenag.   250 ἁπάντηι Sext. (bis),
Hippol. Ref. 10.7: ἕκαστον Simpl. (bis)   252 δέρκευ Clem.
Alex. Strom. 5.15: δέρκου Simpl. Plut.

And inversely, the one separating again, they end up being many,   [B17.10]

To that extent they become, and they do not have a steadfast lifetime;

But insofar as they incessantly exchange their places continually,

To that extent they always are, immobile[1] in a circle.

But come now, listen to my words: for learning will make your mind (*phrenes*) grow.   245

For as I already said, when I was indicating clearly the boundaries of my words,   [B17.15]

Twofold is what I shall say: for at one time they grew to be only one

Out of many, at another time again they separate to be many out of one,

Fire, water, earth, and the immense height of air;

And baleful Strife is separate from them, equivalent everywhere,   250

And Love (*Philotês*) in them, equal in length and in breadth.   [B17.20]

Look you upon her with your mind (*noos*)—and do not sit there with astounded eyes—

She who mortals too think is implanted in their joints (*arthra*),[2]

---

[1] In the masculine, thereby recalling that the elements are gods.

[2] There may be a reference to the penis in particular.

413

τῆι τε φίλα φρονέουσι καὶ ἄρθμια ἔργα
τελοῦσι,

255   Γηθοσύνην καλέοντες ἐπώνυμον ἠδ᾽ Ἀφροδίτην·
[B17.25]   τὴν οὔ τις μετὰ τοῖσιν ἑλισσομένην δεδάηκε
θνητὸς ἀνήρ· σὺ δ᾽ ἄκουε λόγου στόλον οὐκ
ἀπατηλόν.

ταῦτα γὰρ ἰσά τε πάντα καὶ ἥλικα γένναν
ἔασι,
τιμῆς δ᾽ ἄλλης ἄλλο μέδει, πάρα δ᾽ ἦθος
ἑκάστωι,

260   ἐν δὲ μέρει κρατέουσι περιπλομένοιο χρόνοιο.
[B17.30]   καὶ πρὸς τοῖς οὔτ᾽ ἄρ τι ἐπιγίγνεται οὐδ᾽
ἀπολήγει·
εἴ τε γὰρ ἐφθείροντο διαμπερές, οὐκ ἂν ἔ]τ᾽
ἦσα⌊ν⌋. [P. Strasb. a(i), init.]
⌊τοῦτο δ᾽ ἐπαυξήσειε τὸ πᾶν τί κε, καὶ πόθ⌋ε̣ν̣
ἐλ̣⌊θόν;⌋
⌊πῆι δέ κε κἀξαπόλοιτο, ἐπεὶ τῶνδ᾽ οὐδ⌋ὲ̣ν
ἐρῆ⌊μον;⌋

265   ⌊ἀλλ᾽ αὔτ᾽ ἐστιν ταῦτα, δι᾽ ἀλλήλων⌋ γε θέοντα
[B17.35]   ⌊γίγνεται ἄλλοτε ἄλλα καὶ ἠνεκὲ⌋ς αἰὲν ὁμοῖα.
[B17, fin.]

256 μετὰ τοῖσιν Brandis: μετ᾽ ὄσ(σ)οισιν Simpl.
257 λόγου Simpl. DE: λόγων Simpl. F
261 ἄρτι Simpl. DE: ἀρ Simpl. F: ἄρ τ᾽ Janko
262 οὐκ ἂν ἔτ᾽ Pap.: οὐκέτ᾽ ἂν Simpl.

And by whom they have loving thoughts and
    perform deeds of union (*arthmia*),
Calling her 'Joy' as byname and 'Aphrodite';   255
That it is she who is going around among them   [B17.25]
    [i.e. the elements],[3] no mortal man
Knows this. But as for you, listen to the
    undeceitful voyage of my discourse.

For these are all equal and identical in age,
But each one presides over a different honor,
    each one has its own character,
And by turns they dominate while the time   260
    revolves.
And besides these, nothing at all is added nor is   [B17.30]
    lacking;
For if they perished entirely, they would no
    longer be. [beginning of Pap. Str.]
And this whole here, what could increase it, and
    coming from where?
And how could it be completely destroyed, since
    nothing is empty of these?
But these are themselves, but running the ones   265
    through the others
They become now this, now that, and each time   [B17.35]
    are continually similar. [end of B17]

---

[3] The manuscripts have 'in the eyes'; the editors most often
correct the text.

---

264 κἀξαπόλοιτο Martin-Primavesi: καὶ κῆρυξ ἀπόλοιτο
Simpl. (καὶ om. F: κῆρυξ om. ed. Ald.): κἠξαπόλοιτο Diels
265 γε Pap.: δέ Simpl.

[‒ ◡ ◡ | ‒ ◡ ◡ | ‒ ◡ συνερχό]μεθ᾽ εἰς ἕνα κόσμον,

[‒ ◡ ◡ | ‒ ◡ ◡ | ‒ διέφυ πλέ]ον᾽ ἐξ ἑνὸς εἶναι,

⌊ἐξ ὧν πάνθ᾽ ὅσα τ᾽ ἦν ὅσα τ᾽ ἐσθ᾽ ὅ⌋σα τ᾽
    ἔσσετ᾽ ὀπίσσω·

270 ⌊δένδρεά τ᾽ ἐβλάστησε καὶ ἀνέρες⌋ ἠδὲ
    γυναῖκες,

⌊θ⌋ῆρές τ᾽ οἰωνοί ⌊τε καὶ⌋ ὑδατοθρ⌊έμμονες
    ἰχθῦς⌋ [P. Strasb. a(ii)]

⌊κ⌋αί τε θεοὶ δολιχα⌊ίων⌋ες τιμῆισ[ι φέριστοι.

ἐ]ν τῆι δ᾽ ἀίσσοντα [διαμπ]ερὲς οὐδ[αμὰ λήγει
π]υκνῆισιν δίνηισ[ιν ◡ ◡ | ‒ ◡ ◡ | ‒ ◡ ◡] τ . [‒ ‒

275 ν]ωλεμές, οὐδέ πο[τ᾽ | ‒ ◡ ◡ | ‒ ◡ ◡ | ‒ ◡ ◡ | ‒ ‒,

πολλ]οὶ δ᾽ αἰῶνες πρότερ[οι ◡ ◡ | ‒ ◡ ◡ | ‒ ‒,

πρὶν] τούτων μεταβῆνα[ι ◡ | ‒ ◡ ◡ | ‒ ◡ ◡ | ‒ ‒,

πά]ντηι δ᾽ ἀίσσον̣[τ]α διαμ[περὲς οὐδαμὰ λήγει·

οὔ]τε γὰρ ἠέλιος τ[◡ ◡] . ν .[◡ ◡ | οὔτε σελήνη

280 ὁρ]μῆ‹ι› τῆιδε γέμου̣[σά ◡ | ‒ ◡ ◡ | ‒ ◡ ◡ | ‒ ‒,

οὔ]τε τι τῶν ἄλλων [◡ ◡ | ‒ ◡ ◡ | ‒ ◡ ◡ | ‒ ‒

ἀλ]λὰ̣ μεταλλάσσον[τ᾽ ἀίσσ]ε̣ι κύκλωι [ἅπαντηι.

267 συνερχό]μεθ᾽ Pap.[1]: συνερχό]μεν᾽ Pap.[2]: ἀλλ᾽ ἐν μὲν
Φιλότητι συνερχό]μεθ᾽ εἰς ἕνα κόσμον Martin-Primavesi
    268 ἐν δ᾽ Ἔχθρηι γε πάλιν διέφυ πλέ]ον᾽ ἐξ ἑνὸς εἶναι
Martin-Primavesi   269–72a cf. Arist. *Metaph.* B.4 1000a29–
32 (cf. Ps.-Arist. *Mund.* 399b26–28); cf. B21.9–12 DK
    269 ἔσσετ᾽ Pap.: ἔσται Arist. *Metaph.* B4 1000a29
    272 τιμῆισ[ι φέριστοι. Martin-Primavesi ex Simpl. *In Phys.*
33.17 et 159.24
    273 ἐ]ν τῆι Martin-Primavesi: πά]ντηι Trépanier

⟨*But under the rule of Love we come tog*⟩**ether into
one world**

⟨*While under that of Hatred inversely they separate
to be ma*⟩**ny out of one,**

**They, from which come all things that were, that
are, and that will be later:**

Trees have grown [scil. from these], **men and**   270
women,

Wild beasts and birds, water-nourished fish,

And long-lived gods, the greatest in honors.[4]

Under her [scil. Strife's] **rule,**[5] **they incessantly
shoot forth continually**

In dense eddies . . .

Without interruption, and never . . .   275

Many earlier lifetimes . . .

Before from these they go over . . .

⟨*And everywhere they incessantly*⟩ **shoot forth
con**⟨*tinually*⟩

For neither the sun . . .   ⟨. . . *nor the moon*⟩

Filled with this drive . . .   280

And none of the other things . . .

**But exchanging their places, they shoot forth
everywhere in a circle.**

---

[4] Lines 269–72 are cited by Aristotle at *Metaphysics* B4
1000a29–32.

[5] Plutarch (**D98**) gives what is probably a paraphrase of lines
273–287.

---

279 T[ιτά]ν prop. Martin-Primavesi   οὔτε σελήνη suppl.
Janko   280 ὁρ]μῆ⟨ι⟩ Janko: ὁρ]μὴ Primavesi

δὴ τότε] μὲν γὰρ γαῖα [ἀβ]άτη θέει ἠελ[ίου τε
– ◡] τόσην δὴ κα[ί ν]υν ἐπ' ἀνδράσι
τ[εκμήρασθαι·

285 ὣς δ' α]ὕτως τάδ[ε π]άντα δι' ἀλλήλων [θέει αἰεί,
κάλλο]υς τε ἄλλ' [ἔσχη]κε τόπους πλαγ[χθέντ' ◡
◡ | – –·

οὐ δή πω] μεσάτους τ[ι ἐσε]ρχόμεθ' ἐν μ[όνον
εἶναι.

ἀλλ' ὅτ]ε δὴ Νεῖκος [τ' ἀνυ]πέρβατα βέν[θε'
ἵκηται

δ[ίνη]ς, ἐν δὲ μέσ[ηι] Φ[ιλ]ότης στροφά[λιγγι
γένηται,

290 ἐν [τῆι] δὴ τάδε πάντα συνέρχεται ἓν [μόνον
εἶναι.

σπεῦ]δε δ' ὅπως μὴ μοῦνον ἀν' οὔατα [μῦθος
ἵκηται,

ἠδέ] μευ ἀμφὶς ἐόντα κλύων [ν]ημερτ[έα δέρκευ·
δεί]ξω σοι καὶ ἀν' ὄσσε ἵνα μείζονι σώμ[ατι
κύρει,

283 δὴ τό]τε Martin-Primavesi: ἀλλο]τὲ Primavesi
284 σφαῖρα] τόσην Martin-Primavesi
285 [θέει αἰεί Trépanier: [γε δραμόντα Primavesi: [τε θέε-
σκεν Martin-Primavesi: [προθέουσιν Janko
286 πλαγ[χθέντ' ἰδίους τε· Martin-Primavesi: πλαγ[χθέντα
καὶ ἄλλους Janko: πλαγ[χθέντα ἕκαστα Trépanier
292 [ν]ημερτ[έα δέρκευ· Martin-Primavesi: [ν]ημερτ[έα φρά-
ζευ· Janko

For at that time the earth runs untrodden, and
    the sun's
. . .⟩, **as big as men can** ⟨*infer*⟩;
In the same way all these things [scil. the   285
    elements] ⟨*always run*⟩ **through one another,**
And each one, as it wanders, occupies a
    different place . . .
We have ⟨*not yet*⟩ **arrived**[6] **in the center** ⟨*to be*
    only⟩ **one.**
⟨*But when*⟩ **Strife** ⟨*reaches*⟩ **the uncrossable**
    depths
Of the vortex, and Love comes to be in the
    center of the whirling,
Under her dominion all these things [i.e. the   290
    elements] **come together** ⟨*to be only*⟩ **one.**[7]

But make an effort so that ⟨*my word arrives*⟩ **not**
    only at your ears,
And, hearing from me what surrounds us,
    observe what does not deceive.
I shall show you by your eyes too, where they
    encounter a larger body,

---

[6] Perhaps the 'we,' which is sometimes identified with the
fallen divinities of the *Purifications,* simply represents the totality
of all composed things (including Empedocles and his disciple).
But the text of this lacunose line is very uncertain.

[7] **D75** returns to this point after the section beginning in line
291.

π]ρῶτον μὲν ξύνοδόν τε διάπτυξίν τͅε
γενέθλης,]

295 ὅσ[σ]α τε νῦν ἔτι λοιπὰ πέλει τούτοιο τ[όκοιο,
τοῦτο μὲν [ἂν] θηρῶν ὀριπλάγκτων ἀγ[ρότερ'
εἴδη,
τοῦτο δ' ἀν' ἀ[νθρώ]πων δίδυμον φῦμα, [τοῦτο
δ' ἀν' ἀνθέων
ῥιζοφόρων γέννημα καὶ ἀμπελοβάμ[ονα βότρυν.
ἐκ τῶν ἀψευδῆ κόμισαι φρενὶ δείγματα μ[ύθων·

300 ὄψει γὰρ ξύνοδόν τε διάπτυξίν τε γενέθλη͚ς]
πῆι Φιλότης Νεῖκός τε δι͙]άκτορα μη[∪ ∪ | – – [P.
Strasb. c]

[B20.1] [τοῦτο μὲν ἂν βροτέων] μελέων ἀρι͙[δείκετον
ὄγκον·]
[ἄλλοτε μὲν Φιλότητι συν]ερχόμεθ' ε͙ἰς ἓν
ἅπαντα]
[γυῖα, τὰ σῶμα λέλογχε βίου θη]λοῦντος ͚ἐν
ἀκμῆι,]

305 [ἄλλοτε δ' αὖτε κακῆισι διατμηθέντ' ἐρίδεσσιν]
[B20.5] [πλάζεται ἄνδιχ' ἕκαστα περὶ] ῥη͙γμῖνι βίοιο.]
[ὣς δ' αὔτως θάμνοισι καὶ ἰχ͙]θύ[σιν
ὑδρομελάθροις]

296 ἀγ[ρότερ' εἴδη Martin-Primavesi: ἄγ[ρια φῦλα Janko
297 [τοῦτο δ' ἀν' ἀνθέων Janko: [τοῦτο δ' ἀν' ἀγρῶν Martin-
Primavesi   301 πῆι Φιλότης Νεῖκός τε δι]άκτορα μή[δε'
ἔχωσι Primavesi: [. . . ἔργα δι]άκτορα μη[τίσασθαι Martin-
Primavesi: Νείκεος εἵνεκεν ἔργα δι]άκτορα μη[τιόωσας Janko

First the coming together and the unfolding of
    generation,
And all that still remains of this ⟨*birth*⟩:   295
This, among the savage ⟨*kinds*⟩ of mountain-
    wandering wild beasts,
This, among the double race of human beings,
    and this, among the species
Of root-bearing ⟨*flowers*⟩ and the vine-climbing
    ⟨*grape*⟩.
From these things, derive by your mind truthful
    proofs of my ⟨*words*⟩:
For you will see the coming together and   300
    unfolding of generation,
⟨*How Love and Strife . . .*⟩ crossing over.
This [scil. you will see] in the illustrious bulk of   [B20.1]
    mortal limbs:
Sometimes by Love we come together into one,
    all
Limbs that the body has received in the flower
    of blooming life;
Sometimes in turn, cut apart by evil quarrels,   305
Each one wanders separately in the surf of life.   [B20.5]
In the same way for bushes and water-dwelling
    fish

---

302 ἂν βροτέων Martin-Primavesi, Simpl. *In Phys.* 1124.12 AF:
μὲν ἀμβροτέρων Simpl. M: μὲν βροτέων Simpl. edd.: ἂμ βροτέων Bollack   303 συν]ερχόμεθ' Pap.[1]: συν]ερχόμεν' Pap.[2],
Simpl.   304 θηλοῦντος Pap.[ac]: θάλλοντος Pap.[pc]: θαλέθον-
τος Simpl. AM: θαλέοντος Simpl. F

⌊θηρσί τ᾽ ὀρειλεχέεσσιν ἰδὲ πτ⌋ερο⌊βάμοισι
κύμβαις.⌋

308 ὀρειλεχέεσσιν Schneider: ὀρειμελέεσσιν Simpl. (θερσί
τε ῥημελέεσσιν F), Martin-Primavesi

D74 (≠ DK) P. Strasb. gr. Inv. 1665–66, v. 324–30?, ed.
Primavesi 2008; (cf. B76) Simpl. *In Phys.*, pp. 158.1–159.4
(et al.)

<table>
<tr><td>324?</td><td>τοῦτο μὲν ἐν κόγχαισι θαλασσονόμοις</td></tr>
<tr><td>[B76.1]</td><td>βαρυνώτοις,</td></tr>
<tr><td>325?</td><td>ἠδ᾽ ἐν πε]τραίοισι κα[‿ ‿ | – ‿ ‿ | – –·</td></tr>
<tr><td>[B76.3]</td><td>ἔνθ᾽ ὄψει χθόνα χρωτὸς ὑπέρτατα ναιετάουσαν·</td></tr>
<tr><td></td><td>θώρηξ δ᾽ αὖ]τε κραταιν[ώ]των α[‿ | – ‿ ‿ | – –,</td></tr>
<tr><td>[B76.2]</td><td>ναὶ μὴν κηρύκων τε λιθορρίνων χελύων τε</td></tr>
<tr><td></td><td>ὄστρακα κα]ὶ μελίαι κεραῶν ἐλά[φων</td></tr>
<tr><td></td><td>ὀριπλάγκτων.</td></tr>
<tr><td>330?</td><td>ἀλλὰ οὐκ ἂν τελέσαιμ]ι λέγων σύμ[– ‿ ‿ | – –</td></tr>
</table>

325 κα[λύμμαισι, τοῦτο δὲ πίναις Janko   327 ἀ[λίων
τε παγούρων Janko   328 χελύων τε Pap., Plut. *Quaest.*
conv. 618A: χελωνῶν τε Plut. *Fac. orb. lun.* 927E   329 ita
Janko   330 σύμ[παντα γένεθλα Janko

Three Reprises (D75–D77)

D75 (B35) Simpl. *In Cael.*, p. 529.1–15 (v. 1–15); *In*
Phys., pp. 32.13–33.2 (v. 3–17)

And mountain-bedded wild beasts and wing-going birds.

D74 (≠ DK) Strasbourg Papyrus; (cf. B76) Simplicius, *Commentary on Aristotle's* Physics

324?

This, in sea-grazing, heavy-backed seashells, [B76.1]
And in rocky . . .
There you will see the earth living on the 325?
highest level of skin; [B76.3]
⟨*And once more, a breast-plate*⟩ **of strong-backed**
. . .

Yes indeed, of stone-skinned trumpet-shells and [B76.2]
turtles
⟨*The carapaces, and*⟩ **the ashen spears** [i.e. antlers]
of horned stags, ⟨*mountain-wandering.*⟩
⟨*But I could never finish*⟩ **telling** ⟨*all the species.*⟩ 330?

Three Reprises (D75–D77)

D75 (B35) Simplicius, *Commentary on Aristotle's* On the Heavens and *Commentary on Aristotle's* Physics

αὐτὰρ ἐγὼ παλίνορσος ἐλεύσομαι ἐς πόρον
   ὕμνων,
τὸν πρότερον κατέλεξα, λόγῳ λόγον
   ἐξοχετεύων,
κεῖνον· ἐπεὶ Νεῖκος μὲν ἐνέρτατον ἵκετο βένθος
δίνης, ἐν δὲ μέσῃ Φιλότης στροφάλιγγι
   γένηται,
5   ἐν τῇ δὴ τάδε πάντα συνέρχεται ἓν μόνον εἶναι,
οὐκ ἄφαρ, ἀλλὰ θελημὰ συνιστάμεν’ ἄλλοθεν
   ἄλλα.
τῶν δέ τε μισγομένων χεῖτ’ ἔθνεα μυρία
   θνητῶν·
πολλὰ δ’ ἄμειχθ’ ἔστηκε κεραιομένοισιν
   ἐναλλάξ,
ὅσσ’ ἔτι Νεῖκος ἔρυκε μετάρσιον· οὐ γὰρ
   ἀμεμφέως
10   πω πᾶν ἐξέστηκεν ἐπ’ ἔσχατα τέρματα κύκλου,
ἀλλὰ τὰ μέν τ’ ἐνέμιμνε, μελέων τὰ δέ τ’
   ἐξεβεβήκει.
ὅσσον δ’ αἰὲν ὑπεκπροθέοι, τόσον αἰὲν ἐπῄει
ἠπιόφρων Φιλότητος ἀμεμφέος ἄμβροτος ὁρμή·

2 λόγῳ AF: λόγου Karsten   ἐξοχετεύων F: ἐπιχετεύων
A: ἐποχετεύων Brandis   10 πω Cael. F, Phys. F, sed verb.
enclit. in init. hexam. valde inusitatum: τὸ Cael. A: οὔπω Phys.
DE, cf. Phys., p. 33.4: τῶν Diels   13 ἠπιόφρων] ἡ πίφρων
p. 32 ed. Ald.: πίφρων p. 32 DE: ἡ περίφρων p. 32 F

[Reprise 1]

But as for me, coming back, I shall proceed
    toward the path of songs
That I described earlier, drawing out one
    discourse by means of another,
That one [cf. **D73.288**]: **When Strife has reached
    the deepest depth**
**Of the vortex, and Love has come to be in the
    center of the whirl,**
Under her dominion all these [i.e. the elements]   5
    come together to be only one,
**Each one coming from a different place, not
    brusquely, but willingly,**
**And while they were mixing, myriad tribes of
    mortals spread out.**
**But much remained unmixed, alternating with
    the mixtures,**
**Everything that Strife held back suspended. For
    not yet blamelessly**
Had he withdrawn completely to the farthest   10
    limits of the circle,
**But in part he remained in the limbs, in part he
    had gone out from them.**
**And as far as he ran out ahead each time, just so
    far followed it each time**
**The gentle-thinking immortal drive of blameless
    Love.**

αἶψα δὲ θνήτ᾽ ἐφύοντο, τὰ πρὶν μάθον ἀθάνατ᾽
    εἶναι,

15 ζωρά τε τὰ πρὶν ἄκρητα, διαλλάξαντα
    κελεύθους.

τῶν δέ τε μισγομένων χεῖτ᾽ ἔθνεα μυρία
    θνητῶν,

παντοίαις ἰδέῃσιν ἀρηρότα, θαῦμα ἰδέσθαι.

14 δὲ θνήτ᾽ *Cael.* F: δ᾽ ἔθνεά τ᾽ *Cael.* A   15 ἄκρητα
Athen. 10.423F, Plut. *Quaest. conv.* 5.4.1 677D: ἄκριτα Simpl.:
κέκρητο (ι sup. η m. rec.) Arist. *Poet.* 25 1461a23

D76 (≠ DK) P. Strasb. gr. Inv. 1665–66, Frag. d et f, ed.
Primavesi 2008

. . .

ἄν]διχ᾽ ἀπ᾽ ἀλλήλω[ν] πεσέ[ει]ν καὶ π[ότ]μον
    ἐπισπεῖν

πο]λλ᾽ ἀεκαζομέν[ο]ισιν ἀ[να]γκα[ίης ὕ]πο
    λυγρῆς

ση]πο[μ]έ̣νοις. Φιλίην δ᾽ ἐ[ρατ]ὴ̣ν̣ [ἡμῖ]ν νυν
    ἔχουσιν

Ἅρ]πυιαι θανάτοιο πάλοις [ἤδη παρέσ]ονται.

3 Φιλίην δ᾽ ἐ[ρατ]ὴν [ἡμῖ]ν Primavesi, Janko: Φιλίην δὲ [καὶ
E]ὖν[οίη]ν Martin-Primavesi

4 [ἤδη παρέσ]ονται Primavesi, Janko: [ἡμῖν παρέσ]ονται
Martin-Primavesi

And immediately were born as mortals those
    [i.e. the elements] **that earlier had learned to**
    be immortals,
And as blended[1] (?) those that earlier had been   15
    unmixed, exchanging their paths.
And while they were mixing, myriad tribes of
    mortals spread out,
Joined together in forms of all kinds, a wonder
    to see.

[1] The term translated as 'blended' here normally means 'pure'; the meaning 'blended,' required by the context, is attested by an ancient tradition (see e.g. Plutarch, *Quaest. conv.* 5.4.1 677D).

[Continuation of Reprise 1, then
Reprise 2 starting with line 10]

D76 (≠ DK) Strasbourg Papyrus

    < . . . the fate of the limbs is >
To fall separately from one another and to
    encounter their destiny,
Putrefying most unwillingly, under dire
    necessity.
As for us, who now possess desirable Love,
The Harpies will soon be present for us with the
    destinies of death.

5 οἴμοι ὅτι οὐ πρόσθεν με διώλεσε νηλεὲς ἦμαρ,
πρὶν χηλαῖς σχέτλι᾽ ἔργα βορᾶς πέρι
μητίσασθαι·
νῦν δ]ὲ μάτη[ν ἐν] τῶιδε νότ[ωι κατέδ]ευσα
παρειάς·
ἐξικ]νούμε[θα γὰ]ρ πολυβενθ[έα δῖνον], ὅίω,
μυρία τε οὐκ] ἐθέλουσι παρέσσε[ται ἄλγ]εα
θυμῶι
10 ἀνθρώποις.]

10 ἡ]μεῖς δὲ λόγων ἐπιβ[ησόμ]εθ᾽ αὖθις
κείνων· ὁππότ]ε δὴ συνετύγχανε φ[λογ]μὸς
ἀτειρής
– ∪ ∪ ‖ – ∪ ∪]ως ἀνάγων π[ο]λυπήμ[ον]α κρᾶσιν
δὴ τότε – – ζῶι]α φυτάλμια τεκνώθ[η]σαν
– ∪ ∪ ‖ –, τῶν ν]ῦν ἔτι λείψανα δέρκεται Ἠώς.
15 ὁππότ[ε δ᾽ αἰθέρι συμμιχθ]εὶ̣ς τόπον ἐσχάτιο[ν
β]ῆι,
δὴ τό[τε – ∪ ∪ ‖ – ∪ ∪‖ – κλαγ]γῆι καὶ αὐτῆι

5–6 cf. **D34** 7 μάτη[ν ἐν] τῶιδε Martin-Primavesi:
μάτη[ν τού]τωι γε Janko τωιδε Pap.^pc: τωιγε Pap.^ac
8 ἐξικ]νούμε[θα Martin-Primavesi: ἐξικ]νεύμε[θα Janko
10 λόγων ἐπιβ[ησόμ]εθ᾽ Pap.^ac: λόγων ⟨σ᾽⟩ ἐπιβ[ήσομ]εν᾽
Pap.^pc Martin-Primavesi 12 [πᾶσιν ἄμ᾽ ἀλλήλο]ις ἀνάγων π[ο]λυπήμ[ον]α κρῆσιν Janko 13 δὴ τότε suppl.
Primavesi, ζῶι]α Martin-Primavesi: [δὴ τότε καὶ τὰ ζῶι]α Janko
14 παντὶ τρόπωι, τῶν ν]ῦν Janko
15 ita Primavesi: β]ῆι Pap.^1: β]ῆν Pap.^2: [ ] εἰς τόπον ἐσχάτιο[ν β]ῆν Martin-Primavesi: ὁππότ[ε δή γ᾽ αἰθὴρ μιχθ]εὶς
τόπον ἐσχάτιο[ν β]ῆι Janko

Alas, that the pitiless day did not destroy me   5
    earlier, [= **D34.1**]
Before I contrived terrible deeds about feeding
    with my claws! [cf. **D34.2**]
But as it is, in vain have I wetted my cheeks in
    this squall (?) [scil. of tears];[1]
For we are arriving at ⟨*the vortex?*⟩ of enormous
    depth, I suppose,
⟨*And myriads*⟩ of pains will be present to the
    heart of unwilling
⟨*Human beings.*⟩   10

[Reprise 2]

But we shall embark once again upon ⟨*those*⟩   10
Arguments. ⟨*When*⟩ the unwearying flame
    encountered
. . . conducting upward the much-suffering
    mixture
. . . fecund ⟨*living beings*⟩ were engendered
⟨*. . . of which*⟩ even now the Dawn sees the
    remains.
But when, ⟨*mixed with aether,*⟩ it reaches the   15
    farthest place,
Then . . . with crying and screaming

---

[1] If the text has been correctly restored, the metaphor *notos*, a moist wind, perhaps applies to the outburst of the two preceding lines.

---

16 δὴ τό[τε suppl. Primavesi, κλαγ]γῆι Martin-Primavesi: δὴ τό[τ' ἀνέπτοντ' οἰωνοὶ κλα]γγῆι καὶ αὐτῆι Janko: δὴ τό[θ' ἕκαστα διετμήθη κλαγ]γῆι καὶ αὐτῆι Rashed

θεσπε[σίηι, ‿ ‿ | − ‿ ‿ | − κευθ]μῶνα λαχόντα

χορ[τους τ’ − ‿ ‿ | − ‿ ‿ | − ‿ ‿ α]ῦτε περὶ
χθών.

ὡς δ’ [ὁπόταν ‿ ‿ | − ‿ ‿ | − ‿ ‿ | − ‿ ‿ | − −

20 χαλ[κεὺς | − ‿ ‿ | − ‿ ‿ | − ‿ ‿ | − ‿ ‿ | − −

αιδε[‿ | − ‿ ‿ | − ‿ ‿ | − ‿ ‿ | − ‿ ‿ | − −

τη[‿ ‿ | − ‿ ‿ | − ‿ ‿ | − ‿ ‿ | − ‿ ‿ | − −

17 suppl. Primavesi: θεσπε[σίηι· τὰ δ’ ὑπαὶ γαίης κευθ]-
μῶνα λαχόντα Janko: [Ἄτης λει]μῶνα λαχόντα Martin-Primavesi   18 [ ]υτο Pap.¹: [ ]υτε Pap.²: χορ[τους τ’ suppl. Primavesi,
α]ῦτε Martin-Primavesi: χορ[τους τ’ ἐξεγένοντο, ὅπηι εἴλ]υτο
πέρι χθών Janko   19 suppl. Janko   20 suppl. Janko

D77 Simpl. *In Phys.*

a (B21) p. 159.13–26 (v. 1–14) et p. 33.8–17 (v. 3–12) (et
al.)

ἀλλ’ ἄγε, τῶνδ’ ὀάρων προτέρων ἐπιμάρτυρα
δέρκευ,

εἴ τι καὶ ἐν προτέροισι λιπόξυλον ἔπλετο
μορφῆ,

ἠέλιον μὲν θερμὸν ὁρᾶν καὶ λαμπρὸν ἀπάντη,

ἄμβροτα δ’ ὅσσ’ ἴδει τε καὶ ἀργέτι δεύεται
αὐγῆ,

5   ὄμβρον δ’ ἐν πᾶσι δνοφόεντά τε ῥιγαλέον τε·

**Unspeakable . . . those who have been allotted a
refuge
And fodder . . . the earth all around
As ⟨when . . .⟩
A blacksmith . . .** 20

. . .

. . .

D77 Simplicius, *Commentary on Aristotle's* Physics

a (B21)

[Reprise 3]

**But come, consider further witnesses to those
earlier statements,
If anything in what came earlier was defective
in form:
The sun, warm to see and shining everywhere,
All the immortal things** [i.e. probably: clouds[1]]
**moistened with heat and a bright gleam,
And rain for all, dark and icy;** 5

---

[1] This is usually taken to refer to heavenly bodies, but cf.
Picot, *Études philosophiques* 110 (2014): 358–62.

---

3 θερμὸν . . . λαμπρὸν Simpl. bis (. . . θερμὸν 33 F): λαμπρὸν . . . θερμὸν Plut. *Prim. frig.* 13.1 949F: λευκὸν . . .
θερμὸν Arist. *GC* 314b   ὁρᾶν Arist. FJVMW, Simpl. 159 et
33 DE: ὁρᾷ Simpl. 33 F: ὅρα Arist. E¹L Vat gr. 258, Plut.

4 δ' ὅσσ' ἴδει (εἴδει Wackernagel) τε Diels: δ' ὅσσα ἐδεῖτο
Simpl. 159: δὲ ὅσσ' ἔδεται Simpl. 33 DE: δὲ ὅσσε δέ τε Simpl.
33 F   5 δνοφόεντά Arist. FJ¹VM, Plut.: δνοφόοντα Arist.
E¹, Simpl. bis (δνοφόεντά 159 ed. Ald.): ζοφόεντά Arist. HL:
γνοφόεντά Arist. WE²: ζοφέοντά Arist. J²

ἐκ δ' αἴης προρέουσι θέλυμνά τε καὶ στερεωπά.
ἐν δὲ Κότῳ διάμορφα καὶ ἄνδιχα πάντα
  πέλονται,
σὺν δ' ἔβη ἐν Φιλότητι καὶ ἀλλήλοισι ποθεῖται.
ἐκ τούτων γὰρ πάνθ' ὅσα τ' ἦν ὅσα τ' ἔστι καὶ
  ἔσται,
10 δένδρεά τ' ἐβλάστησε καὶ ἀνέρες ἠδὲ γυναῖκες,
θῆρές τ' οἰωνοί τε καὶ ὑδατοθρέμμονες ἰχθῦς,
καί τε θεοὶ δολιχαίωνες τιμῇσι φέριστοι.
αὐτὰ γὰρ ἔστιν ταῦτα, δι' ἀλλήλων δὲ θέοντα
γίγνεται ἀλλοιωπά· τόσον διὰ κρᾶσις ἀμείβει.

6 θέλυμνά τε Sturz: θέλεμνά τε Wilamowitz: θελημά τε
Simpl. 33 D[1]: θέλημά τε 159 DEF, θελημνά τε 33 ED[2], θελή-
ματα 33 F, θελίμνατα 33, θέλιμνά τε 159 ed. Ald.: προρέουσ'
ἐθελυμνά τε Karsten: προρέουσ' ἐθελημά τε Panzerbieter

9 versus saepe citatus cum multis lect. variis quae hic non
singillatim notantur: ἐκ τούτων γὰρ πάνθ' ὅσα τ' ἦν ὅσα τ'
ἔστι καὶ ἔσται Simpl.: ἐξ ὧν πάνθ' ὅσα τ' ἦν ὅσα τ' ἔσται
ὀπίσσω Arist. Metaph. B4 1000a29–30 (E): πάνθ' ὅσα τ' ἦν
ὅσα τ' ἔσθ' ὅσα τ' ἔσται ὀπίσσω Ps.-Arist. Mund. 399b: ἐκ
γὰρ τῶν ὅσα τ' ἦν ὅσα τ' ἔσσεται ὅσσα τ' ἔασιν. Clem. Alex.
Strom. 6.17.3   10 δένδρεα Simpl. 33 DE: δένδρα 33 F ed.
Ald., 159 ed. Ald.   τ' ἐβλάστησε Arist. Metaph, Ps.-Arist
Mund., Simpl. 159: τε βεβλάστηκε Simpl. 33, 159 ed. Ald.

14 τόσον Diels: τογον E: τόγον F: τὰ γὰρ ed. Ald., Martin-
Primavesi (cf. P. Strasb. d12)   διὰ κρᾶσις Diels (ed. Simpl.):
διάκρασις E: διάκρισις D: διάκρυψις ed. Ald.: διὰ κρῆσις
Diels (DK)

b (B26) p. 33.19–34.3 (et al.) [after **D77a**]

ἐν δὲ μέρει κρατέουσι περιπλομένοιο κύκλοιο,

And out of the ground flow forth foundations (?)
   and solid things.
Under Hatred, all things are divided in form
   and are separated,
While under Love they come together and
   desire each other.
For it is out of these that all things come that
   were, all that are and that will be,
Trees have grown [scil. from these], men and   10
   women,
Wild beasts and birds, water-nourished fish,
And long-lived gods, the greatest in honors.
For these are themselves, but, running the ones
   through the others,
They become different in appearance: so much
   exchange does the mixture produce.

b (B26) [after **D77a**]

   And by turns they [i.e. the elements] dominate
      while the circle revolves,

καὶ φθίνει εἰς ἄλληλα καὶ αὔξεται ἐν μέρει
    αἴσης.
αὐτὰ γὰρ ἔστιν ταῦτα, δι’ ἀλλήλων δὲ θέοντα
γίνοντ’ ἄνθρωποί τε καὶ ἄλλων ἔθνεα θηρῶν
ἄλλοτε μὲν Φιλότητι συνερχόμεν’ εἰς ἕνα
    κόσμον,
ἄλλοτε δ’ αὖ δίχ’ ἕκαστα φορούμενα Νείκεος
    ἔχθει,
εἰσόκεν ἓν συμφύντα τὸ πᾶν ὑπένερθε γένηται.
οὕτως ᾗ μὲν ἓν ἐκ πλεόνων μεμάθηκε φύεσθαι,
ἠδὲ πάλιν διαφύντος ἑνὸς πλέον’ ἐκτελέθουσι,
τῇ μὲν γίγνονταί τε καὶ οὔ σφισιν ἔμπεδος
    αἰών·
ᾗ δὲ τάδ’ ἀλλάσσοντα διαμπερὲς οὐδαμὰ λήγει,
ταύτῃ δ’ αἰὲν ἔασιν ἀκίνητοι κατὰ κύκλον.

8 ἐν Arist. *Phys.* 8.1 250b30: om. Simpl.

Testimonia on the Alternation and the
Cycle (D78–D86)

D78 (< A29) Plat. *Soph.* 242d–243a

[ΞΕ.] [. . .] Σικελαί τινες [. . .] Μοῦσαι [. . .] ἐν μέρει
[. . .] τοτὲ μὲν ἓν εἶναί φασι τὸ πᾶν καὶ φίλον ὑπ’
Ἀφροδίτης, τοτὲ δὲ πολλὰ καὶ πολέμιον αὐτὸ αὑτῷ
διὰ νεῖκός τι.

And they decrease and increase into one
    another as it is their turn by destiny.
For these are themselves, but running the ones
    through the others,
They become human beings as well as the tribes
    of wild beasts,
Sometimes coming together, by Love, into one   5
    ordered arrangement (*kosmos*),
Sometimes again each one carried off by the
    hatred of Strife,
Until, grown together (*sumphunta*) in one, the
    whole sinks down [i.e. disappears?].
So insofar as they have learned to grow
    (*phuesthai*) as one out of many
And inversely, when the one grows apart
    (*diaphuntos*), they become many,
To that extent they become, and they do not   10
    have a steadfast lifetime;
But insofar as they do incessantly exchange
    their places continually,
To that extent they always are, immobile in a
    circle.

*Testimonia on the Alternation and the
Cycle (D78–D86)*

D78 (< A29) Plato, *Sophist*

[The stranger from Elea:] Certain Sicilian [. . .] Muses [i.e.
Empedocles] [. . .] say that it is in alternation that at one
time the whole is one and friendly under the dominion of
Aphrodite, at another time many and hostile to itself because of a certain strife [cf. **DOX. T4**].

D79

a (22 A10) Arist. *Cael.* 1.10 279b12–17

γενόμενον μὲν οὖν ἅπαντες εἶναί φασιν, ἀλλὰ γενόμενον οἱ μὲν ἀίδιον, οἱ δὲ φθαρτὸν ὥσπερ ὁτιοῦν ἄλλο
τῶν συνισταμένων, οἱ δ᾽ ἐναλλὰξ ὁτὲ μὲν οὕτως ὁτὲ
δὲ ἄλλως ἔχειν φθειρόμενον,[1] καὶ τοῦτο αἰεὶ διατελεῖν
οὕτως, ὥσπερ Ἐμπεδοκλῆς ὁ Ἀκραγαντῖνος καὶ Ἡράκλειτος ὁ Ἐφέσιος.

[1] φθειρόμενον del. Kassel

b (> A52) Simpl. *In Cael.*, p. 293.15–24

τινὲς δὲ τῶν γενητὸν λεγόντων φθαρτὸν λέγουσι, διχῶς δὲ τοῦτο· οἱ μὲν γὰρ οὕτως φθαρτόν, ὥσπερ
ὁτιοῦν ἄλλο τῶν συνισταμένων ἀτόμων [. . .], οἱ δὲ
ἐναλλὰξ γίνεσθαι καὶ φθείρεσθαι τὸν αὐτὸν καὶ πάλιν γενόμενον πάλιν[1] φθείρεσθαι λέγουσι, καὶ ἀίδιον
εἶναι τὴν τοιαύτην διαδοχήν, ὥσπερ Ἐμπεδοκλῆς τὴν
Φιλίαν λέγων καὶ τὸ Νεῖκος παρὰ μέρος ἐπικρα-
τοῦντα τὴν μὲν συνάγειν τὰ πάντα εἰς ἓν καὶ φθείρειν
τὸν τοῦ Νείκους κόσμον καὶ ποιεῖν ἐξ αὐτοῦ τὸν
Σφαῖρον, τὸ δὲ Νεῖκος διακρίνειν πάλιν τὰ στοιχεῖα
καὶ ποιεῖν τὸν τοιοῦτον κόσμον. ταῦτα δὲ Ἐμπεδοκλῆς σημαίνει λέγων· [. . . = **D73.239–44**].

[1] γενόμενον πάλιν Heiberg (generato eo et iterum Moerbeke): om. ACDE: γίνεσθαι καὶ Ε[2]

D79

a (22 A10) Aristotle, *On the Heavens*

They all say that it [i.e. the world] has been generated, but, once generated, for some it is eternal, for others corruptible like any other assemblage, for still others it undergoes destruction by turns, first in one way and then in another, and this happens forever, as in Empedocles of Agrigentum and Heraclitus of Ephesus.

b (> A52) Simplicius, *Commentary on Aristotle's* On the Heavens

Some of those who say that it [i.e. the world] is generated say that it is corruptible, but this is understood in two ways: for some say that it is corruptible in the same way as anything else composed of atoms assembled together [. . .], while others say that the same thing is generated and destroyed alternately, that after it has been generated again it is destroyed again, and that this succession is eternal, like Empedocles, who says that Love and Strife dominate in turns, the former bringing together all things into one, destroying the world of Strife, and making the Sphere out of it, while Strife once again separates the elements out and creates a world of this sort. This is what Empedocles means when he says [. . . = **D73.239–44**].

D80 (A28) Simpl. *In Phys.*, pp. 25.21–26.4 (< Theophr. Frag. 227A FSH&G)

οὗτος δὲ τὰ μὲν σωματικὰ στοιχεῖα ποιεῖ τέτταρα, πῦρ καὶ ἀέρα καὶ ὕδωρ καὶ γῆν, ἀίδια μὲν ὄντα[1] πλήθει[2] καὶ ὀλιγότητι, μεταβάλλοντα δὲ[3] κατὰ τὴν σύγκρισιν καὶ διάκρισιν, τὰς δὲ κυρίως ἀρχάς, ὑφ᾽ ὧν κινεῖται ταῦτα, Φιλίαν καὶ Νεῖκος. δεῖ γὰρ διατελεῖν ἐναλλὰξ κινούμενα τὰ στοιχεῖα, ποτὲ μὲν ὑπὸ τῆς Φιλίας συγκρινόμενα, ποτὲ δὲ ὑπὸ τοῦ Νείκους διακρινόμενα· ὥστε καὶ ἐξ εἶναι κατ᾽ αὐτὸν τὰς ἀρχάς. καὶ γὰρ ὅπου μὲν ποιητικὴν δίδωσι δύναμιν τῷ Νείκει καὶ τῇ Φιλίᾳ, ὅταν λέγῃ [. . . = **D73.239–40**] [. . .] ποτὲ δὲ τοῖς τέτταρσιν ὡς ἰσόστοιχα συντάττει καὶ ταῦτα, ὅταν λέγῃ [. . . = **D73.248** (τοτὲ δ᾽)–**51**].

[1] post ὄντα inseruit καὶ πεπερασμένα Torstrik, in eundem locum transposuit μεταβάλλοντα δὲ Usener   [2] post πλήθει inseruit δὲ Diels   [3] δὲ del. Diels

D81 (< A46) Arist. *Phys.* 1.4 187a20–26

οἱ δ᾽ ἐκ τοῦ ἑνὸς ἐνούσας τὰς ἐναντιότητας ἐκκρίνεσθαι, ὥσπερ [. . .] ὅσοι [. . .] ἓν καὶ πολλά φασιν εἶναι,[1] ὥσπερ Ἐμπεδοκλῆς καὶ Ἀναξαγόρας· ἐκ τοῦ μίγματος γὰρ καὶ οὗτοι ἐκκρίνουσι τἆλλα. διαφέρουσι δὲ ἀλλήλων τῷ τὸν μὲν περίοδον ποιεῖν τούτων, τὸν δ᾽ ἅπαξ [. . . cf. **ANAXAG. D20**].

[1] εἶναι FIJ[1]: εἶναι τὰ ὄντα EJ[2]

D80 (A28) Simplicius, *Commentary on Aristotle's* Physics

This one [i.e. Empedocles] says that the corporeal elements are four, fire, air, water, and earth, which are eternal, in large or small quantity, but which change according to their union and separation; but the principles properly speaking, by which these move, are Love and Strife. For it is necessary that the elements continue to exchange their places reciprocally, being at one time united by Love, at another time separated by Strife. So that the principles according to him are also six. For in certain passages he attributes the efficient power to Strife and Love, when he says, [. . . = **D73.239–40**], but sometimes he assigns these too to the four as belonging to the same series, when he says, [. . . = **D73.248b–51**].

D81 (< A46) Aristotle, *Physics*

The others [scil. say] that the contraries that are present in the one separate out from it, like [. . .] those who say that there exist the one and the many, like Empedocles and Anaxagoras. For these two also say that the other things separate out from the mixture. But they differ from one another in that the one [i.e. Empedocles] says that these follow each other periodically, while for the other [i.e. Anaxagoras] it is a unique event [. . .].

D82 (A42) Arist. *GC* 2.7 334a5–7

ἅμα δὲ καὶ τὸν κόσμον ὁμοίως ἔχειν φησὶν ἐπί τε τοῦ
Νείκους νῦν καὶ πρότερον ἐπὶ τῆς Φιλίας.

D83 (A42) Arist. *Cael.* 3.2 301a14–20

ἐκ διεστώτων δὲ καὶ κινουμένων οὐκ εὔλογον ποιεῖν
τὴν γένεσιν. διὸ καὶ Ἐμπεδοκλῆς παραλείπει τὴν ἐπὶ
τῆς Φιλότητος· οὐ γὰρ ἂν ἠδύνατο συστῆσαι τὸν
οὐρανὸν ἐκ κεχωρισμένων μὲν κατασκευάζων, σύγκρισιν δὲ ποιῶν διὰ τὴν Φιλότητα· ἐκ διακεκριμένων
γὰρ συνέστηκεν ὁ κόσμος τῶν στοιχείων· ὥστ᾽ ἀναγκαῖον γίνεσθαι ἐξ ἑνὸς καὶ συγκεκριμένου.

D84

a (cf. Nachtrag I, p. 500) Arist. *Phys.* 8.1 250b23–251a5

εἰ δὴ ἐνδέχεταί ποτε μηδὲν κινεῖσθαι, διχῶς ἀνάγκη
τοῦτο συμβαίνειν· ἢ γὰρ ὡς Ἀναξαγόρας λέγει [. . .],
ἢ ὡς Ἐμπεδοκλῆς ἐν μέρει κινεῖσθαι καὶ πάλιν ἠρεμεῖν, κινεῖσθαι μὲν ὅταν ἡ Φιλία ἐκ πολλῶν ποιῇ τὸ
ἓν ἢ τὸ Νεῖκος πολλὰ ἐξ ἑνός, ἠρεμεῖν δ᾽ ἐν τοῖς μεταξὺ χρόνοις, λέγων [. . . = **D77b. 8–12**; cf. **D73.240–
44**]· τὸ γὰρ ʽᾗ δὲ τάδʼ ἀλλάσσονταʼ ἐνθένδε ἐκεῖσε
λέγειν αὐτὸν ὑποληπτέον.

D82 (A42) Aristotle, *On Generation and Corruption*

At the same time, he also says that the world is in the same condition both now, under Strife, and earlier, under Love [cf. **R13**].

D83 (A42) Aristotle, *On the Heavens*

It is not reasonable to conceive of genesis on the basis of things that are separated and in motion. This is why Empedocles omits the one [scil. genesis] under Love. For he could not have arranged the heavens if he had constructed them on the basis of separated things but united them by means of Love. For the world is arranged out of elements that have been separated; so that it is necessary that it be generated from the One and from what is mixed together.

D84

a (cf. Nachtrag I, p. 500) Aristotle, *Physics*

If it is possible that nothing moves at a given time, it is necessary that this happen in one of two ways: for it is either as Anaxagoras says [cf. **EMP. D82**], or else as Empedocles, viz. that there is motion and rest in turns, motion when Love makes the one out of the many or Strife the many out of the one, and rest in the intermediate times, when he says, [. . . = **D77b. 8–12;** cf. **D73.240–44**]. For we must suppose that by the phrase **'but insofar as they** [scil. incessantly] **exchange their places'** he means [scil. a change] from here to there [cf. **R73**].

b (≠ DK) Schol. a et b ad Arist. *Phys.* 8.1.250b28 et 29, *Laur.* 87.7

1 Schol. a ad b28 [τὸ ἕν], fol. 91r, l. 5

τὸν Σφαῖρον τὸν διανοητὸν διάκοσμον

2 Schol. b ad b29 [ἐν τοῖς μεταξύ χρόνοις], fol. 91r, l. 6

παυομένης γὰρ καὶ¹ τῆς Φιλίας μετὰ τοὺς ξ′ χρόνους, οὐκ εὐθὺς ἤρξατο ποιεῖν ἀπόσπασιν τὸ Νεῖκος, ἀλλ᾽ ἠρέμει.

¹ καὶ add. supra lineam prima manus

D85

a (> A38) Arist. *Phys.* 8.1 252a3–10

εἰ δὴ ταῦτ᾽ ἀδύνατα, δῆλον ὡς ἔστιν ἀΐδιος κίνησις, ἀλλ᾽ οὐχ ὁτὲ μὲν ἦν ὁτὲ δ᾽ οὔ· καὶ γὰρ ἔοικε τὸ οὕτω λέγειν πλάσματι μᾶλλον. ὁμοίως δὲ καὶ τὸ λέγειν ὅτι πέφυκεν οὕτως καὶ ταύτην δεῖ νομίζειν εἶναι ἀρχήν, ὅπερ ἔοικεν Ἐμπεδοκλῆς ἂν εἰπεῖν, ὡς τὸ κρατεῖν καὶ κινεῖν ἐν μέρει τὴν Φιλίαν καὶ τὸ Νεῖκος ὑπάρχει τοῖς πράγμασιν ἐξ ἀνάγκης, ἠρεμεῖν δὲ τὸν μεταξὺ χρόνον.

b (≠ DK) Scholia on Aristotle's *Physics*

1

["the one":] the Sphere, the order of the intelligible world.

2

["in the intermediate times":] For when Love too stopped after the sixty periods of time, Strife did not begin immediately to make things break up, but it remained at rest.

D85

a (> A38) Aristotle, *Physics*

If then this [i.e. the perishability of motion] is impossible, it is clear that there is an eternal motion and that it has not existed at one time but not at another: for indeed to speak in this way is more like a fiction [cf. **R74**]. And so too to say that this is how things are by nature and that this must be considered to be a principle, which is what Empedocles seems to have said, supposing that it happens by necessity for things that Love and Strife alternately dominate and cause motion, while during the intermediate time they are in a state of rest.

b (≠ DK) Schol. c ad Arist. *Phys.* 8.1 252a9–10 [ἠρεμεῖν δὲ τὸν μεταξὺ χρόνον], *Laur.* 87.7, fol. 93r, l. 9

. . . καὶ ⟨οὐκ⟩[1] εὐθὺς μετὰ τὴν παρέλευσιν τῶν ξ′ χρόνων ἐν οἷς ἐκράτησεν ἡ Φιλία γενέσθαι διάσπασιν.

  [1] ⟨οὐκ⟩ Rashed

D86 (≠ DK)

a Arist. *Phys.* 8.1 252a31

τὸ δὲ καὶ δι᾽ ἴσων χρόνων [. . . cf. **R12**]

b Schol. d et e ad Arist. *Phys.* 8.1 252a31, *Laur.* 87.7, fol. 93v, l. 20

1 Schol. d ad a31 [δι᾽ ἴσων]

. . . καὶ ι′

2 Schol. e ad a31 [δι᾽ ἴσων χρόνων]

κρατεῖν τὸ Νεῖκος καὶ τὴν Φιλίαν.

b (≠ DK) Scholia on Aristotle's *Physics*

["during the intermediate time they are in a state of rest":] . . . and that the breaking apart happens ‹not› immediately after the passing of the sixty periods of time during which Love has dominated.

D86 (≠ DK)

a Aristotle, *Physics*

The claim that this [scil. alternating predominance of Love and Strife happens] for equal periods of time too [. . . cf. **R13**].

b Scholia on Aristotle's *Physics*

1

["for equal":] . . . and ten.

2

["for equal periods of time":] Strife and Love dominate.

Episodes of the History of the World (D87–D112)

The God Sphairos (the Spherical) (D87–D93)

D87 (ad B29) Simpl. *In Phys.*, p. 1124.2

. . . Σφαῖρον ἔην . . .

D88 (cf. ad B13) Ps.-Arist. *MXG* 2 976b26–27

ὅταν δὲ εἰς μίαν μορφὴν συγκριθῇ, ὥσθ᾿ ἓν εἶναι, οὐδέν, φησί, τό γε

– ◡ ◡ | – ◡ ◡ | – κενεὸν πέλει οὐδὲ περισσόν.

τό γε . . . ⟨οὐ⟩ . . . κενεὸν πέλει οὐδὲ περισσόν Bollack: an οὐδέν ◡ | – ◡ ◡ | – κενεὸν πέλει οὐδὲ περισσόν?

Episodes of the History of the World (D87–D112)[1]

[1] Given that the history of the world for Empedocles is cyclical and that the order of the episodes in the original poem cannot be completely determined, it is possible to locate the rule of Love either at the beginning or at the end. It has seemed to us more illuminating to suggest, by analogy with the narrative of the *Purifications,* that the history of the world is that of a fall followed by a restoration.

The God Sphairos (the Spherical)[1] *(D87–D93)*

[1] *Sphairos* is the masculine name coined by Empedocles to designate the 'spherical' god under the total domination of Love. Simplicius, citing **D87,** notes explicitly that Empedocles also used the term in the neuter.

D87 (ad B29) Simplicius, *Commentary on Aristotle's* Physics

> . . . **he** [or: there] **was Sphairos** . . .

D88 (cf. ad B13) Ps.-Aristotle, *On Melissus, Xenophanes, and Gorgias*

And when the assembling into only one form happens, so that only one thing exists, he says that **it** [i.e. Sphairos] **in any case not at all**[1]

> . . . **is either empty or in excess.**

[1] The terms in boldface doubtless derive from Empedocles, but it is not possible to integrate them with certainty into the verse.

447

D89 (ad B27) Simpl. *In Phys.*, pp. 1183.30–84.1 (et al.)

ἔνθ' οὔτ' Ἠελίοιο διείδεται ὠκέα γυῖα

. . .

οὕτως Ἁρμονίης πυκινῷ κρύφῳ ἐστήρικται
Σφαῖρος κυκλοτερὴς μονίῃ περιγηθέι γαίων.

3 μονίῃ (μονιῇ) περιγηθέι M ed. Ald.: μονιηιπεριγηθει A: μονη [lac. 4 litt.] περιγηθει F   γαίων Simpl. *In. Cael.* p. 591, M. Aur. 12.3: αἰών mss.

D90 (B28) Stob. 1.15.2ab (pp. 144.20–145.1) (et al.)

ἀλλ' ὅ γε πάντοθεν ἶσος <ἔην> καὶ πάμπαν
   ἀπείρων
Σφαῖρος κυκλοτερὴς μονίῃ περιηγέι χαίρων.

1 <ἔην> Diels   2 μονίῃ Diels: μόνῃ Procl. *In Tim.* 160D: μούνῃ Ach.Tat. *Isag.* 6: μιμίης FP   περιηγέι Ach. Tat., Procl.: περιτείθη P (θη in ras): περιτεθῆ F (cf. περιγηθέι Simpl. **D89**)

D91 (B27a) Plut. *Max. c. princ. phil. esse diss.* 2 777C

οὐ στάσις οὐ<δέ τε> δῆρις ἐναίσιμος ἐν
   μελέεσσιν.

versus incerti poetae Empedocli attrib. Wilamowitz   οὐ<δέ τε> Xylander: <ἦν,> οὐ Bergk

D89 (ad B27) Simplicius, *Commentary on Aristotle's* Physics

> There neither the swift limbs of the sun can be
>   distinguished
>   . . . [1]
> So much remains riveted in the dense hiding
>   place of Harmony
> Round Sphairos, exulting in his joyous solitude.

[1] Diels restores the verse missing here (cf. "neither. . .") on the basis of **D96**; but given that the context is not identical, it is possible that **D89** continued differently.

D90 (B28) Stobaeus, *Anthology*

> But he was on all sides equal and entirely
>   without limits,
> Round Sphairos, rejoicing in his circular
>   solitude.

D91 (B27a) Plutarch, *Philosophers Must Especially Converse with Princes*

> Neither dissension nor battle is fitting in his
>   limbs.[1]

[1] This line is transmitted anonymously; Wilamowitz attributed it to Empedocles.

D92 (B29) (Ps.-?) Hipp. *Haer.* 7.29.13

> οὐ γὰρ ἀπὸ νώτοιο δύο κλάδοι ἀίσσονται,
> οὐ πόδες, οὐ θοὰ γοῦν᾽, οὐ μήδεα γεννήεντα,
> ἀλλὰ Σφαῖρος ἔην καὶ ‹πάντοθεν› ἶσος ἑαυτῷ.

2 γοῦν᾽ Duncker-Schneidewin: γούνατ᾽ ms.   3 ‹πάντοθεν› ἶσος ἑαυτῷ Duncker-Schneidewin: ἶσος ἐστὶν αὐτῷ ms.

D93 (B134) Ammon. *In Interp.*, p. 249.7–11 (et al.)

> οὐδὲ γὰρ ἀνδρομέη κεφαλῇ κατὰ γυῖα
>   κέκασται,
> οὐ ‹μὲν› ἀπαὶ νώτοιο δύο κλάδοι ἀίσσονται,
> οὐ πόδες, οὐ θοὰ γοῦν᾽, οὐ μήδεα λαχνήεντα,
> ἀλλὰ φρὴν ἱερὴ καὶ ἀθέσφατος ἔπλετο μοῦνον,
> 5 φροντίσι κόσμον ἅπαντα καταΐσσουσα θοῇσιν.

1 οὐδὲ Olymp. *In Gorg.*, p. 129 Jahn: οὔτε mss., Schol. in
Olymp. (Marc. gr. 196)   2 vers. om. Schol. in Olymp.
‹μὲν› Schneider   νώτοιο Hippol. *Ref.* 7.29.13, cf. **D92**:
νώτων γε mss.   δύο Hipp., cf. **D92**: δύω mss.   ἀίσσονται Hipp., cf. **D92**: ἀίσσουσιν mss.   3 γοῦνα mss.,
corr. Scaliger

D92 (B29) (Ps.-?) Hippolytus, *Refutation of All Heresies*

> For from his back two branches do not shoot
>   forth,
> No feet, no swift knees, no generative organs,
> But he was Sphairos [i.e. spherical], and ‹*ev-
>   erywhere*› equal to himself.

D93 (B134) Ammonius, *Commentary on Aristotle's* On Interpretation

> For his limbs are not furnished with the head of
>   a man either,
> From his back two branches do not shoot forth,
> No feet, no swift knees, no shaggy organs,
> But he was nothing but mind (*phrên*), holy and
>   prodigious,
> Darting forth across the whole world[1] by swift   5
>   thoughts (*phrontides*).[2]

[1] I.e. himself? The term 'world' is applied to Sphairos at **D73.267.**   [2] The reference and context of this fragment are uncertain. Tzetzes attributes these lines to the third book of the poem on nature, which is often identified with the *Purifications;* and so some have thought of a divinity. Ammonius says that Empedocles speaks about Apollo there (**R95**)—hence Picot (http://www.afc.ifcs.ufrj.br/2012/Picot.pdf) identifies the subject as the sun.

Strife Ruptures Sphairos (D94–D95)

D94 (B30) Arist. *Metaph.* B4 1000b14–16 (et al.)

αὐτὰρ ἐπεὶ μέγα Νεῖκος ἐνὶ μελέεσσιν ἐθρέφθη
ἐς τιμάς τ᾽ ἀνόρουσε τελειομένοιο χρόνοιο,
ὅς σφιν ἀμοιβαῖος πλατέος παρελήλαται ὅρκου
. . .

1 αὐτὰρ ἐπεὶ Simpl. *In Phys.*, p. 1184: ἀλλ᾽ ὅτε δὴ Arist. (hinc
Syr.)   ἐθρέφθη mss: ἐρέφθη Simpl.   3 παρελήλαται
A^b: παρελήλατο EJ: παρ᾽ ἐλήλαται Sturz

D95 (B31) Simpl. *In Phys.*, p. 1184.4

πάντα γὰρ ἐξείης πελεμίζετο γυῖα θεοῖο.

The State of the World After Strife
Ruptures Sphairos? (D96)

D96 (cf. B27) Plut. *Fac. orb. lun.* 12 926E

ἔνθ᾽ οὔτ᾽ Ἠελίοιο δεδίσκεται ἀγλαὸν εἶδος
οὐδὲ μὲν οὐδ᾽ αἴης λάσιον δέμας οὐδὲ
θάλασσα.

1 δεδίσκεται Karsten: δεδίττεται mss.: διείδεται Diels (cf.
D89.1)   2 δέμας Karsten: γένος mss.: μένος Bergk

EMPEDOCLES

Strife Ruptures Sphairos (D94–D95)

D94 (B30) Aristotle, *Metaphysics*

But when Strife had grown great in his limbs[1]
And rushed upon his honors, as the time was
fulfilled
That, interchanging, is established for them [i.e.
Strife and Love, or the elements] **by a broad
oath**

. . .

[1] These are the limbs of the god (cf. **D95**), i.e. the elements
that are reunited there.

D95 (B31) Simplicius, *Commentary on Aristotle's* Physics

For all the god's limbs were shaken, one after
another.

The State of the World After Strife
Ruptures Sphairos? (D96)

D96 (cf. B27) Plutarch, *On the Face in the Moon*

There neither has the sun's brilliant form been
fashioned as a disk (?)[1]
Nor the earth's shaggy body nor the sea. [cf.
D73.279–81]

[1] The verb is uncertain. We print Karsten's conjecture *dedis-
ketai* but suggest that this might here be a form not of *deidiskomai*
('greet') or of *deidissomai* ('frighten') but of *diskoomai* ('be
shaped in the form of a disk').

453

The Stages of the Cosmogony (D97–D112)
A General Summary (D97)

D97 (< A30) Ps.-Plut. *Strom.* 10 = Eus. *PE* 1.8.10

Ἐμπεδοκλῆς ὁ Ἀκραγαντῖνος στοιχεῖα τέσσαρα, πῦρ,
ὕδωρ, αἰθέρα, γαῖαν· αἰτίαν δὲ τούτων Φιλίαν καὶ
Νεῖκος. ἐκ πρώτης φησὶ τῆς τῶν στοιχείων κράσεως
ἀποκριθέντα τὸν ἀέρα περιχυθῆναι κύκλῳ, μετὰ δὲ
τὸν ἀέρα τὸ πῦρ ἐκδραμὸν καὶ οὐκ ἔχον ἑτέραν χώραν
ἄνω ἐκτρέχειν ὑπὸ τοῦ περὶ τὸν ἀέρα πάγου. εἶναι δὲ
κύκλῳ περὶ τὴν γῆν φερόμενα δύο ἡμισφαίρια, τὸ μὲν
καθόλου πυρός, τὸ δὲ μικτὸν ἐξ ἀέρος καὶ ὀλίγου πυρός, ὅπερ οἴεται τὴν νύκτα εἶναι. τὴν δὲ ἀρχὴν τῆς
κινήσεως συμβῆναι ἀπὸ τοῦ τετυχηκέναι κατὰ τὸν
ἀθροισμὸν ἐπιβρίσαντος τοῦ πυρός [. . . = **D127,
D134c, D239**].

Initial Disorders (D98–D100)

D98 (ad B27) Plut. *Fac. orb. lun.* 12 926D–927A

[ΛΑ.] ὥσθ᾽ ὅρα καὶ σκόπει, δαιμόνιε, μὴ μεθιστὰς καὶ
ἀπάγων ἕκαστον, ὅπου πέφυκεν εἶναι, διάλυσίν τινα
κόσμου φιλοσοφῇς καὶ τὸ Νεῖκος ἐπάγῃς τὸ Ἐμπεδοκλέους τοῖς πράγμασι, μᾶλλον δὲ τοὺς παλαιοὺς
κινῇς Τιτᾶνας ἐπὶ τὴν φύσιν καὶ Γίγαντας καὶ τὴν
μυθικὴν ἐκείνην καὶ φοβερὰν ἀκοσμίαν καὶ πλημ-
μέλειαν ἐπιδεῖν ποθῇς, χωρὶς τὸ βαρὺ πᾶν καὶ χωρὶς
⟨τιθεὶς⟩[1] τὸ κοῦφον [. . . = **D96**] ὥς φησιν Ἐμπεδο-

EMPEDOCLES

The Stages of the Cosmogony (D97–D112)
A General Summary (D97)

D97 (< A30) Ps.-Plutarch, *Stromata*

Empedocles of Agrigentum says that there are four elements, fire, water, aether [i.e. air], and earth. Their cause [i.e. what acts upon them] is Love and Strife. He says that when the air was separated from the initial mixture of the elements, it spread out in a circle. After the air, the fire, rushing forth and not having any other passage upward, rushed forth from under the crust around the air. There are two hemispheres that move in a circle around the earth; the one is entirely of fire, the other is a mixture of air and a little bit of fire, which he thinks is the night. Motion originated by chance, from the fire that pressed down when it was being massed together [. . .].

Initial Disorders (D98–D100)

D98 (ad B27) Plutarch, *On the Face in the Moon*

[Lamprias, who is defending the Academic philosophers, addresses Apollonides, geometer and astronomer:] So watch out and take care, my dear friend, lest by displacing and removing each thing from where it belongs by nature you accept into your philosophy a dissolution of the world (*kosmos*) and introduce into things the Strife of Empedocles, or rather lest you arouse against nature the ancient Titans and Giants and yearn to see that mythical and terrifying chaos (*akosmia*) and confusion, <putting> everything that is heavy separately and separately what is light, [. . . = **D96**], as Empedocles says: earth had no share in

---

¹ <τιθεὶς> Bernardakis: lac. 8 litt. E, 3–4 B

455

κλῆς, οὐ γῇ θερμότητος μετεῖχεν, οὐχ ὕδωρ πνεύματος, οὐκ ἄνω τι τῶν βαρέων, οὐ κάτω τι τῶν κούφων·
ἀλλ᾽ ἄκρατοι καὶ ἄστοργοι καὶ μονάδες αἱ τῶν ὅλων
ἀρχαί, μὴ προσιέμεναι σύγκρισιν ἑτέρου πρὸς ἕτερον
μηδὲ κοινωνίαν, ἀλλὰ φεύγουσαι καὶ ἀποστρεφόμε-
ναι καὶ φερόμεναι φορὰς ἰδίας καὶ αὐθάδεις οὕτως
εἶχον ὡς ἔχει πᾶν οὗ θεὸς ἄπεστι κατὰ Πλάτωνα, τουτέστιν, ὡς ἔχει τὰ σώματα νοῦ καὶ ψυχῆς ἀπολιπού-
σης, ἄχρις οὗ τὸ ἱμερτὸν ἧκεν ἐπὶ τὴν φύσιν ἐκ προ-
νοίας, Φιλότητος ἐγγενομένης καὶ Ἀφροδίτης καὶ
Ἔρωτος, ὡς Ἐμπεδοκλῆς λέγει καὶ Παρμενίδης καὶ
Ἡσίοδος, ἵνα καὶ τόπους ἀμείψαντα καὶ δυνάμεις ἀπ᾽
ἀλλήλων μεταλαβόντα καὶ τὰ μὲν κινήσεως τὰ δὲ μονῆς ἀνάγκαις ἐνδεθέντα καὶ καταβιασθέντα πρὸς τὸ
βέλτιον, ἐξ οὗ πέφυκεν, ἐνδοῦναι καὶ μεταστῆναι <τά-
ξιν καὶ>[2] ἁρμονίαν καὶ κοινωνίαν ἀπεργάσηται τοῦ
παντός.

[2] <τάξιν καὶ> suppl. Bernardakis: lac. 7 litt. E, 8–9 B: alii alia

D99 (A49)

a Phil. *Prov.* 2.60, p. 86.15–36

 Զաւասար նմին՝ սակայն եւ մասունքն աշխարհիս
կրել երեւին, որպէս ասէ Եմպեդոկլէս: Քանզի իրրեւ
մեկնեալ արփիայն[1] թոյւցեալ էր հոզմոյ եւ հրոյ, եւ էր

[1] յարփիայն Aucher: արփիայն Kingsley: յ expunctum est in
ms. 333 St. Iacobi

heat, nor water in breath, nothing that is heavy was on high, nothing that is light down below; on the contrary, the principles of everything, unmixed, unloving, solitary monads that desire neither mixture nor communion with one another but flee, turn aside, and follow their own self-willed courses, were in the same condition as is everything from which god is absent, as Plato says (*Timaeus* 53b), that is, in the condition of bodies when the mind and soul has left them, until attractiveness arrives to nature from providence, with the arrival of Love, Aphrodite, and Eros, as Empedocles says, and Parmenides [**PARM. D16**], and Hesiod [cf. **COSM. T10**], so that, exchanging their places and receiving their powers from each other, bound by the necessities of motion for the ones and by those of rest for the others, compelled to give in to the better, from which they come by nature, and to change their ⟨order,⟩ they produce the harmony and communion of the whole.

D99 (A49)

a Philo, *On Providence*

But the parts of this world too seem to undergo [scil. something] identical to this, as Empedocles says. For when the aether was separated off, the wind and fire lifted it upward, and it was what it came to be:[1] the heavens,

---

[1] ἔηϐι may render here either a perfect or an aorist form of γίγνομαι.

որ եղև՝ երկին լայն մեծ ի վերայ շուրջ պատ առեալ. իսկ հուր սակաւ մի ի յերկնէ ի ներքս ճառացեալ, եւ սա յարեզական ճառագայթս ածէցաւ: ի մի վայր ընթացեալ եւ խոծեալ հարկիւ իմա երկիր երեւեալ ի մէջ կայր ճառայր: Եւ շուրջ զնովաւ ամենայն ուստեք՝ քանդի իբրու փոքրագոյն էր, յուզի անխլիրտ արփի: Եւ ապա սմա կալոյ ճառոյ պատճառք աստուածով, եւ ոչ շրջանակաւք ի միճեանզ վերայ բազմաւք եղեալ: Որոյ շրջաբերութիւնքն բոլորակաւք ճախարակեցին զնէ: Քանզի շուրջ զնովաւ արզելեալ փակեցաւ լամբար իմա շրջանակ սքանչելի. զի մեծ եւ բազում տեսլեան գաւրութիւն, վասն որոյ ոչ յայսկոյս եւ ոչ յայնկոյս անկեալ սորա:

b Aët. 2.6.3 (Ps.-Plut.; cf. Ps.-Gal.) [ἀπὸ ποίου πρώτου στοιχείου ἤρξατο κοσμοποιεῖν ὁ θεός]

Ἐμπεδοκλῆς τὸν μὲν αἰθέρα πρῶτον διακριθῆναι, δεύτερον δὲ τὸ πῦρ ἐφ᾽ ᾧ τὴν γῆν, ἐξ ἧς ἄγαν περισφιγγομένης τῇ ῥύμῃ τῆς περιφορᾶς ἀναβλύσαι τὸ ὕδωρ· ἐξ οὗ ἀναθυμιαθῆναι[1] τὸν ἀέρα, καὶ γενέσθαι τὸν μὲν οὐρανὸν ἐκ τοῦ αἰθέρος, τὸν δὲ ἥλιον ἐκ τοῦ πυρός, πιληθῆναι δὲ ἐκ τῶν ἄλλων τὰ περίγεια.

[1] ἀναθυμιαθῆναι Gal.: θυμιαθῆναι mss.

broad and vast, encircling [scil. everything] from above;
but the fire, remaining somewhat below the heavens, grew
in turn into sunbeams. The earth, moving quickly to a
single place and condensing out of some necessity, appeared and then remained in the middle. And around it
on every side, since it [i.e. the earth] was smaller,[2] the
aether is agitated without changing its location. Consequently, the cause for its remaining [scil. in its place] is
due to God, and not to the many circles placed over
one another. And the circular revolutions rounded off its
shape, as if on a lathe. For, surrounding it all around, a sort
of torch, a marvelous circle, enclosed it; for large and great
is the power of the form, and it is thanks to this that it [i.e.
the earth] has not fallen to one side or the other.[3]

[2] Or: "since it [i.e. the aether] was lighter."
[3] Translation and notes by Irene Tinti.

b Aëtius

Empedocles says that aether was the first to be separated
out, second fire, followed by earth, which, constricted
tightly by the force of the rotation, released water that
gushed up; out of this, air evaporated, and the sky came
about out of the aether, the sun out of the fire, and the
regions surrounding the earth were compressed out of the
other things.

EARLY GREEK PHILOSOPHY V

D100 (> A66) Tzetz. *In Il.*, p. 42.17–25

κατὰ γὰρ Ἐμπεδοκλέα τὸν φυσικὸν καὶ μετὰ τὸ γῆν
φανῆναι καὶ θάλασσαν ἀτάκτως καὶ ἔτι τὰ στοιχεῖα
κεκίνητο ποτὲ μὲν τοῦ πυρὸς ὑπερνικῶντος καὶ κατα-
φλέγοντος, ὁτὲ δὲ τῆς ὑδατώδους ὑπερβλυζούσης καὶ
κατακλυζούσης ἐπιρροῆς. καὶ τὸν ἥλιον δὲ ὁ αὐτὸς
διὰ τὸ ἄτακτόν φησι τῆς φθορᾶς καὶ ἀστήρικτον τοσ-
οὗτόν γε τῇ ἡμερησίῳ βραδύνειν πορείᾳ, ὅσος νῦν
καιρός ἐστιν ὁ ἑπτάμηνος [. . . = **D179b**].

Places and Exchanges of Places (D101–D112)

D101 (B22) Simpl. *In Phys.*, pp. 160.28–161.7 (et al.)

ἄρθμια μὲν γὰρ ταῦτα ἑαυτῶν πάντα μέρεσσιν,
ἠλέκτωρ τε χθών τε καὶ οὐρανὸς ἠδὲ θάλασσα,
ὅσσα φιν ἐν θνητοῖσιν ἀποπλαχθέντα πέφυκεν.
ὣς δ' αὔτως ὅσα κρᾶσιν ἐπαρκέα μᾶλλον
ἔασιν,
5   ἀλλήλοις ἔστερκται ὁμοιωθέντ' Ἀφροδίτῃ.
ἐχθρὰ <δ' ἃ> πλεῖστον ἀπ' ἀλλήλων διέχουσι
μάλιστα
γέννῃ τε κρήσει τε καὶ εἴδεσιν ἐκμακτοῖσι

1 ἄρθμια DE: ἄρτια F   ταῦτα ἑαυτῶν Diels: ἑαυτὰ
ἑαυτῶν DE: αὐτὰ ἑαυτῶν F   4 κρῆσιν Diels (cf. v. 7)
6 ἔχθρα F: ἔργα DE   <δ' ἃ> Diels   7 κρήσει Diels:
κράσει ed. Ald., Theophr. *Sens.* 16: κρίσει mss.

460

D100 (> A66) Tzetzes, *Commentary on Homer's* Iliad

For according to the natural philosopher Empedocles, even after the earth and sea appeared, the elements still moved in a disorderly fashion, at one time the fire being victorious and kindling things, at another time the watery flow gushing out and flooding. The same man also says that the sun, because of the disorder and instability caused by the destruction, was as slow in its daily travel as the period of seven months is now [. . .].

Places and Exchanges of Places (D101–D112)

D101 (B22) Simplicius, *Commentary on Aristotle's* Physics

For these are all joined in their own parts,
The shining one [i.e. the sun]**, the earth, the sky,**
    and the sea,
Which all by nature wander far from them[1]
    among mortal things.
In the same way, all the things that are, rather,
    receptive of mixture
Love one another, made similar by Aphrodite.   5
Enemies ⟨are those that⟩ **keep most distant from**
    one another
In birth, mixture, and molded forms,

[1] Probably: the elements from which came the great masses of the world, mentioned in the preceding line.

πάντη συγγίνεσθαι ἀήθεα καὶ μάλα λυγρά
Νεικεογεννήτοισιν, ὅτι σφίσι †γένναν ὀργᾶ†.

9 νεικεογεννήτοισιν Stein: νεικεογεννέστησιν mss. (cf.
Simpl. 161.12 τοῖς νεικεογενέσι): Νείκεος ἐννεσίῃσιν Panzerbieter ὀργᾶ] ἔοργεν Diels, alii alia

D102 (B51) Hdn. *Schem. Hom.* 13 (et al.)

Ἐμπεδοκλῆς·

καρπαλίμως δ' ἀνόπαιον ∪ | – ∪ ∪ | – ∪ ∪ | – –

ἐπὶ τοῦ πυρός.

D103 (A35) Ach. Tat. *Introd. Arat.* 4

ὁ δὲ Ἐμπεδοκλῆς οὐ δίδωσι τοῖς στοιχείοις ὡρισμέ-
νους τόπους, ἀλλ' ἀντιπαραχωρεῖν ἀλλήλοις φησίν,
ὥστε καὶ τὴν γῆν μετέωρον φέρεσθαι καὶ τὸ πῦρ τα-
πεινότερον.

D104 (B36) Stob. 1.10.11

τῶν δὲ συνερχομένων ἐξ ἔσχατον ἵστατο
Νεῖκος.

In every way strangers to unification and
 terribly sad,
Because for them, who were born from Strife
 (?), †. . .†.

D102 (B51) Herodian, *Homeric Stylistic Figures*

Empedocles:

Swiftly upward . . .

with regard to fire.[1]

[1] Herodian is illustrating one of the two supposed meanings
('invisible' or 'that rises upward') of the term *anopaia,* which is
found only at *Od.* 1.320. It is impossible to assign this isolated
phrase to a precise thematic context.

D103 (A35) Achilles Tatius, *Introduction to Aratus'* Phaenomena

Empedocles does not assign determinate places to the
elements but says that they yield their place to each other
in turn, so that the earth moves up on high, and the fire
farther down.

D104 (B36) Stobaeus, *Anthology*

**And as they came together, Strife moved away
 the farthest.**

D105 (B53) Arist. *GC* 2.6 334a3

οὕτω γὰρ συνέκυρσε θέων τοτέ, πολλάκι δ'
ἄλλως.

D106 (cf. B59) Simpl. *In Phys.*, p. 327.29

‒ ∪ ∪ | ‒ ∪ ∪ | ‒ ∪ ὅπῃ συνέκυρσεν ἅπαντα

ἅπαντα mss. (et Simpl. *In Phys.*, p. 330): ἕκαστα Simpl. *In Cael.*, p. 586

D107 (B104) Simpl. *In Phys.*, p. 331.14

καὶ καθ' ὅσον μὲν ἀραιότατα ξυνέκυρσε
πεσόντα.

D108 (B54) Arist. *GC* 2.6 334a4–5

αἰθήρ – μακρῇσι κατὰ χθόνα δύετο ῥίζαις.

versus curtus ad init., lac. indic. Diels: post αἰθήρ add. δ' αὖ Diels, τοι vel γὰρ Sturz, ante add. ἀλλ' Diels, alii alia

D109 (B52) Procl. *In Tim.* 3 ad 31b (vol. 2, p. 8.28 Diehl)

πολλὰ δ' ἔνερθ' οὔδεος πυρὰ καίεται ‒ ∪ ∪ | ‒ ‒

ἔνερθεν mss., corr. Sturz

D110 (A68) Sen. *Quaest. nat.* 3.24.1–3

Empedocles existimat ignibus, quos multis locis terra

D105 (B53) Aristotle, *On Generation and Corruption*

> **For it was in this way that it** [scil. aether]
> **happened to run** [or: encountered in its course]
> **sometimes, but often** [scil. it did so]
> **differently.**

D106 (cf. B59) Simplicius, *Commentary on Aristotle's*
Physics

> . . . **in the way that they all chanced** [or: met]

D107 (B104) Simplicius, *Commentary on Aristotle's*
Physics

[a little after **D243**][1]

> **And to the extent that the least dense ones**
> **happened to fall** [or: encountered while falling]

[1] From Simplicius we know the relative location of this line in
the poem. The order presented here is thematic (the motion of
the elements).

D108 (B54) Aristotle, *On Generation and Corruption*

> **Aether sank down under the earth by long**
> **roots.**

D109 (B52) Proclus, *Commentary on Plato's* Timaeus

> **Many fires burn below the ground.**

D110 (A68) Seneca, *Natural Questions*

Empedocles thinks that water is heated by fires that the

opertos tegit, aquam calescere, si subiecti sunt[1] solo per
quod aquis transcursus est. facere solemus dracones et
miliaria et complures formas, in quibus aere tenui fistulas
struimus per declive circumdatas, ut saepe eundem ignem
ambiens aqua per tantum fluat spatii, quantum efficiendo
calori sat est: frigida itaque intrat, effluit calida. idem sub
terra Empedocles existimat fieri.

[1] post sunt *add.* et Φ, *om.* ΔT: sunt ei *Haase, Michaelis*

D111 (A69) Plut. *Prim. frig.* 19 953E

ταυτὶ δὲ τὰ ἐμφανῆ, κρημνοὺς καὶ σκοπέλους καὶ
πέτρας, Ἐμπεδοκλῆς μὲν ὑπὸ τοῦ πυρὸς οἴεται τοῦ ἐν
βάθει τῆς γῆς ἑστάναι καὶ ἀνέχεσθαι διερειδόμενα
φλεγμαίνοντος.

D112 (A69) Ps.-Arist. *Probl.* 24.11 937a11–16 [διὰ τί
ὑπὸ τῶν θερμῶν ὑδάτων μᾶλλον ἢ ὑπὸ τῶν ψυχρῶν
πήγνυνται λίθοι]

πότερον ὅτι τῇ τοῦ ὑγροῦ ἐκλείψει γίνεται λίθος, μᾶλλον δὲ ὑπὸ τοῦ θερμοῦ ἢ τοῦ ψυχροῦ ἐκλείπει τὸ
ὑγρόν, καὶ ἀπολιθοῦται δὴ διὰ τὸ θερμόν, καθάπερ
καὶ Ἐμπεδοκλῆς φησι τάς τε πέτρας καὶ τοὺς λίθους
καὶ τὰ θερμὰ τῶν ὑδάτων γίνεσθαι.

earth keeps covered up in many places, when these lie buried in the ground through which the waters pass. People are accustomed to make water heaters called 'serpents' and 'milestones' or possessing other forms, in which they set thin bronze pipes arranged in a circle and slanting downward, so that the water, circulating around the same fire many times, flows through a space sufficient to heat it. In this way it enters cold and flows out warm. Empedocles thinks that the same thing happens under the earth.

D111 (A69) Plutarch, *On the Principle of Cold*

The cliffs, promontories, and rocks that we see, Empedocles thinks, were formed and rise up by the effect of the fire blazing in the depths of the earth.

D112 (A69) Ps.-Aristotle, *Problems* [Why stones are hardened by hot waters more than by cold ones]

Is it because a stone comes about by the withdrawal of moisture, and moisture withdraws more because of heat than because of cold, and therefore petrification occurs because of heat, as Empedocles says that rocks, stones, and hot waters come about?

Cosmology (D113–D148)
Limits and Orientation of the World (D113–D114)

D113 (B39) Arist. *Cael.* 2.13 294a25–28 (et al.)

εἴπερ ἀπείρονα γῆς τε βάθη καὶ δαψιλὸς αἰθήρ,
ὡς διὰ πολλῶν δὴ γλώσσης ῥηθέντα ματαίως
ἐκκέχυται στομάτων ὀλίγον τοῦ παντὸς
ἰδόντων.

2 ῥηθέντα] ἐλθόντα Clem. Alex. *Strom.* 6.149

D114 (A50) Aët. 2.10.2 (Ps.-Plut.) [τίνα δεξιὰ τοῦ
κόσμου καὶ τίνα ἀριστερά]

Ἐμπεδοκλῆς δεξιὰ μὲν τὰ κατὰ τὸν θερινὸν τροπικόν,
ἀριστερὰ δὲ τὰ κατὰ τὸν χειμερινόν.

Sky and Earth (D115–D120)

D115 (< A1) Diog. Laert. 8.77

[. . .] αὐτὸν δὲ τὸν οὐρανὸν κρυσταλλοειδῆ [. . .].

D116 (Nachtrag I, p. 499) Arist. *Cael.* 2.1 284a24–26

οὔτε [. . .] ὑποληπτέον [. . .] διὰ τὴν δίνησιν θάττονος
τυγχάνοντα φορᾶς τῆς οἰκείας ῥοπῆς ἔτι σῴζεσθαι
τοσοῦτον χρόνον, καθάπερ Ἐμπεδοκλῆς φησιν.

Cosmology (D113–D148)
Limits and Orientation of the World (D113–D114)

D113 (B39) Aristotle, *On the Heavens*

If the depths of the earth as well as the vast
 aether are unlimited,
As what is said in vain that
Flows out from the tongue of the many mouths
 of those who see little of the whole.[1]

[1] Cf. **XEN. D41** (for the earth).

D114 (A50) Aëtius

Empedocles: on the right the parts [scil. of the world] located toward the summer tropic, on the left those toward the winter one.

Sky and Earth (D115–D120)

D115 (< A1) Diogenes Laertius

[. . . scil. he says that] that the sky itself is like a crystal [. . .].

D116 (Nachtrag I, p. 499) Aristotle, *On the Heavens*

Nor [. . .] should one believe [. . .] that it [i.e. the sky], having received because of the vortex a motion more rapid than its own drive, is still preserved for such a long time, as Empedocles says.

D117 (cf. A67) Arist. *Cael.*

a 3.2 300b2–3

[. . .] καθάπερ φησὶν Ἐμπεδοκλῆς τὴν γῆν ὑπὸ τῆς δίνης ἠρεμεῖν.

b 2.13 295a16–21

[. . .] οἱ δ' ὥσπερ Ἐμπεδοκλῆς τὴν τοῦ οὐρανοῦ φορὰν κύκλῳ περιθέουσαν καὶ θᾶττον φερομένην ἢ τὴν τῆς γῆς φορὰν κωλύειν, καθάπερ τὸ ἐν τοῖς κυάθοις ὕδωρ· καὶ γὰρ τοῦτο κύκλῳ τοῦ κυάθου φερομένου πολλάκις κάτω τοῦ χαλκοῦ γινόμενον ὅμως οὐ φέρεται, κάτω πεφυκὸς φέρεσθαι, διὰ τὴν αὐτὴν αἰτίαν.

D118 (A51) Aët. 2.11.2 (Ps.-Plut., Stob.) [περὶ οὐρανοῦ, τίς ἡ τούτου οὐσία]

Ἐμπεδοκλῆς στερέμνιον εἶναι τὸν οὐρανὸν ἐξ ἀέρος συμπαγέντος[1] ὑπὸ πυρὸς κρυσταλλοειδῶς, τὸ[2] πυρῶδες καὶ τὸ ἀερῶδες ἐν ἑκατέρῳ τῶν ἡμισφαιρίων περιέχοντα.

[1] παγέντος Stob.   [2] τὸ om. Plut.

D119 (A50) Aët. 2.31.4 (Stob.) [περὶ τῶν ἀποστημάτων]

Ἐμπεδοκλῆς τοῦ ὕψους τοῦ ἀπὸ τῆς γῆς εἰς ⟨τὸν⟩[1] οὐρανόν, ἥτις ἐστὶν ἀφ' ἡμῶν ἀνάτασις, πλείονα εἶναι τὴν κατὰ τὸ πλάτος διάστασιν, κατὰ τοῦτο τοῦ οὐρα-

470

EMPEDOCLES

D117 (cf. A67) Aristotle, *On the Heavens*

a

[. . .] as Empedocles says that the earth is at rest because of the vortex.

b

[. . .] Others, like Empedocles, [scil. say] that the motion of the sky, moving in a circle and more rapidly than the motion of the earth, prevents the latter, like what happens to water in cups. For it is for the same reason that this latter too, although it often ends up being below the bronze, all the same does not move when the cup is moved in a circle, even though its nature is to move downward.

D118 (A51) Aëtius

Empedocles: the sky is solid, made of air that has been solidified like crystal by fire, and it surrounds the fiery and the airy regions in each of the two hemispheres.

D119 (A50) Aëtius

Empedocles: larger than the height from the earth to the sky that hangs over us is the distance in breadth, the sky

---

[1] εἰς ⟨τὸν⟩ Diels: εἰς P²: οἷον FP¹

νοῦ μᾶλλον ἀναπεπταμένου διὰ τὸ ᾠῷ παραπλησίως
τὸν κόσμον κεῖσθαι.

D120 (A58) Aët. 2.8.2 (Ps.-Plut.) [τίς ἡ αἰτία τοῦ τὸν
κόσμον ἐγκλιθῆναι]

Ἐμπεδοκλῆς τοῦ ἀέρος εἴξαντος τῇ τοῦ ἡλίου ὁρμῇ
ἐγκλιθῆναι τὰς ἄρκτους, καὶ τὰ μὲν βόρεια ὑψωθῆναι
τὰ δὲ νότια ταπεινωθῆναι, καθ' ὃ καὶ τὸν ὅλον κόσμον.

The Heavenly Bodies (D121)

D121 Aët. (Ps.-Plut.) [τίς ἡ οὐσία τῶν ἄστρων, πλα-
νητῶν καὶ ἀπλανῶν, καὶ πῶς συνέστη]

a (A53) 2.13.2

Ἐμπεδοκλῆς πύρινα ἐκ τοῦ πυρώδους, ὅπερ ὁ ἀὴρ[1] ἐν
ἑαυτῷ περιέχων ἐξανέθλιψε κατὰ τὴν πρώτην διάκρισιν.

[1] ἀὴρ Mm: αἰθήρ Plut. Π

b (A54) 2.13.11

Ἐμπεδοκλῆς τοὺς μὲν ἀπλανεῖς ἀστέρας συνδεδέσθαι
τῷ κρυστάλλῳ, τοὺς δὲ πλανήτας ἀνεῖσθαι.

being more extended in this direction since the world has a shape similar to an egg.

D120 (A58) Aëtius

Empedocles: the air having yielded to the drive of the sun, the poles became inclined and the north went up while the south went down, and the whole world correspondingly.

The Heavenly Bodies (D121)

D121 Aëtius

a (A53)

Empedocles: they [i.e. the heavenly bodies, the planets and the fixed stars] are fiery and come from the fiery element, which the air that surrounded it in itself extruded upward during the first separation.

b (A54)

Empedocles: the fixed stars are fastened onto the crystalline [scil. vault], while the planets are unfastened.

The Sun (D122–D133)
Nature of the Sun (D122–D125)

D122 (B38) Clem. Alex. *Strom.* 5.48.3

εἰ δ' ἄγε τοι λέξω ∪ ∪ | – πρῶθ' ἥλιον ἀρχήν,
ἐξ ὧν δῆλ' ἐγένοντο τὰ νῦν ἐσορῶμεν ἅπαντα,
γαῖά τε καὶ πόντος πολυκύμων ἠδ' ὑγρὸς ἀήρ,
Τιτὰν ἠδ' αἰθὴρ σφίγγων περὶ κύκλον ἅπαντα.

1 versus curtus   εἰ δ'] εἶτ' Koetschau   ⟨νῦν⟩ τοι
⟨ἐγὼ⟩ Mayor, τοι ⟨μὲν ἐγὼ⟩ Potter   ⟨πάντων⟩ πρῶθ'
Sylburg   ἥλιον mss.: ἥλικα τ' Diels   2 δῆλ' H. Weil:
δὴ ms.

D123 (B44) Plut. *Pyth. orac.* 12 400B

ἀνταυγεῖ πρὸς Ὄλυμπον ἀταρβήτοισι
προσώποις.

ἀταρβήτοις mss., corr. Wyttenbach

D124 (B41) *Etym. Mag.* 426.54–427.1 s.v. ἥλιος (et al.)

ἀλλ' ὁ μὲν ἁλισθεὶς μέγαν οὐρανὸν
ἀμφιπολεύει.

ἀλλ' ὁ μὲν *Etym. Mag.*, *Etym. Gud.* 241.22   μέγαν
Etym. Gud. 241.22: μέσον *Etym. Mag.*, *Etym. Gud.* 241.46

The Sun (D122–D133)
Nature of the Sun (D122–D125)

D122 (B38) Clement of Alexandria, *Stromata*

> But come, I shall tell you, ⟨*beginning?*⟩ **first with
> the sun,**[1]
> **From what all the things that we now look upon
> became visible,**
> **Earth and sea with many waves and moist air,**
> **The Titan and Aether, gripping all things in a
> circle.**[2]

[1] This line is missing some syllables, but it is unlikely that the meaning is much affected.　　[2] The sun ('Titan') and the aether are the two aspects of one and the same reality, the former being only the concentrated reflection of the latter (cf. the following note).

D123 (B44) Plutarch, *On the Pythian Oracles*

> It [i.e. the sun] **shines back toward Olympus with
> fearless countenance.**

D124 (B41) *Etymologicum Magnum*

> But he [i.e. the sun, *hêlios*], **concentrated
> (*halistheis*),**[1] **moves in a circle around the vast
> sky.**

[1] The name of the sun is etymologized; the concentration is that of the aether reflected onto the vault of the sky by the earth (cf. **D126–D127**).

D125 (B40) Plut. *Fac. orb. lun.* 2 920C

ἥλιος ὀξυβελὴς ἠδ᾽ ἱλάειρα σελήνη

ὀξυμελὴς mss., corr. Turnebus   λάιρα mss., corr.
Turnebus: ⟨ἡ⟩ ἱλάειρα Wilamowitz

The Sun and Its Course (D126–D130)

D126 (A56) Aët.

a 2.20.13 (Ps.-Plut.) [περὶ οὐσίας ἡλίου]

Ἐμπεδοκλῆς δύο ἡλίους, τὸν μὲν ἀρχέτυπον, πῦρ ἐν
τῷ ἑτέρῳ ἡμισφαιρίῳ τοῦ κόσμου πεπληρωκὸς τὸ
ἡμισφαίριον, ἀεὶ καταντικρὺ τῇ ἀνταυγείᾳ ἑαυτοῦ τε-
ταγμένον· τὸν δὲ φαινόμενον, ἀνταύγειαν ἐν τῷ ἑτέρῳ
ἡμισφαιρίῳ τῷ τοῦ ἀέρος τοῦ θερμομιγοῦς πεπληρω-
μένῳ ἀπὸ κυκλοτεροῦς τῆς γῆς κατ᾽ ἀνάκλασιν ἐγ-
γιγνομένην εἰς τὸν Ὄλυμπον[1] τὸν κρυσταλλοειδῆ,
συμπεριελκομένην δὲ τῇ κινήσει τοῦ πυρίνου· ὡς δὲ
βραχέως εἰρῆσθαι συντεμόντα, ἀνταύγειαν εἶναι τοῦ
περὶ τὴν γῆν πυρὸς τὸν ἥλιον.

   [1] ὄλυμπον Mansfeld ex vers. Arab.: ἥλιον Plut.

b Aët. 2.21.2 (Stob.) [περὶ μεγέθους ἡλίου]

Ἐμπεδοκλῆς ἴσον τῇ γῇ τὸν κατὰ τὴν ἀνταύγειαν.

   post ἴσον add. δὲ Stob.

D125 (B40) Plutarch, *On the Face in the Moon*

Sharp-shooting sun and mild moon

The Sun and Its Course (D126–D130)

D126 (A56) Aëtius

a

Empedocles: there are two suns: the one is the archetype, the fire in one of the two hemispheres of the world, which has filled that hemisphere and is always located opposite its own reflection; and the other is the one that appears, the reflection in the other hemisphere filled with air mixed with fire, produced by the reflection of the round earth upon the crystalline Olympus [i.e. the vault of the sky], and drawn along conjointly by the motion of the fiery element. And to summarize it briefly, the sun is the reflection of the fire surrounding the earth.

b

Empedocles: the one [scil. sun] produced by reflection is equal to the earth.

D127 (< A30) Ps.-Plut. *Strom.* 10 = Eus. *PE* 1.8.10

[. . . = **D97**] ὁ δὲ ἥλιος τὴν φύσιν οὐκ ἔστι πῦρ, ἀλλὰ τοῦ πυρὸς ἀντανάκλασις ὁμοία τῇ ἀφ᾽ ὕδατος γινομένη [. . . = **D134c**].

D128 (< A1) Diog. Laert. 8.77

καὶ τὸν μὲν ἥλιόν φησι πυρὸς ἄθροισμα μέγα καὶ τῆς σελήνης μείζω.

D129 (A50) Aët. 2.1.4 (Stob.) [περὶ κόσμου]

Ἐμπεδοκλῆς τὸν τοῦ ἡλίου περίδρομον εἶναι περιγραφὴν τοῦ πέρατος τοῦ κόσμου.

D130 (A58) Aët. 2.23.3 (Ps.-Plut., Stob.) [περὶ τροπῶν ἡλίου]

Ἐμπεδοκλῆς ὑπὸ τῆς περιεχούσης αὐτὸν σφαίρας κωλυόμενον ἄχρι παντὸς εὐθυπορεῖν καὶ ὑπὸ των τροπικῶν κύκλων.

The Night (D131)

D131 (B48) Plut. *Quaest. Plat.* 8.3 1006F

νύκτα δὲ γαῖα τίθησιν ὑφισταμένη φάεσσι

ὑφισταμένη] ἐφισταμένη Scaliger: ὑφισταμένοιο coni. Diels

478

D127 (< A30) Ps.-Plutarch, *Stromata*

[. . .] The sun by its nature is not fire, but the reflection of fire, similar to the one produced by water [. . .].

D128 (< A1) Diogenes Laertius

And he says that the sun is a large aggregate of fire and that it is larger than the moon.

D129 (A50) Aëtius

Empedocles: the circular course of the sun is the circumference of the limit of the world.

D130 (A58) Aëtius

Empedocles: it [i.e. the sun] is prevented by the sphere surrounding it and by the tropical circles from following its path straight to the end.

The Night (D131)

D131 (B48) Plutarch, *Platonic Questions*

The earth makes the night by opposing its [i.e. the sun's] **rays**

The Solar Eclipse (D132–D133)

D132 (B42) Plut. *Fac. orb. lun.* 16 929C

– ◡ ◡ | – ◡ ◡ | – ◡ ἀπεσκέδασεν δέ οἱ αὐγάς
†ἔστε αἶαν† καθύπερθεν, ἀπεσκνίφωσε δὲ γαίης
τόσσον ὅσον τ’ εὖρος γλαυκώπιδος ἔπλετο
μήνης.

1 ἀπεσκεύασε mss., corr. Xylander: ἀπεστέγασεν Diels: ἀπ-
εσκίασεν Bergk   2 ἔστε αἶαν mss.: ἔστ’ ἂν ἴῃ Diels: ἐς
γαῖαν Xylander

D133 (A59) Aët. 2.24.7 (Stob.) [περὶ ἐκλείψεως ἡλίου]

ἔκλειψιν δὲ γίνεσθαι σελήνης αὐτὸν ὑπερχομένης.

The Moon (D134–D142)
Nature and Shape of the Moon (D134–D135)

D134

a (A60) Aët. 2.25.15 [περὶ οὐσίας σελήνης]

Ἐμπεδοκλῆς ἀέρα συνεστραμμένον νεφοειδῆ, πεπη-
γότα ὑπὸ πυρός, ὥστε σύμμικτον.

b (A60) Plut. *Fac. orb. lun.* 5 922C

καὶ γὰρ Ἐμπεδοκλεῖ δυσκολαίνουσι πάγον ἀέρος χα-
λαζώδη ποιοῦντι τὴν σελήνην ὑπὸ τῆς τοῦ πυρὸς
σφαίρας περιεχόμενον [. . .].

EMPEDOCLES

The Solar Eclipse (D132–D133)

D132 (B42) Plutarch, *On the Face in the Moon*

> **It** [i.e. the lunar body] **scattered his** [i.e. the sun's] **rays**
> †**All the way to the earth**†[1] **from above, and it obscured as much**
> **Of the earth as was the breadth of the gray-eyed moon.**

[1] The turn of phrase is not archaic, and the idea does not square well with the explanation of an eclipse.

D133 (A59) Aëtius

[Empedocles:] an eclipse [scil. of the sun] comes about when the moon passes under it.

The Moon (D134–D142)
Nature and Shape of the Moon (D134–D135)

D134

a (A60) Aëtius

Empedocles: it [i.e. the moon] is congealed air, cloud-like, solidified by fire, so that it is a mixture.

b (A60) Plutarch, *On the Face in the Moon*

For they [i.e. the Stoics] are annoyed with Empedocles because he posits that the moon is a mass of air congealed like hail, surrounded by the sphere of fire [. . .].

481

c (< A30) Ps.-Plut. *Strom.* 10 = Eus. *PE* 1.8.10

[. . . = **D127**] σελήνην δέ φησιν συστῆναι καθ᾽ ἑαυτὴν
ἐκ τοῦ ἀποληφθέντος ἀέρος ὑπὸ τοῦ πυρός· τοῦτον
γὰρ παγῆναι, καθάπερ καὶ τὴν χάλαζαν· τὸ δὲ φῶς
αὐτὴν ἔχειν ἀπὸ τοῦ ἡλίου [. . . = **D239**].

D135

a (A60) Plut. *Quaest. Rom.* 101 288B

τὸ γὰρ φαινόμενον σχῆμα τῆς σελήνης, ὅταν ᾖ δι-
χόμηνος, οὐ σφαιροειδὲς ἀλλὰ φακοειδές ἐστι καὶ
δισκοειδές, ὡς δ᾽ Ἐμπεδοκλῆς οἴεται, καὶ τὸ ὑποκεί-
μενον.

b (< A1). Diog. Laert. 8.77

[. . .] φησι [. . .] τὴν δὲ σελήνην δισκοειδῆ [. . .].

Distance of the Moon (D136–D137)

D136 (A61) Aët. 2.31.1 (Ps.-Plut., Stob.) [περὶ τῶν ἀπο-
στημάτων]

Ἐμπεδοκλῆς διπλάσιον ἀπέχειν τὴν σελήνην ἀπὸ τοῦ
ἡλίου ἤπερ ἀπὸ τῆς γῆς.[1]

---

[1] ἀπέχειν. . . γῆς Plut: ἀπέχειν τῆς σελήνης ἀπὸ γῆς ἤπερ
ἀπὸ τοῦ ἡλίου Stob.: ἀπέχειν τὸν ἥλιον ἀπὸ τῆς γῆς ἤπερ
τὴν σελήνην Diels

c (< A30) Ps.-Plutarch, *Stromata*

He says that the moon is in itself made of air that has been blocked by the fire; for this [i.e. the air] became solidified, like hail. Its light it has from the sun.

D135

a (A60) Plutarch, *Roman Questions*

The apparent form of the moon when it is full is not that of a sphere but of a lentil and a quoit, as Empedocles thinks that its form really is.

b (< A1) Diogenes Laertius

He says [. . .] and that the moon has the form of a quoit [. . .].

Distance of the Moon (D136–D137)

D136 (A61) Aëtius

Empedocles: the moon is twice as far from the sun as from the earth.

D137 (< B46) Plut. *Fac. orb. lun.* 9 925B

[. . .] τῆς δὲ γῆς τρόπον τινὰ ψαύει καὶ περιφερομένη πλησίον

ἅρματος ὡς πέρι χνοίη ἑλίσσεται – ∪ ∪ | – –[1]

φησὶν Ἐμπεδοκλῆς

ἢ †τε περὶ† ἄκραν . . .[2]

[1] ὡς πέρι χνοίη ἑλίσσεται Panzerbieter: ὥσπερ ἴχνος ἀνελίσσεται mss.   [2] post ἄκραν lac. XVII lit. E, XXV B, παρ' ἄκρην ‹νύσσαν (vel γαῖαν)› ἐλαυνομένη Diels

Light of the Moon (D138–D141)

D138 (B47) *Coll. locut. util.* s.v. ἀγής = Anecd. Gr. 1.337.15 Bekker

ἀθρεῖ μὲν γὰρ ἄνακτος ἐναντίον ἀγέα κύκλον.

ἄθρει mss., corr. Karsten   ἀγέα Bollack: ἀγέα edd.

D139 (B45) Ach. Tat. *Introd. Arat.* 16

κυκλοτερὲς περὶ γαῖαν ἑλίσσεται ἀλλότριον φῶς.

D140 (B43, ad B42) Plut. *Fac. orb. lun.* 16 929D–E

ἀπολείπεται τοίνυν [. . .] τὸ τοῦ Ἐμπεδοκλέους ἀνακλάσει τινὶ τοῦ ἡλίου πρὸς τὴν σελήνην γίνεσθαι τὸν

D137 (< B46) Plutarch, *On the Face in the Moon*

[. . .] it [i.e. the moon] touches the earth in a certain sense and revolves near it,

as the chariot's nave whirls around,

says Empedocles,

which †. . .† the farthest . . .

Light of the Moon (D138–D141)

D138 (B47) *Collection of Useful Terms*

For she [i.e. the moon] **watches opposite the luminous circle of the ruler** [i.e. the sun].

D139 (B45) Achilles Tatius, *Introduction to Aratus'* Phaenomena

Circular, she [i.e. the moon] **turns around the earth her borrowed light.**

D140 (B43, ad B42) Plutarch, *On the Face in the Moon*

There only remains then [. . .] Empedocles' theory, that it is by a kind of reflection of the sun onto the moon that the

ἐνταῦθα φωτισμὸν ἀπ' αὐτῆς. ὅθεν οὐδὲ[1] θερμὸν οὐδὲ
λαμπρὸν ἀφικνεῖται πρὸς ἡμᾶς, ὥσπερ ἦν εἰκὸς ἐξ-
άψεως καὶ μίξεως ⟨δυοῖν⟩[2] φώτων γεγενημένης ἀλλ'
οἷον αἵ τε φωναὶ κατὰ τὰς ἀνακλάσεις ἀμαυροτέραν
ἀναφαίνουσι τὴν ἠχὼ τοῦ φθέγματος αἵ τε πληγαὶ
τῶν ἀφαλλομένων βελῶν μαλακώτεραι προσπίπτου-
σιν,

ὡς αὐγὴ[3] τύψασα σεληναίης κύκλον εὐρύν

ἀσθενῆ καὶ ἀμυδρὰν ἀνάρροιαν ἴσχει πρὸς ἡμᾶς, διὰ
τὴν κλάσιν ἐκλυομένης τῆς δυνάμεως.

[1] οὐδὲν Emperius   [2] ⟨δυοῖν⟩ Pohlenz: lac. 4 litt. E, 2–3 B:
⟨δύο⟩ Reinhardt et Raingeard, ⟨τῶν⟩ Bernardakis   [3] αὐτὴ
mss., corr. Xylander

D141 (B43) Phil. *Prov.* 2.70, p. 92.24–33

Իսկ լուսնի նշոյլ ո՛չ արդեաւք ընդունայն կարծեալ է,
թէ յարեզակնէ ըստ նախախնամութեան իմ առեալ
լինի զլոյսն, այլ ոչ որպէս ի հայելւոյ՝ որ առանկանի
ի նմա՝ ըստատրեցաւ կերպարան ընդունէլ: Ըստ որում
Եմպեդոկլէս, Լոյս ընկալեալ՝ լուսնային բոլորն մեծ եւ
լայն, վաղվաղակի դարձեալ անդրէն շրջեցաւ հասեալ
յերկին ընթանալով:

illumination is produced that comes here from it. That is also why it does not reach us hot nor bright, as would be likely if there were a kindling and mixture of ‹two› lights; but just as the reflection of voices weakens the echo of the sound, and the blows of projectiles that ricochet strike more softly,

> **So too the ray that strikes the broad circle of the moon**

reaches us in a reflux that is weak and faint, since its power has been dissolved by the reflection.

D141 (B43) Philo, *On Providence*

Indeed, is it not true that the brilliance of the moon is thought, without reason, to have received its light from the sun in accordance with some [scil. decree of] Providence, rather than being naturally disposed to receive the image that falls on it, as on a mirror? Accordingly, Empedocles [scil. says], "Having received light, the lunar globe, big and large, immediately turned back again, reaching the sky in its course."[1]

[1] An alternative interpretation, less likely (especially with this punctuation) but not impossible, of the Armenian text as attested in Aucher (1822) would be, "The light, having reached the lunar globe, big and large, immediately turned back again, reaching the sky in its course." (Translation and note by Irene Tinti)

A Limit between Two Worlds? (D142)

D142 (< A62) (Ps.-?) Hippol. *Ref.* 1.4.3

καὶ ὥσπερ ὁ Ἐμπεδοκλῆς πάντα τὸν καθ᾽ ἡμᾶς τόπον
ἔφη κακῶν μεστὸν εἶναι καὶ μέχρι μὲν σελήνης τὰ
κακὰ φθάνειν ἐκ τοῦ περὶ γῆν τόπου ταθέντα, περαι-
τέρω δὲ μὴ χωρεῖν, ἅτε καθαρωτέρου τοῦ ὑπὲρ τὴν
σελήνην παντὸς ὄντος τόπου [. . . cf. **HER. R49**].

Atmospheric Phenomena (D143–D146)

D143 (cf. B149) Plut. *Quaest. conv.* 5.8.2 683E

νεφεληγερέτην [cf. **R4**]

D144 (< A65) Aët. 3.8.1 (Ps.-Plut.) [περὶ χειμῶνος καὶ
θέρους]

Ἐμπεδοκλῆς [. . .] χειμῶνα μὲν γίνεσθαι τοῦ ἀέρος
ἐπικρατοῦντος τῇ πυκνώσει καὶ εἰς τὸ ἀνωτέρω βια-
ζομένου, θερείαν δὲ τοῦ πυρός, ὅταν εἰς τὸ κατωτέρω
βιάζηται.

D145 (< A64) Olymp. *In Meteor.*, p. 102.1–3

καὶ τί τὸ κινοῦν αὐτοὺς λοξὴν κίνησιν; ὅτι οὐ τὸ γεῶ-
δες καὶ τὸ πυρῶδες τὴν ἐναντίαν κινούμενα κίνησιν,
ὡς Ἐμπεδοκλῆς ᾤετο [. . .].

A Limit between Two Worlds? (D142)

D142 (< A62) (Ps.-?) Hippolytus, *Refutation of All Heresies*

And as Empedocles said that the whole region near us is full of evils, and that evils spread as far as the moon, extending outward from the region around the earth, but do not go any farther, since the whole region beyond the moon is purer [. . .].[1]

---

[1] It is difficult to determine what in this testimonium reflects an Aristotelianizing reading.

Atmospheric Phenomena (D143–D146)

D143 (cf. B149) Plutarch, *Table Talk*

. . . **cloud-gatherer** [i.e. air] . . .

D144 (< A65) Aëtius

Empedocles [. . .]: winter comes about when the air dominates because of its density and is forced upward, and summer when it is fire, whenever it is forced downward.

D145 (< A64) Olympiodorus, *Commentary on Aristotle's* Meteorology

And what is it that imparts an oblique motion to them [i.e. the winds]? Because it is not the fact that the earthy element and the fiery one are moving in opposite directions, as Empedocles thought [. . .].

D146 (A63)

a Arist. *Meteor.* 2.9 369b12–14

[. . .] τινὲς λέγουσιν ὡς ἐν τοῖς νέφεσιν ἐγγίνεται πῦρ. τοῦτο δ' Ἐμπεδοκλῆς μέν φησιν εἶναι τὸ ἐμπεριλαμβανόμενον τῶν τοῦ ἡλίου ἀκτίνων [. . .].

b Aët. 3.3.7 (Stob.) [περὶ βροντῶν, ἀστραπῶν, κεραυνῶν, πρηστήρων τε καὶ τυφώνων]

Ἐμπεδοκλῆς ἔμπτωσιν φωτὸς εἰς νέφος ἐξείργοντος τὸν ἀνθεστῶτα ἀέρα, οὗ τὴν μὲν σβέσιν καὶ τὴν θραῦσιν κτύπον ἀπεργάζεσθαι, τὴν δὲ λάμψιν ἀστραπήν· κεραυνὸν δὲ τὸν τῆς ἀστραπῆς τόνον.

The Sea (D147)

D147

a (cf. B55) Arist. *Meteor.* 2.3 357a25

[. . .] εἴ τις εἰπὼν ἱδρῶτα τῆς γῆς εἶναι τὴν θάλατταν[1] [. . .] καθάπερ Ἐμπεδοκλῆς.

[1] versus frustulum γῆς ἱδρῶτα (θάλασσαν) fingunt plerique edd.

b (B56) Heph. *Ench.* 1, p. 2.13

ἃλς ἐπάγη ῥιπῇσιν ἐωσμένος ἠελίοιο.

ἐπάγη ex ἐπάγει corr. P: ἐπάγει ADI

D146 (A63)

a Aristotle, *Meteorology*

[. . .] some people say [scil. about lightning] that fire comes to be in the clouds. Empedocles says that it is some rays of the sun that are enclosed within them [. . .].

b Aëtius

Empedocles: it is light that, falling onto a cloud, repels the air in front of it; its extinguishing and pulverization causes the noise, while its flash causes the lightning; and the thunderbolt is the intensity of the lightning.

The Sea (D147)

D147

a (cf. B55) Aristotle, *Meteorology*

[. . .] if someone says that the sea is the **sweat of the earth** [. . .] like Empedocles.

b (B56) Hephaestion, *Handbook*

The salt solidified, pressed by the blows of the sun.

c (A66) Aët. 3.16.3 (Ps.-Plut.) [περὶ θαλάττης, πῶς συνέστηκεν καὶ πῶς ἐστι πικρά]

Ἐμπεδοκλῆς ἱδρῶτα τῆς γῆς ἐκκαιομένης ὑπὸ τοῦ
ἡλίου διὰ τὴν ἐπὶ τὸ πλεῖον πίλησιν.

d (A66) Philo *Prov.* 2.61, pp. 86.37–87.4

Եւ ապա յաղագս ծովուն պատճառս ասելով՝ ասէ,
պնդեցելը այնր †որ ըմբռնեցեալ յանկութիւնն էր
սափչին†, մանաւանդ կարկուտքն ի վեր ձնշեալք
աղտաղտուկ ջուր: Քանզի որ միանգամ յերկրի
խոնաւութիւն է՛ ի նստաստ եւ ի հովտագոյն տեղիսն
նորա սիրտաց՝ ի միմեանց վերայ ստեպ ստեպ հողմոցն
շրջանակաւք զաւրէն կապոց իՖ հզաւրագունից
ձնշեցեալ:

Why Does the Magnet Attract Iron? (D148)

D148 (< A89) Alex. (?) *Quaest.* 2.23, p. 72.9

Ἐμπεδοκλῆς μὲν ταῖς ἀπορροίαις ταῖς ἀπ᾽ ἀμφοτέρων
καὶ τοῖς πόροις τοῖς τῆς λίθου συμμέτροις οὖσιν ταῖς
ἀπὸ τοῦ σιδήρου τὸν σίδηρον φέρεσθαι λέγει πρὸς
τὴν λίθον· αἱ μὲν γὰρ ταύτης ἀπόρροιαι τὸν ἀέρα τὸν
ἐπὶ τοῖς τοῦ σιδήρου πόροις ἀπωθοῦσί τε καὶ κινοῦσι
τὸν ἐπιπωματίζοντα αὐτούς· τούτου δὲ χωρισθέντος
ἀθρόᾳ ἀπορροίᾳ ῥεούσῃ τὸν σίδηρον ἕπεσθαι· φερο-

c (A66) Aëtius

Empedocles: it [scil. the sea] is the sweat of the earth, which has been burned up by the sun because of an increased compression.

d (A66) Philo, *On Providence*

And then, speaking about the causes of the sea, he says, "after the solidification of what had been received into the fall of (?),[1] in particular, hail, being compressed, [scil. produced] salty water. For all moisture on the earth tends to collect in its low and depressed places, while the winds press [scil. the liquids or, possibly, themselves] onto one another incessantly, in circles, like strong bonds."

[1] The sequence որ ընբրնեցեալ յանկութիւնն էր սապիշին is highly problematic, and the translation proposed here must be considered purely indicative. The question mark signals the position of the hapax or corrupted form սապիշին in the text. (Note and translation by Irene Tinti.)

Why Does the Magnet Attract Iron? (D148)

D148 (< A89) Alexander of Aphrodisias, *Problems and Solutions (Questions) on Nature*

Empedocles says that iron moves toward the stone [scil. of Heracles, i.e. the magnet] because of the effluences that come from both of them and the passages in the stone, which fit the iron's. For the latter's effluences repel the air located on the passages of the iron and displace that [scil. air] which covers them. Once this air has been removed, the iron follows the dense flux that is flowing out. The ef-

μένων δὲ τῶν ἀπ᾽ αὐτοῦ ἀπορροιῶν ἐπὶ τοὺς τῆς λίθου
πόρους, διὰ τὸ συμμέτρους τε αὐτοῖς εἶναι καὶ ἐναρ-
μόζειν καὶ τὸν σίδηρον σὺν ταῖς ἀπορροίαις ἕπεσθαί
τε καὶ φέρεσθαι.

Genesis and Structure of Living
Beings (D149–D256)
The Stages of Phylogenesis (D149–D151)

D149 (B59) Simpl. *In Cael.*, p. 587.20–23 (et al.)

αὐτὰρ ἐπεὶ κατὰ μεῖζον ἐμίσγετο δαίμονι
    δαίμων,
ταῦτά τε συμπίπτεσκον, ὅπῃ συνέκυρσεν
    ἕκαστα,
ἄλλα τε πρὸς τοῖς πολλὰ διηνεκῆ ἐξεγένοντο.

2 ἕκαστα mss.: ἄπαντα Simpl. *In Cael.*, p. 327 et p. 330

D150 (< A70) Aët. 5.26.4 (Ps.-Plut.) [πῶς ηὐξήθη τὰ
φυτὰ καὶ εἰ ζῷα]

Ἐμπεδοκλῆς πρῶτα τὰ δένδρα τῶν ζῴων ἐκ γῆς ἀνα-
δῦναί φησι πρὶν τὸν ἥλιον περιαπλωθῆναι καὶ πρὶν
ἡμέραν καὶ νύκτα διακριθῆναι [. . . = **D245**].

D151 (A72) Aët. 5.19.5 (Ps.-Plut.) [περὶ ζῴων γενέσεως,
πῶς ἐγένοντο ζῷα καὶ εἰ φθαρτά]

Ἐμπεδοκλῆς τὰς πρώτας γενέσεις τῶν ζῴων καὶ φυ-

fluences that come from this latter move toward the passages in the stone, the iron too follows them and moves along with the effluences because they fit them and are adapted to them.

Genesis and Structure of Living
Beings (D149–D256)
The Stages of Phylogenesis (D149–D151)

D149 (B59) Simplicius, *Commentary on Aristotle's* On the Heavens

> **But when a divinity was mixed more with a** [scil. different] **divinity,**
> **These** [scil. the divine elements] **would come together, according to how each one happened to be,**[1]
> **And many other things came to be born besides these, continuously.**

[1] Or: 'encountered' (cf. **D105–D107**).

D150 (< A70) Aëtius

Empedocles says that trees were the first living beings to rise up out of the earth, before the sun began its circular movement and before the day and night were separated [. . . = **D245**].

D151 (A72) Aëtius

Empedocles: the first generations of animals and plants

τῶν μηδαμῶς ὁλοκλήρους γενέσθαι, ἀσυμφυέσι δὲ
τοῖς μορίοις διεζευγμένας, τὰς δὲ δευτέρας συμφυο-
μένων τῶν μερῶν εἰδωλοφανεῖς, τὰς δὲ τρίτας τῶν
ἀλληλοφυῶν·[1] τὰς δὲ τετάρτας οὐκέτι ἐκ τῶν ὁμοίων[2]
οἷον ἐκ γῆς καὶ ὕδατος, ἀλλὰ δι᾽ ἀλλήλων ἤδη, τοῖς
μὲν πυκνωθείσης[3] ⟨τῆς⟩[4] τροφῆς, τοῖς δὲ καὶ τῆς εὐ-
μορφίας τῶν γυναικῶν ἐπερεθισμὸν τοῦ σπερματικοῦ
κινήματος ἐμποιησάσης. τῶν δὲ ζῴων πάντων τὰ
γένη διακριθῆναι διὰ τὰς ποιὰς κράσεις· τὰ μὲν[5] οἰ-
κειότερον[6] εἰς τὸ ὕδωρ τὴν ὁρμὴν ἔχειν,[7] τὰ δ᾽ εἰς ἀέρα
ἀναπτῆναι,[8] ἕως ἂν[9] πυρῶδες ἔχῃ τὸ[10] πλέον, τὰ δὲ
βαρύτερα ἐπὶ τὴν γῆν, τὰ δ᾽ ἰσόμοιρα τῇ κράσει πᾶσι
τοῖς †θώραξι[11] πεφωνηκέναι.[12]†

[1] ἀλληλοφυῶν mss.: ὁλοφυῶν Karsten   [2] ὁμοίων mss.:
οἰκείων Reiske: στοιχείων coni. Diels: ὁμοιομερῶν Diels
[3] post πυκνωθείσης hab. mss. τοῖς δὲ καὶ τοῖς ζῴοις, del.
Diels ut gloss.   [4] ⟨τῆς⟩ Diels   [5] μὲν ⟨ὑγρὰ⟩ Diels
[6] οἰκειότερα mss., corr. Diels   [7] ἔχει mss., corr. Diels
[8] ἀναπνεῖν mss., corr. Diels   [9] ἕως ἂν ΜΠ: ὥς ἂν m:
ὅσα ἂν Reiske   [10] τὸ om. m   [11] χωρίοις Diels
[12] ξυμπεφωνηκέναι Reiske: σύμφωνα εἶναι Diels

Wandering Parts and Monsters (D152–D156)

D152 (ad B61) Simpl. *In Phys.*, pp. 371.33–372.9

ὥσπερ Ἐμπεδοκλῆς κατὰ τὴν τῆς Φιλίας ἀρχήν φησι
γενέσθαι ὡς ἔτυχε μέρη πρῶτον τῶν ζῴων, οἷον κε-
φαλὰς καὶ χεῖρας καὶ πόδας, ἔπειτα συνιέναι ταῦτα

were not at all born as complete entities, but were disconnected, with parts that had not grown together; the second ones, when the parts had grown together, had the appearance of phantasms (*eidôlophaneis*); the third ones, when the parts had grown in conformity with one another (*allêlophueis*); the fourth ones no longer came from similar things, like earth and water, but henceforth from each other, in some cases because of the thickening of their food, in others too because the women's beauty caused an excitation of the spermatic movement. The species of all the animals became distinguished by virtue of the varieties of their mixtures: some had a drive toward water, with which they had a greater affinity; others flew up into the air until they possessed more of the fiery element; heavier ones [scil. went] onto the ground; and those whose mixture was in equilibrium with their whole †chest made sounds†.[1]

---

[1] The final words are presumably corrupt, as their meaning does not seem appropriate.

Wandering Parts and Monsters (D152–D156)

D152 (ad B61) Simplicius, *Commentary on Aristotle's* Physics

Thus Empedocles says that at the beginning of Love there were born first, as it happened by chance, the parts of animals, like heads, hands, and feet, and that later these came together,

βουγενῆ ἀνδρόπρῳρα, τὰ δ' ἔμπαλιν
ἐξανατέλλειν[1] [= **D156.2**]

"ἀνδρογενῆ" δηλονότι "βούπρῳρα," τουτέστιν ἐκ βοὸς
καὶ ἀνθρώπου. καὶ ὅσα μὲν οὕτω συνέστη[2] ἀλλήλοις
ὥστε δύνασθαι τυχεῖν σωτηρίας, ἐγένετο ζῷα καὶ
ἔμεινεν διὰ τὸ ἀλλήλοις ἐκπληροῦν τὴν χρείαν, τοὺς
μὲν ὀδόντας τέμνοντάς τε καὶ λεαίνοντας τὴν τροφήν,
τὴν δὲ γαστέρα πέττουσαν, τὸ δὲ ἧπαρ ἐξαιματοῦν.
καὶ ἡ μὲν τοῦ ἀνθρώπου κεφαλὴ τῷ ἀνθρωπίνῳ
σώματι συνελθοῦσα σῴζεσθαι ποιεῖ τὸ ὅλον, τῷ δὲ
τοῦ βοὸς οὐ συναρμόζει καὶ διόλλυται· ὅσα γὰρ μὴ
κατὰ τὸν οἰκεῖον συνῆλθε λόγον, ἐφθάρη. τὸν αὐτὸν
δὲ τρόπον καὶ νῦν πάντα συμβαίνει.

[1] ἐξανέτελλον Karsten   [2] σύνεστιν mss., corr. emenda-
tor Ambrosiani

D153 (B58) Simpl. *In Cael.*, p. 587.18–19

ἐν ταύτῃ οὖν τῇ καταστάσει 'μουνομελῆ' ἔτι τὰ γυῖα
ἀπὸ τῆς τοῦ Νείκους διακρίσεως ὄντα ἐπλανᾶτο τῆς
πρὸς ἄλληλα μίξεως ἐφιέμενα.

D154 (B57) Simpl. *In Cael.*, p. 586.12 (v. 1) et 587.1–2
(v. 2–3) (et al.)

ᾗ πολλαὶ μὲν κόρσαι ἀναύχενες ἐβλάστησαν,

Races of man-prowed cattle, while others sprang up inversely [= **D156.2**],

(evidently these latter are 'races of cattle-prowed men' [cf. **D156.3**]), that is, composites of cattle and human beings. And all the parts that were assembled with one another in such as way as to be capable of surviving became animals and continued to exist because they satisfied each other's needs, the teeth cutting and chewing the food, the stomach digesting it, the liver turning it into blood. And a human head, coming together with a human body, ensures the survival of the whole, but with a cow's [scil. body] it is not adapted and is destroyed. For whatever did not come together according to an appropriate relation perished. It is in the same way that everything happens now too.

D153 (B58) Simplicius, *Commentary on Aristotle's* On the Heavens

Therefore in this situation [scil. when Strife had not yet completely retreated], the limbs, still **'solitary-membered'** because of the separation caused by Strife, were wandering, desiring to mix with one another.

D154 (B57) Simplicius, *Commentary on Aristotle's* On the Heavens

From it [scil. the earth] **blossomed many faces without necks,**

---

1 πολλαὶ Arist. *Cael.* 3.2 300b30 E et *GA* 1.17 722b20, Simpl. *In Cael.* et *In Cat.* 337.2: πολλῶν Arist. *Cael.* JH, Arist. *An.* 3.6 430a29

499

γυμνοὶ δ' ἐπλάζοντο βραχίονες εὔνιδες ὤμων,
ὄμματά τ' οἶ' ἐπλανᾶτο πενητεύοντα μετώπων.

3 οἶ' Peyron: οἷα D: οἷα AE

D155 (B60) Plut. *Adv. Col.* 28 1123B

εἰλίποδ' ἀκριτόχειρα ∪ | – ∪ ∪ | – ∪ ∪ | – –

D156 (B61) Ael. *Nat. anim.* 16.29 (et al.)

πολλὰ μὲν ἀμφιπρόσωπα καὶ ἀμφίστερνα
    φύεσθαι,
βουγενῆ ἀνδρόπρωρα, τὰ δ' ἔμπαλιν
    ἐξανατέλλειν
ἀνδροφυῆ βούκρανα, μεμειγμένα τῇ μὲν ἀπ'
    ἀνδρῶν
τῇ δὲ γυναικοφυῆ, σκιεροῖς ἠσκημένα γυίοις.

1 ἀμφίστερν' ἐφύοντο Karsten   2 ἐξανατέλλειν Simpl.
In Phys. 372.1: ἐξανατείνειν mss.: ἐξανέτελλον Karsten
    3 ἀπ' Karsten: ὑπ' mss.   4 σκιεροῖς mss.: χλιεροῖς Kar-
sten, διεροῖς Panzerbieter, στείροις vel σκιροῖς Diels, alii alia

The First Birth of Humans (D157–D158)

D157 (B62) Simpl. *In Phys.*, pp. 381.31–382.3 (et al.)

νῦν δ' ἄγ', ὅπως ἀνδρῶν τε πολυκλαύτων τε
    γυναικῶν
ἐννυχίους ὅρπηκας ἀνήγαγε κρινόμενον πῦρ,

500

Naked arms wandered about, bereft of
   shoulders,
And eyes roamed about alone, deprived of
   brows.

D155 (B60) Plutarch, *Against Colotes*

Foot-whirling, with undistinguishable hands . . .

D156 (B61) Aelian, *On the Nature of Animals*

Many grew double of face and double of chest,
Races of man-prowed cattle, while others
   sprang up inversely,
Creatures of cattle-headed men, mixed here
   from men,
There creatures of women fitted with shadowy
   genitals.

The First Birth of Humans (D157–D158)

D157 (B62) Simplicius, *Commentary on Aristotle's*
Physics

Come then: how fire, separating off, drew
   upward the nocturnal saplings
Of much-weeping men and women—

---

2 ἐννυχίους] ἐμμυχίους Panzerbieter

τῶνδε κλύ· οὐ γὰρ μῦθος ἀπόσκοπος οὐδ'
    ἀδαήμων.
οὐλοφυεῖς μὲν πρῶτα τύποι χθονὸς ἐξανέτελλον,
5   ἀμφοτέρων ὕδατός τε καὶ ἴδεος αἶσαν ἔχοντες·
τοὺς μὲν πῦρ ἀνέπεμπε θέλον πρὸς ὁμοῖον
    ἱκέσθαι,
οὔτε τί πω μελέων ἐρατὸν δέμας ἐμφαίνοντας
οὔτ' ἐνοπὴν οἷόν τ' ἐπιχώριον ἀνδράσι γυῖον.

5 ἴδεος Diels: εἴδεος mss.: οὔδεος Sturz   8 οἷόν τ᾽ Diels:
οἷα τ᾽ E: οὔτ᾽ F: οὔτ᾽ αὖ ed. Ald.: οὔτ᾽ οὖν Wilamowitz   γυῖον
Stein: γύων EF: γήρυν ed. Ald.

D158 (B67) Gal. *In Hipp. Epid.* 6.2.46, pp. 119.17–120.2

ἐν γὰρ θερμοτέρῳ τοκὰς ἄρρενος ἔπλετο γαῖα·
καὶ μέλανες διὰ τοῦτο καὶ ἀνδρωδέστεροι
    ἄνδρες
καὶ λαχνήεντες μᾶλλον ∪ ∪ | – ∪ ∪ | – –

1 τοκὰς ἄρρενος Diels: τὸ κατ᾽ ἄρρενα mss.   γαῖα
Deichgräber: γαίης mss.: γαστήρ Diels   2 ἀνδρωδέστε-
ροι] ἁδρομελέστεροι Karsten

Hear this. For my tale is not aimless nor
   ignorant.
First, complete [or: rough] outlines sprang up
   from the earth
Possessing a share of both, of water as of heat.   5
These fire sent upward, wishing to reach what
   was similar to it;
As yet they displayed neither the lovely
   framework of limbs
Nor the voice and the organ that is native to
   men.

D158 (B67) Galen, *Commentary on Hippocrates'* Epidemics

For it was in its warmer part that the earth was
   productive of the male;
And that is why men are swarthy and more
   manly
And more hirsute too.

The Stages of Ontogenesis: Reproduction and Embryology (D158–D188)
Menstruation and the Female Reproductive Organ (D159–D161)

D159 (B66) Schol. in Eur. 18 (vol. 1, p. 249.24 Schwartz)

⟨εἰς⟩ σχιστοὺς λειμῶνας – ∪ ∪ – Ἀφροδίτης

⟨εἰς⟩ Diels   σχιστοὺς] ἔχεις τούς B

D160 (< B153) Hesych. s.v. βαυβώ

βαυβώ: [. . .] σημαίνει δὲ καὶ κοιλίαν ὡς παρ’ Ἐμπεδοκλεῖ.

D161 (< A80) Soran. *Gyn.* 1.21.1–3

τοῦτο δὲ[1] ἑκάστη κατὰ τὴν ἰδίαν ἀπαντᾷ[2] προθεσμίαν,
καὶ οὐ ⟨λαμβάνει⟩[3] κατὰ τὰς αὐτὰς ⟨περιόδους⟩,[4]
ὥσπερ ὁ Διοκλῆς ⟨φησιν⟩,[5] πάσας,[6] καὶ πάλιν Ἐμπεδοκλῆς, ἐλαττουμένου τοῦ φωτὸς τῆς σελήνης.

[1] δὲ ⟨ἐν⟩ Rose   [2] ἄπαντα ms., corr. Dietz
[3] ⟨λαμβάνει⟩ Ilberg: lac. 8 litt. ms.: οὐ⟨κ ἀεὶ⟩ Kalbfleisch
[4] ⟨περιόδους⟩ Kalbfleisch: lac. 8 litt. ms.
[5] ⟨φησιν⟩ Ilberg   [6] πάσας ms.: πάσαις edd.

The Stages of Ontogenesis: Reproduction and
Embryology (D159–D188)
Menstruation and the Female Reproductive
Organ (D159–D161)

D159 (B66) Scholia on Euripides' *Phoenician Women*

⟨To⟩ **the cleft meadows** . . . **of Aphrodite**

D160 (‹ B153) Hesychius

'Baubô': [. . .] it also means 'womb,' as in Empedocles.

D161 (‹ A80) Soranus, *Gynecology*

This [i.e. menstruation] happens to each woman at the time that is right for her and it does not ⟨affect⟩ them all at the same ⟨time⟩, as Diocles [scil. of Carystos] ⟨asserts⟩, and again Empedocles, viz. when the light of the moon decreases.

Sexual Union (D162)

D162 (B64) Plut. *Quaest nat.* 21 917C

τῷ δ᾽ ἐπὶ καὶ πόθος εἶσι δι᾽ ὄψιος ἀμμιμνήσκων

versus valde corruptus   δ᾽ ἐπὶ . . . εἶσι Karsten: δέ
τι . . . εἴτε mss.   δι᾽ ὄψιος Wyttenbach: διὰ πέψεως
mss.   ἀμμιμνήσκων Diels: ἀμμίσγων mss. plerique: ἄμ-
ματα μίσγων Diels 1901

The Development of the Embryo (D163–D184)
Nourishment of the Embryo (D163)

D163 (< A79) Soran. *Gyn.* 1.57.3–4

ἐμφύεσθαι δὲ ταῦτα Ἐμπεδοκλῆς μὲν εἰς τὸ ἧπαρ
οἴεται [. . .].

Formation of Its Parts (D164–D169)

D164 (B63) Arist. *GA* 1.18 722b12–13 et 4.1 764b3

ἀλλὰ διέσπασται μελέων φύσις· ἡ μὲν ἐν
ἀνδρός
. . .

versum sequentem Diels ita temptavit: ἡ δ᾽ ἐνὶ θηλείης δίχ᾽
ἑκάστη σπέρματι κεύθει

Sexual Union (D162)

D162 (B64) Plutarch, *Natural Questions*

**To him too approaches desire, reminding him
by vision (?)[1]**

[1] This line is very corrupt, its text, meaning, and context all
quite uncertain. We place it here on the hypothesis that it may be
referring to sexual attraction.

The Development of the Embryo (D163–D184)
Nourishment of the Embryo (D163)

D163 (< A79) Soranus, *Gynecology*

Empedocles thinks that these vessels [scil. the four vessels
of the umbilical cord] are naturally attached to the liver
[. . .].[1]

[1] The number of vessels must surely be attributed to Soranus,
not to Empedocles.

Formation of Its Parts (D164–D169)

D164 (B63) Aristotle, *Generation of Animals*

**But the birth of the limbs is divided into two:
the one in the man's** [scil. probably: seed]
   . . .

D165 (A83) Aët. 5.21.1 (Ps.-Plut.) [ἐν πόσῳ χρόνῳ μορφοῦται τὰ ζῷα ἐν τῇ γαστρὶ ὄντα]

Ἐμπεδοκλῆς ἐπὶ μὲν τῶν ἀνθρώπων[1] ἄρχεσθαι τῆς διαρθρώσεως ἀπὸ ἕκτης καὶ τριακοστῆς, τελειοῦσθαι δὲ τοῖς μορίοις ἀπὸ πεντηκοστῆς μιᾶς δεούσης.

[1] ἀνθρώπων ΜΠ: ἀρρένων m

D166 (< A83) Athen. Cilic. in Oribas. *Coll. med.* Libri incerti 16.4 (*CMG* 6.2.2, p. 106.4–7 Raeder)

συμφωνεῖ δὲ τοῖς χρόνοις τῆς παντελοῦς τῶν ἐμβρύων διακρίσεως καὶ ὁ φυσικὸς Ἐμπεδοκλῆς, ‹καί›[1] φησιν ὅτι θᾶσσον διαμορφοῦται τὸ ἄρρεν τοῦ θήλεος, καὶ τὰ ἐν τοῖς δεξιοῖς τῶν ἐν τοῖς εὐωνύμοις.

[1] ‹καί› Daremberg

D167 (< A84) Cens. *Die nat.* 6.1

Empedocles [. . .] ante omnia cor iudicavit increscere, quod hominis vitam maxime contineat.

D168 (B68) Arist. *GA* 4.8 777a10

μηνὸς ἐν ὀγδοάτου δεκάτῃ πύον ἔπλετο λευκόν.

D169 (B153a) Theon Sm. *Exp.*, p. 104.1

. . . ἐν ἑπτὰ . . . ἑβδομάσιν . . .

D165 (A83) Aëtius

Empedocles: in the case of human beings, the beginning
of the articulation [scil. of the embryo] takes place starting
on the thirty-sixth day, and the completion of the parts
starting on the forty-ninth.

D166 (< A83) Athenaeus of Cilicia in Oribasius, *Medical
Compilations*

The natural philosopher Empedocles too agrees [scil.
probably: with Diocles of Carystus] regarding the duration of the complete articulation of embryos [scil. ca. the
thirty-sixth day for the first articulation and ca. the forty-
fourth for its complete articulation], ⟨and⟩ he says that the
male is formed more quickly than the female, and those
on the right side more quickly than those on the left.

D167 (< A84) Censorinus, *The Birthday*

Empedocles [. . .] thought that the heart develops before
all the other parts, because it is this on which the life of
man depends most of all.

D168 (B68) Aristotle, *Generation of Animals*

On the tenth day of the eighth month, it [i.e. the
blood] **became white pus.**

D169 (B153a) Theon of Smyrna, *On Mathematics Useful
for Understanding Plato*

. . . in seven . . . hebdomads . . .

First Respiration (D170)

D170 Aët.

a (cf. A74) 5.15.3 (Ps.-Plut.; cf. Ps.-Gal.) [εἰ τὸ ἔμβρυον ζῷον]

Ἐμπεδοκλῆς εἶναι[1] μὲν ζῷον τὸ ἔμβρυον ἀλλ᾽ ἄπνουν[2] ὑπάρχειν ἐν τῇ γαστρί [. . .].

[1] μὴ ante εἶναι del. Karsten   [2] ἄπνουν Diels (cf. Gal. 119): ἔμπνουν mss.: μὴ ἔμπνουν Karsten

b (< A74) 4.22.1 (Ps.-Plut.) [περὶ ἀναπνοῆς]

Ἐμπεδοκλῆς τὴν πρώτην ἀναπνοὴν τοῦ πρώτου ζῴου γενέσθαι τῆς ⟨μὲν⟩[1] ἐν τοῖς βρέφεσιν ὑγρασίας ἀποχώρησιν λαμβανούσης, πρὸς δὲ τὸ παρακενωθὲν ἐπεισόδου τοῦ ἐκτὸς ἀερώδους γινομένης εἰς τὰ παρανοιχθέντα τῶν ἀγγείων· τὸ δὲ μετὰ τοῦτο ἤδη τοῦ ἐμφύτου θερμοῦ τῇ πρὸς τὸ ἐκτὸς ὁρμῇ τὸ ἀερῶδες ὑπαναθλίβοντος, τὴν ἐκπνοήν, τῇ δ᾽ εἰς τὸ ἐντὸς ἀνθυποχωρήσει τῷ ἀερώδει τὴν ἀντεπείσοδον παρεχομένου, τὴν εἰσπνοήν [. . . = **D202**].

[1] ⟨μὲν⟩ Diels

Determination of the Sex of the Embryo (D171–D176)

D171 (ad B63) Arist. *GA* 1.18 722b10–12

φησὶ γὰρ ἐν τῷ ἄρρενι καὶ τῷ θήλει οἷον σύμβολον ἐνεῖναι, ὅλον δ᾽ ἀπ᾽ οὐδετέρου ἀπιέναι, [. . . = **D164**].

510

First Respiration (D170)

D170 Aëtius

a (cf. A74)

Empedocles: the embryo is a living being but it does not breathe in the belly [. . .].[1]

> [1] The part omitted here is practically identical to **D170b.**

b (< A74)

Empedocles: the first inhalation of the first living being came about when the liquid in the embryos withdrew and the external airy element entered from outside via the openings of the vessels into the empty space that resulted. Afterward, exhalation [scil. came about] when the innate heat expelled the airy element by its impulse outward, inhalation when it provided the airy element with a reverse passage inward by withdrawing in the opposite direction [. . .].

Determination of the Sex of the Embryo (D171–D176)

D171 (ad B63) Aristotle, *Generation of Animals*

He says that in the male and in the female there is something like a fragment of the same piece, and that the whole does not come from either of them: [. . . = **D164**].

D172 (B65) Arist. *GA* 1.18 723a24–26

ἐν δ᾽ ἐχύθη καθαροῖσι· τὰ μὲν τελέθουσι
   γυναῖκες,
ψύχεος ἀντιάσαντα ∪ | – ∪ ∪ | – ∪ ∪ | – –

post ἀντιάσαντα suppl. e.g. τὰ δ᾽ ἔμπαλιν ἄρρενα θερμοῦ
Diels

D173 Arist.

a (< A81) *GA* 4.1 764a1–6

οἱ δ᾽ ἐν τῇ μήτρᾳ, καθάπερ Ἐμπεδοκλῆς· τὰ μὲν γὰρ
εἰς θερμὴν ἐλθόντα τὴν ὑστέραν ἄρρενα γίνεσθαί
φησι,[1] τὰ δ᾽ εἰς ψυχρὰν θήλεα, τῆς δὲ θερμότητος καὶ
τῆς ψυχρότητος τὴν τῶν καταμηνίων αἰτίαν εἶναι ῥύ-
σιν, ἢ ψυχροτέραν οὖσαν ἢ θερμοτέραν, καὶ ἢ παλαι-
οτέραν ἢ προσφατωτέραν [. . . cf. **R19**].

   [1] φασι P

b (< 28 A52) *PA* 2.2 648a31

[. . . = **PARM. D43**] Ἐμπεδοκλῆς δὲ τοὐναντίον.

D174 (A81) Aët. 5.7.1 (Ps.-Plut.) [πῶς ἄρρενα γεννᾶται
καὶ θήλεα]

Ἐμπεδοκλῆς ἄρρενα καὶ θήλεα γίνεσθαι παρὰ θερ-
μότητα καὶ ψυχρότητα· ὅθεν ἱστορεῖται τοὺς μὲν πρώ-

D172 (B65) Aristotle, *Generation of Animals*

> **On pure** [scil. seeds?] **they** [i.e. male semen] **were**
> **poured; some end up as women,**
> **Having encountered the cold** . . .

D173 Aristotle

a (< A81) *Generation of Animals*

The others say that it [i.e. the differentiation of the sexes] occurs in the womb, like Empedocles. For he says that what penetrates into a warm uterus becomes male, what into a cold one female, and that the cause of the warmth or coldness is the flow of the menstrual fluids, which is colder or warmer, and older or more recent [. . . cf. **R19**].

b (< 28 A52) *Parts of Animals*

[. . .] Empedocles the opposite [scil. of Parmenides, cf. **PARM. D43**].

D174 (A81) Aëtius

Empedocles: males and females are born because of warmth and coldness. This is why he reports that the first

τους ἄρρενας πρὸς ἀνατολῇ καὶ μεσημβρίᾳ γεγενῆσθαι μᾶλλον ἐκ τῆς γῆς, τὰς δὲ θηλείας πρὸς ταῖς
ἄρκτοις.

D175 (< A81) Cens. *Die nat.* 6.6

ex[1] dextris partibus profuso semine mares gigni, at e laevis
feminas Anaxagoras Empedoclesque consentiunt [. . . =
D180].

   [1] et CPV, *corr. Jahn*

D176 (< A81) Cens. *Die nat.* 6.10

id ipsum ferme Empedocles videtur sensisse; nam causas
quidem, cur divideretur, non posuit, partiri[1] tantummodo
ait, et si utrumque sedes aeque calidas occupaverit,
utrumque marem nasci, si frigidas aeque, utramque
feminam;[2] si vero alterum calidiorem, alterum frigidio-
rem, dispari sexu partum futurum.

   [1] partiri *Jahn*: partim *CPV al.*: partum *V²RBBW edd.*: partus
BE   [2] frigidas utrumque feminas *G*

Other Anatomical Features (D177)

D177 (< B97) Arist. *PA* 1.1 640a19–22

[. . .] Ἐμπεδοκλῆς [. . .] εἴρηκε [. . .] ὑπάρχειν πολλὰ
τοῖς ζῴοις διὰ τὸ συμβῆναι οὕτως ἐν τῇ γενέσει οἷον
καὶ τὴν ῥάχιν τοιαύτην ἔχειν ὅτι στραφέντος καταχθῆναι συνέβη.

males were born from the earth toward the east and south, females toward the north.

D175 (< A81) Censorinus, *The Birthday*

Anaxagoras [cf. **ANAXAG. D86**] and Empedocles agree in saying that males are born from sperm diffused on the right side and females on the left side [. . .].

D176 (< A81) Censorinus, *The Birthday*

Empedocles seems to have thought just about the same thing [scil. as **HIPPO D13**]; for he did not indicate the reason it [scil. the seed] is divided, but merely said that it splits into two parts and that if both occupy places that are equally warm, then both will be born males; if equally cold, then both females; but if one [scil. occupies] a warmer one and the other a colder one, then the offspring will be of different sexes.

Other Anatomical Features (D177)

D177 (< B97) Aristotle, *Parts of Animals*

[. . .] Empedocles [. . .] says that the cause of many characteristics in animals is that they happened in this way accidentally during their development, for example that their **spinal column** has a certain shape because it accidentally broke when it [i.e. the embryo] twisted.

Viability (D178–D179)

D178

a (A75) Aët. 5.18.1 [διὰ τί ἑπταμηνιαῖα γόνιμα]

Ἐμπεδοκλῆς ὅτε ἐγεννᾶτο τὸ τῶν ἀνθρώπων γένος ἐκ
τῆς γῆς, τοσαύτην γενέσθαι τῷ μήκει τοῦ χρόνου διὰ
τὸ βραδυπορεῖν τὸν ἥλιον τὴν ἡμέραν, ὁπόση νῦν
ἐστιν ἡ δεκάμηνος· προϊόντος δὲ τοῦ χρόνου τοσαύτην γενέσθαι τὴν ἡμέραν, ὁπόση νῦν ἐστιν ἡ ἑπτάμη-
νος· διὰ τοῦτο καὶ τὰ δεκάμηνα[1] καὶ τὰ ἑπτάμηνα, τῆς
φύσεως τοῦ κόσμου οὕτω μεμελετηκυίας, αὔξεσθαι ἐν
μιᾷ ἡμέρᾳ[2] †ᾗ τίθεται νυκτὶ†[3] τὸ βρέφος.

[1] γόνιμα post δεκάμηνα del. Diels   [2] post ἡμέρᾳ lac.
indic. Diels   [3] τῇ τότε καὶ νυκτὶ Reiske: ᾗ τίκτεται νῦν
Xylander: τε καὶ νυκτὶ Wyttenbach

b (≠ DK) Tzetz. *In Il.*, p. 42

[. . . = **D100**] διὰ δὴ τοῦτό φησιν ζῳογονεῖσθαι καὶ
τῶν βρεφῶν τὰ ἑπτάμηνα.

D179 (< B69) Procl. *In Remp.* 2.34.26

ὅτι καὶ ὁ Ἐμπεδοκλῆς οἶδεν τὸν διπλοῦν τῶν γεννή-
σεων χρόνον· διὸ καὶ τὰς γυναῖκας καλεῖ **διγόνους**
[. . .].

Viability (D178–D179)

D178

a (A75) Aëtius

Empedocles: when the race of human beings was born from the earth, the day lasted for as long a time as ten months last now because the sun moved slowly, but as time went on the day came to last as long as seven months do now [cf. **D100**]. This is why both ten-month embryos and seven-month ones, since the nature of the world took care to arrange matters in this way, grow in a single day †in which† the embryo †is placed at night†.

b (≠ DK) Tzetzes, *Commentary on Homer's* Iliad

[. . .] He says that it is for this reason [scil. that a day originally lasted for seven months] that seven-month babies are born alive too.

D179 (< B69) Proclus, *Commentary on Plato's* Republic

Empedocles also knows the two times of births; that is why he calls women **"double-bearing"** [. . .].

Resemblances (D180–D182)

D180 (< A81) Cens. *Die nat.* 6.6

[. . . = **D175**] quorum opiniones [. . .] de similitudine
liberorum dispariles; super qua re Empedocles disputata
ratione[1] talia profert:[2] si par calor in parentum seminibus
fuit, patri similem marem procreari; si frigus,[3] feminam
matri similem. quodsi[4] patris calidius erit et frigidius
matris, puerum fore, qui matris vultus repraesentet; at si
calidius matris, patris autem fuerit frigidius, puellam
futuram, quae patris reddat similitudinem.

[1] disputata ratione CPV: disputatione W: disputata ratio Q[3]
mg., nonnulli edd.   [2] talis profertur mss., corr. Sallmann
[3] frigus <i>Jahn:</i> frigidus <i>PV:</i> figidus <i>C</i>   [4] quodsi ⟨semen⟩
Sallmann

D181 (A81) Aët. 5.11.1 (Ps.-Plut.) [πόθεν γίνονται τῶν
γονέων αἱ ὁμοιώσεις ἢ τῶν προγόνων]

Ἐμπεδοκλῆς ὁμοιότητας γίνεσθαι κατ᾽ ἐπικράτειαν
τῶν σπερματικῶν γόνων, ἀνομοιότητας δὲ τῆς ἐν τῷ
σπέρματι[1] θερμασίας ἐξατμισθείσης.

[1] τῷ σπέρματι ΜΠ: τοῖς σπέρμασι m

D182 (A81) Aët. 5.12.2 (Ps.-Plut.) [πῶς ἄλλοις ὅμοιοι
γίνονται οἱ γεννώμενοι καὶ οὐ τοῖς γονεῦσιν]

Ἐμπεδοκλῆς τῇ κατὰ τὴν σύλληψιν φαντασίᾳ τῆς

Resemblances (D180–D182)

D180 (< A81) Censorinus, *The Birthday*

[. . .] their [i.e. Anaxagoras' and Empedocles'] opinions [. . .] differ regarding the similarity of children. On this subject, Empedocles says the following, after having examined the question: if the seeds of both parents were equally warm, then a male similar to the father is generated; if they were cold, a female similar to the mother. But if the father's was warmer and the mother's colder, that it will be a boy who reproduces his mother's face; and if his mother's is warmer and his father's is colder, it will be a girl who shows a resemblance to her father.

D181 (A81) Aëtius

Empedocles: similarities [scil. with parents and ancestors] come about as a result of the preponderance of the spermatic seeds, dissimilarities when the heat in the sperm evaporates.

D182 (A81) Aëtius

Empedocles: [scil. the reason why some children are born resembling other people and not their parents is that] the

γυναικὸς μορφοῦσθαι τὰ βρέφη· πολλάκις γὰρ ἀν-
δριάντων καὶ εἰκόνων ἠράσθησαν γυναῖκες, καὶ ὅμοια
τούτοις ἀπέτεκον.

Anomalies (D183–D184)

D183 (A81) Aët. 5.10.1 (Ps.-Plut.) [πῶς δίδυμα καὶ
τρίδυμα γίνεται]

Ἐμπεδοκλῆς δίδυμα καὶ τρίδυμα γίνεσθαι κατὰ πλεονασμὸν καὶ περισχισμὸν τοῦ σπέρματος.

D184 (A81) Aët. 5.8.1 (Ps.-Plut.) [πῶς τέρατα γίνεται]

Ἐμπεδοκλῆς τέρατα γίνεσθαι παρὰ πλεονασμὸν
σπέρματος ἢ παρ᾽ ἔλλειψιν ἢ παρὰ τὴν τῆς κινήσεως
ταραχὴν ἢ παρὰ τὴν εἰς πλείω διαίρεσιν ἢ παρὰ τὸ
ἀπονεύειν.

Sterility of Mules (D185–D186)

D185 (< B92) Arist. GA 2.8 747a34–b3

Ἐμπεδοκλῆς δ᾽ αἰτιᾶται τὸ μίγμα τὸ τῶν σπερμάτων
γίνεσθαι πυκνὸν ἐκ μαλακῆς τῆς γονῆς οὔσης ἑκα-
τέρας· συναρμόττειν γὰρ τὰ κοῖλα τοῖς πυκνοῖς ἀλλήλων, ἐκ δὲ τῶν τοιούτων γίνεσθαι ἐκ μαλακῶν
σκληρόν, ὥσπερ τῷ καττιτέρῳ μιχθέντα τὸν χαλκόν
[. . .= **R22**].

shape of embryos is determined by the imagination of the woman at the moment of conception. For women have often fallen in love with statues and portraits and have given birth to children resembling them.

Anomalies (D183–D184)

D183 (A81) Aëtius

Empedocles: twins and triplets are born according to the excess and splitting apart of the sperm.

D184 (A81) Aëtius

Empedocles: abnormal offspring are born from an excess of sperm or from a lack thereof, or from a disturbance of its motion, or from its division into many parts, or from its being deviated.

Sterility of Mules (D185–D186)

D185 (< B92) Aristotle, *Generation of Animals*

Empedocles attributes the cause [scil. of the sterility of mules] to the fact that the mixture of the seeds becomes dense, each of the two seeds out of which it is made being soft; for the hollow parts and the dense ones fit together into each other,[1] and out of seeds of this sort, the hard comes about from soft ones, like bronze mixed with tin [. . .].

[1] The situation described here seems to correspond to the normal case, by contrast with the particular situation in which the two seeds are soft.

D186 (A82) Aët. 5.14.2 (Ps.-Plut.) [διὰ τί αἱ ἡμίονοι στεῖραι]

Ἐμπεδοκλῆς διὰ τὴν σμικρότητα καὶ ταπεινότητα καὶ στενότητα τῆς μήτρας, κατεστραμμένως προσπεφυκυίας τῇ γαστρί, μήτε τοῦ σπέρματος εὐθυβολοῦντος εἰς αὐτὴν μήτε, εἰ καὶ φθάσειεν, αὐτῆς ἐκδεχομένης.

*Two Probable References to the Reproduction of
Plants and Fishes (D187–D188)*

D187 (B72) Athen. *Deipn.* 8.10 334B

πῶς καὶ δένδρεα μακρὰ καὶ εἰνάλιοι καμασῆνες

D188 (B74) Plut. *Quaest. conv.* 5.10.4 685F

φῦλον ἄμουσον ἄγουσα πολυσπερέων
καμασήνων.

πολυσπορέων Karsten

*Physiology of Living Beings (D189–D256)
Parts and Secretions (D189–D200)
A General Summary (D189)*

D189 (A78) Aët. 5.22.1 (Ps.-Plut.; cf. Ps.-Gal.) [ἐκ ποίων συνίσταται στοιχείων ἕκαστον τῶν ἐν ἡμῖν γενικῶν μορίων]

Ἐμπεδοκλῆς τὰς μὲν σάρκας γεννᾶσθαι ἐκ τῶν ἴσων[1]

D186 (A82) Aëtius

Empedocles: [scil. the sterility of mules] is because of the smallness, drooping, and narrowness of the womb, which is attached to the abdomen slantwise, so that neither does the sperm strike directly upon it nor, even if it does at first, is it accepted by it.

Two Probable References to the Reproduction of Plants and Fishes (D187–D188)

D187 (B72) Athenaeus, *Deipnosophists*

How high trees and the poles (*kamasênes*)[1] **of the sea** [i.e. fish]

[1] The term *kamasênes,* a neologism, evokes the elongated, stick-like shape of fish.

D188 (B74) Plutarch, *Table Talk*

Leading the Museless [i.e. mute] **tribe of many-seeded fish** (*kamasênes*).

Physiology of Living Beings (D189–D256)
Parts and Secretions (D189–D200)
A General Summary (D189)

D189 (A78) Aëtius

Empedocles: the flesh is born from the four elements

---

[1] ἔσω MII, corr. Wyttenbach

τῇ κράσει τεττάρων στοιχείων· τὰ δὲ νεῦρα πυρὸς
⟨καὶ⟩ γῆς ὕδατι διπλασίονι μιχθέντων·[2] τοὺς δ' ὄνυ-
χας τοῖς ζῴοις γεννᾶσθαι τῶν νεύρων καθὸ τῷ ἀέρι
συνέτυχε περιψυχθέντων· ὀστᾶ δὲ δυεῖν[3] μὲν ὕδατος
καὶ τῶν ἴσων[4] γῆς, τεττάρων δὲ πυρός,[5] τοσούτων[6]
συγκραθέντων μερῶν· ἱδρῶτα καὶ δάκρυον γίνεσθαι
τοῦ αἵματος τηκομένου καὶ παρὰ τὸ λεπτύνεσθαι διαχεομένου.[7]

    [2] locus incertus: πυρὸς ⟨καὶ⟩ γῆς ὕδατι διπλασίονι μιχθέ-
ντων Bernardakis ex Gal.: πυρὸς (om. lac. VII litt. m) γῆς τὰ
διπλασίονα μιχθέντα mss.   [3] δυεῖν Diels: δοκεῖν mss.
[4] τῶν ἴσων Diels: τῆς ἔσω mss.: τῶν ἴσων ἀέρος Wyttenbach
[5] post πυρὸς hab. mss. γῆς, del. Lachenaud: καὶ γῆς Wyttenbach   [6] τοσούτων Wyttenbach: τούτων mss.   [7] αἵματος . . . διαχεομένου Diels ex Gal.: σωματικοῦ οὕτως mss.: post
οὕτως pos. lac. Lachenaud

Blood and Flesh (D190–D191)

D190 (B98) Simpl. *In Phys.*, p. 32.6–10

ἡ δὲ χθὼν τούτοισιν ἴση συνέκυρσε μάλιστα,
Ἡφαίστῳ τ' ὄμβρῳ τε καὶ αἰθέρι παμφανόωντι,
Κύπριδος ὁρμισθεῖσα τελείοις ἐν λιμένεσσιν,
εἴτ' ὀλίγον μείζων εἴτε πλέον ἐστὶν ἐλάσσων·
  5 ἐκ τῶν αἷμά τε γέντο καὶ ἄλλης εἴδεα σαρκός.

    1 μάλιστα] μιγεῖσα Karsten   3 ὁρμισθεῖσα F: ὁρμη-
σθεῖσα DE ed. Ald.: ὁρμισθεῖσι Stein   4 μείζων DE: μεῖζον F   πλέον ἐστὶν] πλεόνεσσιν Panzerbieter   ἐλάσσων
DE: ἔλασσον F

when they are present in equal proportions in the mixture; the tendons, when fire ‹and› earth are mixed with a double quantity of water (?); the nails are born to animals when the tendons have cooled down to the degree that they have encountered the air; bones, two parts of water and the same amount of earth, four of fire, these parts having been mixed together in these proportions; sweat and tears come about when the blood is liquefied and is diffused by becoming less dense.

Blood and flesh (D190–D191)

D190 (B98) Simplicius, *Commentary on Aristotle's Physics*

> **And earth, approximately equal to these** [scil. in
>   quantity], **encountered them—**
> **Hephaistos, rain, and all-illuminating aether,**
> **Anchored in the perfect harbors of Cypris—**
> **Or else a little bit more, or, rather, less;**
> **Out of these were born blood and the other**   5
>   **forms of flesh.**

5 αἷμά τε γέντο Sturz: αἵματ᾽ ἔγεντο E: αἷμα τέγεντο D: αἵματ᾽ ἐγένοντο F

D191 (B85) Simpl. *In Phys.*, p. 331.7

ἡ δὲ φλὸξ ἱλάειρα μινυνθαδίης τύχε γαίης.

ἡ δὲ F: ἡ δὴ D: ἤδη E   φλόξ om. E   τύχε E: ψύχε
DF: τύχεν αὐγῆς Stein

Bones (D192–D193)

D192 (B96) Simpl. *In Phys.*, p. 300.21–24 (et al.)

ἡ δὲ χθὼν ἐπίηρος ἐν εὐστέρνοις χοάνοισι
τὼ δύο τῶν ὀκτὼ μερέων λάχε Νήστιδος
    αἴγλης,
τέσσαρα δ' Ἡφαίστοιο· τὰ δ' ὀστέα λευκὰ
    γένοντο
Ἁρμονίης κόλλησιν ἀρηρότα θεσπεσίηθεν.

1 εὐστέρνοις D (et Arist. *An.* 410a4): εὐτύκτοις EF
2 τὼ Steinhardt: τὰς Simpl. DE, Arist. P: τὰ Arist. Fᵇ: Simpl.
F: τῶν Arist. cett.

D193 (< 464 Bollack) Mich. Eph. *In PA*, p. 29.9–10

[. . .] ὀστεογενῆ τὸν μυελὸν Ἐμπεδοκλῆς λέγει.

D191 (B85) Simplicius, *Commentary on Aristotle's* Physics

And she, mild flame, received a bit of earth.[1]

[1] Simplicius cites this line with reference to the parts of animals in general.

Bones (D192–D193)

D192 (B96) Simplicius, *Commentary on Aristotle's* Physics

And kindly earth in her broad-breasted
    crucibles
Received two parts, out of eight, of the
    gleaming of Nestis
And four of Hephaestus.[1] **And they became**
    white bones
Fitted together marvelously by Harmony's
    adhesives.

[1] Air is missing in these lines; Ps.-Simplicius, in his commentary on Aristotle's *De anima* (p. 68.12–14), attempts to derive it from the epithet of Nestis, which would owe its gleam to the air.

D193 (≠ DK) Michael of Ephesus, *Commentary on Aristotle's* Parts of Animals

[. . .] Empedocles says that the marrow is a product of the bone.

Tears (D194)

D194 (cf. A78) Plut. *Quaest. nat.* 20 917A

ἔνιοι δέ φασιν ὥσπερ γάλακτος ὀρρὸν τοῦ αἵματος
ταραχθέντος ἐκκρούεσθαι τὸ δάκρυον, ὡς Ἐμπεδοκλῆς.

Other Parts (D195–D200)

D195 (B70) Ruf. Ephes. *Part. corp.* 229

τὸ δὲ βρέφος περιέχεται χιτῶσι, τῷ μὲν λεπτῷ καὶ
μαλακῷ· 'ἀμνίον' αὐτὸν Ἐμπεδοκλῆς καλεῖ.

D196 (B150) Plut. *Quaest. conv.* 5.8.2 683E

– ∪ ∪ | – ∪ ∪ | – ∪ ∪ | – πολυαίματον ἧπαρ [cf.
R4]

D197 (B83) Plut. *Fort.* 3 98D

– ∪ ∪ | – ∪ ∪ | – ∪ ∪ | – ∪ ∪ αὐτὰρ ἐχίνοις
ὀξυβελεῖς χαῖται νώτοις ἐπιπεφρίκασιν.

1 ἐχίνοις Vulcobius: ἐχῖνος mss.

D198 (B82) Arist. *Meteor.* 4.9 387b4–6

ταὐτὰ τρίχες καὶ φύλλα καὶ οἰωνῶν πτερὰ
    πυκνά
καὶ λεπίδες γίγνονται ἐπὶ στιβαροῖσι μέλεσσιν.

Tears (D194)

D194 (cf. A78) Plutarch, *Natural Questions*

Some people, like Empedocles, say that tears are expelled from the blood when it is agitated, as whey is from milk.

Other Parts (D195–D200)

D195 (B70) Rufus of Ephesus, *On the Names of the Parts of the Body*

The embryo is enveloped by membranes, one of them thin and soft; Empedocles calls it **'amnios'** ('of lamb').

D196 (B150) Plutarch, *Table Talk*

> . . . **liver with much blood**

D197 (B83) Plutarch, *On Fortune*

> . . . **but in hedgehogs,**
> **Sharp-pointed hairs bristle on their backs.**

D198 (B82) Aristotle, *Meteorology*

> **Hairs, leaves, the dense feathers of birds, are**
> **the same,**
> **And scales on sturdy limbs.**

---

2 λεπίδες] φλονίδες Karsten ex φολιδονίδες Olymp. *In Meteor.*, p. 335.21

D199 (B73) Simpl. *In Cael.*, p. 530.6–7 [a little after **D61**]

ὡς δὲ τότε χθόνα Κύπρις, ἐπεί τ᾽ ἐδίηνεν ἐν
  ὄμβρῳ,
εἴδεα ποιπνύουσα θοῷ πυρὶ δῶκε κρατῦναι.

2 εἴδεα F: εἰ δὲ A: αἰθέρ᾽ Stein: ἴδεα Diels   ποιπνύουσα
F: ἀποπνοιοῦσα A: ἐπιπνείουσα Panzerbieter   θοῷ A:
θεῶ F

D200 (B75) Simpl. *In Cael.*, p. 530.9 (v. 1–2) et *In Phys.*,
p. 331.9 (v. 2) [after **D199**]

τῶν δ᾽ ὅσ᾽ ἔσω μὲν πυκνά, τὰ δ᾽ ἔκτοθι μανὰ
  πέπηγε,
Κύπριδος ἐν παλάμῃσι πλάδης τοιῆσδε
  τυχόντα
. . .

1 ὅσ᾽ Karsten: ὅσσ᾽ AF   2 πλάδης Simpl. *In Cael.*:
πλάσης *In Phys.* E: πλάσιος *In Phys.* ed. Ald.: om. 4 litt. lac.
rel. *In Phys.* D: πλάδης . . . τυχόντα om. lac. 25 litt. rel. *In
Phys.*F

Functions (D201–D244)
Respiration (D201–D202)

D201

a (B100) Arist. *Resp.* 7 473b9–474a6

ὧδε δ᾽ ἀναπνεῖ πάντα καὶ ἐκπνεῖ· πᾶσι λίφαιμοι

D199 (B73) Simplicius, *Commentary on Aristotle's* On the Heavens [a little after **D61**][1]

**And as Cypris then, when she had moistened
  the earth in rain,
Bustling about gave the forms to swift fire to
  strengthen them.**

[1] From Simplicius we know the relative location of this line in the poem. The order presented here is thematic.

D200 (B75) Simplicius, *Commentary on Aristotle's* On the Heavens and *Commentary on Aristotle's* Physics [after **D199**]

**Of these, all those whose internal texture has
  become dense, and their exterior is loose,
Having received from Cypris' hands this kind of
  moisture**

. . .

Functions (D201–D244)
Respiration (D201–D202)

D201

a (B100) Aristotle, *On Respiration*

It is in this way that all [scil. probably: living
  beings] **inhale and exhale: for all,**

1 δίαιμοι M

σαρκῶν σύριγγες πύματον κατὰ σῶμα
  τέτανται,
καί σφιν ἐπὶ στομίοις πυκναῖς τέτρηνται
  ἄλοξιν
ῥινῶν ἔσχατα τέρθρα διαμπερές, ὥστε φόνον
  μέν
5 κεύθειν, αἰθέρι δ' εὐπορίην διόδοισι τετμῆσθαι.
ἔνθεν ἔπειθ' ὁπόταν μὲν ἀπαίξῃ τέρεν αἷμα,
αἰθὴρ παφλάζων καταΐσσεται οἴδματι μάργῳ,
εὖτε δ' ἀναθρώσκῃ, πάλιν ἐκπνέει, ὥσπερ ὅταν
  παῖς
κλεψύδρῃ παίζῃσι δι' εὐπετέος χαλκοῖο·
10 εὖτε μὲν αὐλοῦ πορθμὸν ἐπ' εὐειδεῖ χερὶ θεῖσα
εἰς ὕδατος βάπτῃσι τέρεν δέμας ἀργυφέοιο,
οὐκέτ' ἐς ἄγγοσδ' ὄμβρος ἐσέρχεται, ἀλλά μιν
  εἴργει
ἀέρος ὄγκος ἔσωθε πεσὼν ἐπὶ τρήματα πυκνά,
εἰσόκ' ἀποστεγάσῃ πυκινὸν ῥόον· αὐτὰρ
  ἔπειτα
15 πνεύματος ἐλλείποντος ἐσέρχεται αἴσιμον ὕδωρ.

4 τέρθρα L: τέθρα PSXZ: lac. M   φανὸν bPZ
6 ἐπαίξῃ PSZ²: ἐπάξῃ MZ¹   8 ἀναθρώσκει mss., corr.
Karsten   ἐκπνεῖ mss., corr. Diels   9 κλεψύδρη Diels:
κλεψύδρην mss.   παίζῃσι Diels: παίζῃσι il: παίζουσι a:
παίζουσα bP   δι' εὐπετέος LX: δι' εὐπετέοις S: δι' εὐπα-
γέος P: διιπετέος MZil: διειπετέος Diels   12 οὐκέτ' ἐς nos:
οὐδέτ' ἐς bP: οὐδ' ὅτι εἰς MZ¹: οὐδ' ὅτ' ἐς ilZ^pc: οὐδεὶς
Wilamowitz   ἄγγοσδ'] ἄγγος ἔτ' X: ἄγγος P: ἄργος δ' M:
ἄργος ἔτ' Z¹

Channels of flesh, which the blood leaves,
    extend to the surface of their bodies;
And at the openings, the furthest limits of their
    skin (*rhinôn*)[1]
Are perforated through and through with dense
    furrows, so that the blood
Lies hidden, while easy access is cut by these   5
    passages for the air (*aithêr*).
When from here the delicate blood then rushes
    backward,
The air (*aithêr*), boiling, rushes after it in a
    raging surge,
But when it [i.e. the blood] leaps back, the other
    is exhaled again—just as when a child
Plays with a clepsydra of handy copper:
When she places the opening of the pipe against   10
    her well-formed hand
And dips it into the delicate body of silvery
    water,
Liquid no longer enters into the container, but
    it is prevented from doing so
By the mass of air (*aêr*) falling from inside upon
    the dense holes,
As long as she restrains the thick flow [scil. of
    air]; but then,
When the breath is lacking, water enters in the   15
    predetermined amount.

---

[1] The term is sometimes thought to refer here only to the
nostrils.

---

13 αἰθέρος Stein   15 ἐκλείποντος MZil   αἴσιμον
PSX: αὔξιμον aLZ

ὡς δ’ αὔτως ὅθ’ ὕδωρ μὲν ἔχῃ κατὰ βένθεα
   χαλκοῦ
πορθμοῦ χωσθέντος βροτέῳ χροῒ ἠδὲ πόροιο,
αἰθὴρ δ’ ἐκτὸς ἔσω λελιημένος ὄμβρον ἐρύκει
ἀμφὶ πύλας ἠθμοῖο δυσηχέος, ἄκρα κρατύνων,
20   εἰσόκε χειρὶ μεθῇ· τότε δ’ αὖ πάλιν, ἔμπαλιν ἢ
   πρίν,
πνεύματος ἐμπίπτοντος ὑπεκθέει αἴσιμον ὕδωρ.
ὡς δ’ αὔτως τέρεν αἷμα κλαδασσόμενον διὰ
   γυίων,
ὁππότε μὲν παλίνορσον ἐπαΐξειε μυχόνδε,
αἰθέρος εὐθὺς ῥεῦμα κατέρχεται οἴδματι θῦον,
25   εὖτε δ’ ἀναθρῴσκῃ, πάλιν ἐκπνέει ἶσον ὀπίσσω.

17 χρωσθέντος aPS   18 ἐρύκει mss.: ἐρύκῃ Diels
19 ἠθμοῖο PSXZ: ἰσθμοῖο LM   κραταίνων S: τιταίνων a
21 ἐκπίπτοντος MZ   23 ἐπαΐξειε bP: ἐπάξειεν MZ:
ἀπαΐξειε Stein   24 αἰθέρος MZ: ἕτερον bP   οἶδμα
τίταινον a   25 ἐκπνέει Diels: ἐκπνεῖ bP: πνεῖ Z: om. M

b (ad B100) Arist. *Resp.* 13 473b1–8

γίνεσθαι δέ φησι τὴν ἀναπνοὴν καὶ ἐκπνοὴν διὰ τὸ
φλέβας εἶναί τινας, ἐν αἷς ἔνεστι μὲν αἷμα, οὐ μέντοι
πλήρεις εἰσὶν αἵματος, ἔχουσι δὲ πόρους εἰς τὸν ἔξω
ἀέρα, τῶν μὲν τοῦ σώματος μορίων ἐλάττους, τῶν δὲ
τοῦ ἀέρος μείζους· διὸ τοῦ αἵματος πεφυκότος κινεῖσθαι ἄνω καὶ κάτω, κάτω μὲν φερομένου εἰσρεῖν τὸν
ἀέρα καὶ γίνεσθαι ἀναπνοήν, ἄνω δ’ ἰόντος ἐκπίπτειν
θύραζε καὶ γίνεσθαι τὴν ἐκπνοήν, παρεικάζων τὸ
συμβαῖνον ταῖς κλεψύδραις [. . . = **D201a**].

In the same way, when she keeps the water in
    the depths of the copper vessel,
Blocking with her mortal skin the opening and
    the passage,
The air (*aithêr*) outside, desiring to come inside,
    repels the liquid
Around the gates of the dull-sounding sieve,
    dominating the surface,
Until she lets go with her hand; then again   20
    inversely, in reverse of earlier,
The breath now falling into it, the water runs
    out in the destined amount.
In the same way the delicate blood, trembling
    through the limbs,
When, turning back, it leaps toward the nooks
    inside,
At once the flow of air (*aithêr*) pursues it,
    rushing in its surge,
But when it leaps back, it exhales again, in the   25
    same amount, backward.

b (ad B100) Aristotle, *On Respiration*

He says that inhalation and exhalation occur because there
are certain vessels that contain blood but are not full of
blood, but possess passages toward the air outside that
are smaller than the particles of this body [i.e. blood] but
larger than those of the air. That is why when blood, which
by nature moves upward and downward, is borne downward, the air flows inside and inhalation occurs, but when
it goes upward it [i.e. the air] is expelled outward and
exhalation occurs, comparing moreover what happens
with clepsydras: [. . . = **D201a**].

535

D202 (< A74) Aët. 4.22.1 (Ps.-Plut.) [περὶ ἀναπνοῆς]

Ἐμπεδοκλῆς [. . . = **D170b**] τὴν δὲ νῦν κατέχουσαν
φερομένου τοῦ αἵματος[1] ὡς πρὸς τὴν ἐπιφάνειαν καὶ
τὸ ἀερῶδες διὰ τῶν ῥινῶν ταῖς ἑαυτοῦ ἐπιρροίαις ἀν-
αθλίβοντος κατὰ[2] τὴν ἐκχώρησιν αὐτοῦ γίνεσθαι τὴν
ἐκπνοήν, παλινδρομοῦντος δὲ καὶ τοῦ ἀέρος ἀντεπεισιόντος[3] εἰς τὰ διὰ τοῦ αἵματος ἀραιώματα τὴν εἰσπνοήν. ὑπομιμνήσκει δ᾽ αὖ τὸ[4] ἐπὶ τῆς κλεψύδρας.

[1] αἵματος ΜΠ: ὕδατος m   [2] καὶ mss., corr. Voss
[3] ἀντεπεισιόντος Mm: -αχθέντος Π   [4] αὖ τὸ nos: αὐτὸ
mss.: τὸ Diels

Nutrition and Growth (D203–D205)

D203 Aët.

a (< A95) 4.9.14 (Stob.) [εἰ ἀληθεῖς αἱ αἰσθήσεις]

[. . .] Ἐμπεδοκλῆς ἐλλείψει τροφῆς τὴν ὄρεξιν.

post ὄρεξιν lac. posuit Diels (*Dox.*)

b (A77) 5.27.1 (Ps.-Plut.) [περὶ τροφῆς καὶ αὐξήσεως]

Ἐμπεδοκλῆς τρέφεσθαι μὲν τὰ ζῷα διὰ τὴν ὑπόστασιν τοῦ οἰκείου,[1] αὔξεσθαι δὲ διὰ τὴν παρουσίαν τοῦ
θερμοῦ, μειοῦσθαι δὲ καὶ φθίνειν διὰ τὴν ἔκλειψιν
ἑκατέρων· τοὺς δὲ νῦν ἀνθρώπους τοῖς πρώτοις συμ-
βαλλομένους βρεφῶν ἐπέχειν τάξιν.

[1] οἰκείου ⟨ὑγροῦ⟩ Usener

D202 (< A74) Aëtius

Empedocles: [. . .] as for that [scil. respiration] prevailing now, exhalation occurs when the blood moves toward the surface and, pushing out through the orifices[1] the airy element compressed by its effluences, causes its expulsion; and inhalation when it [i.e. the blood] runs back and the air enters in turn into the less dense parts of the blood. He mentions moreover what happens in the case of the clepsydra.

[1] *Rhines* here surely designates not only the nostrils but also, more generally, the cutaneous orifices, cf. **D201a.1–4.**

Nutrition and Growth (D203–D205)

D203 Aëtius

a (< A95)

[. . .] Empedocles: appetite [scil. comes] from lack of food.[1]

[1] This notice is found in a chapter entitled "Whether sensations are truthful," in a section specifically dedicated to the sensations of pleasure and pain (cf. **PARM. D58**); it may be lacunose.

b (A77)

Empedocles: animals are nourished by the depositing of what is appropriate, grow by the presence of heat, and decrease and perish by the lack of both of these. And the humans of nowadays, compared with the first ones, have the rank of those who are newborn.[1]

[1] Originally, one day was equivalent to seven months; cf. **D100, D178a.**

D204 (< A66) Ael. *Nat. anim.* 9.64

καὶ Ἐμπεδοκλῆς δὲ ὁ Ἀκραγαντῖνος λέγει τι εἶναι
γλυκὺ ἐν τῇ θαλάττῃ ὕδωρ, οὐ πᾶσι δῆλον, τρόφιμον
δὲ τῶν ἰχθύων. καὶ τὴν αἰτίαν τοῦδε τοῦ ἐν τῇ ἅλμῃ
γλυκαινομένου λέγει φυσικήν, ἣν ἐκεῖθεν εἴσεσθε.

D205 (< A77) Ps.-Galen. *Def. med.* 99

Ἐμπεδοκλῆς δὲ σήψει [scil. τὰς πέψεις τῆς τροφῆς
φησι γίνεσθαι].

Sleep and Death (D206)

D206 Aët.

a (< A85) 5.25.4 (Ps.-Plut.) [ὁποτέρου ἐστὶν ὕπνος ἢ
θάνατος, ψυχῆς ἢ σώματος]

Ἐμπεδοκλῆς τὸν θάνατον γεγενῆσθαι διαχωρισμὸν[1]
τοῦ πυρώδους,[2] ἐξ ὧν[3] ἡ σύγκρισις τῷ ἀνθρώπῳ[4] συν-
εστάθη [. . . = **R29**]· ὕπνον δὲ γίνεσθαι διαχωρισμὸν[5]
τοῦ πυρώδους.

---

[1] διαχωρισμῷ Bernardakis   [2] πυρώδους ‹καὶ γεώ-
δους› Reiske   [3] ὧν MΠ: οὗ m   [4] τῷ ἀνθρώπῳ om. m
[5] διαχωρισμῷ Bernardakis

D204 (< A66) Aelian, *On the Nature of Animals*

And Empedocles of Agrigentum too [scil. like Democritus, Aristotle, and Theophrastus] says that there is some sweet water in the sea that is not manifest to all but that nourishes the fish. And he gives a natural explanation of this sweetness in salt water that you will find below.[1]

[1] The corresponding passage has not been preserved.

D205 (< A77) Ps.-Galen, *Medical Definitions*

Empedocles [scil. says that the digestion of food occurs] by putrefaction.

Sleep and Death (D206)

D206 Aëtius

a (< A85)

Empedocles: death occurred as the separation of the fiery element from the ones out of which the mixture is composed for the human being [. . .]; and sleep occurs as the separation of the fiery element.

EARLY GREEK PHILOSOPHY V

b (A85) 5.24.2 (Ps.-Plut) [πῶς ὕπνος γίνεται καὶ θάνα-
τος]

Ἐμπεδοκλῆς τὸν μὲν ὕπνον κατὰ ψύξιν[1] τοῦ ἐν τῷ
αἵματι θερμοῦ σύμμετρον γίνεσθαι, κατὰ δὲ παντελῆ
θάνατον.

[1] κατὰ ψύξιν ΜΠ: καταψύξει m

Sensation and Thought: The General
Principle (D207–D212)

D207 (B109) Arist. *An.* 1.2 404b13–15 (et al.)

γαίῃ μὲν γὰρ γαῖαν ὀπώπαμεν, ὕδατι δ᾽ ὕδωρ,
αἰθέρι δ᾽ αἰθέρα δῖον, ἀτὰρ πυρὶ πῦρ ἀίδηλον,
στοργὴν δὲ στοργῇ, νεῖκος δέ τε νείκεϊ λυγρῷ.

2 ἠέρι δ᾽ ἠέρα Sext. Emp. 1.302   δῖον V²WXy: δία S:
δίαν cett., Sext. Emp. *Adv. Math.* 7.120 NLE: θεῖον Arist.
Metaph. B4 1000b7 A[b]

D208 (B89) Plut. *Quaest. nat.* 19 916D

γνοὺς ὅτι πάντων εἰσὶν ἀπορροαί, ὅσσ᾽
ἐγένοντο.

D209 (< A92) Plat. *Men.* 76c–d

[. . . = **GORG. D45**] [ΣΩ.] οὐκοῦν λέγετε ἀπορροάς
τινας τῶν ὄντων κατὰ Ἐμπεδοκλέα;

540

b (A85)

Empedocles: sleep occurs by a moderate cooling of the heat in the blood, death by a complete one.

Sensation and Thought: The General Principle (D207–D212)

D207 (B109) Aristotle, *On the Soul*

> **For it is by earth that we see earth, by water water,**
> **By aether divine aether, and by fire destructive fire,**
> **And fondness by fondness, and strife by baleful strife.**

D208 (B89) Plutarch, *Natural Questions*

> **Knowing that there are effluences of all the things that have come about.**

D209 (< A92) Plato, *Meno*

[. . .] [Socrates:] Do you people [scil. you and Gorgias; cf. **GORG. D45a**] not say, following Empedocles, that there are certain effluences emanating from the things that are?

[ΜΕ.] σφόδρα γε.

[ΣΩ.] καὶ πόρους εἰς οὓς καὶ δι᾽ ὧν αἱ ἀπορροαὶ πορεύονται;

[ΜΕ.] πάνυ γε.

[ΣΩ.] καὶ τῶν ἀπορροῶν τὰς μὲν ἁρμόττειν ἐνίοις τῶν πόρων, τὰς δὲ ἐλάττους ἢ μείζους εἶναι;

[ΜΕ.] ἔστι ταῦτα.

D210 (A87) Arist. *GC* 1.8 324b26–35

τοῖς μὲν οὖν δοκεῖ πάσχειν ἕκαστον διά τινων πόρων εἰσιόντος τοῦ ποιοῦντος ἐσχάτου καὶ κυριωτάτου, καὶ τοῦτον τὸν τρόπον ὁρᾶν καὶ ἀκούειν ἡμᾶς φασι καὶ τὰς ἄλλας αἰσθήσεις αἰσθάνεσθαι πάσας. ἔτι δὲ ὁρᾶσθαι διά τε ἀέρος καὶ ὕδατος καὶ τῶν διαφανῶν, διὰ τὸ πόρους ἔχειν ἀοράτους μὲν διὰ μικρότητα, πυκνοὺς δὲ καὶ κατὰ στοῖχον, καὶ μᾶλλον ἔχειν τὰ διαφανῆ μᾶλλον. οἱ μὲν οὖν ἐπί τινων οὕτω διώρισαν, ὥσπερ καὶ Ἐμπεδοκλῆς, οὐ μόνον ἐπὶ τῶν ποιούντων καὶ πασχόντων, ἀλλὰ καὶ μίγνυσθαί φασιν[1] ὅσων οἱ πόροι σύμμετροι πρὸς ἀλλήλους εἰσίν.

[1] φασιν EFHV: φησιν LWJ: φασὶ corr. ex φησὶ Μ (ut vid.)

D211 (< A86) Theophr. *Sens.* 2 et 7

[2] [. . . cf. **DOX. T15**] περὶ ἑκάστης δὲ τῶν κατὰ μέρος οἱ μὲν ἄλλοι σχεδὸν ἀπολείπουσιν, Ἐμπεδοκλῆς δὲ πειρᾶται καὶ ταύτας ἀνάγειν εἰς τὴν ὁμοιότητα.

[7] Ἐμπεδοκλῆς δὲ περὶ ἁπασῶν ὁμοίως λέγει καὶ

[Meno:] Certainly.

[Socrates:] And passages into which and through which the effluences pass?

[Meno:] Yes indeed.

[Socrates:] And among the effluences, some fit some of the passages, while others are too small or too big?

[Meno:] That is so.

D210 (A87) Aristotle, *On Generation and Corruption*

Some people think that each thing is affected when the last agent, which is the agent in the proper sense, enters through certain passages, and they say that it is in this way that we see, hear, and employ all the other sensations. Moreover, one sees through air, water, and transparent bodies because these possess passages, invisible because of their smallness, that are close-set and aligned; and the more transparent the body, the more of these it possesses. So it is in this way that some people have defined things with regard to certain processes, like Empedocles, not only with regard to agents and what is affected, but they also assert that everything of which the passages are proportioned to one another is mixed.

D211 (< A86) Theophrastus, *On Sensations*

[2] [. . .] As for each of the particular [scil. sensations], the other people [i.e. those who explain by similarity, essentially Parmenides] ignore them almost entirely, while Empedocles tries to refer these too to similarity.

[7] Empedocles speaks about all of them [i.e. sensations]

φησι τῷ ἐναρμόττειν εἰς τοὺς πόρους τοὺς ἑκάστης
αἰσθάνεσθαι· διὸ καὶ οὐ δύνασθαι τὰ ἀλλήλων κρίνειν, ὅτι τῶν μὲν εὐρύτεροί πως,[1] τῶν δὲ στενώτεροι
τυγχάνουσιν οἱ πόροι πρὸς τὸ αἰσθητόν, ὡς τὰ μὲν
οὐχ ἁπτόμενα διευτονεῖν,[2] τὰ δ' ὅλως εἰσελθεῖν οὐ δύνασθαι [. . . = **D218**].

[1] πως Diels: πρὸς mss.: ὄντες Wimmer   [2] διεκπνεῖν
coni. Usener

D212 (cf. A90, < 28 A47) Aët. 4.9.6 (Stob.) [εἰ ἀληθεῖς
αἱ αἰσθήσεις]

[. . .] Ἐμπεδοκλῆς [. . .] παρὰ τὰς συμμετρίας τῶν
πόρων τὰς κατὰ μέρος αἰσθήσεις γίνεσθαι τοῦ οἰκείου, τῶν αἰσθητῶν ἑκάστου ἑκάστῃ ἐναρμόττοντος.

Vision (D213–D225)
The Configuration of the Eye and the
Mechanism of Vision (D213–D221)

D213 (B86) Simpl. In Cael., p. 529.23

ἐξ ὧν ὄμματ' ἔπηξεν ἀτειρέα δῖ' Ἀφροδίτη.

D214 (B87) Simpl. In Cael., p. 529.25

γόμφοις ἀσκήσασα καταστόργοις Ἀφροδίτη

in the same way, and says that sensation occurs by the adaptation to the passages of each of the senses; that is why they cannot distinguish each other's objects, because the passages of the ones are too broad, those of the others too narrow in relation to the perceptible, so that some things pass straight through without touching, while others cannot penetrate at all.

D212 (cf. A90, < 28 A47) Aëtius

[. . .] Empedocles [. . .]: the particular perceptions, which bear on an object proper to them, occur by the commensurability of the passages, each of the perceptibles being adapted to each one [scil. of the particular perceptions].

Vision (D213–D225)
The Configuration of the Eye and the
Mechanism of Vision (D213–D221)

D213 (B86) Simplicius, *Commentary on Aristotle's* On the Heavens

> **From which** [scil. the elements] **divine Aphrodite constructed the unyielding eyes.**

D214 (B87) Simplicius, *Commentary on Aristotle's* On the Heavens

> **Having constructed** [scil. the eyes] **with loving pegs, Aphrodite**

545

D215 (B84) Arist. *Sens.* 2 437b26–438a3

ὡς δ᾽ ὅτε τις πρόοδον νοέων ὡπλίσσατο λύχνον
χειμερίην διὰ νύκτα πυρὸς σέλας αἰθομένοιο,
ἅψας, παντοίων ἀνέμων λαμπτῆρας ἀμοργούς,
οἵ τ᾽ ἀνέμων μὲν πνεῦμα διασκιδνᾶσιν ἀέντων,
5   φῶς δ᾽ ἔξω διαθρῷσκον, ὅσον ταναώτερον ἦεν,
λάμπεσκεν κατὰ βηλὸν ἀτειρέσιν ἀκτίνεσσιν·
ὡς δὲ τότ᾽ ἐν μήνιγξιν ἐεργμένον ὠγύγιον πῦρ
λεπτῆσίν ⟨τ᾽⟩ ὀθόνῃσι λοχάζετο κύκλοπα
κούρην,
αἳ δ᾽ ὕδατος μὲν βένθος ἀπέστεγον
ἀμφιναέντος,
10   πῦρ δ᾽ ἔξω δίεσκεν, ὅσον ταναώτερον ἦεν.

1 πρόσοδον SW¹   3 ἀμουργούς bPAᶜ   5 φῶς b:
πῦρ aP   7 ἐεργμένον LPUX: ἐέρμενον S¹W: ἐελμένον a
8 ⟨τ᾽⟩ Diels   ὀθόνῃσι (ὀθόνοισιν X) b: χθονήῃσι a: χοάνη-
σιν P   λοχάζετο a: ἐχέατο (ἐχείατο L) bP: λοχεύσατο
Förster   post 8 add. Blass versum αἳ χοάνῃσι δίαντα τε-
τρήατο θερπεσίῃσιν rest. ex P 437b30, cf. 438a1   9 ἀμφὶ
καέντος M: ἀμφιναάοντος LX   10 δίεσκεν Gallavotti: δίε-
σκον P: διαθρῷσκον ab

D216 (B88) Arist. *Poet.* 21 1458a5 (et al.)

| – ∪ ∪ | – ∪ ∪ | – μία γίγνεται ἀμφοτέρων ὄψ.

ὄψ Strab. 8, p. 364: ὁης vel ὁης mss.

---

[1] Others understand "both" to refer to earth and water.

D215 (B84) Aristotle, *On Sensation*

Just as when, thinking of setting forth, someone
 arms a lamp,
A gleam of bright fire across the stormy night,
Lighting [or: assembling] a lamp-case to protect it
 against all kinds of winds,
Which scatters the breath of the blowing winds
While the light, leaping outward as far as   5
 possible,
Shines beyond the threshold with its unyielding
 rays—
In the same way, the ancient fire, confined in
 membranes and delicate linens,
Lay in wait for the round-eyed maiden [i.e. the
 opened pupil]:[1]
These protected it against the depth of water
 flowing around,
While the fire gushed through outward as far as   10
 possible.[2]

[1] Rashed in Stern-Gillet and Corrigan (2007) pp. 31–32 inserts **D214** between lines 7 and 8 and translates, "Thus, after Aphrodite had fitted the ogygian fire enclosed in membranes with pegs of love, she poured (*ekheuato*) round-eyed Korê in filmy veils. . . ."   [2] Or adopting *diathrôskon* from most of the manuscripts (cf. line 5) and supposing that the citation is interrupted before the main verb: "While the fire, leaping outward as far as possible . . ."

D216 (B88) Aristotle, *Poetics*

 . . . the vision of 'both' [scil. eyes] becomes
one.[1]

D217 (B95) Simpl. *In Cael.*, p. 529.26–27

καὶ τὴν αἰτίαν λέγων τοῦ τοὺς μὲν ἐν ἡμέρᾳ, τοὺς δὲ ἐν νυκτὶ κάλλιον ὁρᾶν,

Κύπριδος

φησίν,

ἐν παλάμῃσιν ὅτε ξὺμ πρῶτ᾽ ἐφύοντο.

D218 (< A86) Theophr. *Sens.* 7–8

[7] [. . . = **D211**] πειρᾶται δὲ καὶ τὴν ὄψιν λέγειν, ποία τίς ἐστι· καί φησι τὸ μὲν ἐντὸς αὐτῆς εἶναι πῦρ ‹καὶ ὕδωρ›,[1] τὸ δὲ περὶ αὐτὸ γῆν καὶ ἀέρα, δι᾽ ὧν διέναι[2] λεπτὸν ὂν καθάπερ τὸ ἐν τοῖς λαμπτῆρσι φῶς. τοὺς δὲ πόρους ἐναλλὰξ κεῖσθαι τοῦ τε πυρὸς καὶ τοῦ ὕδατος, ὧν τοῖς μὲν τοῦ πυρὸς τὰ λευκά, τοῖς δὲ τοῦ ὕδατος τὰ μέλανα γνωρίζειν· ἐναρμόττειν γὰρ ἑκατέροις[3] ἑκάτερα. φέρεσθαι δὲ τὰ χρώματα πρὸς τὴν ὄψιν διὰ τὴν ἀπορροήν. [8] συγκεῖσθαι δ᾽ οὐχ ὁμοίως, ‹ἀλλὰ τὰς μὲν μᾶλλον ἐκ τῶν ὁμοίων›[4] τὰς δ᾽ ἐκ τῶν ἀντικειμένων, καὶ ταῖς μὲν ἐν μέσῳ, ταῖς δ᾽ ἐκτὸς εἶναι τὸ πῦρ, διὸ καὶ τῶν ζῴων τὰ μὲν ἐν ἡμέρᾳ,[5] τὰ δὲ νύκτωρ μᾶλλον ὀξυωπεῖν· ὅσα μὲν πυρὸς ἔλαττον ἔχει μεθ᾽ ἡμέραν· ἐπανισοῦσθαι γὰρ αὐτοῖς[6] τὸ ἐντὸς φῶς ὑπὸ τοῦ ἐκτός· ὅσα δὲ τοῦ ἐναντίου νύκτωρ· ἐπαναπληροῦσθαι γὰρ καὶ τούτοις τὸ ἐνδεές. ἐν δὲ τοῖς ἐναντίοις

D217 (B95) Simplicius, *Commentary on Aristotle's* On the Heavens

Explaining the reason why some see better by day, others at night, he says,

When at the hands of Cypris they [i.e. probably: the eyes] **first grew together.**

D218 (< A86) Theophrastus, *On Sensations*

[7] [. . .] But he also tries to explain what sight specifically is; and he says that what is inside it is fire ⟨and water⟩, and what surrounds it is earth and air, across which this passes through because of its fineness, as does the light in lamps [cf. **D215**]. The passages of fire and of water are arranged so as to alternate; it is by the passages of fire that bright things are perceived, by those of water dark things, for each kind adapts to both respectively. And colors are brought to sight by the effluence. [8] But they [i.e. the organs of sight] are not constituted in the same way ⟨but the ones come more from what is similar,⟩ the others from the opposites; and for some the fire is in the center, for others outside. This is also why some animals have sharper sight by day, others at night: those that have less fire, by day, for their inner light is compensated by the external one; those that have less of the opposite element, at night, for their lack too is compensated by an addition. And both

---

¹ ⟨καὶ ὕδωρ⟩ Diels   ² δϊὸν mss., corr. Wimmer
³ ἑκατέραις mss., corr. Schneider   ⁴ ⟨ἀλλὰ τὰς μὲν ἐκ τῶν ὁμοίων⟩ coni. Diels (μᾶλλον add. nos): ⟨τὰς ὄψεις ἀλλὰ τὰς μὲν ἐκ τῶν αὐτῶν⟩ Schneider   ⁵ ἐν ἡμέρα P: ἥμερα rescr. F: μεθ᾽ ἡμέραν Stephanus   ⁶ αὐτῷ mss., corr. Schneider

⟨ἐναντίως⟩[7] ἑκάτερον· ἀμβλυωπεῖν μὲν γὰρ καὶ οἷς
ὑπερέχει τὸ πῦρ, ἐπεὶ αὐξηθὲν[8] ἔτι μεθ᾽ ἡμέραν ἐπι-
πλάττειν καὶ καταλαμβάνειν τοὺς τοῦ ὕδατος πόρους·
οἷς[9] δὲ τὸ ὕδωρ, ταὐτὸ τοῦτο γίνεσθαι νύκτωρ· καταλαμβάνεσθαι γὰρ τὸ πῦρ ὑπὸ τοῦ ὕδατος. ⟨γίγνεσθαι
δὲ ταῦτα⟩[10] ἕως ἂν τοῖς μὲν ὑπὸ τοῦ ἔξωθεν φωτὸς
ἀποκριθῇ τὸ ὕδωρ, τοῖς δ᾽ ὑπὸ τοῦ ἀέρος τὸ πῦρ·
ἑκατέρων γὰρ ἴασιν εἶναι τὸ ἐναντίον. ἄριστα δὲ κεκρᾶσθαι καὶ βελτίστην εἶναι τὴν ἐξ ἀμφοῖν ἴσων
συγκειμένην[11] [. . . = **D226**].

7 ⟨ἐναντίως⟩ Diels   8 ἐπαυξηθὲν mss., corr. Usener
9 ὧν mss., corr. Schneider   10 add. Usener   11 συγ-
κειμένων mss., corr. Stephanus

D219 (< A91) Arist. *GA* 5.1 779b15–19

τὸ μὲν οὖν ὑπολαμβάνειν τὰ μὲν γλαυκὰ πυρώδη,
καθάπερ Ἐμπεδοκλῆς φησι, τὰ δὲ μέλανα[1] πλεῖον
ὕδατος ἔχειν ἢ πυρός, καὶ διὰ τοῦτο τὰ μὲν ἡμέρας
οὐκ ὀξὺ βλέπειν, τὰ γλαυκά, δι᾽ ἔνδειαν ὕδατος, θάτερα δὲ νύκτωρ δι᾽ ἔνδειαν πυρός [. . .].

1 μέλανα] μελανόμματα PS: μεγαλόμματα Y

D220 (A90) Aët. 4.13.4 (Stob.) [περὶ ὁράσεως]

Ἐμπεδοκλῆς καὶ πρὸς τὸ διὰ τῶν ἀκτίνων καὶ πρὸς
τὸ διὰ τῶν εἰδώλων ἐκδοχὰς παρέχεται· πλείους δὲ
πρὸς ⟨τὸ⟩[1] δεύτερον· τὰς γὰρ ἀπορροίας ἀποδέχεται.

of these processes depend upon contraries ‹in a contrary manner›. For those that have an excess of fire see also more dimly, since, increased further by day, it spreads out over the passages of water and covers them; while for those with an excess of water, the same thing happens at night (for the fire is covered by the water). ‹And this happens› until for the ones the water is removed by the external light and for the others the fire is removed by the air. For the remedy comes for each of them from the opposite. The one [scil. organ of sight] that is composed of both elements in the same quantity is the one that is best mixed and is the best one.

D219 (‹ A91) Aristotle, *Generation of Animals*

To suppose that blue ones [i.e. eyes] are of fiery nature, as Empedocles says, while black ones have more water than fire, and that this is why the ones, those that are blue, do not see sharply by day, because of a lack of water, and the others at night, because of a lack of fire [. . .].

D220 (A90) Aëtius

Empedocles offers explanations both in terms of rays [scil. coming from the eye] and in terms of images. But the more numerous ones are according to the latter. For he accepts effluences.

---

¹ ‹τὸ› Diels

D221 (< A57) Arist. *Sens.* 6 446a26–28

[. . .] Ἐμπεδοκλῆς φησιν ἀφικνεῖσθαι πρότερον τὸ
ἀπὸ[1] τοῦ ἡλίου φῶς εἰς τὸ μεταξὺ πρὶν πρὸς[2] τὴν ὄψιν
ἢ[3] ἐπὶ τὴν γῆν [. . .].

[1] ἀπὸ aP: om. b   [2] πρὸς om. X   [3] ἢ om. S[1]UWX

Colors (D222–D224)

D222 (A92) Aët. 1.15.3 (Stob.) [περὶ χρωμάτων]

Ἐμπεδοκλῆς χρῶμα εἶναι ἀπεφαίνετο τὸ τοῖς πόροις
τῆς ὄψεως ἐναρμόττον. τέτταρα δὲ τοῖς στοιχείοις
ἰσάριθμα, λευκόν, μέλαν, ἐρυθρόν, ὠχρόν.[1]

[1] ὠχρόν] χλωρόν coni. Burchard

D223 (A69a) Theophr. *Sens.* 59

Ἐμπεδοκλῆς δὲ καὶ περὶ τῶν χρωμάτων καὶ ὅτι τὸ
μὲν λευκὸν τοῦ πυρός, τὸ δὲ μέλαν τοῦ ὕδατος.

D224 (B94) Plut. *Quaest. nat.* 39

Cur aqua in summa parte alba, in fundo vero nigra
spectatur? an quod profunditas nigredinis mater est, ut
quae solis radios prius quam ad eam descendant, obtundat
et labefactet? [. . .] Quod ipsum et Empedocles approbat:

et niger in fundo fluvii color exstat ab umbra
atque cavernosis itidem spectatur in antris.

D221 (< A57) Aristotle, *On Sensation*

[. . .] Empedocles says that the light coming from the sun arrives in the intermediate space first before it reaches eyesight or arrives on the earth [. . .].

Colors (D222–D224)

D222 (A92) Aëtius

Empedocles asserted that color is what is adapted to the passages of sight. There are four, the same number as the elements: white, black, red, and yellow.

D223 (A69a) Theophrastus, *On Sensations*

Empedocles also [scil. speaks] about colors and [scil. says] that white belongs to fire, black to water.

D224 (B94) Plutarch, *Natural Questions*

Why is water seen to be white near the surface but black at the bottom? Is it because the depth is a source of blackness, so that it blunts and weakens the rays of the sun before they reach down to it? [. . .] This is the very opinion that Empedocles too approves:

> And the black color at the bottom of a river derives
>   from the shadow
> And is seen in the same way in hollow caverns.[1]

[1] The text is known only from this Latin translation.

Mirrors (D225)

D225 (A88) Aët. 4.14.1 (Stob.) [περὶ κατοπτρικῶν ἐμ-
φάσεων]

Ἐμπεδοκλῆς κατ᾽ ἀπορροίας τὰς συνισταμένας μὲν
ἐπὶ τῆς ἐπιφανείας τοῦ κατόπτρου, πιλουμένας δ᾽ ὑπὸ
τοῦ ἐκκρινομένου ἐκ τοῦ κατόπτρου πυρώδους καὶ τὸν
προκείμενον ἀέρα, εἰς ὃν φέρεται τὰ ῥεύματα, συμ-
μεταφέροντος.

Hearing (D226–D228)

D226 (< A86, B99) Theophr. *Sens.* 9

[. . . = **D218**] τὴν δ᾽ ἀκοὴν ἀπὸ τῶν ἔξωθεν[1] γίνεσθαι
ψόφων· ὅταν γὰρ[2] ὑπὸ τῆς φωνῆς κινηθῇ, ἠχεῖν[3] ἐντός·
ὥσπερ γὰρ εἶναι κώδωνα τῶν ἴσων[4] ἤχων[5] τὴν ἀκοὴν
ἣν προσαγορεύει σάρκινον ὄζον· κινουμένη[6] δὲ παί-
ειν τὸν ἀέρα πρὸς τὰ στερεὰ καὶ ποιεῖν ἦχον [. . . =
D229].

---

[1] ἔσωθεν coni. Karsten   [2] γὰρ mss.: ὁ ἀὴρ Diels: γὰρ
‹ὁ ἀὴρ› Kranz   [3] κινηθὲν ἠχεῖ F: κινηθὲν ἠχῇ P: corr.
Schneider: κινηθεὶς ἠχῇ coni. Diels   [4] ἴσων] ἔσω
Schneider: ἔσωθεν et εἰσιόντων coni. Diels   [5] κώδωνά τιν᾽
ἔσω ἠχοῦντα coni. Diels   [6] κινουμένης et κινούμενον
coni. Diels

D227 (A93) Aët. 4.16.1 (Ps.-Plut.) [περὶ ἀκοῆς]

Ἐμπεδοκλῆς τὴν ἀκοὴν γίνεσθαι κατὰ πρόσπτωσιν

Mirrors (D225)

D225 (A88) Aëtius

Empedocles: [scil. images in mirrors occur] by effluences that collect on the surface of the mirror and condense because of the fiery matter which is detached from the mirror and carries off along with it the air lying before it, toward which the effluences are borne.

Hearing (D226–D228)

D226 (< A86, B99) Theophrastus, *On Sensations*

[. . .] Hearing has its origin in external sounds: for whenever it is shaken by a noise, it resonates inside. For the organ of hearing, which he calls **'a branch of flesh,'** is like a bell producing the same resonances: once it is shaken, it strikes the air against its solid walls and causes the resonance.

D227 (A93) Aëtius

Empedocles: hearing occurs when a breath falls against

πνεύματος τῷ χονδρώδει, ὅπερ φησὶν ἐξηρτῆσθαι ἐντὸς τοῦ ὠτὸς κώδωνος δίκην αἰωρούμενον καὶ τυπτό-
μενον.

D228 (B49) Plut. *Quaest. conv.* 720E

> νυκτὸς ἐρημαίης ἀλαώπιδος – ∪ ∪ | – –

ἐρεμναίης coni. Nauck   ἀγλαώπιδος mss., corr. Xylander

Smelling (D229–D232)

D229 (< A86) Theophr. *Sens.* 9

[. . . = **D226**] ὄσφρησιν δὲ γίνεσθαι τῇ ἀναπνοῇ· διὸ
καὶ μάλιστα ὀσφραίνεσθαι τούτους, οἷς σφοδροτάτη
τοῦ ἄσθματος ἡ κίνησις· ὀσμὴν δὲ πλείστην ἀπὸ τῶν
λεπτῶν καὶ τῶν κούφων ἀπορρεῖν [. . . = **D233**].

D230 (A94) Aët. 4.17.2 (Ps.-Plut.) [περὶ ὀσφρήσεως]

Ἐμπεδοκλῆς ταῖς ἀναπνοαῖς ταῖς ἀπὸ τοῦ πνεύμονος
συνεισκρίνεσθαι τὴν ὀδμήν· ὅταν γοῦν ἡ ἀναπνοὴ
βαρεῖα γίνηται, κατὰ τραχύτητα μὴ συναισθάνεσθαι,
ὡς ἐπὶ τῶν ῥευματιζομένων.

D231 (B102) Theophr. *Sens.* 22

> ὧδε μὲν οὖν πνοιῆς τε λελόγχασι πάντα καὶ
> ὀσμῶν.

1 πνοῆς mss., corr. Stephanus

the cartilaginous part of which he says that, hanging suspended inside the ear, it oscillates and is struck like a bell.

D228 (B49) Plutarch, *Table Talk*

Of the lonely, blind-eyed night . . . [1]

[1] Plutarch cites this expression in the course of a discussion on the possibility of hearing at night, when seeing is impossible. It is possible, but not certain, that the context in Empedocles was the same.

Smelling (D229–D232)

D229 (< A86) Theophrastus, *On Sensations*

[. . .] Smelling comes about by respiration: that is why those people have a more highly developed sense of smell whose movement of breathing is more vigorous; as for the odor, the strongest one emanates from fine and light bodies [. . .].

D230 (A94) Aëtius

Empedocles: odor penetrates together with the inhalations due to the lungs: so that when inhalation becomes labored, there is no accompanying perception because of its roughness, as is the case with people who suffer from the flu.

D231 (B102) Theophrastus, *On Sensations*

Thus all things have received a share of breath and of odors.

D232 (B101) Plut. *Curios.* 11 520F et *Quaest. nat.* 23 917E (v. 1); Ps.-Alex. *Probl.* 4.102, p. 22.7 (v. 2)

κέρματα θηρείων μελέων μυκτῆρσιν ἐρευνῶν
– ‿ ‿ ὅσσ' ἀπέλειπε ποδῶν ἁπαλῇ περὶ ποίᾳ

hos duo versus separatim transmissos Diels collocavit sed dubitavit num continui fuerint   1 κέρματα Anon. *Comm. in Plat. Theat., CPF* 1/1 p. 145: τέρματα Plut. 520ᴱ: πέλματα Emperius: κλέμματα Plut. 917ᴱ, Est. 145, u γ: κόμματα Plut. 917ᴮ: κέρματα Plut. 917ᴱ O   λεχέων Karsten

2 <ζώονθ'> ante ὅσσ' rest. Diels   ὡς Alex., corr. Nauck πολῶν coni. Usener

Taste and Touch (D233–D234)

D233 (< A86) Theophr. *Sens.* 9

[. . . = **D229**] περὶ δὲ γεύσεως καὶ ἁφῆς οὐ διορίζεται καθ' ἑκατέραν[1] οὔτε πῶς οὔτε δι' ἃ γίγνονται, πλὴν τὸ κοινὸν ὅτι τῷ ἐναρμόττειν τοῖς πόροις[2] αἴσθησίς ἐστιν [. . . = **D235**].

[1] ἑκατέραν Schneider: ἑτέραν mss.   [2] τῷ συναρμόττειν τοὺς πόρους F et (nisi quod τὸ habet) P, corr. Diels

D234 (< A94) Arist. *Sens.* 4 441a3–6

ἡ μὲν οὖν τοῦ ὕδατος φύσις βούλεται ἄχυμος εἶναι. ἀνάγκη δ' ἢ ἐν αὐτῷ τὸ ὕδωρ ἔχειν τὰ γένη τῶν χυμῶν ἀναίσθητα διὰ μικρότητα, καθάπερ Ἐμπεδοκλῆς φησιν [. . . = **R18**].

D232 (B101) Plutarch, *On Curiosity* and *Natural Questions;* Ps.-Alexander, *Problems*

> [scil. a dog] **Seeking with its nostrils the bits of the limbs of wild beasts**
> . . . **that they have left behind from their paws on the tender grass**[1]

[1] The two lines of this fragment are transmitted independently.

Taste and Touch (D233–D234)

D233 (< A86) Theophrastus, *On Sensations*

[. . .] As for taste and touch, he does not define each one separately, nor does he explain in what way or by what cause they occur, except for the feature they share that perception is due to the adaptation of the passages [. . .].

D234 (< A94) Aristotle, *On Sensation*

Water tends by nature to be tasteless. But it is necessary either that water have within itself the [scil. different] kinds of flavors in a form that is imperceptible because of their smallness, as Empedocles says [. . . = **R18**].

Pleasure and Pain (D235–D236)

D235 (< A86) Theophr. *Sens.* 9

[. . . = **D233**] ἥδεσθαι δὲ τοῖς ὁμοίοις κατὰ ⟨τά⟩ τε[1]
μόρια καὶ τὴν κρᾶσιν, λυπεῖσθαι δὲ τοῖς ἐναντίοις
[. . . = **D237**].

---

[1] κατὰ ⟨τά⟩ τε Philippson, κατὰ τὰ στοιχεῖα coni. Diels

D236 (A95) Aët.

a 4.9.15 (Stob.) [περὶ αἰσθήσεως καὶ αἰσθητῶν καὶ εἰ
ἀληθεῖς αἱ αἰσθήσεις]

Ἐμπεδοκλῆς τὰς ἡδονὰς γίνεσθαι τοῖς μὲν ὁμοίοις,[1]
κατὰ δὲ τὸ ἐλλεῖπον πρὸς τὴν ἀναπλήρωσιν, ὥστε τῷ
ἐλλείποντι ἡ ὄρεξις τοῦ ὁμοίου· τὰς δ' ἀλγηδόνας τοῖς
ἐναντίοις, ἠλλοτριῶσθαι[2] γὰρ πρὸς ἄλληλα[3] ὅσα διαφέρει κατά τε τὴν σύγκρισιν καὶ τὴν τῶν στοιχείων
κρᾶσιν.

---

[1] post ὁμοίοις hab. mss. τῶν ὁμοίων, secl. Karsten: ⟨ἐκ⟩ τῶν
ὁμοίων Meineke   [2] ἢ ἀλλοτριοῦσθαι ms., corr. Meineke
[3] ἄλλα ms., corr. Karsten

b 5.28.1 (Ps.-Plut.) [πόθεν αἱ ὀρέξεις γίνονται τοῖς
ζῴοις καὶ αἱ ἡδοναί]

Ἐμπεδοκλῆς τὰς μὲν ὀρέξεις γίνεσθαι τοῖς ζῴοις
κατὰ τὰς ἐλλείψεις τῶν ἀποτελούντων ἕκαστον στοι-

Pleasure and Pain (D235–D236)

D235 (< A86) Theophrastus, *On Sensations*

[. . .] The sensation of pleasure is caused by what is similar, in terms of parts[1] and their mixture, that of pain by contraries [. . .].

[1] Meaning uncertain. Diels suggests reading 'elements' instead of 'parts.'

D236 (A95) Aëtius

a

Empedocles: pleasures occur by what is similar, as a result of a lack, for what would fill it, so that the desire, in what has the lack, is for what is similar. Pains come about by contraries; for all things that differ with regard to the mixture and the blending of the elements are alien to one another.

b

Empedocles: desires occur in animals as a result of a lack of the elements that fill each of them, pleasures from what

χείων, τὰς δὲ ἡδονὰς ἐξ οἰκείου κατὰ τὰς τῶν συγγενῶν καὶ ὁμοίων κράσεις,[1] τὰς δὲ ὀχλήσεις καὶ τὰς ⟨ἀλγηδόνας ἐξ ἀνοικείου⟩.[2]

[1] ὑγροῦ καὶ τὰς τῶν κινδύνων καὶ ὁμοίων κινήσεις mss., corr. Diels   [2] suppl. Diels

Thought (D237–D244)

D237 (< A86) Theophr. *Sens.* 9–11

[. . . = **D233**] ὡσαύτως δὲ λέγει καὶ περὶ φρονήσεως καὶ ἀγνοίας. [10] τὸ μὲν γὰρ φρονεῖν εἶναι τοῖς ὁμοίοις, τὸ δ' ἀγνοεῖν τοῖς ἀνομοίοις, ὡς ἢ ταὐτὸν ἢ παραπλήσιον ὂν τῇ αἰσθήσει τὴν φρόνησιν. διαριθμησάμενος γὰρ ὡς ἕκαστον ἑκάστῳ γνωρίζομεν ἐπὶ τέλει προσέθηκεν ὡς [. . . = **D241**]. διὸ καὶ τῷ αἵματι μάλιστα φρονεῖν· ἐν τούτῳ γὰρ μάλιστα κεκρᾶσθαι ἐστὶ[1] τὰ στοιχεῖα τῶν μερῶν.

[11] ὅσοις μὲν οὖν ἴσα καὶ παραπλήσια μέμικται καὶ μὴ διὰ πολλοῦ μηδ' αὖ μικρὰ μηδ' ὑπερβάλλοντα τῷ μεγέθει, τούτους φρονιμωτάτους εἶναι καὶ κατὰ τὰς αἰσθήσεις ἀκριβεστάτους, κατὰ λόγον δὲ καὶ τοὺς ἐγγυτάτω τούτων, ὅσοις δ' ἐναντίως, ἀφρονεστάτους. καὶ ὧν μὲν μανὰ καὶ ἀραιὰ κεῖται τὰ στοιχεῖα, νωθροὺς καὶ ἐπιπόνους· ὧν δὲ πυκνὰ καὶ κατὰ μικρὰ τεθραυσμένα, τοὺς δὲ τοιούτους ὀξέως φερομένους[2]

[1] ἐστὶ secl. Mullach: πάντα coni. Usener

is appropriate as a result of the mixtures of things that are akin and similar, and displeasures and ⟨pains out of what is inappropriate⟩.

Thought (D237–D244)

D237 (< A86) Theophrastus, *On Sensations*

[. . .] [10] He speaks in the same way about thinking and ignorance. For one thinks by means of what is similar, while one does not know because of what is dissimilar, since for him thinking is either identical with perception or very similar to it. For after having indicated by means of an enumeration that we know each thing by the same, he adds at the end: [. . . = **D241**]. This is why it is by means of the blood that one thinks best; for, among the parts [scil. of the body], it is in this one that the elements can achieve the best mixture.

[11] So the people in whom they are mixed in equal quantity, in a homogeneous manner and without large disparities, when moreover they are neither small nor too big, these are the ones who think the best and are most precise in the use of the senses, and in the same way, proportionally, those who are closest to these conditions; while those who are in the opposite condition are the ones who think least well: those in whom the elements are rarefied and loosely dispersed are sluggish and laborious; while those in whom the elements are dense and crowded closely together get carried away quickly and launch themselves

---

καὶ πολλοῖς[3] ἐπιβαλλομένους ὀλίγα ἐπιτελεῖν διὰ τὴν
ὀξύτητα τῆς τοῦ αἵματος φορᾶς. οἷς δὲ καθ᾽ ἕν τι
μόριον ἡ μέση κρᾶσίς ἐστι, ταύτῃ σοφοὺς ἑκάστους
εἶναι· διὸ τοὺς μὲν ῥήτορας ἀγαθούς, τοὺς δὲ τεχνί-
τας, ὡς τοῖς μὲν ἐν ταῖς χερσί, τοῖς δὲ ἐν τῇ γλώττῃ
τὴν κρᾶσιν οὖσαν· ὁμοίως δ᾽ ἔχειν καὶ κατὰ τὰς ἄλλας δυνάμεις [. . . = **R25**].

3 πολλὰ mss., corr. Wimmer

D238 Aët. 4.5.8 et 12 (Ps.-Plut., Stob.) [τί τὸ τῆς ψυχῆς
ἡγεμονικὸν καὶ ἐν τίνι ἐστίν]

a (A97)

Ἐμπεδοκλῆς ἐν τῇ τοῦ αἵματος συστάσει.

b (< A96)

[. . .] Ἐμπεδοκλῆς [. . .] ταὐτὸν νοῦν καὶ ψυχήν[1] [. . .].

1 νοῦν . . . ψυχήν Diels: νοῦς . . . ψυχὴ mss.

D239 (< A30) Ps.-Plut. *Strom.* 10 = Eus. *PE* 1.8.10

[. . . = **D134c**] τὸ δὲ ἡγεμονικὸν οὔτε ἐν κεφαλῇ οὔτε
ἐν θώρακι, ἀλλ᾽ ἐν αἵματι· ὅθεν καθ᾽ ὅ τι ἂν μέρος τοῦ
σώματος πλεῖον[1] ᾖ παρεσπαρμένον[2] τὸ ἡγεμονικόν,
οἴεται κατ᾽ ἐκεῖνο προτερεῖν τοὺς ἀνθρώπους.

1 πλεῖον ANV, om. BO   2 παρεσπαρμένον AV: παρ-
εσπασμένον B: παρασπασμένον ON

upon many projects but complete only few of them because of the rapidity of the motion of their blood. And those in whom the mixture is moderate in a specific limb are proficient in that regard: it is for this reason that some people are good orators, others artisans, since the latter have the mixture in their hands, the former in their tongue. And the same applies to the other talents.

D238 Aëtius

a (A97)

Empedocles: it [scil. the directing organ of the soul is located] in the composition of the blood.

b (< A96)

[. . .] Empedocles [. . .]: the intellect and the soul are the same thing [. . .].

D239 (< A30) Ps.-Plutarch, *Stromata* = Eusebius, *Evangelical Preparation*

[. . .] The directing organ is neither in the head nor in the chest, but in the blood; so that he thinks that men excel in whatever part of the body the directing organ is more disseminated.

D240 (B105) Porph. in Stob. 1.49.53

αἵματος ἐν πελάγεσσι τεθραμμένη ἀντιθορόντος,
τῇ τε νόημα μάλιστα κικλήσκεται ἀνθρώποισιν·
αἷμα γὰρ ἀνθρώποις περικάρδιόν ἐστι νόημα.

1 τεθραμμένη Grotius (ad κραδίη referens): τετραμμένα
mss. ἀντιθορόντος Scaliger: ἀντιθρῶντος FP¹: ἀντιθορῶν-
τος P² 2 κικλήσκεται mss.: κυκλίσκεται Heeren

D241 (B107) Theophr. *Sens.* 10

ἐκ τούτων ⟨γὰρ⟩ πάντα πεπήγασιν ἁρμοσθέντα
καὶ τούτοις φρονέουσι καὶ ἥδοντ᾽ ἠδ᾽ ἀνιῶνται.

1 ⟨γὰρ⟩ Karsten: lacunam 14 litt. P: om. (in mrg. ζήτει) F
2 ἥδονται καὶ PF, corr. Karsten

D242 (B103) Simpl. *In Phys.*, p. 331.12

τῇδε μὲν οὖν ἰότητι Τύχης πεφρόνηκεν ἅπαντα.

οὖν DE: om. F

D243 (B106) Arist. *Metaph.* Γ5 1009b18–19 (et al.)

πρὸς παρεὸν γὰρ μῆτις ἀέξεται ἀνθρώποισιν.

ἀέξεται E¹, Arist. *An.* 427a23 CW: ἐναύξεται AᵇJE², *An.* E¹:
αὔξεται *An.* SU: δέξεται *An.* X¹

D240 (B105) Porphyry in Stobaeus, *Anthology*

[scil. probably: the heart] **Nourished in the seas of back-springing blood,**
Where above all is located what humans call thought:
For the blood around the heart is for humans their thought.

D241 (B107) Theophrastus, *On Sensations*

⟨For⟩ **it is out of these** [i.e. the elements] **that all things are adjusted and assembled,**
And it is by them that they think and feel pleasure and pain.

D242 (B103) Simplicius, *Commentary on Aristotle's* Physics

It is in this way that, by the will of Fortune, all things think.

D243 (B106) Aristotle, *Metaphysics*

For it is with regard to what is present that intelligence ⟨*mêtis*⟩ **grows in humans.**

D244 (B108)

a Arist. *Metaph.* Γ5 1009b20–21 (et al.)

ὅσσον ‹τ᾽› ἀλλοῖοι μετέφυν, τόσον ἄρ σφισιν
  αἰεί
καὶ τὸ φρονεῖν ἀλλοῖα παρίσταται – ∪ ∪ | – –

1 ‹τ᾽› Stein: ‹γ᾽› Sturz: ‹δ᾽› Diels   2 τὸ φρονεῖν mss.:
φρονέειν Karsten   παρίσταται Arist. *An.* 427a25: παρί-
στατο Arist. *Metaph.*

b Philop. *In An.*, p. 486.13–15

ὁ γὰρ Ἐμπεδοκλῆς τὰς διαφορὰς τῶν ὀνειράτων λέγων φησὶν ὅτι ἐκ τῶν μεθ᾽ ἡμέραν ἐνεργηγμάτων αἱ
νυκτεριναὶ γίνονται φαντασίαι· ταύτην δὲ τὴν φαντα-
σίαν φρόνησιν καλεῖ ἐν οἷς φησιν· [. . . = **244a**].

Plants (D245–D256)

D245 (‹ A70) Aët. 5.26.4 (Ps.-Plut.; cf. Ps.-Gal.) [πῶς
ηὐξήθη τὰ φυτὰ καὶ εἰ ζῷα]

Ἐμπεδοκλῆς [. . . = **D150**] διὰ δὲ συμμετρίαν[1] τῆς
κράσεως τὸν τοῦ ἄρρενος καὶ τοῦ θήλεος περιέχειν
λόγον· αὔξεσθαι δ᾽ ἀπὸ[2] τοῦ ἐν τῇ γῇ θερμοῦ διαιρομένου,[3] ὥστε γῆς εἶναι μέρη, καθάπερ καὶ τὰ ἔμβρυα
τὰ ἐν τῇ γαστρὶ τῆς μήτρας μέρη· τοὺς δὲ καρποὺς
περιττεύματα[4] εἶναι τοῦ[5] ἐν τοῖς φυτοῖς ὕδατος καὶ πυ-
ρός· καὶ τὰ μὲν ἐλλιπὲς ἔχοντα τὸ ὑγρόν, ἐξικμαζομέ-

D244 (B108)

a Aristotle, *Metaphysics*

**And to the extent that what they are becomes
    different, to the same extent each time
It happens to them also to think** (*phronein*)
    different things . . .

b Philoponus, *Commentary on Aristotle's* On the Soul

Empedocles, speaking about the differences among
dreams, says that nocturnal mental images come about
from daytime activities. He calls this mental image
'thought' (*phronêsis*) when he says, [. . . = **D244a**].

See also **R25**

Plants (D245–D256)

D245 (< A70) Aëtius

Empedocles: [. . .] and because of the equilibria of their
mixture, they [i.e. trees] include the principle of the male
and that of the female. They grow from the heat in the
earth that separates, so that they are parts of the earth, just
as embryos in the belly are parts of the womb. As for fruits,
they are excesses of water and fire in the plants. Those that
lack moisture due to its evaporation during the summer

---

¹ συμμετρίας mss.: corr. Diels   ² ὑπὸ Gal.

³ διαιρομένου Bernardakis: διαιρουμένου ΜΠ: ἀραιομένου
m: διαιρόμενα Diels   ⁴ περιττεύματα Gal.: περιττώματα
Plut.   ⁵ τοῦ om. Plut.

νου αὐτοῦ τῷ θέρει, φυλλορροεῖν, τὰ δὲ πλεῖον⁶ παραμένειν, ὥσπερ ἐπὶ τῆς δάφνης καὶ τῆς ἐλαίας καὶ τοῦ
φοίνικος· τὰς δὲ διαφορὰς τῶν χυμῶν παραλλαγὰς
τῆς ⟨γῆς⟩⁷ πολυμερείας καὶ τῶν φυτῶν⁸ γίνεσθαι, δια-
φόρους⁹ ἑλκόντων¹⁰ τὰς ἀπὸ τοῦ τρέφοντος¹¹ ὁμοιομε-
ρείας, ὥσπερ ἐπὶ τῶν ἀμπέλων· οὐ γὰρ αἱ διαφοραὶ
τούτων χρηστὸν τὸν¹² οἶνον ποιοῦσιν, ἀλλ᾽ αἱ τοῦ τρέ-
φοντος¹³ ἐδάφους.

⁶ πλείονα mss., corr. Wyttenbach   ⁷ ⟨γῆς⟩ Diels
⁸ φυτῶν Gal.: χυμῶν m: αἰτίων ΜΠ   ⁹ διαφόρους
Bergk: διαφορὰς mss.   ¹⁰ ἑλκόντων Gal.: ἐχόντων mss.
¹¹ τρέφοντος Π: τρέφεσθαι Μ   ¹² χρηστικὸν mss.,
corr. Diels   ¹³ ἐκ τοῦ τρέφεσθαι mss., corr. Wyttenbach

D246 (A70) Plut. *Quaest. conv.* 6.2.2 688A

τηρεῖται δὲ τοῖς μὲν φυτοῖς ἀναισθήτως ἐκ τοῦ περιέχοντος, ὥς φησιν Ἐμπεδοκλῆς, ὑδρευομένοις τὸ
πρόσφορον [. . .].

D247 (> A73) Theophr. *CP* 1.21.5

οὕτω γὰρ εὐθὺς καὶ τὴν φύσιν γεννᾶν ὡς ὑπὸ μὲν τοῦ
ὁμοίου φθειρομένων διὰ τὴν ὑπερβολὴν, ὑπὸ δὲ τοῦ
ἐναντίου σῳζομένων οἷον εὐκρασίας τινὸς γινομένης,
ὥσπερ καὶ Ἐμπεδοκλῆς λέγει περὶ τῶν ζῴων· τὰ γὰρ
ὑπέρπυρα τὴν φύσιν ἄγειν εἰς τὸ ὑγρόν.

lose their leaves, but most of them keep them, as in the case of the laurel, olive, and palm. The differences among the juices come about from the variations of the numerous parts ⟨of the earth⟩ and of the plants, which extract from what nourishes them different similar parts, as in the case of vines. For it is not the differences among these that make wine good, but those of the soil that nourishes them.

D246 (A70) Plutarch, *Table Talk*

As for plants [scil. in contrast with human beings], their [scil. nature] is preserved because, without there being perception, they draw from their environment, as Empedocles says, the water that they need [. . .].

D247 (> A73) Theophrastus, *Causes of Plants*

Thus nature generates them [i.e. plants] directly, as though they perished by the similar through an excess and were preserved by the contrary because of a certain good mixture, as Empedocles says about living beings: that nature leads those with too much fire toward moisture.

D248 (cf. ad B77) Plut. *Quaest. conv.* 3.2.2 649D

ἔνιοι μὲν οὖν ὁμαλότητι κράσεως οἴονται παραμένειν
τὸ φύλλον· Ἐμπεδοκλῆς δὲ πρὸς τούτῳ καὶ πόρων
τινὰ συμμετρίαν αἰτιᾶται¹ τεταγμένως καὶ ὁμαλῶς
τὴν τροφὴν διιέντων ὥστ' ἀρκούντως² ἐπιρρεῖν. τοῖς
δὲ φυλλοροοῦσιν οὐκ ἔστι διὰ μανότητα τῶν ἄνω καὶ
στενότητα τῶν κάτω πόρων, ὅταν οἱ μὲν μὴ ἐπιπέμ-
πωσιν οἱ δὲ <μὴ>³ φυλάττωσιν ἀλλ' ὀλίγον⁴ λαβόντες
ἄθρουν⁵ ἐκχέωσιν, ὥσπερ ἐν ἀνδήροις τισὶν οὐχ ὁμα-
λοῖς· τὰ δ' ὑδρευόμεν' ἀεὶ τὴν τροφὴν διαρκῆ⁶ καὶ
σύμμετρον ἀντέχει, καὶ παραμένει ἀγήρω καὶ χλοερά.

¹ αἰᾶται mss., corr. Aldus
² ὥστε σαρκούντων mss., corr. Xylander
³ <μὴ> Vulcobius   ⁴ ὀλίγην coni. Wyttenbach
⁵ ἄθρουν λαβόντες mss., transp. Reiske
⁶ διαρκῆ gγ: διαρκεῖ T

D249 (cf. ad B79) Arist. *GA* 1.23 731a1–6

ἐν δὲ τοῖς φυτοῖς μεμιγμέναι αὗται αἱ δυνάμεις εἰσί,
καὶ οὐ κεχώρισται τὸ θῆλυ τοῦ ἄρρενος, διὸ καὶ γεννᾷ
αὐτὰ ἐξ αὑτῶν, καὶ προίεται οὐ γονὴν ἀλλὰ κύημα τὰ
καλούμενα σπέρματα. καὶ τοῦτο καλῶς λέγει Ἐμπεδοκλῆς ποιήσας· [= **D254**]. τό τε γὰρ ὠὸν κύημά ἐστι
[. . .].

D248 (cf. ad B77) Plutarch, *Table Talk*

Some people think that leaves persist because of the regularity of the mixture. But Empedocles also attributes the cause to a certain adaptation of the passages that permit nourishment to enter in an orderly and regular manner, so that it arrives in sufficient quantity. But this is not possible for deciduous trees, because the upper passages are loose and the lower ones are tight, when the latter do not send it up and the former ⟨do not⟩ keep it, but having received only a little they release it in abundance, as happens with some flowerbeds that present irregularities. But plants that are always well watered with a sufficient and adapted nourishment persist, so that they endure without getting old and remain green.[1]

> [1] Or: "But plants that are always well watered always conserve a sufficient and adapted nourishment and endure . . ."

D249 (cf. ad B79) Aristotle, *Generation of Animals*

In plants, these powers [scil. the two sexes] are mingled and the female is not separated from the male; this is why they generate by themselves and emit not a generative seed but a fetus, which people call the kernels. And this, Empedocles says it well in his poem: [. . . = **D254**]. For the egg is a fetus [. . .].

D250 (cf. A70) Nic. Dam. *Plant.*, ed. Drossaart Lulofs

a 1.3, p. 127(cf. Ps.-Arist. *Plant.* 1.1 815a15–21)

أما أنكساغورس وهمفدوقلس فزعما أن للنبات شهوة وحسا وغما ولذة [. . .]
وأما همفدوقلس فزعم أن ذكوره وإناثه مختلطة. [. . .]

b p. 449.66–451.2

[. . .] דקליס יניח שיש להם זכרים ונקבות. ולמה שראה שכלם עושים פרי
אמר שהזכר והנקבה מעורבים יחד.

c 1.10, p. 129 (cf. Ps.-Arist. *Plant.* 1.1 815b16–17)

فأما أنكساغورس وهمفدوقلس وديمقراطيس فزعموا أن للنبات عقلا وفهما.

d 1.47, p. 141

وقد جود همفدوقلس في قوله إن الشجر الطوال لا تولد فراخا لأن الشيء النابت
إنما ينبت من جزء البزر ويصير ما ‹بقي› فيه في بدء الأمر غذاء الأصل
والسبب والنابتة تتحرك على المكان.

‹بقَى› Drossaart Lulofs

e 57, p. 221

ولهذا يكون قول أمبادقلس أصوب إن النبات تولد والعالم ناقص فلما تولد
الحيوان.

D250 (cf. A70) Nicolaus of Damascus, *On Plants*

a

Now, Anaxagoras and Empedocles assert that plants have desire and sensation, pain and pleasure, [. . .] and Empedocles asserts that their males and females are mingled together.

b

[. . .] Empedocles allowed that they have males and females, and because he had observed that all of them bear fruit, he declared that the males and females were combined together.

c

Anaxagoras, Empedocles and Democritus maintained that plants possess reason and understanding.

d

Empedocles was right when he said, "Tall trees do not bring forth young," because what sprouts does so from a part of the seed only, and ‹the remainder› becomes first the nutriment of the root and the cause, and the sprout is moved on the spot.

e

For that reason [scil. that animals are superior to plants] Empedocles' statement is correct, that the plants were generated when the world was incomplete, and when it was perfected, animals were generated.[1]

[1] Texts **a, c, d** (modified), and **e** (modified) translated by H. J. Drossaart Lulofs, **b** by Elisa Coda.

D251 (B77) Plut. *Quaest. conv.* 3.2.2 649C

. . . *ἐμπεδόφυλλον* . . .

cf. app. ad **D253**

D252 (cf. ad B78) Theophr. *CP* 1.13.2

. . . *ἐμπεδόκαρπα* . . .

cf. app. ad **D253**

D253 (B78) Theophr. *CP* 1.13.2

καρπῶν ἀφθονίῃσι κατ' ἠέρα πάντ' ἐνιαυτόν

ex *ἐμπεδόφυλλον* (**D251**) et *ἐμπεδόκαρπα* (**D252**) finxit
Karsten versum *δένδρεα δ' ἐμπεδόφυλλα καὶ ἐμπεδόκαρπα*
τεθήλει quod Diels (qui corr. *τεθήλεν*) ante hunc versum prae-
fixit   *καρπῶν*] *μήλων* Karsten   *κατῆρα* mss., corr.
Sturz: *κατήρεα* Scaliger: *κατήορα* Lobeck

D254 (B79) Theophr. *CP* 1.7.1 (et al.)

οὕτω δ' ᾠοτοκεῖ μακρὰ δένδρεα πρῶτον ἐλαίας.

μακρὰ Theophr., Arist. *GA* 731a5 Z: *μικρὰ* Arist. PSY

D255 (B80) Plut. *Quaest. conv.* 5.8.2 683D

οὕνεκεν ὀψίγονοί τε σίδαι καὶ ὑπέρφλοια μῆλα

D251 (B77) Plutarch, *Table Talk*

. . . **with abiding foliage** . . .

D252 (cf. ad B78) Theophrastus, *Causes of Plants*

. . . **with abiding fruits** . . .

D253 (B78) Theophrastus, *Causes of Plants*

**With abundances of fruits for the whole year
because of the air**

D254 (B79) Aristòtle, *Generation of Animals*

Thus the tall[1] trees lay their eggs, olives, first.

[1] 'Small' is also transmitted.

D255 (B80) Plutarch, *Table Talk*

**That is why pomegranate trees produce late and
their fruit is thick-skinned[1]**

[1] Or: "that is why late-born pomegranate trees and thick-
skinned apples."

D256 (B81) Plut. *Quaest. nat.* 2 912C

οἶνος ἀπὸ φλοιοῦ πέλεται σαπὲν ἐν ξύλῳ ὕδωρ.

ἀπὸ] ὑπὸ Xylander

The End of the Poem on Nature? (D257)

D257 (B110) (Ps.-?) Hipp. *Haer.* 7.29.26 (et al.)

εἰ γάρ κέν σφ' ἀδινῇσιν ὑπὸ πραπίδεσσιν
    ἐρείσας
εὐμενέως καθαρῇσιν ἐποπτεύσῃς μελέτῃσιν,
ταῦτά τέ σοι μάλα πάντα δι' αἰῶνος
    παρέσονται,
ἄλλα τε πόλλ' ἀπὸ τῶνδ' ἐκτήσεαι· αὐτὰ γὰρ
    αὔξει
5   ταῦτ' εἰς ἦθος ἕκαστον, ὅπῃ φύσις ἐστὶν
    ἑκάστῳ.
εἰ δὲ σύ γ' ἀλλοίων ἐπορέξεαι οἷα κατ' ἄνδρας
μυρία δειλὰ πέλονται ἅ τ' ἀμβλύνουσι
    μερίμνας,
ἦ σ' ἄφαρ ἐκλείψουσι περιπλομένοιο χρόνοιο

1 κέν σφ' ἀδινῇσιν Duncker-Schneidewin: καὶ ἐν σφαδίνη-
σιν ms.: καὶ σφ' ἀδινῇσιν Bollack
2 ἐποπτεύσῃς Duncker-Schneidewin: ἐποπτεύεις ms.
3 τε Duncker-Schneidewin: δέ ms.   4 τῶνδ' ἐκτήσεαι
Diels: τῶνδεκτ .. ηται ms.: τῶνδε κτήσεαι Marcovich: τῶν κε-
κτήσεαι Meineke   5 ἔθος ms., corr. Miller

D256 (B81) Plutarch, *Natural Questions*

> Wine is water flowing from the bark and
>   putrefied in the wood.

The End of the Poem on Nature? (D257)

D257 (B110) (Ps.-?) Hippolytus, *Refutation of all Heresies*

> For if, leaning upon your firm organs of thought
>   (*prapides*),
> With pure efforts you gaze upon them
>   benevolently,
> They [i.e. the elements] will all be present to you
>   throughout your lifetime
> And many other good things will come to you
>   from them. For these themselves
> Are what makes each thing grow in one's   5
>   character, according to each person's nature.
> But if you yourself covet different things, such
>   as those that among men are
> Countless miseries that blunt their thoughts,
> Certainly they will abandon you quickly, as the
>   time revolves,

---

6 σὺ τἄλλ᾽ οἵων ἐπιρέξεις ms., corr. Duncker-Schneidewin

7 δῆλα ms., corr. Duncker-Schneidewin   ἅ τ᾽ Diels: τά
τ᾽ ms.   μερίμνας Duncker-Schneidewin: μέριμναι ms.

8 ἣ σ᾽ Meineke: σῆς ms.   περιπλομένοιο Miller: περι-
πλομένοις ms.

σφῶν αὐτῶν ποθέοντα φίλην ἐπὶ γένναν
  ἱκέσθαι·
10 πάντα γὰρ ἴσθι φρόνησιν ἔχειν καὶ νώματος
  αἶσαν.

9 γένναν ms., corr. Miller
10 νώματος αἶσαν Sext. Emp. *Adv. Math.* 8.286 (νώ. . . . .
N): γνωματοσισον Hipp. 7.29.24: γνώμην ἴσην Hipp. 6.12.1

Two Corrupt Texts (D258–D259)

D258 (B5) Plut. *Quaest. conv.* 8.8.1 728E

[. . . = **R45**] †στέγουσαι φρενὸς ἀλλ᾽ ὅπερ ἐλάσσω†

στεγάσαι Diels   ἀλλ᾽ ὅπερ] ἔλλοπος Wyttenbach   εἴσω Diels, ἄσσον Bollack

D259 (B32) Ps.-Arist. *Lin.* 972b29

†διὸ δεῖ ὀρθῶς†

δύω δέει ἄρθρον dub. Diels coll. vers. Marciani Rotae
(*articulis constat semper iunctura duobus*)

In their desire to rejoin the race that is theirs.
For know that all things feel (*phronêsis*) **and**   10
   have their share of thought (*noêma*).

Two Corrupt Texts (D258–D259)

D258 (B5) Plutarch, *Table Talk*

†. . .†[1]

[1] Diels' much-emended text would mean 'to cover inside of your voiceless breast.'

D259 (B32) Ps.-Aristotle, *On Indivisible Lines*

  †. . .†[1]

[1] Diels' doubtfully offered conjectural restoration would mean 'the joint binds two.'

EMPEDOCLES [31 DK]

R

The Philosopher-Poet (R1–R4)

R1 Arist.

a (A22) *Poet.* 1 1447b17–19

οὐδὲν δὲ κοινόν ἐστιν Ὁμήρῳ καὶ Ἐμπεδοκλεῖ πλὴν τὸ μέτρον, διὸ τὸν μὲν ποιητὴν δίκαιον καλεῖν, τὸν δὲ φυσιολόγον μᾶλλον ἢ ποιητήν.

b (< A1) *De poetis* in Diog. Laert. 8.57

[. . . = **R5a**] ἐν δὲ τῷ Περὶ ποιητῶν φησιν [Arist. Frag. 70 Rose] ὅτι καὶ Ὁμηρικὸς ὁ Ἐμπεδοκλῆς καὶ δεινὸς περὶ τὴν φράσιν γέγονεν, μεταφορητικός τε ὢν καὶ τοῖς ἄλλοις τοῖς περὶ ποιητικὴν ἐπιτεύγμασι χρώμενος.

c (< A25) *Rhet.* 3.5 1407a31–35

τρίτον μὴ ἀμφιβόλοις· ταῦτα δέ, ἂν μὴ τἀναντία προαιρῆται, ὅπερ ποιοῦσιν ὅταν μηθὲν μὲν ἔχωσι λέγειν,

EMPEDOCLES

The Philosopher-Poet (R1–R4)

R1 Aristotle

a (A22) *Poetics*

Homer and Empedocles have nothing in common except for the meter. That is why it is right to call the former a poet and the other a natural philosopher rather than a poet.

b (< A1) *On Poets*

In his book *On Poets,* he [i.e. Aristotle] says that Empedocles was Homeric and possessed powerful diction, since he was good at metaphors and used the other successful poetic devices.

c (< A25) *Rhetoric*

Thirdly [scil. good style avoids] ambiguities, unless one deliberately chooses the opposite, which is what people do

προσποιῶνται δέ τι λέγειν· οἱ γὰρ τοιοῦτοι ἐν ποιήσει[1] λέγουσι ταῦτα, οἷον Ἐμπεδοκλῆς.

[1] προαιρέσει Victorius, προσποιήσει Morelius

R2 Cic.

a (< A25) *De orat.* 1.50.217

[. . .] dicantur ei[1] quos physicos Graeci nominant idem
poetae, quoniam Empedocles physicus egregium poema
fecerit.

[1] et *ms., corr. Bake*

b (≠ DK) *Lael.* 24

Agrigentium quidem doctum quemdam virum carminibus
Graecis vaticinatum ferunt, quae in rerum natura totoque
mundo constarent quaeque moverentur, ea contrahere
amicitiam, dissipare discordiam.

R3

a (> A24) Quintil. *Inst. or.* 1.4.4

[. . .] nec ignara philosophiae cum propter plurimos
in omnibus fere carminibus locos ex intima naturalium
quaestionum subtilitate repetitos, tum vel propter Empedoclea in Graecis, Varronem ac Lucretium in Latinis, qui
praecepta sapientiae versibus tradiderunt.

who have nothing to say but pretend to be saying something. People like this say these things in poetry, like Empedocles.

R2 Cicero

a (< A25) *On the Orator*

[. . .] those people whom the Greeks call 'natural philosophers' (*phusikoi*) may be called poets too, since Empedocles, the natural philosopher, composed an outstanding poem.

b (≠ DK) *On Friendship*

They say that a certain learned man from Agrigentum sang prophetically in Greek poems that friendship draws together all the things that are at rest in nature and the whole world and all the things that are in motion, and that strife drives them apart.

R3

a (> A24) Quintilian, *Training in Oratory*

[. . .] Nor [scil. will the study of language and literature be perfect] if it is ignorant of philosophy, not only because there are many passages, in almost all poems, that are based on recondite points of natural philosophy, but also because of Empedocles among the Greeks as well as Varro and Lucretius among the Latins, who have transmitted the precepts of wisdom in verses.

585

b (< A24) Lact. *Div. inst.* 2.12.4

[. . .] Empedocles, quem nescias utrumne inter poetas an inter philosophos numeres, quia de rerum natura versibus scripsit ut aput Romanos Lucretius et Varro [. . .].

R4 (ad B80) Plut. *Quaest. conv.* 5.8.2 683D–E

τὰ δὲ μῆλα καθ' ἥντινα διάνοιαν ὁ σοφὸς 'ὑπέρφλοια' [cf. **D255**] προσειρήκοι, διαπορεῖν, καὶ μάλιστα τοῦ ἀνδρὸς οὐ καλλιγραφίας ἕνεκα τοῖς εὐπροσωποτάτοις τῶν ἐπιθέτων, ὥσπερ ἀνθηροῖς χρώμασι, τὰ πράγματα γανοῦν εἰωθότος, ἀλλ' ἕκαστον οὐσίας τινὸς ἢ δυνάμεως δήλωμα ποιοῦντος, οἷον 'ἀμφιβρότην χθόνα' [**D20**] τὸ τῇ ψυχῇ[1] περικείμενον σῶμα, καὶ 'νεφεληγερέτην' [**D143**] τὸν ἀέρα καὶ 'πολυαίματον' [**D196**] τὸ ἧπαρ.

---

[1] τὴν ψυχὴν ms., corr. Turnebus

Empedocles and Rhetoric (R5)

R5

a (< A1) Diog. Laert. 8.57

Ἀριστοτέλης δ' ἐν τῷ Σοφιστῇ φησι [Frag. 65 Rose] πρῶτον Ἐμπεδοκλέα ῥητορικὴν εὑρεῖν, Ζήνωνα δὲ διαλεκτικήν.

b (< A24) Lactantius, *Divine Institutions*

[. . .] Empedocles, of whom one does not know whether he should be counted among the poets or among the philosophers, since he wrote about the nature of things in verses, like Lucretius and Varro among the Romans [. . .].

R4 (ad B80) Plutarch, *Table Talk*

[Scil. for my part I said that] I did not know what the sage's [scil. Empedocles'] intention was when he called apples **'thick-skinned'** [= **D255**], especially since that man did not have the habit of prettifying things with extremely fair-faced epithets like flowery colors, merely for the sake of beautiful writing, but instead he used every expression to indicate some essence or power, for example when he calls the body that surrounds the soul **'man-enveloping earth'** [**D20**], the air **'cloud-gatherer'** [**D143**], and the liver **'with much blood'** [**D196**].

See also **XEN. R28b**

Empedocles and Rhetoric (R5)

R5

a (< A1) Aristotle in Diogenes Laertius

Aristotle says in his *Sophist* that Empedocles was the first person to have discovered rhetoric, and Zeno dialectic.

b (A19) Quintil. *Inst. or.* 3.1.8

nam primus post eos, quos poetae tradiderunt, movisse
aliqua circa rhetoricen Empedocles dicitur. artium autem
scriptores antiquissimi Corax et Tisias Siculi, quos in-
secutus est vir eiusdem insulae Gorgias Leontinus, Empe-
doclis, ut traditur, discipulus.

The Earliest Mention of Empedocles (R6)

R6 (< A71) Hipp. *Vet. med.* 20

λέγουσι δέ τινες ἰητροὶ καὶ σοφισταὶ ὡς οὐκ εἴη
δυνατὸν¹ ἰητρικὴν εἰδέναι, ὅστις μὴ οἶδεν ὅ τί ἐστιν
ἄνθρωπος [. . .]. τείνει τε² αὐτοῖσιν ὁ λόγος ἐς φιλοσο-
φίην, καθάπερ Ἐμπεδοκλέης ἢ ἄλλοι, οἳ περὶ φύσιος
γεγράφασιν, ἐξ ἀρχῆς ὅ τί ἐστιν ἄνθρωπος, καὶ ὅπως
ἐγένετο πρῶτον, καὶ ὁπόθεν συνεπάγη. ἐγὼ δὲ τοῦτο
μέν, ὅσα τινὶ εἴρηται ἢ σοφιστῇ ἢ ἰητρῷ ἢ γέγραπται
περὶ φύσιος, ἧσσον νομίζω τῇ ἰητρικῇ τέχνῃ προσ-
ήκειν ἢ τῇ γραφικῇ, νομίζω δὲ περὶ φύσιος γνῶναί τι
σαφὲς οὐδαμόθεν ἄλλοθεν εἶναι ἢ ἐξ ἰητρικῆς.

---

¹ δυνατὸς Kühlewein   ² τε M: δὲ A

b (A19) Quintilian, *Training in Oratory*

After those whose names the poets transmit, Empedocles is said to have been the first person to make some beginnings in rhetoric. But the most ancient authors of treatises were the Sicilians Corax and Tisias, followed by a man of the same island, Gorgias of Leontini, a disciple of Empedocles, according to tradition [cf. **GORG. P5**].

The Earliest Mention of Empedocles (R6)

R6 (< A71) Hippocrates, *Ancient Medicine*

Some doctors and experts (*sophistai*) say that it is impossible for anyone to know medicine who does not know what a human being is [. . .]. But what they are talking about belongs to philosophy (*philosophiê*), like Empedocles and other people who have written about nature—what a human is from the beginning, how he came about at first and what things he is constituted of. But as for me, I think that whatever has been said or written by some expert (*sophistês*) or doctor about nature belongs less to the art of medicine than it does to that of painting [or: of writing], and I think that there is no other source than medicine in order to have clear knowledge about nature [= **MED. T7b**].

EARLY GREEK PHILOSOPHY V

Empedocles in Plato (R7)
An Aristophanic Parody of Empedocles'
Phylogenesis of Human Beings (R7)

R7 (≠ DK) Plat. *Symp.* 189d5–7, 189e5–190a4, 190b5–c1, 190c6–d4, 191a6–b1, 191b5–d5

[ΑΡ.] δεῖ δὲ πρῶτον ὑμᾶς μαθεῖν τὴν ἀνθρωπίνην φύσιν καὶ τὰ παθήματα αὐτῆς. ἡ γὰρ πάλαι ἡμῶν φύσις οὐχ αὑτὴ ἦν ἥπερ νῦν, ἀλλ᾽ ἀλλοία. [. . .] [189e5] ἔπειτα ὅλον ἦν ἑκάστου τοῦ ἀνθρώπου τὸ εἶδος στρογγύλον, νῶτον καὶ πλευρὰς κύκλῳ ἔχον, χεῖρας δὲ τέτταρας εἶχε, καὶ σκέλη τὰ ἴσα ταῖς χερσίν, καὶ πρόσωπα δύ᾽ ἐπ᾽ αὐχένι κυκλοτερεῖ, ὅμοια πάντῃ· κεφαλὴν δ᾽ ἐπ᾽ ἀμφοτέροις τοῖς προσώποις ἐναντίοις κειμένοις μίαν, καὶ ὦτα τέτταρα, καὶ αἰδοῖα δύο, καὶ τἆλλα πάντα ὡς ἀπὸ τούτων ἄν τις εἰκάσειεν. [. . .] [190b5] ἦν οὖν τὴν ἰσχὺν δεινὰ καὶ τὴν ῥώμην, καὶ τὰ φρονήματα μεγάλα εἶχον, ἐπεχείρησαν δὲ τοῖς θεοῖς [. . .], καὶ ὃ λέγει Ὅμηρος περὶ Ἐφιάλτου τε καὶ Ὤτου, περὶ ἐκείνων λέγεται, τὸ εἰς τὸν οὐρανὸν ἀνάβασιν ἐπιχειρεῖν ποιεῖν, ὡς ἐπιθησομένων τοῖς θεοῖς. [. . .] [190c6] μόγις δὴ ὁ Ζεὺς ἐννοήσας λέγει ὅτι "δοκῶ μοι," ἔφη, "ἔχειν μηχανήν, ὡς ἂν εἶέν τε ἄνθρωποι[1] καὶ παύσαιντο τῆς ἀκολασίας ἀσθενέστεροι γενόμενοι. νῦν μὲν γὰρ αὐτούς," ἔφη, "διατεμῶ δίχα ἕκαστον, [. . .] καὶ ἅμα μὲν ἀσθενέστεροι ἔσονται, ἅμα δὲ χρησιμώτεροι ἡμῖν διὰ τὸ πλείους τὸν ἀριθμὸν

EMPEDOCLES

Empedocles in Plato (R7)
An Aristophanic Parody of Empedocles'
Phylogenesis of Human Beings (R7)

R7 (≠ DK) Plato, *Symposium*

[Aristophanes:] First of all you must learn about human nature and its vicissitudes. For long ago our nature was not the same as it is now but was of a different sort. [. . .] [189e5] then, the shape of every human being was completely spherical, with the back and sides circular, and every one had four arms, and legs equal in number to their arms, and two faces, similar in every way, set upon a cylindrical neck. There was a single head for the two faces placed on opposite sides, four ears, two genitals, and all the rest as one could guess from these. [. . .] [190b5] Their strength and power were terrible, and they had extreme ideas; they made an attempt upon the gods [. . .] and the same story as what Homer says about Ephialtes and Otus [*Il.* 5.385; *Od.* 11.305] is told about them, that they made an attempt to mount to heaven in order to attack the gods. [. . .][190c6] Hardly had Zeus thought about it before he said, "I think that I have found a plan by which humans will become weaker and will stop their uncontrolled violence but will continue to exist. I will cut each one in half, [. . .] and in this way they will become not only weaker but also more useful for us, since their number will be in-

---

1 ἄνθρωποι mss., corr. Voegelin

γεγονέναι· καὶ βαδιοῦνται ὀρθοὶ ἐπὶ δυοῖν σκελοῖν."
[. . .] [191a5] ἐπειδὴ οὖν ἡ φύσις δίχα ἐτμήθη, ποθοῦν
ἕκαστον τὸ ἥμισυ τὸ αὑτοῦ συνῄει,² καὶ περιβάλλον-
τες τὰς χεῖρας καὶ συμπλεκόμενοι ἀλλήλοις, ἐπιθυ-
μοῦντες συμφῦναι, ἀπέθνῃσκον ὑπὸ λιμοῦ καὶ τῆς
ἄλλης ἀργίας διὰ τὸ μηδὲν ἐθέλειν χωρὶς ἀλλήλων
ποιεῖν. [. . .] [191b5] ἐλεήσας δὲ ὁ Ζεὺς ἄλλην μηχανὴν
πορίζεται, καὶ μετατίθησιν αὐτῶν τὰ αἰδοῖα εἰς τὸ
πρόσθεν—τέως γὰρ καὶ ταῦτα ἐκτὸς εἶχον, καὶ ἐγέν-
νων καὶ ἔτικτον οὐκ εἰς ἀλλήλους ἀλλ' εἰς γῆν, ὥσπερ
οἱ τέττιγες—μετέθηκέ τε οὖν οὕτω αὐτῶν εἰς τὸ πρόσθεν καὶ διὰ τούτων τὴν γένεσιν³ ἐν ἀλλήλοις ἐποίη-
σεν, διὰ τοῦ ἄρρενος ἐν τῷ θήλει, τῶνδε ἕνεκα, ἵνα ἐν
τῇ συμπλοκῇ ἅμα μὲν εἰ ἀνὴρ γυναικὶ ἐντύχοι, γεν-
νῷεν καὶ γίγνοιτο τὸ γένος, ἅμα δ' εἰ καὶ ἄρρην ἄρρενι, πλησμονὴ γοῦν γίγνοιτο τῆς συνουσίας καὶ
διαπαύοιντο καὶ ἐπὶ τὰ ἔργα τρέποιντο καὶ τοῦ ἄλλου
βίου ἐπιμελοῖντο. ἔστι δὴ οὖν ἐκ τόσου ὁ ἔρως ἔμφυ-
τος ἀλλήλων τοῖς ἀνθρώποις καὶ τῆς ἀρχαίας φύσεως
συναγωγεὺς καὶ ἐπιχειρῶν ποιῆσαι ἓν ἐκ δυοῖν καὶ
ἰάσασθαι τὴν φύσιν τὴν ἀνθρωπίνην. ἕκαστος οὖν
ἡμῶν ἐστιν ἀνθρώπου σύμβολον, ἅτε τετμημένος
ὥσπερ αἱ ψῆτται, ἐξ ἑνὸς δύο· ζητεῖ δὴ ἀεὶ τὸ αὑτοῦ
ἕκαστος σύμβολον.

² ξυνῄει T: ξυνεῖναι B: del. Rettig
³ γέννησιν Vermehren

creased; and they will walk upright on two legs." [. . .] [191a5] Then when their natural shape had been cut in half, each half desired its other half and went after it, and throwing their arms around one another and embracing each other in their desire to coalesce, they were dying of starvation and more generally of inactivity, since they did not want to do anything separately from one another. [. . .] [191b5] Zeus took pity upon them and devised another plan: he moved their genitals to the front—for until then they had had these too on their outside, and they procreated and gave birth not on each other but on the earth, like crickets. So in this way he moved them to their front and made these the means for their procreation inside one another, by the male inside the female, so that if a male embraced a female, they would procreate and the species would be reproduced; but if a male embraced a male, there would at least be satisfaction and relief because of the sexual union, and after they had finished they would turn to their work and take care of the rest of their life. So ever since then, sexual desire has been implanted in human beings for one another; it reunites our ancient natural shape and attempts to make one out of two and to heal human nature. So each of us is a half of a human being, since we have been cut in half like flat-fishes, made two out of one. And each one is always seeking his missing half.

EARLY GREEK PHILOSOPHY V

A Parallel with Heraclitus

See **D78** and **DOX. T4**

*Criticisms by Aristotle and the
First Peripatetics (R8–R25)
Comparison with Anaxagoras*

See **ANAXAG. D95e, R8, R15, R16, R23[35]; EMP.
D81, D84**

The Elements Ought to Generate Each Other (R8)

R8 (≠ DK)

a Arist. *GC* 1.1 315a3–19

Ἐμπεδοκλῆς μὲν οὖν ἔοικεν ἐναντία λέγειν καὶ πρὸς
τὰ φαινόμενα καὶ πρὸς αὐτὸν αὑτός. ἅμα μὲν γὰρ οὔ
φησιν ἕτερον ἐξ ἑτέρου γίνεσθαι τῶν στοιχείων οὐδέν, ἀλλὰ τἆλλα πάντα ἐκ τούτων, ἅμα δ' ὅταν εἰς ἓν
συναγάγῃ τὴν ἅπασαν φύσιν πλὴν τοῦ Νείκους, ἐκ
τοῦ ἑνὸς γίγνεσθαι πάλιν ἕκαστον· ὥστ' ἐξ ἑνός τινος
δῆλον ὅτι διαφοραῖς τισι χωριζομένων καὶ πάθεσιν
ἐγένετο τὸ μὲν ὕδωρ τὸ δὲ πῦρ, καθάπερ λέγει τὸν μὲν
ἥλιον λευκὸν καὶ θερμόν, τὴν δὲ γῆν βαρὺ καὶ σκλη-
ρόν· ἀφαιρουμένων οὖν τούτων τῶν διαφορῶν (εἰσὶ
γὰρ ἀφαιρεταὶ γενόμεναί γε) δῆλον ὡς ἀνάγκη γίνεσθαι καὶ γῆν ἐξ ὕδατος καὶ ὕδωρ ἐκ γῆς, ὁμοίως δὲ
καὶ τῶν ἄλλων ἕκαστον, οὐ τότε μόνον ἀλλὰ καὶ νῦν,

594

EMPEDOCLES

A Parallel with Heraclitus

See **D78** and **DOX. T4**

*Criticisms by Aristotle and the
First Peripatetics (R8–R25)
Comparison with Anaxagoras*

See **ANAXAG. D95e, R8, R15, R16, R23[35]; EMP.
D81, D84**

The Elements Ought to Generate Each Other (R8)

R8 (≠ DK)

a Aristotle, *On Generation and Corruption*

Thus Empedocles seems to contradict both the phenomena and himself. For at the same time as he says that none of the elements can come about from another one but that all other things come about from these, he also says, when he collects all of nature except for Strife into one unity, that each thing comes about once again from the one [cf. **D75**]; so that it is manifest that it is out of some one entity (things separating by virtue of certain differences and affections), that water and fire have come about, just as he says that the sun is brilliant and hot, and the earth heavy and hard. Thus, when these differences disappear (for they are capable of disappearing, since they have come about), it is manifest that earth necessarily comes about from water and water from earth, and the same for each of the others, not only then, but now too, the change hap-

μεταβάλλοντά γε τοῖς πάθεσιν. ἔστι δ' ἐξ ὧν εἴρηκε
δυνάμενα προσγίνεσθαι καὶ χωρίζεσθαι πάλιν, ἄλλως τε καὶ μαχομένων ἀλλήλοις ἔτι τοῦ Νείκους καὶ
τῆς Φιλίας, διόπερ καὶ τότε ἐξ ἑνὸς ἐγεννήθησαν—οὐ
γὰρ δὴ πῦρ γε καὶ γῆ καὶ ὕδωρ ὄντα ἓν ἦν τὸ πᾶν.

b Schol. f et g ad Arist. *GC* 1.1 315a6–8, *Laur.* 87.7

1 Schol. f ad a6 [εἰς ἕν], fol. 201r, l. 22

Σφαῖρον
. . . ἵνα γένηται ὁ διανοητὸς κόσμος τῆς φιλίας ἐπι-
κρατησάσης.

2 Schol. g ad a7–8 [ἐκ τοῦ ἑνὸς γίνεσθαι πάλιν
ἕκαστον], fol. 201v, l. 1

. . . διακρίσει μετὰ ρ' χρόνους
. . . Νείκους ἐπικρατήσαντος
. . . σύμπ(αν)

The Elements Ought to Have
Indivisible Parts (R9–R10)

R9 (A43a) Arist. *Cael.* 3.6 305a1–4

εἰ δὲ στήσεταί που ἡ διάλυσις, ἤτοι ἄτομον ἔσται τὸ[1]
σῶμα ἐν ᾧ ἵσταται, ἢ διαιρετὸν μὲν οὐ μέντοι διαι-

[1] τι E[2]

596

pening at the level of the affections. And from what he says it follows that they are capable of combining and separating in turn, especially when Strife and Love are still fighting against each another; this is why things came about then out of the One—for certainly, if fire, earth, and water existed, the whole was not one.

b Scholia on Aristotle's *On Generation and Corruption*[1]

1

["into one unity":]
the Sphere
... so that the intelligible world can come about under the domination of Love.

2

["that each thing comes about once again from the one":]
... by separation after one hundred periods of time
... under the domination of Strife
... the whole

[1] These scholia, which we reproduce following the passage that they comment on, essentially concern Empedocles' cycle; cf. **D84–D86**.

The Elements Ought to Have
Indivisible Parts (R9–R10)

R9 (A43a) Aristotle, *On the Heavens*

If the dissolution is to stop somewhere, then either the body at which it stops will be indivisible, or else it will be

ρεθησόμενον οὐδέποτε, καθάπερ ἔοικεν Ἐμπεδοκλῆς βούλεσθαι λέγειν.

R10 (A43) Arist. *GC* 2.7 334a26–31

ἐκείνοις τε γὰρ τοῖς λέγουσιν ὡς Ἐμπεδοκλῆς τίς ἔσται τρόπος; ἀνάγκη γὰρ σύνθεσιν εἶναι καθάπερ ἐκ πλίνθων καὶ λίθων τοῖχος· καὶ τὸ μίγμα δὴ τοῦτο[1] ἐκ σωζομένων μὲν ἔσται τῶν στοιχείων, κατὰ μικρὰ δὲ παρ᾽ ἄλληλα συγκειμένων· οὕτω δὴ σὰρξ καὶ τῶν ἄλλων ἕκαστον.

[1] τοῦτο E[1]LJM: τὸ ἐν FHJ[1]VWE

What Is the Cause of Motion? (R11–R13)

R11 Arist. *Metaph.*

a (< A37) A4 985a21–29

[. . .] καὶ Ἐμπεδοκλῆς ἐπὶ πλέον μὲν τούτου χρῆται τοῖς αἰτίοις, οὐ μὴν οὔθ᾽ ἱκανῶς, οὔτ᾽ ἐν τούτοις εὑρίσκει τὸ ὁμολογούμενον. πολλαχοῦ γοῦν αὐτῷ ἡ μὲν Φιλία διακρίνει τὸ δὲ Νεῖκος συγκρίνει. ὅταν μὲν γὰρ εἰς τὰ στοιχεῖα διίστηται τὸ πᾶν ὑπὸ τοῦ Νείκους, τότε τὸ πῦρ εἰς ἓν συγκρίνεται καὶ τῶν ἄλλων στοιχείων ἕκαστον· ὅταν δὲ πάλιν ὑπὸ τῆς Φιλίας συνίωσιν εἰς τὸ ἕν, ἀναγκαῖον ἐξ ἑκάστου τὰ μόρια διακρίνεσθαι πάλιν.

divisible but will never actually be divided, as Empedocles seems to have meant.

R10 (A43) Aristotle, *On Generation and Corruption*

For those who speak as Empedocles does, what will be their way [scil. of explaining generation]? For necessarily it will be an assemblage, like a wall made out of bricks and stones; and this mixture will be made out of elements that have been conserved and whose little parts are assembled next to one another—thus indeed flesh and each of the other things.

What Is the Cause of Motion? (R11–R13)

R11 Aristotle, *Metaphysics*

a (< A37)

[. . .] and Empedocles has recourse to causes more than he [i.e. Anaxagoras] does, but he does not do so sufficiently, and he does not manage to discover coherence in these either. For in him, Love divides and Strife joins in many passages. For when the whole separates into the elements under the effect of Strife, at that time the fire is combined into one, as is each of the other elements; and when inversely they come together into one under the effect of Love, it is necessary that the parts separate again from each of them.

b (< 318 Bollack) α2 994a3–8

οὔτε γὰρ ὡς ἐξ ὕλης τόδ᾽ ἐκ τοῦδε δυνατὸν ἰέναι εἰς[1]
ἄπειρον (οἷον σάρκα μὲν ἐκ γῆς, γῆν δ᾽ ἐξ ἀέρος,
ἀέρα δ᾽ ἐκ πυρός, καὶ τοῦτο μὴ ἵστασθαι), οὔτε ὅθεν
ἡ ἀρχὴ τῆς κινήσεως (οἷον τὸν μὲν ἄνθρωπον ὑπὸ[2]
τοῦ ἀέρος κινηθῆναι, τοῦτον δ᾽ ὑπὸ τοῦ ἡλίου, τὸν δὲ
ἥλιον ὑπὸ τοῦ Νείκους, καὶ τούτου μηδὲν εἶναι πέρας).

[1] ἰέναι εἰς Aᵇ: εἶναι ἐπ᾽ E   [2] ὑπὸ E: ἐκ Aᵇ

R12 (≠ DK) Arist. *Phys.* 8.1 252a27–32

εἰ δὲ προσοριεῖται τὸ ἐν μέρει, λεκτέον ἐφ᾽ ὧν οὕτως,
ὥσπερ ὅτι ἔστιν τι ὃ συνάγει τοὺς ἀνθρώπους, ἡ Φιλία, καὶ φεύγουσιν οἱ ἐχθροὶ ἀλλήλους· τοῦτο γὰρ
ὑποτίθεται καὶ ἐν τῷ ὅλῳ εἶναι· φαίνεται γὰρ ἐπί τινων οὕτως. τὸ δὲ καὶ δι᾽ ἴσων χρόνων δεῖται λόγου
τινός.

R13

a (> A42) Arist. *GC* 2.6 333b35–334a9

ἔτι δὲ καὶ φαίνεται κινούμενα· διέκρινε μὲν γὰρ τὸ
Νεῖκος, ἠνέχθη δ᾽ ἄνω ὁ αἰθὴρ οὐχ ὑπὸ τοῦ Νείκους,
ἀλλ᾽ ὁτὲ μέν φησιν ὥσπερ ἀπὸ τύχης [. . . = **D105**],
ὁτὲ δέ φησι πεφυκέναι τὸ πῦρ ἄνω φέρεσθαι, ὁ δ᾽
αἰθήρ, φησί, "μακρῇσι κατὰ χθόνα δύετο ῥίζαις"

b (≠ DK)

For it is not possible that this come from that, as from its matter, to infinity (for example flesh from earth, earth from air, air from fire, and that this not cease), and it is not possible either for the origin of motion (for example that the man is moved by the air, the air by the fire, this latter by the sun, and the sun by Strife, and that there not be any limit to this).

R12 (≠ DK) Aristotle, *Physics*

If he had to define further [scil. than by appealing to necessity] the alternation [scil. of the domination of Love and of Strife], then he would have to say in which cases things happen this way, saying for example that there is something that brings humans together, namely Love, while enemies flee from one another; for he presumes that this is what happens in the universe too, for it is observed that in certain cases things happen this way. As for the idea of equal periods of time [cf. **D86**], this too requires some explanation.

R13

a (> A42) Aristotle, *On Generation and Corruption*

Moreover, it is manifest that they [i.e. the elements] move [scil. by themselves]. For indeed Strife has separated; but it is not under the effect of Strife that the aether has been borne upward, but sometimes he says that it is as though by chance [. . . = **D105**], sometimes he says that fire has a natural tendency to move upward, while the aether, as he says, **"sank down under the earth by long roots"**

[**D108**]. ἅμα δὲ καὶ τὸν κόσμον ὁμοίως ἔχειν φησὶν ἐπί τε τοῦ Νείκους νῦν καὶ πρότερον ἐπὶ τῆς Φιλίας. τί οὖν ἐστι τὸ κινοῦν πρῶτον καὶ αἴτιον τῆς κινήσεως; οὐ γὰρ δὴ ἡ Φιλία καὶ τὸ Νεῖκος.

b (≠ DK) Schol. i et j ad Arist. *GC* 1.1 334a6–7, *Laur.* 87.7

1 Schol. i ad a6 [τὸν κόσμον . . . ὁμοίως . . . ἔχειν], fol. 236v, l. 2

τὰ δ᾽ στοιχεῖα . . . εὐτάκτως . . . κινεῖσθαι . . .

2 Schol. j ad a6–7 [ἐπί τε τοῦ Νείκους νῦν καὶ πρότερον ἐπὶ τῆς Φιλίας], fol. 236v, l. 2

ἀλλ᾽ ἐπεί ποτε καὶ ἅπαξ ἐκινήθησαν ὑπὸ τοῦ Νείκους ἕως εἰς τοὺς ξ΄ χρόνους, τί τὸ αἴτιον τῆς κινήσεως;

Why Is the Earth Immobile? (R14)

R14 (< 202 Bollack) Arist. *Cael.* 2.13 295a29–b3

ἔτι δὲ πρὸς Ἐμπεδοκλέα κἂν ἐκεῖνό τις εἴπειεν. ὅτε γὰρ τὰ στοιχεῖα διειστήκει χωρὶς ὑπὸ τοῦ Νείκους, τίς αἰτία τῇ γῇ τῆς μονῆς ἦν; οὐ γὰρ δὴ καὶ τότε αἰτιάσεται τὴν δίνην. ἄτοπον δὲ καὶ τὸ μὴ συννοεῖν ὅτι πρότερον μὲν διὰ τὴν δίνησιν ἐφέρετο τὰ μόρια τῆς γῆς πρὸς τὸ μέσον· νῦν δὲ διὰ τίν᾽ αἰτίαν πάντα

[**D108**]. At the same time, he also says that the world is in the same condition both now, under Strife, and earlier, under Love. Then what is the first mover and the cause of motion? For this certainly cannot be Love and Strife.

b (≠ DK) Scholia on Aristotle's *On Generation and Corruption*[1]

1

["the world . . . in the same condition . . . is":]
the four elements . . . well-ordered . . . move.

2

["both now, under Strife, and earlier, under Love":]
but since at some time and only one time they [i.e. the four elements] were set in motion by Strife for the sixty periods of time [scil. of the growth of Strife], what is the cause of the motion?

[1] See the note on **R8b,** above.

Why Is the Earth Immobile? (R14)

R14 (≠ DK) Aristotle, *On the Heavens*

One could also make the following objection against Empedocles: when the elements were separated from one another under the effect of Strife, what was the cause of the earth's immobility? For he will certainly not assign the cause to the vortex at that time too. It is also absurd not to consider this: earlier, the parts of the earth were borne toward the center because of the rotation; but at present,

603

τὰ βάρος ἔχοντα φέρεται πρὸς αὐτήν; οὐ γὰρ ἥ γε
δίνη πλησιάζει πρὸς ἡμᾶς. ἔτι δὲ καὶ τὸ πῦρ ἄνω
φέρεται διὰ τίν' αἰτίαν; οὐ γὰρ διά γε τὴν δίνην. εἰ
δὲ τοῦτο φέρεσθαί που πέφυκεν, δῆλον ὅτι καὶ τὴν
γῆν οἰητέον [. . . = **R15a**].

Heaviness and Lightness (R15)

R15 Arist. *Cael.*

a (< 202 Bollack) Arist. *Cael.* 2.13 295b3–4

[. . . = **R14**] ἀλλὰ μὴν οὐδὲ τῇ δίνῃ γε τὸ βαρὺ καὶ
κοῦφον ὥρισται [. . .].

b (59 A68) Arist. *Cael.* 4.2 309a19–21

ἔνιοι μὲν οὖν τῶν μὴ φασκόντων εἶναι κενὸν οὐδὲν
διώρισαν περὶ κούφου καὶ βαρέος, οἷον Ἀναξαγόρας
καὶ Ἐμπεδοκλῆς.

Light (R16)

R16 (cf. A57) Arist. *An.* 2.7 418b20–26

καὶ οὐκ ὀρθῶς Ἐμπεδοκλῆς, οὐδ' εἴ τις ἄλλος οὕτως
εἴρηκεν, ὡς φερομένου τοῦ φωτὸς καὶ τεινομένου[1] ποτὲ
μεταξὺ τῆς γῆς καὶ τοῦ περιέχοντος, ἡμᾶς δὲ λανθά-
νοντος· τοῦτο γάρ ἐστι καὶ παρὰ τὴν τοῦ λόγου[2] ἐνάργειαν[3] καὶ παρὰ τὰ φαινόμενα· ἐν μικρῷ μὲν γὰρ δια-

---

[1] τεινομένου CVe: γιγνομένου cett.

for what reason are all heavy bodies borne toward it [i.e. the earth]? For the vortex, to be sure, does not come near to us. Moreover, for what reason is fire borne upward? For this is surely not because of the vortex. And if it is its nature to be borne somewhere, then evidently one must think this about the earth as well. [. . .].

Heaviness and Lightness (R15)

R15 Aristotle, *On the Heavens*

a (≠ DK)

[. . .] But certainly it is not by the vortex either that heavy and light are defined.

b (59 A68)

Some of those people who deny the existence of the void have not given any definition of light and heavy, like Anaxagoras [= **ANAXAG. D59**] and Empedocles.

Light (R16)

R16 (cf. A57) Aristotle, *On the Soul*

Empedocles is mistaken, as is anyone else who might have spoken as he did, in saying that the light moves and sometimes extends between the earth and what surrounds it [scil. the universe] without our noticing. For this contradicts both the clarity of reasoning and the observed facts: for if the distance were small we might not notice, but to

---

2 τοῦ λόγου plerique: ἐν τῷ λόγῳ SUX
3 ἐνάργειαν Py: ἐνέργειαν CWe: ἀλήθειαν SUVX

στήματι λάθοι ἄν, ἀπ' ἀνατολῆς δ' ἐπὶ δυσμὰς τὸ
λανθάνειν μέγα λίαν τὸ αἴτημα.

Plants and Fruits (R17–R18)

R17 (> A70) Arist. *An.* 2.4 415b28–416a9

Ἐμπεδοκλῆς δ' οὐ καλῶς εἴρηκε τοῦτο, προστιθεὶς
τὴν αὔξησιν συμβαίνειν τοῖς φυτοῖς, κάτω μὲν συρ-
ριζουμένοις¹ διὰ τὸ τὴν γῆν οὕτω φέρεσθαι κατὰ φύσιν, ἄνω δὲ διὰ τὸ ‹τὸ›² πῦρ ὡσαύτως. οὔτε γὰρ τὸ
ἄνω καὶ κάτω καλῶς λαμβάνει (οὐ γὰρ ταὐτὸ πᾶσι
τὸ ἄνω καὶ κάτω καὶ τῷ παντί, ἀλλ' ὡς ἡ κεφαλὴ τῶν
ζῴων, οὕτως αἱ ῥίζαι τῶν φυτῶν [. . .])· πρὸς δὲ τούτοις
τί τὸ συνέχον εἰς τἀναντία φερόμενα τὸ πῦρ καὶ τὴν
γῆν; διασπασθήσεται γάρ, εἰ μή τι ἔσται τὸ κωλύον
[. . .].

¹ συρριζουμένοις Cᵉ: ῥιζουμένοις PW: ῥιζουμένων SUVX
² ‹τὸ› Ross

R18 (cf. A94) Arist. *Sens.* 4 441a10–14

τούτων δ' ὡς μὲν Ἐμπεδοκλῆς λέγει λίαν εὐσύνοπτον
τὸ ψεῦδος· ὁρῶμεν γὰρ μεταβάλλοντας ὑπὸ τοῦ θερμοῦ τοὺς χυμοὺς ἀφαιρουμένων τῶν περικαρπίων¹ εἰς
τὸν ἥλιον² καὶ πυρουμένων,³ ὡς οὐ τῷ ἐκ τοῦ ὕδατος
ἕλκειν τοιούτους γιγνομένους, ἀλλ' ἐν αὐτῷ τῷ περι-
καρπίῳ μεταβάλλοντας [. . .].

claim that we did not notice from sunrise to sunset is to ask far too much.

Plants and Fruits (R17–R18)

R17 (> A70) Aristotle, *On the Soul*

Empedocles did not speak correctly when he adds that growth occurs downward for plants because they are rooted and earth moves in this direction by nature, and upward because the same applies to fire. For on the one hand he does not correctly conceive up and down: for up and down are not the same for all things and for the universe, but what the head is for animals, the roots are for plants [. . .]. On the other hand, what is it that holds together fire and earth, since they are moving in opposite directions? For they will become disconnected, unless there is something that prevents this [. . .].

R18 (cf. A94) Aristotle, *On Sensation*

Among these [scil. theories of taste], Empedocles' error is easy to see [cf. **D235**]. For we see that flavors change by the effect of heat when pericarpal fruits that have been picked are exposed to the sun and are warmed by it, which shows that they do not become such because they come from water, but because the change takes place in the fruit itself [. . .].

---

[1] κάρπων coni. Thurot   [2] εἰς τὸν ἥλιον del. Bitterauf
[3] πυρρουμένων coni. G. R. T. Ross

EARLY GREEK PHILOSOPHY V

Animal Physiology (R19–R23)

R19 (< A81) Arist. *GA* 4.1 764a12–15

τοῦτο γὰρ ὡς ἀληθῶς Ἐμπεδοκλῆς ῥᾳθυμότερον ὑπείληφεν οἰόμενος ψυχρότητι καὶ θερμότητι διαφέρειν
μόνον ἀλλήλων, ὁρῶν ὅλα τὰ μόρια μεγάλην ἔχοντα
διαφορὰν τήν τε τῶν αἰδοίων καὶ τὴν τῆς ὑστέρας.

R20 (B97) Arist. *PA* 1.1 640a18–22

ἡ γὰρ γένεσις ἕνεκα τῆς οὐσίας ἐστίν, ἀλλ᾽ οὐχ ἡ
οὐσία ἕνεκα τῆς γενέσεως. διόπερ Ἐμπεδοκλῆς οὐκ
ὀρθῶς εἴρηκε λέγων ὑπάρχειν πολλὰ τοῖς ζῴοις διὰ
τὸ συμβῆναι οὕτως ἐν τῇ γενέσει, οἷον καὶ τὴν ῥάχιν
τοιαύτην ἔχειν, ὅτι στραφέντος καταχθῆναι συνέβη
[. . .].

R21 (> A73) Arist. *Resp.* 14 477a32–b7 et b12–17

Ἐμπεδοκλῆς δ᾽ οὐ καλῶς τοῦτ᾽ εἴρηκε, φάσκων τὰ
θερμότατα καὶ πῦρ ἔχοντα πλεῖστον τῶν ζῴων ἔνυδρα
εἶναι, φεύγοντα τὴν ὑπερβολὴν τῆς ἐν τῇ φύσει θερμότητος, ὅπως, ἐπειδὴ τοῦ ψυχροῦ καὶ τοῦ ὑγροῦ ἐλ-
λείπει, κατὰ τὸν τόπον ἀνασῴζηται,[1] ἐναντίον[2] ὄντα·
θερμὸν γὰρ εἶναι τὸ ὑγρὸν ἧττον τοῦ ἀέρος. ὅλως μὲν

---

[1] ἀνασῴζη τὰ MZ[1]: ἀνισάζη τὰ L   [2] ἐναντίον Ross:
ἐναντία mss.

608

Animal Physiology (R19–R23)

R19 (< A81) Aristotle, *Generation of Animals*

To tell the truth, Empedocles conceived these matters too lazily, when he thought that they [i.e. male and female] differ from one another only by coldness and warmth [cf. **D173a**], even though he saw that the bodily parts in their totality present a great difference, that existing between the genital organ and the uterus.

R20 (B97) Aristotle, *Parts of Animals*

Generation is for the sake of the substance, and not the substance for the sake of generation. That is why Empedocles has not spoken correctly when he says that the cause of many characteristics in animals is that it happened in this way accidentally during their development, for example that their **spinal column** has a certain shape because it accidentally broke when it [i.e. the embryo] twisted [cf. **D177**] [. . .].

R21 (> A73) Aristotle, *On Respiration*

Empedocles has not spoken correctly when he claims that the animals that are warmest and have the most fire are the aquatic ones, since they are fleeing the excess warmth of their natural constitution, since it lacks coldness and wetness, in order to be preserved by an environment that is opposite to them [cf. **D247**]; for wetness is less warm than air. In general, then, it is impossible to understand

οὖν ἄτοπον πῶς ἐνδέχεται γενόμενον ἕκαστον αὐτῶν
ἐν τῷ ξηρῷ μεταβάλλειν τὸν τόπον εἰς τὸ ὑγρόν (σχεδὸν γὰρ καὶ ἄποδα τὰ πλεῖστα αὐτῶν ἐστιν) [. . .]·
περὶ δ᾽ ἧς αἰτίας εἴρηκεν Ἐμπεδοκλῆς, τῇ μὲν ἔχει τὸ
ζητούμενον λόγον, οὐ μὴν ὅ γέ φησιν ἐκεῖνος ἀληθές.
τῶν μὲν γὰρ ἕξεων τοὺς τὰς ὑπερβολὰς ἔχοντας οἱ
ἐναντίοι τόποι καὶ ὧραι σῴζουσιν, ἡ δὲ φύσις ἐν τοῖς
οἰκείοις σῴζεται μάλιστα τόποις.

R22 (> B92) Arist. *GA* 2.8 747a24–29 et 34–b8

[. . .] τὸ δὲ τῶν ἡμιόνων γένος ὅλον ἄγονόν ἐστιν. περὶ
δὲ τῆς αἰτίας, ὡς μὲν λέγουσιν Ἐμπεδοκλῆς καὶ Δημόκριτος, λέγων ὁ μὲν οὐ σαφῶς, Δημόκριτος δὲ γνω-
ρίμως μᾶλλον, οὐ καλῶς εἰρήκασιν. λέγουσι γὰρ ἐπὶ
πάντων ὁμοίως τὴν ἀπόδειξιν τῶν παρὰ τὴν συγγέ-
νειαν συνδυαζομένων. [. . . = **ATOM. D178**] Ἐμπεδοκλῆς δ᾽ αἰτιᾶται τὸ μίγμα τὸ τῶν σπερμάτων γίνεσθαι πυκνὸν ἐκ μαλακῆς τῆς γονῆς οὔσης ἑκατέρας·
συναρμόττειν γὰρ τὰ κοῖλα τοῖς πυκνοῖς ἀλλήλων, ἐκ
δὲ τῶν τοιούτων γίνεσθαι ἐκ μαλακῶν σκληρόν,
ὥσπερ τῷ καττιτέρῳ μιχθέντα τὸν χαλκόν, λέγων οὔτ᾽
ἐπὶ τοῦ χαλκοῦ καὶ τοῦ καττιτέρου τὴν αἰτίαν ὀρθῶς
[. . .] οὔθ᾽ ὅλως ἐκ γνωρίμων ποιούμενος τὰς ἀρχάς.
τὰ γὰρ κοῖλα καὶ τὰ στερεὰ ἁρμόττοντα ἀλλήλοις
πῶς ποιεῖ τὴν μίξιν, οἷον οἴνου καὶ ὕδατος; τοῦτο γὰρ
ὑπὲρ ἡμᾶς ἐστι τὸ λεγόμενον.

how each of them, born on dry land, could have changed
its place for a wet one (for most of them have no feet)
[. . .]. As for the cause of which Empedocles speaks, what
he is looking for is certainly reasonable, but what he himself says is not true. For while, among dispositions, opposite environments and seasons preserve those that suffer from an excess, nature itself is preserved most of all in
those environments that are best adapted to it.

R22 (> B92) Aristotle, *Generation of Animals*

[. . .] the whole race of mules is sterile. But about the
cause, Empedocles and Democritus have not spoken correctly, the former speaking unclearly, but Democritus
more understandably. For they argue in a similar way
about all [scil. the animals] that mate outside their species.
[. . .] Empedocles attributes the cause to the fact that the
mixture of the seeds becomes dense, each of the two seeds
out of which it is made being soft; for the hollow parts and
the dense ones fit together into each other, and out of
seeds of this sort, the hard comes about from soft ones,
like bronze mixed with tin. But he does not explain the
cause correctly in the case of bronze and tin either [. . .]
and in general he does not derive his principles from
known facts. For how does the reciprocal fitting together
of the hollow parts and the solid ones produce the mixture,
between wine and water for example? What he says is over
our heads.

R23 (> A78) Ps.-Arist. *Spirit.* 9 485b26–29

διὸ καὶ Ἐμπεδοκλῆς αἰτίαν[1] ἁπλῶς τὴν τοῦ ὀστοῦ φύσιν ‹. . .›[2] εἴπερ ἅπαντα τὸν αὐτὸν λόγον ἔχει τῆς
μίξεως, ἀδιάφορα ἐχρῆν ἵππου καὶ λέοντος καὶ ἀνθρώπου εἶναι.

---

[1] λίαν Ross: μίαν Neustadt: an αἰτιᾶται?   [2] spat. aliquot
litt. Z: ἐπεὶ suppl. Ross, οὐ καλῶς, ἐπεὶ Jaeger

Theory of Sensation (R24–R25)

R24 (< A91) Arist. *Sens.* 2 437b10–14

[. . .] ἐπεὶ εἴ γε πῦρ ἦν, καθάπερ Ἐμπεδοκλῆς φησὶ
[. . .], καὶ συνέβαινε τὸ ὁρᾶν ἐξιόντος ὥσπερ ἐκ λαμ-
πτῆρος τοῦ φωτός, διὰ τί οὐ καὶ ἐν τῷ σκότει ἑώρα
ἂν ἡ ὄψις;

R25 (< A86) Theophr. *Sens.* 12–24

[General difficulties]

[. . . = **D237**] [12] Ἐμπεδοκλῆς μὲν οὖν οὕτως οἴεται
καὶ τὴν αἴσθησιν γίνεσθαι καὶ τὸ φρονεῖν. ἀπορήσειε
δ' ἄν τις ἐξ ὧν λέγει πρῶτον μέν, τί διοίσει τὰ ἔμ-
ψυχα πρὸς τὸ[1] αἰσθάνεσθαι τῶν ἄλλων. ἐναρμόττει
γὰρ καὶ τοῖς τῶν ἀψύχων πόροις· ὅλως γὰρ ποιεῖ τὴν
μίξιν τῇ συμμετρίᾳ τῶν πόρων· διόπερ ἔλαιον μὲν καὶ
ὕδωρ οὐ μίγνυσθαι, τὰ δὲ ἄλλα ὑγρὰ καὶ περὶ ὅσων
δὴ καταριθμεῖται τὰς ἰδίας κράσεις. ὥστε πάντα τε

R23 (> A78) Ps.-Aristotle, *On Breath*

That is why Empedocles ‹assigns (?)› the cause of the
nature of bone in a general manner: if indeed all possess
a mixture presenting the same proportion [cf. **D192**],
then the horse's, the lion's, and the human being's would
have to be indistinguishable.

Theory of Sensation (R24–R25)

R24 (< A91) Aristotle, *On Sensation*

[. . .] for if it [i.e. the eye] were of fire, as Empedocles says
[. . .], and if vision occurred when light is emitted as from
a lantern [cf. **D215**], then why would sight not perceive
in darkness too?

R25 (< A86) Theophrastus, *On Sensations*

[General difficulties]

[. . .] [12] Well then, it is in this way that Empedocles
thinks that sensation and thinking occur. On the basis of
what he says one could raise a first difficulty: in what regard will animate beings differ from others, regarding
sensation? For there is adaption to the passages in inani-
mate beings too: for he explains the mixture by commensurability of the passages in a general manner. This is why
[scil. according to him] oil and water do not mix, unlike
other liquids and all the bodies of which he enumerates
the particular mixtures [cf. **D69**]. As a result, all things will

---

¹ τῷ mss., corr. Schneider

αἰσθήσεται καὶ ταὐτὸ ἔσται μίξις καὶ αἴσθησις καὶ
αὔξησις· πάντα γὰρ ποιεῖ τῇ συμμετρίᾳ τῶν πόρων,
ἐὰν μὴ προσθῇ τινα διαφοράν.

[13] ἔπειτα ἐν αὐτοῖς τοῖς ἐμψύχοις τί μᾶλλον αἰσθήσεται τὸ ἐν τῷ ζῴῳ πῦρ ἢ τὸ ἐκτός, εἴπερ ἐναρμότ-
τουσιν ἀλλήλοις; ὑπάρχει γὰρ καὶ ἡ συμμετρία καὶ
τὸ ὅμοιον. ἔτι δὲ ἀνάγκη διαφοράν τινα ἔχειν, εἴπερ
αὐτὸ μὲν μὴ δύναται συμπληροῦν τοὺς πόρους, τὸ δ'
ἔξωθεν ἐπεισιόν· ὥστ' εἰ ὅμοιον ἦν πάντῃ καὶ πάντως,
οὐκ ἂν ἦν αἴσθησις. ἔτι δὲ πότερον οἱ πόροι κενοὶ
ἢ πλήρεις; εἰ μὲν γὰρ κενοί, συμβαίνει διαφωνεῖν
ἑαυτῷ, φησὶ γὰρ ὅλως οὐκ εἶναι κενόν· εἰ δὲ πλήρεις,
ἀεὶ ἂν αἰσθάνοιτο τὰ ζῷα· δῆλον γὰρ ὡς ἐναρμόττει,
καθάπερ φησί, τὸ ὅμοιον.

[14] καίτοι κἂν αὐτὸ τοῦτό τις διαπορήσειεν, εἰ δυνατόν ἐστι τηλικαῦτα μεγέθη γενέσθαι τῶν ἑτερογενῶν,
ὥστ' ἐναρμόττειν, ἄλλως τε κἂν συμβαίνῃ,[2] καθάπερ
φησί,[3] τὰς ὄψεις ὧν ἀσύμμετρος ἡ κρᾶσις ὁτὲ μὲν ὑπὸ
τοῦ πυρός, ὁτὲ δὲ ὑπὸ τοῦ ἀέρος ἐμπλαττομένων τῶν
πόρων ἀμαυροῦσθαι. εἰ δ' οὖν ἐστι καὶ τούτων συμμετρία καὶ πλήρεις οἱ πόροι τῶν μὴ[4] συγγενῶν, πῶς,
ὅταν αἰσθάνηται, καὶ ποῦ ταῦτα ὑπεξέρχεται; δεῖ γάρ
τινα ἀποδοῦναι μεταβολήν. ὥστε πάντως ἔχει[5] δυσ-
κολίαν· ἢ γὰρ κενὸν ἀνάγκη ποιεῖν, ἢ ἀεὶ τὰ ζῷα

    [2] καὶ συμβαίνει mss., corr. Schneider   [3] φασί mss.,
corr. Schneider   [4] μὲν mss., corr. Schneider   [5] ἔχειν
mss., corr. Stephanus

perceive, and mixture, sensation, and growth will be the same thing (for he explains everything by the commensurability of the passages), unless he adds some difference. [13] Then, in the case of animate beings themselves, why will the fire in an animal perceive more than the fire outside, given that they are adapted to each other? For commensurability as well as similarity are present. Moreover, there must necessarily be some difference, if indeed it [i.e. the internal fire] is not able to fill the passages, while the fire that penetrates from outside can; so that if it were similar in every way and everywhere, perception would not happen. Moreover, are the passages empty or full? For if they are empty, it follows that he contradicts himself, for he says that absolutely there exists no void. But if they are full, then living beings would perceive all the time; for it is clear that what is similar adapts, as he says.

[14] But one could also raise a difficulty on this particular point: whether it is possible among heterogeneous elements for magnitudes of such a size to be formed that they adapt, especially if it happens, as he says, that eyes whose mixture is not commensurable are weakened when the passages are obstructed, sometimes by fire, sometimes by air? And if there is commensurability for these elements too, and the passages are filled with elements of a different kind, then how, when there is sensation, and where do these elements escape? For one must admit [or: explain] a certain change. So that in any case there is a difficulty: for it is necessary either to admit the void, or else that living beings are always perceiving all things, or else that

αἰσθάνεσθαι πάντων, ἢ τὸ μὴ συγγενὲς ἁρμόττειν οὐ
ποιοῦν αἴσθησιν οὐδ᾽ ἔχον μεταβολὴν οἰκείαν τοῖς
ἐμποιοῦσιν.

[15] ἔτι δὲ εἰ καὶ μὴ ἐναρμόττοι[6] τὸ ὅμοιον, ἀλλὰ μόνον ἅπτοιτο, καθ᾽ ὁτιοῦν εὔλογον αἴσθησιν γίνεσθαι·
δυοῖν γὰρ τούτοιν ἀποδίδωσι τὴν γνῶσιν τῷ τε ὁμοίῳ
καὶ τῇ ἁφῇ, διὸ καὶ τὸ ἁρμόττειν εἴρηκεν· ὥστ᾽ εἰ τὸ
ἔλαττον ἅψαιτο τῶν μειζόνων, εἴη ἂν αἴσθησις. ὅλως
τε[7] κατά γε ἐκεῖνον ἀφαιρεῖται καὶ τὸ ὅμοιον, ἀλλὰ ἡ
συμμετρία μόνον ἱκανόν. διὰ τοῦτο γὰρ οὐκ αἰσθάνεσθαί[8] φησιν ἀλλήλων, ὅτι τοὺς πόρους ἀσυμμέτρους
ἔχουσιν· εἰ δ᾽ ὅμοιον ἢ ἀνόμοιον τὸ ἀπορρέον, οὐδὲν
ἔτι προσαφώρισεν. ὥστε ἢ οὐ τῷ ὁμοίῳ ἡ αἴσθησις
ἢ οὐ διά τινα ἀσυμμετρίαν οὐ[9] κρίνουσιν, ἀπάσας
⟨τ᾽⟩[10] ἀνάγκη τὰς αἰσθήσεις καὶ πάντα τὰ αἰσθητὰ
τὴν αὐτὴν ἔχειν φύσιν.

[16] ἀλλὰ μὴν οὐδὲ τὴν ἡδονὴν καὶ λύπην ὁμολογουμένως ἀποδίδωσιν ἥδεσθαι μὲν ποιῶν τοῖς ὁμοίοις,
λυπεῖσθαι δὲ τοῖς ἐναντίοις· 'ἐχθρὰ' γὰρ εἶναι, διότι[11]
[. . . = **D101.6–7**]. αἰσθήσεις γάρ τινας ἢ μετ᾽ αἰσθήσεως ποιοῦσι τὴν ἡδονὴν καὶ τὴν λύπην, ὥστε οὐχ
ἅπασι[12] γίνεται τοῖς ὁμοίοις. ἔτι εἰ τὰ συγγενῆ μάλιστα ποιεῖ τὴν ἡδονὴν ἐν τῇ ἁφῇ, καθάπερ φησί, τὰ

---

[6] ἐναρμόττει mss., corr. Stephanus   [7] δὲ coni. Schneider
[8] αἰσθάνεσθαί Diels: αἰσθάνεταί mss.: αἰσθάνονταί Stephanus
[9] οὖ mss., corr. Schneider   [10] ⟨τ᾽⟩ Usener   [11] διὸ mss.,
corr. Usener   [12] ἅπασα coni. Schneider

an element of a different kind adapts without producing sensation and also without undergoing the change appropriate to the elements that produce it.

[15] Moreover, even if what is similar did not adapt but only made contact, it would follow logically that sensation would come about in any case. For he explains knowledge in these two ways, viz. by similarity and by contact; that is why he used the term 'adapts'; consequently, if something smaller makes contact with things that are larger, there would be sensation; and in general, on his view, similarity is abolished, and commensurability suffices by itself. For if they [scil. the elements] do not perceive each other, as he says, the reason is that they have incommensurable passages. As for whether the effluence is similar or dissimilar, he has not supplied a further clarification. In consequence, either sensation does not happen by similarity or else it is not because of a lack of commensurability that they do not discern, and by necessity all sensations and all perceptibles have the same nature.

[16] But neither does he give a coherent account of pleasure and pain, when he explains pleasure by what is similar and pain by what is contrary (for these are **'enemies,'** since [. . . = **D101.6–7**]. For people consider pleasure and pain as kinds of sensations or else as something accompanying sensation, so that it is not in all cases that it [i.e. sensation] occurs from what is similar. Moreover, if it is above all by contact that things of the same kind cause pleasure, as he says, then what has developed together by nature would feel the greatest pleasure and in general

σύμφυτα μάλιστ᾽ ἂν ἥδοιτο καὶ ὅλως αἰσθάνοιτο· διὰ
τῶν αὐτῶν γὰρ ποιεῖ τὴν αἴσθησιν καὶ τὴν ἡδονήν.
[17] καίτοι πολλάκις αἰσθανόμενοι λυπούμεθα κατ᾽
αὐτὴν τὴν αἴσθησιν, ὡς ⟨δ᾽⟩¹³ Ἀναξαγόρας φησίν,
ἀεί· πᾶσαν γὰρ αἴσθησιν εἶναι μετὰ λύπης.

13 ⟨δ᾽⟩ Wimmer

[Difficulties concerning the particular senses]
[Vision]

ἔτι δ᾽ ἐν ταῖς κατὰ μέρος·¹ συμβαίνει γὰρ τῷ ὁμοίῳ
γίνεσθαι τὴν γνῶσιν· τὴν γὰρ ὄψιν ὅταν ἐκ πυρὸς καὶ
τοῦ ἐναντίου συστήσῃ, τὸ μὲν λευκὸν καὶ τὸ μέλαν
δύναιτ᾽ ἂν τοῖς ὁμοίοις γνωρίζειν, τὸ δὲ φαιὸν καὶ
τἄλλα χρώματα τὰ μικτὰ πῶς; οὔτε γὰρ τοῖς τοῦ πυρὸς οὔτε τοῖς τοῦ ὕδατος πόροις οὔτ᾽ ἄλλοις ποιεῖ
κοινοῖς² ἐξ ἀμφοῖν· ὁρῶμεν δ᾽ οὐδὲν ἧττον ταῦτα τῶν
ἁπλῶν.
[18] ἀτόπως δὲ καὶ ὅτι τὰ μὲν ἡμέρας, τὰ δὲ νύκτωρ
μᾶλλον ὁρᾷ· τὸ γὰρ ἔλαττον πῦρ ὑπὸ τοῦ πλείονος
φθείρεται, διὸ καὶ πρὸς τὸν ἥλιον καὶ ὅλως τὸ καθαρὸν οὐ δυνάμεθ᾽ ἀντιβλέπειν. ὥστε ὅσοις ἐνδεέστερον
τὸ φῶς, ἧττον ἐχρῆν ὁρᾶν μεθ᾽ ἡμέραν· ἢ εἴπερ τὸ
ὅμοιον συναύξει, καθάπερ φησί, τὸ δὲ ἐναντίον φθεί-
ρει καὶ κωλύει, τὰ μὲν λευκὰ μᾶλλον ἐχρῆν ὁρᾶν
ἅπαντας μεθ᾽ ἡμέραν καὶ ὅσοις ἔλαττον καὶ ὅσοις
πλεῖον τὸ φῶς, τὰ δὲ μέλανα νύκτωρ. νῦν δὲ πάντες
ἅπαντα μεθ᾽ ἡμέραν μᾶλλον ὁρῶσι πλὴν ὀλίγων

would perceive the most; for it is by the same causes that he explains sensation and pleasure.

[17] And yet often when we have a sensation we feel pain by reason of the sensation itself—as Anaxagoras says, always, since, he says, every sensation is accompanied by pain [cf. **ANAXAG. D79**].

[Difficulties concerning the particular senses]
[Vision]

And again, in the case of the particular sensations. For it happens that knowledge is produced by what is similar; so that vision, given that he composes it out of fire and its opposite, could doubtless recognize white and black by what is similar, but how could it do this for gray and the other mixed colors? For it does not do this by the passages of fire nor by those of water nor by others shared in common by both of them; but we do not see these [scil. colors] any less than the simple ones.

[18] Absurd too is [scil. his explanation for the fact] that some see better during the day, others by night; for the lesser fire is destroyed by the greater one, which is why we cannot look directly at the sun nor in general at pure [scil. light]. So that those who are more lacking in light should see less during the day; or if it is true that what is similar makes things grow, as he says, while the opposite destroys and prevents, then all, whether they have less light or more, should see white things more during the day and black things at night. But in fact all see all things better during the day, except for a few animals. For these latter

---

ζῴων· τούτοις δ᾽ εὔλογον τοῦτ᾽ ἰσχύειν τὸ οἰκεῖον
πῦρ, ὥσπερ ἔνια καὶ τῇ χρόᾳ διαλάμπει[3] μᾶλλον τῆς
νυκτός.

[19] ἔτι δ᾽ οἷς ἡ κρᾶσις ἐξ ἴσων, ἀνάγκη συναύξεσθαι
κατὰ μέρος ἑκάτερον· ὥστ᾽ εἰ πλεονάζον κωλύει θάτερον ὁρᾶν, ἁπάντων ἂν εἴη παραπλησία πως ἡ διάθεσις. ἀλλὰ τὰ μὲν τῆς ὄψεως πάθη χαλεπώτερον ἔσται
διελεῖν.

---

[3] διαλάμπειν mss., corr. Stephanus

[Other sensations]
[General criticisms]

τὰ δὲ περὶ τὰς ἄλλας αἰσθήσεις πῶς κρίνωμεν[1] τῷ
ὁμοίῳ; τὸ γὰρ ὅμοιον ἀόριστον. οὔτε γὰρ ψόφῳ τὸν
ψόφον οὔτ᾽ ὀσμῇ τὴν ὀσμὴν οὔτε τοῖς ἄλλοις τοῖς
ὁμογενέσιν, ἀλλὰ μᾶλλον ὡς εἰπεῖν τοῖς ἐναντίοις.
ἀπαθῆ γὰρ δεῖ τὴν αἴσθησιν προσάγειν· ἤχου δὲ
ἐνόντος ἐν ὠσὶν ἢ χυλῶν ἐν γεύσει καὶ ὀσμῆς ἐν
ὀσφρήσει κωφότεραι πᾶσαι γίνονται ‹καὶ›[2] μᾶλλον
ὅσῳ ἂν πλήρεις ὦσι τῶν ὁμοίων, εἰ μή τις λεχθείη
περὶ τούτων διορισμός.

[20] ἔτι δὲ τὸ περὶ τὴν ἀπορροήν, καίπερ οὐχ ἱκανῶς
λεγόμενον περὶ μὲν τὰς ἄλλας ὅμως ἔστι πως ὑπολαβεῖν, περὶ δὲ τὴν ἁφὴν καὶ γεῦσιν οὐ ῥᾴδιον. πῶς γὰρ
τῇ ἀπορροῇ κρίνωμεν[3] ἢ πῶς ἐναρμόττον[4] τοῖς πόροις
τὸ τραχὺ καὶ τὸ λεῖον; μόνου γὰρ δοκεῖ τῶν στοιχείων

it is reasonable [scil. to suppose] that it is their own fire
that has this strength, like the skin of certain animals that
shines more at night.

[19] Moreover, among those beings in which the mixture
is composed of equal parts, it is necessary that each part
grows in turn, so that if the one, by its preponderance,
prevents the other from seeing, the disposition of sight
would be about the same for all. But in any case it will be
rather difficult to explain the properties of sight.

[Other sensations]
[General criticisms]

As for the objects of the other sensations, how will we
discern them by what is similar? For 'similar' is undefined.
For it is not by sound that we perceive sound, nor by odor
odor, nor by ones of the same kind [scil. other phenom-
ena], but rather, so to speak, it is by contraries; for it is
necessary to present the organ of sensation without its
being affected. But if there is a resonance in the ears or
tastes on the palate or a smell in the nostrils, they all become more blunted, ⟨and⟩ the more so the more they
become filled with what is similar, unless one makes some
further distinction about these things.

[20] Moreover, regarding the effluence, although what is
said about it is insufficient, all the same one can conceive
it, more or less, with regard to the other [scil. senses]; but
about touch and taste this is not at all easy. For how do we
discern the rough and the smooth by effluence, or in what
way will there be adaptation to the passages? For it seems

---

1 κρίνομεν mss., corr. Stephanus   2 ⟨καὶ⟩ Diels
3 κρίνομεν mss., corr. Stephanus   4 ἐναρμόττον P: -ειν F

τοῦ πυρὸς ἀπορρεῖν, ἀπὸ δὲ τῶν ἄλλων οὐδενός. ἔτι
δ᾽ εἰ ἡ φθίσις διὰ τὴν ἀπορροήν, ᾧπερ χρῆται κοινο-
τάτῳ σημείῳ, συμβαίνει δὲ⁵ καὶ τὰς ὀσμὰς ἀπορροῇ
γίνεσθαι, τὰ πλείστην ἔχοντα ὀσμὴν τάχιστ᾽ ἐχρῆν
φθείρεσθαι.⁶ νῦν δὲ σχεδὸν ἐναντίως ἔχει· τὰ γὰρ
ὀσμωδέστατα τῶν φυτῶν καὶ τῶν ἄλλων ἐστὶ χρο-
νιώτατα. συμβαίνει δὲ καὶ ἐπὶ τῆς Φιλίας ὅλως μὴ
εἶναι αἴσθησιν ἢ ἧττον διὰ τὸ συγκρίνεσθαι τότε καὶ
μὴ ἀπορρεῖν.

⁵ συμβαίνει δὲ Diels: συμβαίνειν mss., del. Wimmer
⁶ φθείρειν mss., corr. Schneider

[Sound and smell]

[21] ἀλλὰ περὶ μὲν τὴν ἀκοὴν ὅταν ἀποδῷ τοῖς ἔσωθεν γίνεσθαι ψόφοις, ἄτοπον τὸ οἴεσθαι δῆλον εἶναι
πῶς ἀκούουσιν, ἔνδον ποιήσαντα¹ ψόφον ὥσπερ κώ-
δωνος.² τῶν μὲν γὰρ ἔξω δι᾽ ἐκεῖνον³ ἀκούομεν, ἐκείνου
δὲ ψοφοῦντος διὰ τί; τὸ⁴ γὰρ αὐτὸ λείπεται ζητεῖν.
ἀτόπως δὲ καὶ τὸ περὶ τὴν ὄσφρησιν εἴρηκεν. πρῶτον
μὲν γὰρ οὐ κοινὴν αἰτίαν ἀπέδωκεν· ἔνια μὲν γὰρ
ὅλως οὐδ᾽ ἀναπνέει τῶν ὀσφραινομένων. ἔπειτα τὸ
μάλιστα ὀσφραίνεσθαι τοὺς πλεῖστον ἐπισπωμένους
εὔηθες· οὐδὲν γὰρ ὄφελος μὴ ὑγιαινούσης ἢ μὴ
ἀνεῳγμένης πως τῆς αἰσθήσεως. πολλοῖς δὲ συμβαίνει πεπληρῶσθαι⁵ καὶ ὅλως μηδὲν αἰσθάνεσθαι. πρὸς

¹ ποιήσαντος Wimmer   ² κώδωνας mss., corr. Sturz
³ ἐκεῖνον Schneider: ἐκεῖνα mss.: ἐκείνου Usener

that among the elements it is only fire that produces an effluence, but not any of the other ones. Moreover, if being destroyed occurs because of the effluence (which he uses very often as a proof), and if odors too happen to come about by an effluence, then of necessity those bodies that release the strongest odor would be destroyed most quickly. But in fact what happens is almost the opposite: among plants and other things, it is the ones with the strongest odor that last the longest. In addition, in the reign of Love there would be no perception at all, or less, since at that time things are united and do not produce an effluence.

[Sound and smell]

[21] Now, regarding hearing, when he explains that it happens by virtue of internal sounds, it is absurd to suppose that the way in which people hear has been clarified if one locates the sound on the inside, like that of a bell. For regarding the sounds that come from outside, it is by this means that we hear these, but by what means do we hear what makes a sound on the inside? For the same problem still remains to be resolved. Absurd, too, is what he says about smell. For first, he does not provide a cause that would be in common. For some of the beings that perceive odor do not breathe at all. Then it is foolish to say that those who inhale the most perceive odor most keenly; for this is of no use, if the organ of sensation is not healthy or open in a certain way; and it happens that many are blocked and do not perceive at all. And, what is more,

δὲ τούτοις οἱ δύσπνοοι καὶ οἱ πονοῦντες καὶ οἱ καθεύ-
δοντες μᾶλλον ἂν αἰσθάνοιντο τῶν ὀσμῶν· τὸν πλεῖστον γὰρ ἕλκουσιν ἀέρα. νῦν δὲ συμβαίνει τοὐναντίον.

[22] οὐ γὰρ ἴσως καθ᾽ αὑτὸ τὸ ἀναπνεῖν αἴτιον τῆς
ὀσφρήσεως, ἀλλὰ κατὰ συμβεβηκός, ὡς ἔκ τε τῶν
ἄλλων ζῴων μαρτυρεῖται καὶ διὰ τῶν εἰρημένων πα-
θῶν· ὁ δ᾽ ὡς ταύτης οὔσης τῆς αἰτίας καὶ ἐπὶ τέλει
πάλιν εἴρηκεν ὥσπερ ἐπισημαινόμενος [. . . = **D231**].
οὐκ ἀληθὲς ‹δὲ›⁶ οὐδὲ τὸ μάλιστα ὀσφραίνεσθαι τῶν
κούφων, ἀλλὰ δεῖ καὶ ὀσμὴν ἐνυπάρχειν. ὁ γὰρ ἀὴρ
καὶ τὸ πῦρ κουφότατα μέν, οὐ ποιοῦσι δὲ αἴσθησιν
ὀσμῆς.

⁶ ‹δὲ› Schneider

[Thought]

[23] ὡσαύτως δ᾽ ἄν τις καὶ περὶ τὴν φρόνησιν ἀπορή-
σειεν, εἰ γὰρ¹ τῶν αὐτῶν ποιεῖ καὶ τὴν αἴσθησιν. καὶ
γὰρ ἅπαντα μεθέξει τοῦ φρονεῖν. καὶ ἅμα πῶς ἐνδέχεται καὶ ἐν ἀλλοιώσει καὶ ὑπὸ τοῦ ὁμοίου γίνεσθαι
τὸ φρονεῖν; τὸ γὰρ ὅμοιον οὐκ ἀλλοιοῦται τῷ ὁμοίῳ.
τὸ δὲ δὴ τῷ αἵματι φρονεῖν καὶ παντελῶς ἄτοπον·
πολλὰ γὰρ τῶν ζῴων ἄναιμα, τῶν δὲ ἐναίμων² τὰ περὶ
τὰς αἰσθήσεις ἀναιμότατα τῶν μερῶν. ἔτι καὶ ὀστοῦν
καὶ θρὶξ αἰσθάνοιτ᾽ ἄν, ἐπεὶ οὖν³ ἐξ ἁπάντων ἐστὶ τῶν

¹ εἴπερ olim coni. Diels (cf. *DG*, app.): εἴ γ᾽ ἀπὸ Usener, ἐκ
γὰρ vel εἰ διὰ Schneider   ² ἀναίμων mss., corr. Schneider

those people who breathe with difficulty, the ones who are working hard, and those who are asleep would perceive odors better, for they are the ones who inhale the most air. But in fact it is the opposite that happens.

[22] For probably it is not in itself that respiration is the cause of smell, but by accident, as the evidence of the other animals and the phenomena just mentioned indicate. But he has said it again, as though this were the cause, at the end as well, as though to set his seal upon it: [. . . = **D231**]. And it is not true either that it is most of all light bodies that are smelled, but there must be some odor present in them as well. For air and fire are the lightest things, to be sure, but they do not produce a sensation of odor.

[Thought]

[23] In the same way, one could also raise difficulties about thought, if indeed he considers it to arise from the same things as sensation. For all things will then have a share in thinking. And how is it possible that thinking should occur at the same time both in virtue of an alteration and by means of what is similar? For what is similar is not altered by what is similar. As for the claim that it is by means of blood that thought takes place, this is completely absurd: for many animals have no blood, and among those that have blood the parts of the body related to sensations have the least blood in them. Moreover, bone and hair would perceive, since therefore they too are composed out of all the elements. And the result is that to think, to perceive, and to feel pleasure [scil. on the one hand], and to experi-

---

3 γοῦν Wimmer

στοιχείων. καὶ συμβαίνει ταὐτὸ[4] εἶναι τὸ φρονεῖν καὶ
αἰσθάνεσθαι καὶ ἥδεσθαι καὶ <τὸ>[5] λυπεῖσθαι καὶ[6]
ἀγνοεῖν· ἄμφω γὰρ ποιεῖ τοῖς ἀνομοίοις. ὥσθ' ἅμα τῷ
μὲν ἀγνοεῖν ἔδει γίνεσθαι λύπην, τῷ δὲ φρονεῖν ἡδονήν.

[24] ἄτοπον δὲ καὶ τὸ τὰς δυνάμεις ἑκάστοις ἐγγίνεσθαι διὰ τὴν ἐν τοῖς μορίοις τοῦ αἵματος σύγκρασιν,
ὡς ἢ τὴν γλῶτταν αἰτίαν τοῦ εὖ λέγειν <οὖσαν ἢ>[7]
τὰς χεῖρας τοῦ δημιουργεῖν, ἀλλ' οὐκ ὀργάνου τάξιν
ἔχοντα. διὸ καὶ μᾶλλον ἄν τις ἀποδοίη τῇ μορφῇ τὴν
αἰτίαν ἢ τῇ κράσει τοῦ αἵματος, ἢ χωρὶς διανοίας
ἐστίν· οὕτως γὰρ ἔχει καὶ ἐπὶ τῶν ἄλλων ζῴων.

[4] τοῦτο mss., corr. Stephanus   [5] <τὸ> Schneider
[6] post καὶ hab. mss. τὸ, del. Wimmer
[7] <οὖσαν ἢ> Diels

[General conclusion]
Ἐμπεδοκλῆς μὲν οὖν ἔοικεν ἐν πολλοῖς διαμαρτάνειν.

The Handbook of Aëtius: Examples of Summaries
Marked by Various Later Philosophical
Problematics (R26–R30)

R26 (A47) Aët. 1.5.2 (Ps.-Plut.) [εἰ ἓν τὸ πᾶν]

Ἐμπεδοκλῆς δὲ κόσμον μὲν ἕνα, οὐ μέντοι τὸ πᾶν
εἶναι τὸν κόσμον ἀλλ' ὀλίγον τι τοῦ παντὸς μέρος, τὸ
δὲ λοιπὸν ἀργὴν ὕλην.

ence pain and to be ignorant [scil. on the other hand] would be identical (for both of them he explains by what is dissimilar): so that ignorance would have to be accompanied by pain, and thinking by pleasure.

[24] So too it is absurd to claim that capabilities develop in each one because of the mixture of the blood in the parts of its body, as though the tongue were the cause of eloquence, or the hands that of craftsmanship, and they did not have instead the rank of an instrument. For this reason it would be better to attribute the cause to the shape rather than to the mixture of the blood, which is deprived of thought. And the same applies to the other animals as well.

[General conclusion]

So it seems that Empedocles was mistaken on many points.

The Handbook of Aëtius: Examples of Summaries Marked by Various Later Philosophical Problematics (R26–R30)

R26 (A47) Aëtius

Empedocles: the world is one, but the world is not the whole but a small part of the whole, while the rest is inert matter.[1]

[1] The distinction between the world and the whole is Stoic.

R27 (A43) Aët. 1.13.1 (Ps.-Plut., Stob.) [περὶ ἐλαχίστων]

Ἐμπεδοκλῆς πρὸ τῶν τεσσάρων στοιχείων θραύ-
σματα ἐλάχιστα, οἰονεὶ στοιχεῖα πρὶν στοιχείων,
ὁμοιομερῆ ὅ ἐστι στρογγύλα.[1]

   [1] ὅ ἐστι στρογγύλα om. Stob., del. Sturz

R28 Aët.

a (< A32) 1.7.28 (Stob.) [τίς ὁ θεός]

‹Ἐμπεδοκλῆς›[1] τὸ ἕν, καὶ τὸ μὲν ἓν τὴν ἀνάγκην,
ὕλην δὲ αὐτοῦ[2] τὰ τέσσαρα στοιχεῖα, εἴδη δὲ τὸ Νεῖκος καὶ τὴν Φιλίαν[3] [. . .].

   [1] add. Heeren: ‹Ἐμπεδοκλῆς τὸν σφαῖρον καὶ›Wachsmuth,
‹Ἐμπεδοκλῆς σφαιροειδῆ καὶ ἀίδιον καὶ ἀκίνητον τὸ ἓν›
Diels   [2] αὐτοῦ Wachsmuth: αὐτῆς mss.   [3] φιλίαν corr. P[2]:
φιλονεικίαν F: φινεικίαν P[1]

b (A45) Aët. 1.26.1 (Ps.-Plut.) [περὶ οὐσίας ἀνάγκης]

Ἐμπεδοκλῆς οὐσίαν ἀνάγκης αἰτίαν χρηστικὴν τῶν
ἀρχῶν καὶ τῶν στοιχείων.

R29 (< A85) Aët. 5.25.4 (Ps.-Plut.) [ὁποτέρου ἐστὶν
ὕπνος ἢ θάνατος, ψυχῆς ἢ σώματος]

Ἐμπεδοκλῆς τὸν θάνατον γεγενῆσθαι διαχωρισμὸν
τοῦ πυρώδους, ἐξ ὧν ἡ σύγκρισις τῷ ἀνθρώπῳ συν-
εστάθη· ὥστε κατὰ τοῦτο κοινὸν εἶναι τὸν θάνατον
σώματος καὶ ψυχῆς· [. . . cf. **D206a**].

R27 (A43) Aëtius

Empedocles: before the four elements there are smallest sparks, like elements before the elements, homoeomers, that is, spherical.

R28 Aëtius

a (< A32)

‹Empedocles:› [scil. god is] the one. And the one is necessity, and its matter the four elements, its forms Strife and Love [. . .].

b (A45)

Empedocles: the essence of necessity is a cause that uses the principles and the elements.

R29 (< A85) Aëtius

Empedocles: death occurred as the separation of the fiery element from the ones out of which the mixture is composed for the human being. So that from this point of view it [i.e. death] is in common for the body and the soul [. . .].

___

app. cf. ad **D206a**

R30 (< 28 A49) Aët. 4.9.1 (Stob.) [εἰ ἀληθεῖς αἱ αἰσθήσεις καὶ φαντασίαι]

[. . .] Ἐμπεδοκλῆς [. . .] ψευδεῖς εἶναι τὰς αἰσθήσεις.

Empedocles Among the Epicureans (R31–R35)
Lucretius' Praise (R31)

R31 (> A21) Lucr. 1.712–733

712   adde etiam qui [. . .]
      et qui quattuor ex rebus posse omnia rentur
715   ex igni terra atque anima procrescere et imbri.
      quorum Acragantinus cum primis Empedocles est,
      insula quem triquetris terrarum gessit in oris,
      quam fluitans circum magnis anfractibus aequor
      Ionium glaucis aspargit virus ab undis
720   angustoque fretu rapidum mare dividit undis
      Aeoliae terrarum oras a finibus eius.
      hic est vasta Charybdis et hic Aetnaea minantur
      murmura flammarum rursum se colligere iras,
      faucibus eruptos iterum vis ut vomat ignis
725   ad caelumque ferat flammai fulgura rursum.
      quae cum magna modis multis miranda videtur
      gentibus humanis regio visendaque fertur
      rebus opima bonis, multa munita virum vi,

720 undans *Lachmann*
721 Aeoliae *Heinsius*: haeliae *OQ*: haeoliae *O¹G*: Italiae *L*
724 eructans *Brieger*   vomat *Lambinus*: omniat *OQG*

R30 (< 28 A49) Aëtius

[. . .] Empedocles [. . .]: sensations are deceptive.

Empedocles Among the Epicureans (R31–R35)
Lucretius' Praise (R31)

R31 (> A21) Lucretius, *On the Nature of Things*

Add those who [. . .]	712
And those who think that it is from four things that all can	
Grow, from fire, earth, air, and water.	715
Among these, the foremost is Empedocles of Agrigentum,	
Whom in its triangular shores an island bore	
Around which the Ionian Sea, flowing in mighty circuits	
Scatters the salty brine of its green waves,	
And by a narrow strait the swift sea divides with its waters	720
The shores of the Aeolian land from the limits of that island.	
Destructive Charybdis is here, and here the rumblings of Aetna	
Threaten that its wrathful flames are gathering again,	
So that once again its violence might pour forth fires bursting from its throat	
And carry the lightnings of its flame back to the sky.	725
This mighty region, which seems wondrous in many ways to many	
Human populations and is said to be worth visiting,	
Rich in good things, fortified by a huge force of men,	

nil tamen hoc habuisse viro praeclarius in se
730 nec sanctum magis et mirum carumque videtur.
carmina quin etiam divini pectoris eius
vociferantur et exponunt praeclara reperta,
ut vix humana videatur stirpe creatus.

A Positive Use of One Verse of the
Purifications *(R32)*

R32 (ad B118) Sext. Emp. *Adv. Math.* 11.96

ἀλλ᾽ εἰώθασί τινες τῶν ἀπὸ τῆς Ἐπικούρου αἱρέσεως
[ad Frag. 398 Usener] [. . .] λέγειν ὅτι φυσικῶς καὶ ἀδι-
δάκτως τὸ ζῷον φεύγει μὲν τὴν ἀλγηδόνα, διώκει δὲ
τὴν ἡδονήν· γεννηθὲν γοῦν καὶ μηδέπω τοῖς κατὰ δόξαν δουλεῦον ἅμα τῷ ῥαπισθῆναι[1] ἀσυνήθει ἀέρος
ψύξει ἔκλαυσέ τε καὶ ἐκώκυσεν [cf. **D14**].

[1] ῥιπισθῆναι Usener

Two Criticisms . . . (R33–R34)

R33 (≠ DK) Lucr. 1.734–747

hic tamen et supra quos diximus inferiores
735 partibus egregie multis multoque minores,
quamquam multa bene ac divinitus invenientes

Nonetheless seems to have possessed nothing more
  illustrious than this man,
Nothing more sacred, more admirable, and more   730
  precious.
Indeed, the songs arising from his divine heart
Speak loudly and declare illustrious discoveries,
So that he scarcely seems to have been born of
  human stock.[1]

[1] Elsewhere (2.1081–82) Lucretius virtually translates
D73.296–97.

A Positive Use of One Verse of the
Purifications *(R32)*

R32 (ad B118) Sextus Empiricus, *Against the Ethicists*

But some members of the school of Epicurus [. . .] have
the custom of saying that it is by nature and without having
been taught that an animal flees pain and pursues pleasure; thus when it has just been born and has not yet become enslaved by opinion it **"wept and wailed"** at the
moment it was lashed by the air's **"unaccustomed"** cold
[cf. **D14**].

Two Criticisms . . . (R33–R34)

R33 (≠ DK) Lucretius, *On the Nature of Things*

Nonetheless, he and those who, I said earlier, were
  much inferior
To him in many regards and were far below him,   735
Although, by making many fine discoveries by divine
  inspiration,

ex adyto tamquam cordis responsa dedere
sanctius et multo certa ratione magis quam
Pythia quae tripodi a Phoebi lauroque profatur,
740   principiis tamen in rerum fecere ruinas
et graviter magni magno cecidere ibi casu.
primum quod motus exempto rebus inani
constituunt et res mollis rarasque relinquunt,
aera solem ignem terras animalia frugis
745   nec tamen admiscent in eorum corpus inane;
deinde quod omnino finem non esse secandis
corporibus faciunt neque pausam stare fragori
[. . .]

741 casu O^1: cauu O: causa QU
744 solem] rorem *Christ*   ignem] imbrim *Bailey*
747 faciunt *Laur. XXXV.31*: facient *OQU*

R34 (≠ DK) Diog. Oen. 42.II–III et V Smith

[Col. II] [. . .] μεταβαίνειν [φη]|σὶ τὰς ψυχὰς ἐκ σω-
μά|των εἰς σώματα με|τὰ τὸ τὰ πρῶτα διαφθα|[5]ρῆ-
ναι καὶ ἐπ᾽ ἄπειρον τοῦ|το γείνεσθαι, ὥσπερ οὐ|κ
ἐροῦντος αὐτῷ τινος· | ῾Ἐνπεδόκλεις, εἰ μὲν | οὖ[ν]
δύνανται καθ᾽ ἑαυ|[10]τὰς [α]ἱ ψυχαὶ μένειν μη|δὲ †κ
. τΛκλεις† σύρειν | εἰς ζ[ώ]ου φύσιν καὶ τού|του χάριν
μεταφέρειν | [α]ὐτάς, τί σοι δύναται ἡ | [Col. III] μετά-
βασις; ἐν γὰ[ρ τῷ] | μεταξὺ χρόνῳ, δι᾽ ο[ὗ τὸ] | μετα-

omnia suppl. Smith exceptis III.1, 8, 9, 10, 12 (εἰς), 13 Usener;
2, 3–4, 7, 11, 12 (μεταβιβάζων) William; V.3–4 (ἄμεινον)

They gave oracular responses, as it were from the
    shrine of the heart,
In a more holy and much more certain way than
The Pythia who speaks forth from Phoebus' tripod
    and laurel,
Nonetheless, concerning the beginnings of things,   740
    they have come to ruin
And, great as they were, they have crashed heavily
    with a great fall:
First because they accept motion but suppress the
    void
And suppose that things are soft and porous,
Air, sun, fire, earth, animals, plants,
But nonetheless they do not mix void into their   745
    bodies;
Then, they do not set any end to the division
Of bodies and give no respite to their fragmentation
[. . .]

R34 (≠ DK) Diogenes of Oenoanda, Epicurean inscription

[Col. II] . . . he says that the souls transmigrate from some
bodies to other bodies after the first ones have been destroyed and that this continues to infinity, as though no one
asked him, "Empedocles, if on the one hand souls are able
to subsist by themselves and you do not ‹have› to drag
them into the nature of a living being and to transfer them
for this reason, [Col. III] then what good is transmigration
for you? For during the intermediate time during which

Gomperz; 4 (γὰρ), 5 Herberdey-Kalinka; 8 Usener; 11 (ὑπῆρχε
τὸ) rest. Cousin; 13 Casanova; 14 William   Col. II.11 sensus
exiget ὀφείλεις vel sim.: alii alia, cf. Smith ad loc.

βαίνειν αὐτα[ῖς γεί]|νεται ζώου φύσιν [δι]|[5]έχον, τὸ
πᾶν ταραχθ[ῇ]|σονται. εἰ δὲ μη[δαμῶς] | ἔχουσι μένειν
ἄ[νευ] | σώματος, τί μά[λιστα] | ἑαυτῷ παρέχει[ς
πρά]|[10]γματα, μᾶλλον [δὲ ἐ]|κείναις, σύρω[ν αὐτὰς]
|καὶ μεταβιβάζ[ων εἰς] | ἕτερον ἐξ ἑτέρου [ζῷ]|ον;
καὶ ταῦτα πο . . . [Col. V] ἄ]|[μεινον γ]ὰρ ἁπλῶς
ἀ|[5]φθάρτους [ἦν] τὰς ψυ|χὰς καθ’ ἑαυτὰς ποιεῖν καὶ
μὴ εἰς μα|κρὸν ἐνβαλεῖν αὐτὰ[ς] | περίπλουν, ἵνα σου
τὸ | [10] πανέσχατον σεμνό|τερον ὑπῆρχε τὸ ψεῦσ|μα.
ἢ σοὶ μέν, Ἐνπε|δόκλεις, ἀπιστήσομε[ν] | τὰς μετα-
βάσεις τα[ύ|τας] [. . .].”

. . . and Plutarch’s Reply to a Third One (R35)

R35 (> ad B8) Plut. *Adv. Col.* 10–11 1111F–1112B

ὁ δὲ Κωλώτης [. . .] πάλιν ἐξάπτεται τοῦ Ἐμπεδοκλέους ταὐτὸ πνέοντος· [. . . = **D53,** with textual variants].
ταῦτ’ ἐγὼ μὲν οὐχ ὁρῶ καθ’ ὅ τι πρὸς τὸ ζῆν ὑπεναν-
τιοῦται[1] τοῖς ὑπολαμβάνουσι μήτε γένεσιν τοῦ μὴ
ὄντος εἶναι μήτε φθορὰν τοῦ ὄντος, ἀλλ’ ὄντων τινῶν
συνόδῳ πρὸς ἄλληλα τὴν γένεσιν διαλύσει δ’ ἀπ’ ἀλλήλων τὸν θάνατον ἐπονομάζεσθαι. ὅτι γὰρ ἀντὶ τῆς
γενέσεως εἴρηκε τὴν φύσιν, ἀντιθεὶς τὸν θάνατον
αὐτῇ[2] δεδήλωκεν ὁ Ἐμπεδοκλῆς. εἰ δ’ οἱ μίξεις τὰς
γενέσεις τιθέμενοι τὰς δὲ φθορὰς διαλύσεις οὐ ζῶσιν
οὐδὲ δύνανται ζῆν, τί ποιοῦσιν ἕτερον οὗτοι; καίτοι ὁ
μὲν Ἐμπεδοκλῆς τὰ στοιχεῖα κολλῶν καὶ συναρμότ-

---

[1] ὑπεναντιοῦσθαι mss., corr. Xylander

the transmigration takes place, ⟨interrupting⟩ the nature of a living being, they will be thrown into complete disorder. But if on the other hand they are not able at all to subsist without a body, why do you worry yourself, and even more them, by dragging them and displacing them from one living being to another? . . . [Col. V] For it would have been better to make the souls simply indestructible by themselves and not to send them out on a great voyage, in which case your last error would have been worthier. Or else, Empedocles, we shall refuse to believe you regarding these transmigrations [. . .].

. . . and Plutarch's Reply to a Third One (R35)

R35 (> ad B8) Plutarch, *Against Colotes*

Colotes [. . .] once again attacks Empedocles who expresses the same idea [scil. as Democritus, the object of Colotes' preceding attack] [. . . = **D53**]. I myself do not see in what way it is an obstacle to living if one supposes that there is neither birth of what does not exist nor destruction of what does exist, and that what people call 'birth' occurs by the reunification with one another of certain things that exist, and what people call 'death' happens by their dissolution. For the fact that Empedocles said 'nature' (*phusis*) in place of 'birth' (*genesis*) he has made clear by opposing 'death' to it. But if those people who posit that births are mixtures and that destructions are dissolutions do not live and are not capable of living, what do they do that is different? And what is more, by combining and fitting together the elements by heat, softness, and

---

2 ἀστὴρ mss., corr. Xylander

των θερμότησι καὶ μαλακότησι καὶ ὑγρότησι μῖξιν
αὐτοῖς καὶ συμφυίαν ἑνωτικὴν ἀμωσγέπως ἐνδίδωσιν,
οἱ δὲ τὰς ἀτρέπτους καὶ ἀσυμπαθεῖς ἀτόμους εἰς τὸ
αὐτὸ συνελαύνοντες [. . .].

A Lost Latin Poem on Empedocles (R36)

R36 (A27) Cic. *Ad Q.* 2.9.3

Lucreti poemata ut scribis ita sunt: multis luminibus
ingenii, multae tamen[1] artis; sed cum veneris, virum te
putabo, si Sallusti Empedoclea legeris, hominem non
putabo.

[1] etiam *Orelli*

Empedocles Among the Skeptics (R37–R39)
Mockery by Timon of Phlius (R37)

R37 (< A1) Diog. Laert. 8.67

οὐ παρῆκέ τ’[1] οὐδὲ τοῦτον ὁ Τίμων, ἀλλ’ ὧδε[2] αὐτοῦ
καθάπτεται λέγων [Frag. 42 Di Marco]

καὶ Ἐμπεδοκλῆς ἀγοραίων
ληκητὴς[3] ἐπέων· ὅσα δ’ ἔσθενε, τόσσα διεῖλεν[4]
ἄρχων[5] ὃς διέθηκ’ ἀρχὰς ἐπιδευέας ἄλλων.

[1] τ’ BP[1]: δ’ FP[4]:   [2] ἀλλ’ ὧδε rec.: ἄλλω δ’ (vel δὲ) BF:
ἄλλων δ’ P[4]   [3] ληκητὴς BP[1]F: κηλητὴς rec.   [4] τόσσα
διεῖλεν Apelt: τοσσάδε εἷλεν BPF: τοσσάδ’ ἔειλεν Diels
[5] ἀρχῶν Sturz

moisture, Empedocles confers upon them in one way or another a unifying mixture and cohesion, while those who drive together inflexible and impassive atoms [. . .].

A Lost Latin Poem on Empedocles (R36)

R36 (A27) Cicero, *Letters to His Brother Quintus*

The poems of Lucretius are just as you describe them, with many brilliant passages demonstrating his talent, but nonetheless displaying his great artistry. But when you come, I will think you are manly if you can read Sallust's *Empedoclea*—but I won't think you're human.

Empedocles Among the Skeptics (R37–R39)
Mockery by Timon of Phlius (R37)

R37 (< A1) Diogenes Laertius

Timon did not let him [i.e. Empedocles] escape either, but he attacks him like this, saying,

> . . . and Empedocles, bawler of
> Vulgar verses; as far as his strength permitted, he
> divided everything,
> A commander who established principles in need of
> other principles.

A Radical Skeptical Interpretation (R38)

R38 (≠ DK) Cic. *Acad.* 2.14

[. . .] et tamen isti physici raro admodum, cum haerent aliquo loco, exclamant quasi mente incitati, Empedocles quidem ut interdum mihi furere videatur, abstrusa esse omnia, nihil nos sentire nihil cernere nihil omnino quale sit posse reperire [. . .].

A Criticism: Humans and Animals (R39)

R39 (ad B136 et B137) Sext. Emp. *Adv. Math.* 9.127–30

[127] οἱ μὲν οὖν περὶ τὸν Πυθαγόραν καὶ τὸν Ἐμπεδοκλέα καὶ τὸ λοιπὸν τῶν Ἰταλῶν πλῆθός φασι μὴ μόνον ἡμῖν πρὸς ἀλλήλους καὶ πρὸς τοὺς θεοὺς εἶναί τινα κοινωνίαν, ἀλλὰ καὶ πρὸς τὰ ἄλογα τῶν ζῴων. ἓν γὰρ ὑπάρχει[1] πνεῦμα τὸ διὰ παντὸς τοῦ κόσμου διῆκον ψυχῆς τρόπον, τὸ καὶ ἑνοῦν ἡμᾶς πρὸς ἐκεῖνα. [128] διόπερ καὶ κτείνοντες αὐτὰ καὶ ταῖς σαρξὶν αὐτῶν τρεφόμενοι ἀδικήσομέν τε καὶ ἀσεβήσομεν ὡς συγγενεῖς ἀναιροῦντες. ἔνθεν καὶ παρήνουν οὗτοι οἱ φιλόσοφοι ἀπέχεσθαι τῶν ἐμψύχων, καὶ ἀσεβεῖν ἔφασκον τοὺς ἀνθρώπους

βωμὸν ἐρεύθοντας μακάρων θερμοῖσι φόνοισιν.

---

[1] ὑπάρχειν ed. Gen.

EMPEDOCLES

A Radical Skeptical Interpretation (R38)

R38 (≠ DK) Cicero, *Prior Academics*

[. . .] and yet those natural philosophers of yours, when they get stuck on some point, occasionally cry out as though they were mentally excited—Empedocles, indeed, in such a way that he sometimes seems to me to be raving mad—that all things are concealed, that we perceive nothing, distinguish nothing, are incapable of knowing the true nature of anything at all [. . .] [cf. **D42**].

A Criticism: Humans and Animals (R39)

R39 (ad B136 et B137) Sextus Empiricus, *Against the Natural Philosophers*

[127] Pythagoras, Empedocles, and most of the other Italians say that there exists for us a community not only with regard to one another and with regard to the gods, but also with regard to the irrational animals. For there exists a single breath that penetrates through the whole world like a soul, which also unifies us with them. [128] That is why if we kill them and feed on their flesh we will be committing an injustice and an impiety, as if we were killing our relatives. This is why these philosophers urged that we abstain from living beings and said that those men were committing an impiety

who redden the altar of the blessed with hot blood.[1]

---

[1] Some scholars think that this anonymous verse comes from a *Hieros logos* ('Sacred Discourse') attributed to Pythagoras (cf. **PYTHS. R46**).

[129] καὶ Ἐμπεδοκλῆς πού φησιν [. . . = **D28**] καὶ [. . . = **D29**].

[130] ταῦτα δὴ παρήνουν οἱ περὶ τὸν Πυθαγόραν, πταίοντες· οὐ γὰρ εἰ ἔστι τι[2] διῆκον δι᾽ ἡμῶν τε καὶ ἐκείνων πνεῦμα, εὐθὺς ἔστι τις ἡμῖν δικαιοσύνη πρὸς τὰ ἄλογα τῶν ζῴων.

----

[2] τὸ mss., corr. ed. Gen.

The Stoic Reception (R40–R42)
Explicit Traces (R40–R41)

R40 (≠ DK) Gal. *Plac. Hipp. Plat.*

a 3.3.25 (< Chrys. Frag. 906, vol. 2, p. 255.15–20 SVF)

[. . .] οὕτως ἐξ Ὀρφέως καὶ Ἐμπεδοκλέους [. . .] καὶ ἑτέρων ποιητῶν ἐπῶν μνημονεύει παμπόλλων ὁμοίαν ἐχόντων ἀτοπίαν [. . .].

b 3.5.22 (< Chrys. Frag. 884, vol. 2, p. 237.23–25 SVF)

ἀρξάμενος οὖν ἀπό τινος Ἐμπεδοκλείου ῥήσεως ἐξηγεῖταί τε αὐτὴν καί τινων κατὰ τὴν ἐξήγησιν ἀξιολογωτέρων ἄρχεται λόγων, ἐν οἷς ἐστι καὶ ὁ περὶ τῆς φωνῆς [. . .].

R41 (< A31) (Ps.-?) Hipp. *Haer.* 1.3.1–2

οὗτος τὴν τοῦ παντὸς ἀρχὴν Νεῖκος καὶ Φιλίαν ἔφη· καὶ τὸ τῆς μονάδος νοερὸν πῦρ τὸν θεόν, καὶ συν-

[129] And Empedocles says somewhere, [. . . = **D28**] and [. . . = **D29**].

[130] This is what the disciples of Pythagoras urged—in error: for it is not because there is a breath penetrating us and them that we have a relation of justice with regard to the irrational animals.

The Stoic Reception (R40–R42)
Explicit Traces (R40–R41)

R40 (≠ DK) Galen, *On the Opinions of Hippocrates and Plato*

a

[. . .] so too he [i.e. Chrysippus] cites from Orpheus, Empedocles, [. . .] and other poets very many lines that are just as irrelevant[1] [. . .].

[1] Because they do not mean what Chrysippus wants to make them say, viz. that the soul is located in the chest.

b

So starting with a passage from Empedocles, he [i.e. Chrysippus] interprets it, and in the course of his interpretation he broaches some rather noteworthy arguments, including the one about speech [. . .].

R41 (< A31) (Ps.-?) Hippolytus, *Refutation of All Heresies*

This man said that the principle of everything is Strife and Love, and that god is the intellectual fire of the monad,

εστάναι ἐκ πυρὸς τὰ πάντα καὶ εἰς πῦρ ἀναλυθήσε-
σθαι·[1] ᾧ[2] σχεδὸν καὶ οἱ Στωικοὶ συντίθενται δόγματι,
ἐκπύρωσιν προσδοκῶντες. μάλιστα δὲ πάντων συγ-
κατατίθεται τῇ μετενσωματώσει [. . . = **D13**].

[1] ἀναλυθήσασθαι O   [2] ᾧ LO: ὡς Bb

Implicit Traces (R42)

R42 (ad B2 et B3) Sext. Emp. *Adv. Math.* 7.115–16,
120–25

[115] Ἐμπεδοκλῆς δὲ ὁ Ἀκραγαντῖνος κατὰ μὲν τοὺς
ἁπλούστερον δοκοῦντας αὐτὸν ἐξηγεῖσθαι ἐξ κριτήρια τῆς ἀληθείας παραδίδωσιν. δύο γὰρ δραστη-
ρίους τῶν ὅλων ἀρχὰς ὑποθέμενος, Φιλίαν καὶ Νεῖκος,
ἅμα τε τῶν τεσσάρων μνησθεὶς ὡς ὑλικῶν, γῆς τε καὶ
ὕδατος καὶ ἀέρος καὶ πυρός, πάντων[1] ταῦτα[2] ἔφη κριτήρια τυγχάνειν. [116] παλαιὰ γάρ τις [. . .] ἄνωθεν
παρὰ τοῖς φυσικοῖς κυλίεται δόξα περὶ τοῦ τὸ ὅμοια
τῶν ὁμοίων εἶναι γνωριστικά· [. . .] [120] [. . .] ἔοικε καὶ
ὁ Ἐμπεδοκλῆς ταύτῃ συμπεριφέρεσθαι, ἔξ τε οὐσῶν
τῶν τὰ πάντα συνεστακυιῶν ἀρχῶν λέγειν ἰσάριθμα
ταύταις ὑπάρχειν τὰ κριτήρια, δι᾽ ὧν γέγραφε [121]
[. . . = **D207**], ἐμφαίνων ὡς γῆν μὲν καταλαμβανόμεθα
μετουσίᾳ γῆς, ὕδωρ δὲ κατὰ μετοχὴν ὕδατος, ἀέρα δὲ
μετουσίᾳ τοῦ ἀέρος, καὶ ἐπὶ πυρὸς τὰ ἀνάλογον. [122]
ἄλλοι δὲ ἦσαν οἱ λέγοντες κατὰ τὸν Ἐμπεδοκλέα κρι-

and that all things come from fire and will be dissolved into fire—a doctrine to which the Stoics too subscribe by and large, since they expect the conflagration (*ekpurôsis*) [cf. **R100**]. But what he approves above all is metempsychosis (*metensômatôsis*) [. . . = **D13**].

See also **D134b, R100**

Implicit Traces (R42)

R42 (ad B2 and B3) Sextus Empiricus, *Against the Logicians*

[115] Empedocles of Agrigentum, according to those who seem to give the simplest interpretation of him, proposes six criteria of the truth. For having posited, with regard to the universe, two active principles, Love and Strife, and having also mentioned the four—earth, water, air, and fire—as being material, he said that these are the criteria of all things. [116] For there is an ancient [. . .] opinion that has circulated since times immemorial among the natural philosophers, that like knows like. [. . .] [120] [. . .] Empedocles seems to adhere to this doctrine and to say that, there being six principles from which all things are made, the number of criteria is equal to these, when he writes [121] [. . . = **D207**], declaring that we grasp the earth because we participate in earth, water because we have a share in water, air because we participate in air, and analogously for fire. [122] But there have been others [scil.

---

[1] πάντων N: πλάσας LE𝄴: πάσας Fabricius

[2] ταύτας Fabricius

τήριον εἶναι τῆς ἀληθείας οὐ τὰς αἰσθήσεις ἀλλὰ τὸν
ὀρθὸν λόγον, τοῦ δὲ ὀρθοῦ λόγου τὸν μέν τινα θεῖον
ὑπάρχειν τὸν δὲ ἀνθρώπινον· ὧν τὸν μὲν θεῖον ἀνέξοι-
στον εἶναι, τὸν δὲ ἀνθρώπινον ἐξοιστόν. [123] λέγει δὲ
περὶ μὲν τοῦ μὴ ἐν ταῖς αἰσθήσεσι τὴν κρίσιν τἀλη-
θοῦς ὑπάρχειν οὕτως· [. . . = **D42.1–8a**]. [124] περὶ δὲ
τοῦ μὴ εἰς τὸ παντελὲς ἄληπτον εἶναι τὴν ἀλήθειαν,
ἀλλ᾽ ἐφ᾽ ὅσον ἱκνεῖται ὁ ἀνθρώπινος λόγος ληπτὴν
ὑπάρχειν, διασαφεῖ τοῖς προκειμένοις ἐπιφέρων [. . .
= **D42.8b–9**]. καὶ διὰ τῶν ἑξῆς ἐπιπλήξας τοῖς πλέον
ἐπαγγελλομένοις γιγνώσκειν παρίστησιν, ὅτι τὸ δι᾽
ἑκάστης αἰσθήσεως λαμβανόμενον πιστόν ἐστι, τοῦ
λόγου τούτων ἐπιστατοῦντος, καίπερ πρότερον κατα-
δραμὼν τῆς ἀπ᾽ αὐτῶν πίστεως. [125] φησὶ γὰρ [. . .
= **D44**].

The Pythagorean-Platonic Tradition (R43–R67)
Empedocles and Pythagoras (R43)

R43 (ad B129) Porph. *VP* 30–31 (et al.)

[. . .] τούτοις καὶ Ἐμπεδοκλῆς μαρτυρεῖ λέγων περὶ
αὐτοῦ· [. . . = **D38**]. τὸ γὰρ ‘περιώσια’ καὶ ‘τῶν ὄντων
λεύσσεσκεν ἕκαστα’ καὶ ‘πραπίδων πλοῦτον’ καὶ τὰ
ἐοικότα ἐμφαντικὰ μάλιστα τῆς ἐξαιρέτου καὶ ἀκρι-
βεστέρας παρὰ τοὺς ἄλλους διοργανώσεως ἔν τε τῷ
ὁρᾶν καὶ τῷ ἀκούειν καὶ τῷ νοεῖν τοῦ Πυθαγόρου.

surely: Stoics] who said that according to Empedocles it is not sensations that are the criterion of the truth but correct reason, and that of this correct reason the one is divine, the other human; and of these the one, the divine one, cannot be expressed, while the other, the human one, can. [123] This is the way he says that the discernment of the true does not reside in sensations: [. . . = **D42.1–8a**]; [124] but that the truth is not completely ungraspable but that, within the limits to which human reason can attain, it is graspable, he makes this clear by adding to the preceding verses [. . . = **D42.8b–9**]. And in what follows, attacking those who pride themselves on knowing more, he establishes that what is grasped by each sensation is reliable if reason controls them, despite the fact that earlier he had attacked the belief that comes from them. [125] For he says, [. . . = **D44**].

The Pythagorean-Platonic Tradition (R43–R67)
Empedocles and Pythagoras (R43)

R43 (ad B129) Porphyry, *Life of Pythagoras*

[. . .] Empedocles bears witness to this [scil. that Pythagoras listened to the celestial harmony, cf. **PYTH. a P33**] when he says about him, [. . . = **D38**]. For the expressions **'beyond measure,' 'he saw each one of all the things that are,' 'wealth of organs of thought,'** and other similar ones indicate above all the existence of an extraordinary organic faculty in Pythagoras, one more precise than other people's with regard to seeing, hearing, and thinking.

*Pythagorizing Appropriations of Lines
of Empedocles (R44–R45)*

R44 (< 44 A29) Sext. Emp. *Adv. Math.* 7.92

[. . .] καθάπερ ἔλεγε καὶ ὁ Φιλόλαος [. . . = **D207**].

R45 (cf. ad B5) Plut. *Quaest. conv.* 8.8.1 728E

[. . .] ἔλεγε δὲ τῆς ἐχεμυθίας τοῦτο γέρας εἶναι τοὺς
ἰχθῦς καλεῖν ‹ἔλλοπας›[1] [. . .], καὶ τὸν ὁμώνυμον ἐμοὶ
τῷ Παυσανίᾳ Πυθαγορικῶς παραινεῖν τὰ δόγματα
[. . . = **D258**].

[1] ‹ἔλλοπας› Xylander

*A Justification, Possibly of Pythagorean Origin,
for Empedocles' Claim to Be a God (R46)*

R46 (≠ DK) Sext. Emp. *Adv. Math.* 1.302–3

καὶ μὴν ὡς ἐν τούτοις ἐστὶ τυφλός, οὕτω κἂν τοῖς
περὶ αὐτῶν γραφεῖσι ποιήμασιν, οἷον Ἐμπεδοκλέους
λέγοντος [. . . = **D4.4–5a**] καὶ πάλιν [. . . = **D5**]. ὁ μὲν
γὰρ γραμματικὸς καὶ ὁ ἰδιώτης ὑπολήψονται κατ᾽
ἀλαζονείαν καὶ τὴν πρὸς τοὺς ἄλλους ἀνθρώπους
ὑπεροψίαν ταῦτ᾽ ἀνεφθέγχθαι τὸν φιλόσοφον, ὅπερ
ἀλλότριόν ἐστι τοῦ κἂν μετρίαν ἕξιν ἐν φιλοσοφίᾳ
ἔχοντος, οὐχ ὅτι γε τοῦ τοσούτου ἀνδρός· ὁ δὲ ἀπὸ
φυσικῆς ὁρμώμενος θεωρίας, σαφῶς γινώσκων ὅτι

Pythagorizing Appropriations of Lines of
Empedocles (R44–R45)

R44 (< 44 A29) Sextus Empiricus, *Against the Logicians*

[. . .] as Philolaus said too: [. . . = **D207**].[1]

1 These lines are cited by Aristotle as being by Empedocles.

R45 (cf. ad B5) Plutarch, *Table Talk*

[. . .] He [scil. an unknown author] said that it was a pre-rogative of [scil. Pythagorean, cf. **PYTH. b T11**] silence to call fish <mute> (*ellopos*) [. . .] and that it was as a Pythagorean that my namesake [viz. the speaker in Plutarch's dialogue is named Empedocles] recommended his doctrines to Pausanias [. . .].

A Justification, Possibly of Pythagorean[1] Origin,
for Empedocles' Claim to Be a God (R46)

R46 (≠ DK) Sextus Empiricus, *Against the Professors*

Just as he [i.e. the grammarian] is blind in the case of these [scil. technical treatises in prose], so too in that of the poems written on these subjects, as when Empedocles says [. . . = **D4.4–5a**], and again [. . . = **D5**]. For the grammarian and the ordinary man will think that the philosopher has said this out of boastfulness and contempt for other men, something that is foreign to anyone who has even only a moderate condition in philosophy, let alone to such a great man. But whoever takes natural science as his starting point, since he knows well that the doctrine that

1 But Diels attributes it to Posidonius.

ἀρχαῖον ὅλως τὸ δόγμα ἐστί, τοῖς ὁμοίοις τὰ ὅμοια
γιγνώσκεσθαι, ὅπερ ἀπὸ Πυθαγόρου δοκοῦν κατελη-
λυθέναι κεῖται μὲν καὶ παρὰ Πλάτωνι ἐν τῷ Τιμαίῳ,
εἴρηται δὲ πολὺ πρότερον ὑπ᾽ αὐτοῦ Ἐμπεδοκλέους
[. . . = **D207**], συνήσει ὅτι ὁ Ἐμπεδοκλῆς θεὸν ἑαυτὸν
προσηγόρευσεν [cf. **D4.4**], ἐπεὶ μόνος καθαρὸν ἀπὸ
κακίας τηρήσας τὸν νοῦν καὶ ἀνεπιθόλωτον τῷ ἐν
ἑαυτῷ θεῷ τὸν ἐκτὸς θεὸν κατείληφεν.

The Exile of the Daemons as the Tribulations
of the Soul (R47–R55)

R47 (≠ DK) Plut. *Esu carn.* 1.7 996B

οὐ χεῖρον δ᾽ ἴσως καὶ προανακρούσασθαι καὶ προ-
αναφωνῆσαι τὰ τοῦ Ἐμπεδοκλέους·[1] ἀλληγορεῖ γὰρ
ἐνταῦθα τὰς ψυχάς, ὅτι φόνων καὶ βρώσεως σαρκῶν
καὶ ἀλληλοφαγίας δίκην τίνουσαι σώμασι θνητοῖς
ἐνδέδενται.

[1] post Ἐμπεδοκλέους lac. ind. Stephanus

R48 (ad B115 et B119) Plut. *Exil.* 17 607C

ὁ δ᾽ Ἐμπεδοκλῆς ἐν ἀρχῇ τῆς φιλοσοφίας προανα-
φωνήσας [. . . = **D10.1, 3, 5, 6, 13**], οὐχ ἑαυτόν,[1] ἀλλ᾽
ἀφ᾽ ἑαυτοῦ πάντας ἀποδείκνυσι μετανάστας ἐνταῦθα
καὶ ξένους καὶ φυγάδας ἡμᾶς ὄντας. "οὐ γὰρ αἷμα"

[1] ἑαυτὸν ⟨μόνον⟩ Giesecke

650

like is known by like is quite ancient—since it is thought to come from Pythagoras, is also found in Plato in the *Timaeus,* and was enunciated much earlier by Empedocles himself [. . . = **D207**]—will understand that Empedocles called himself a god [cf. **D4.4**] because, since he alone had kept his spirit pure of evil and uncontaminated, he had comprehended the god outside himself by means of the god within him.

The Exile of the Daemons as the Tribulations of the Soul (R47–R55)

R47 (≠ DK) Plutarch, *On the Eating of Flesh*

It is surely not worse to declaim as a musical prelude and as a preface the verses of Empedocles.[1] For he says allegorically there that the souls become bound to mortal bodies because they are being punished for having committed murder, consumed meat, and eaten each other.

[1] Editors generally indicate after the first phrase a lacuna that would have contained a citation of **D10.** But Empedocles' proem was so famous that Plutarch could have alluded to it without quoting it.

R48 (ad B115 and B119) Plutarch, *On Exile*

Empedocles, having proclaimed as a prelude at the beginning of his philosophy [. . . = **D10.1, 3, 5, 6, 13**], reveals that not he himself, but, starting from himself, all of us have changed our place of habitation in coming here and are foreigners and exiles. For what he is saying is, "Oh

φησίν "ἡμῖν οὐδὲ πνεῦμα συγκραθέν, ὦ ἄνθρωποι,
ψυχῆς οὐσίαν καὶ ἀρχὴν παρέσχεν, ἀλλ' ἐκ τούτων
τὸ σῶμα συμπέπλασται, γηγενὲς καὶ θνητόν," τῆς δὲ
ψυχῆς ἀλλαχόθεν ἡκούσης δεῦρο, τὴν γένεσιν ἀπο-
δημίαν ὑποκορίζεται τῷ πραοτάτῳ τῶν ὀνομάτων. τὸ
δ' ἀληθέστατον, φεύγει καὶ πλανᾶται θείοις ἐλαυνομένη δόγμασι καὶ νόμοις, εἶθ' ὥσπερ ἐν νηὶ[2] σάλον
ἐχούσῃ πολύν, καθάπερ φησὶν ὁ Πλάτων, "ὀστρέου
τρόπον" ἐνδεδεμένη τῷ σώματι διὰ τὸ μὴ μνημονεύειν
μηδὲ ἀναφέρειν

ἐξ οἵης τιμῆς τε καὶ ὅσσου μήκεος ὄλβου [**D15**]

μεθέστηκεν, οὐ Σάρδεων Ἀθήνας οὐδὲ Κορίνθου Λῆ-
μνον ἢ Σκῦρον ἀλλ' οὐρανοῦ καὶ σελήνης γῆν ἀμει-
ψαμένη καὶ τὸν ἐπὶ γῆς βίον [. . .].

[2] νήσῳ mss., corr. Sieveking

R49 (ad B122) Plut. *Tranquil. an.* 15–16 474B

ἀλλὰ μᾶλλον, ὡς Ἐμπεδοκλῆς, διτταί τινες ἕκαστον
ἡμῶν γινόμενον παραλαμβάνουσι καὶ κατάρχονται
μοῖραι καὶ δαίμονες· [. . . = **D21**] ὥστε τούτων ἑκάστου
σπέρματα τῶν παθῶν ἀνακεκραμένα δεδεγμένης
ἡμῶν τῆς γενέσεως καὶ διὰ τοῦτο πολλὴν ἀνωμαλίαν
ἐχούσης, εὔχεται μὲν ὁ νοῦν ἔχων τὰ βελτίονα, προσ-
δοκᾷ δὲ καὶ θάτερα, χρῆται δ' ἀμφοτέροις τὸ ἄγαν
ἀφαιρῶν.

humans, it is not blood or breath mixed together that has supplied us with the substance and principle of our soul; it is the body, earthborn and mortal, that is fashioned from these"; as for the soul, which has come here from somewhere else, he euphemistically calls its birth a 'voyage' with the gentlest of terms. But the truth is that it flees and wanders, driven by divine decrees and laws, and then, as though on a ship that is being mightily buffeted, it is bound to the body "like an oyster," as Plato says [*Phaedrus* 250c], because it does not remember nor consider

far from what honor and from what abundance of bliss [D15]

it departed when it left, not Sardis for Athens nor Corinth for Lemnos or Scyros, but the heaven and moon for the earth and for life on the earth [. . .].

R49 (ad B122) Plutarch, *On the Tranquility of the Soul*

But it is rather, as Empedocles [scil. says], that two destinies and divinities seize hold of each of us and rule us when we are born [. . . = **D21**], so that since our birth has received the mixed seeds of both of these conditions, and for this reason possesses much irregularity, our mind wishes to have the better ones but also watches out for the others, and makes use of both of them, excluding their excess.

EARLY GREEK PHILOSOPHY V

R50 (ad B115 et B120) Plot. *Enn.* 4.8.1

[. . .] ἀπορῶ, πῶς ποτε καὶ νῦν καταβαίνω, καὶ ὅπως
ποτέ μοι ἔνδον ἡ ψυχὴ γεγένηται τοῦ σώματος [. . .
cf. **HER. R88**]. Ἐμπεδοκλῆς τε εἰπὼν ἁμαρτανούσαις
νόμον εἶναι ταῖς ψυχαῖς πεσεῖν ἐνταῦθα καὶ αὐτὸς
"φυγὰς θεόθεν" γενόμενος ἥκειν **"πίσυνος μαινομένῳ
νείκει"** [**D10.13–14**] τοσοῦτον παρεγύμνου, ὅσον καὶ
Πυθαγόρας, οἶμαι, καὶ οἱ ἀπ' ἐκείνου ἠνίττοντο περί
τε τούτου περί τε πολλῶν ἄλλων. τῷ δὲ παρῆν καὶ διὰ
ποίησιν οὐ σαφεῖ εἶναι. λείπεται δὴ ἡμῖν ὁ θεῖος
Πλάτων, ὃς πολλά τε καὶ καλὰ περὶ ψυχῆς εἶπε [. . .]·
καὶ τὸ σπήλαιον αὐτῷ, ὥσπερ Ἐμπεδοκλεῖ τὸ ἄντρον
[cf. **D16**], τόδε τὸ πᾶν—δοκῶ μοι—λέγει [. . .].

R51 (ad B126) Porph. in Stob. 1.49.60 (< 382 F22–26
Smith)

αὐτῆς γὰρ τῆς μετακοσμήσεως εἱμαρμένη καὶ φύσις
ὑπὸ Ἐμπεδοκλέους δαίμων ἀνηγόρευται,

σαρκῶν ἀλλογνῶτι περιστέλλουσι χιτῶνι [**D19**]

καὶ μεταμπίσχουσα τὰς ψυχάς.

R52 (ad B121) Synes. *Provid.* 1 1.3–4

δύο δὲ ἡ τοῦ κόσμου φύσις παρέχεται, τὴν μὲν φω-
τοειδῆ, τὴν δὲ ἀειδῆ· [. . .] [4] κεῖται δὲ Θέμιδος νόμος
ἀγορεύων ψυχαῖς, ἥτις ἂν ὁμιλήσασα τῇ τῶν ὄντων

R50 (ad B115 and B120) Plotinus, *The Descent of the Soul into Bodies*

[. . .] I am puzzled how it can happen that I am descending now, and how my soul could ever come to be within a body [. . .]. Empedocles too, when he said that for souls that have committed a sin there is a law, that they must fall here, and that he himself became **"an exile from the divine"** and came here because he **"relied on insane Strife"** [**D10.13–14**], was merely revealing explicitly exactly what Pythagoras, I suppose, and his followers indicated allegorically on this subject and on many others; moreover, he is not clear because he is writing poetry. So we are left with the divine Plato, who said many fine things about the soul [. . .] and his 'cave' [*Republic* 7.514a], like Empedocles' 'cave' [cf. **D16**], seems to me to designate this universe [. . .].

R51 (ad B126) Porphyry in Stobaeus, *Anthology*

The destiny and nature of this cosmic reconfiguration are called by Empedocles a divinity

> **enveloping** [scil. them] **in an unfamiliar cloak of flesh [D19]**

and putting new clothes on the souls.

R52 (ad B121) Synesius, *On Providence*

[1] The nature of the world has two [scil. sources], one of them luminous, the other indistinct [. . .]. [4] A law of Themis has been laid down proclaiming to souls that any

ἐσχατιᾷ τηρήσῃ τὴν φύσιν, καὶ ἀμόλυντος διαγένη-
ται, ταύτην δὴ[1] τὴν αὐτὴν ὁδὸν αὖθις ἀναρρυῆναι, καὶ
εἰς τὴν οἰκείαν ἀναχυθῆναι πηγήν, ὥσπερ γε καὶ τὰς
ἐκ τῆς ἑτέρας μερίδος τρόπον τινὰ ἐξορμησαμένας,[2]
φύσεως ἀνάγκῃ ἐς τοὺς συγγενεῖς αὐλισθῆναι κευθ-
μῶνας [. . . = **D24.2–3**, with textual variants].

[1] δὴ edd. Lond. Harley 6322: δεῖ mss.   [2] τρόπον τινὰ
ἐξορμησαμένας mss. plerique: χρόνον τινὰ ἐξορχησαμένας
cett.

R53 (ad B121 et B158) Hierocl. *In Carm. Aur.* 24.2–3

[2] κάτεισι γὰρ καὶ ἀποπίπτει τῆς εὐδαίμονος χώρας
ὁ ἄνθρωπος, ὡς Ἐμπεδοκλῆς φησιν ὁ Πυθαγόρειος
[. . . = **D10.13b–14**]. ἄνεισι δὲ καὶ τὴν ἀρχαίαν ἕξιν
ἀπολαμβάνει, εἰ φύγοι τὰ περὶ γῆν καὶ τὸν

ἀτερπέα χῶρον [**D24.1**],

ὡς ὁ αὐτὸς λέγει,

ἔνθα Φόνος τε Κότος τε καὶ ἄλλων ἔθνεα
    Κηρῶν [**D24.2**],

εἰς ὃν οἱ [3] ἐκπεσόντες

Ἄτης ἂν λειμῶνα κατὰ σκότος ἠλάσκουσιν
    [**D24.3**].

ἡ δὲ ἔφεσις τοῦ φεύγοντος τὸν τῆς Ἄτης λειμῶνα

one of them that, having spent time in the very bottom of what exists, preserves its nature and maintains itself unpolluted, flows back once again along the same path and spills back into its own source, just as those that have escaped somehow from the other portion inhabit by a necessity of nature underground places that are akin to them: [. . . = **D24.2–3**].

R53 (ad B121 and B158) Hierocles, *Commentary on Pythagoras'* Golden Verses

[2] For man descends and falls away from the happy region, as Empedocles the Pythagorean says, [. . . = **D10.13b–14**]. But he ascends and takes on his ancient disposition once again if he flees the terrestrial region and the

> **joyless place,** [**D24.1**]

as the same man says,

> **where Murder, Rage, and the tribes of the other Death-divinities** [scil. are, **D24.2**],

where those have fallen who

> **wander in darkness along the meadow of Destruction** [**D24.3**].

The desire of the man who flees the meadow of Destruc-

πρὸς τὸν τῆς ἀληθείας ἐπείγεται λειμῶνα, ὃν ἀπολι-
πὼν τῇ ὁρμῇ τῆς πτερορρυήσεως εἰς γήινον ἔρχεται
σῶμα ὀλβίου αἰῶνος ἀμερθείς. τούτοις δὲ καὶ ὁ Πλάτων ἐστὶ σύμφωνος περὶ μὲν τῆς καθόδου ταυτὶ λέ-
γων· [. . . = Plat. *Phaedr.* 248c5–8].

R54 (≠ DK) Procl. *In Tim.* 3 *ad* 34b–c (vol. 2, p. 116.18–
29 Diehl)

ἐπειδὴ δὲ καὶ αἴσθησιν ἔχομεν καὶ τὰ αἰσθητὰ πρὸ
ὀμμάτων ἐστὶν ἡμῶν,[1] εἰκῇ τε ζῶμεν[2] καὶ κατὰ τὸ
προστυχὸν καί, ὅ φασι, κάτω κάρα ποιούμεθα τὴν
τῶν ὄντων κρίσιν. ὃ καὶ Ἐμπεδοκλῆς ἡμῶν κατοδυ-
ρόμενος ἔφη· [. . . = **D42.2**]. πολλὰ γὰρ ἐμπίπτοντα
τοῖς ὄντως ἡμῖν δειλοῖς, ὡς φυγάσι θεόθεν γενομένοις
[cf. **D10.13b**], ἀμβλύνει τὴν τῶν ὄντων θεωρίαν.
ἐπειδὴ δέ, ὥσπερ καὶ οὗτος ὁ φιλόσοφος εἶπεν, ἔξωθεν ἐφῆκεν ἡμῖν τοῦτο τὸ προστυχὸν καὶ τὸ εἰκαῖον,
διὰ τοῦτο καὶ ὁ Πλάτων μετέχειν ἡμᾶς αὐτῶν εἶπεν,
ἀλλ᾽ οὐκ ἀπὸ τῆς οὐσίας ἡμῶν ἀνεγείρεσθαι ταῦτα.

[1] ἡμῖν coni. Diehl   [2] ζητῶμεν P

R55 (≠ DK) Herm. *In Phaedr.*, p. 160.14–15

ἀπέρχονται οὖν, φησί, τουτέστι φεύγουσιν ἐπὶ τὸ
ἄθεον καὶ σκοτεινόν, **φυγὰς θεόθεν καὶ ἀλήτης** [=
D10.13b].

tion is eagerly directed toward the meadow of Truth, which he left because of the impulse of molting when he entered into an earthly body, deprived of the blessed lifetime. Plato too is of this opinion, when he says about the descent, [. . . = *Phaedrus* 248c5–8].

R54 (≠ DK) Proclus, *Commentary on Plato's* Timaeus

But since we possess sensation and since the perceptibles are also before our eyes, we live at random and as a function of whatever happens, and, as they say, we judge the things that exist "with our heads upside down." This is what Empedocles too said when he lamented our fate [. . . = **D42.2**]. For the many things that befall us, miserable as we truly are, since we are "exiles from the divine," [cf. **D10.13**] blunt our contemplation of the things that are. But since, as this philosopher has also said, it is from outside that it [i.e. the divinity] has sent upon us this happenstance and randomness [cf. **D42.2, 5–6?**], for this reason Plato too says that we only "participate" in them but that it is not from our own essence that they arise.

R55 (≠ DK) Hermias, *Commentary on Plato's* Phaedrus

They [i.e. the souls] depart, he says [i.e. Plato, *Phaedrus* 248b], that is, they flee in exile toward what is godless and dark, **"an exile from the divine and a wanderer"** [**D10.13**].

Cavern and Meadow (R56–R57)

R56 (cf. ad B120) Porph. *Antr.* 8

ἀφ᾽ ὧν οἶμαι ὁρμώμενοι καὶ οἱ Πυθαγόρειοι καὶ μετὰ
τούτους Πλάτων ἄντρον καὶ σπήλαιον τὸν κόσμον
ἀπεφήναντο. παρά τε γὰρ Ἐμπεδοκλεῖ αἱ ψυχοπομποὶ δυνάμεις λέγουσιν [. . . = **D16**] [. . .] παρά τε Πλάτωνι ἐν τῷ ἑβδόμῳ τῆς Πολιτείας λέγεται [*Rep.* 7.514a].

R57 (ad B121) Procl. *In Remp.* 2.157.9–158.3

τὸν μὲν οὖν λειμῶνα καὶ διὰ τούτων οἶμαι δηλοῖ τῶν
ῥημάτων ⟨ὅτι⟩[1] τὸν δικαστικόν, ὥσπερ ἐν τῷ Γοργίᾳ
[*Gorg.* 523b], τόπον ἀποκαλεῖ. [. . .] ὃν ἀπεδείκνυμεν
ἔμπροσθεν [cf. 2.133.2 Kroll] ἐναργῶς αὐτὸν εἶναι τὸν
αἰθέρα τὸν οὐρανοῦ καὶ γῆς ὅλης μέσον καὶ οὐχὶ τῶν
ἐγκοίλων μόνων τῆς γῆς. ἔστι μὲν οὖν ὁ λειμὼν οὗτος
ταύτην ἔχων τὴν ἐπωνυμίαν ὡς ἀρχὴ τῆς τῶν ῥευ-
στῶν φύσεως καὶ τῶν ἐν ὑγρῷ τρεφομένων περιοχὴ
πάντων λόγων τε γενεσιουργῶν καὶ ζωῆς ὑλικῆς
ἀστάτως κινουμένης τόπος· τοιοῦτοι γὰρ οἱ λειμῶνες
ὑδρηλοί τινες καὶ ἀνθέων καὶ ἄλλων τοιούτων γέμον-
τες. τοῦτον Ἐμπεδοκλῆς ἰδὼν τὸν λειμῶνα παντοίων
αὐτὸν εἶναι κακῶν πλήρη καὶ εἶπεν καὶ εἰπὼν ἀνώμω-
ξεν· [. . . = **D24**]. μισοφαὴς γὰρ οὗτος ὁ χῶρος [*Or.
Ch.* 181] ὡς καὶ τὸ σκότος ἐν αὐτῷ ἐγένετο, καὶ τῆς
τίσεως κακούργῳ παντί.[2]

---

[1] ⟨ὅτι⟩ Reitzenstein   [2] παντὶ ⟨αἴτιος⟩ coni. Kroll

EMPEDOCLES

Cavern and Meadow (R56–R57)

R56 (cf. ad B120) Porphyry, *On the Cave of the Nymphs*

I think that it is on the basis of these verses [i.e. a hymn to Apollo, otherwise unknown] that the Pythagoreans, and after them Plato, declared that the world is a cave and a cavern. For both in Empedocles the powers that escort the souls say [. . . = **D16**], [. . .] and in Plato, in Book Seven of the *Republic*, it is said: [. . . = *Republic* 7.514a].

R57 (ad B121) Proclus, *Commentary on Plato's* Republic

Well then, I think that with these words [scil. *Republic* 10 614d3–e3] he [i.e. Plato] too is indicating that he calls the meadow the place of judgment, just as in the *Gorgias* [i.e. 523b]. [. . .] we clearly showed earlier that it [i.e. this place] is the aether located in the middle between the heavens and the whole earth, and not only between the heavens and the hollows of the earth. Now then, this prairie derives its name from the fact that it is the source of the nature of fluids, that it contains everything that is nourished in moisture, and that it is the place of the generative principles and of material life, which moves irregularly. For this is what meadows are like, watered and full of flowers and of other things like this. When Empedocles saw this meadow he said that it was full of all kinds of evils and saying this he cried out in mourning, [. . . = **D24**[1]]. For this region "hates the light" [*Chaldaic Oracles* 181], since the darkness too was born in it, and [scil. since it is the region] of punishment for every evildoer.

---

[1] The citation contains a line that is very probably inauthentic; cf. app. crit. ad. loc.

The Bursting of the Sphere as the Fall (R58–R61)

R58 (≠ DK) Iambl. *An.* in Stob. 1.49.37 (1.375.2–11 Wachsmuth)

καὶ οὗτοι μὲν προυποκειμένων τῶν ἀτάκτων καὶ πλημ-
μελῶν κινημάτων ἐπεισιέναι φασὶν ὕστερα τὰ κατα-
κοσμοῦντα αὐτὰ καὶ διατάττοντα καὶ τὴν συμφωνίαν
ἀπ᾽ ἀμφοτέρων οὕτως συνυφαίνουσι, κατὰ μὲν Πλω-
τῖνον τῆς πρώτης¹ ἑτερότητος, κατ᾽ Ἐμπεδοκλέα δὲ
τῆς πρώτης² ἀπὸ τοῦ θεοῦ φυγῆς, καθ᾽ Ἡράκλειτον
[. . . cf. **HER. R91**], κατὰ δὲ τοὺς Γνωστικοὺς [. . .],
κατ᾽ Ἀλβῖνον [. . .], αἰτίας γιγνομένης τῶν καταγωγῶν
ἐνεργημάτων.

¹⁻² πρώτης secl. Wachsmuth

R59 (> ad B115 PPF) Asclep. *In Metaph.*, p. 197.15–24

. . . ¹ ὁ Ἐμπεδοκλῆς, τί ἐστιν αἴτιον τῆς ἁπλῶς κινήσεως; οὐ γὰρ δεῖ λέγειν ἁπλῶς ὅτι οὕτως πέφυκεν,
ἐπεὶ οὕτω πάντα ῥᾷστα ἐπιλύεσθαι. λέγομεν οὖν ὃ
πολλάκις εἴρηται, ὅτι πάντα ταῦτα συμβολικῶς ἔλεγεν ὁ Ἐμπεδοκλῆς· οὔτε γὰρ τὸν Σφαῖρον ὑπετίθετο
φθείρεσθαι, ὥς φησιν, οὔτε δὲ τὸν αἰσθητὸν κόσμον,
ἀλλὰ διὰ τούτων ἐδήλου τὴν ἄνοδον καὶ τὴν κάθοδον
τῆς ψυχῆς. διὸ ἔλεγεν [. . . = **D10.13–14,** with textual
variants]. ἔστι γὰρ καὶ ἐν τῷ Σφαίρῳ διάκρισις, εἴ γε
πολλὰ νοητά, ἀλλὰ καλύπτεται ὑπὸ τῆς ἀφράστου
ἑνώσεως. καὶ ἐν τῷ αἰσθητῷ δέ ἐστιν ἕνωσις, ἀλλὰ
μᾶλλον ἐπικρατεῖ ἡ διάκρισις.

The Bursting of the Sphere as the Fall (R58–R61)

R58 (≠ DK) Iamblichus, *On the Soul* in Stobaeus, *Anthology*

They [i.e. different groups of Platonists] say that irregular and chaotic motions existed earlier, and that the causes of order and arrangement were introduced later, and that in this way they weave together harmony out of both of them. According to Plotinus [cf. *Enn.* 6.1.1] it is the first alterity that is responsible for causing the descents, according to Empedocles it is the first exile away from god, according to Heraclitus [. . .], according to the Gnostics [. . .], according to Albinus [. . .].

R59 (≠ DK) Asclepius, *Commentary on Aristotle's* Metaphysics

⟨. . .⟩ Empedocles, what is the cause of motion in general? For one should not simply say that it is this way by nature, since everything is resolved too easily in this way. Hence we say, as we have often said, that Empedocles said all these things symbolically. For he did not suppose that the Sphere was destroyed, as he says it, and not the perceptible world either, but he was indicating by means of these expressions the ascent and descent of the soul. That is why he said, [. . . = **D10.13–14**]. For there is separation within the Sphere too, since there is a plurality of intelligibles, but it is hidden by the ineffable unification; and there is unification in the perceptible too, but dissociation dominates more.

---

[1] lac. 7 litt. AD, coni. τίθεται Hayduck

R60 (≠ DK) Olymp. *In Gorg.* 35.12

κοινωνεῖν γὰρ ἀδύνατος] ἡ γὰρ κοινωνία φιλία τίς
ἐστιν· ἡ δὲ φιλία ὡς οἱ σοφοί φασιν, ὅ ἐστιν οἱ Πυθαγόρειοι καὶ ὁ Ἐμπεδοκλῆς φάσκων τὴν φιλίαν
ἑνοῦν τὸν Σφαῖρον, ἑνοποιός ἐστιν· ἡ γὰρ φιλία πρὸς
τῇ μιᾷ τῶν πάντων ἐστὶν ἀρχῇ, εἴγε ἐκεῖ ἕνωσις πανταχοῦ καὶ οὐδαμοῦ διάκρισις· ὁ οὖν ἄδικος παντὶ
ἐχθρός ἐστι καὶ οὐδενὶ κοινωνεῖ.

R61 (≠ DK) Procl. *In Parm.* 2.723.15–724.8

[. . .] ὃ καὶ Ἐμπεδοκλῆς ὕστερον ἑωρακώς, ἅτε Πυθαγόρειος καὶ αὐτὸς ὤν, Σφαῖρον ἀπεκάλει πᾶν τὸ νοητὸν ὡς ἡνωμένον ἑαυτῷ, καὶ εἰς ἑαυτὸν συννεῦον¹ διὰ²
τὸν καλλοποιὸν καὶ ἑνοποιὸν τοῦ κάλλους θεόν· πάντα
γὰρ ἐρῶντα ἀλλήλων καὶ ἐφιέμενα ἀλλήλων ἥνωται
πρὸς ἄλληλα αἰωνίως, καὶ ἔστιν αὐτῶν ὁ ἔρως νοητὸς
καὶ ἡ συνουσία καὶ ἡ σύγκρασις ἄφραστος. οἱ δέ γε
πολλοί, φυγάδες ἀπὸ τῆς ἑνώσεως ὄντες καὶ τῆς τῶν
ὄντων μονάδος, ἐπὶ δὲ τὸ πλῆθος κατασυρόμενοι διὰ
τὴν ἐν αὐτοῖς ζωὴν μεριστὴν οὖσαν καὶ διῃρημένην,
[. . .] αὐτὰ τὰ πολλὰ κεχωρισμένα τῆς ἑαυτῶν ἑνότητος ἐλάμβανον [. . .].

¹ συννεύειν ΑΣ (συννεύει F), corr. Cousin   ² διὰ post
ἑνοποιὸν ΑΣ, huc transp. Cousin

R60 (≠ DK) Olympiodorus, *Commentary on Plato's Gorgias*

"For he is not capable of sharing" [*Gorgias* 507e5]: for sharing is a kind of friendship, and friendship, as the sages say (that is, the Pythagoreans, and Empedocles, who says that friendship [i.e. Love] unifies the Sphere), creates unity; for, besides the principle of all things [i.e. the Sphere], there is also friendship, if indeed it is true that there is unification everywhere and separation nowhere. Thus the unjust man is hateful to everyone and shares with no one.

R61 (≠ DK) Proclus, *Commentary on Plato's* Parmenides

[. . .] what Empedocles, since he himself was a Pythagorean too [scil. like Parmenides] saw later [scil. that there exist two levels of reality]; so he called the totality of the intelligible 'Sphere' since it is unified in itself, and inclines toward itself because of the god of beauty, the god that produces beauty and unity.[1] For all things that love one another and desire one another have been unified with one another forever, and their desire is intelligible, and their union and mixture are ineffable. But most people, being exiles from unification and from the monad of the things that are, being dragged toward multiplicity by the life in them, which is divisible and dissociated, [. . .] have grasped multiplicity itself separate from the unity that belongs to them [. . .].

[1] Proclus is probably referring in this way to Love, which Empedocles also calls Aphrodite.

Empedocles and Vegetarianism (R62–R65)

R62 (≠ DK) Plut. *Esu carn.* 2.3 997D–E

ποῖον οὖν οὐ πολυτελὲς δεῖπνον, εἰς ὃ¹ θανατοῦταί τι
ἔμψυχον; μικρὸν ἀνάλωμα ἡγούμεθα ψυχήν; οὔπω
λέγω τάχα μητρὸς ἢ πατρὸς ἢ φίλου τινὸς ἢ παιδός,
ὡς ἔλεγεν Ἐμπεδοκλῆς [cf. **D29**], ἀλλ᾽ αἰσθήσεώς γε²
μετέχουσαν [. . .]. σκόπει δ᾽ ἡμᾶς πότεροι βέλτιον ἐξ-
ημεροῦσι τῶν φιλοσόφων, οἱ καὶ τέκνα καὶ φίλους
καὶ πατέρας καὶ γυναῖκας ἐσθίειν κελεύοντες ὡς ἀπο-
θανόντας, ἢ Πυθαγόρας καὶ Ἐμπεδοκλῆς ἐθίζοντες
εἶναι καὶ πρὸς τὰ ἀλλογενῆ³ δικαίους.

¹ post εἰς ὃ habent mss. οὐ, del. Xylander   ² τε mss.,
corr. Xylander   ³ ἀλλογενῆ Pohlenz: ἄλλα μέρη mss.:
ἄλλα γένη Xylander

R63 (103 Bollack) Plut. *Soll. anim.* 7 964D–E

ἐπεὶ τό γε μὴ παντάπασι καθαρεύειν ἀδικίας τὸν ἄνθρωπον οὕτω τὰ ζῷα μεταχειριζόμενον Ἐμπεδοκλῆς
καὶ Ἡράκλειτος ὡς ἀληθὲς προσδέχονται, πολλάκις
ὀδυρόμενοι καὶ λοιδοροῦντες τὴν φύσιν, ὡς ἀνάγκην
καὶ πόλεμον οὖσαν, ἀμιγὲς δὲ μηδὲν μηδ᾽ εἰλικρινὲς
ἔχουσαν ἀλλὰ διὰ πολλῶν καὶ δικαίων¹ παθῶν περαι-
νομένην· ὅπου καὶ τὴν γένεσιν αὐτὴν² ἐξ ἀδικίας συν-
τυγχάνειν λέγουσι, τῷ θνητῷ συνερχομένου τοῦ ἀθα-
νάτου, καὶ τρέφεσθαι³ τὸ γεννώμενον⁴ παρὰ φύσιν
μέλεσι⁵ τοῦ γεννήσαντος ἀποσπωμένοις.

EMPEDOCLES

Empedocles and Vegetarianism (R62–R65)

R62 (≠ DK) Plutarch, *On the Eating of Flesh*

What kind of meal would not be expensive for which a living being is killed? Do we consider life to be a small expense? I am not yet speaking about that of a mother or father or of some friend or a child, as Empedocles said [cf. **D29**], but of what at least possesses sensation [. . .]. But consider which of the two groups of philosophers is better at making us gentle, those [i.e. the Cynics] who bid us eat our children, our friends, our fathers, our wives, since they are dead, or else Pythagoras and Empedocles, who accustom us to exercise justice with regard to other species too?

R63 (≠ DK) Plutarch, *On the Cleverness of Animals*

Empedocles and Heraclitus accept as true the idea that man is not entirely pure of injustice, given that he treats animals as he does; they often complain and vilify nature as being necessity and war [cf. **HER. D63–D64**], as not possessing anything unmixed and pure, and as acting by means of many just [or perhaps: unjust] sufferings. Hence they say that generation itself results from an injustice, as what is immortal encounters what is mortal, and that what is born is nourished against nature by the limbs ripped away from its parent [cf. **D29**].

---

1 καὶ δικαίων mss.: κἀδίκων Leonicus

2 αὐτὴν] αὐτῆς kFZBII, αὐτῇ υ

3 τέρπεσθαι mss., corr. Bachet de Méziriac

4 γενόμενον mss., corr. Reiske   5 μέρεσι coni. Emperius

R64 (ad B128) Porph. *Abst.* 2.20

τὰ μὲν ἀρχαῖα τῶν ἱερῶν νηφάλια παρὰ πολλοῖς ἦν
[. . .]. μαρτυρεῖται δὲ ταῦτα [. . .] καὶ παρ᾽ Ἐμπεδοκλέους, ὃς περὶ τῆς θεογονίας διεξιὼν καὶ περὶ τῶν
θυμάτων[1] παρεμφαίνει λέγων [. . . cf. **D25**].

[1] περί τε τῶν θυμάτων καὶ περὶ τῆς θεογονίας διεξιὼν
mss., corr. Bernays

R65 (cf. ad B139) Porph. *Abst.* 2.31

πάντων μὲν οὖν ἴσως ἦν κράτιστον εὐθὺς[1] ἀποσχέ-
σθαι· ἐπεὶ δ᾽ ἀναμάρτητος οὐδείς, λοιπὸν ⟨δὴ⟩ ἀκεῖσθαι[2] τοῖς ὕστερον διὰ τῶν καθαρμῶν τὰς πρόσθε
περὶ τὴν τροφὴν[3] ἁμαρτίας. τοῦτο δὲ ὁμοίως γένοιτ᾽
ἄν, εἰ πρὸ ὀμμάτων ποιησάμενοι τὸ δεινὸν ἀνευφημή-
σαιμεν κατὰ τὸν Ἐμπεδοκλέα λέγοντες [. . . = **D34**, cf.
D74.5–6].

[1] εὐθὺς λοιπὸν mss., corr. Reiske   [2] λοιπὸν ἀνακεῖ-
σθαι mss.: ⟨δὴ⟩ Nauck, ἀκεῖσθαι Ruhnken   [3] τῆς τροφῆς
mss., corr. Reiske

A Mention of Empedocles' Daemons in a
Discussion about Oracles (R66)

R66 (≠ DK) Plut. *Def. orac.*

a 16 418E

καὶ ὁ Ἡρακλέων "τὸ μὲν ἐφεστάναι τοῖς χρηστη-

R64 (ad B128) Porphyry, *On Abstinence*

Ancient ritual libations were wineless among many peoples [. . .]; evidence for this is found [. . .] also in Empedocles, who in the course of his exposition of the theogony also speaks in passing about sacrifices, saying, [. . . cf. **D25**].

R65 (cf. ad B139) Porphyry, *On Abstinence*

Doubtless the best thing of all would be to refrain from the start. But since no one is without sin, all that remains for those who live later is to remedy, by means of purifications (*katharmoi*), earlier sins regarding nourishment. And this would happen likewise if, setting the horror before our eyes, we shouted out, saying, like Empedocles, [. . . = **D34,** cf. **D76.5–6**].

A Mention of Empedocles' Daemons in a
Discussion about Oracles (R66)

R66 (≠ DK) Plutarch, *The Obsolescence of Oracles*

a

And Heracleon said, "To set in charge of the oracles not

ρίοις," εἶπε, "μὴ θεοὺς οἷς ἀπηλλάχθαι τῶν περὶ γῆν
προσῆκόν ἐστιν, ἀλλὰ δαίμονας ὑπηρέτας θεῶν, οὐ
δοκεῖ μοι κακῶς ἀξιοῦσθαι· τὸ δὲ τοῖς δαίμοσι τούτοις
μονονουχὶ δράγδην[1] λαμβάνοντας ἐκ τῶν ἐπῶν τῶν
Ἐμπεδοκλέους ἁμαρτίας καὶ ἄτας καὶ πλάνας θεη-
λάτους ἐπιφέρειν, τελευτῶντας δὲ καὶ θανάτους ὥσπερ
ἀνθρώπων ὑποτίθεσθαι, θρασύτερον ἡγοῦμαι καὶ
βαρβαρικώτερον."

[1] ῥάγδην mss., corr. Wyttenbach

b 17 419A

"ἀλλὰ φαύλους μέν," ἔφη, "δαίμονας οὐκ Ἐμπεδοκλῆς μόνον, ὦ Ἡρακλέων, ἀπέλιπεν, ἀλλὰ καὶ Πλάτων
καὶ Ξενοκράτης καὶ Χρύσιππος· ἔτι δὲ Δημόκριτος
εὐχόμενος 'εὐλόγχων εἰδώλων' τυγχάνειν, ᾗ δῆλος ἦν
ἕτερα δυστράπελα καὶ μοχθηρὰς γιγνώσκων ἔχοντα
προαιρέσεις τινὰς καὶ ὁρμάς."

c 20 420D

"ὃ μέντοι μόνον ἀκήκοα τῶν Ἐπικουρείων λεγόντων
πρὸς τοὺς εἰσαγομένους ὑπ' Ἐμπεδοκλέους δαίμονας,
ὡς οὐ δυνατὸν εἶναι φαύλους καὶ ἁμαρτητικοὺς ὄντας
μακαρίους καὶ μακραίωνας, πολλὴν τυφλότητα τῆς
κακίας ἐχούσης καὶ τὸ περιπτωτικὸν τοῖς ἀναιρετι-
κοῖς, εὔηθές ἐστιν. [. . .]"

gods, for whom it is fitting that they be remote from terrestrial matters, but instead daemons, who are servants of the gods, does not seem to me to be a bad idea. But to attribute to these daemons sins, crimes, and god-sent wanderings, drawing them from Empedocles' verses as it were by handfuls, and to attribute to them an end and death like that of humans—this I consider too audacious and barbaric."

b

[Philip replies:] "Empedocles is not the only one who has transmitted to us bad daemons: so have Plato, Xenocrates, and Chrysippus too. And Democritus too, when he wishes to encounter 'propitious images' [**ATOM. D154**], clearly knows of other ones that are difficult and possess wicked intentions and impulses."

c

[Ammonius:] "The only thing that the Epicureans, as far as I have heard, say regarding the daemons introduced by Empedocles, namely that it is not possible for them to be wicked and sinful, given that they are 'happy' and 'long-lived' [cf. **D60.8, D73.272, D77.12**]—since evil is accompanied by great blindness and a tendency to expose oneself to destruction—is silly. [. . .]"

A Humorous Application of the
Exile of the Daemons (R67)

R67 (≠ DK) Plut. *Vit. aer. alien.* 830F–831A

ὁ δ' ἅπαξ ἐνειληθεὶς μένει χρεώστης διὰ παντός, ἄλλον ἐξ ἄλλου μεταλαμβάνων ἀναβάτην, ὥσπερ ἵππος
ἐγχαλινωθείς· ἀποφυγὴ δ' οὐκ ἔστιν ἐπὶ τὰς νομὰς
ἐκείνας καὶ τοὺς λειμῶνας, ἀλλὰ πλάζονται καθάπερ
οἱ θεήλατοι καὶ οὐρανοπετεῖς ἐκεῖνοι τοῦ Ἐμπεδοκλέους δαίμονες· [. . . = **D10.9–12**]—τοκιστὴς ἢ πραγ-
ματευτὴς Κορίνθιος, εἶτα Πατρεύς, εἶτ' Ἀθηναῖος,
ἄχρι ἂν ὑπὸ πάντων περικρουόμενος εἰς τόκους δια-
λυθῇ καὶ κατακερματισθῇ.

Empedocles in Simplicius (R68–R79)
The Transmission of the Fragments of
Empedocles: Some Examples (R68–R70)

R68 (cf. ad B17, B21, B22, B23, B26) Simpl. *In Phys.*,
pp. 157.25–161.20

ὁ δὲ Ἐμπεδοκλῆς τὸ ἓν καὶ τὰ πολλὰ τὰ πεπερασμένα καὶ τὴν κατὰ περίοδον ἀποκατάστασιν καὶ τὴν
κατὰ σύγκρισιν καὶ διάκρισιν γένεσιν καὶ φθορὰν
οὕτως ἐν τῷ πρώτῳ τῶν Φυσικῶν παραδίδωσι· [. . . =
D73.233–66]. ἐν δὴ τούτοις ἓν μὲν τὸ ἐκ πλειόνων
φησὶ τῶν τεττάρων στοιχείων, καὶ ποτὲ μὲν τῆς Φιλίας δηλοῖ ἐπικρατούσης, ποτὲ δὲ τοῦ Νείκους. ὅτι

EMPEDOCLES

A Humorous Application of the
Exile of the Daemons (R67)

R67 (≠ DK) Plutarch, *That One Should Not Borrow*

The man who is ensnared once remains a debtor forever, exchanging one rider for another, like a horse once it has been bridled. There is no escape to those pastures and meadows, but they wander like those daemons of Empedocles who are chased by the gods and fallen from heaven [. . . = **D10.9–12**]—a borrower or businessman from Corinth, then from Patras, then from Athens, until, assailed by everyone from every side, he is destroyed and completely reduced to the interest owed.

Empedocles in Simplicius (R68–R79)
The Transmission of the Fragments of
Empedocles: Some Examples (R68–R70)

R68 (cf. ad B17, B21, B22, B23, B26) Simplicius, *Commentary on Aristotle's* Physics

Empedocles transmits the doctrines of the one, of limited multiplicity, of periodic restoration, and of generation and corruption by assembly and division in the first book of his *Physics:* [. . . = **D73.233–66**]. In these lines, he calls 'one' what comes from the plurality of the four elements, and he indicates that this occurs sometimes when Love dominates and sometimes when Strife does. For the fact that

γὰρ οὐδέτερον τούτων τελέως ἀπολείπει, δηλοῖ τὸ
πάντα ἴσα εἶναι καὶ ἥλικα κατὰ τὴν γένναν [cf.
D73.258] καὶ τὸ μηδὲν ἐπιγίνεσθαι μηδ᾽ ἀπολήγειν
[cf. **D73.261**]. πολλὰ δὲ τὰ πλείονα ἐξ ὧν τὸ ἕν· οὐ
γὰρ ἡ Φιλία τὸ ἕν ἐστιν, ἀλλὰ καὶ τὸ Νεῖκος εἰς τὸ
ἓν τελεῖ. πλείονα δὲ ἄλλα εἰπὼν ἐπάγει ἑκάστου τῶν
εἰρημένων τὸν χαρακτῆρα, τὸ μὲν πῦρ ἥλιον καλῶν,
τὸν δὲ ἀέρα αὐγὴν καὶ οὐρανόν, τὸ δὲ ὕδωρ ὄμβρον
καὶ θάλασσαν. λέγει δὲ οὕτως· [. . . = **D77a**]. καὶ παράδειγμα δὲ ἐναργὲς παρέθετο τοῦ ἐκ τῶν αὐτῶν γίνεσθαι τὰ διάφορα· [. . . = **D60**]. καὶ ὅτι μὲν τὰ πολλὰ
ταῦτα ἐν τῷ γενητῷ κόσμῳ θεωρεῖ, καὶ οὐ μόνον τὸ
Νεῖκος ἀλλὰ καὶ τὴν Φιλίαν, δῆλον ἐκ τοῦ καὶ δένδρα
καὶ ἄνδρας καὶ γυναῖκας καὶ τὰ θηρία ἐκ τούτων λέγειν γεγονέναι [cf. **D60.6–7**]· ὅτι δὲ εἰς ἄλληλα μετα-
βάλλει, δηλοῖ λέγων [. . . = **D77b.1–2**]. ὅτι δὲ τῇ δια-
δοχῇ τὸ ἀίδιον ἔχει καὶ τὰ γινόμενα καὶ φθειρόμενα,
ἐδήλωσεν εἰπών [. . . = **D73.243–44**]. καὶ ὅτι διττὸν καὶ
οὗτος αἰνίττεται διάκοσμον, τὸν μὲν νοητὸν τὸν δὲ
αἰσθητόν, καὶ τὸν μὲν θεῖον τὸν δὲ ἐπίκηρον, ὧν ὁ μὲν
παραδειγματικῶς ἔχει ταῦτα, ὁ δὲ εἰκονικῶς, ἐδήλωσε
μὴ μόνον τὰ γενητὰ καὶ φθαρτὰ λέγων ἐκ τούτων
συνεστάναι, ἀλλὰ καὶ τοὺς θεούς, εἰ μὴ ἄρα τις τοῦτο
κατὰ τὴν Ἐμπεδοκλέους συνήθειαν ἐξηγήσαιτο. καὶ

---

[1] Cf. **D77b.5–7**.

[2] 'Sun,' 'gleam,' and 'rain' appear in the lines that Simplicius
cites from Empedocles, but not 'sky.'

neither of these two completely disappears is indicated by
the facts that "all are equal and identical in age" [cf.
D73.258] and that "nothing is added nor is lacking" [cf.
D73.261]. "Multiple" is the plurality from which the One
comes; for it is not Love that is the One, but Strife too
leads to the One.[1] Then, after he has said many other
things, he adds the character proper to each of the things
that he has mentioned, calling the fire 'sun,' the air 'gleam'
and 'sky,' and the water 'rain' and 'sea.' He speaks as follows: [. . . = **D77a**].[2] And he has supplied a clear illustra-
tion of the fact that different things come from the same
ones: [. . . = **D60**]. And the fact that he considers this
multiplicity in the generated world, and not only Strife but
Love too, is clear from the fact that he says that trees, men,
women, and animals are born from these things [cf.
D60.6–7]. And the fact that they are transformed into
each other, he indicates by saying, [. . . = **D77b.1–2**]. And
the fact that the things that come to be and perish possess
eternity by virtue of their succession, he has made clear
by saying, [. . . = **D73.243–44**]. And the fact that he too
[scil. like Anaxagoras] is referring allegorically to a double
organization of the world, the one intelligible and the
other perceptible, the one divine and the other mortal, of
which the one possesses these things [i.e. the elements] in
the mode of a paradigm, the other in the mode of an image
[cf. **R76–R79**], he has made this clear by saying that not
only the things that come to be and perish come from
these things, but also the gods—unless one interprets this
in terms of Empedocles' usage. And one could think that

ἐκ τούτων δὲ ἄν τις τὸν διττὸν αἰνίττεσθαι διάκοσμον
οἴοιτο· [. . . = **D101**]. καὶ γὰρ ὅτι καὶ ἐν τοῖς θνητοῖς
ἥρμοσται ταῦτα, δεδήλωκεν, ἐν δὲ τοῖς νοητοῖς μᾶλλον ἥνωται καὶ [. . . = **D101.5**], καὶ ὅτι κἂν πανταχοῦ,
ἀλλὰ τὰ μὲν νοητὰ τῇ Φιλίᾳ ὡμοίωται, τὰ δὲ αἰσθητὰ
[10] ὑπὸ τοῦ Νείκους κρατηθέντα καὶ ἐπὶ πλέον δια-
σπασθέντα ἐν τῇ κατὰ τὴν κρᾶσιν γενέσει ἐν ἐκμα-
κτοῖς καὶ εἰκονικοῖς εἴδεσιν [cf. **D101.7**] ὑπέστησαν
τοῖς Νεικεογενέσι καὶ ἀήθως ἔχουσι πρὸς τὴν ἔνωσιν[1]
τὴν πρὸς ἄλληλα. ὅτι δὲ καὶ οὗτος κατὰ σύγκρισίν
τινα καὶ διάκρισιν τὴν γένεσιν ὑπέθετο, δηλοῖ τὰ εὐθὺς ἐν ἀρχῇ παρατεθέντα [. . . = **D73.233b** (τοτὲ)–**34**]
καὶ ἐκεῖνο μέντοι τὸ τὴν γένεσιν καὶ τὴν φθορὰν μηδὲν ἄλλο εἶναι, [. . . = **D53.3**], καὶ "σύνοδον διάπτυξίν
τε γενέσθαι †αἴης†"[2] [cf. **D73.300**].

[1] ἔνωσιν E ed. Ald.: γένεσιν F   [2] αἴης DEF: αἴσης ed.
Ald.: γενέθλης P. Strasb. (= **D73.300**)

R69 (cf. ad B85, B103, B104) Simpl. *In Phys.*, pp. 330.31–
331.16

ὅτι δὲ εἶχον ἔννοιάν τινα περὶ τῶν κατὰ τύχην συμ-
βαινόντων, δηλοῖ τὸ χρῆσθαι ἐνίοτε τῷ ὀνόματι,
ὥσπερ Ἐμπεδοκλῆς οὐκ ἀεὶ τὸν ἀέρα ἀνωτάτω ἀπο-
κρίνεσθαί φησιν, ἀλλ' ὅπως ἂν τύχῃ. λέγει γοῦν ἐν
τῇ κοσμοποιίᾳ ὡς [. . . = **D105,** with textual variations],
καὶ ἐν ἄλλοις [. . . = **D106**], καὶ τὰ μόρια τῶν ζῴων
ἀπὸ τύχης γενέσθαι τὰ πλεῖστά φησιν, ὡς ὅταν λέγῃ

he is referring allegorically to a double organization of the world on the basis of the following lines: [. . . = **D101**]. For the fact that these things are fitted together in mortal things too, he has made clear, but that among intelligible ones they are more unified and [. . . = **D101.5**]; and that even if they are everywhere, the intelligibles are made similar by Love, while the perceptibles, which have been dominated by Strife and are torn apart more in their birth, by virtue of the mixture, in **"molded forms"** [= **D101.7**] and in the mode of images, serve as basis for the things born from Strife, which are not accustomed to mutual unification. But the fact that he posited generation as a function of assembly and separation is indicated by the passage cited at the beginning: [. . . = **D73.233b–34**], as well as by this one, that genesis and corruption are nothing else than [. . . = **D53.3**], and that there is a **"coming together and unfolding of** †. . .†**"** [cf. **D73.300**].

R69 (cf. ad B85, B103, B104) Simplicius, *Commentary on Aristotle's* Physics

The fact that they [i.e. the ancient natural philosophers] had a certain idea about what happens by chance is made clear by the fact that they sometimes use the word, like Empedocles, who says that the air is not always separated upward, but as it happens. For he says in the cosmogony [. . . = **D105**], and elsewhere [. . . = **D106**], and he says that most of the parts of animals have come about by

[. . . = **D190.1**, with textual variations], καὶ πάλιν [. . . = **D191**], καὶ ἐν ἄλλοις [. . . = **D200.2**]. καὶ πολλὰ ἄν τις εὕροι ἐκ τῶν Ἐμπεδοκλέους Φυσικῶν τοιαῦτα παρατεθέσθαι, ὥσπερ καὶ τοῦτο· [. . . = **D242**], καὶ μετ᾽ ὀλίγον [. . . = **D107**]. ἀλλ᾽ οὗτος μὲν ἐπὶ σμικροῖς τῇ τύχῃ καταχρῆσθαι δοκῶν ἥττονος ἂν εἴη ἐπιστάσεως ἄξιος, τί ποτ᾽ ἔστιν ἡ τύχη μὴ παραδούς [. . .].

R70 (cf. ad B35, B71, B73, B75, B86, B87, B95) Simpl. *In Cael.*, pp. 528.29–530.11

ἀλλ᾽ ἐβιάζετο, μᾶλλον δὲ ἐβιάσθη νομίζων τὸν κόσμον τοῦτον ὑπὸ μόνου τοῦ Νείκους κατὰ τὸν Ἐμπεδοκλέα γενέσθαι. μήποτε δέ, κἂν ἐπικρατῇ ἐν τούτῳ τὸ Νεῖκος ὥσπερ ἐν τῷ Σφαίρῳ ἡ Φιλία, ἀλλ᾽ ἄμφω ὑπ᾽ ἀμφοῖν λέγονται γίνεσθαι. καὶ τάχα οὐδὲν κωλύει παραθέσθαι τινὰ τῶν τοῦ Ἐμπεδοκλέους ἐπῶν τοῦτο δηλοῦντα· [. . . = **D75.1–15**]. ἐν τούτοις δηλοῦται ὅτι ἐν τῇ ἁπλῇ[1] διακοσμήσει ὑποστέλλεται μὲν τὸ Νεῖκος, ἡ δὲ Φιλότης ἐπικρατεῖ, ὅταν ἐν μέσῃ τῇ στροφάλιγγι, τουτέστι τῇ δίνῃ, γένηται [cf. **D75.4**], ὥστε καὶ τῆς Φιλότητος ἐπικρατούσης ἔστιν ἡ δίνη, καὶ ὅτι τὰ μὲν τῶν στοιχείων ἄμικτα μένει ὑπὸ τοῦ Νείκους, τὰ δὲ μιγνύμενα ποιεῖ τὰ θνητὰ καὶ[2] ζῷα καὶ φυτά, διότι[3] πάλιν διαλύεται τὰ μιγνύμενα. ἀλλὰ καὶ περὶ γενέσεως τῶν ὀφθαλμῶν τῶν σωματικῶν τούτων λέγων ἐπήγαγεν [. . . = **D213**], καὶ μετ᾽ ὀλίγον [. . . =

chance, as when he says [. . . = **D190.1**], and again [. . . = **D191**], and elsewhere [. . . = **D200.2**]. And one could cite many passages of this sort from Empedocles' *Physics,* like this one too [. . . = **D242**], and a little later [. . . = **D107**]. But since he does not seem to have had recourse to chance except in minor cases, it is doubtless not worth lingering on this, since he did not transmit a doctrine of what chance is [. . .].

R70 (cf. ad B35, B71, B73, B75, B86, B87, B95) Simplicius, *Commentary on Aristotle's* On the Heavens

He [i.e. Alexander] committed violence, or rather he suffered it, since he thought that according to Empedocles this world comes about as a result of Strife alone. But perhaps, even if Strife dominates in this world just as Love does in the Sphere, both of them are said to come about as a result of the action of both of them. And perhaps nothing prevents us from citing some of Empedocles' verses that show this: [. . . = **D75.1–15**]. In these verses he shows that in the simple organization (?) of the world Strife retreats and Love dominates, when she arrives in the center of the **whirl** [cf. **D75.4**], that is of the vortex, so that the vortex exists when Love dominates too; and [scil. he shows] that those elements that do not mix remain under Strife, while the ones that do mix make mortal things, both animals and plants, because of which the mixtures dissolve once again. And speaking about the generation of these bodily eyes he has continued, [. . . = **D213**];

---

1 ἁπλῇ A: αὐτῇ F   2 καὶ A: om. F
3 διότι] δίχα τε Karsten

D214], καὶ τὴν αἰτίαν λέγων τοῦ τοὺς μὲν ἐν ἡμέρᾳ, τοὺς δὲ ἐν νυκτὶ κάλλιον ὁρᾶν [. . . = **D217**]. ὅτι δὲ περὶ τούτων λέγει τῶν ἐν τούτῳ τῷ κόσμῳ, ἄκουε τούτων τῶν ἐπῶν· [. . . = **D61**], καὶ μετ᾽ ὀλίγα⁴ [. . . = **D199**], καὶ πάλιν [. . . = **D200**]. ταῦτ᾽ ἐξ ὀλίγων τῶν εὐθὺς προσπεσόντων ἐπῶν ἀναλεξάμενος παρεθέμην.

⁴ ὀλίγον F

Replies by Simplicius to Aristotle and the Peripatetics (R71–R75)

R71 (≠ DK) Simpl. *In Cael.*, pp. 528.5–14 et 530.12–26

τέτρασι δὲ χρῆται ἐπιχειρήμασιν, ὧν τὸ πρῶτον ἀσαφῶς ἀπηγγέλθαι δοκεῖ. "ὅτε γάρ," φησί, "τὰ στοιχεῖα διειστήκει χωρὶς ὑπὸ τοῦ Νείκους, τίς αἰτία τῇ γῇ τῆς μονῆς ἦν; οὐ γὰρ δὴ καὶ τότε αἰτιάσεται τὴν δίνην." δοκεῖ τοίνυν λέγειν ὅτε τὰ στοιχεῖα διειστήκει ὑπὸ τοῦ Νείκους ὡς ἄλλην τινὰ κατάστασιν παρὰ τὴν νῦν¹ ἐκείνην λέγων τὴν ὑπὸ τοῦ Νείκους γινομένην. καίτοι ὑπὸ τοῦ Νείκους διακρίνοντος τὰ στοιχεῖα τοῦτον λέγει γίνεσθαι τὸν κόσμον ὁ Ἐμπεδοκλῆς, ὥσπερ ὑπὸ τῆς Φιλίας συναγούσης καὶ ἑνούσης αὐτὰ τὸν Σφαῖρον. πῶς δὲ ἐν τῇ τοῦ Νείκους ἐπικρατείᾳ, εἴπερ αὕτη ἐστίν, οὐ φησὶν εἶναι τὴν δίνην; [. . .] μήποτε δὲ τοῦ Ἐμπεδοκλέους ὡς ποιητοῦ μυθικώτερον

¹ τὴν νῦν F: τὸν νοῦν A

and a little later [. . . = **D214**], and, explaining the reason why some see better by day, others at night, [. . . = **D217**]. But the fact that he is speaking about the things that are in this world, hear this in these lines: [. . . = **D61**]; and a little later, [. . . = **D199**]; and again, [. . . = **D200**]. I chose these lines to cite from the few that immediately presented themselves.

Replies by Simplicius to Aristotle and the Peripatetics (R71–R75)

R71 (≠ DK) Simplicius, *Commentary on Aristotle's* On the Heavens

He [i.e. Aristotle] makes four objections, of which the first one does not seem to be expressed clearly. For he says, "when the elements were separated from one another under the effect of Strife, what was the cause of the earth's immobility? For he will certainly not assign the cause to the vortex at that time too" [*On the Heavens* 2.13 295a30–32] [cf. **R14**]. So he seems to be saying, "when the elements were separated from one another under the effect of Strife" on the idea that there exists some other state besides the one that comes about now under the effect of Strife. And yet Empedocles says that this world here comes about under the effect of Strife, which separates the elements, just as the Sphere comes about under the effect of Love, which brings them together and unifies them. So how can he say that there is no vortex during the domination of Strife, given that it [scil. this domination] exists? [. . .] But, since Empedocles, as a poet, speaks in a

παρὰ μέρος τὴν ἐπικράτειαν αὐτῶν λέγοντος [. . . = **D73.239–40**], ὁ Ἀριστοτέλης τῷ μυθικωτέρῳ τούτῳ ἀποχρησάμενος ἐρωτᾷ τοὺς τὴν δίνην τῆς μονῆς τῆς γῆς αἰτιωμένους· "ὅτε τὰ στοιχεῖα διειστήκει χωρὶς ὑπὸ τοῦ Νείκους,[2] ἐπειδὴ τότε ἀμίκτων ὄντων οὐκ ἦν σύνταξις τῷ οὐρανῷ πρὸς τὴν γῆν, μᾶλλον δὲ ἀμίκτων ὄντων τῶν στοιχείων οὔπω οὐδὲ ὁ οὐρανὸς ἦν κατὰ τὴν τοιαύτην ὑπόθεσιν, ἡ δὲ γῆ ἦν, εἴπερ ἀίδια τὰ στοιχεῖα, ὡς ὑποτίθενται, τίς αἰτία τότε τῇ γῇ τῆς μονῆς ἦν; οὐ γὰρ δὴ καὶ τότε αἰτιάσεται τὴν δίνην." εἴποι δὲ ἄν, οἶμαι, Ἐμπεδοκλῆς, ὅτι οὐκ ἔστιν ὅτε χωρὶς διειστήκει τὰ στοιχεῖα μὴ καὶ τῆς πρὸς ἄλληλα συντάξεως αὐτῶν οὔσης· οὐ γὰρ ἂν ἦν στοιχεῖα· ἀλλ' ὁ λόγος τὴν φύσιν τῶν πραγμάτων ἀναπτύξαι βουλόμενος, καὶ γένεσιν τῶν ἀγενήτων καὶ διάκρισιν τῶν ἡνωμένων καὶ ἕνωσιν τῶν διακεκριμένων ὑποτίθεται.

[2] ‹τίς ἡ αἰτία τότε τῇ γῇ τῆς μονῆς ἦν;› post νείκους Karsten ex infra transp.

R72 (≠ DK) Simpl. *In An.*, p. 202.25–30

οὐ μὲν Ἐμπεδοκλέα ἢ Ὅμηρον ἐπὶ ταύτης θετέον τῆς δόξης, κἂν ὁ Ἀριστοτέλης τῷ παχυμερῶς λεγομένῳ ἐφιστάνων ἐλέγχῃ τὰ καὶ ἄλλως ἀκούεσθαι δυνά-

[1] This thesis is derived from Plat. *Theaet.* 151e. Aristotle approaches Empedocles in citing side-by-side **D243** and **D244** on the one hand, and Hom. *Od.* 18.136 on the other (cf. **MOR. T8b**),

rather mythical fashion about their alternating dominance [. . . = **D73.239–40**], perhaps Aristotle, taking advantage of this rather mythical presentation, is asking those who assign to the vortex the cause of the earth's immobility: "when the elements were separated from one another under the effect of Strife, given that they were not mixed at this time and that there was no ordered relationship between the heaven and the earth, but that rather, as they were not mixed, there did not yet even exist a heaven according to this hypothesis, but that by contrast the earth existed, since the elements are eternal, as they posit them—what was the cause of the earth's immobility at that time? For he will certainly not assign the cause to the vortex at that time too." Empedocles would have answered, I suppose, that there was not any time when the elements were separated from one another without there also being an ordered relationship among them. For otherwise they would not be elements. But this argument, which wishes to deploy the nature of things, posits the genesis of what is ungenerated, the separation of what is unified, and the unification of what is separated.

R72 (≠ DK) Simplicius, *Commentary on Aristotle's* On the Soul

Empedocles and Homer should not be attached to this view [scil. that knowledge is identical to sensation[1]], even if Aristotle, stopping at an inexact assertion, refutes something that can also be understood differently. For one

as he does at *Metaph.* Γ5 1009b18–20. For the association between Empedocles and Homer in related contexts, see also **DOX. T2; PROT. R12**.

μενα. ἀκούσειε μὲν γὰρ ἄν τις αἰσθητὸν εἶναι τὸ
παρόν [cf. **D243**]· οὐ μὲν ἢ ὑπὸ Ἐμπεδοκλέους οὕτως
εἴρηται, ἢ τὸ ἀληθὲς ὧδε ἔχει. ἡ γὰρ μῆτις οὐ τοῖς
αἰσθητοῖς ἀλλὰ τοῖς νοητοῖς αὐτῇ παροῦσιν ἀεὶ εἰς
τὴν ἑαυτῆς ἐπιδίδωσι τελειότητα [. . .].

R73 (≠ DK) Simpl. *In Phys.*, pp. 1124.19–1125.25

παραθέμενος δὲ ὁ Ἀριστοτέλης τὰ τοῦ Ἐμπεδοκλέους
ἔπη, ἐν οἷς αὐτὸν οἴεται τήν τε κίνησιν καὶ τὴν ἀκινησίαν παραδιδόναι, τὴν μὲν κίνησιν κατὰ τὴν γένεσιν θεωρεῖ τοῦ τε ἑνὸς ἐκ τῶν πολλῶν καὶ τῶν πολλῶν
ἐκ τοῦ ἑνός, σαφῶς καὶ τοῦ Ἐμπεδοκλέους εἰπόντος
[. . . = **D73.242**]. ὅτι γὰρ τῇ γενέσει κίνησις σύνεστιν
εἴρηται πρότερον, τὴν δὲ ἀκινησίαν ἔοικεν ὁ Ἐμπεδοκλῆς ἐνορᾶν κατὰ τὴν ἀίδιον ταυτότητα τῆς εἰς ἄλληλα τοῦ ἑνὸς καὶ τῶν πολλῶν μεταβολῆς· τοιοῦτον
γὰρ τὸ [. . . = **D73.243–44**]. ὁ δὲ Ἀλέξανδρος οἶδεν μὲν
καὶ τοῦτον τὸν νοῦν, φησὶ δὲ μὴ κατὰ τοῦτον ἐκδέχε-
σθαι τὸν Ἀριστοτέλην, ἀλλὰ καὶ ταῦτα περὶ τῆς μεταβολῆς ἀκούειν, ὅταν λέγῃ· 'ἧ δὲ τάδ' ἐνθένδ' ἀλλάσσοντα' [**D73.243**], τουτέστιν εἰς τάδε ἐκ τῶνδε
μεταβάλλοντα οὐ λήγει. κατὰ τὴν ἄμειψιν ταύτην καὶ
τὴν εἰς ἄλληλα ἐν μέρει μεταβολὴν καὶ ταύτῃ ἀίδιά
ἐστι, τουτέστιν ἀίδιος αὐτῶν ἡ εἰς ἄλληλα μεταβολή.
ἰδίᾳ μὲν γὰρ οὐθέτερον τῶν γινομένων ὑπὸ τοῦ Νείκους καὶ τῆς Φιλίας ἐκ τῶν στοιχείων ἀίδιόν ἐστιν
οὐδὲ ἔμπεδος αὐτοῖς ὁ αἰών [**D73.242**], ἡ μέντοι εἰς

could understand "what is present" [cf. **D243**] as the perceptible. But neither is this what Empedocles said nor is this how things are in truth. For intelligence does not add its own perfection to perceptibles but to the intelligibles that are present to it [. . .].

R73 (≠ DK) Simplicius, *Commentary on Aristotle's Physics*

Aristotle, having cited the verses of Empedocles in which he supposes him to be teaching both motion and lack of motion [*Phys.* 8.1 250a29, cf. **D84a**], sees motion in the genesis of the one out of the many and of the many out of the one, since Empedocles for his part has clearly said, [. . . = **D73.242**]. For I said earlier that motion coexists with genesis, and as for the absence of motion, Empedocles seems to see this in the eternal identity of the change of the one and the many into each other. For this is what is meant by [. . . = **D73.243–44**]. Alexander knows this interpretation too, but he says that Aristotle does not take it in this way but understands these verses too as bearing on change, when he says, **'but insofar as they incessantly exchange their places'** [**D73.243**] from here, that is, to change from this state to that state: by virtue of this exchange and alternating transformation into each other, they are eternal in this way too, that is, their transformation into each other is eternal. For it is peculiar that nothing of what is engendered as much by Strife as by Love out of the elements be eternal and that **'they do not have a steadfast lifetime'** [**D73.242**], while their trans-

ἄλληλα αὐτῶν μεταβολὴ ἀΐδιος· τοῦτο γὰρ σημαίνει
τὸ **αἰὲν ἔασι** [**D73.244**]. ταῦτα κατὰ λέξιν εἰπὼν ὁ
Ἀλέξανδρος ἐπάγει· "εἶτα ἐπὶ τούτοις εἴη ἂν ἰδίᾳ λεγόμενον τὸ **ἀκίνητοι κατὰ κύκλον** [**D73.244**], τουτέστιν ἀκίνητα γενόμενα καθ᾽ ἑκάστην περίοδον καὶ
καθ᾽ ἑκάστην τελειότητα, ἣν κύκλον λέγει."

μήποτε δὲ ἀπίθανος ἡ ἀπόστασις τοῦ **ἀκίνητοι
κατὰ κύκλον**, ἅμα δὲ καὶ ἀδιανόητος· δεῖται γὰρ τοῦ
αἰὲν ἔασιν. ἀλλὰ μᾶλλον ῥητέον οὕτως ἀκούειν τὸν
Ἀριστοτέλην, ὅτι καθ᾽ ὅσον μὲν εἰς ἄλληλα ἀεὶ μετα-
βάλλει, ἀΐδιος αὐτῶν ἡ μεταβολὴ καὶ ἡ κίνησις, καθ᾽
ὅσον δὲ ἐνθένδε ἐκεῖσε μεταβάλλοντα τάδε γίνεται,
οἷον ἐκ πολλῶν ἓν ἢ ἐξ ἑνὸς πολλά, καὶ μετὰ τὴν
μεταβολὴν ἵσταται ποτὲ μὲν εἰς τὸ ἓν εἶναι ποτὲ δὲ
εἰς τὸ πολλά, ταύτῃ κατὰ περιόδους ἀεὶ μετὰ τὴν
μεταβολὴν ἀποκαθιστάμενα εἰς τὸ τοῦ ἑνὸς ἢ τὸ τῶν
πολλῶν εἶδος ἀκίνητά ἐστι κατὰ τὴν περίοδον ἐκείνην,
ἕως ἂν πάλιν μεταβάλλειν ἄρξηται. φαίνεται δὲ καὶ
ὁ Θεμίστιος ταύτης τῆς ἐννοίας ἐχόμενος [*in Phys.*,
p. 209.17–20]· τὴν γὰρ ἠρεμίαν ἐν τοῖς μεταξὺ τῶν
μεταβολῶν χρόνοις γίνεσθαί φησι.

R74 (> ad B27, B30, B3) Simpl. *In Phys.*, pp. 1183.21–
1184.18

πλάσματι ἐοικέναι εἰπὼν τὸ λέγειν, ὅτι ὀτὲ μὲν ἦν
κίνησις, ὀτὲ δὲ οὔ, διὰ τὸ μὴ ἔχειν αἰτίαν ἀποδοῦναι
τούτου, ἐφεξῆς φησιν ὅτι καὶ τὸ λέγειν ὅτι πέφυκεν

formation into each other is eternal. For this is what is meant by **'they always are'** [**D73.244**]. This is an exact quotation from Alexander, who continues, "Moreover it would be peculiar if it were to these that the expression **'immobile in a circle'** [**D73.244**] applied, that is that they were immobile in each period and every time that the state of perfection is reached, what he calls a **'circle.'**"

But perhaps it is implausible to separate the phrase **'immobile in a circle'** and at the same time inconceivable: for one needs the phrase **'they always are.'** And it is better to say that Aristotle understands that, to the extent that they are always changing into each other, their change and motion are eternal, but to the extent that these things are generated by changing from here to there, i.e. from the many to the one or from the one to the many, and that after the change there is a stop sometimes in being one, sometimes in being many, in this way, always returning periodically after the change to the form of the One or to that of the many, they are immobile during this period, until the motion begins once again. And Themistius clearly adheres to this view; for he says that rest occurs during the periods of time between the changes.

R74 (> ad B27, B30, B31) Simplicius, *Commentary on Aristotle's* Physics

Having said that to say that at one time there is motion, at another not, resembles a fiction since he can not give a reason for this [cf. **D86a**], he [i.e. Aristotle] then says that

οὕτω, καὶ ταύτην ὡς ἀρχὴν καὶ αἰτίαν ἀποδιδόναι,
ὁμοίως πλασματῶδές ἐστιν. τοῦτο δὲ "ἔοικεν Ἐμπεδοκλῆς ἂν εἰπεῖν," ὅτε λέγει ὅτι "τὸ κρατεῖν καὶ κινεῖν
ἐν μέρει τὴν Φιλίαν καὶ τὸ Νεῖκος ἐξ ἀνάγκης ὑπάρχει τοῖς πράγμασιν," εἰ δὲ καὶ τοῦτο, καὶ τὸ ἠρεμεῖν
ἐν τῷ μεταξὺ χρόνῳ· τῶν γὰρ ἐναντίων κινήσεων
ἠρεμία μεταξύ ἐστιν.

Εὔδημος δὲ τὴν ἀκινησίαν ἐν τῇ τῆς Φιλίας ἐπικρατείᾳ κατὰ τὸν Σφαῖρον ἐκδέχεται [Frag. 110 Wehrli],
ἐπειδὰν ἅπαντα συγκριθῇ, [. . . = **D89.1**], ἀλλ᾿, ὥς
φησιν, [. . . = **D89.3–4,** with textual variants]. ἀρξαμένου
δὲ πάλιν τοῦ Νείκους ἐπικρατεῖν τότε πάλιν κίνησις
ἐν τῷ Σφαίρῳ γίνεται· [. . . = **D95**].

τί δὲ διαφέρει τοῦ 'ὅτι πέφυκεν οὕτως' τὸ 'ἐξ ἀνάγκης' λέγειν αἰτίαν μὴ προστιθέντα; ταῦτα δὲ Ἐμπεδοκλῆς ἔοικε λέγειν ἐν τῷ [. . . = **D73.260**] καὶ ὅτ᾿
ἀνάγκην τῶν γινομένων αἰτιᾶται [. . . = **D10.1–2,** with
textual variants]. διὰ γὰρ τὴν ἀνάγκην καὶ τοὺς ὅρκους
τούτους ἑκάτερον παρὰ μέρος ἐπικρατεῖν φησι. λέγει
δὲ καὶ ταῦτα Ἐμπεδοκλῆς ἐπὶ τῆς τοῦ Νείκους ἐπι-
κρατείας· [. . . = **D95**]. ταῦτα οὖν φησὶ χωρὶς αἰτίας
λεγόμενα οὐδὲν ἄλλο λέγειν ἐστὶν ἢ πέφυκεν οὕτω.

R75 (> ad B57) Simpl. *In Cael.*, pp. 586.5–12, 586.25–
587.26

καὶ ἄλλο ἄτοπον ἐπάγει τοῖς ἄτακτον κίνησιν πρὸ τοῦ
κόσμου λέγουσιν, ὃ διὰ βραχυλογίαν ἀσαφέστερον

to say that things are like this by nature, and to define this as the principle and cause, is just as fictional. This is what is meant by "what Empedocles would seem to have said," when he says that "it happens by necessity for things that Love and Strife alternately dominate and cause motion" [*Phys.* 252a7–9], and if this is the case, it is also the case for rest in the intermediate period. For rest is intermediate between the contrary motions.

Eudemus interprets the immobility during the dominance of Love as referring to the Sphere, when all things are gathered together [. . . = **D89.1**], but, as he says, [. . . = **D89.3–4,** with textual variants]. And when Strife begins to dominate again, then motion in the Sphere begins again: [. . . = **D95**].

But how does saying "by necessity" differ from "because this is how things are by nature" if one does not add the cause? And this is what Empedocles seems to mean in the phrase [. . . = **D73.260**], and when he makes necessity responsible for the things that come about: [. . . = **D10.1– 2,** with textual variants]. For he says that it is because of necessity and these oaths that each of these two dominates in turn. And Empedocles also says this about the dominance of Strife: [. . . = **D95**]. This, then, is what he [i.e. Aristotle] is saying: the cause not being indicated, this means nothing else than "this is how things are by nature."

R75 (> ad B57) Simplicius, *Commentary on Aristotle's* On the Heavens

And against those who accept a disordered motion before the world [scil. the Atomists and Plato], he [i.e. Aristotle] mentions yet another absurdity, which seems rather ob-

δοκεῖ. ἐρωτᾷ δέ, πότερον οὐχ οἷά τε ἦν τότε οὕτω κινεῖσθαι ἀτάκτως, ὥστε "καὶ μίγνυσθαι τοιαύτας μίξεις ἔνια, ἐξ ὧν συνίσταται τὰ κατὰ φύσιν συνιστά-
μενα σώματα, οἷον ὀστᾶ καὶ σάρκες" καὶ ὅλως τὰ τῶν
ζῴων μέρη καὶ τῶν φυτῶν καὶ αὐτὰ τὰ ζῷα καὶ τὰ
φυτά, "καθάπερ Ἐμπεδοκλῆς γίνεσθαί φησιν ἐπὶ τῆς
Φιλότητος λέγων"· [. . . = **D154.1**]. [. . .] [586.25] τὸ δὲ
"καθάπερ Ἐμπεδοκλῆς γίνεσθαί φησιν ἐπὶ τῆς Φιλότητος" ὁ μὲν Ἀλέξανδρος ὡς μίξεως παράδειγμα
ἀκούει, ἐξ ἧς συνίσταται τὰ κατὰ φύσιν σώματα, καὶ
συναίρεσθαι δοκεῖ τῷ λόγῳ αὐτοῦ τὸ ἐπὶ τῆς Φιλότητος τοῦτο λέγεσθαι μίξεως αἰτίας οὔσης ὥσπερ τοῦ
Νείκους διακρίσεως. πῶς δὲ ἂν εἴη μίξεως σημαντι-
κὸν ἡ "ἀναύχενος κόρση" [cf. **D154.1**] καὶ τἆλλα τὰ
ὑπὸ τοῦ Ἐμπεδοκλέους λεγόμενα ἐν τούτοις· [. . . =
D154.2–3], καὶ πολλὰ ἄλλα, ἅπερ οὐκ ἔστι μίξεως
παραδείγματα, ἐξ ἧς τὰ κατὰ φύσιν συνίσταται;

μήποτε οὖν εἰπὼν ὁ Ἀριστοτέλης "πότερον οὐχ οἷά
τε ἦν κινούμενα ἀτάκτως καὶ μίγνυσθαι τοιαύτας μίξεις ἔνια, ἐξ ὧν συνίσταται τὰ κατὰ φύσιν συνιστά-
μενα σώματα" ἐπήγαγε "καθάπερ Ἐμπεδοκλῆς γίνεσθαί φησιν," τουτέστι κινούμενα ἀτάκτως μίγνυσθαι·[1]
τὸ γὰρ πλανᾶσθαι καὶ τὸ πλάζεσθαι ἄτακτον κίνησιν
δηλοῖ.

καὶ πῶς ταῦτα, φαίη ἄν τις, "ἐπὶ τῆς Φιλότητος
γίνεσθαι" λέγει ὁ Ἀριστοτέλης, δι' ἣν πάντα ἓν γίνε-

---

[1] μίγνυσθαι A: μὴ μίγνυσθαι DE

scure because it is stated elliptically. He asks whether it might not be possible that the disordered motion at that time "also produced certain mixtures such that out of them came the bodies that are formed by nature, like bones and flesh" [*On the Heavens* 3.2 300b27–29], and generally speaking the parts of animals and of plants, and the animals and plants themselves, "as Empedocles says that they were born at the time of Love, saying" [. . . = **D154.1**] [*On the Heavens* 3.2 300b29–31]. [. . .] [586.25] Alexander understands the phrase 'as Empedocles says that they are born at the time of Love' as an example of mixture from which are formed the bodies in conformity with nature, and the phrase 'at the time of Love' seems to him to agree with his argument, since Love is the cause of mixture, just as Strife is of separation. But how would the 'faces without necks' [cf. **D154.1**] signify mixture, and the other things Empedocles mentions in the following verses [. . . = **D154.2–3**], and many other things that are not examples of a mixture out of which bodies in conformity with nature are formed?

So perhaps Aristotle, having said, "whether it might not be possible that the disordered motion at that time produced certain mixtures such that out of them came the bodies that are formed by nature," continued, "as Empedocles says that they were born," that is, that things that move without order are mixed. For 'to wander' and 'to go astray' [*planasthai, plazesthai,* cf. **D154.2**] indicate a disordered motion.

But, someone might say, how can Aristotle say that this occurs 'at the time of Love,' when Empedocles says that

σθαι ὁ Ἐμπεδοκλῆς φησιν· [. . . = **D75.5**]; μήποτε οὖν
οὐκ ἐν τῇ ἐπικρατείᾳ τῆς Φιλίας ταῦτα λέγει γενέσθαι
ὁ Ἐμπεδοκλῆς, ὡς ἐνόμισεν Ἀλέξανδρος, ἀλλὰ τότε,
ὅτε οὔπω τὸ Νεῖκος "πᾶν ἐξέστηκεν ἐπ' ἔσχατα τέρματα κύκλου" [**D75.10–13**]. ἐν ταύτῃ οὖν τῇ καταστάσει "μουνομελῆ" ἔτι τὰ γυῖα ἀπὸ τῆς τοῦ Νείκους
διακρίσεως ὄντα ἐπλανᾶτο τῆς πρὸς ἄλληλα μίξεως
ἐφιέμενα. "αὐτὰρ ἐπεὶ κατὰ μεῖζον ἐμίσγετο δαίμονι
δαίμων" [**D149.1**], ὅτε τοῦ Νείκους ἐπεκράτει λοιπὸν
ἡ Φιλότης, "ταῦτά τε συμπίπτεσκον" [. . . = **D149.2–
3**].

ἐπὶ τῆς Φιλότητος οὖν ὁ Ἐμπεδοκλῆς ἐκεῖνα εἶπεν,
οὐχ ὡς ἐπικρατούσης ἤδη τῆς Φιλότητος, ἀλλ' ὡς
μελλούσης ἐπικρατεῖν, ἔτι δὲ τὰ ἄμικτα καὶ [25] μονό-
γυια δηλούσης.

Simplicius' Own Interpretation (R76–R79)

R76 (≠ DK) Simpl. *In Cael.*, p. 294.7–13

ὅτι δὲ οἱ θεολόγοι οὐχ ὡς ἀπὸ χρονικῆς ἀρχῆς, ἀλλ'
ὡς ἀπὸ αἰτίας ποιητικῆς λέγουσι τὴν γένεσιν τοῦ κόσμου καὶ ταύτην μυθικῶς ὥσπερ καὶ τὰ ἄλλα, πρό-
δηλον. Ἐμπεδοκλῆς δὲ ὅτι δύο κόσμους ἐνδείκνυται,
τὸν μὲν ἡνωμένον καὶ νοητόν, τὸν δὲ διακεκριμένον
καὶ αἰσθητόν, καὶ ὅτι καὶ ἐν τούτῳ τῷ κόσμῳ τὴν
ἕνωσιν ὁρᾷ καὶ τὴν διάκρισιν, ἐν ἄλλοις οἶμαι με-
τρίως ἐκ τῶν αὐτοῦ δεδειχέναι ῥημάτων.

through it all things become one: [. . . = **D75.5**]? Perhaps then Empedocles is not saying that this happens under the domination of Love, as Alexander thought, but at the time when Strife had not yet **"withdrawn completely to the farthest limits of the circle"** [**D75.10–13**]. In this situation, then, the limbs that resulted from the separation caused by Strife were wandering, **"isolated parts"** desiring to mix with each other. **"But as a divinity was mixed more with a divinity"** [**D149.1**], when, once Love dominated over Strife, **"These** [scil. the divine elements] **would come together"** [. . . = **D149.2–3**].

So Empedocles said that these events occurred at the time of Love, in the sense not that Love was already dominating, but that it was going to dominate and was still bringing to light things that were unmixed and [25] isolated parts.

Simplicius' Own Interpretation (R76–R79)

R76 (≠ DK) Simplicius, *Commentary on Aristotle's* On the Heavens

It is evident that the theologians speak of the coming into being of the universe understanding this not from a temporal beginning but from an efficient cause, and that they speak of it mythically, just as they speak of everything else. And the fact that Empedocles indicates two worlds, the one unified and intelligible, the other separated and perceptible, and that he sees unification and separation in this world here too, I think that I have shown this sufficiently in other passages, relying upon his own words [cf. the end of **R68**].

R77 (≠ DK) Simpl. *In Phys.*, p. 31.18–23

ἀλλὰ δὴ καὶ Ἐμπεδοκλῆς περί τε τοῦ νοητοῦ κόσμου
καὶ περὶ τοῦ αἰσθητοῦ διδάσκων καὶ ἐκεῖνον τούτου
ἀρχέτυπον παράδειγμα τιθέμενος ἐν ἑκατέρῳ μὲν ἀρχὰς καὶ στοιχεῖα τὰ τέτταρα ταῦτα τέθεικε πῦρ ἀέρα
ὕδωρ καὶ γῆν, καὶ ποιητικὰ αἴτια τὴν Φιλίαν καὶ τὸ
Νεῖκος, πλὴν ὅτι τὰ μὲν ἐν τῷ νοητῷ τῇ νοητῇ ἑνώσει
κρατούμενα διὰ Φιλίας μᾶλλον συνάγεσθαί φησι, τὰ
δὲ ἐν τῷ αἰσθητῷ ὑπὸ τοῦ Νείκους μᾶλλον διακρίνεσθαι.

R78 (≠ DK) Simpl. *In Phys.*, pp. 31.31–32.3

ὅτι γὰρ οὐχ ὡς οἱ πολλοὶ νομίζουσι Φιλία μὲν μόνη
κατ᾽ Ἐμπεδοκλέα τὸν νοητὸν ἐποίησε κόσμον, Νεῖκος
δὲ μόνον τὸν αἰσθητόν, ἀλλ᾽ ἄμφω πανταχοῦ οἰκείως[1]
θεωρεῖ, ἄκουσον αὐτοῦ τῶν ἐν τοῖς Φυσικοῖς λεγομένων, ἐν οἷς καὶ τῆς ἐνταῦθα δημιουργικῆς συγκρά-
σεως τὴν Ἀφροδίτην ἤτοι τὴν Φιλίαν αἰτίαν φησί·
[. . .]. λέγει οὖν πολλαχοῦ μὲν ταῦτα καὶ ἐν τούτοις δὲ
τοῖς ἔπεσιν [. . . = **D190, D75.3–17, D77a3–12, D75,
D77b**, cited at pp. 32.35–34.3].

[1] ὁμοίως coni. Torstrik

R79 (cf. ad B20 et B29) Simpl. *In Phys.*, pp. 1123.25–
1124.18

δεύτερος δὲ τρόπος ὁ κατ᾽ Ἐμπεδοκλέα παρὰ μέρος

R77 (≠ DK) Simplicius, *Commentary on Aristotle's* Physics

But Empedocles, whose teaching too [scil. like Parmenides', cf. **PARM. R16–R18**], bears on both the intelligible world and the perceptible one and posits the former as the archetypal model of the latter, has placed in both of them, as principles and elements, these four—fire, air, water, and earth—and as efficient causes Love and Strife, except that he says that the elements ruled in the intelligible world by the intelligible unification are assembled more by Love, while those in the perceptible world are divided more by Strife.

R78 (≠ DK) Simplicius, *Commentary on Aristotle's* Physics

The fact that it is not the case, as most people think, that Love alone created the intelligible world [i.e. the Sphere] according to Empedocles, and Strife alone the perceptible world, but that he considers both of them everywhere, as is appropriate—listen to what he says about this in the lines of his *Physics* in which he says that Aphrodite, i.e. Love, is the cause of the demiurgic mixture of here too: [. . .] He says this in many passages and in particular in the following verses: [. . . **D190, D75.3–17, D77a3–12, D75, D77b,** cited at pp. 32.35–34.3].

R79 (cf. ad B20 et B29) Simplicius, *Commentary on Aristotle's* Physics

The second way [scil. of conceiving things when one does not admit the eternity of motion] is that of Empedocles,

κίνησιν ποιοῦντα καὶ ἠρεμίαν. ὑπέθετο γὰρ οὗτος τόν
τε νοητὸν καὶ τὸν αἰσθητὸν κόσμον ἐκ τῶν αὐτῶν
στοιχείων τῶν τεττάρων συνεστῶτας, τὸν μὲν παραδειγματικῶς δηλονότι τὸν δὲ εἰκονικῶς, καὶ ποιητικὰ
αἴτια τοῦ μὲν νοητοῦ τὴν Φιλίαν διὰ τῆς ἑνώσεως τὸν
Σφαῖρον ποιοῦσαν, ὃν καὶ θεὸν ἐπονομάζει (καὶ οὐδε-
τέρως ποτὲ καλεῖ [. . . = **D87**]), τοῦ δὲ αἰσθητοῦ τὸ
Νεῖκος, ὅταν ἐπικρατῇ μὴ τελέως, διὰ τῆς διακρίσεως
τὸν κόσμον τοῦτον ποιοῦν. δυνατὸν δὲ καὶ ἐν τούτῳ
τῷ κόσμῳ τήν τε ἕνωσιν ὁρᾶν καὶ τὴν διάκρισιν, τὴν
μὲν κατὰ τὸν οὐρανόν, ὃν ἄν τις καὶ Σφαῖρον καὶ θεὸν
εἰκότως καλέσειε, τὴν δὲ κατὰ τὸ ὑπὸ σελήνην, ὃ
μάλιστα τοῦ κοσμεῖσθαι δεόμενον κόσμος καλεῖται
κυριώτερον. δυνατὸν δὲ καὶ ἐν τῷ ὑπὸ σελήνην ἄμφω
θεωρεῖν τήν τε ἕνωσιν καὶ τὴν διάκρισιν ἀεὶ μὲν
ἄμφω, ἄλλοτε δὲ ἄλλην ἐν ἄλλοις καὶ ἄλλοις μέρεσιν
ἢ ἐν ἄλλοις καὶ ἄλλοις χρόνοις ἐπικρατοῦσαν. καὶ
γὰρ καὶ ἐνταῦθα τὸ Νεῖκος καὶ τὴν Φιλίαν παρὰ
μέρος ἐπικρατεῖν ἐπί τε ἀνθρώπων καὶ ἰχθύων καὶ
θηρίων καὶ ὀρνέων ὁ Ἐμπεδοκλῆς φησι τάδε γράφων·
[. . . = **D73.302–8**].

Empedocles in Christian Authors (R80–R89)
The Quasi-Christian Empedocles of Clement of
Alexandria (R80–R85)

R80 (> ad B145) Clem. Alex. *Protr.* 2.27.3

ταύτῃ τοι ἡμεῖς οἱ τῆς ἀνομίας υἱοί ποτε διὰ τὴν φι-

who posits an alternation of motion and rest. For he assumed that both the intelligible world [i.e. the Sphere] and the perceptible world are composed out of the same four elements, the former, evidently, in the mode of a paradigm, the latter in the mode of an image, and that the efficient causes are, for the intelligible world, Love, which by unification produces the Sphere, which he also calls 'god' (and sometimes speaks of in the neuter [. . . = **D87**]), and, for the perceptible world, Strife, when it dominates incompletely, producing this world here by separation. But it is possible to see in this world here too unification and separation, the former in the heavens, which one might appropriately call "Sphere" and "god," the latter in the sublunar region, which, needing most of all to be ordered, is called "world" (*kosmos*) more properly. And it is possible to observe both of them, unification and separation, in the sublunar region too, now the one dominating, now the other, in different areas or in different periods of time. For the fact that here too Strife and Love dominate in turns, regarding humans, fish, animals, and birds, Empedocles says this when he writes as follows: [. . . = **D73.302–8**].

Empedocles in Christian Authors (R80–R89)
The Quasi-Christian Empedocles of Clement of
Alexandria (R80–R85)

80 (> ad B145) Clement of Alexandria, *Protreptic*

In this way we who were once the sons of lawlessness have

λανθρωπίαν τοῦ λόγου νῦν υἱοὶ γεγόναμεν τοῦ θεοῦ·
ὑμῖν δὲ καὶ ὁ ὑμέτερος ὑποδύεται[1] ποιητὴς ὁ Ἀκραγαντῖνος Ἐμπεδοκλῆς· [. . . = **D30**].

[1] ἀποδύεται Schwartz

R81 (> ad B119) Clem. Alex. *Strom.* 4.13.1

ὅθεν εἰκότως καλούμενος ὁ γνωστικὸς ὑπακούει ῥα-
δίως καὶ τῷ τὸ σωμάτιον αἰτοῦντι φέρων προσδίδωσι
καὶ τὰ πάθη, προαποδυόμενος τοῦ σαρκίου ταῦτα,
οὐχ ὑβρίζων τὸν πειράζοντα, παιδεύων δέ, οἶμαι, καὶ
ἐλέγχων ἐξ οἵης τιμῆς καὶ οἵου μήκεος ὄλβου [**D15**],
ὥς φησιν Ἐμπεδοκλῆς, ὧδε ἐλθὼν[1] μετὰ θνητῶν ἀνα-
στρέφεται.

[1] ἐλθὼν Stählin: λιπὼν ms.: λοιπὸν Potter: <τοιάδε> λιπὼν
Lowth

R82 (> ad B146) Clem. Alex. *Strom.* 4.149.8–150.1

τούτῳ δυνατὸν τῷ τρόπῳ τὸν γνωστικὸν ἤδη γενέσθαι
θεόν· "ἐγὼ εἶπα· θεοί ἐστε καὶ υἱοὶ ὑψίστου." φησὶ δὲ
καὶ ὁ Ἐμπεδοκλῆς τῶν σοφῶν τὰς ψυχὰς θεοὺς γίνεσθαι ὧδέ πως γράφων· [. . . = **D39**].

R83 (cf. ad B114) Clem. Alex. *Strom.* 5.9.1

καί μοι σφόδρα ἐπαινεῖν ἔπεισι τὸν Ἀκραγαντῖνον
ποιητὴν ἐξυμνοῦντα τὴν πίστιν ὧδέ πως· [. . . = **D6**].

now become the sons of God thanks to the love of the Word for human beings. And your poet too, Empedocles of Agrigentum, plays this role (?) for you: [. . . = **D30**].

R81 (> ad B119) Clement of Alexandria, *Stromata*

The man who knows, when he bears this name [scil. *gnôs-tikos*] correctly, yields easily and, putting his poor little body at the disposition of the one who asks for it, he offers him his sufferings too, first stripping away these things from the carnal element; he does not insult the one who is putting him to the test, but teaches him, I think, and shows him **"from what honor and what abundance of bliss"** [**D15**] [scil. he is deprived?], as Empedocles says, coming he passes his life among mortals in this way.

R82 (> ad B146) Clement of Alexandria, *Stromata*

It is in this way that the man who knows (*gnôstikos*) can already become a god: "I have said: you are gods and sons of the Highest" [Ps. 81:6]. And Empedocles too says that the souls of the sages become gods, writing as follows: [. . . = **D39**].

R83 (cf. ad B114) Clement of Alexandria, *Stromata*

And it occurs to me to praise greatly the poet of Agrigentum, who celebrates faith in the following way: [. . . = **D6**].

R84 (ad B147) Clem. Alex. *Strom.* 5.122.3

ἢν δὲ ὁσίως καὶ δικαίως διαβιώσωμεν, μακάριοι μὲν
ἐνταῦθα, μακαριώτεροι δὲ μετὰ τὴν ἐνθένδε ἀπαλλα-
γήν, οὐ χρόνῳ τινὶ τὴν εὐδαιμονίαν ἔχοντες, ἀλλὰ ἐν
αἰῶνι ἀναπαύεσθαι δυνάμενοι [. . . = **D40**], ἡ φιλόσοφος Ἐμπεδοκλέους λέγει ποιητική.

R85 (> A14) Clem. Alex. *Strom.* 6.30.1–4

Ἐμπεδοκλῆς τε ὁ Ἀκραγαντῖνος Κωλυσανέμας ἐπε-
κλήθη. λέγεται οὖν ἀπὸ τοῦ Ἀκράγαντος ὄρους πνέον-
τός ποτε ἀνέμου βαρὺ καὶ νοσῶδες τοῖς ἐγχωρίοις,
ἀλλὰ καὶ ταῖς γυναιξὶν αὐτῶν ἀγονίας αἰτίου γινομένου, παῦσαι τὸν ἄνεμον· διὸ καὶ αὐτὸς ἐν τοῖς ἔπεσι
γράφει· [. . . = **D43.3–5**]. παρακολουθεῖν τε αὐτῷ ἔλεγεν[1] [. . . cf. **D4.10, 12**]. ἄντικρυς γοῦν ἰάσεις τε καὶ
σημεῖα καὶ τέρατα ἐπιτελεῖν τοὺς δικαίους ἐκ τῶν
ἡμετέρων πεπιστεύκασι γραφῶν.

   [1] ἔλεγον ms., corr. Hervet

Empedocles as a Pagan (R86–R89)
Criticisms of Metempsychosis (R86–R87)

R86 (> ad B137) Orig. *Cels.* 5.49

ὅρα δὲ καὶ τὴν διαφορὰν τοῦ αἰτίου τῆς τῶν ἐμψύχων
ἀποχῆς τῶν ἀπὸ τοῦ Πυθαγόρου καὶ τῶν ἐν ἡμῖν
ἀσκητῶν. ἐκεῖνοι μὲν γὰρ διὰ τὸν περὶ ψυχῆς μετεν-

R84 (ad B147) Clement of Alexandria, *Stromata*

If we live our whole lives piously and justly, we shall be blessed here, and even more after our departure from here, for we shall not possess happiness for a certain period of time only, but we shall be able to rest in eternity— [. . . = **D40**], says the philosophical poetry of Empedocles.

R85 (> A14) Clement of Alexandria, *Stromata*

Empedocles of Agrigentum was called 'Wind-stopper' [cf. **P16[60]**]. So it is said that once when a violent and unhealthy wind was blowing from the mountain of Agrigentum upon the inhabitants and was also causing sterility among their women, he stopped the wind. That is why he himself writes in his verses, [. . . = **D43.3–5**]; and he says that people followed him, [. . . = **D4.10, 12**]. Well, the fact that righteous men perform cures, omens, and prodigies—it is precisely on the basis of our Scriptures that they have the assurance of this.

Empedocles as a Pagan (R86–R89)
Criticisms of Metempsychosis (R86–R87)

R86 (> ad B137) Origen, *Against Celsus*

Look at how different the reason is for abstinence from living beings, between Pythagoras' disciples and our ascetics. For the former abstain from living beings because of

σωματουμένης μῦθον ἐμψύχων ἀπέχονται· καί τις[1]
[. . . = **D29.1–2,** with textual variants]· ἡμεῖς δὲ κἂν τὸ
τοιοῦτο πράττωμεν, ποιοῦμεν αὐτό, ἐπεὶ ὑπωπιάζομεν
τὸ σῶμα καὶ δουλαγωγοῦμεν [. . .].

[1] καὶ τίς Koetschau

R87 (≠ DK) Herm. *Irris.* 4

ὅταν δὲ ἐμαυτὸν ἴδω, φοβοῦμαι τὸ σῶμα καὶ οὐκ οἶδα
ὅπως αὐτὸ καλέσω, ἄνθρωπον ἢ κύνα ἢ λύκον ἢ ταῦ-
ρον ἢ ὄρνιν ἢ ὄφιν ἢ δράκοντα ἢ χίμαιραν· εἰς πάντα
γὰρ τὰ θηρία ὑπὸ τῶν φιλοσοφούντων μεταβάλλο-
μαι, χερσαῖα ἔνυδρα πτηνὰ πολύμορφα ἄγρια τι-
θασσὰ ἄφωνα εὔφωνα ἄλογα λογικά· νήχομαι ἵπτα-
μαι ἔρπω θέω καθίζω. ἔτι δὲ ὁ[1] Ἐμπεδοκλῆς καὶ
θάμνον με ποιεῖ.

[1] ἔστι δὲ ὁ mss., corr. Menzel: ἔστι δὲ ὅτε Wolf

Empedocles in the Refutation of
All Heresies *(R88–R89)*
*The Gnostic Empedocles of Marcion and
His Disciples (R88)*

R88 (> ad B131) (Ps.-?) Hipp. *Haer.* 7.29.1–3 et 31.2–4

[29.1–3] Μαρκίων δὲ ὁ Ποντικὸς πολὺ τούτων μανι-
κώτερος, τὰ πολλὰ τῶν πλειόνων παραπεμψάμενος
ἐπὶ τὸ ἀναιδέστερον ὁρμήσας δύο ἀρχὰς τοῦ παντὸς

the myth of the metempsychosis of the soul; and someone [scil. says,] [. . . = **D29.1–2**]. But we, even if we act in the same way, we do so because we mortify the body and treat it as a slave [. . .].

R87 (≠ DK) Hermias, *Derision of Gentile Philosophers*

When I look at myself, I am afraid of my body and I do not know what to call it, human, dog, wolf, bull, bird, snake, dragon, or chimera. For I am transformed by the philosophers into all kinds of animals, terrestrial, aquatic, winged, polymorphic, wild, domestic, mute, voiced, irrational, rational. I swim, I fly, I crawl, I run, I sit. And what is more, Empedocles turns me into a bush too [cf. **D13.2**].

Empedocles in the Refutation of All Heresies *(R88–R89)*
The Gnostic Empedocles of Marcion and His Disciples (R88)

R88 (> ad B131) (Ps.-?) Hippolytus, *Refutation of All Heresies*

[29.1–3] Marcion of Pontus, much more insane than them [i.e. the Gnostics Basilides and Saturnilus], after rejecting much of what most people believe and rushing off into greater shamelessness, posited two principles of the uni-

ὑπέθετο, ἀγαθόν ⟨θεόν⟩[1] τινα λέγων καὶ τὸν ἕτερον
πονηρόν· καὶ αὐτὸς δὲ νομίζων καινόν τι παρεισαγα-
γεῖν σχολὴν ἐσκεύασεν ἀπονοίας γέμουσαν καὶ κυνι-
κοῦ βίου, ὧν τις μάχιμος·[2] οὗτος[3] νομίζων λήσεσθαι
τοὺς πολλούς ὅτι μὴ Χριστοῦ τυγχάνοι μαθητὴς ἀλλ᾽
Ἐμπεδοκλέους πολὺ αὐτοῦ[4] προγενεστέρου τυγχάνον-
τος, ταὐτὰ[5] ὁρίσας ἐδογμάτισε δύο εἶναι τὰ τοῦ παντὸς αἴτια, Νεῖκος καὶ Φιλίαν. [. . .]

[31.2–4] τρίτην φάσκων δίκαιον εἶναι ἀρχὴν καὶ μέ-
σην ἀγαθοῦ καὶ κακοῦ τεταγμένην, οὐδ᾽ οὕτως[6] δὴ[7] ὁ
Πρέπων τὰς[8] Ἐμπεδοκλέους διαφυγεῖν ἴσχυσε δόξας.
κόσμον γάρ φησιν εἶναι ὁ Ἐμπεδοκλῆς τὸν ὑπὸ τοῦ
Νείκους διοικούμενον τοῦ πονηροῦ καὶ ἕτερον νοητὸν
τὸν ὑπὸ τῆς Φιλίας, καὶ εἶναι ταύτας τὰς διαφερού-
σας ἀρχὰς δύο ἀγαθοῦ καὶ κακοῦ, μέσον δὲ εἶναι τῶν
διαφόρων ἀρχῶν δίκαιον λόγον, καθ᾽ ὃν συγκρίνεται
τὰ διῃρημένα ὑπὸ τοῦ Νείκους καὶ προσαρμόζεται
κατὰ τὴν Φιλίαν τῷ ἑνί. τοῦτον δὲ αὐτὸν τὸν δίκαιον
λόγον τὸν τῇ Φιλίᾳ συναγωνιζόμενον Μοῦσαν ὁ Ἐμπεδοκλῆς προσαγορεύων,[9] καὶ αὐτὸς αὐτῷ[10] συναγω-
νίζεσθαι παρακαλεῖ, λέγων ὧδέ πως· [. . . = **D7**].

---

[1] ⟨θεόν⟩ Marcovich   [2] μάχλος coni. Miller, μανικός
Duncker-Schneidewin   [3] ὅτι ms., corr. Miller: ὃς Marcovich
[4] αὐτῷ ms., corr. Cruice   [5] ταῦτα ms., corr. Duncker-
Schneidewin   [6] οὗτος ms., corr. Duncker-Schneidewin
[7] δὲ ms., corr. Miller   [8] τῆς ms., Duncker-Schneidewin
[9] προσαγορεύει Marcovich   [10] αὐτῷ ms., corr. Miller

verse, one good god and another evil one. And as he himself thought that he had introduced a novelty, he founded a school filled with madness and a Cynic way of life, for he was combative. This man, thinking that most people would not notice that he was a disciple not of Christ but of Empedocles, who belonged to a much earlier time than he did, made the same definitions and taught that there are two causes of the universe, Strife and Love. [. . .]

[31.2–4] Prepon [i.e. a disciple of Marcion] asserted that there is a third, just principle, located in the middle between good and evil, but not even in this way did he manage to escape Empedocles' opinions. For Empedocles says that there is a world administered by wicked Strife and another, intelligible one, administered by Love, and that these are the two different principles, of good and of evil, but that in the middle of the different principles is located just reason (*logos*), in virtue of which what is divided by Strife is assembled and fitted together to the one in conformity with Love. This just reason (*logos*), which is an ally with Love in its combat, Empedocles calls a Muse, and he calls upon her to be his ally in his combat, speaking as follows: [. . . = **D7**].

EARLY GREEK PHILOSOPHY V

The Presentation of Empedocles' Doctrine in the
Refutation of All Heresies *(R89)*

R89 (cf. A33 et ad B16, B29, B110, B115, B131) (Ps.-?)
Hipp. *Haer.* 7.29.3–31.4

[29.3] τί γάρ φησιν ὁ Ἐμπεδοκλῆς περὶ τῆς τοῦ κόσμου διαγωγῆς εἰ καὶ προείπομεν, ἀλλά γε καὶ νῦν
πρὸς τὸ ἀντιπαραθεῖναι τῇ τοῦ κλεψιλόγου αἱρέσει οὐ
σιωπήσομαι.

[The physical system (1)]

[4] οὗτός φησιν εἶναι τὰ πάντα στοιχεῖα, ἐξ ὧν ὁ κόσμος συνέστηκε καὶ ἔστιν, ἕξ, δύο μὲν ὑλικά, γῆν καὶ
ὕδωρ, δύο δὲ ὄργανα, οἷς τὰ ὑλικὰ κοσμεῖται καὶ
μεταβάλλεται, πῦρ καὶ ἀέρα, δύο δὲ τὰ ἐργαζόμενα
τοῖς ὀργάνοις τὴν ὕλην καὶ δημιουργοῦντα, Νεῖκος
καὶ Φιλίαν, λέγων ὧδέ πως· [citation and exegesis of
D57; cf. **R92**].

[8] καὶ ἡ μὲν Φιλία εἰρήνη τίς ἐστι καὶ ὁμόνοια καὶ
στοργὴ ἕνα τέλειον[1] κατηρτισμένον εἶναι προαιρου-
μένη τὸν κόσμον, τὸ δὲ Νεῖκος ἀεὶ διασπᾷ τὸν ἕνα
καὶ κατακερματίζει ἢ ἀπεργάζεται ἐξ ἑνὸς πολλά.
[9] ἔστι μὲν οὖν τὸ μὲν Νεῖκος αἴτιον τῆς κτίσεως
πάσης, ὅ φησιν 'οὐλόμενον' εἶναι [**D73.250**], τουτέστιν ὀλέθριον· μέλει γὰρ αὐτῷ ὅπως διὰ παντὸς
αἰῶνος ἡ κτίσις αὕτη[2] συνεστήκῃ[3] καὶ ἔστι πάντων
τῶν γεγονότων τῆς γενέσεως δημιουργὸς καὶ ποιητὴς
τὸ Νεῖκος τὸ ὀλέθριον, τῆς δὲ ἐκ τοῦ κόσμου τῶν

The Presentation of Empedocles' Doctrine in the
Refutation of All Heresies *(R89)*

R89 (cf. A33 and ad B16, B29, B110, B115, B131) (Ps.-?)
Hippolytus, *Refutation of All Heresies*

[29.3] For as for what Empedocles says about how the
world is conducted [cf. **R41, R88**], even if I have stated it
earlier [cf. 6.25.2–4], I shall not pass it over in silence now
either, in order to compare it with the sect of the plagiarist
[i.e. Marcion].

[The physical system (1)]

[4] He says that all the elements from which the world has
been constituted and composed are six: two that act as
matter, earth and water; two as instruments thanks to
which the material ones are organized and transformed,
fire and air; and two work on the matter thanks to these
instruments and fashion it, Strife and Love. He speaks as
follows: [citation and exegesis of **D57**; cf. **R92**].

[8] And Love is a kind of peace and unanimity and fond-
ness that chooses that the world be one, perfect, well adjusted; Strife by contrast always tears apart [scil. the
world], which is one, chops it into pieces, or makes many
out of one. [9] Thus Strife is the cause of all creation; he
says that it is **'baleful'** [**D73.250**], that is, destructive, for
it matters to him that this creation continue throughout
all eternity. And destructive Strife is the demiurge and
craftsman of the birth of all the things that are born, while

---

¹ τέλειον ‹καὶ› Miller
Duncker-Schneidewin
Schneidewin

² αὕτη Cruice: αὐτὴ ms.: αὐτὴ
³ συνέστηκε ms., corr. Duncker-
Schneidewin

γεγονότων ἐξαγωγῆς καὶ μεταβολῆς καὶ εἰς τὸ ἕν[4]
ἀποκαταστάσεως ἡ Φιλία· [10] [. . .]. τὸ δὲ πῦρ ‹καὶ
τὸ ὕδωρ›[5] καὶ ἡ γῆ καὶ ὁ ἀὴρ θνήσκοντα καὶ ἀνα-
βιοῦντα. [11] ὅταν μὲν γὰρ ἀποθάνῃ τὰ[6] ὑπὸ τοῦ
Νείκους γινόμενα, παραλαμβάνουσα αὐτὰ ἡ Φιλία
προσάγει καὶ προστίθησι καὶ προσοικειοῖ τῷ παντί,
ἵνα μένῃ τὸ πᾶν ἕν, ὑπὸ τῆς Φιλίας ἀεὶ διακοσμούμε-
νον μονοτρόπως καὶ μονοειδῶς. [12] ὅταν δὲ ἡ Φιλία
ἐκ πολλῶν ποιήσῃ τὸ ἓν καὶ τὰ διεσπασμένα προσοι-
κειώσῃ[7] τῷ ἑνί, πάλιν τὸ Νεῖκος ἀπὸ τοῦ ἑνὸς ἀποσπᾷ
καὶ ποιεῖ πολλά, τουτέστι πῦρ, ὕδωρ, γῆν, ἀέρα, τά
‹τ᾽›[8] ἐκ τούτων γεννώμενα ζῷα καὶ φυτὰ καὶ ὅσα
μέρη τοῦ κόσμου κατανοοῦμεν. [13] καὶ περὶ μὲν τῆς
τοῦ κόσμου ἰδέας, ὁποία τίς ἐστιν ὑπὸ τῆς Φιλίας
κοσμουμένη, λέγει τοιοῦτόν τινα τρόπον· [. . . = **D92**;
cf. **D93.2–3**].

---

[4] τὸν ἕνα ms., corr. Sauppe   [5] ‹καὶ τὸ ὕδωρ› Duncker-
Schneidewin   [6] τὰ Wendland: ταῦτα ms.   [7] προσοι-
κειώσῃ Roeper: προοικονομήσει ms.: προσοικονομήσῃ Miller:
προσοικοδομήσῃ Marcovich   [8] ‹τ᾽› Marcovich: ‹καὶ› τὰ
coni. Sauppe

[The case of Empedocles]

[14] καὶ τοῦτό ἐστιν ὃ λέγει περὶ τῆς ἑαυτοῦ γεννή-
σεως ὁ Ἐμπεδοκλῆς· "**τῶν καὶ ἐγώ εἰμι, φυγὰς θεόθεν καὶ ἀλήτης**" [= corrupted citation of **D10.13**],
τουτέστι θεὸν καλῶν τὸ ἓν καὶ τὴν ἐκείνου ἑνότητα,
ἐν ᾧ ἦν πρὶν ὑπὸ τοῦ Νείκους ἀποσπασθῆναι καὶ
γενέσθαι ἐν τοῖς πολλοῖς τούτοις τοῖς κατὰ τὴν τοῦ

Love is the cause of the departure out of the world of the things that are born and of their transformation and restoration in the One [10] [. . .]. Fire, ‹water,› earth, and air die and are reborn. [11] For when the things generated by Strife die, Love takes them over and leads, adds, and assimilates them to the whole, so that the whole remain one, and eternally organized by Love in the mode of unicity and of unity. [12] But when Love makes one out of the many and assimilates to the One the things that have been torn apart, then in turn Strife tears them away from the One and makes them many, that is fire, water, earth, air, and what is born out of these: animals, plants, and all the parts of the world that we perceive. [13] And regarding what the configuration of the world is as it is organized by Love, he speaks as follows: [. . . = **D92;** cf. **D93.2–3**].

[The case of Empedocles]
[14] And this is what Empedocles says about his own birth: **"Of them, I too am one, an exile from the divine and a wanderer"** [**D10.13**], that is, calling 'god' the one and unity, in which he existed before he was torn away by Strife and was born amidst this multiplicity here which belongs

Νείκους διακόσμησιν· [15] **Νείκει** γάρ φησι [. . . = corrupted citation of **D10.14**], ‹Νεῖκος μαι›νόμενον¹ καὶ τετα‹ρα›γμένον² καὶ ἄστατον τὸν δημιουργὸν το‹ῦ›δε³ τοῦ κόσμου ὁ Ἐμπεδοκλῆς ἀποκαλῶν. αὕτη γάρ ἐστιν ἡ καταδίκη καὶ ἀνάγκη τῶν ψυχῶν, ὧν ἀποσπᾷ τὸ Νεῖκος ἀπὸ τοῦ ἑνὸς καὶ δημιουργεῖ καὶ ἐργάζεται, λέγων τοιοῦτόν τινα τρόπον· [citation and paraphrase of **D10**].

¹ ‹Νεῖκος μαι›νόμενον Duncker-Schneidewin
² τετα‹ρα›γμένον Miller
³ τὸ δὲ ms., corr. Roeper: τό‹ν›δε Miller

[Moral consequences (1)]

[22] διὰ τὴν τοιαύτην οὖν τοῦ ὀλεθρίου Νείκους δια-κόσμησιν τοῦδε τοῦ μεμερισμένου κόσμου πάντων¹ ἐμψύχων ὁ Ἐμπεδοκλῆς τοὺς ἑαυτοῦ μαθητὰς ἀπέχε-σθαι παρακαλεῖ· εἶναι γάρ φησι τὰ σώματα τῶν ζῴων τὰ ἐσθιόμενα ψυχῶν κεκολασμένων οἰκητήρια· καὶ ἐγκρατεῖς εἶναι τοὺς τῶν τοιούτων λόγων ἀκροω-μένους τῆς πρὸς γυναῖκα ὁμιλίας διδάσκει, ἵνα μὴ συνεργάζωνται καὶ συνεπιλαμβάνωνται τῶν ἔργων ὧν δημιουργεῖ τὸ Νεῖκος, τὸ τῆς Φιλίας ἔργον λύον ἀεὶ καὶ διασπῶν. [23] τοῦτον εἶναί φησιν ὁ Ἐμπεδο-κλῆς νόμον μέγιστον τῆς τοῦ παντὸς διοικήσεως, λέ-γων ὧδέ πως· [. . . = **D10.1–2**] ἀνάγκην καλῶν τὴν ἐξ ἑνὸς εἰς πολλὰ κατὰ τὸ Νεῖκος καὶ ἐκ πολλῶν εἰς ἓν κατὰ τὴν Φιλίαν μεταβολήν·

to the organization of Strife: [15] for he says, **"on Strife"**
[... = corrupted citation of **D10.14**], Empedocles calling
the demiurge of this world **'insane'** (disturbed and unstable) ‹**'Strife'**.› For such is the condemnation and torture of the souls that Strife tears away from the one and
creates and fashions—he speaks as follows: [citation and
paraphrase of **D10**].

[Moral consequences (1)]

[22] It is therefore because of this sort of organization by
destructive Strife of this divided world that Empedocles
calls upon his disciples to abstain from all living beings.
For he says that the bodies of animals that are eaten are
the dwellings of souls that have been punished. And he
teaches those who listen to such arguments to refrain from
intercourse with a woman, so that they will not associate
with and collaborate in the works that Strife creates, which
always dissolves and tears apart the work of Love. [23]
Empedocles says that this is the greatest law of the organization of the whole, when he speaks as follows: [... =
D10.1–2], calling 'Necessity' the change of one into many
according to Strife and that of many into one according to
Love.

---

1 πάντως Klostermann: πάντων ‹τῶν› coni. Wendland

[The physical system (2)]

θεοὺς δέ, ὡς ἔφην, τέσσαρας μὲν θνητούς, πῦρ, ὕδωρ,
γῆν, ἀέρα, δύο δὲ ἀθανάτους, ἀγενήτους,[1] πολεμίους
ἑαυτοῖς διὰ παντός, τὸ Νεῖκος καὶ τὴν Φιλίαν· [24] καὶ
τὸ μὲν Νεῖκος ἀδικεῖν διὰ παντὸς καὶ πλεονεκτεῖν καὶ
ἀποσπᾶν τὰ τῆς Φιλίας καὶ ἑαυτῷ προσνέμειν, τὴν δὲ
Φιλίαν ἀεὶ καὶ διὰ παντός, ἀγαθήν τινα οὖσαν καὶ
τῆς ἑνότητος ἐπιμελουμένην, τὰ ἀπεσπασμένα τοῦ
παντὸς καὶ βεβασανισμένα καὶ κεκολασμένα ἐν τῇ
κτίσει ὑπὸ τοῦ δημιουργοῦ ἀνακαλεῖσθαι καὶ προσ-
άγειν[2] καὶ ἓν ποιεῖν.[3] [25] τοιαύτη[4] τις ἡ κατὰ τὸν Ἐμπεδοκλέα ἡμῖν ἡ τοῦ κόσμου γένεσις καὶ φθορὰ καὶ
σύστασις ἐξ ἀγαθοῦ καὶ κακοῦ συνεστῶσα φιλοσο-
φεῖται.

[1] ἀγενήτους corr. Wendland: ἀγεννήτους mss.   [2] προσ-
άγειν ⟨τῷ παντὶ⟩ Marcovich   [3] ἓν ποιεῖν Duncker-
Schneidewin: ἐμποιεῖν ms.   [4] τοιαύτη ⟨δή⟩ Marcovich

[The third power]

[29.25] εἶναι δέ φησι καὶ νοητὴν[1] τρίτην τινὰ δύναμιν,
ἣν καὶ ἐκ τούτων ἐπινοεῖσθαι δύνασθαι, λέγων ὧδέ
πως· [. . . = **D257**].

[1] καινὸν τὴν ms., corr. Miller

[Moral consequences (2)]

[30.3] κωλύεις γαμεῖν, τεκνοῦν, ⟨. . .⟩[1] ἀπέχεσθαι βρω-
μάτων, ὧν ὁ θεὸς ἔκτισεν εἰς μετάληψιν τοῖς πιστοῖς
καὶ ἐπεγνωκόσι τὴν ἀλήθειαν· τοὺς Ἐμπεδοκλέους
λανθάνεις διδάσκων Καθαρμούς.[2] [4] ἑπόμενος γὰρ ὡς

[The physical system (2)]

As for the gods, as I have said, there are four mortal ones, fire, water, earth, and air, and two immortal ones, ungenerated, eternally enemies of each other, Strife and Love. [24] And Strife eternally commits injustice, is greedy, tears apart the works of Love and attributes them to itself, while Love, which is good and cares for unity, restores each time and eternally what has been torn away from the whole and tortured and punished in creation by the demiurge, and calls upon it and leads it forward and unifies it. [25] Such is the generation and destruction of the world and its condition constituted from good and evil, such as Empedocles' philosophy presents it to us.

[The third power]

[29.25] He says that there also exists a third, intelligible power, which can be conceived on the basis of these [i.e. verses], when he speaks as follows: [. . . = **D257**].

[Moral consequences (2)]

[30.3] [Speaking to Marcion:] You forbid marriage, procreation, ‹. . . and you demand (?)› abstinence from the food that God created to be received by the faithful and those who confess the truth [cf. 1 Tim. 4:3]. You do not realize that you are teaching Empedocles' *Purifications* [or: purifications]. [4] For you follow him truly on all top-

---

¹ an ‹ἀπαιτεῖς›?   ² ‹εἶτ᾽ οὐ› τοὺς . . . Καθαρμούς; Marcovich

ἀληθῶς κατὰ πάντα τούτῳ τὰ βρώματα παραιτεῖσθαι
τοὺς ἑαυτοῦ μαθητὰς διδάσκεις, ἵνα μὴ φάγωσι σῶμά
τι λείψανον ψυχῆς ὑπὸ τοῦ δημιουργοῦ κεκολασμένης·
λύεις τοὺς ὑπὸ τοῦ θεοῦ συνηρμοσμένους γάμους τοῖς
Ἐμπεδοκλέους ἀκολουθῶν δόγμασιν, ἵνα σοι φυλα-
χθῇ τὸ τῆς Φιλίας ἔργον ἓν ἀδιαίρετον. διαιρεῖ γὰρ ὁ
γάμος κατὰ Ἐμπεδοκλέα τὸ ἓν καὶ ποιεῖ πολλά, κα-
θὼς ἀπεδείξαμεν.

Allegorical Interpretations (R90–R100)
Disparate Interpretations of the Names of the
Elements in D57 (R90–R92)

R90 (< A33) Aët. 1.3.20 (Ps.-Plut.; cf. Stob.) [περὶ τῶν
ἀρχῶν τί εἰσιν]

φησὶ δ᾽ οὕτως· [. . . = **D57**]. Δία μὲν γὰρ λέγει τὴν
ζέσιν καὶ τὸν αἰθέρα, Ἥρην δὲ **φερέσβιον** τὸν ἀέρα,
τὴν δὲ γῆν τὸν Ἀϊδωνέα,[1] Νῆστιν δὲ καὶ **κρούνωμα
βρότειον** οἱονεὶ τὸ σπέρμα καὶ τὸ ὕδωρ.

[1] Ἥρην . . . Ἀϊδωνέα] Ἥρην δὲ φερέσβιον τὴν γῆν, ἀέρα
δὲ τὸν Ἀϊδωνέα, ἐπειδὴ φῶς οἰκεῖον οὐκ ἔχει, ἀλλὰ ὑπὸ ἡλίου
καὶ σελήνης καὶ ἄστρων καταλάμπεται Stob.

R91 (< A1) Diog. Laert. 8.76

φησὶ δ᾽ οὕτω· [. . . = **D57.2–3**], Δία μὲν τὸ πῦρ λέγων,
Ἥρην δὲ τὴν γῆν, Ἀϊδωνέα δὲ τὸν ἀέρα, Νῆστιν δὲ
τὸ ὕδωρ.

ics when you teach your disciples to refuse meats so that they do not eat any body, the remains of a soul that has been punished by the demiurge; when you dissolve the marriages that have been fitted together by God, following Empedocles' teachings, so that the action of Love remain one and indivisible. For according to Empedocles marriage divides the one and makes it many, as we have shown.

Allegorical Interpretations (R90–R100)
Disparate Interpretations of the Names of the
Elements in D57 (R90–R92)

R90 (< A33) Aëtius

He says this [scil. about the principles]: [. . . = **D57**]. For he calls boiling and aether **'Zeus,'** air **'life-giving Hera,'** earth **'Aidoneus,'**[1] and **'Nêstis'** and **'mortal fountain'** are the seed and water.

[1] In the version in Stobaeus, Hera is identified with the earth and Aidoneus with the air "because it does not have its own light but is illuminated by the sun, the moon, and the stars."

R91 (< A1) Diogenes Laertius

He says this: [. . . = **D57.2–3**], calling fire **'Zeus,'** earth **'Hera,'** air **'Aidoneus,'** water **'Nêstis.'**

R92 (< A33) (Ps.-?) Hipp. *Haer.* 7.29.5–6

[. . . cf. **R89 [29.4]**] [5] Ζεύς ἐστι τὸ πῦρ, Ἥρη δὲ φερέσβιος ἡ γῆ ἡ φέρουσα τοὺς πρὸς τὸν βίον καρ-
πούς, Ἀϊδωνεὺς δὲ ὁ ἀήρ, ὅτι πάντα δι᾿ αὐτοῦ βλέπον-
τες μόνον αὐτὸν οὐ καθορῶμεν, Νῆστις δὲ τὸ ὕδωρ·
μόνον γὰρ τοῦτο ὄχημα τροφῆς αἴτιον γινόμενον
πᾶσι τοῖς τρεφομένοις, αὐτὸ καθ᾿ αὐτὸ τρέφειν οὐ δυνάμενον τὰ τρεφόμενα. [6] εἰ γὰρ ἔτρεφε, φησίν, οὐκ
ἄν ποτε λιμῷ κατελήφθη τὰ ζῷα, ὕδατος ἐν τῷ κόσμῳ
πλεονάζοντος ἀεί. διὰ τοῦτο ‘Νῆστιν’ καλεῖ τὸ ὕδωρ,
ὅτι τροφῆς αἴτιον γινόμενον τρέφειν οὐκ εὐτονεῖ τὰ
τρεφόμενα [. . .].

Other Allegories Relating to Divinities (R93–R97)

R93 (B19) Plut. *Prim. frig.* 16 952B

καὶ ὅλως τὸ μὲν πῦρ διαστατικόν ἐστι καὶ διαιρετικόν, τὸ δ᾿ ὕδωρ κολλητικὸν καὶ σχετικόν, τῇ ὑγρότητι
συνέχον καὶ πιέζον· ᾗ καὶ παρέσχεν Ἐμπεδοκλῆς
ὑπόνοιαν, ὡς τὸ μὲν πῦρ "Νεῖκος οὐλόμενον" [**D62a,
73.250**], "σχεδύνην δὲ Φιλότητα" [**D62b**] τὸ ὑγρὸν
ἑκάστοτε προσαγορεύων.

R94 (ad B27 Diels PPF) Ach. Tat. *Introd. Arat.* 6

στρέφεται δὲ τὸ πᾶν αὐτὸ περὶ αὐτὸ ὁσημέραι καὶ

R92 (< A33) (Ps.-?) Hippolytus, *Refutation of All Heresies*

[. . .] [5] Zeus is fire; life-giving Hera the earth that bears fruits for the sake of life; Aidoneus the air, because we see all things through it but it is the only thing that we do not see; Nêstis is water. For this vehicle is only the cause of nourishment for everything that is nourished, but by itself it is not capable of nourishing what is nourished. [6] For if it nourished, he says, living beings would never die of hunger, since water is always abundantly present in the world. That is why he calls water **'Nêstis'** [i.e. "not eating"] because although it is the cause of nourishment it does not have the power to nourish what is nourished.

Other Allegories Relating to Divinities (R93–R97)

R93 (B19) Plutarch, *On the Principle of Cold*

And in general fire has the power to separate and to divide, water to unify and to retain, by means of its moisture holding together and compressing; Empedocles gave this allegorical expression, each time calling fire **'baleful Strife'** [**D62a, 73.250**] and moisture **'Love that holds together'** [**D62b**].

R94 (≠ DK) Achilles Tatius, *Introduction to Aratus' Phaenomena*

The whole turns around itself every day and every hour,

EARLY GREEK PHILOSOPHY V

ὧραι, καθὸ καὶ ὁ Ἀκραγαντῖνός[1] φησι [. . . = **D90.2**],
'Σφαῖρον'[2] μὲν καλέσας τὴν σφαῖραν, ὡς καὶ Ὅμηρος
ἕσπερον[3] τὴν ἑσπέραν, 'κυκλοτερῆ'[4] δὲ διὰ τὸ σφαιροειδές, 'μονίαν'[5] δὲ 'περιηγέα' τῆς στροφῆς τὴν μονήν.

[1] ἀσκραῖος ms., corr. Maass   [2] σφαῖραν ms., corr.
Maass   [3] ἑσπέριον ms., corr. Maass   [4] καὶ ante κυκλοτερῆ hab. ms., secl. Maass   [5] μανίαν ms., corr. Maass

R95 (ad B134) Ammon. *In Interp.*, p. 249.1–11

[. . .] ὁ Ἀκραγαντῖνος σοφὸς ἐπιρραπίσας[1] τοὺς περὶ
θεῶν ὡς ἀνθρωποειδῶν ὄντων παρὰ τοῖς ποιηταῖς λε-
γομένους μύθους, ἐπήγαγε προηγουμένως μὲν περὶ
Ἀπόλλωνος, περὶ οὗ ἦν αὐτῷ προσεχῶς[2] ὁ λόγος,
κατὰ δὲ τὸν αὐτὸν τρόπον καὶ περὶ τοῦ θείου παντὸς
ἁπλῶς ἀποφαινόμενος [. . . = **D93**], διὰ τοῦ 'ἱερὴ' καὶ
τὴν ὑπὲρ νοῦν αἰνιττόμενος αἰτίαν [. . .].

[1] ἐπιρραπίζων M   [2] προσεχὴς A

R96 (< A23) Men. Rh. *Div. Epid.* 1, pp. 333.12–14,
337.1–7

φυσικοὶ δὲ οἵους οἱ[1] περὶ Παρμενίδην[2] καὶ Ἐμπεδοκλέα ἐποίησαν,[3] τίς ἡ τοῦ Ἀπόλλωνος φύσις, τίς ἡ τοῦ
Διός, παρατιθέμενοι. [. . .] εἰσὶ δὲ τοιοῦτοι,[4] ὅταν
Ἀπόλλωνος ὕμνον λέγοντες ἥλιον αὐτὸν εἶναι φάσκω-
μεν, καὶ περὶ τοῦ ἡλίου τῆς φύσεως διαλεγώμεθα, καὶ
περὶ Ἥρας ὅτι ἀήρ, καὶ Ζεὺς τὸ θερμόν· οἱ γὰρ

just as the man from Agrigentum says [. . . = **D90.2**], calling the Sphere [*sphaira*] 'Sphairos' as Homer says *hespe-
ros* for *hespera* [i.e. the evening], 'round' because of its
sphericity, and 'circular solitude' (*monia*) because of the
constancy (*monê*) of its turning.

R95 (ad B134) Ammonius, *Commentary on Aristotle's*
On Interpretation

[. . .] the sage of Agrigentum, after having inveighed
against the myths told by the poets about gods supposed
to be of human form, continued, first of all about Apollo
(whom in particular his discourse concerned) but also in
the same way about all divinity in general, declaring [. . .
= **D93**], indicating allegorically with the word **'holy'** the
cause that is superior to the intellect [. . .].

R96 (< A23) Menander Rhetor, *On Epideictic Speeches*

Physical are the ones [i.e. hymns] that Parmenides and
Empedocles composed, explaining what Apollo's nature
is, what Zeus'. [. . .] It is ones of this sort, whenever, reciting a hymn to Apollo, we declare that he is the sun, and
discuss the nature of the sun, and [scil. we say] that Hera
is the air, and Zeus heat. For hymns of this sort are a form

---

1 τοι ὅσοι ms., corr. Bursian

2 παρὰ πᾶν μέρος ms., corr. Heeren

3 ἐτίμησαν ms., corr. Bernhardy

4 τοιοῦτοι edd.: de ms. non liquet

τοιοῦτοι ὕμνοι φυσιολογικοί. καὶ χρῶνται δὲ τῷ τοιούτῳ τρόπῳ Παρμενίδης τε καὶ Ἐμπεδοκλῆς ἀκριβῶς
[. . .].

R97 (cf. ad B123) Corn. *Theol.*, p. 30.2–8

οὗτοι δ᾽ ἂν εἶεν διαφοραὶ τῶν ὄντων. ὡς γὰρ Ἐμπεδοκλῆς φυσικῶς ἐξαριθμεῖται [. . . = **D22**] καὶ πολλὰς
ἄλλας,[1] τὴν εἰρημένην ποικιλίαν τῶν ὄντων αἰνιττόμενος [. . .].

[1] ἄλλαι πολλαὶ Osann

A Categorial Interpretation of
Empedocles' Cycle (R98)

R98 (65 Mansfeld-Primavesi) Schol. in Arist. *Cat.* 6a36,
p. 310

ὁ δὲ Ἀλέξανδρος, δεικνὺς ὅτι φυσικῇ τάξει προετάγη-
σαν, τοῦτο πιστοῖ μὲν καὶ τὸν Ἐμπεδοκλέα παρ-
ιστῶν δοξάζοντα πρώτως μὲν στοιχεῖα δ᾽, ἐν οἷς
εὐθὺς τὸ ποσόν· εἶτα συνερχόμενα καὶ εἰρηνεύοντα, ἐν
ᾧ ἡ σχέσις ἐν ᾗ τὰ πρός τι, τὸν νοητὸν ἀνελεῖν διά-
κοσμον· Νεῖκος δὲ πάλιν σχόντα, ὅπερ κατὰ τὰς ποι-
ότητάς ἐστιν ἐν ᾧ τὸ ποιόν, τὰ ὑπὸ τὴν αἴσθησιν
ἐμφαίνεσθαι.

of natural philosophy. Parmenides and Empedocles make use of this kind in a precise way [. . .].

R97 (cf. ad B123) Cornutus, *Greek Theology*

They [scil. the Titans] will be the differences among beings. For just as Empedocles enumerates, as a natural philosopher [. . . = **D22**], and many others, indicating allegorically the great diversity of beings mentioned earlier [. . .].

*A Categorical Interpretation
of Empedocles' Cycle (R98)*

R98 (≠ DK) Scholia on Aristotle's *Categories*

Alexander, having shown that they [scil. the categories of the relative and of quality] were previously arranged [scil. by Aristotle] in a natural order,[1] confirms this by citing as a witness Empedocles too, whose opinion is [scil. that there are] first of all four elements, in which quantity is found first of all; then the intelligible order of the world suppresses [scil. them] while they are coming together and are in a state of peace, which is the moment of the state of things (*skhesis*) in which the relatives[2] are located; and then receiving Strife again, which, in virtue of the qualities [scil. the respective qualities of the four elements], is the moment [scil. in which is located] quality, they render manifest the things that fall under sensation.

---

[1] The scholiast is discussing the fact that in Aristotle's *Categories,* the chapter on the relatives (7) precedes the one on quality (8), while the initial enumeration (beginning of chapter 4) follows the order quantity-quality-relatives.   [2] The scholium transposes Alexander's argument into Neoplatonic terms.

An Allegorical Interpretation of an
Obscure Fragment (R99)

R99 (> ad B143) Theon Sm. *Exp.*, p. 15.7–14

κατὰ ταὐτὰ δὴ καὶ ἡ τῶν Πλατωνικῶν[1] λόγων παρά-
δοσις τὸ μὲν πρῶτον ἔχει καθαρμόν τινα, οἷον τὴν ἐν
τοῖς προσήκουσι μαθήμασιν ἐκ παίδων συγγυμνα-
σίαν.[2] ὁ μὲν γὰρ Ἐμπεδοκλῆς **"κρηνάων ἄπο πέντε**
ταμόντα"[3] φησι **"ἀτειρέι[4] χαλκῷ"** [**D35**] δεῖν ἀπορρύ-
πτεσθαι·[5] ὁ δὲ Πλάτων ἀπὸ πέντε μαθημάτων δεῖν
φησι ποιεῖσθαι τὴν κάθαρσιν· ταῦτα δ' ἐστὶν ἀριθμη-
τική, γεωμετρία, στερεομετρία, μουσική, ἀστρονομία.

---

[1] πολιτικῶν ms., corr. Hiller   [2] ἡ . . . συγγυμνασία
ms., corr. Hiller   [3] ταμόντα ms.ᵃᶜ, ἀνιμῶντα ms.ᵖᶜ, cf.
Picot, *Organon* 41 (2009), 64f.   [4] ἀτειρέι dett. quidam:
ἀκηρέι lect. incerta in ms. (in ras.)   [5] ἀποκρύπτεσθαι ms.ᵃᶜ

An Obscure Interpretation, or a
Confusion? (R100)

R100 (≠ DK) Clem. Alex. *Strom.* 5.103.6

[103.6] οὐ παραπέμπομαι καὶ τὸν Ἐμπεδοκλέα, ὃς φυσικῶς οὕτως τῆς τῶν πάντων ἀναλήψεως μέμνηται,
ὡς ἐσομένης ποτὲ εἰς τὴν τοῦ πυρὸς οὐσίαν μεταβολῆς.

An Allegorical Interpretation of an
Obscure Fragment (R99)

R99 (> ad B143) Theon of Smyrna, *On Mathematics Useful for Understanding Plato*

In the same way too [scil. as for initiation to the mysteries] the transmission of Plato's teachings implies first of all a kind of purification, viz. training in the appropriate mathematics starting from boyhood. For Empedocles says that it is necessary to cleanse oneself, **"Cutting from five sources . . . with unwearying (?) bronze"** [**D35**]. But Plato says that it is necessary to purify oneself on the basis of five mathematical disciplines: arithmetic, geometry, stereometry, music, and astronomy.

An Obscure Interpretation, or a
Confusion? (R100)

R100 (≠ DK) Clement of Alexandria, *Stromata*

I do not omit Empedocles, who mentions the regeneration of all things from a physical point of view in the idea that one day there will be a change into the substance of fire [cf. **R41**].

Empedocles in the Literature of the
Imperial Period (R101–R103)
A Parody (R101)

R101 (≠ DK) Luc. *Icaromen.* 13

[13] [. . .] ἐπεὶ γὰρ αὐτὴν μὲν ἐγνώρισα τὴν γῆν ἰδών,
τὰ δ᾿ ἄλλα οὐχ οἷός τε ἦν καθορᾶν ὑπὸ τοῦ βάθους
ἄτε τῆς ὄψεως μηκέτι ἐφικνουμένης, πάνυ μ᾿ ἠνία τὸ
χρῆμα καὶ πολλὴν παρεῖχε τὴν ἀπορίαν. κατηφεῖ δὲ
ὄντι μοι καὶ ὀλίγου δεῖν δεδακρυμένῳ ἐφίσταται κατ-
όπιν ὁ σοφὸς Ἐμπεδοκλῆς, ἀνθρακίας τις ἰδεῖν καὶ
σποδοῦ πλέως καὶ κατωπτημένος· κἀγὼ μὲν ὡς εἶ-
δον,—εἰρήσεται γάρ—ὑπεταράχθην καί τινα σελη-
ναῖον δαίμονα ᾠήθην ὁρᾶν· ὁ δέ, "θάρρει," φησίν, "ὦ
Μένιππε, 'οὔτις τοι θεός εἰμι, τί μ᾿ ἀθανάτοισιν
ἐίσκεις;' ὁ φυσικὸς οὗτός εἰμι Ἐμπεδοκλῆς· ἐπεὶ γὰρ
ἐς τοὺς κρατῆρας ἐμαυτὸν φέρων ἐνέβαλον, ὁ καπνός
με ἀπὸ τῆς Αἴτνης ἁρπάσας δεῦρο ἀνήγαγε, καὶ νῦν
ἐν τῇ σελήνῃ κατοικῶ ἀεροβατῶν τὰ πολλὰ καὶ σι-
τοῦμαι δρόσον. ἥκω τοίνυν σε ἀπολύσων τῆς παρού-
σης ἀπορίας· ἀνιᾷ γάρ σε, οἶμαι, καὶ στρέφει τὸ μὴ
σαφῶς τὰ ἐπὶ γῆς ὁρᾶν [. . .]."

Empedocles in the Literature of the Imperial Period (R101–R103)
A Parody (R101)

R101 (≠ DK) Lucian, *Icaromenippus*

[13] [. . .] Since I had recognized the earth itself when I saw it, but I was not able to see anything else on account of the height, because my sight no longer reached far enough, this matter bothered me a lot and I had no idea what to do. I was discouraged and almost in tears when suddenly the sage Empedocles stood behind me, black as a coal, covered with ashes, and thoroughly roasted [cf. **P29[69]**]. When I saw him I was—I have to admit it—somewhat troubled, and I thought I was seeing some lunar demon [cf. **PYTH. a P35**]. But he said to me, "Be of good courage, Menippus, 'I am not a god [cf. **D4.4**], why do you liken me to the immortals?' [Homer, *Od.* 16.187] I am Empedocles, the natural philosopher (*phusikos*). When I went to the crater and threw myself in, the smoke seized me and carried me from Aetna to here, and now I live on the moon, walking for the most part on the air and dining on dew. So now I have come to free you from your present difficulty. For I think that this bothers and torments you, not to be able to see clearly what is happening on the earth [. . .]."[1]

---

[1] Empedocles goes on to suggest to Menippus that he use the wing of an eagle—the only bird able to look directly at the sun—in order to benefit from its keen sight.

Eros in the Rhetoric of Wedding Speeches:
Empedoclean Inspiration? (R102)

R102

a (≠ DK) Men. Rh. *Div. epid.* 400.31–401.3

τὰ δὲ μετὰ τὰ προοίμια ἔστω περὶ τοῦ θεοῦ τοῦ γάμου
λόγος ὥσπερ θετικὸς καθόλου τὴν ἐξέτασιν περιέχων
ὅτι καλὸν ὁ γάμος, ἄρξῃ δὲ ἄνωθεν, ὅτι μετὰ τὴν
λύσιν τοῦ χάους εὐθὺς ὑπὸ τῆς φύσεως ἐδημιουργήθη
ὁ γάμος, εἰ δὲ βούλει, ὡς Ἐμπεδοκλῆς φησι, καὶ <ὁ>[1]
Ἔρως.

[1] <ὁ> Bursian

b (≠ DK) Procop. *Mel. et Ant.* 3–4 et 6 (p. 58 Amato)

[3] τῆς ἑορτῆς δὲ τὴν πρόφασιν, ἀρχὴν τοῦ λόγου
ποιήσομαι, τὸν Γάμον[1] ὑμῖν ἀφηγούμενος, ὃν πατέρα
ἀνδρῶν τε θεῶν τε πρὸ τοῦ Διὸς εἰκότως ἂν ἔφησαν.
τοῦ γὰρ Χάους ὄντος—καὶ γὰρ ἦν πάλαι Χάος πρὶν
φανεὶς ὁ Γάμος κατέπαυσε—καὶ τῆς τῶν ὅλων φύσεως σαλευομένης ἀπαύστῳ φορᾷ καὶ τῶν στοιχείων
ἐπ᾽ ἄλληλα φερομένων ἐμπλήκτῳ ῥοπῇ (οἰδούσης
γῆς, πλημμυράντων ὑδάτων, ἀντωθοῦντος ἀέρος, τοῦ
πυρὸς ἐπιφλέγοντος), ἀλλήλοις ἐμβαλλόντων, ὠθου-
μένων, νικώντων, καὶ τῆς ὕλης ἀτάκτοις μεταχωρού-
σης πηδήμασι, [. . .] τούτων οὕτως ἐχόντων καὶ πρὸς
ἑαυτὴν ἀεὶ πολεμούσης τῆς φύσεως, ἐπέστη Γάμος·

Eros in the Rhetoric of Wedding Speeches:
Empedoclean Inspiration? (R102)

R102

a (≠ DK) Menander Rhetor, *On Epideictic Speeches*

After the proems there should be a positive discussion
concerning the god of marriage, including a general investigation of the idea that marriage is a fine thing. You should
begin at the beginning, saying that marriage was contrived
by nature immediately after the dissolution of chaos, and,
if you wish, as Empedocles says, Eros too.

b (≠ DK) Procopius of Gaza, *Speech for the Most Elo-
quent Meles and the Most Honorable Antonina*

[3] On account of this ceremony, I shall begin my speech
by telling you of Gamos [i.e. the god of weddings], whom
they could have called suitably the father of men and of
gods, rather than Zeus. For when Chaos existed—and
Chaos once existed before Gamos appeared and put an
end to him—and the nature of the universe was in turmoil
with incessant motion and the elements were rushing toward one another with an unbalanced impulse (with the
earth swelling, the waters overflowing, the air repelling,
the fire blazing), attacking one another, being repelled,
conquering, and matter changing places with disordered
leaps, [. . .]—things being in this condition and nature
incessantly warring against itself, there arose Gamos: har-

---

1 Γάμον Corcella: γὰρ ms.

ἁρμονία συνέστη, σπονδαὶ παρῆλθον καὶ πρὸς τάξιν
ἡ μάχη μεθίστατο. [4] κάτω μὲν εἵλκετο γῆ, τὸ δὲ πῦρ
ἀνωθεῖτο μετέωρον, ἀὴρ δέ τι μέσον ἐπλήρου καὶ
πρὸς τὸ κοῖλον ἐχώρει τὰ ῥεύματα. ὁ οὐρανὸς δὲ μέσα
πάντα φέρων ἀπαύστοις περιέσφιγγε δινήμασι·² [. . .]
[6] ἐν τούτοις Ἔρως ἐχόρευεν, δεδιὼς μὴ φθαρείη τὰ
φανέντα καὶ μὴ γένοιτο δεύτερα καὶ λάθη φύσις ἀρ-
χαία πρὸς ἑαυτὴν ὀλισθήσασα [. . .].

² δινεύμασι coni. Amato

A Poetic Doxography (R103)

R103 (≠ DK) Claud. *Car.* 17.72–74

alter in Aetnaeas casurus sponte favillas
dispergit revocatque deum rursusque receptis
nectit amicitiis quidquid discordia solvit.

Two Pseudepigraphic Poetic
Compositions (R104–R105)

R104 (< B155) Diog. Laert. 8.43

Ἱππόβοτός γέ τοί φησι [Frag. 14 Gigante] λέγειν
Ἐμπεδοκλέα·

Τήλαυγες,¹ κλυτὲ κοῦρε Θεανοῦς Πυθαγόρεω τε.

¹ τηλαυγῆ vel sim. mss., corr. Bentley

mony was created, a truce was established, and battle was replaced by order. [4] The earth was dragged downward, the fire was pushed upward, air filled the intermediate space and the liquids flowed down into the cavities. The heavens, bearing all things in the middle, rotated with incessant whirlings [. . .] [6] Among these [i.e. the animals], Eros danced, fearing lest what had appeared be destroyed and lest a second birth come about and the ancient nature return to itself without being noticed [. . .].[1]

1 Empedocles is not named, but Procopius' text follows Menander's recommendations (**R102a**), and certain features of its description of the primitive chaos are similar to those in Plutarch (**D98**).

A Poetic Doxography (R103)

R103 (≠ DK) Claudian, *On the Consulship of Manlius Theodorus*

Another, about to jump voluntarily into Aetnas'
    flames,
Disperses god and calls him back together, and in
    renewed bonds of
Love he connects all that Strife has separated.

Two Pseudepigraphic Poetic
Compositions (R104–R105)

R104 (< B155) Diogenes Laertius

Hippobotus reports that Empedocles said,

Telauges, listen, son of Theano and of Pythagoras.[1]

1 Cf. **P10–P12.**

R105 (B156) Diog. Laert. 8.61

ἀλλὰ καὶ ἐπίγραμμα [*Anth. Gr.* 7.508 (Simonidi attrib.)]
εἰς αὐτὸν ἐποίησε·

Παυσανίην ἰητρὸν ἐπώνυμον Ἀγχίτεω υἱόν
    φῶτ᾿ Ἀσκληπιάδην πατρὶς ἔθρεψε Γέλα,
ὃς πολλοὺς μογεροῖσι μαραινομένους καμάτοισιν
    φῶτας ἀπέστρεψεν Φερσεφόνης ἀδύτων.

2 τόνδ᾿ Ἀ. Π. ἔθαψε Anth.   3 ὃς πλείστους κρυεραῖσι
μ. ὑπὸ νούσοις Anth.   4 ἀδύτων] θαλάμων Anth.

Empedocles in The Assembly of
Philosophers *(R106)*

R106 (≠ DK) *Turba Phil.* Sermo IV, p. 52.1–2, 3–8, 11–
22 Plessner

dixit: significo posteris quod aer est tenue aquae et quod
non separatur ab ea; quod si non esset, terra sicca super
aquam humidam non maneret. [. . .]

dixit quod aer absconditus in aqua, quae sub terra est,
est qui fert terram, ne mergatur in aquam, quae est sub
terra, et prohibet ne terram humectet aqua. aer igitur
factus est complectens et inter diversa separans, aquam sc.
et terram, ac inter adversaria, aquam sc. et ignem, factus
est igitur concordans et separans, ne se invicem destruant.

R105 (B156) Diogenes Laertius

But he also composed an epigram about him:

> Pausanias, of byname 'doctor,' son of Anchitus,
>   Mortal man of the Asclepiads, was raised by his
>   fatherland Gela—
> He who turned back many mortal men who were
>   wasting away with terrible sufferings
> From the innermost sanctuary of Persephone.[1]

1 Pausanias' name means 'he who stops pains.' Medical writings were also attributed to Empedocles, cf. **P25–P26.**

Empedocles in The Assembly of Philosophers (R106)

R106 (≠ DK) *The Assembly of Philosophers*

He (i.e. Pandolfus,[1] scil. Empedocles) said: I declare to posterity that air is the most rarefied water and that it is not separated from it. If it did not exist, the earth would not remain dry above the moist water [. . .].

He said that the air hidden within the water that is found below the earth is what supports the earth so that it does not fall into the water that is found below the earth and what prevents the water from moistening the earth. Thus air was established as an entity that encompasses and that causes separation among things that are different, viz. water and earth, and that causes both harmony and separation among things that are contraries, viz. water and fire, so that they do not destroy each other. [. . .] The example

1 Empedocles' name in this Latin text (*Pandolfus*) is the result of a common confusion between *qaf* and *fa* in Arabic.

[. . .] exemplum eius est ovum, in quo quatuor coniuncta sunt. eius cortex apparens est terra et albedo aqua; cortex vero tenuissima cortici iuncta est separans inter terram et aquam, sicut significavi vobis, quod aer est separans terram ab aqua. rubeum quoque ovi est ignis; cortex, qui rubeum continet, est aer aquam separans ab igne, et utrumque unum et idem est. aer tamen frigida separans, terram videlicet et aquam, ab invicem, spissior est aere altiore. aer vero altior est rarior et subtilior; est namque igni propinquior aere inferiore. in ovo igitur facta sunt quator: terra, aqua, aer et ignis; saliens autem punctus, his exceptis quatuor, in medio rubei qui est pullus. ideoque omnes philosophi in hac excellentissima arte ovum descripserunt ipsumque exemplum suo operi posuerunt.

of this is the egg, in which four things are united. Its visible shell is the earth and the white is the water; the very thin membrane that adheres to the shell is what causes separation between earth and water, as I have indicated to you that air is what separates the earth from the water. Then the yolk of the egg is the fire: the film that contains the yolk is the air that separates the water from the fire: the two are one and the same thing. Only, the air that separates the cold elements, viz. earth and water, from each other is denser than the upper air. The upper air, by contrast, is more rarefied and more subtle; it is likewise nearer to the fire than the lower air is. Thus there are four things in the egg: earth, water, air, and fire; the leaping point in the middle of the yolk, which is the chick, is outside of these four. For this reason, all the philosophers in this exquisite art [i.e. alchemy] have described the egg and have chosen it as an example for their work.

PHILOSOPHY AND MEDICINE

23. ALCMAEON [ALCM.]

The only evidence available for situating Alcmaeon chronologically is a (problematic) sentence in Aristotle's *Metaphysics,* from which it can be inferred that Alcmaeon was young, or at any rate still alive, when Pythagoras was already aged. The fact that Alcmaeon addressed his treatise to three men who belonged to the first generation of Pythagoreans (**D4**) suggests a date of composition at the end of the sixth or the beginning of the fifth century BC.

The question to what extent Alcmaeon was 'Pythagorean' depends on the meaning attributed to this designation (see the General Introduction to Chapters 10–18). Croton, which was Alcmaeon's native city, was the center of the most important Pythagorean political association (*hetairia*), but it was also celebrated for its doctors. Most of the fragments and testimonia regarding Alcmaeon concern the human body and its functions. It seems clear that Alcmaeon figured as a precursor in the field of human physiology. His cosmological and speculative dimension is more difficult to grasp. The pairs of contraries played a fundamental role in his doctrine, and this is the aspect by which he is connected with the Pythagorean school, even though the contraries occupy a central place in other natural philosophers.

BIBLIOGRAPHY

Editions

At the time of this writing (2016), there is no edition of the fragments of Alcmaeon besides that in Diels-Kranz.

Studies

J. Mansfeld. "Alcmaeon: *'Physikos'* or Physician? With Some Remarks on Calcidius 'On Vision' Compared to Galen," in J. Mansfeld and L. M. de Rijk, eds., *Kephalaion: Studies in Greek Philosophy and Its Continuation Offered to Professor C. J. de Vogel* (Assen, 1975), pp. 26–38.

OUTLINE OF THE CHAPTER

P

D

ALCMAEON [24 DK]

P

Chronology (P1)

P1 (< A3) Arist. *Metaph.* A5 986a29–30

[. . . cf. **D5**] καὶ γὰρ ἐγένετο τὴν ἡλικίαν¹ Ἀλκμαίων ἐπὶ² γέροντι Πυθαγόρᾳ³ [. . .].

    ¹ ἐγένετο τὴν ἡλικίαν om. Aᵇ, secl. edd.   ² ⟨νέος⟩ ἐπὶ Diels   ³ ἐπὶ γέροντι Πυθαγόρᾳ om. Aᵇ, secl. edd.

Family (P2)

P2 (< A1) Diog. Laert. 8.83

ἦν δὲ Πειρίθου υἱός, ὡς αὐτὸς ἐναρχόμενος τοῦ συγγράμματός φησιν [. . . = **D4**].

ALCMAEON

P

Chronology (P1)

P1 (< A3) Aristotle, *Metaphysics*

[. . .] Alcmaeon attained maturity[1] when Pythagoras was an old man [. . .].

  [1] Or, with the addition proposed by Diels: "Alcmaeon was young . . ." (cf. Iamblichus, *Life of Pythagoras* 104). Many editors believe that the words "attained . . . old man" do not belong to Aristotle and were introduced later into the text of the *Metaphysics*.

Family (P2)

P2 (< A1) Diogenes Laertius

He was the son of Peirithus, as he himself says at the beginning of his treatise [**D4**] [. . .].

Pythagorean Affiliations (P3)

P3 (< A1) Diog. Laert. 8.83

Ἀλκμαίων Κροτωνιάτης. καὶ οὗτος Πυθαγόρου διήκουσε.

An Apothegm (P4)

P4 (< B5) Clem. Alex. *Strom.* 6.16.2–3

Ἀλκμαίωνος γὰρ τοῦ Κροτωνιάτου [. . .] "ἐχθρὸν ἄνδρα ῥᾷον φυλάξασθαι ἢ φίλον [. . .]."

Pythagorean Affiliations (P3)

P3 (<A1) Diogenes Laertius

Alcmaeon of Croton. He too [*scil.* like Empedocles, Epicharmus, and Archytas] studied with Pythagoras.

See also **PYTH. b T30[1]**

An Apothegm (P4)

P4 (< B5) Clement of Alexandria, *Stromata*

Alcmaeon of Croton [. . .]: "It is easier to protect yourself against an enemy than against a friend [. . .]."

ALCMAEON [24 DK]

D

Alcmaeon's Writings (D1–D3)

D1

a (<A1) Diog. Laert. 8.83

δοκεῖ δὲ πρῶτος φυσικὸν λόγον συγγεγραφέναι, καθά φησι Φαβωρῖνος ἐν Παντοδαπῇ ἱστορίᾳ [Frag. 79 Amato].

b (A2) Clem. Alex. *Strom.* 1.78.3

Ἀλκμαίων γοῦν Περίθου Κροτωνιάτης πρῶτος φυσικὸν λόγον συνέταξεν.

D2 (A2) Gal. *Elem. Hipp.* 1.9.27 (p. 134.16–19 De Lacy)

τὰ γὰρ τῶν παλαιῶν ἅπαντα Περὶ φύσεως ἐπιγέγραπται, τὰ Μελίσσου, τὰ Παρμενίδου, τὰ Ἐμπεδοκλέους Ἀλκμαίωνός τε καὶ Γοργίου καὶ Προδίκου καὶ τῶν ἄλλων ἁπάντων.

ALCMAEON

D

Alcmaeon's Writings (D1–D3)

D1

a (< A1) Diogenes Laertius

He seems to have been the first person to have written a treatise of natural philosophy, as Favorinus says in his *Miscellaneous History*.

b (A2) Clement of Alexandria, *Stromata*

Alcmaeon of Croton, son of Perithus, was the first person to compose a discourse about nature.

D2 (A2) Galen, *On the Elements According to Hippocrates*

For all of the writings of the ancients are entitled *On Nature:* those of Melissus, Parmenides, Empedocles, Alcmaeon as well as of Gorgias, Prodicus, and all the others.[1]

---

[1] The generic title *On Nature* (*Peri phuseôs*) is not original; it makes its first appearance toward the end of the fifth century BC in order to designate a group of writings that had come to be perceived as belonging to a shared project, that of 'research on nature' (*historia peri phuseôs*, cf. Plato, *Phaedo* 96a, **SOC. D7**).

D3 (< A1) Diog. Laert. 8.83

καὶ τὰ πλεῖστά γε τὰ ἰατρικὰ λέγει, ὅμως δὲ καὶ φυσιολογεῖ ἐνίοτε λέγων, "δύο τὰ πολλά ἐστι τῶν ἀνθρωπίνων."

The Beginning of the Treatise (D4)

D4 (< A1, B1) Diog. Laert. 8.83

[. . . = **P2**] ὡς αὐτὸς ἐναρχόμενος τοῦ συγγράμματός φησιν· "Ἀλκμαίων Κροτωνιήτης τάδε ἔλεξε Πειρίθου υἱὸς Βροτίνῳ καὶ Λέοντι καὶ Βαθύλλῳ περὶ τῶν ἀφανέων· περὶ τῶν θνητῶν σαφήνειαν μὲν θεοὶ ἔχοντι, ὡς δὲ ἀνθρώποις τεκμαίρεσθαι . . . "

The Opposites (D5)

D5 (< A3) Arist. *Metaph.* A5 986a27–b2

[. . . cf. **PYTHS. ANON. D6**] ὅνπερ τρόπον ἔοικε καὶ Ἀλκμαίων ὁ Κροτωνιάτης ὑπολαβεῖν, καὶ ἤτοι οὗτος παρ᾽ ἐκείνων ἢ ἐκεῖνοι παρὰ τούτου παρέλαβον τὸν λόγον τοῦτον· [. . . = **P1**] ἀπεφήνατο δὲ παραπλησίως τούτοις· φησὶ γὰρ εἶναι δύο τὰ πολλὰ τῶν ἀνθρωπίνων [= **D3**], λέγων τὰς ἐναντιότητας οὐχ ὥσπερ οὗτοι διωρισμένας ἀλλὰ τὰς τυχούσας, οἷον λευκὸν μέλαν, γλυκὺ πικρόν, ἀγαθὸν κακόν, μέγα μικρόν. οὗτος μὲν οὖν ἀδιορίστως ἀπέρριψε περὶ τῶν λοιπῶν,

D3 (< A1) Diogenes Laertius

For the most part, he speaks about medical matters; but all the same he also sometimes speaks about nature, saying, **"most of the things involving humans are two."**

The Beginning of the Treatise (D4–D5)

D4 (< A1, B1) Diogenes Laertius

[. . .] he himself says at the beginning of his treatise: **"Alcmaeon of Croton, the son of Peirithus, has said the following to Brotinus, Leon, and Bathyllus about things that are not manifest: about mortal things the gods possess certainty, but as humans,** [scil. one must?] **conclude on the basis of signs."**[1]

   [1] Text and construction uncertain.

The Opposites (D6)

D5 (< A3) Aristotle, *Metaphysics*

Alcmaeon of Croton seems to have thought in the same way [scil. as certain Pythagoreans], and either he took this conception over from them or else they took it over from him. For [. . .] Alcmaeon's mode of expression is very similar to theirs. For he states that **most of the things involving humans are two,** speaking of contraries that are not, as theirs are, determinate, but instead are taken randomly, like white and black, sweet and bitter, good and evil, large and small. Regarding the others [scil. pairs of opposites], he spoke at random without determining

οἱ δὲ Πυθαγόρειοι καὶ πόσαι καὶ τίνες αἱ ἐναντιώσεις
ἀπεφήναντο.

Astronomical Doctrines (D6–D8)

D6 (< A4) Aët. 2.16.2 (Ps.-Plut.; cf. Stob.) [περὶ τῆς τῶν
ἀστέρων φορᾶς καὶ κινήσεως]

Ἀλκμαίων [. . .] τοὺς πλανήτας τοῖς ἀπλανέσιν ἀπὸ[1]
δυσμῶν ἐπ’ ἀνατολὰς ἀντιφέρεσθαι.

  [1] ἀπλανέσιν ἀπὸ Stob.: ἀπλανέσιν ἐναντίως, ἀπὸ γὰρ Plut.

D7 (A4) Aët. 2.22.4 (Stob.) [περὶ σχήματος ἡλίου]

Ἀλκμαίων πλατὺν εἶναι τὸν ἥλιον.

D8 (< A4) Aët. 2.29.3 (Stob.) [περὶ ἐκλείψεως σελήνης]

Ἀλκμαίων [. . .] κατὰ τὴν τοῦ σκαφοειδοῦς στροφὴν
καὶ τὰς περικλίσεις.

Soul and Heavenly Bodies (D9–D10)

D9 (A12) Arist. An. 1.2 405a29–b1

παραπλησίως δὲ τούτοις καὶ Ἀλκμαίων ἔοικεν ὑπολαβεῖν περὶ ψυχῆς· φησὶ γὰρ αὐτὴν ἀθάνατον εἶναι διὰ
τὸ ἐοικέναι τοῖς ἀθανάτοις· τοῦτο δ’ ὑπάρχειν αὐτῇ ὡς
ἀεὶ κινουμένῃ· κινεῖσθαι γὰρ καὶ τὰ θεῖα πάντα συν-
εχῶς ἀεί, σελήνην, ἥλιον, τοὺς ἀστέρας καὶ τὸν οὐρανὸν ὅλον.

them, while the Pythagoreans declared how many contraries there are and what they are.

Astronomical Doctrines (D6–D8)

D6 (A4) Aëtius

Alcmaeon [. . .]: the planets move in the opposite direction from the fixed stars, from west to east.

D7 (A4) Aëtius

Alcmaeon: the sun is flat.

D8 (< A4) Aëtius

Alcmaeon [. . .]: [scil. the lunar eclipse occurs] by virtue of the rotation of the bowl-shaped body and its inclinations.

Soul and Heavenly Bodies (D9–D10)

D9 (A12) Aristotle, *On the Soul*

Alcmaeon too seems to have had a conception about the soul similar to these [scil. those who explain the nature of the soul with reference to its mobility, Thales, Diogenes of Apollonia, and Heraclitus]. For he says that it is immortal because it resembles the immortals. This belongs to it because it is always in motion. For everything that is divine always moves continually: the moon, the sun, the heavenly bodies, and the whole heavens.

749

D10 (< A1) Diog. Laert. 8.83

ἔφη δὲ καὶ τὴν ψυχὴν ἀθάνατον, καὶ κινεῖσθαι αὐτὴν
συνεχὲς ὡς τὸν ἥλιον.

The Cognitive Faculties (D11–D19)
Humans and Animals (D11)

D11 (< A5) Theophr. *Sens.* 25

[. . . cf. **DOX. T15[25]**] Ἀλκμαίων μὲν πρῶτον ἀφορίζει
τὴν πρὸς τὰ ζῷα διαφοράν. ἄνθρωπον γάρ φησι τῶν
ἄλλων διαφέρειν ὅτι μόνος¹ ξυνίησι, τὰ δ᾽ ἄλλα αἰ-
σθάνεται μὲν οὐ ξυνίησι δέ, ὡς ἕτερον ὂν τὸ φρονεῖν
καὶ αἰσθάνεσθαι, [. . .] ἔπειτα περὶ ἑκάστης λέγει.

¹ μόνον mss., corr. Zeller

Hearing (D12)

D12

a (< A5) Theophr. *Sens.* 25

ἀκούειν μὲν οὖν φησι τοῖς ὠσίν, διότι κενὸν ἐν αὑτοῖς
ἐνυπάρχει· τοῦτο γὰρ ἠχεῖν. φθέγγεσθαι δὲ τῷ κοίλῳ,¹
τὸν ἀέρα δ᾽ ἀντηχεῖν.

¹ τοῦτο γὰρ ἠχοῦν φθέγγεσθαι διὰ τὸ κοῖλον Diels

D10 (< A1) Diogenes Laertius

He said that the soul is immortal and that it moves continually like the sun.

See also **R3**

The Cognitive Faculties (D11–D19)
Humans and Animals (D11)

D11 (< A5) Theophrastus, *On Sensations*

[. . .] Alcmaeon begins by determining the difference with regard to animals. For he says that a human being differs from the others because he is the only one that understands, while the others perceive but do not understand,[1] since he considers that thinking and perceiving differ from one another [. . .]. Then he speaks about each one [scil. of the sensations].

---

[1] Diels thinks that his sentence is a verbal citation (B1a).

Hearing (D12)

D12

a (< A5) Theophrastus, *On Sensations*

He says that hearing occurs by the ears, since there is void in them; for this resounds (and a sound is produced by what is hollow), and air makes an echo in response.

b (< A6) Aët. 4.16.2 (Ps.-Plut.; cf. Stob.) [περὶ ἀκοῆς]

Ἀλκμαίων ἀκούειν ἡμᾶς τῷ κενῷ τῷ ἐντὸς τοῦ ὠτός· τοῦτο γὰρ εἶναι τὸ διηχοῦν κατὰ τὴν τοῦ πνεύματος ἐμβολήν·[1] πάντα γὰρ τὰ κενὰ[2] ἠχεῖ.

[1] ἐμβολήν Plut.: εἰσβολήν Stob.   [2] κενὰ Plut.: κοῖλα Stob.

Respiration and Smelling (D13–D14)

D13

a (< A5) Theophr. *Sens.* 25

ὀσφραίνεσθαι δὲ ῥισὶν ἅμα τῷ ἀναπνεῖν ἀνάγοντα[1] τὸ πνεῦμα πρὸς τὸν ἐγκέφαλον.

[1] ἀνάγοντας coni. Usener

b (< A8) Aët. 4.17.1 (Ps.-Plut.) [περὶ ὀσφρήσεως]

[. . . = **D19b**] τούτῳ οὖν ὀσφραίνεσθαι ἕλκοντι διὰ τῶν ἀναπνοῶν τὰς ὀσμάς.

D14 (< A7) Arist. *HA* 1.11 492a14–15

Ἀλκμαίων [. . .] φάμενος ἀναπνεῖν τὰς αἶγας κατὰ τὰ ὦτα [. . . cf. **R2**].

b (< A6) Aëtius

Alcmaeon: we hear by means of the void inside the ear. For this is what resounds when a breath strikes it. For all empty things resound.

Respiration and Smelling (D13–D14)

D13

a (< A5) Theophrastus, *On Sensations*

Smelling occurs by the nostrils, at the same time as breathing occurs, by making the breath rise up to the brain.

b (< A8) Aëtius

[. . .] It is thus by this [scil. the brain], which attracts odors by means of acts of breathing, that odors are perceived.

D14 (< A7) Aristotle, *History of Animals*

Alcmaeon [. . .] asserting that goats breathe by their ears [. . .].

Taste (D15)

D15

a (< A5) Theophr. *Sens.* 25

γλώττῃ δὲ τοὺς χυμοὺς κρίνειν· χλιαρὰν γὰρ οὖσαν
καὶ μαλακὴν τήκειν τῇ θερμότητι· δέχεσθαι δὲ καὶ
διαδιδόναι[1] διὰ τὴν μανότητα καὶ ἀπαλότητα.[2]

> [1] δεδέχθαι et διδόναι mss., corr. Schneider   [2] τῆς ἀπα-
> λότητος mss., corr. Wimmer

b (A9) Aët. 4.18.1 (Ps.-Plut.) [περὶ γεύσεως]

Ἀλκμαίων τῷ ὑγρῷ καὶ τῷ χλιαρῷ τῷ ἐν τῇ γλώττῃ
πρὸς τῇ μαλακότητι διακρίνεσθαι τοὺς χυμούς.

Sight (D16–D17)

D16 (< A5) Theophr. *Sens.* 26

ὀφθαλμοὺς δὲ ὁρᾶν διὰ τοῦ πέριξ ὕδατος· ὅτι δ' ἔχει
πῦρ δῆλον εἶναι, πληγέντος γὰρ ἐκλάμπειν· ὁρᾶν δὲ
τῷ στίλβοντι καὶ τῷ διαφανεῖ, ὅταν ἀντιφαίνῃ, καὶ
ὅσῳ[1] ἂν καθαρώτερον ᾖ μᾶλλον.

> [1] ὅσον mss., corr. Schneider

Taste (D15)

D15

a (< A5) Theophrastus, *On Sensations*

It is by means of the tongue that flavors are distinguished; for being tepid and soft, it melts because of heat, and it receives and transmits because of its porosity and softness.

b (A9) Aëtius

Alcmaeon: it is by means of the moisture and tepid warmth in the tongue, besides its softness, that flavors are distinguished.

Sight (D16–D17)

D16 (< A5) Theophrastus, *On Sensations*

The eyes see thanks to the peripheral water. But it is clear that it [scil. the eye] contains fire, for when it is struck it flashes. But it sees by means of what is brilliant and is transparent when it reflects, and does so all the more the purer it is.

D17 (A10) Aët. 4.13.12 (Stob.) [περὶ ὁράσεως καὶ κατοπτρικῶν ἐμφάσεων]

Ἀλκμαίων κατὰ τὴν τοῦ διαφανοῦς ἀντίληψιν.[1]

[1] ἀντίλαμψιν coni. Diels

Touch (D18)

D18 (< A5) Theophr. *Sens.* 26

περὶ δὲ ἁφῆς οὐκ εἴρηκεν οὔτε πῶς οὔτε τίνι γίνεται.

The Brain (D19)

D19

a (< A5) Theophr. *Sens.* 26

ἁπάσας δὲ τὰς αἰσθήσεις συνηρτῆσθαί πως πρὸς τὸν ἐγκέφαλον, διὸ καὶ πηροῦσθαι[1] κινουμένου καὶ μεταλλάττοντος τὴν χώραν· ἐπιλαμβάνειν γὰρ τοὺς πόρους, δι᾽ ὧν αἱ αἰσθήσεις.

[1] πληροῦσθαι mss., corr. Koraïs

b (< A8) Aët. 4.17.1 (Ps.-Plut.) [περὶ ὀσφρήσεως]

Ἀλκμαίων ἐν τῷ ἐγκεφάλῳ εἶναι τὸ ἡγεμονικόν· [. . . = **D13b**].

D17 (A10) Aëtius

Alcmaeon: [scil. vision occurs] by the apprehension of what is transparent.

See also **R6**

Touch (D18)

D18 (< A5) Theophrastus, *On Sensations*

Regarding touch he has not said either how it occurs or by what means.

The Brain (D19)

D19

a (< A5) Theophrastus, *On Sensations*

All of the sense organs are connected in some way to the brain, and that is why they are impaired when it is altered or changes place. For this obstructs the passages which the sensations traverse.

b (< A8) Aëtius

Alcmaeon: the directing part is in the brain [. . .].

Seed and Embryology (D20–D29)
The First Production of the Seed (D20)

D20 (< A15) Arist. *HA* 1.1 581a14–16

ἅμα δὲ καὶ ἡ τρίχωσις τῆς ἥβης ἄρχεται, καθάπερ
καὶ τὰ φυτὰ τὰ μέλλοντα σπέρμα φέρειν ἀνθεῖν
πρῶτον Ἀλκμαίων φησὶν ὁ Κροτωνιάτης.

Origin of the Seed (D21–D23)

D21 (A13) Aët. 5.3.3 (Ps.-Plut.) [τίς ἡ οὐσία τοῦ σπέρματος;]

Ἀλκμαίων ἐγκεφάλου μέρος.

D22 (< A13) Cens. *Die nat.* 5.3

sed hanc opinionem nonnulli refellunt, ut [. . .] Alcmaeon
Crotoniates; hi enim post gregum contentionem[1] non
medullis modo, verum et adipe multaque carne mares
exhauriri respondent.

[1] crebram coitionem *ed. Ald.*: contentam initionem *Barth*

D23 (< A13) Cens. *Die nat.* 5.4

illud quoque ambiguam facit inter auctores opinionem,
utrumne ex patris tantummodo semine partus nascatur
[. . .] an etiam ex matris, quod [. . .] Alcmaeoni [. . .] visum
est [. . . = **D26**].

ALCMAEON

Seed and Embryology (D20–D29)
The First Production of the Seed (D20)

D20 (< A15) Aristotle, *History of Animals*

The growth of hair at puberty begins at the same time
[scil. as the first production of seed, viz. at twice seven
years], as Alcmaeon of Croton says that plants that are
about to produce seed begin to bloom.

Origin of the Seed (D21–D23)

D21 (A13) Aëtius

Alcmaeon: [scil. the seed is] a part of the brain.

D22 (< A13) Censorinus, *The Birthday*

This opinion [scil. that the seed comes from the marrow]
is rejected by some, like [. . .] Alcmaeon of Croton: they
object that after the [scil. reproductive] effort of the flocks,
the males are drained not only of their marrow but also of
their fat and of much of their flesh.

D23 (< A13) Censorinus, *The Birthday*

The following point too produces two opinions among the
authorities who discuss it: whether the child is born only
from the father's seed [. . .] or also from the mother's, as
[. . .] Alcmaeon [. . .] believed.

Sterility (D24)

D24 (B3) Aët. 5.14.1 (Ps.-Plut.) [διὰ τί αἱ ἡμίονοι στεῖραι]

Ἀλκμαίων τῶν ἡμιόνων τοὺς μὲν ἄρρενας ἀγόνους παρὰ τὴν λεπτότητα τῆς θορῆς, ὅ ἐστι σπέρματος,[1] ‹ἢ›[2] ψυχρότητα· τὰς δὲ θηλείας παρὰ τὸ μὴ ἀναχάσκειν τὰς μήτρας, ὅ ἐστιν ἀναστομοῦσθαι.[3] οὕτω γὰρ αὐτὸς εἴρηκεν.

[1] ὅ ἐστι σπέρματος om. Gal., del. Diels   [2] ‹ἢ› Diels
[3] ὅ ἐστιν ἀναστομοῦσθαι om. Gal., del. Diels

Determination of the Sex (D25)

D25 (A14) Cens. *Die nat.* 6.4

nam ex quo parente seminis amplius fuit, eius sexum repraesentari dixit Alcmaeon.

Development of the Embryo (D26–D27)

D26 (< A13) Cens. *Die nat.* 5.4

[. . . = **D23**] de conformatione autem partus nihilo minus definite se scire Alcmaeon confessus est, ratus neminem posse perspicere quid primum in infante formetur.

Sterility (D24)

D24 (B3) Aëtius

Alcmaeon: in mules, the males are sterile because of the thinness ⟨or⟩ coldness of the **emission,** that is, of the seed, the females because their wombs do not **gape open,** that is, become dilated. For this is how he himself expressed it.

Determination of the Sex (D25)

D25 (A14) Censorinus, *The Birthday*

Alcmaeon said that the sex of that parent is reproduced whose seed is more abundant.

Development of the Embryo (D26–D27)

D26 (< A13) Censorinus, *The Birthday*

But regarding the formation of the embryo, Alcmaeon acknowledged that he knew less than nothing for certain, for he thought that no one was able to perceive what was formed first in an unborn baby.[1]

[1] If this testimonium is not to contradict the following one, the moment of initial formation (**D26**) must be distinguished from that of completion (**D27**).

761

D27 (A13) Aët. 5.17.3 (Ps.-Plut.) [τί πρῶτον τελεσιουρ-
γεῖται ἐν γαστρί]

Ἀλκμαίων τὴν κεφαλήν, ἐν ᾗ ἐστι τὸ ἡγεμονικόν.

Nourishment of the Embryo (D28–D29)

D28 (A17) Aët. 5.16.3 (Ps.-Plut.) [πῶς τρέφεται τὰ ἔμ-
βρυα]

Ἀλκμαίων δι᾽ ὅλου τοῦ σώματος τρέφεσθαι· ἀναλαμ-
βάνειν γὰρ αὐτό, ὥσπερ σπογγιά,[1] τὰ ἀπὸ τῆς τροφῆς θρεπτικά.

   [1] σπογγιά Mm: -άν Π

D29 (< A16) Arist. *GA* 3.2 752b22–26

τοῖς δ᾽ ὄρνισι τοῦτο ποιεῖ ἡ φύσις ἐν τοῖς ᾠοῖς, τοὐναντίον μέντοι ἢ οἵ τ᾽ ἄνθρωποι οἴονται καὶ Ἀλκμαίων
φησὶν ὁ Κροτωνιάτης. οὐ γὰρ τὸ λευκόν ἐστι γάλα,
ἀλλὰ τὸ ὠχρόν.

Health and Sickness (D30)

D30 (B4) Aët. 5.30.1 (Ps.-Plut.; cf. Stob.) [περὶ ὑγείας
καὶ νόσου καὶ γήρως], p. 248 Runia

Ἀλκμαίων τῆς μὲν ὑγείας εἶναι συνεκτικὴν ⟨τὴν⟩[1]
ἰσονομίαν τῶν δυνάμεων, ὑγροῦ, ξηροῦ, ψυχροῦ, θερ-

   [1] ⟨τὴν⟩ Diels

D27 (A13) Aëtius

Alcmaeon: the head, in which the directing part is located [scil. is the first part to take on its definitive shape in the womb].

Nourishment of the Embryo (D28–D29)

D28 (A17) Aëtius

Alcmaeon: it [i.e. the embryo] is nourished by the whole body. For like a sponge it absorbs the nutritional portions of the nourishment.

D29 (< A16) Aristotle, *Generation of Animals*

In birds, nature produces this [scil. milk] in the eggs, but in the opposite way from what people think and from what Alcmaeon of Croton says: for it is not the white that is the milk, but the yellow.

Health and Sickness (D30)

D30 (B4) Aëtius

Alcmaeon says that what maintains health is the **equality** (*isonomia,* literally: equality before the law) of the powers, of the moist and dry, cold and hot, bitter and sweet, and the

μοῦ, πικροῦ, γλυκέος καὶ τῶν λοιπῶν· τὴν δ' ἐν αὐτοῖς
μοναρχίαν νόσου ποιητικήν, φθοροποιὸν γὰρ ἑκα-
τέρου μοναρχία. καὶ νόσον συμπίπτειν[2] ὡς μὲν ὑφ' οὗ[3]
ὑπερβολῇ θερμότητος ἢ ψυχρότητος, ὡς δ' ἐξ ἧς διὰ
πλῆθος τροφῆς[4] ἢ ἔνδειαν, ὡς δ' ἐν οἷς ἢ αἷμα ἢ μυελὸν[5] ἢ ἐγκέφαλον· ἐγγίνεσθαι[6] δὲ τούτοις ποτὲ κἀκ[7]
τῶν ἔξωθεν αἰτιῶν, ὑδάτων ποιῶν ἢ χώρας ἢ κόπων
ἢ ἀνάγκης ἢ τῶν τούτοις παραπλησίων.[8] τὴν δὲ
ὑγείαν τὴν σύμμετρον τῶν ποιῶν κρᾶσιν.[9]

2 νόσον συμπίπτειν Diels e Psell. *Resp. diff. quaest.* p. 66
Boissonade: νόσων αἰτία Plut.: λέγει δὲ τὰς νόσους συμπίπτειν Stob.   3 ὑφ' οὗ Stob.: ὑφ' ἔξω Plut.   4 τροφῆς
Stob., om. Plut.   5 ἢ μυελὸν Stob.: ἐνδέον Plut.: ἔνδον
Lachenaud   6 ἐγγίνεσθαι Diels: γίνεσθαι Stob.   7 κἀκ
corr. Diels: καὶ ὑπὸ Stob.   8 ἐγγίνεσθαι . . . παραπλησίων om. Plut.   9 τὴν δὲ ὑγείαν . . . κρᾶσιν om. Stob.

Sleep and Death (D31–D32)

D31 (B2) Ps.-Arist. *Probl.* 17.3

τοὺς ἀνθρώπους φησὶν Ἀλκμαίων διὰ τοῦτο ἀπόλλυσθαι, ὅτι οὐ δύνανται τὴν ἀρχὴν τῷ τέλει προσάψαι.

D32 (A18) Aët. 5.24.1 (Ps.-Plut.) [πότερου ἐστὶν ὕπνος
καὶ θάνατος, ψυχῆς ἢ σώματος]

Ἀλκμαίων ἀναχωρήσει τοῦ αἵματος εἰς τὰς αἱμόρ-
ρους[1] φλέβας ὕπνον γίνεσθαί φησι, τὴν δ' ἐξέγερσιν
διάχυσιν, τὴν δὲ παντελῆ ἀναχώρησιν θάνατον.

other ones [scil. opposites], while the **monarchy** of only one among them causes sickness, for the monarchy of one of the two [scil. terms of a pair] is destructive for the other. And sickness occurs, with regard to the agent, from excess of heat or cold; with regard to the [scil. material] origin, from abundance or lack of nourishment; and with regard to place, blood, marrow, or the brain; it is also sometimes produced by external causes, certain kinds of water, the country, blows, dearth, and other causes similar to these, while health is the proportionate mixture of the qualities.[1]

[1] This notice is written in a language that is clearly anachronistic (note especially the terminology of the causes); the second part is attributed to Herophilus in the Arabic translation of the text of Ps.-Plutarch. Nevertheless, we suggest that the fundamental ideas may go back to Alcmaeon, as well as the terms *isonomia* and *monarchia,* with their implied political metaphor.

Sleep and Death (D31–D32)

D31 (B2) Ps.-Aristotle, *Problems*

Alcmaeon says that humans die because they are not able **to attach the beginning to the end.**[1]

[1] Diels considers the whole phrase, beginning "humans," to be a verbal citation.

D32 (A18) Aëtius

Alcmaeon says that it is by the blood's withdrawal into the blood vessels that sleep occurs, that its diffusion is awakening, and that its complete withdrawal is death.

---

[1] ὁμόρους (vel - ρρους) mss., corr. Reiske

Plants (D33)

D33 (≠ DK) Nic. Dam. *Plant.* 1.44, p. 141 Drossaart
Lulofs (cf. Ps.-Arist. *Plant.* 1.2 817a27–28)

[. . .] قال رجل يقال له القماون إن الأرض أم النبات والشمس أبوه.

Plants (D33)

D33 (≠ DK) Nicolaus of Damascus, *On Plants*

[. . .] a man called Alcmaeon says that the earth is the mother of plants and the sun is their father.[1]

1 Translated by H. J. Drossaart Lulofs.

ALCMAEON [24 DK]

R

Earliest Attestation: Isocrates

See **DOX. T6**

Aristotle on Alcmaeon (R1–R2)
An Aristotelian Treatise on Alcmaeon (R1)

R1 (cf. ad A3) Diog. Laert. 5.25 (= Arist.)

Πρὸς τὰ Ἀλκμαίωνος α΄.

Aristotle Disagrees with Alcmaeon on a
Point of Zoology (R2)

R2 (< A7) Arist. *HA* 1.11 492a14–15

Ἀλκμαίων γὰρ οὐκ ἀληθῆ λέγει, φάμενος ἀναπνεῖν
τὰς αἶγας κατὰ τὰ ὦτα.

The Platonization of Alcmaeon (R3–R4)

R3 (A12) Aët. 4.2.2 (Stob.) [περὶ ψυχῆς]

Ἀλκμαίων φύσιν αὐτοκίνητον κατ᾽ ἀίδιον κίνησιν καὶ

ALCMAEON

Earliest Attestation: Isocrates

See **DOX. T6**

Aristotle on Alcmaeon (R1–R2)
An Aristotelian Treatise on Alcmaeon (R1)

R1 (cf. ad A3) Diogenes Laertius [list of Aristotle's writings]

Against [or: *On*] *Alcmaeon's Doctrines,* one book.

Aristotle Disagrees with Alcmaeon on a
Point of Zoology (R2)

R2 (< A7) Aristotle, *History of Animals*

Alcmaeon is not right when he asserts that goats breathe by their ears.

See also **D29**

The Platonization of Alcmaeon (R3–R4)

R3 (A12) Aëtius

Alcmaeon: [*scil.* the soul is] a nature that moves itself with

769

διὰ τοῦτο ἀθάνατον αὐτὴν καὶ προσεμφερῆ τοῖς θείοις ὑπολαμβάνει.

R4 (A12) Clem. Alex. *Protr.* 66.2

ὁ γάρ τοι Κροτωνιάτης Ἀλκμαίων θεοὺς ᾤετο τοὺς ἀστέρας εἶναι ἐμψύχους ὄντας.

An Epicurean Polemic (R5)

R5 (A12) Cic. *Nat. deor.* 1.27

Crotoniates autem Alcmaeo, qui soli et lunae reliquisque sideribus animoque praeterea divinitatem dedit, non sensit sese mortalibus rebus inmortalitatem dare.

Alcmaeon and Dissection: A (Probably Anachronistic) Attribution (R6)

R6 (< A10) Calcid. *In Tim.* 246 (pp. 474.31–476.2 Bakhouche)

[. . .] oculi natura [. . .] de qua cum plerique alii tum Alcmaeo Crotoniensis, in physicis exercitatus quique primus exectionem aggredi est ausus, [. . .] multa et praeclara in lucem protulerunt [. . .].

an eternal motion [cf. Plato, *Phaedrus* 245c], and it is for this reason that he thinks that it is immortal and similar to divine things [cf. **D9**].

R4 (A12) Clement of Alexandria, *Proptreptic*

Alcmaeon of Croton thought that the heavenly bodies are gods endowed with a soul.

An Epicurean Polemic (R5)

R5 (A12) Cicero, *On the Nature of the Gods*

Alcmaeon of Croton, who attributed divinity to the sun, the moon, and all the other heavenly bodies, and besides those to the soul, did not understand that he was attributing immortality to things that are mortal.

Alcmaeon and Dissection: A (Probably Anachronistic) Attribution (R6)

R6 (< A10) Calcidius, *Commentary on Plato's* Timaeus

[. . .] the nature of the eye [. . .] about which, together with many others, Alcmaeon of Croton, an expert on questions regarding nature, and the first person to dare to perform a dissection [. . .], brought to light many remarkable things.[1]

[1] The following anatomical description (reproduced by DK) certainly goes back to the Hellenistic medical writer Herophilus of Alexandria. Nonetheless, some scholars think that Alcmaeon himself might have performed a dissection.

24. HIPPO [HIPPO]

The tradition that calls Hippo a Pythagorean is explicit among late authors and is doubtless implied by the names of the cities he is said to have come from. He certainly belongs to a generation later than that of Alcmaeon (probably toward the middle of the fifth century BC, if Cratinus was alluding to him in one of his comedies, cf. **DRAM. T15–T16**). As in the case of Alcmaeon, Hippo's connection with the Pythagorean movement depends on just what one means by 'Pythagorean.' In any case, Hippo's medical interests are evident. Although our basis for forming a judgment on him is very limited, it is quite possible that Hippo does not deserve Aristotle's scathing condemnation of him; indeed, it is highly likely that it was Hippo's doctrines that inspired Aristotle's reconstruction of Thales' possible arguments in favor of water as a principle (cf. **THAL. R32**].

BIBLIOGRAPHY

Editions

At the time of this writing (2015), there is no edition of the fragments of Hippo besides that in Diels-Kranz.

OUTLINE OF THE CHAPTER

HIPPO [38 DK]

P

Conflicting Reports on His Native City (P1–P6)

P1 (< A1) Iambl. *VP* 267

Σάμιοι [. . .] Ἵππων [cf. **PYTH. b T30[18]**].

P2 Cens. *Die nat.*

a (A1) 5.2

Hipponi vero Metapontino, sive, ut Aristoxenus auctor est [Frag. 21 Wehrli], Samio [. . . = **D9**].

b (< A16) 7.2

Hippon Metapontinus [. . . = **D17**].

P3 (< B4) Claud. Mam. *Statu an.* 7, p. 121.14

Hippon Metapontinus [. . . = **P7, R8**].

mettapontinus *G*: tarentinus *cett.*

HIPPO

P

Conflicting Reports on His Native City (P1–P6)

P1 (< A1) Iamblichus, *Life of Pythagoras*
From Samos: [. . .] Hippo.

P2 Censorinus, *The Birthday*
a (A1)
Hippo of Metapontum or, on the authority of Aristoxenus, of Samos [. . .].

b (< A16)
Hippo of Metapontum [. . .].

P3 (< B4) Claudianus Mamertus, *On the State of the Soul*
Hippo of Metapontum [. . .].

P4 (A1) Sext. Emp. *Pyrrh. Hyp.* 3.30

Ἵππων δὲ ὁ Ῥηγῖνος [. . . = **D4**].

P5 (< A3) (Ps.-?) Hippol. *Ref.* 1.16

Ἵππων δὲ ‹ὁ›¹ Ῥηγῖνος [. . . = **D1**].

¹ ‹ὁ› Wolf

P6 (< A11) Anon. Lond. 11.23–24

Ἵππ[ων δ]ὲ ὁ Κροτω|νιάτης [. . . = **D8**].

leg. et suppl. Diels

A Pythagorean? (P7)

P7 (< B4) Claud. Mam. *Stat. an.* 7, p. 121.14

Hippon [. . . = **P3**] ex eadem schola Pythagorae [. . . = **R8**].

P4 (A1) Sextus Empiricus, *Outlines of Pyrrhonism*
Hippo of Rhegium [. . .].

P5 (< A3) (Ps.-?) Hippolytus, *Refutation of All Heresies*
Hippo of Rhegium [. . .].

P6 (< A11) Anonymous of London
Hippo of Croton [. . .].

A Pythagorean? (P7)

P7 (< B4) Claudianus Mamertus, *On the State of the Soul*
Hippo [. . .], from the same school of Pythagoras [. . .].

See also **P1**

HIPPO [38 DK]

D

A General Summary of His Doctrine (D1)

D1 (< A3) (Ps.-?) Hippol. *Ref.* 1.16

Ἵππων δὲ [. . . = **P5**] ἀρχὰς ἔφη ψυχρὸν τὸ ὕδωρ καὶ
θερμὸν τὸ πῦρ. γεννώμενον δὲ τὸ πῦρ ὑπὸ ὕδατος[1]
κατανικῆσαι[2] τὴν τοῦ γεννήσαντος δύναμιν συστῆσαί
τε τὸν κόσμον. τὴν δὲ ψυχὴν ποτὲ μὲν ἐγκέφαλον λέγει,[3] ποτὲ δὲ ὕδωρ· καὶ γὰρ[4] τὸ σπέρμα εἶναι τὸ φαινόμενον ἡμῖν ἐξ ὑγροῦ, ἐξ οὗ φησι ψυχὴν γίνεσθαι.

[1] ‹τοῦ› ὕδατος Marcovich   [2] κατανικῆσαι T: -σαν
LOB
[3] λέγει Zeller: ἔχειν mss.   [4] γὰρ Bakhuizen: παρὰ mss.

The Principle(s) (D2–D5)

D2 (< A4) Simpl. *In Phys.*, p. 23.22

Θαλῆς [. . .] καὶ Ἵππων [. . . = **R3**] ὕδωρ ἔλεγον τὴν
ἀρχὴν [. . .].

HIPPO

D

A General Summary of His Doctrine (D1)

D1 (< A3) (Ps.-?) Hippolytus, *Refutation of All Heresies*

Hippo [. . .] said that the principles are cold, viz. water, and hot, viz. fire. The fire generated by water overcame the power of what generated it and constituted the world order. Sometimes he says that the soul is the brain, sometimes water; for semen, which manifests itself to us, [scil. comes] from moisture, and it is from this [i.e. the seed] that, he says, the soul is produced.

The Principle(s) (D2–D5)

D2 (< A4) Simplicius, *Commentary on Aristotle's* Physics

Thales [. . .] and Hippo [. . .] said that water is the principle [. . .].

779

D3 (A6) Alex. Aphr. *In Metaph.*, p. 26.21–22

Ἵππωνα ἱστοροῦσιν ἀρχὴν ἁπλῶς τὸ ὑγρὸν ἀδιορίστως ὑποθέσθαι, οὐ διασαφήσαντα πότερον ὕδωρ, ὡς Θαλῆς, ἢ ἀήρ, ὡς Ἀναξιμένης καὶ Διογένης.

D4 (< A5) Sext. Emp. *Pyrrh. Hyp.* 3.30

Ἵππων δὲ [. . . = **P4**] πῦρ καὶ ὕδωρ.

D5 (< A6) Ioan. Diac. Galen. *in Theog.* 116, p. 305 Flach

[. . .] ὁ δὲ τὴν γῆν, ὡς Ἵππων [. . . = **R4**].

The Soul (D6–D8)

D6 (31 A4) Arist. *An.* 1.2 405b1–5

τῶν δὲ φορτικωτέρων καὶ ὕδωρ τινὲς ἀπεφήναντο, καθάπερ Ἵππων· πεισθῆναι δ' ἐοίκασιν ἐκ τῆς γονῆς, ὅτι πάντων ὑγρά. καὶ γὰρ ἐλέγχει τοὺς αἷμα φάσκοντας τὴν ψυχήν, ὅτι ἡ γονὴ οὐχ αἷμα.

D7 (A10) Aët. 4.3.9 (Stob.) [εἰ σῶμα ἡ ψυχὴ καὶ τίς ἡ οὐσία αὐτῆς]

Ἵππων ἐξ ὕδατος τὴν ψυχήν.

D3 (A6) Alexander of Aphrodisias, *Commentary on Aristotle's* Metaphysics

They report that Hippo simply posited moisture as principle in an undifferentiated way, without clarifying whether it was water, like Thales, or air, like Anaximenes and Diogenes.

D4 (< A5) Sextus Empiricus, *Outlines of Pyrrhonism*

Hippo [. . .]: fire and water.

D5 (< A6) John Diaconus Galenus, *Allegories on Hesiod's* Theogony

[. . .] another [scil. positing as anterior to all other things] the earth, like Hippo [. . .].

The Soul (D6–D8)

D6 (31 A4) Aristotle, *On the Soul*

Among the more vulgar ones [scil. who have written on the soul], some have also asserted that it [i.e. the soul] is water, like Hippo. They seem to have been convinced by the case of seed, because that of all [scil. animals] is moist. For he objects to those who say that the soul is blood [cf. **EMP. D238**] that the seed is not blood.

D7 (A10) Aëtius

Hippo: the soul comes from water.

D8 (A11) Anon. Lond. 11.23–43

Ἴππ[ων δ]ὲ ὁ Κροτω|νιάτης οἴεται ἐν ἡμῖν οἰκείαν
εἶναι ὑγρότη||[25]τα, καθ᾽ [ἣ]ν καὶ αἰσθανόμεθα καὶ |
[ζ]ῶμεν· ὅταν μὲν οὖν οἰκείως ἔχῃ | ἡ τοιαύτη ὑγρότης,
ὑγιαίνει τὸ ζῷον, | ὅταν δὲ ἀναξηρανθῇ, ἀναισθητεῖ
τε | τὸ ζῷον καὶ ἀποθνῄσκει. διὰ δὴ τοῦτο | [30] [κ]αὶ
οἱ [γέ]ρ[ο]ντες ξηροὶ καὶ ἀναίσθητοι, ὅτι | χωρὶς
ὑγρότητος· ἀναλόγως δὴ τὰ πέλ|ματα ἀναίσθητα, ὅτι
ἄμοιρα ὑγρότητος. | καὶ ταῦτα μὲν ἄχρι τούτου φη-
σίν. ἐν ἄλλωι | δὲ βυβλίῳ αὐ[τὸ]ς ἀνὴρ λέγει τὴν
κα|[35]τωνομασ[μ]έ[ν]ην ὑγρότητα μεταβάλ|λειν δι᾽
ὑπ[ερβο]λὴν θερμότητος καὶ | δι᾽ ὑπερβολὴν ψυχρό-
τητος καὶ νόσ[ο]υς | ἐπιφέρειν. μεταβάλλειν δέ, φη-
σιν, αὐτὴν | ἢ ἐπὶ τὸ πλεῖον ὑγρὸν ἢ ἐπὶ τὸ ξηρό||[40]
τερον ἢ ἐπὶ τὸ παχυμερέστερον | ἢ ἐπὶ τὸ λεπτομερέ-
στερον ἢ εἰς [ἕτ]ερα. καὶ τοιούτως νοσολογεῖ |, τὰς δὲ
νόσους τὰς γινομένας | οὐχ ὑπαγορεύει.

plurima rest. et corr. Diels

Reproduction (D9–D12)

D9 (A12) Cens. *Die nat.* 5.2

Hipponi [. . . = **P2a**] ex medullis profluere semen videtur,
idque eo probari, quod post admissionem pecudum si quis
mares interimat,[1] medullas utpote exhaustas non reperiat.

[1] mares interimat *Jahn*: mare (-res C^2) sint perimat *CP*: mares
perimat (-atur *H*) *V*

D8 (A11) Anonymous of London

Hippo of Croton thinks that there is within us our own moisture [25], thanks to which we both perceive and live. Hence when such a moisture is in its appropriate condition, the living creature is healthy, but when it dries out, the living creature does not perceive and dies. And this is why [30] old men too are dry and do not perceive, because they are deprived of moisture; and analogously, the soles of the feet do not perceive, because they have no share in moisture. And this is what he says up to this point. In another book, the same man says that [35] what he calls moisture is transformed by excess of heat and by excess of cold, and produces illnesses; it is transformed, he says, into moister or drier [40], or into denser or more rarefied, or into other conditions, and it in this way that he explains the cause of illnesses, but he does not enumerate the illnesses that occur.

Reproduction (D9–D12)

D9 (A12) Censorinus, *The Birthday*

Hippo [. . .] believes that semen flows from the marrow and proves this by the fact that if, after male livestock has been admitted to the females, the males are slaughtered, one does not find their marrow, since it has been exhausted.

D10 (A13) Aët. 5.5.3 (Ps.-Plut.)

Ἵππων προίεσθαι μὲν σπέρμα τὰς θηλείας οὐχ ἥκιστα τῶν ἀρρένων, μὴ μέντοι εἰς ζῳογονίαν τοῦτο
συμβάλλεσθαι διὰ τὸ ἐκτὸς πίπτειν τῆς ὑστέρας·
ὅθεν ὀλίγας[1] προίεσθαι πολλάκις δίχα τῶν ἀνδρῶν[2]
σπέρμα, καὶ μάλιστα τὰς[3] χηρευούσας. καὶ εἶναι τὰ
μὲν ὀστᾶ παρὰ τοῦ ἄρρενος τὰς δὲ σάρκας παρὰ τῆς
θηλείας.[4]

[1] ⟨οὐκ⟩ ὀλίγας Wyttenbach: ἐνίας Diels   [2] ἀνδρῶν
ΜΠ: ἀρρένων m   [3] τὰς μάλιστα mss., corr. Wyttenbach
[4] καὶ . . . θηλείας secl. Kranz

D11 (A14)

a Aët. 5.7.3 (Ps.-Plut.) [πῶς ἄρρενα γεννᾶται καὶ θή-
λεα]

Ἵππῶν[1] παρὰ τὸ συνεστὸς καὶ ἰσχυρὸν ἢ[2] παρὰ τὸ
ῥευστικόν τε καὶ ἀσθενέστερον σπέρμα.

[1] Ἱππῶναξ mss., corr. Diels   [2] ἢ ante καὶ hab. mss.,
transp. Diels

b Cens. *Die nat.* 6.4

ex seminibus autem tenuioribus feminas, ex densioribus
mares fieri Hippon adfirmat.

D10 (A13) Aëtius

Hippo: females do not emit seed any less than males do, but it makes no contribution to reproduction because it falls outside of the uterus; whence it happens that a few females often emit seed independently of the males, especially widows. And the bones come from the male, the flesh from the female.

D11 (A14)

a Aëtius

Hippo[1]: [scil. males and females come] from seed that is solid and strong, or fluid and weaker.

[1] The mss. read "Hipponax"; Diels refers the indication to Hippo.

b Censorinus, *The Birthday*

Hippo affirms that females are produced from more rarefied seeds, males from denser ones.

785

D12 (A14) Aët. 5.7.7 (Ps.-Plut.) [πῶς ἄρρενα γεννᾶται καὶ θήλεα]

Ἵππων,¹ εἰ μὲν ἡ γονὴ κρατήσειεν, ἄρρεν· εἰ δ᾽ ἡ τροφή, θῆλυ.

¹ Ἱππῶναξ mss., corr. Diels

Growth of the Embryo and Child (D13–D17)

D13 (< A18) Cens. *Die nat.* 6.9

[. . .] de geminis, qui ut aliquando nascantur, modo seminis fieri Hippon ratus est: id enim cum amplius est quam uni satis fuit, bifariam deduci.¹

¹ deduci] diduci *IBW*

D14 (A17) Cens. *Die nat.* 6.3

at Diogenes et Hippon existimarunt esse in alvo prominens quiddam, quod infans ore adprehendat et¹ ex eo alimentum ita trahat ut, cum editus est, ex matris uberibus.

¹ et V²: *om. rell.*

D15 (A15) Cens. *Die nat.* 6.1

Hippon vero caput, in quo est animi¹ principale.

¹ animi] cum *HQILU*

D12 (A14) Aëtius

Hippo:[1] if the seed dominates, male; if the nourishment does, female.

[1] The mss. read "Hipponax"; Diels refers the indication to Hippo.

Growth of the Embryo and Child (D13–D17)

D13 (< A18) Censorinus, *The Birthday*

[. . .] concerning twins, who are born now and then, Hippo thought it depends on the amount of seed: if there is more than would have been enough for one child, it is divided into two.

D14 (A17) Censorinus, *The Birthday*

But Diogenes [cf. **DIOG. D32a**] and Hippo thought that there exists in the belly [scil. of the mother] a protrusion that the infant takes in its mouth and from which it draws nourishment in the same way as, after it is born, it does from its mother's breasts.

D15 (A15) Censorinus, *The Birthday*

But Hippo [scil. says that the first part to develop] is the head, in which the principle of the soul is located.

D16 (> A16) Cens. *Die nat.* 9.2

[. . . = **DIOG. D31b**] vel[1] Hippon, qui diebus LX infantem scribit formari, et quarto mense carnem fieri concretam, quinto ungues capillumve[2] nasci, septimo iam hominem esse perfectum.

[1] vel] *ut IGU*   [2] capillumque *H*: -live *OIL*: -losve *GB*

D17 (< A16) Cens. *Die nat.* 7.2–4

Hippon [. . . = **P2b**] a septimo ad decimum mensem nasci posse aestimavit. nam septimo partum iam esse maturum eo, quod in omnibus numerus septenarius plurimum possit, siquidem septem formemur[1] mensibus, additisque alteris recti consistere incipiamus, et post septimum mensem dentes nobis innascantur, idemque post septimum cadant annum, quarto decimo autem pubescere soleamus. [3] sed hanc a septem mensibus incipientem maturitatem usque ad decem perductam,[2] ideo quod in aliis omnibus haec eadem natura est, ut septem mensibus annisve tres aut menses aut anni ad consummationem[3] accedant. [4] nam dentes septem mensum infanti nasci et maxime decimo perfici mense, septimo anno primos eorum excidere, decimo ultimos; post quartum decimum annum nonnullos, sed omnes intra septimum decimum annum pubescere.

[1] formemur] formentur *QGL*: -antur *I*: a partu formentur dentes *Q*[3]   [2] perductam] perduci *H*: perductam ⟨putat⟩ *Giusta*   [3] consummationem] confirmationem *QIG*

D16 (> A16) Censorinus, *The Birthday*

[. . .] or Hippo, who writes that the embryo is formed in sixty days, and the flesh becomes solid in the fourth month, the nails or hair appear in the fifth, and the human being is fully developed in the seventh.

D17 (< A16) Censorinus, *The Birthday*

Hippo [. . .] thought that birth could occur between the seventh and the tenth month. For a child born in the seventh month is already completed by reason of the fact that in all things the number seven has the greatest power, since we are formed in seven months and when another seven are added we begin to stand upright, and after the seventh month our teeth start to grow and after the seventh year they fall out, and in the fourteenth [scil. year] we usually reach puberty. [3] But this maturation, which begins at seven months and lasts until ten [scil. months], is of the same nature as in all other things: to the seven months or years are added either three months or three years to reach completeness: [4] for teeth start to grow when an infant is seven months old and finish at the latest in the tenth one; the first of them fall out in the seventh year, the last ones in the tenth one; some children reach puberty at the end of the fourteenth year, but all do so before the beginning of the seventeenth year.

Botany (D18)

D18 Theophr. *HP*

a (A19) (1.3.5)

πᾶν γὰρ ἄγριον καὶ ἥμερόν φησιν Ἵππων γίνεσθαι
τυγχάνον ἢ μὴ τυγχάνον θεραπείας. ἄκαρπα δὲ καὶ
κάρπιμα καὶ ἀνθοφόρα καὶ ἀνανθῆ παρὰ τοὺς τόπους
καὶ τὸν ἀέρα τὸν περιέχοντα· τὸν αὐτὸν δὲ τρόπον καὶ
φυλλοβόλα καὶ ἀείφυλλα.

b (< A19) (3.2.2)

καίτοι φησὶν Ἵππων ἅπαν καὶ ἥμερον καὶ ἄγριον εἶναι, καὶ θεραπευόμενον μὲν ἥμερον μὴ θεραπευόμενον
δὲ ἄγριον [. . . = **R2**].

The Waters of the Earth (D19)

D19 (< B1) Schol. Genav. in *Il.* 21.195

Ἵππων· τὰ γὰρ ὕδατα πινόμενα πάντα ἐκ τῆς θαλάσσης ἐστίν· οὐ γὰρ δή που[1] τὰ φρέατα βαθύτερα ἢ
ἢ[2] θάλασσά ἐστιν ἐξ ὧν[3] πίνομεν· οὕτω γὰρ οὐκ
⟨ἂν⟩[4] ἐκ τῆς θαλάσσης τὸ ὕδωρ εἴη, ἀλλ᾽ ἄλλοθέν
ποθεν· νῦν δὲ ἡ θάλασσα βαθυτέρα ἐστὶ τῶν ὑδάτων. ὅσα οὖν καθυπέρθεν τῆς θαλάσσης ἐστί, πάντα ἀπ᾽ αὐτῆς ἐστιν.

Botany (D18)

D18 Theophrastus, *History of Plants*

a (A19)

Hippo says that every [scil. plant] may be wild or domestic, depending on whether or not it receives cultivation, and that the question whether it is fruitless or fruit-bearing, or flowering or nonflowering, varies according to the places and the surrounding air, and so too whether it is deciduous or evergreen.

b (< A19)

But Hippo says that every [scil. plant] is both domestic and wild, and that if it is cultivated it is domestic, but if it is not cultivated it is wild [. . .].

The Waters of the Earth (D19)

D19 (< B1) Geneva Scholia on Homer's *Iliad*

Hippo: **"All potable water comes from the sea. For the wells from which we drink are surely not deeper than the sea is. For if they were, the water would not come from the sea but from somewhere else. But as it is, the sea is deeper than the waters. Hence whatever waters are above the sea all come from it."**

---

¹ πως ms., corr. Diels, qui που ‹εἰ› scrips. ² ἢ ἡ Wilamowitz: ἤν mss.   ³ ὧν Wilamowitz: ἢς ms. Nicole   ⁴ ‹ἂν›

791

The Earth Floats on Water (D20)

D20 (< 11 A13) Simpl. *In Phys.*, p. 23.28–29

[. . . cf. **DOX. 14**] τὴν γῆν ἐφ᾽ ὕδατος ἀπεφήναντο κεῖσθαι [. . .].

The Earth Floats on Water (D20)

D20 (< 11 A13) Simplicius, *Commentary on Aristotle's* Physics

[. . .] they [scil. Thales and Hippo] stated that the earth rests on water [. . .].

HIPPO [38 DK]

R

A Possible Parody of Hippo in Cratinus

See **DRAM. T15–T16**

Aristotle's Contempt for Hippo (R1)

R1 (A7) Arist. *Metaph.* A3 984a3–5

Ἵππωνα μὲν γὰρ οὐκ ἄν τις ἀξιώσειε θεῖναι μετὰ
τούτων διὰ τὴν εὐτέλειαν αὐτοῦ τῆς διανοίας [. . .].

*Theophrastus' Balanced Judgment on
Hippo's Botany (R2)*

R2 (< A19) Theophr. *HP* 3.2.2

[. . . = **D18b**] τῇ μὲν ὀρθῶς λέγων τῇ δὲ οὐκ ὀρθῶς.
ἐξαμελούμενον γὰρ ἅπαν χεῖρον γίνεται καὶ ἀπαγρι-
οῦται, θεραπευόμενον δὲ οὐχ ἅπαν βέλτιον, ὥσπερ
εἴρηται.

HIPPO

R

See **DRAM. T15–T16**

A Possible Parody of Hippo in Cratinus

Aristotle's Contempt for Hippo (R1)

R1 (A7) Aristotle, *Metaphysics*

One would not think that Hippo deserves to be placed next to these [i.e. Thales and the early mythic cosmologists], given the shoddiness of his thought [. . .].

Theophrastus' Balanced Judgment on Hippo's Botany (R2)

R2 (< A19) Theophrastus, *History of Plants*

[. . .] On the one hand, what he says is correct, on the other it is not: for while everything that is neglected deteriorates and becomes wild, not everything that is cultivated becomes better, as I have said.

Hippo's Reputation as an Atheist (R3–R7)

R3 (< A4) Simpl. *In Phys.*, p. 23.22

[. . .] καὶ Ἵππων, ὃς δοκεῖ καὶ ἄθεος γεγονέναι [. . . = **D2**].

R4 (< A6) Ioan. Diac. Galen. *in Theog.* 116, p. 305

[. . . = **D5**] Ἵππων ὁ ἄθεος [. . .].

R5 (A8) Philop. *In An.*, p. 88.23–24

οὗτος ἄθεος ἐπεκέκλητο δι᾽ αὐτὸ τοῦτο, ὅτι τὴν τῶν πάντων αἰτίαν οὐδενὶ ἄλλῳ ἢ τῷ ὕδατι ἀπεδίδου.

R6

a (B2) Alex. *In Metaph.*, p. 27.1–4

τοῦτο δὲ λέγοι ἂν περὶ αὐτοῦ [cf. **R1**], ὅτι ἄθεος ἦν· τοιοῦτο γὰρ καὶ τὸ ἐπὶ τοῦ τάφου αὐτοῦ ἐπίγραμμα

   Ἵππωνος τόδε σῆμα, τὸν ἀθανάτοισι θεοῖσιν
    ἶσον ἐποίησεν μοῖρα καταφθίμενον.

b (≠ DK) Alex. *In Metaph.*, p. 26 (app.)

Ἵππων τὴν αὐτὴν ἔσχε δόξαν Θαλῇ, ἀρχὴν λέγων καὶ αἰτίαν τῶν ὄντων τὸ ὕδωρ· φησὶ δὲ ὅτι οὐ δίκαιόν ἐστι συντάττειν τοῦτον τοῖς φυσικοῖς διὰ τὴν εὐτέλειαν

Hippo's Reputation as an Atheist (R3–R7)

R3 (< A4) Simplicius, *Commentary on Aristotle's* Physics

[. . .] Hippo, who seems to have been an atheist [. . .].

R4 (< A6) John Diaconus Galenus, *Allegories on Hesiod's* Theogony

[. . .] Hippo the atheist [. . .].

R5 (A8) Philoponus, *Commentary on Aristotle's* On the Soul

He was called 'atheist' for this very reason, that he assigned the cause of all things to nothing else than to water.

R6

a (B2) Alexander of Aphrodisias, *Commentary on Aristotle's* Metaphysics

He [i.e. Aristotle] may be saying this [cf. **R1**] about him because he was an atheist; for this is the sort of epigram found on his tomb:

> This is the tomb of Hippo, whom Fate made equal
>   To the immortal gods when he died.

b (≠ DK) Alexander of Aphrodisias, *Commentary on Aristotle's* Metaphysics

Hippo was of the same opinion as Thales: he said that water is the principle and cause of the things that are. He [i.e. Aristotle] says that it is not just to rank this man to-

αὐτοῦ τῆς διανοίας. οὐκ εἶπε δὲ τῆς δόξης (ὕδωρ γὰρ
καὶ αὐτὸς ἐδόξαζεν ὡς Θαλῆς) ἀλλὰ διὰ τὴν ἀθεότητα·
θεὸν γὰρ οὐ προεστήσατο τῶν ὄντων δημιουργόν· διὸ
καὶ ἀπέπτυσε πρὸς αὐτὸν [. . .].

c (≠ DK) Asclep. *In Metaph.*, p. 25.16–18

Ἵππωνα μὲν γὰρ οὐ δίκαιον τάττειν μετὰ τούτων, καὶ
αὐτὸν ὑπολαβόντα τὸ ὕδωρ εἶναι τὴν ἀρχήν, διὰ τὸ
εὐτελὲς[1] τῆς διανοίας αὐτοῦ· ἄθεος γάρ ἐστιν. οὐ λέγει
γὰρ ἄλλο τι εἶναι παρὰ τὰ φαινόμενα φυσικὰ πράγματα.

   [1] ἀτελές ABCD

R7 Clem. Alex. *Protr.*

a (A8) 2.24. 2

[. . .] θαυμάζειν ἔπεισί μοι ὅτῳ τρόπῳ Εὐήμερον τὸν
Ἀκραγαντῖνον καὶ Νικάνορα τὸν Κύπριον καὶ Ἵππωνα καὶ Διαγόραν[1] τὸν Μήλιον [. . .] καί τινας ἄλλους συχνούς, σωφρόνως βεβιωκότας καὶ καθεωρα-
κότας ὀξύτερόν που τῶν λοιπῶν ἀνθρώπων τὴν ἀμφὶ
τοὺς θεοὺς τούτους πλάνην, ἀθέους ἐπικεκλήκασιν
[. . .].

   [1] Διαγόραν καὶ Ἵππωνα ms., corr. Diels

gether with the natural philosophers because of the shoddiness of his thought. He was not saying this about his opinion (for Thales himself had the same opinion about water), but because of his atheism (for he did not place a god as demiurge over the things that are). And this is why he has expressed loathing for him [. . .].

c (≠ DK) Asclepius, *Commentary on Aristotle's* Metaphysics

For it is not fair to put together in the same rank with these [i.e. Thales and the earliest mythic cosmologists] Hippo, who also assumes that water is the principle, by reason of the shoddiness of his thought; for he is an atheist. For he says that no other thing exists besides the physical entities that appear to us.[1]

[1] The words from "for he is" to the end appear in a slightly different formulation in Ps.-Alexander, *Commentary on Aristotle's* Metaphysics, p. 462.29 (= 38 A9 DK).

R7 Clement of Alexandria, *Protreptic*

a (A8)

I am astonished at the way in which they have called atheists Euhemerus of Acragas, Nicanor of Cyprus, Hippo, Diagoras of Melos, [. . .] and many others, who lived moderately and looked down more acutely than other men upon the errors regarding these gods [. . .].

b (B2) 4.55.1

οὐ νέμεσις τοίνυν οὐδὲ Ἵππωνι ἀπαθανατίζοντι τὸν
θάνατον τὸν ἑαυτοῦ· ὁ Ἵππων οὗτος ἐπιγραφῆναι
ἐκέλευσεν τῷ μνήματι τῷ ἑαυτοῦ τόδε τὸ ἐλεγεῖον·
[citation of the epitaph mentioned in **R6a**].

A Neopythagorean Pseudepigraphic Text? (R8)

R8 (< B4) Claud. Mamert. *Statu an.* 7, p. 121.14–18

Hippon [. . . = **P3, P7**] praemissis pro statu sententiae
suae insolubilibus argumentis de anima sic pronuntiat:
"longe aliud anima, aliud corpus est, quae corpore et
torpente viget et caeco videt et mortuo vivit [. . .]."

b (B2)

There is no reason to feel indignant at Hippo either, who immortalized his own death. This Hippo ordered that the following elegy be inscribed on his tomb [citation of the epitaph mentioned in **R6a**].

See also **DRAM. T15**

A Neopythagorean Pseudepigraphic Text? (R8)

R8 (< B4) Claudianus Mamertus, *On the State of the Soul*

Hippo [. . .], after having put forward incontrovertible arguments about the soul in support of his own position, speaks as follows: "The soul is one thing, the body is another very different one; it is vigorous even when the body is lethargic, it sees even when it is blind, and it lives even when it is dead [. . .]."

See **PYTHS. R47**